RACE and CRIME

THIRD EDITION

For my loving parents, Daphne and Patrick Gabbidon,
who continue to be supportive of all my endeavors.

—SLG

To my ancestors for paving the way.

—HTG

RACE and CRIME

THIRD EDITION

Shaun L. Gabbidon | Helen Taylor Greene

Penn State Harrisburg   *Texas Southern University*

Los Angeles | London | New Delhi
Singapore | Washington DC

SAGE

Los Angeles | London | New Delhi
Singapore | Washington DC

FOR INFORMATION:

SAGE Publications, Inc.
2455 Teller Road
Thousand Oaks, California 91320
E-mail: order@sagepub.com

SAGE Publications Ltd.
1 Oliver's Yard
55 City Road
London EC1Y 1SP
United Kingdom

SAGE Publications India Pvt. Ltd.
B 1/I 1 Mohan Cooperative Industrial Area
Mathura Road, New Delhi 110 044
India

SAGE Publications Asia-Pacific Pte. Ltd.
3 Church Street
#10-04 Samsung Hub
Singapore 049483

Acquisitions Editor: Jerry Westby
Editorial Assistant: Laura Cheung
Production Editor: Laureen Gleason
Copy Editor: Diana Breti
Typesetter: C&M Digitals (P) Ltd.
Proofreader: Annette R. Van Deusen
Indexer: Julie Grayson
Cover Designer: Edgar Abarca
Marketing Manager: Terra Schultz
Permissions Editor: Karen Ehrmann

Printed in the United States of America

Library of Congress Cataloging-in-Publication Data

Gabbidon, Shaun L., 1967-

Race and crime / Shaun L. Gabbidon, Helen Taylor Greene. — 3rd ed.

p. cm.
Includes bibliographical references and index.

ISBN 978-1-4522-0260-0 (pbk.)

1. Crime and race—United States.
2. Criminal justice, Administration of—United States.
3. Discrimination in criminal justice administration—United States.
4. Minorities—United States.
I. Greene, Helen Taylor, 1949- II. Title.

HV6789.G32 2013
364.973089—dc23 2011041244

SFI Certified Sourcing
www.sfiprogram.org
SFI-00453

This book is printed on acid-free paper.

12 13 14 15 16 10 9 8 7 6 5 4 3 2 1

Brief Contents

Detailed Contents

Preface to the Third Edition

"Justice is Blind" represents the basic motto and principle of our criminal justice system. It symbolizes equity in the administration of justice and represents our basic rights in a free society.

For many in the minority community, however, society is not that free and justice is far from blind. Justice in many cases has perfect 20/20 vision that distinguishes people on the basis of race, ethnicity, gender, religious beliefs and social and economic status.

—National Organization of Black Law
Enforcement Executives (2001, p. 4)

Welcome to the third edition of *Race and Crime*. We are excited that the first two editions were positively received by students and instructors and that the book continues to be one of the standard texts used in courses related to race, ethnicity, and crime. For this edition, we have updated each chapter and also devoted attention to the increasing societal focus on immigration. As in the earlier editions, we provide information on crime and justice trends in the appropriate chapters. We have also included critical thinking questions in the Boxes in each chapter as well as Internet Exercises at the end of each chapter. Both give students an opportunity to reflect on historical and contemporary issues and familiarize themselves with relevant information available. (Note that the credits for the boxes and other items appear in a Credits and Sources section toward the end of the book.) This edition includes coverage of several timely topics, such as biosocial theory, violent victimizations, immigrant policing, and juveniles sentenced to "death in prison."

Race and crime is a contemporary issue in many societies where there is a diverse population and racial and ethnic minorities (Gabbidon, 2009; Kalunta-Crumpton, 2010). Since the colonial era, race and crime in America have been inextricably linked; there has been a belief that minorities, especially Blacks, are more criminal. At first, support for this belief was the result of racist ideologies that labeled minorities as both "criminal" and "inferior." More recently, support for this erroneous belief was based on the disproportionate number of racial and ethnic minorities who are arrested and imprisoned. After the 1960s, the relationship between race and crime became more ambiguous as we learned about the role of justice practitioners and their use of discretion. Early in this century, as reported crime, arrests, and victimizations decrease, incarceration rates continue to be a concern.

The opening quotation captures the beliefs of many racial and ethnic minorities about justice in the United States in the past and present. Whites, who form the majority of the U.S.

population, are less likely to believe there is discrimination in the administration of justice. Because the news media usually focus on persons who commit crimes, especially serious crimes like murder and rape, it is easy to lose sight of the fact that the majority of Americans, regardless of their race or ethnicity, are law-abiding citizens. It seems that we have just as easily lost sight of the historical context of race and crime in the United States. Why do racial minorities, most of whom are law-abiding citizens, continue to be labeled criminals? The study of race and crime has a long history in the discipline of criminology and the study of criminal justice. In the 19th century, positivist scholars (those who explained crime using biological, sociological, or psychological factors) deemed the physical characteristics of racial minorities and some white ethnics to be associated with crime (Gabbidon, 2010; Gabbidon & Taylor Greene, 2005).

Early criminology texts devoted whole chapters to race and crime that not only presented crime figures, but also sought to explain the trends related to race and crime (Gabbidon & Taylor Greene, 2001). Interestingly, contemporary criminology textbooks do not devote as much attention to race and crime as did earlier texts (Gabbidon & Taylor Greene, 2001). Even many of the early textbooks omitted many important topics like slave patrols, lynching, race riots, and legal segregation, which often resulted in socially disorganized communities. More recently, despite a strong argument for studying race and crime put forth by LaFree and Russell (1993), only a handful of comprehensive books on this topic are available (Barak, Flavin, & Leighton, 2010; Gabbidon, 2010; Mann, 1993; Tarver, Walker, & Wallace, 2002; Walker, Spohn, & Delone, 2012).

Most of the early scholarly research on race that is available refers primarily to Blacks. This is due, at least in part, to the fact that until recently, Blacks were the largest minority group in the United States and therefore the most visible. It is also related to the (over) representation of Blacks in official data on crime and justice. Another important factor in the focus on Blacks probably has to do with their foray into higher education, especially into the discipline of criminology. Most majority scholars were uninterested in studying race and crime. Blacks, in contrast, were interested. Throughout the 20th century, even before the emergence of Black criminologists, many Black scholars at historically Black colleges and universities were studying Black issues, including crime (Taylor Greene & Gabbidon, 2000). It is only recently that other minorities have received increased attention. At the same time, Latinos are now the largest minority group and also have more scholars interested in race, ethnicity, and crime; as a result, more research is being published on this group. This does not mean that other racial and ethnic groups have not been subjected to differential treatment in society and the administration of justice. It means that the historical record of their experiences is less complete. Notably, although interest in Latino and Native American crime has increased, the research on Asian Americans and crime is still limited.

Despite more research, books, and government documents about race and crime, we are still unable to explain and adequately address the continuous pattern of overrepresentation of some minorities in arrest and victimization statistics, corrections, persons under sentence of death, and juvenile delinquency. We believe that prior attempts to make sense of the disproportionate number of minorities in the administration of justice are incomplete because they fail to consider relevant historical information.

One of our goals in writing this book was to put the study of race and crime in a more complete historical context. This remains one of our key goals in this third edition. Another goal is to examine several contemporary issues relevant to understanding race and crime.

To achieve these goals, we utilize a limited-systems approach to examine policing, courts, sentencing, the death penalty, and corrections in the past and the present. An additional chapter examines the juvenile justice system. We include an issues approach to focus on several contemporary challenges in the study of race and crime, including hate/bias crimes, immigration and crime, racial profiling, sentencing disparities, wrongful convictions, felon disenfranchisement, disproportionate minority confinement, minority female delinquency, juveniles and life without parole, and delinquency prevention. We include the major racial and ethnic groups in the United States—Asians, Blacks, Latinos/as, Native Americans, and Whites—although not as much information is available on all groups.

Various terms are used to refer to these groups. Some are the terms preferred in present-day usage, whereas others also are utilized to preserve their temporal context, especially in direct quotations. For example, you will see Blacks referred to as *Negroes, African Americans,* and *colored;* Native Americans referred to as *American Indians;* and Latinos referred to as *Hispanics.*

The book is divided into nine chapters that present historical details and contemporary information on both the administration of justice and related issues. Chapter 1 provides an overview of race and crime. It begins with a discussion of what many have referred to as the "invention of race." It also provides an overview of race and DNA databases. The remainder of the chapter highlights the historical experiences of Native Americans, African Americans, White ethnics, Latino Americans, and Asian Americans. The chapter pays particular attention to how crime has intersected with each of their experiences. Chapter 2 examines the extent of crime and victimization. It includes an overview of the history of the collection of crime data in the United States, a discussion of the limitations of crime statistics, the reported extent of crime and victimization for various racial groups, and an analysis of hate crime statistics. Chapter 3 presents theoretical perspectives on race and crime and provides a discussion of biological, sociological, subcultural, and nontraditional theoretical perspectives, including the colonial model and counter-colonial criminology.

Chapters 4 through 9 examine race and several key components of the administration of justice: police, courts, sentencing, the death penalty, corrections, and juvenile justice. An overview of policing in the United States is presented in Chapter 4. Minority employment data and an analysis of the history of race and policing are also presented. Contemporary issues presented in this chapter include citizen satisfaction with the police, police deviance (brutality and use of excessive force), immigration and policing, and community policing. Chapter 5 examines the history of race and the courts in America and how race impacts various facets of the American court system (i.e., bail, legal counsel, plea bargaining, etc.). A portion of the chapter also looks at the promise of drug courts.

Chapter 6 includes historical information and a comprehensive discussion of sentencing disparities. The chapter provides an overview of the sentencing process, along with a discussion of sentencing philosophies and contemporary issues related to race and sentencing. Chapter 7 examines race and the death penalty. Following an examination of the key Supreme Court death penalty cases, the chapter examines the history of the death penalty in America and also public opinion on the death penalty. Other contemporary issues discussed include the Capital Jury Project, wrongful convictions, and the death penalty moratorium movement. Chapter 8 provides a review of the history of corrections and the overrepresentation of racial minorities in jails and prisons. The chapter also examines prison gangs, explanations for racial disparities in corrections, prisoner reentry concerns, and felon disenfranchisement.

The issue of race and juvenile justice is presented in Chapter 9. The chapter presents an overview of juvenile justice in the United States and the historical context of race effects in juvenile justice, an explanation of the extent of juvenile delinquency and victimization, and a discussion of several contemporary issues, including disproportionate minority confinement, minority female delinquency, life without parole, and delinquency prevention. The book ends with a concluding chapter that provides a brief reflection on the findings from the various chapters. The chapter also discusses prospects for study and the future of race and crime.

Overall, as with prior editions of the text, we envision this one as an addition to the body of knowledge in the area of race and crime. With our historical emphasis, we hope those who read this work leave with an appreciation for the similar historical experiences of most American racial and ethnic groups. We also hope that readers will see how race and ethnicity have mattered and continue to matter in the administration of justice.

Acknowledgments

There are numerous individuals who have assisted us in the completion of this project. First, we would like to express our appreciation to our editor, Jerry Westby, for his continued support and encouragement. We especially thank Erim Sarbuland, Catherine Chilton, Diana Breti, and the entire SAGE team for their assistance in the completion of this manuscript. We thank the following original reviewers for their constructive comments and suggestions that produced a well-received first edition: Mary Atwell, Radford University; Stephanie Bush-Baskette, Rutgers-Newark University; Charles Crawford, Western Michigan University; Alex del Carmen, University of Texas Arlington; Roland Chilton, University of Massachusetts, Amherst; Martha L. Henderson, The Citadel; D. Kall Loper, University of North Texas; Mike Males, University of California, Santa Cruz; Michael A. McMorris, Comstock Park, MI; Karen Parker, University of Delaware; Charles Reasons, Central Washington University; Katheryn Russell-Brown, University of Florida; Adina Schwartz, John Jay College of Criminal Justice; Susan F. Sharp, University of Oklahoma; Shirley Williams, New Jersey City University; Bill Wells, Southern Indiana University; and Ernest Uwazie, California State University, Sacramento.

For the second edition, we thank the following reviewers who provided great suggestions to improve the text: Tony Barringer, Florida Gulf Coast University; Dawn Beicher, Illinois State University; Lorenzo Boyd, Fayetteville State University; Roland Chilton, University of Massachusetts, Amherst; Ben Fleury-Steiner, University of Delaware; Kareem Jordan, University of Central Florida; Peter C. Kratcoski, Kent State University; Everette Penn, University of Houston, Clear Lake; Carolyn Petrosino, Bridgewater State College; Robert Sigler, University of Alabama; and Ernest Uwazie, California State University, Sacramento.

The following reviewers provided useful suggestions for the third edition: Jonathon A. Cooper, Arizona State University; Francisco J. Alatorre, Arizona State University; Tony A. Barringer, Florida Gulf Coast University; Francis M. Williams, Plymouth State University; Christine Martin, University of Illinois at Chicago; Peter C. Kratcoski, Kent State University; Stephanie R. Bush-Baskette, Rutgers University; Tara N. Tripp, Temple University; Ernest Uwazie, California State University, Sacramento; and Patricia Warren, Florida State University.

Professor Gabbidon would like to thank his family for their continued encouragement and support. At Penn State, he would like to thank Dr. Steve Peterson, Director, School of Public Affairs, who has provided a supportive environment for conducting research in which the possibilities continue to seem endless. During the completion of the three editions of this work, the assistance of several research assistants proved invaluable. Specifically, Nora Carerras, Nancy McGee, Patricia Patrick, Leslie Kowal, Matthew Nelson, and Grace Monjardo are acknowledged for their contributions. My son, Jini Gabbidon, is acknowledged for his efforts organizing the references into one file. Finally, Dr. Gabbidon would like to acknowledge his mentor and intellectual partner, Dr. Helen Taylor Greene, for her continued guidance and support.

Dr. Greene would like to thank her family for their continued support and appreciation of her scholarly endeavors. She thanks Dr. Gabbidon, her co-author, for his vision and commitment to the study of race and crime, and for inspiring her to persevere no matter what. She also thanks her colleagues at Texas Southern University and elsewhere for their support. She gives special thanks to Mr. Jason Williams and Ms. Kashley Brown, who assisted with revisions to the third edition, and Ms. Palencia Lewis, who assisted with preparation of several tables in Chapters 2 and 4.

Overview of Race and Crime

Because skin color is socially constructed, it can also be reconstructed. Thus, when the descendants of the European immigrants began to move up economically and socially, their skins apparently began to look lighter to the whites who had come to America before them. When enough of these descendants became visibly middle class, their skin was seen as fully white. The biological skin color of the second and third generations had not changed, but it was socially blanched or whitened.

—Herbert J. Gans (2005)

At a time when the United States is more diverse than ever, with the minority population topping 100 million (one in every three U.S. residents; U.S. Census Bureau, 2010), the notion of **race** seems to permeate almost every facet of American life. Certainly, one of the more highly charged aspects of the race dialogue relates to crime. Before embarking on an overview of race and crime, we must first set the parameters of the discussion, which include relevant definitions and the scope of our review. When speaking of race, it is always important to remind readers of the history of the concept and some current definitions.

The idea of race originated 5,000 years ago in India, but it was also prevalent among the Chinese, Egyptians, and Jews (Gossett, 1963). Although François Bernier (1625–1688) is usually credited with first classifying humans into distinct races, Carolus Linnaeus (1707–1778) invented the first system of categorizing plants and humans. It was, however, Johan Frederich Blumenbach (1752–1840) who developed the first taxonomy of race. In his 1795 work, "On the Natural Variety of Mankind," Blumenbach separated the inhabitants of the earth into five races: Ethiopian (African or Negroid), Mongolian (Asian), American (Native American), and Malaysian (Pacific Islander). When categorizing the fifth group, Whites, Blumenbach coined the term *Caucasian* (Feagin & Booher Feagin, 2012). Relying on Blumenbach's work, European scholars created a categorization that led to the belief that the differences among the groups were biological—and from the beginning Europeans placed themselves at the apex of the racial hierarchy (Feagin & Booher Feagin, 2012). It is widely believed, however, that the biological differences among racial groups are attributable to the patterns of their migration out of Africa (Dulaney, 1879; Shane, 1999; see Figure 1.1).

Figure 1.1

Migration Patterns
Out of Africa

Source: Shane
(1999, p. 6A).

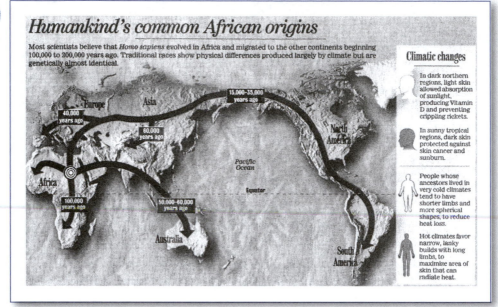

Today, social scientists refer to race as a "social construct." Gallagher (1997) writes that "race and ethnicity are social constructions because their meanings are derived by focusing on arbitrary characteristics that a given society deems socially important. Race and ethnicity are social products based on cultural values; they are not scientific facts" (p. 2). Another relevant definition has been provided by Flowers (1988): "Race . . . refers to a group of persons characterized by common physical and/or biological traits that are transmitted in descent" (p. xiv). Finally, the U.S. Census Bureau (2000) has added the following:

> The concept of race . . . reflects self-identification by people according to the race or races with which they most closely identify. These categories are sociopolitical constructs and should not be interpreted as being scientific or anthropological in nature.

Thus, there is no shortage of definitions that refer to race as a social construct. Increasingly, however, some scholars—relying on scientific discoveries in the natural sciences—are beginning to challenge the notion of race as a social construct (Sesardic, 2010; J. P. Wright, 2009).

❖ Race, DNA, Criminal Justice Databases, and Civil Rights Concerns

Recent criminal justice investigations involving the use of DNA evidence have challenged the notion that there are no biological differences between races. These cases have relied on DNA to identify the race of a perpetrator (D. H. Simons, 2003). In one instance, skeptical police investigators had a scientist conduct a sample test to illustrate support for the science behind the use of DNA to identify the race of the suspect. Specifically, the investigators sent a molecular biologist 20 DNA samples to test for racial identity; after conducting his analysis, the molecular biologist correctly identified the race of all 20 samples. He later helped investigators solve the case by identifying the offender as Black, not White, as had been previously thought (Newsome, 2007).

The general collection and use of DNA has not been without controversy. The American Civil Liberties Union (ACLU) has recently articulated three general concerns about forensic DNA databases. First, they believe the use of such databases can result in an invasion of medical privacy. In particular, they believe that DNA data "might be used by employers, insurers, and others for invidious genetic discrimination—against both the individual who supplied the DNA and also their immediate family members, who have similar DNA" (Schwartz, 2011, p. 1). Thus, there is concern about the FBI's Combined DNA Index System (CODIS). Contrary to the belief of some, the DNA information collected by the FBI does provide information on "medically relevant" genes. Second, the ACLU believes that the use of forensic DNA databases represents an invasion of bodily integrity. To collect the information for the database, officials often place a swab in a person's mouth; if the person refuses, he or she is often forced to comply. Schwartz (2011) notes that the government can get around forcibly taking the DNA by covertly taking DNA that is shed onto objects citizens have handled (e.g., soda cans). Potentially, the government could secretly seize the DNA of all Americans (p. 3). The ACLU's third concern related to DNA databases is their racially disparate impact. Here, the ACLU takes the position that because "African Americans and Hispanics are arrested, prosecuted, and convicted—often wrongly—at a far higher rate than Caucasians," they are likely to be disparately impacted by DNA databases (Schwartz, 2011). In addition to these general concerns, the ACLU is also concerned about familial DNA testing.

Familial DNA testing occurs when the DNA of the suspect is only a partial match. This can result in police questioning the immediate and extended family of the suspect, which has the potential to criminalize entire families—especially families of color (De Gruy, 2010; Schwartz, 2011). Given that people of color are more likely to be arrested and incarcerated, familial DNA testing has the potential to contribute to racial injustice in the administration of justice.

There is clearly a delicate balance that needs to be struck when collecting DNA data. In the United Kingdom, for example, there are now 5 million profiles in their Police National Computer (PNC), which was a 40% increase in just two years. Currently, the United States has nearly double that figure, with 9 million people in the FBI's CODIS database (Schwartz, 2011). The reality is that the successful use of DNA databases is spurring the increased use of DNA evidence in the criminal justice field—in the United States and abroad. The real challenge ahead is how to balance privacy concerns with public safety concerns (Kazemian, Pease, & Farrington, 2011; Tseloni & Pease, 2011).

❖ Race, Ethnicity, and the 2010 U.S. Census

Even though the debate about the existence of distinct races persists, the U.S. Census Bureau continues to track national data on race/ethnicity. In fact, the 2010 census collected these data, which became the standard practice during the first decennial census in 1790 (Humes, Jones, & Ramirez, 2011). Figure 1.2 shows the form that was used to ask questions pertaining to race and ethnicity on the 2010 census. The form illustrates the separation of race and ethnicity. This practice dates to 1997, when the federal government mandated that "race and Hispanic origin (ethnicity) are separate and distinct concepts and that when collecting these data via self-identification, two different questions must be used" (Humes et al., 2011, p. 2).

Figure 1.2

Reproduction of the Questions on Hispanic Origin and Race From the 2010 Census

Source: U.S. Census Bureau, 2010 Census questionnaire.

→ **NOTE: Please answer BOTH Question 5 about Hispanic origin and Question 6 about race. For this census, Hispanic origins are not races.**

5. Is this person of Hispanic, Latino, or Spanish origin?
   ☐ **No**, not of Hispanic, Latino, or Spanish origin
   ☐ Yes, Mexican, Mexican Am., Chicano
   ☐ Yes, Puerto Rican
   ☐ Yes, Cuban
   ☐ Yes, another Hispanic, Latino, or Spanish origin — *Print origin, for example Argentinean, Colombian, Dominican, Nicaraguan, Salvadoran, Spaniard, and so on.* ⬃

   [ ]

6. What is this person's race? *Mark* ☒ *one or more boxes.*
   ☐ White
   ☐ Black, African Am., or Negro
   ☐ American Indian or Alaska Native — *Print name of enrolled or principal tribe.* ⬃

   [ ]

   ☐ Asian Indian   ☐ Japanese   ☐ Native Hawaiian
   ☐ Chinese   ☐ Korean   ☐ Guamanian or Chamorro
   ☐ Filipino   ☐ Vietnamese   ☐ Samoan
   ☐ Other Asian — *Print race, for example, Hmong, Laotian, Thai, Pakistani, Cambodian, and so on.* ⬃   ☐ Other Pacific Islander — *Print race, for example, Fijian, Tongan, and so on.* ⬃

   [ ]

   ☐ Some other race — *Print race.* ⬃

   [ ]

Typically, Hispanics/Latinos are referred to as an ethnic group. The term ***ethnicity*** comes from the Greek word *ethnos*, which means "nation." Generally, ethnic groups are defined by their similar genetic inheritances or some identifiable traits visible among most members of a particular group. Ethnic groups are also generally held together by a common language, culture, group spirit (nationalism or group solidarity), or geography (most typically originate from the same region; Marger, 1997). Therefore, most scholars generally see the terms *race* and *ethnicity* as culturally relevant rather than biologically relevant.

We follow the U.S. Census Bureau racial/ethnic categories and separate the American population into five groups: Native Americans, Whites, African Americans, Hispanic/Latino Americans, and Asian Americans. We also use the definitions for each of the groups outlined in the 2010 Census. We acknowledge that there are limitations to these categories. First, these categories do not take into account the ethnic variation within each race. For example, Table 1.1 provides a breakdown of the U.S. population by Hispanic/Latino origin and race. As you can see in Table 1.2, there are a number of ethnic groups within the racial classification "Hispanic or Latino Americans." This is true of other races as well. Another example is the category "African American/Black." There is also ethnic diversity within this category; it often encompasses people from the Caribbean (e.g., Jamaica, Haiti), African countries, and other parts of the world. Because each of these groups has had a unique experience in America, it is, at times, presumptive for researchers to assume that the experience of one

Table 1.1

Population by Hispanic or Latino Origin and by Race for the United States: 2000 and 2010

(For information on confidentiality protection, nonsampling error, and definitions, see *www.census.gov/prod/cen2010/doc/pl94-171 pdf*)

Hispanic or Latino origin and race	2000		2010		Change, 2000 to 2010	
	Number	Percentage of total population	Number	Percentage of total population	Number	Percent
HISPANIC OR LATINO ORIGIN AND RACE						
Total population	281,421,906	100.0	308,745,538	100.0	27,323,632	9.7
Hispanic or Latino	35,305,818	12.5	50,477,594	16.3	15,171,776	43.0
Not Hispanic or Latino ..	246,116,088	87.5	258,267,944	83.7	12,151,856	4.9
White alone	194,552,774	69.1	196,817,552	63.7	2,264,778	1.2
RACE						
Total population	281,421,906	100.0	308,745,538	100.0	27,323,632	9.7
One Race......................	274,595,678	97.6	299,736,465	97.1	25,140,787	9.2
White	211,460,626	75.1	223,553,265	72.4	12,092,639	5.7
Black or African American	34,658,190	12.3	38,929,319	12.6	4,271,129	12.3
American Indian and Alaska Native	2,475,956	0.9	2,932,246	0.9	456,292	18.4
Asian	10,242,998	3.6	14,674,252	4.8	4,431,254	43.3
Native Hawaiian and Other Pacific Islander	398,835	0.1	540,013	0.2	141,178	35.4
Some Other Race	15,359,073	5.5	19,107,368	6.2	3,748,295	24.4
Two or More Races[1].......	6,826,228	2.4	9,009,073	2.9	2,182,845	32.0

Sources: U.S. Census Bureau. *Census 2000 Redistricting Data (Public Law 94-171) Summary File.* Tables PL1 and PL2; and *2010 Census Redistricting Data (Public Law 94-171) Summary File.* Tables PI and P2.

1. In Census 2000, an error in data processing resulted in an overstatement of the Two or More Races population by about 1 million people (about 15 percent) nationally, which almost entirely affected race combinations involving Some Other Race. Therefore, data users should assess observed changes in the Two or More Races population and race combinations involving Some Other Race between Census 2000 and Census 2010 with caution. Changes in specific race combinations not involving Some Other Race, such as White *and* Black or African American or White *and* Asian, generally should be more comparable.

Table 1.2

Hispanic or Latino Origin Population by Type: 2000 and 2010

(For information on confidentiality protection, nonsampling error, and definitions, see *www.census.gov/prod/cen2010/doc/sf1.pdf*)

Origin and type	2000		2010		Change, 2000 to 2010[1]	
	Number	Percent of total	Number	Percent of total	Number	Percent
HISPANIC OR LATINO ORIGIN						
Total.................................	281,421,906	100.0	308,745,538	100.0	27,323,632	9.7
Hispanic or Latino	35,305,818	12.5	50,477,594	16.3	15,171,776	43.0
Not Hispanic or Latino	246,116,088	87.5	258,267,944	83.7	12,151,856	4.9
HISPANIC OR LATINO BY TYPE						
Total	35,305,818	100.0	50,477,594	100.0	15,171,776	43.0
Mexican	20,640,711	58.5	31,798,258	63.0	11,157,547	54.1
Puerto Rican	3,406,178	9.6	4,623,716	9.2	1,217,538	35.7
Cuban	1,241,685	3.5	1,785,547	3.5	543,862	43.8
Other Hispanic or Latino ..	10,017,244	28.4	12,270,073	24.3	2,252,829	22.5
Dominican (Dominican Republic)	764,945	2.2	1,414,703	2.8	649,758	84.9
Central American (excludes Mexican)	1,686,937	4.8	3,998,280	7.9	2,311,343	137.0
Costa Rican	68,588	0.2	126,418	0.3	57,830	84.3
Guatemalan	372,487	1.1	1,044,209	2.1	671,722	180.3
Honduran	217,569	0.6	633,401	1.3	415,832	191.1
Nicaraguan	177,684	0.5	348,202	0.7	170,518	96.0
Panamanian	91,723	0.3	165,456	0.3	73,733	80.4
Salvadoran	655,165	1.9	1,648,968	3.3	993,803	151.7
Other Central American[2] .	103,721	0.3	31,626	0.1	−72,095	−69.5
South American	1,353,562	3.8	2,769,434	5.5	1,415,872	104.6
Argentinean	100,864	0.3	224,952	0.4	124,088	123.0
Bolivian	42,088	0.1	99,210	0.2	57,142	135.8
Chilean	68,849	0.2	126,810	0.3	57,961	84.2
Colombian	470,684	1.3	908,734	1.8	438,050	93.1
Ecuadorian	260,559	0.7	564,631	1.1	304,072	116.7

Origin and type	2000		2010		Change, 2000 to 2010[1]	
	Number	**Percent of total**	**Number**	**Percent of total**	**Number**	**Percent**
Paraguayan	8,769	—	20,023	—	11,254	128.3
Peruvian	233,926	0.7	531,358	1.1	297,432	127.1
Uruguayan	18,804	0.1	56,884	0.1	38,080	202.5
Venezuelan.	91,507	0.3	215,023	0.4	123,516	135.0
Other South American[3] ...	57,532	0.2	21,809	—	−35,723	−62.1
Spaniard........................	100,135	0.3	635,253	1.3	535,118	534.4
All other Hispanic or Latino[4].............................	6,111,665	17.3	3,452,403	6.8	−2,659,262	−43.5

Sources: U.S. Census Bureau, *Census 2000 Summary File 1 and 2010 Census Summary File 1.*

— Percentage rounds to 0.0.

1. The observed changes in Hispanic origin counts between Census 2000 and the 2010 Census could be attributed to a number of factors. Demographic change since 2000, which includes births and deaths in a geographic area and migration in and out of a geographic area, will have an impact on the resulting 2010 Census counts. Some changes in the Hispanic origin question's wording and format since Census 2000 could have influenced reporting patterns in the 2010 Census. Additionally, changes to the Hispanic origin edit and coding procedures could have impacted the 2010 counts. These factors should especially be considered when observing changes for detailed Hispanic groups.

2. This category includes people who reported Central American Indian groups, "Canal Zone," and "Central American."

3. This category includes people who reported South American Indian groups and "South American."

4. This category includes people who reported "Hispanic" or "Latino" and other general terms.

African/Black American is representative of so many diverse groups. Nevertheless, although we are aware of the problems with these classifications, the research and data we review follow this classification approach. Second, and relatedly, with the use of the multiracial category in the 2000 census, the lines between racial groups have become rather blurred. Table 1.1 illustrates that, in 2010, more than 9 million Americans considered themselves multiracial and self-identified with two or more races (up from about 7.8 million in 2000). This increasing trend adds to the considerable limitations of population and crime data (this topic is discussed further in Chapter 2).

❖ Race, Ethnicity, and Population Trends

The 2010 U.S. Census provides the most recent data on the racial and ethnic dynamics of America. The 2010 census reported more than 308 million residents in the United States. The figures also confirmed earlier estimates that the minority population had topped 100 million. The Hispanic/Latino population, as was observed in population estimates earlier in the decade, continues to be the largest minority population and now represents 16% (50.5 million) of the U.S. population. Interestingly, their rise in population from 2000 to 2010, as outlined in Table 1.2, accounted for more than 50% of the increase in the U.S. population during the decade (Ennis, Rios-Vargas, & Albert, 2011). This increase in the Hispanic/Latino population has been largely fueled by the increasing number of Mexicans in the United States. Specifically, there were approximately 11 million more persons of Mexican descent in the United States in 2010 than there were a decade earlier. This trend has resulted in concerns not only about immigration in general but also illegal immigration. Border states, including Arizona, Texas, and California, have especially taken notice of this trend and reacted with legislation to stem the rising number of illegal immigrants. These states and others have enacted numerous measures to restrict the benefits (e.g., medical, educational) and rights (e.g., due process) of illegal immigrants in their states (Huntington, 2004; MacDonald, 2004). Other states have followed suit, contributing to a national debate on the best way to reduce the number of illegal immigrants in the United States. Ironically, later in the chapter it will become clear that such fears are not new.

Given the rapidly changing demographics of the United States, in past years, some have called for the discontinuance of the term ***minority*** (Texeira, 2005). In place of *minority*, which some believe is a "term of oppression" or a term that seeks to minimize the collective aspirations of a group, the term ***people of color*** has been suggested (Texeira, 2005). Whatever the term to be used, if current estimates are correct, it is clear that one day racial and ethnic groups now considered to be minorities will become nearly half the U.S. population (U.S. Census Bureau, 2004). In fact, estimates are that Whites will represent only 50% of the population in 2050, with Hispanics/Latinos representing nearly a quarter of the population and other racial and ethnic minorities comprising the remainder of the populace (U.S. Census Bureau, 2004). In addition to the varying population figures, Table 1.3 provides some sociodemographic information on several racial/ethnic groups.

Table 1.3

Sociodemographic Characteristics of Select Racial/Ethnic Groups

Category	White	Black/African American	Hispanic/Latino	Asian	Total Population Average
Education					
High school or higher 2009	87.10%	84.10%	61.9%	88.20%	86.70%
4 year or higher 2009	29.90%	19.30%	13.20%	52.30%	29.50%
Individuals below poverty 2009	9.40%	25.80%	25.30%	12.50%	14.30%
Median per capita income (dollars) 2009	30,941	18,135	15,063	18,653	26,530
Unemployed 2009	8.50%	14.80%	12%	7.30%	9.30%

❖ Prejudice and Discrimination

Even with the growth in the minority population, prejudice and discrimination remain a central concern. **Prejudice** is a negative attitude toward a particular group. This is usually in the form of stereotypes that often result in people making negative generalizations about an entire group. Discrimination is the "unequal treatment of a person or persons based on group membership" (Healey, 2007, p. 20). As you can imagine, having prejudicial attitudes toward a particular group, in many instances, can lead to discriminatory actions in areas such as employment, housing, and the criminal justice system. Thus, determining whether prejudice and discrimination permeate the criminal justice system is critical to understanding the role of race in justice system outcomes.

The remainder of this chapter provides a brief historical overview of each major racial/ethnic group, highlighting the complex history of race in America and how this history is intertwined with race, crime, and the criminal justice system. Readers should keep in mind that our historical review is not meant to be comprehensive. Rather, we see our review as illustrating that concerns regarding race and crime are not new and have been the norm since distinctive racial and ethnic groups from across the globe arrived in America.

❖ Historical Antecedents of Race and Crime in America

Native Americans

Prior to the arrival of Europeans in the Americas, the native people had existed on the continent for thousands of years. It is believed that they originated from eastern Asia. More specifically, it is believed that they have been in North America for the last 30,000 years, having crossed over from Asia into America on glaciers that, due to warming trends, later melted (Polk, 2006, pp. 3–4). Over time, they built complex societies throughout the Americas. Even so, on arrival in the Americas (South America and the West Indies), it is clear from their actions that Christopher Columbus and his followers viewed the native people (then referred to as "Indians," now referred to as "Native Americans") as inferior (H. J. Clarke, 1992). The brutality that followed has been painstakingly documented by firsthand observers of the massacres (De Las Casas, 1552/1993). Sale (1990) has suggested that prior to the arrival of Europeans there were about 15 million Native Americans in North America. According to Healey (2003), nearly four centuries later, in 1890, only 250,000 remained. Today, there are nearly 4.5 million American Indians/Alaskan Natives in the United States. Nonetheless, considering the historical decimation of the Native American population, some criminologists have viewed their massacre as genocide (Barak, Flavin, & Leighton, 2010).

Although some have categorized all Native Americans into one group, they represent "a diverse array of nations, with major differences in population, economies, polities, language, and customs" (Feagin & Booher Feagin, 2012, p. 139). It has been noted that their societies were more advanced than those of the Europeans who colonized them. Consequently, Europeans borrowed much from Native American agriculture and pharmacology. Furthermore, some have noted that "Benjamin Franklin, Thomas Jefferson, and other colonial leaders admired and were influenced by the democratic institutions of certain indigenous nations such as the Iroquois. Even the symbol of the United States, an eagle clutching arrows, was copied from Iroquois symbols" (Feagin & Booher Feagin, 2012, p. 146).

During their initial contact with Europeans, Native Americans assisted the newcomers with advice on how to survive in their new environment. However, once colonists became comfortable with the surroundings, they began to displace, enslave, and destroy Native American societies. In time, massacres of Native Americans became commonplace throughout the colonies, but once the Constitution was ratified (with little mention of Native Americans), treaties were enacted with the aim of ending massacres and also protecting Native American lands from further pillage. But the government did not honor the treaties. Such actions were sanctioned at the highest levels, with presidents such as Andrew Jackson encouraging the defiance of Supreme Court rulings related to Native Americans. From 1790 to the mid-1800s, there were more than 300 treaties signed between Whites and Native Americans, most of which were not honored. As a result, conflicts persisted, which led to concerns regarding "criminal aggression" and the subsequent enactment of another approach: removal. Healey (2003) wrote,

> East of the Mississippi, the period of open conflict was brought to a close by the Indian Removal Act of 1830, which dictated a policy of forced emigration to the tribes. The law required all eastern tribes to move to new lands west of the Mississippi. Some of the affected tribes went without resistance, others fought, and still others fled to Canada rather than move to a new territory. (p. 190)

This infamous "Trail of Tears," as it became known, resulted in the death of thousands of Native Americans. Nearly 40 years later, in 1867, the Doolittle Committee, which was investigating several recent massacres of Native Americans, found that much of the aggression by Native Americans around that time had occurred in response to White aggression (Harjo, 2002).

The same year of this massive removal of Native Americans, the Bureau of Indian Affairs (BIA) was established to handle matters related to this population. Following the creation of the BIA, the agency had to deal with the competing aims of the federal government. On the one hand, the government created the agency to help Native Americans; on the other hand, the military had a policy of "genocidal extermination." Nearly 60 years after the creation of the BIA, the 1887 Dawes Act provided that individual families be provided with reservation lands. While well meaning, as Feagin and Booher Feagin (2012) observed, "This policy resulted in a large-scale land sale to Whites. Through means fair and foul, the remaining 140 million acres of Indian lands were further reduced to 50 million acres by the 1930s" (p. 146). In the early part of the 20th century, the government tried to assimilate Native Americans by sending them to Indian boarding schools that were Christian-based and were used to indoctrinate Native Americans into American culture. During this process, Native Americans were forced to abandon their native language and customs. The attempt to assimilate Native Americans culminated during the 1920s with the passage of the Indian Citizenship Act of 1924, which granted all Native Americans citizenship. The end of this period saw Native Americans calling for new policies, one of which came in the form of the 1934 Indian Reorganization Act. The Act, which essentially ended the Dawes Act, "Was intended to establish Indian civil and cultural rights, allow for semi-autonomous tribal governments, and foster better economic development on reservations" (Feagin & Booher Feagin, 2012, p. 147).

As with all legislation, there were problems. Most notably, Native Americans saw this Act as giving too much power to the secretary of the interior. In addition, many Native Americans believed the Act violated their sovereignty, or their right to govern themselves, provided by previously enacted treaties.

The second half of the 20th century spurred more attempts by Native Americans to shed governmental control. In the early 1950s, Congress enacted legislation called *termination*, which "call[ed] for an end to the reservation system and to the special relationships between the tribes and the federal government" (Healey, 2004, p. 134). This process also negated previous treaties, a policy that was vigorously opposed by Native Americans. In addition, based on the specifics of the policy, "Tribes would no longer exist as legally recognized entities, and tribal lands and other resources would be placed in private hands" (Healey, 2004, p. 134). Because of this policy, many Native Americans moved to urban areas.

The decades following the enactment of the termination policy saw increasing opposition from Native Americans. After about 25 years, the policy was repealed. In 1975, the Indian Self-Determination and Education Assistance Act "increased aid to reservation schools and Native American students and increased the tribes' control over the administration of the reservations, from police forces to schools and road maintenance" (Healey, 2004, p. 136). This Act provides much of the basis on which many tribes now operate. Recent federal legislation has enabled some tribes to open gambling facilities on reservations, which, according to the National Indian Gaming Commission (n.d.), generated more than $26 billion in revenues in 2009. Other tribes have invested in additional ways to generate revenue (e.g., tax-free cigarette sales). Native Americans' move to self-determination also has resulted in suits against the federal government seeking reparations for past broken treaties. With 561 recognized tribes, Native Americans remain a notable presence in the United States.

African Americans

African Americans are another group that has had a long and arduous relationship with the United States. With the Native American population nearly completely decimated because of brutality, enslavement, and diseases that were brought to the Americas by the Spanish, Bartolome De Las Casas, the priest who accompanied Columbus to America, sought a way to stem their extermination.

De Las Casas' idea centered on not ending the slave system, but instead replacing the Native Americans with another labor force: Africans. Of De Las Casas' thinking, Finger (1959) wrote,

> Having heard that the Negroes of the Portuguese colonies in Africa were more robust than the natives of the West Indies Islands, he [De Las Casas] recommended that Black slaves be imported to take the place of Indians in server tasks of the plantations and mines. (p. 716)

Finger (1959) also described the results of De Las Casas' suggestion:

> A terrible traffic in human flesh ensued. Portuguese raiders carried the Africans from their homes, and English sailors conveyed them across the Atlantic. Spanish, Portuguese, and later English slave-owners worked the poor Black men as though they possessed no natural rights as human beings. (pp. 716–717)

As with the decimation of the Native American population, the slave trade involving Africans has been viewed as genocidal and referred to as the "African holocaust" (H. J. Clarke, 1992).

It is disputable as to when Africans initially arrived in the colonies. Some suggest that Africans arrived in America long before their arrival in the 1600s as indentured servants and slaves (Goodwin, 2008; Van Sertima, 1976). But the prevailing historical account describes Africans arriving in America in 1619 as a result of piracy (Higginbotham, 1996). When a slave ship carrying Africans headed to the West Indies was taken over by pirates and ran out of supplies, the pirates landed in Jamestown, Virginia, where they sold the Africans for food and supplies. It is important to note that, prior to their movement into perpetual slavery, Africans had existed much like the other citizens in the colony. Thus, from their arrival in 1619 to the 1660s, Africans were not considered slaves in colonial America; they were able to fulfill indentures and were fairly integrated into the life of the colony. After 1660, however, colonial legislation made it clear that Africans were to be considered slaves.

McIntyre (1992) believes the leaders of the colony came to a juncture where they needed to decide the best way to further the economic fortunes of its citizens, and they came up with several potential options. The first involved the continued use of the indentured servant system for Blacks and Whites. Second, the colonists, like the Spaniards earlier, thought about enslaving the Native Americans. Third, both Native Americans and Blacks could be enslaved. Fourth, the colonists could create a free labor system for Blacks, Whites, Indians, and immigrants. Eventually, they chose the fifth option: the enslavement of Blacks. McIntyre (1992) has suggested that this was the case because Whites had the option to appeal for protection from the British monarchy; in addition, they could appeal to general White public opinion. Enslaving Native Americans did not appeal to the colonists because besides feeling that they would not hold up under slave conditions, they were aware that the natives were familiar with the terrain, which would have permitted easy escape. For the next two centuries, African Americans would serve as the primary labor force keeping the Southern economy afloat.

Although much of the slave system was kept intact by "plantation justice," there was little interference in these matters from outside developing criminal justice institutions, except when slaves escaped or there was a slave revolt. In times of escapes, slave owners cooperated by enlisting **slave patrols** to ensure slaves were quickly captured and returned to their owners. Similarly, when slave revolts occurred, slave owners worked together to expeditiously bring a close to the uprisings that threatened the stability of the slave system (H. Aptheker, 1943/1993). Slave owners were so committed to quelling escapes and revolts that they enacted widespread "slave codes" to reduce their likelihood. Describing the slave codes, Russell (1998) wrote,

> Slave codes embodied the criminal law and procedure applied against enslaved Africans. The codes, which regulated slave life from cradle to grave, were virtually uniform across states—each with the overriding goal of upholding chattel slavery. The codes not only enumerated the applicable law but also prescribed the social boundaries for slaves—where they could go, what types of activity they could engage in, and what type of contracts they could enter into. Under the codes, the harshest criminal penalties were reserved for those acts that threatened the institution of slavery (e.g., the murder of someone White or a slave insurrection). The slave codes also penalized Whites who opposed slavery. (pp. 14–15)

In addition to the slave codes, Whites used psychology to keep the slave system intact. Claude Anderson (1994) wrote that "this process was designed to instill in Blacks strict discipline, a sense of inferiority, belief in the slave owners' superior power, acceptance of the owners' standards and a deep sense of a slave's helplessness and dependence" (p. 165). Moreover, Anderson noted that "the slave owners strove to cut Blacks off from their own history, culture, language, and community, and to inculcate White society's value system" (p. 165).

Another telling dynamic during the slave era was the way in which punishment was exacted for crimes committed by African Americans in comparison with Whites. After reviewing nearly every appellate case on antebellum slavery and race relations from 1630 to 1865, A. Leon Higginbotham, the late jurist and scholar, formulated his "Ten Precepts of American Slavery Jurisprudence" (Higginbotham, 1996; see Box 1.1). These precepts describe the foundations on which justice was distributed during this era. Most notably, to maintain the slave system, White supremacy called for little justice to be distributed to African Americans, whereas Whites were indifferent to their own criminal activity. This was most pronounced in the crime of rape. Whites might rape Black women with impunity; however, if Blacks so much as looked at White women in an unacceptable way, they were subjected to severe beatings. Table 1.4 highlights the differential punishments for African American and White crimes during the slave era.

Table 1.4

Criminal Punishments by Race in Slave Era Virginia

Crime	White Offender	Black Slave Offender
Murder (White victim) Petit treason (murder of slave owner)	Maximum penalty: death	Death
Murder (Black victim)	Rarely prosecuted	If prosecuted, whipping, hard labor, or death
Rape (White victim)	No crime	No crime, exile, or death (If rape of free Black woman, penalty could be death)
Assault (White victim)	1–10 years (if done with intent to kill)	Whipping, exile, mutilation, or death

The 1700s brought similar race and crime concerns. Some Whites, however, continued to show indifference toward their own criminal activity. Although the slave system began to expand under the encouragement of the colonial aristocracy, the slave trade began to be shunned in the international community. Subsequently, there was a movement to stop the trade, although slavery continued for those slaves already in America. Du Bois (1891) wrote about the movement to stop the slave trade as having four periods, and these were tied to large-scale efforts by Whites to circumvent the law. Du Bois wrote that there were varying levels of commitment to this initiative. The compromise of the Constitutional convention allowed the slave trade to continue until 1808; however, Du Bois's research showed that Whites never took the prohibition seriously, considering the large numbers of persons who were actively involved in trading slaves even with the threat of imprisonment.

BOX 1.1

The 10 Precepts of American Slavery Jurisprudence

1. *Inferiority:* Presume, preserve, protect, and defend the ideal of the superiority of Whites and the inferiority of Blacks.

2. *Property:* Define the slave as the master's property, maximize the master's economic interest, disregard the humanity of the slave except when it serves the master's interest, and deny slaves the fruits of their labor.

3. *Powerlessness:* Keep Blacks—whether slave or free—as powerless as possible so they will be submissive and dependent in every respect, not only to the master, but to Whites in general. Limit Blacks' accessibility to the courts and subject Blacks to an inferior system of justice with lesser rights and protections and greater punishments. Utilize violence and the powers of government to ensure the submissiveness of Blacks.

4. *Racial "purity":* Always preserve White male sexual dominance. Draw an arbitrary racial line and preserve White racial purity as thus defined. Tolerate sexual relations between White men and Black women; punish severely relations between White women and non-White men. As to children who are products of interracial sexual relations, the freedom or enslavement of the Black child is determined by the status of the mother.

5. *Manumission and free Blacks:* Limit and discourage **manumission**; minimize the number of free Blacks in the state. Confine free Blacks to a status as close to slavery as possible.

6. *Family:* Recognize no rights of the Black family; destroy the unity of the Black family; deny slaves the right of marriage; demean and degrade Black women, Black men, Black parents, and Black children, and then condemn them for their conduct and state of mind.

7. *Education and culture:* Deny Blacks any education, deny them knowledge of their culture, and make it a crime to teach those who are slaves how to read and write.

8. *Religion:* Recognize no rights of slaves to define or practice their own religions, choose their own religious leaders, or worship with other Blacks. Encourage them to adopt the religion of the White master, and teach them that God, who is White, will reward the slave who obeys the commands of his master here on earth. Use religion to justify the slave's status on earth.

9. *Liberty–resistance:* Limit Blacks' opportunity to resist, bear arms, rebel, or flee; curtail their freedom of movement, freedom of association, and freedom of expression. Deny Blacks the right to vote and to participate in government.

10. *By any means possible:* Support all measures, including the use of violence, that maximize the profitability of slavery and that legitimize racism. Oppose, by the use of violence if necessary, all measures that advocate the abolition of slavery or the diminution of White supremacy.

Du Bois found that when the U.S. government signed the Treaty of Ghent in 1814, it further committed to ending the international slave trade. As a part of this commitment, participating nations were asked to engage in searches of vessels abroad; however, the U.S. was unwilling to agree to this stipulation. Hence, many ships that flew the American flag were not American; they were slave traders who sought refuge by using the American flag. Du Bois also noted that even after the **death penalty** was instituted for slave trading, he found few instances when Whites had been convicted, much less executed, for being connected to the slave trade. In the end, this early form of White crime in America, which was particularly tied to the ruling class of slaveholders in the South, was allowed to persist because Whites were unwilling to give up the financial benefit derived from the slave trade and system (C. Anderson, 1994; E. Williams, 1944).

During the mid-1850s, there was a crisis brewing regarding slavery. Although a civil war seemed imminent, the North and South tried to delay the inevitable. Of particular concern during this period was the acquisition of territories in the southwest portion of the United States. The debate centered on which states should be slave states—if any at all. Predictably, Northerners argued to keep such states free, whereas Southerners wanted to preserve the institution of slavery, so they argued the reverse. Vigorous debate led to the well-known Compromise of 1850, which essentially gave each side a portion of what it wanted. For example, California entered the Union as a Free State, while other territories would enter the Union without mention of slavery (Franklin & Moss, 2000). One of the provisions of the Compromise led to the enactment of the Fugitive Slave Law of 1850.

A revision of the 1793 Fugitive Slave Act, the Fugitive Slave Law (or Act) of 1850 was structured to ensure the return of runaway slaves. The Act called for the appointment of numerous commissioners who were authorized to hire deputies who all could "enlist the aid of bystanders or posses to enforce the act" (Kennedy, 1997, p. 83). Furthermore, monetary incentives were tied to this process. For example, "commissioners would be paid a fee of $5 in each case in which he determined that a slave master was *not* [emphasis added] entitled to an alleged fugitive slave, and would be paid a fee of $10 in each case in which he determined that a master was entitled to the accused person" (Kennedy, 1997, pp. 83–84). Finally, to illustrate the seriousness with which the enforcement of the Act was to be taken, there was a stipulation that if a U.S. Marshall refused or neglected to execute warrants issued by commissioners, he would be fined $1,000 (Kennedy, 1997). The enactment of this Act and other provisions of the Compromise still could not stop the move toward civil war. Thus, not long after the notorious 1857 Dred Scott decision that continued to increase the tensions between North and South, the country headed into the Civil War in 1861.

Following the Emancipation Proclamation in 1863, which freed the slaves in the Confederate states, and the enactment of the Thirteenth Amendment in 1865, which ended slavery throughout the United States, many African Americans chose to remain in the South. Others dreamed of migrating north and starting anew. Unfortunately, Southern landowners were unwilling to part so easily with their former free labor force. Therefore, following emancipation, they enacted the **Black codes**. These codes were an assortment of laws that targeted poor Whites and African Americans. Some scholars have argued that the laws were specifically created so that a significant number of African Americans could be returned to plantation owners through the **convict-lease system** (Du Bois, 1901/2002; Myers, 1998; Oshinsky, 1996). The convict-lease system allowed states to lease convict labor to private landowners. Although some poor Whites also were caught up in this legal system, most of those being leased out to Southern landowners were African Americans. Before long, whereas previously they had engaged only in trivial offenses, African Americans began to engage in more bold and brutal offenses, which shocked Southern Whites who had created the system (Du Bois, 1901/2002).

Prior to the Civil War, primarily Whites had been incarcerated in Southern penal institutions, and one product of the massive changes in the South was the increasing number of African Americans found in prisons. Following this period, along with the convict-lease system, states such as Mississippi ran notorious state prisons that put the prisoners to work. Parchman Farm was one of the most infamous (Oshinsky, 1996). The Reconstruction Era also brought the formal advent of hate groups. Groups such as the Knights of White Camellia, the Constitutional Union Guards, the Pale Faces, the White Brotherhood, the Council of Safety, the '76 Association, and the infamous Knights of the Ku Klux Klan were all formed to ensure White supremacy ruled in the South following Emancipation and the passage of the Thirteenth Amendment in 1865, which officially abolished slavery. These groups wreaked havoc on African American and other citizens, who were targets of their hatred. **Lynching** became the means used to intimidate and handle those who challenged the racist White power structure (see Figure 1.3). It is generally accepted that, between 1882 and 1930, "At least three thousand Black men, women, and children were murdered by White gangs during this era of the lynch mob, and this toll does not count other racially motivated murders or Black deaths from race riots" (Beck & Tolnay, 1995, p. 121). These indiscriminate killings of African Americans (and some Native Americans and Spanish-speaking minorities), usually by hanging, were typically carried out to avenge some unsubstantiated crime committed by an African American or other "undesirable" minority against a White person (Zangrando, 1980). In most instances, rape was alleged to justify these horrific actions.

The Ku Klux Klan emerged as the leading hate organization. In an effort to suppress African American economic equality and pride, the Klan beat African Americans for minor things, such as "Black women . . . dressing in brightly-colored clothes, and men for being impolite, talking back to Whites or failing to say 'Yes Sir'" (Katz, 1986, p. 39). In many jurisdictions, Klan activities were condoned by local law enforcement. As a result, many African Americans lost faith in the justice system and stopped reporting crimes altogether (Katz, 1986).

On the eve of the 20th century, the *Plessy v. Ferguson* (1896) "separate but equal" decision was hailed by Southern bigots. This decision was significant in that it gave Whites legal support to enforce some of their ideas concerning White supremacy and the separation of the races. Furthermore, this decision enabled law enforcement officials to take action against African Americans who sought basic services now reserved for Whites. Du Bois (1899) clearly saw the danger of state-sanctioned segregation, writing,

> [Another] cause of Negro crime is the exaggerated and unnatural separation in the South of the best classes of Whites and Blacks. A drawing of the color line, that extends to street-cars, elevators, and cemeteries, which leaves no common ground of meeting, no medium for communication, no ties of sympathy between two races who live together, and whose interests are at bottom one—such a discrimination is more than silly, it is dangerous. (p. 1357)

Ten years after the turn of the 20th century, African Americans were primarily Southern. Meier and Rudwick (1970) observed that "approximately three out of four lived in rural areas and nine out of ten lived in the South" (p. 213). The "Great Migration," however, changed the landscape of the North and South. By the 1950s, "Negroes were mainly an urban population, almost three fourths of them being city-dwellers" (Meier & Rudwick, 1970, p. 213). During this era, African Americans crowded into Northern cities in search of job opportunities; what they found, however, were overcrowded urban areas with assorted European immigrants either seeking similar opportunities or already established in the low-skill, low-wage jobs that African Americans had hoped to receive.

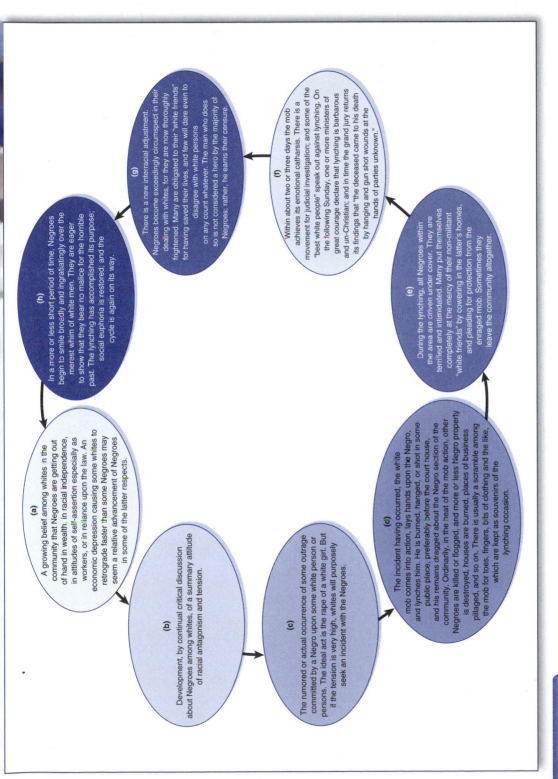

Figure 1.3

Oliver Cox's Lynching Cycle

Source: Adapted from Cox (1945).

(a) A growing belief among whites in the community that Negroes are getting out of hand in wealth, in racial independence, in attitudes of self-assertion especially as workers, or in reliance upon the law. An economic depression causing some whites to retrograde faster than some Negroes may seem a relative advancement of Negroes in some of the latter respects.

(b) Development, by continual critical discussion about Negroes among whites, of a summary attitude of racial antagonism and tension.

(c) The rumored or actual occurrence of some outrage committed by a Negro upon some white person or persons. The ideal act is the rape of a white girl. But if the tension is very high, whites will purposely seek an incident with the Negroes.

(d) The incident having occurred, the white mob comes into action, lays hands upon the Negro, and lynches him. He is burned, hanged, or shot in some public place, preferably before the court house, and his remains dragged about the Negro section of the community. Ordinarily, in the heat of the mob action, other Negroes are killed or flogged, and more or less Negro property is destroyed, houses are burned, places of business pillaged, and so on. There is usually a scramble among the mob for toes, fingers, bits of clothing and the like, which are kept as souvenirs of the lynching occasion.

(e) During the lynching, all Negroes within the area are driven under cover. They are terrified and intimidated. Many put themselves completely at the mercy of their non-militant "white friends" by cowering in the latter's homes, and pleading for protection from the enraged mob. Sometimes they leave the community altogether.

(f) Within about two or three days the mob achieves its emotional catharsis. There is a movement for judicial investigation; and some of the "best white people" speak out against lynching. On the following Sunday, one or more ministers of great courage declare that lynching is barbarous and un-Christian; and in time the grand jury returns its findings that "the deceased came to his death by hanging and gun shot wounds at the hands of parties unknown."

(g) There is a new interracial adjustment. Negroes become exceedingly circumspect in their dealing with whites, for they are now thoroughly frightened. Many are obligated to their "white friends" for having saved their lives, and few will dare even to disagree with white persons on any count whatever. The man who does so is not considered a hero by the majority of Negroes; rather, he earns their censure.

(h) In a more or less short period of time, Negroes begin to smile broadly and ingratiatingly over the merast whim of white men. They are eager to show that they bear no malice for the horrible past. The lynching has accomplished its purpose; social euphoria is restored; and the cycle is again on its way.

17

African American women were able to secure employment in domestic service, where, unfortunately, White men often sexually assaulted them. Writing of the dilemma this posed, scholar activist Angela Davis (1981) noted,

> From Reconstruction to the present, Black women household workers have considered sexual abuse perpetrated by the "man of the house" as one of their major occupational hazards. Time after time they have been victims of extortion on the job, compelled to choose between sexual submission and absolute poverty for themselves and their families. (p. 91)

African American men who did find work were also relegated to menial jobs and, from 1890 to 1930, were often used as strikebreakers (Massey & Denton, 1993). Their role as strikebreakers often led to racial violence in the North, which repeatedly culminated in race riots. From 1900 to 1919, there was a steady stream of race riots throughout the North. The riots continued into the 1920s, with Whites resisting integration "by any means necessary." As Massey and Denton (1993) documented,

> A wave of bombings followed the expansion of Black residential areas in the cities throughout the north. In Chicago, fifty-eight homes were bombed between 1917 and 1921, one every twenty days; and one Black real estate agent, Jesse Binga, had his home and office bombed seven times in one year. (p. 35)

Devastating riots followed in Tulsa, Oklahoma in 1921 (Hirsch, 2002) and Rosewood, Florida in 1923 (Russell, 1998). Because of the continuing racial tensions related to labor competition and integration attempts, race riots persisted well into the 1960s (Grimshaw, 1969).

In the 1930s, the "Scottsboro Boys" drew international attention to the plight of African Americans. The case involved several African American boys who were traveling in a freight train with several White boys and two White girls. After a fight ensued, the White boys were ejected from the train. At the next stop in Scottsboro, Alabama, the girls got off the train and claimed they had been gang-raped by the nine African American boys. Playing on the worst fears of Southern White men, the girls' accusations resulted in a mob being quickly formed in anticipation of the lynching of the boys (Carter, 1969). With the protection of law enforcement, however, the boys made it to trial. Following several trials, the boys were found guilty and received the death penalty. Although it was later revealed that the claims were a hoax, the boys spent the better part of their youth and early adulthood incarcerated for crimes they didn't commit.

During the 1930s and 1940s, there was continued interest in the subject of crime among African Americans. In the last edition of his landmark text, *Principles of Criminology* (1947), pioneering criminologist Edwin Sutherland devoted a chapter to "crime in relation to race and nativity." He first noted that, much like today, African Americans were "arrested, convicted, and committed to prisons approximately three times as frequently as White persons" (Sutherland, 1947, p. 121). Sutherland also cautioned that some of these statistics "probably reflect a bias against all of the minority races but especially against the Negro" (p. 121).

By the early 1950s, African Americans and other ethnic groups were still struggling to survive in an increasingly segregated and hostile America. Some turned to crime, whereas others turned to the United Nations for assistance. In 1951, African Americans petitioned the United Nations and charged the U.S. government with genocide against African Americans (Patterson, 1951/1970). Although the United Nations did not respond to the petition, African

Americans had made the commitment to try to change their position within American society. This movement was given a further push by the 1955 kidnapping and slaying of Emmett Till in Mississippi.

The shocking and brutal killing of the 14-year-old boy for "disrespecting" a White woman spurred a movement that picked up steam with the Montgomery boycott, which started on December 5, 1955. The civil rights movement showed the national and international communities the depth of racial hatred and interracial strife in America. The demonstrations that defined the movement were seen by millions on TV, and the brutality of the police toward nonviolent demonstrators spoke to the oppressive role the police played in the African American and other minority communities.

By the 1960s, according to figures from Tuskegee Institute (Zangrando, 1980), lynchings were rare events; however, Whites had successfully used the practice to discourage any serious level of integration. Therefore, although Thurgood Marshall and his colleagues were successful in the landmark *Brown v. Board of Education* (1954) case, minority communities did not substantially change for decades. Because of "the White strategy of ghetto containment and tactical retreat before an advancing color line" (Massey & Denton, 1993, p. 45), substantial underclass communities were in existence by the 1970s. This bred a level of poverty and despair that fostered the continuation of the African American criminal classes and organized crime. The riots of the 1960s were a response to the long-standing troublesome conditions in some of these cities (National Advisory Commission on Civil Disorders, 1968).

When African Americans (especially those that comprised a growing middle class) were finally able to take advantage of the opportunities forged by the civil rights movement and desegregation, many of them left inner-city areas (an event known as "Black flight"). Unfortunately, they had brought an important level of stability to those communities. As a result of this exodus, those communities are now composed of what Wilson (1987) describes as "the truly disadvantaged." They are heavily dependent on the underground economy for survival (see Venkatesh, 2006, 2008), which has likely contributed to the overrepresentation of African Americans throughout the U.S. criminal justice system.

In the mid part of the first decade of the 2000s, the plight of the **truly disadvantaged** was brought to the forefront of American consciousness with the 2005 Hurricane Katrina fiasco, in which the government—at all levels—failed to provide an adequate response to the needs of poor and mostly Black New Orleans residents (Dyson, 2006; Potter, 2007). Moreover, in the absence of government response, citizens who took matters into their own hands have been portrayed as criminals (Russell-Brown, 2006). Although research has been inconclusive as to whether crime has increased in cities where evacuees were relocated, this truly disadvantaged population continues to be stereotyped and faces few options to survive in the aftermath of the devastation left by Hurricane Katrina.

Even with the many struggles encountered by African Americans and other Black ethnic groups, and the historical fixation on their criminality, they have contributed to every aspect of American life, from the toiling of the soil in the South and factory work in the North to produce the wealth that made America what it is, to the innumerable scientific, musical, and artistic contributions that are now considered staples of American culture.

White Ethnics

During the early 1600s, while the slave trade in South America and the West Indies was going on, the British colonized parts of what would later become the American colonies.

This led to many of the same kinds of conflicts with Native Americans that the Spanish had quelled with unimaginable brutality. Although the British saw the colonies as somewhere they could send criminals and other undesirables, they also saw opportunity for monetary gain, so they encouraged immigration to the colonies. Some came freely, whereas others used indentures to get themselves to the New World. These arrangements allowed them to work for a period of time to pay for their travel expenses to the colonies. Once their indentures were completed, immigrants were free to pursue whatever opportunities they desired. In addition to British immigrants, Germans and Italians were among the first to immigrate to America. Many began to arrive in the early 1600s, settling first in New Amsterdam (New York) and later in Pennsylvania (Sowell, 1981). Given this rich history of European immigration to the United States, we briefly review the history of several **White ethnic** groups. Although our review does not cover every White ethnic group that immigrated to America, we provide discussions of several of the major groups. We begin with an overview of the experience of German Americans. This is followed by a review of the experiences of Italian Americans, Irish Americans, Jewish Americans, and Arab Americans. As you will see, many of these groups have similar stories regarding their reason for making the long journey to America. In addition, many have had nearly identical experiences on their arrival in America.

German Americans

Faust (1927) places the first German in America at the time of Leif Eriksson's pioneering journey that landed him in North America 500 years prior to Columbus's arrival. Among Eriksson's crew was a German named Tyrker, who "is credited with discovering grapes in North America and therefore also naming the new land Vineland" (Rippley, 1976, p. 22). Not until the 1500s was there a settlement of Germans in America. Located in Port Royal, South Carolina, the settlement was composed of Huguenots (French Protestants) and Alsatian and Hessian Protestants (both of German origin). The settlement, however, was destroyed by the Spaniards, and thus only lasted four years, from 1562 to 1566. The next wave of German immigrants arrived with the first settlers in Jamestown in 1607. Often referred to as the "Dutch," which is likely "a linguistic slip that occurred because the word 'Dutch' so closely resembles a German's designation for himself, *Deutsch*" (Rippley, 1976, p. 24), they were often mistreated during the early colonial period. Consequently, they sympathized with the plight of Native Americans and "chose to remain with the Indians, preferring their friendship to that of the 'gentlemen' of Jamestown" (Faust, 1927, p. 8).

In the late 1600s, 13 German families arrived in Philadelphia and represented the beginning of mass German immigration to the United States (Coppa & Curran, 1976). Many of these immigrants came at the urging of William Penn, who told them of the religious freedoms in his colony of Pennsylvania (Sowell, 1981). Others came as a result of the disarray in their homeland. Of this, Coppa and Curran (1976) wrote, "The havoc wrought by the Thirty Years' War (1618–1648) devastated Germany for many decades: commerce declined; industry was crippled; and intellectual life sustained a deep if not mortal blow" (p. 45). The German population also increased because of the use of indentures to get them to America. Hence, those who wanted to immigrate to America signed contracts that paid their way. As one might imagine, this was shady business. Sowell (1981) writes that

> the indentured servants were preyed upon by the dishonest. Some ship captains provided inadequate food or sold them into longer periods of bondage than actually

required to work off the cost off their transportation. Germans who could not under-stand English were particularly vulnerable. (p. 49)

As a consequence of all these events, by the time of the Revolutionary War, there were about 225,000 German Americans in the colonies (Rippley, 1976, p. 29).

Immigration from Germany in the 1800s began slowly, but because of continuing issues in the homeland, Germans continued to hear from other groups of the promise of America. As such, around the 1830s, the number of German immigrants rose again and continued to increase throughout the 19th century. By the 1900 census, there were more than 2.6 mil-lion Germans in America (Faust, 1927). These formidable numbers made them a significant force in American culture and politics. They were outstanding farmers and glassmakers and have been credited with setting up the first paper mill. Culturally, they incorporated German chocolate cake, coleslaw, sauerkraut, hotdogs, and hamburgers into American life. Well-known Germans such as Albert Einstein, Babe Ruth, Lou Gehrig, and Presidents Hoover and Eisenhower, among others, helped shape sports, science, and political life in America.

Given their large numbers in the American colonies following the Revolutionary War, Germans, unlike some other ethnic groups, were accepted early in the development of the country. Consequently, throughout the 1800s and 1900s, there were few bumps along the path toward full **assimilation**. An exception to this was during World War I, when America went to war with Germany. The anti-German sentiment was strong, but as Sowell (1981) notes, the animus was not restricted to Germans in Germany:

> Anti-German feeling among Americans was not confined to Germany, but extended quickly to the whole German culture and to German Americans, many of whom were sympathetic to their former homeland. German books were removed from the shelves of American libraries, German-language courses were canceled from the public schools, readers and advertisers boycotted German-American newspapers. (p. 65)

Anti-German sentiment returned with World War II; however, it never approached the level of World War I. Also, it was Japanese Americans who caught the ire of patriotic Americans. After World War II, German Americans further assimilated by intermarriage and their increasing advancement within key institutions in American society. Today, Germans are no longer a distinct Census category. In fact, looking back at their history, they have long been considered a significant segment of the White American population.

Italian Americans

Centuries after Christopher Columbus "discovered" the New World other Italians would take advantage of his discovery by immigrating to the American colonies. Although few in num-ber, Italians were among the earliest immigrants to arrive in colonial America. The small numbers were not simply because of the disinterest in immigrating to America. Some juris-dictions, such as Maryland, only allowed the settlement of immigrants from Britain (Iorizzo & Mondello, 2006). But as a result of labor shortages, these laws started to disappear in the colonies. By 1648, Maryland had also changed its practice and passed legislation that "encouraged French, Dutch and Italians to come to its shores" (Iorizzo & Mondello, 2006, p. 26). To further encourage immigration to the colonies, in 1649 the Toleration Act was passed, which ensured religious freedom for Catholics. From the 1600s through the mid-1800s, immigration from Italy was steady but, mirroring the trend of other White ethnic groups, really picked up in the late 1800s. Those Italians who immigrated were trying to escape the turmoil in their homeland or simply looking for better economic opportunities. Among them were not only poor people, but various artists and political dissidents who were middle class and others who were revolutionaries. Settling mostly in northern cities, they contributed to the diversity of cities such as Boston, New York, and Philadelphia (Iorizzo & Mondello, 2006).

By 1920, more than 4 million Italians had arrived in the United States. This was not necessarily a welcome development. Leading up to this period, during the late 1800s and early 1900s, heavy anti-Italian sentiment had resulted in numerous killings and hangings (Marger, 1997). Therefore, to stem Italian immigration to the United States, the Immigration Act of 1924 placed a stringent quota on the number of Italians who could immigrate to the country. In 1929, that number "was only 5,802, compared with 65,721 for British Immigrants" (Feagin & Booher Feagin, 2012, p. 98). Similar to the experience of other ethnic immigrant groups, their religion, Catholicism, also became a point of contention, along with stinging stereotypes, which, as noted in the experience of other ethnic groups, have often been created to demonize new immigrants. Italians were perceived by many to be "dangerous" and "inferior" to other European immigrants. The perception was enhanced by the image of the Italian Mafia (also referred to as the "Black Hand"; Marger, 1997).

The belief that Italians were heavily involved in organized crime likely originated from the fact that many of the immigrants came from Sicily, where the mafia was a social institution. However, in America, Italian organized crime became an obsession. The terms *organized crime* and *mafia* became synonymous with Italians. They were considered a lawless race. One congressional report described them as morally deficient, excitable, superstitious, and vengeful (Iorizzo & Mondello, 2006). These negative and racist characterizations were clearly unfair considering that the Irish, German, Jewish, and Polish immigrants had preceded them in organized criminal activity (Iorizzo & Mondello, 2006). In fact, as Sowell (1981) has aptly noted, "Organized crime was an existing American institution, and the Italian Americans had to literally fight their way into it" (p. 125). Despite the prevailing criminal stereotype, in the early part of the 20th century, Italians had "*lower* [emphasis added] crime rates than other Americans" (Sowell, 1981, p. 125). Although Italians eventually assimilated into American society and are presently subsumed under the White racial category, some of the early stereotypes remain.

Irish Americans

According to Meagher (2005), "The first Irishman came to America in 1584 as part of Sir Walter Raleigh's ill-fated expedition to the Outer Banks of North Carolina" (p. 1). Later, the Irish came in great numbers to America, looking for opportunities to escape extreme poverty in Ireland. Meagher has noted that 60% of those who came in the 17th century did so by way of indentures. Others were given the option of leaving Ireland instead of serving a prison sentence for a criminal conviction. Those who came in the mid-1800s as a result of the potato famine in Ireland, which killed (through starvation and disease) an estimated 1 million people, contributed to the exponential increase of Irish Americans. For example, during the 100-year period from 1820 to 1920, about 5 million Irish arrived in America (Meagher, 2005). They settled in areas throughout the country; however, many landed in northern states such as New York, Massachusetts, Pennsylvania, and Illinois. In addition, by the early 1860s, one-third of the Irish population could be found in the western and midwestern parts of the United States. Wherever the Irish settled, because of the prevailing nativist views and their predominantly Catholic backgrounds (some were Protestant), they often were ostracized and relegated to the worst areas of cities.

Historians have generally agreed that few immigrant groups have encountered such harsh conditions as did the Irish in 19th-century America. Many of them brought alcohol and fighting habits to American shores. As a result, they often caught the attention of police officials, who called police vans "paddy wagons" because so many Irish were occupants. In some cities, such as New York, the areas where the Irish dominated were some of the toughest.

The highly acclaimed 2002 movie *Gangs of New York* depicts the immigration of the Irish to New York during a period when there was a strong sense of resentment and hate directed toward immigrants. Largely based on actual events, the movie shows how ethnic antagonism between the native population (English) and newest immigrant group (Irish) resulted in brutal gang wars. The Irish are portrayed as a criminogenic ethnic group who bring their bad habits to an already overcrowded and notorious district of New York. The movie culminates with the "Draft Riots," which were provoked by ethnic tensions and Whites who objected to being drafted into the Union army to fight for the liberation of African American slaves, while they themselves were struggling to survive. Prior to the September 11, 2001, terrorist attack on the World Trade Center buildings, the Draft Riot was considered the single event to have caused the largest loss of life in New York City history (more than 1,000 deaths).

Not until the second- and third-generation families did the Irish truly start to become a part of the American social fabric. In fact, during the early and mid-20th century, they became major contributors to the arts and were prominently featured in major motion pictures. Nevertheless, they were still faced with challenges.

Restrictive immigration quotas in the 1920s also hit them hard, and there were still barriers in place that restricted them from reaching their full potential occupationally. For example, Irish women, unlike other White ethnic females, had to take jobs as domestic servants to make ends meet. As noted previously with the experience of Black female domestics, these were dangerous jobs that often resulted in sexual harassment, rape, or, out of desperation, a descent into prostitution (Meagher, 2005). Nevertheless, large numbers of them headed to college, and research shows that in the 1920s and 1940s, they were as successful as the native-born European immigrants. By 1960, "Irish occupational status exceeded national averages and was higher than every other white ethnic group except Jews" (Meagher, 2005, p. 132). In short, after initial resistance to their presence in America, the Irish had fulfilled the promise of the "American Dream." It is significant that despite the resistance to their presence in America, the Irish were able to swiftly rise out of the doldrums of their early American experience. This is likely attributable to the fact that, as time went on, the Irish became integrated into the fabric of American society and assimilated into the status of White Americans (T. W. Allen, 1994; Ignatiev, 1996).

Jewish Americans

Interestingly, the first Jews who arrived in America were of Hispanic origin. In 1654, 23 Sephardic Jews from Spain and Portugal arrived in New Amsterdam (Finkelstein, 2007). Their arrival in the New World began with controversy. On arrival, they were sued by the captain of the ship that brought them to America because their fares had not been paid. To pay their fares, "The court ordered two of the new arrivals imprisoned and the belongings of all 23 passengers sold at auction" (Finkelstein, 2007, p. 31). Moreover, the governor of New

Amsterdam, Peter Stuyvesant, wanted them to leave. In short, he viewed Jews as repugnant and originating from a "deceitful race" (Finkelstein, 2007, p. 31). Stuyvesant was so anti-Semitic that he banned Jews from building a synagogue and restricted their enlistment in the military. Thus, the first American synagogue was not built until the 1720s. Henceforth, Jews began to branch out and started to become somewhat more accepted within American society. This was fostered by the advent of American Freemasonry, in which Christians and Jews interacted. Although discrimination remained a part of the Jewish American landscape, Article VI of the U.S. Constitution, which banned religious discrimination, provided some respite for Jews who aspired to public office.

The 19th century saw a considerable increase in the Jewish presence in America. Whereas there were only 3,000 Jews in America in 1820, 40 years later there were 200,000 (Finkelstein, 2007). Tied together by religious and cultural traditions, many arrived from Russia, Poland, and other Eastern European countries, where they had long been persecuted for their religious beliefs and customs. To preserve their culture, in 1843, 12 German Jews gathered in a New York café and founded B'nai B'rith, which means "Sons of the Covenant." The mission of the organization was ambitious, but it laid the grounds for an organization that, by 1861, was "operating in every major Jewish community in America" (Sachar, 1993, p. 71). The mission of the organization was as follows:

> Uniting Israelites in the work of promoting their highest interests and those of humanity; of developing and elevating the mental and moral character of the people of our faith; of inculcating the purest principles of philanthropy, honor, and patriotism; of supporting science and art; of alleviating the wants of the victims of persecution; providing for, protecting and assisting the widow and orphan on the broadest principles of humanity. (Finkelstein, 2007, p. 64)

Recounting Jewish history, Feagin and Booher Feagin (2012) write,

> From the Egyptian and Roman persecutions in ancient times to massacres in Spain in the 1400s to brutal pogroms in Russia in the 1880s to German Nazi massacres, Jews might be regarded as the most widely oppressed racial or ethnic group in world history. (p. 115)

Seeking relief from persecution in European countries, Jews continued to arrive in America en masse. In the 40 years from 1880 to 1920, 2 million Jews arrived in America. As the persecution continued, many more arrived and eventually assimilated into the American way of life while maintaining their Jewish traditions. However, coinciding with this significant wave of immigration was an increase in anti-Semitism. Describing this turbulent period for Jews, Finkelstein (2007) writes, "Much of this was fueled by the stereotypes brought over from Europe by the large numbers of newly arrived Christian immigrants. Jews faced growing restrictions in housing, employment, and education" (p. 79).

During the first quarter of the 20th century, the mass immigration and squalid living conditions of Jews resulted in abundant numbers of Jewish youth hanging out on the streets. This produced rising juvenile delinquency rates, which became the target of a number of Jewish organizations. In a similar vein, whereas the 1920s and 1930s were periods of considerable Jewish progress, Brodkin Sacks (1997) noted that Jewish success in organized crime was also critical to their upward mobility. She specifically mentioned that "Arnold Rothstein transformed crime from a haphazard, small-scale activity into a well-organized and well-financed business operation. Consider also Detroit's Purple Gang, Murder Incorporated in New York, and a host of other big-city Jewish gangs in organized crime" (p. 399). These illicit activities were also found among other ethnic groups striving to move up the social ladder, albeit through criminality, in urban areas.

The period also saw quotas established restricting the number of Jews who could attend prestigious universities such as Harvard. Thus, although they were progressing in terms of their status in American society, there remained barriers to full assimilation. Jews, however, continued to be successful in educational pursuits and small businesses. In 1921, Albert Einstein won the Nobel Prize in Physics, and Jews were among the most successful immigrants. Because of their success in education, Finkelstein (2007) notes that "by the end of World War II . . . most Jews had established themselves firmly into the middle class, with large numbers employed in 'economically secure' jobs as civil servants: Teachers, accountants, lawyers, and medical professionals" (pp. 129–130). As a result, many moved out of the ghettos and into the suburbs, where they were largely unwelcome. In time, however, Jews assimilated and were also categorized as White Americans (Brodkin, 1999; Brodkin Sacks, 1997).

Each of the aforementioned White ethnic groups came to America seeking prosperity but was immediately thrust into dire socioeconomic conditions. In many instances, crime provided the means to rise above their condition (Bell, 1960; Light, 1977). Initially, each group was labeled criminal, but after a period of decades, most were able to rise out of their situations and assimilate into America—as White Americans (Gans, 2005). In recent years, some Whites have become concerned about their status as White Americans. This has led to a variety of nativist movements. These movements have suggested that Whites are becoming a racially oppressed group. Box 1.2 reviews the concerns being expressed by some Whites. One group that is currently classified by the U.S. Census Bureau as White American that, in the last decade, has had a divergent experience from other White ethnics is Arab Americans. We provide a brief overview of their experience in the next section.

BOX 1.2

Are Whites Racially Oppressed?

(CNN)—They marched on Washington to reclaim civil rights.

They complained of voter intimidation at the polls.

They called for ethnic studies programs to promote racial pride.

They are, some say, the new face of racial oppression in this nation—and their faces are white.

"We went from being a privileged group to all of a sudden becoming whites, the new victims," says Charles Gallagher, a sociologist at La Salle University in Pennsylvania who researches white racial attitudes and was baffled to find that whites see themselves as a minority.

"You have this perception out there that whites are no longer in control or the majority. Whites are the new minority group."

Call it racial jujitsu: A growing number of white Americans are acting like a racially oppressed majority. They are adopting the language and protest tactics of an embattled minority group, scholars and commentators say.

(Continued)

(Continued)

They point to these signs of racial anxiety:

- A recent Public Religion Research Institute poll found 44% of Americans surveyed identify discrimination against whites as being just as big as bigotry aimed at blacks and other minorities. The poll found 61% of those identifying with the Tea Party held that view, as did 56% of Republicans and 57% of white evangelicals.
- More colleges are offering courses in "Whiteness Studies" as white Americans cope with becoming what one commentator calls a "dispossessed majority group."
- A Texas group recently formed the "Former Majority Association for Equality" to offer college scholarships to needy white men. Colby Bohannan, the group's president, says white men don't have scholarship options available to minorities. "White males are definitely not a majority" anymore, he says.
- U.S. Census Bureau projections that whites will become a minority by 2050 are fueling fears that whiteness no longer represents the norm. This fear has been compounded by the recent recession, which hit whites hard.
- Conservative talk-show host Rush Limbaugh argued in a radio show that Republicans are an "oppressed minority" in need of a "civil rights movement" because its members willingly sit in the "back of the bus" and "are afraid of the fire hoses and the dogs."
- Fox talk-show host Glenn Beck led a march on Washington (attended primarily by white people) to "restore honor" and once called President Obama a racist with a "deep-seated hatred for white people and white culture." He later said he regretted making that comment.
- Conservative news outlets ran a number of stories last summer highlighting an incident from the 2008 elections, in which activists from the New Black Panther Party appeared to be intimidating voters at a polling place. Those claims were never proven.

Mass rallies in Washington, voter intimidation at the polls, creating ethnic studies programs at colleges to promote racial self-awareness—it sounds like a script from a civil rights documentary.

But not everyone buys that script. Mona Charen, a conservative columnist for the National Review, challenges that view with this question: If more white Americans feel like an embattled minority, why did they elect President Barack Obama?

"Did they become racist after electing the first black president?" she asks.

Charen says the United States today is "incredibly tolerant and open."

Sure, she says, there are individuals who nurture racial animosity, but most Americans deserve praise for looking past race.

The proof, she says, isn't just in the fact that the nation elected its first black president. She cites the rise of more interracial couples.

"When I grew up, it was incredibly rare to see interracial couples," she says. "People would turn their heads on the streets. Now it's so common that no one notices it anymore."

When White Is No Longer the Norm

The notion that many white Americans feel anxious about their race is not new. Today, however, economic anxieties are feeding those racial fears, says Tim Wise, author of "White Like Me."

Wise says the recession hit blue-collar, white Americans hard, financially and psychologically.

Many white Americans have lived under the assumption that if they worked hard, they would be rewarded. Now more white Americans are sharing unemployment lines with "those people"—black and brown, Wise says.

"For the first time since the Great Depression, white Americans have been confronted with a level of economic insecurity that we're not used to," he says. "It's not so new for black and brown folks, but for white folks, this is something we haven't seen since the Depression."

Economic insecurity is what Colby Bohannan says convinced him to form the "Former Majority Association for Equality." The association is awarding $500 scholarships to five deserving white men because they aren't eligible for scholarships reserved for women and minorities, he says.

"Living in America, you hear about this minority or that minority, but it's never been used in the same sense for Caucasian Americans," Bohannan says. "There was no one for white males until we came around."

Bohannan says the formation of his group was not motivated by racism, nor will it accept donations from hate groups.

"We're not trying to promote racial bigotry," Bohannan says. "All we're about is helping college students trying to better their lives who happen to be white males."

Some white Americans not only feel ignored in higher education; they feel excluded by popular culture.

The face of America is changing, says Wise, author of "White Like Me." American culture has become so multicultural that many of the nation's icons—including celebrities, sports heroes, and other leaders—are people of color.

"The very definition of being an American is going through a profound change," Wise says. "We can no longer take it for granted that we (whites) are the dictionary definition of an American."

This racial unease is more pronounced among older white Americans, who grew up in an era where America's icons were virtually all white, Wise says.

"The idea that we're losing our country is something that's not going to have a lot of resonance for someone under 30," Wise says. "These are white folks who don't remember the country that their parents are talking about."

With white no longer the norm, more white Americans are hitting the books to ask a question that few felt a need to ask before: What does it mean to be white?

"Whiteness Studies" began popping up in a few isolated academic institutions in the 1990s. Now such programs can be found in places such as the University of Wisconsin and the University of Utah. These courses examine what whiteness has meant during different periods of American history.

For many decades, white people saw themselves as individuals, not as members of a race, says Matt Wray, a sociologist at Temple University in Pennsylvania, who writes books about white studies.

"We are often offended if someone calls attention to our race as shaping how we view the world," says Wray, author of "Not Quite White." "We don't like to be pigeon-holed that way. Non-white Americans are seldom afforded this luxury of seeing themselves as individuals, disconnected from any race."

Still, Wray says anxiety among whites over their place in America is nothing new. Some 19th century whites worried about slave revolts. During segregation, some worried about blacks they labeled as "uppity Negroes."

"Whites have never really felt terribly secure in their majority status," he says. "It's often said that it is lonely at the top, but it's also an anxious place to be, because you live in constant fear of falling."

"Diversity Is Not Strength"

Some white commentators are unapologetic about this racial anxiety.

Peter Brimelow, author of "Alien Nation: Common Sense About America's Immigration Disaster," asserts that much of white America's anxiety derives from living under a black president and changing demographics.

Diversity, he says, "is not strength."

Brimelow's website, VDARE.COM, has been described as a hate site by the Southern Poverty Law Center, a group that tracks extremist groups in the U.S.

Some may see him as extreme, but Brimelow argues in his columns that more white Americans are moving toward his stance on immigration and other issues.

He cites as proof the rise of the Tea Party movement and the racial makeup of Beck's march on Washington. He says more whites recognize, even if it's only on a subliminal level, that they have common interests to defend.

"Of course, they would deny this, quite sincerely, if you put it to them because the idea of whites defending their interests as whites is quite new," he says. "Americans are trained to think that any explicit defense of white interests is 'racist.'"

(Continued)

(Continued)

James Edwards, host of the "Political Cesspool" radio show, isn't shy about naming those interests. He says white Americans have become the "dispossessed majority" and that coming demographic changes may turn the United States into a "Third-World flophouse."

Edwards, who is considered a white nationalist by the Southern Poverty Law Center, says whites must organize like other stigmatized groups.

"There is nothing wrong for Jewish organizations to promote the self-interest of Jews or black organizations to promote the interest of blacks," he says. "There is no organization to stand up to advance the interests of the dispossessed majority."

Those white interests have been compromised by what he sees as the "preferential treatment" blacks have received in the job market to compensate for slavery, Edwards says.

"Whatever mistakes might have been made in our pasts, they have not only been corrected, but they've been overcompensated for," he says.

Now whites are victims of pervasive racism, Edwards says.

"They're the victims of it every day. Anything a white conservative does that a liberal doesn't like is called racism."

Both Brimelow and Edwards reject outright the Southern Poverty Law Center's description of their organizations as extremist.

"It's Not a Race Issue, It's a Principle"

Ginger Howard is a white Southerner who doesn't feel dispossessed. She attended Beck's rally last summer and described it as a religious event, not a political one.

"It was such an amazing event to be with such like-minded people," she says.

Beck says he held the rally to reclaim the civil rights movement "from politics." He held the rally on the anniversary of the 1963 March on Washington, where the Rev. Martin Luther King Jr. delivered his "I Have a Dream Speech."

Howard says she attended because she wanted to raise money for U.S. troops and protest against government dependency.

"It's not a race issue, it's a principle issue," says Howard, owner of the Ginger Howard Selections clothing store in Atlanta, Georgia.

Chris Plante, a conservative talk show host, says white racial anxiety isn't a race issue but a smokescreen by leftists. Plante says they yell racism to avoid talking about Obama's "unpopular liberal expansion" of the federal government.

Plante, who says he grew up in a Chicago home with a picture of Martin Luther King, Jr. on the wall, attended both Beck's rally and a follow-up rally by Jon Stewart, host of the *Daily Show*.

Stewart and fellow Comedy Central host Stephen Colbert held their "March to Keep Fear Alive" on the National Mall two months after Beck's rally. Stewart said he held the rally for people tired of the media portraying America as a divided country.

"The Beck crowd was no more white than the Jon Stewart rally, but nobody in the news media described the Stewart crowd as overwhelmingly white," Plante says.

"Hunkering Down"

One prominent observer of American culture suggests all Americans—white, black and every other minority—should be concerned about the future.

Robert Putnam, author of the celebrated book "Bowling Alone," says his studies of multiracial neighborhoods in America suggest that more diversity doesn't initially create more tolerance. It can erode community.

In his 2007 book, "E Pluribus Unum: Diversity and Community in the Twenty-first Century," Putnam says his studies of diverse communities show that in the short run, its members tend to expect the worst, distrust neighbors and withdraw.

"Residents of all races tend to 'hunker down,' " Putnam writes. "Trust (even of one's own race) is lower, altruism and community cooperation rarer, friends fewer."

Is this America's future?

Dueling mass rallies in Washington? Dueling complaints of racial persecution? Dueling versions of ethnic history?

It doesn't have to be, says Gallagher, the La Salle University sociologist.

Gallagher points out that the United States has accommodated massive change before. Women were once thought too emotional to vote, interracial couples were outlawed, blacks enslaved.

He says his children won't see race the same way that he or other generations did. They won't see diversity as a weakness.

It'll just be a way of life.

"Like it or not, the country is going to look more like it should—more brown folks, more yellow folks, more gay folks, more mixed folks," he says.

It's easy to be pessimistic, he says, but his profession teaches him to look past the headlines.

"When you take the long view of human history, change is slow, but change happens."

Do you believe that whites are a racially oppressed group in America? Provide arguments in support of your position.

Arab Americans

Arab Americans have a long history in the United States. Before reviewing their experience, it is important that readers understand that the terms *Arab Americans* and *Muslim Americans* are not synonymous. In other words, not all Muslims are Arab. And similarly, not all Arab Americans are Muslims. Arab Americans are a cultural group in the United States, and Muslim Americans are those persons from all races and ethnic backgrounds who follow the Islamic religious tradition. Our focus here is on Arab Americans, who are people from Lebanon, Egypt, Syria, Palestine, Jordan, and a host of other Middle Eastern countries. Orfalea (2006) separates the Arab American experience into three significant waves of immigration. The first wave commenced in 1878 and continued through 1924. There are multiple reasons given for why Arabs immigrated to the United States in the late 19th century. It has been suggested that economics, political conflict, religious strife, and the pursuit of fortune contributed to Arab immigration to America. Not unlike other **white immigrants**, Arab Americans viewed the United States as having "streets of gold" (p. 51). These varying motivations resulted in approximately 200,000—mostly Christian—Arab Americans in the country during the 1920s (Feagin & Booher Feagin, 2012; Kayyali, 2006).

Just as the immigration of other ethnic groups was reduced by legislation, Arab Americans were also affected by the notorious 1924 Immigration Act that severely restricted the total immigration to the United States to fewer than 160,000 (Federal Reserve Archival System for Economic Research, n.d.). The second wave of Arab American immigration followed World War II and spanned the years 1947 to 1966. With the relaxing of immigration policies, Arabs fled war-torn areas in the Middle East. Some came as political refugees in the 1950s and 1960s when the United States passed the Refugee Relief Act that was targeted at Palestinian refugees. In total, 6,000 Palestinians made use of this Act (Kayyali, 2006). The late 1960s saw the third wave of Arab immigration to the United States. Following the Arab defeat in the 1967 Six-Day War against Israel, Arabs became "disillusioned and pessimistic about the future of the Arab world and chose to move to the United States and other non-Arab countries" (p. 33). This resulted in more than 400,000 Arab immigrants arriving in the United States between the 1960s and the 1990s (p. 33).

On the surface, the Arab American story mirrors that of other White ethnics, as they also had to endure negative stereotypes leveled at them by other more established immigrant groups. The Arab American story was considerably altered following the events of September 11, 2001 (hereafter 9/11). While other groups quietly assimilated into whiteness, the 9/11 terrorist attacks returned Arab Americans to the status of a recognizable minority (Jamal & Naber, 2008). The racial animus that had previously targeted minority groups such as Blacks and Latinos also targeted Arab Americans (and Muslim Americans) because of the Middle Eastern backgrounds of the 9/11 terrorists. In particular, Arab Americans were perceived to be the group most likely to engage in terrorist activities; therefore, citizens and policing officials alike were supportive of racial profiling of people of Middle Eastern descent. This led to the harassment of Arab Americans and to the term *flying while Arab,* which refers to the additional scrutiny Arab Americans are perceived to receive when traveling by airplane (Baker, 2002; Schildkraut, 2009). Despite this recent harassment directed at them, the approximately 3.5 million Arab Americans remain a vital force in the United States.

> ### Quick Facts
>
> - 89% of Arab American adults have at least a high school diploma
> - 45% have a bachelor's degree or more
> - 5% are unemployed
> - In 2008, their median household income was $56,331
>
> *Source:* Arab American Institute (2011).

Latino Americans

Prior to the 2000 census, the term *Hispanic* was used to refer to persons from Mexico, Puerto Rico, Cuba, and Central and South America. Feagin and Booher Feagin (2012) noted that the term *Latino* emerged because it "recognizes the complex Latin American origins of these groups. It is a Spanish-language word preferred by many Spanish-speaking scholars, activists, and others" (p. 209). Our review of their history focuses on the two largest ethnic groups under the Latino category: Mexicans and Puerto Ricans. The data presented earlier in Table 1.2 clearly illuminate the diversity of the American Latino population.

Mexicans

Between 1500 and 1853, the Spanish conquered and ruled Mexico. For much of this period, Mexicans were exploited for their labor by the Spanish. Many Mexicans became Americans with the annexation of Texas. Following the Mexican-American War (1846–1848) and the Treaty of Guadalupe Hidalgo (1848), Mexicans had the option to stay in the United States or return to Mexico. According to Feagin and Booher Feagin (2012), although many returned, others stayed in America.

Sowell (1981) wrote that Mexicans immigrated to America in three great waves. The first wave of Mexicans came to America by railroad—and ironically, over the years, railroads became one of the largest employers of Mexicans. Specifically, they were employed "as construction workers, as watchmen, or as laborers maintaining the tracks. Many lived in boxcars or in shacks near the railroads—primitive settlements that were the beginning of many Mexican-American communities today" (p. 249). Before World War I, other industries employing Mexicans were agriculture and mining. Mexican workers in America were paid considerably more than they were in Mexico. As a result, there was a steady flow of seasonal workers crossing the Mexican border to earn money to take back home to Mexico. Labor shortages caused by World War I resulted in formalized programs to encourage such practices. About 500,000 Mexicans came to America to work during this period (Tarver, Walker, & Wallace, 2002). Beginning in this period, Mexicans also were subject to negative stereotypes, such as being considered "dirty," "ignorant," and lacking standards of appropriate behavior (Sowell, 1981). Even so, they were tolerated because of the dire need for their labor. With the arrival of the Depression, "Fears of the unemployed created an anti-immigrant movement, and immigration laws were modified to deport the 'undesirables' and restrict the numbers of foreign-contract laborers" (Tarver et al., 2002, p. 54).

About the same time of the notorious Scottsboro cases, the federal government, under the direction of President Herbert Hoover, commissioned the first national crime commission. Commonly referred to as the "Wickersham Report," for its director, George Wickersham, the commission's report, published in 1931, covered almost every aspect of American criminal justice. The report included a review of the state of Mexicans and crime; it found that there were varying levels of crime among Mexicans in California and Texas. In general, however, the report noted that, like African Americans, Mexicans were treated with considerable prejudice by the justice system (Abbott, 1931). The report suggested that the criminality of the Mexicans was overstated. There was also brief mention of Filipinos, who were overrepresented in offenses related to gambling, and Japanese, who were "among the most law abiding of all population groups" (p. 415).

The second wave of Mexican immigrants came to the United States during World War II. Another war had resulted in another labor shortage, which produced the **Bracero Program**, which brought in thousands of agricultural workers. *Bracero* is a Spanish term that was used to describe guest workers coming from Mexico to the United States. By the end of the Bracero Program in 1964, 5 million Mexican workers had been imported into this country (Tarver et al., 2002, p. 54).

The third wave of Mexican immigration is tied to the various immigration laws from the 1970s to the present, which have sought to protect, defend, or curtail Mexican immigration to the United States. One such law, the Immigration Reform and Control Act of 1986, provided temporary residency for some illegal aliens. Furthermore, those who had come to America before 1982 were given permanent resident status. According to Tarver et al. (2002),

> This Act had an enormous impact on Mexican immigration, with 1,655,842 people entering the United States during the decade of the 1980s. Since the first decade of the twentieth century, this was the largest number of immigrants from a single country. (p. 55)

Another law aimed at Mexican illegal immigration is the Illegal Immigration Reform and Immigrant Responsibility Act of 1996. In addition to shoring up the borders in California and Texas, the Act "increased the number of investigators monitoring workplace employment of aliens, passport fraud, and alien smuggling" (Tarver et al., 2002, p. 55). Today, because of the estimated 11 million illegal immigrants in America (Hsu, 2010), the fears concerning illegal immigration continue with the passage of Arizona's Immigration Bill SB 1070 in 2010. Most notably, the bill requires immigrants to carry their alien registration information and provides law enforcement officials with the discretion to question persons who they believe are illegal immigrants.

After the law was passed, there were suits challenging its constitutionality. In particular, immediately before the law was to take effect, a judge issued an injunction against the enforcement of the section of the Act allowing law enforcement to question citizens about their residency status. In addition,

> U.S. District Judge Susan Bolton also blocked provisions of the law making it a crime to fail to apply for or carry alien registration papers or "for an unauthorized alien to solicit, apply for, or perform work," and a provision "authorizing the warrantless arrest of a person" if there is reason to believe that person might be subject to deportation. ("Legal battle looms," 2010)

It is apparent from this type of legislation that some Americans believe the heavy influx of Mexicans is changing the fabric of the country. Box 1.3 discusses recent legislation in Alabama targeting illegal immigrants. Besides concerns about job competition and the strain on social services caused by considerable illegal immigration, Americans have continued their fascination with the perceived connection between immigration and crime (Hickman & Suttorp, 2008; Higgins, Gabbidon, & Martin, 2010; Martinez & Valenzuela, 2006; Stowell, 2007). As you should know by now, this fear-based fascination is not new—it is the American way (Martinez, 2006).

BOX 1.3

Alabama Sets Nation's Toughest Immigration Law

By Peggy Gargis

Birmingham, Ala (Reuters)—Republican Governor Robert Bentley on Thursday signed into law a crackdown on illegal immigration in Alabama that both supporters and critics consider the toughest in the nation.

The measure will require public schools to determine the citizenship status of students—a provision not included in an Arizona law that has been at the forefront of actions by several states to curb illegal immigration.

Under the Alabama law, police must detain someone they suspect of being in the country illegally if the person cannot produce proper documentation when stopped for any reason.

It also will be a crime to knowingly transport or harbor someone who is in the country illegally. The law imposes penalties on businesses that knowingly employ someone without legal resident status. A company's business license could be suspended or revoked.

The law, which is scheduled to take effect September 1, requires businesses to use a database called E-Verify to confirm the immigration status of new employees.

"We have a real problem with illegal immigration in this country," Bentley said after signing the law. "I campaigned for the toughest immigration laws, and I'm proud of the Legislature for working tirelessly to create the strongest immigration bill in the country."

Several states have enacted immigration restrictions, even though the U.S. government considers it to be a federal issue.

Immigration rights advocates called the new law "draconian " and vowed to challenge it in court. Rights organizations have sued to block similar measures in Arizona, Utah, Indiana and Georgia. The U.S. Justice Department also sued over Arizona's law.

"This law is an outrageous throw-back to the pre-Civil Rights era," said Cecillia Wang, director of the American Civil Liberties Union's Immigrants' Rights Project. Alabama was at the center of some of the bitter struggles over the civil rights of African Americans during the 1960s.

After Arizona passed its controversial measure last year, the courts blocked implementation of a provision allowing police to check the immigration status of people there.

But the U.S. Supreme Court recently endorsed a separate Arizona law requiring employers to use E-Verify. The court also ruled that Arizona could suspend or revoke business licenses of those companies that knowingly hire illegal immigrants.

Will Students Be Afraid?

Alabama's law is unique in requiring public schools to determine, by review of birth certificates or sworn affidavits, the legal residency status of students.

"We fear that it will, in effect, ban the student through fear and harassment," said Shay Farley, legal director of Alabama Appleseed, a nonprofit policy and legal advocacy organization.

Farley said there is also concern about the increased financial burden on schools to collect the information.

The Alabama bill passed the state House of Representatives and Senate by large margins before landing on Bentley's desk. Republicans took over majority control of both chambers of the Alabama legislature last year for the first time in 136 years.

Some farmers in the U.S. South are worried that new immigration restrictions could limit access to farm workers. But Gene Armstrong, mayor of Allgood, Alabama, a small community where the Hispanic population has grown to almost 50 percent, is not worried.

"We managed in the past without illegal immigrants to pick the tomatoes here, and I haven't heard anyone say that if we sent them all home nobody would be left to do that work," Armstrong said.

"When you have 9 percent unemployment, I think that some people who might not have wanted those jobs previously might reconsider."

Do you support Alabama's new immigration law? If not, how would you modify the law?

Puerto Ricans

The island of Puerto Rico was colonized by the Spanish in the late 1400s. Not until 1897, however, did Puerto Ricans gain their independence. However, the Spanish-American War resulted in the U.S. taking over the island in 1898. In the 1950s, Puerto Rico became a commonwealth of the United States, granting Puerto Ricans more independence in their governance. From 1945 to the 1970s, the high unemployment rate resulted in one in three Puerto Ricans leaving the island (Feagin & Booher Feagin, 2012). Significant numbers of Puerto Ricans headed to New York and other states, such as New Jersey and Delaware. Thus, after having only 2,000 Puerto Ricans in New York in 1900, there was significant Puerto Rican immigration to the United States, which resulted in an increase to 70,000 in 1940 and 887,000 by 1960 (Feagin & Booher Feagin, 2012). Upon their arrival, as with other immigrants who headed to the "promised land," they were faced with high levels of unemployment and poverty. In fact, these dire circumstances resulted in what has been referred to as "circular migration." That is, after the opportunities they were seeking did not materialize, Puerto Ricans would head home, but then return because of the lack of opportunities in Puerto Rico. Mirroring the experience of other racial and ethnic groups, over time, Puerto Ricans were also saddled with negative stereotypes, such as "lazy," "submissive," "violent," and "criminal." Moreover, because they cannot always "pass" as White, they have been unable to assimilate like some other ethnic groups. As a result of their varying skin tones and backgrounds, they often are categorized as either White or Black.

A Brief Note on Other Latino Americans

Cubans are also a notable segment of the Latino population. With much of their immigration coming after Fidel Castro's takeover of the government in 1959, they currently number about 1.7 million. Combined, South Americans from the Dominican Republic, El Salvador, and Colombia also represent another substantial portion of the Latino population. Given these figures, it is no wonder that Latinos have become the largest minority group in the United States. They have also, however, suffered from some of the same crime-related concerns as other ethnic groups before them. Notably, however, they have not experienced the same levels of crime and violence as African Americans (Martinez, 2002; Martinez, Stowell, & Lee, 2010). This may reflect the fact that many Latinos have come to the United States specifically seeking opportunities for employment, with a willingness to take the most undesirable jobs in the labor market. For many, these jobs provide much more financial compensation than the available employment in the various Latin American countries from which a substantial portion of Latino immigrants originate. Nevertheless, some Latinos have drifted into gangs and other criminal activities as a way to survive in America. Unfortunately, their criminal activities have been exaggerated by the news media and Hollywood, which has resulted in continuing stereotypes (Martinez, Lee, & Nielsen, 2001; see Box 1.4).

BOX 1.4

Nation's First Multilingual Poll Uncovers Tensions Among the Largest Ethnic Groups in America

Washington—The nation's first multilingual poll of Black, Hispanic, and Asian Americans has uncovered serious tensions among these ethnic groups, including mistrust and significant stereotyping, but a majority of each group also said they should put aside differences and work together to better their communities.

The poll, which was released today during a news conference at the National Press Club, was sponsored by New America Media (NAM) and nine ethnic media outlets who are founding members of the organization.

"This extraordinary poll reveals some unflattering realities that exist in America today," said Sandy Close, Executive Editor and Director of NAM, the nation's first and largest collaboration of ethnic news media. "The sponsors of the poll strongly believe the best way to move forward is by identifying the problems and initiating a dialogue that can bring ethnic groups closer together in their fight for equality and against discrimination."

Broadly, the poll of 1,105 African American, Asian American, and Hispanic adults found that the predominantly immigrant populations—Hispanics and Asians—expressed far greater optimism about their lives in America, concluding that hard work is rewarded in this society. By contrast, more than 60% of the African Americans polled do not believe the American Dream works for them. Blacks also described themselves as more segregated from the rest of America than the other groups.

The poll found that friction between ethnic and racial groups, which at times has erupted into highly publicized incidents around the country, is clearly rooted in the mistrust that the groups harbor towards each other, as well as the sentiment that other groups are mistreating them or are detrimental to their own future. For instance, 44% of Hispanics and 47% of Asians are "generally afraid of African Americans because they are responsible for most of the crime." Meanwhile, 46% of Hispanics and 52% of African Americans believe "most Asian business owners do not treat them with respect." And half of African

Americans feel threatened by Latin American immigrants because "they are taking jobs, housing, and political power away from the Black community."

Moreover, the three groups seem more trusting of Whites than of each other. The poll found that 61% of Hispanics, 54% of Asians, and 47% of African Americans would rather do business with Whites than members of the other two groups.

"The poll reaffirms that while race relations between ethnic groups and Whites grab the headlines, there are also serious racial problems between minority groups in America," said Sergio Bendixen, who is an expert on Hispanic and multilingual polling. "Blacks feel they are left out of the American Dream and are being displaced by newcomers, and each group buys into the negative stereotypes about the other two. What's clear is the need to dissolve this friction. The poll results show that the overwhelming majority of ethnic Americans want that positive outcome."

Specifically, the poll also found that:

- A majority of Hispanics and a significant percentage of Asians believe in the concept that every American has an equal opportunity to succeed. By contrast, the majority of Black respondents—66%—disagreed with that notion.
- Blacks overwhelmingly believe the criminal justice system favors the rich and powerful; most Hispanics and an even larger majority of Asians disagree.
- A large majority of each group believes that they should put aside their differences and work together on issues affecting their communities; they also say the country would be better if more from all three groups were in positions of authority at universities, businesses, media, and government.
- All three groups are optimistic about the future. Strong majorities of each group believe that racial tensions will ease over the next 10 years.

Further, Ms. Close said the poll found "a shared appreciation" for each group's cultural and political contributions. "Hispanics and Asians recognize that African Americans led the fight for civil rights and against discrimination, forging a better future for the other groups," she said. "Asian Americans and African Americans say Hispanic culture has enriched the quality of their lives. African Americans and Hispanics perceive Asian Americans as role models when it comes to family and educational values."

Poll respondents sent mixed messages to the ethnic media, which many depend on for news about their community. While criticizing the ethnic media's coverage of race relations, particularly other groups outside their own community, all three groups maintained that the ethnic media must play a vital role by strengthening intergroup communication and helping to break negative stereotypes.

The ethnic media is embracing their challenge to do better. "The poll is part of our campaign to address mutual misunderstandings, of which there are many," said Sok Jeong, editor of the *Korea Times.* "The poll is a call to action for ethnic media to expand coverage of our mutual communities and help our readers gain a better understanding of the other ethnic groups."

About the Poll

The poll of 1,105 African American, Asian American, and Hispanic adults was conducted by telephone during the months of August and September, 2007. The sample was designed to be representative of the adult population of the three major racial and ethnic minorities in the United States. Hispanic respondents were interviewed in English or Spanish, and Asian American respondents were interviewed in English, Mandarin, Cantonese, Korean, Vietnamese, or Tagalog. RDD (Random Digit Dialing) methodology was employed in areas of the country that have significant (10% or more) African American, Asian American, and Hispanic populations.

Why do Hispanics and Asians perceive Blacks to be responsible for most of the crime? Why are Whites perceived to be the most trustworthy racial/ethnic group?

Asian Americans

Asian Americans provide another interesting case study of ethnic group acculturation in America. Like Latinos, they belong to a number of ethnic groups, such as Filipino, Korean, Japanese, and Vietnamese. Table 1.5 provides an overview of the population of the various Asian American groups. We begin our review with a brief discussion of the Chinese American experience.

Chinese Americans

According to Daniels (1988), there were Chinese in America as early as the late 1700s. Not until the California gold rush of the mid-1850s was there any significant Chinese immigration to America: Between 1849 and 1882, nearly 300,000 Chinese came to America (Daniels, 1988). The **Chinese Exclusion Act of 1882** limited immigration until the 1940s. Most of the early Chinese immigrants were male (90%) and came to work in America temporarily. However, they came in significant enough numbers to represent nearly 10% of California's population between 1860 and 1880 (Daniels, 1988). Those who did stay were subjected to considerable violence due to anti-Chinese sentiment. Chinatowns had existed since the arrival of the Chinese in America; they embraced these areas because there they were free to maintain their culture without fear of hostility—although some areas occupied exclusively by Chinese inhabitants were "shabby looking, vice-infested, and violence prone" (Sowell, 1981, p. 141).

The Chinese were quite successful as laborers as well as in independent businesses such as restaurants and laundries (Daniels, 1988; Sowell, 1981). Yet, as with other immigrant groups, the Chinese were not immune to engaging in illegal activities. Daniels (1988) wrote

Table 1.5

Asian American Population, 2010

Asian Origin	Population	Percentage of Asian Population	Percentage of Total U.S. Population
Asian Indian	2,843,391	19.38	0.92
Chinese	3,347,229	22.81	1.08
Filipino	2,555,923	17.42	0.83
Japanese	763,325	5.20	0.25
Korean	1,423,784	9.70	0.46
Vietnamese	1,548,449	10.55	0.50
Other Asian	2,192,151	14.94	0.71
Total Asian Population:	14,674,252	100.00	4.75
Total U.S. Population	308,745,538		

that prostitution and gambling flourished in the "bachelor society" created by the dearth of Asian women in America. In 1870, "More than 75% of the nearly 3,000 Chinese women workers in the United States identified themselves as prostitutes" (Perry, 2000, p. 104). Brothels and opium-smoking establishments became popular among both Asians and Whites. Regarding opium use among early Chinese immigrants, Mann (1993) suggested that 35% of the Chinese immigrants smoked opium regularly, which "led to the first national campaign against narcotics" (p. 59), and the subsequent legislation was aimed at "excluding Chinese participation in American society" (p. 59). On the participation of the Chinese in these illegal activities, Daniels (1988) noted, "Since all of these activities were both lucrative and illegal, it seems clear that police and politicians in the White community were involved in sanctioning and profiting from them" (p. 22).

Eventually, following the pattern of other immigrants, Asian organized crime emerged, and secret societies such as "tongs" were formed. Describing these organizations, Perry (2000) indicated that such societies were originally created to assist Asian men in adjusting to America. But, as Perry notes, over time, many evolved into criminal organizations or developed links with Chinese "triads." Consequently, the tongs came to dominate prostitution, along with gambling, drugs, and other vice crimes. So, in addition to providing sexual outlets, they also created other opportunities for recreation and escapist behavior. Despite the profits reaped by Whites from the legal and illicit activities of the Chinese, heavy anti-Chinese sentiment persisted in California, which led to numerous negative campaigns against the population. Pointing to the roots of this negative sentiment, Sowell (1981) wrote, "The Chinese were both non-White and non-Christian, at a time when either trait alone was a serious handicap. They looked different, dressed differently, ate differently, and followed customs wholly unfamiliar to Americans" (pp. 136–137). Once they began to receive jobs in competition with Whites, they became targets of increasing violence and, in several instances, were massacred. By and large, the Chinese were generally relegated to the most menial and "dirty" occupations, such as mining, laying railroad tracks, and agricultural work. As a result of the Chinese Exclusion Act of 1882, unlike other ethnic minorities, the Chinese population decreased from the late 1880s through the mid-1940s. Since then, their numbers have increased, and they have remained the largest segment of the Asian American population. Until the last 30 years of the 20th century, Japanese Americans represented the second-largest group among Asians in the United States. Several other Asian groups have now surpassed them in population (most notably, Filipinos). We briefly review the Japanese American experience below.

Japanese Americans

Before arriving on the shores of North America in the last quarter of the 19th century, a considerable contingent of Japanese workers (30,000) arrived in Hawaii. They were contract workers who came to the island to provide much-needed labor for sugar plantations and "to serve as a counterweight to the relatively large number of Chinese in the islands" (Daniels, 1988, pp. 100–101). Like the Chinese before them, the Japanese also arrived on North American shores as a result of labor needs, and the relatively small number of Japanese men who made it to America (about 2,200 by 1890) filled the continuing need for laborers on California farms (Daniels, 1988). Like the Chinese and other groups, some Japanese immigrants turned to illicit activities, such as prostitution and other petty crimes, to survive.

Over time, the number of Japanese in America began to increase, with 24,326 in 1900, 72,157 in 1910, and nearly 127,000 by 1940. Mirroring the experience of the

Chinese, anti-Japanese sentiment arose in the United States, culminating with the arrival of World War II. During World War II, negative sentiment toward the Japanese reached new heights; they were hated and mistrusted by many Americans. Once the attack on Pearl Harbor occurred, in December, 1941, life for Japanese Americans would never be the same. In February, 1942, President Roosevelt issued Executive Order 9066 (Dinnerstein & Reimers, 1982). The order, which was upheld by the Supreme Court, required that all Japanese from the West Coast be rounded up and placed in camps called **relocation centers**. In all, about 110,000 were rounded up on five days' notice and were told they could take only what they could carry. The camps were nothing more than prison facilities with armed military police on patrol watching for escapes.

Photo 1.1

Japanese American internees await processing in 1942.

Following the war, the Japanese population remained low in the United States due to immigration restrictions that were not lifted until the 1960s. At that time, Japanese Americans represented 52% of the Asian American population. However, over the next 20 years, the number of Japanese who immigrated to America declined. This trend was largely a result of the increased need for labor in Japan, which stunted the immigration of the Japanese to America (Takaki, 1989). The Japanese who were already here or among those who came after stringent quotas were lifted in the 1960s would go on to become some of the most successful immigrants. Today, economic indicators related to income and unemployment levels all reveal a positive trend for Japanese Americans. Nonetheless, Japanese Americans are still targets of discrimination. Two other Asian groups whose numbers have increased over the last few decades are Filipinos and Koreans. We provide brief overviews of their American experiences in the next section.

Filipinos and Koreans

Filipinos have been in the United States since the 1700s. But, as you might expect, much of their most significant immigration to the United States occurred in the 19th and 20th centuries. Many headed to plantations in Hawaii due to labor shortages. Unfortunately, when they arrived in America, they encountered violent attacks from Whites. In California, they competed with White farm workers; besides receiving lower wages than their counterparts, they were the target of continuing violence. In fact, in 1929 and 1930, there were brutal riots that were brought on by anti-Filipino sentiment (Feagin & Booher Feagin, 2012). During this same time, the 1924 immigration law restricted the number of Filipinos who could enter the country to 50 (Kim, 2001). Since this early period, although their population has increased precipitously, they remain the targets of violence, and in post-9/11 America, some have been targeted as potential terrorists.

Like Filipino Americans, Korean Americans headed to Hawaii in the early part of the 20th century to fill labor shortages. Koreans also followed other Asian groups to California. In the case of Koreans, the place of choice was San Francisco. Limited by immigration restrictions, much of Korean immigration followed World War II. Not until 1965 were the stringent immigration restrictions lifted. This policy change coincided with more Koreans (mostly from South Korea) arriving in America. Looking for opportunities, Koreans headed to inner-city communities, where they set up dry cleaners and convenience stores. Unfortunately, the relations between Koreans and urban residents are tenuous at best: Koreans are resented for entering largely African American communities and "setting up shop," as some have noted. Therefore, besides feeling that they were mistreated by clerks in Korean establishments, some have felt that such businesses should be owned by community members. This sentiment spilled over in the Los Angeles riot of 1992 (Kim, 1999). There, tensions remain between the two communities, but the dialogue continues. In 2007, Korean Americans again received negative attention because the perpetrator of the Virginia Tech massacre was an immigrant from South Korea.

Asian Indians

Asian Indians are the second most populous Asian group in America. They began to arrive from India and other South Asian countries in the United States in the early 1800s, but only 17,000 made it to American shores between 1820 and 1965 (Schaefer, 2011). Many of these early immigrants were employed in railroad and agricultural industries on the West Coast (Feagin & Booher Feagin, 2012). Following the easing of immigration restrictions, the number of Asian Indian immigrants began to rise. In particular, the need for skilled workers resulted in the immigration of highly educated and skilled Asian Indians. Many initially headed to northeastern states such as New York; however, after the rise of Silicon Valley, California quickly became the destination of choice for many of the more technologically savvy Asian Indians. In addition to the highly skilled and educated immigrants from India, there is also a contingent of Asian Indians who are heavily engaged in the service sector occupations including driving taxi cabs, managing motels, and operating convenience stores (Schaefer, 2011). Their success in the professions has resulted in many Asian Indians moving directly to suburban areas, as opposed to urban areas where most immigrants normally begin their ascension up the rungs of American society (Feagin & Boohler Feagin, 2012). Asian Indians clearly represent one of the true immigrant success stories.

In closing, the difference between Asians and ethnic groups who came to be classified as White is that, although they have attained high levels of achievement, Asians have never fully assimilated. This leaves them, as one author put it, "as perpetual outsiders" (Perry, 2000). Like African Americans, Native Americans, and some Latinos, Asian Americans have maintained a distinct racial categorization in the Census. L. A. Gould (2000) has suggested that physical characteristics unique to their race (e.g., skin color, facial characteristics, size) have barred them from full assimilation and acceptance in America.

Despite not being able to fully assimilate, Asian Americans have been labeled the ***model minority*** because of their success in education. Some see their success as proof that all groups can succeed if they "put their best foot forward." Others see this label as problematic (Wu, 2002), noting that all Asians are not equally successful. For example, as Perry (2000) noted, "Koreans and Vietnamese consistently lag behind Chinese, Japanese, and Asian Indians on most indicators of socioeconomic status" (p. 100). Furthermore, the continuing discrimination in employment, income, and education is masked by the model minority label. Nevertheless, over the last century, Asian Americans have been a productive force in the United States.

❖ Conclusion

Since the categorization of races in the late 1700s, societies have, unfortunately, used the social construct to divide populations. In America, the notion of race was not of considerable use until the 1660s, when color was one of the deciding factors in the creation of the slave system. It was at this time in history that the category "White" began to take on increased importance.

Along with "Whiteness" came racism, which justified the system from the point of view of the dominant population. For the next two and a half centuries, as more White ethnic immigrants came to the United States looking for opportunities, they were looked down on as well. However, at some point, each group was allowed to fully assimilate and truly "become White," and over time, the stereotypes with which they had been identified eventually dissipated (see Table 1.6). In the case of Native Americans, African Americans, Asians, and Latinos, however, this process has been more difficult because of distinct physical traits that have limited their ability to fully assimilate. Recent years have also seen an increasing intolerance of Arab Americans following 9/11.

Table 1.6

Early Stereotypes of Racial and Ethnic Minorities* (1600s–1900s)

Native American	Irish	Jewish	African American	Mexican American	Puerto Rican	Chinese/Japanese
childlike	temperamental	too intelligent	bad odor	lazy	emotional	devious
cruel	dangerous	crafty	lazy	backward	lazy	corrupt
thieves	quarrelsome	clumsy	criminal	lawless	criminal	dirty
wild beasts	idle		apelike	violent		crafty
exotic	apelike			shiftless		docile
powerful				improvident		dangerous

*All groups were thought to be "biologically inferior" to the native White population.

Our review of the historical antecedents of race and crime in America has revealed that, over the past few centuries, although the level of crime in each group has varied over time, most racial/ethnic groups have committed the same kinds of offenses and have had similar offenses perpetrated against them by the dominant culture. Initially, Whites criminally brutalized Native Americans and African Americans. As time went on, ethnic immigrants such as the Germans, Italians, and Irish, also were subjected to harsh treatment and sometimes violence. As these "White ethnic" groups assimilated into the populace, they, in turn, became part of the oppressive White population, continuing at times to engage in racial violence against other minority groups.

In short, the history of race and crime in America is a story of exploitation, violence, and, in the case of most racial/ethnic groups, the common use of crime as a way to ascend from the lower rungs of American society. The next chapter examines official crime and victimization data for the various races.

Discussion Questions

1. Explain the origin of race and its implications for race and crime.

2. Do you believe there are distinct races?

3. What role has the law played in the experiences of the groups portrayed in the chapter? Provide some examples using specific laws.

4. How does slavery intersect with the study of race and crime?

5. What role does "Whiteness" play in understanding race and crime?

Internet Exercises

1. Visit the U.S. Bureau of the Census Web site (http://www.census.gov) and provide another logical way of categorizing the various groups in American society.

2. Visit The DNA Initiative website (http://www.dna.gov/) and view some of the advances in DNA identification in crime solving.

3. Visit the U.S. National Archives and Records Administration (http://www.archives .gov/) website and view some of the tools people use to investigate their racial/ ethnic heritage.

Internet Sites

The DNA Initiative: http://www.dna.gov/

U.S. Bureau of the Census: http://www.census.gov

Ellis Island: http://www.nps.gov/elis/index.htm

Extent of Crime and Victimization

Present statistics which pretend to report the criminal behavior of minority ethnic and racial groups both reflect and perpetuate a large number of errors and myths, which can be, in their most innocent form, misleading, and, in their least innocent, both vicious and malevolent.

—Geis (1972, p. 61)

Race and crime have been inextricably linked throughout American history. As noted in Chapter 1, early stereotypes of some Americans implied their criminality. Over time, beliefs about the inferiority and criminality of certain groups, including African Americans, Native Americans, White immigrants, and others, fostered the eugenics movement of the early 20th century and the "law and order" campaigns that came later. Although not created to do so, crime data often are used to support (erroneous) beliefs about minorities and crime. Between 1850 and the early 1900s, census data about convicted persons were the primary source of criminal statistics. At that time, distinctions were made between foreign and native-born convicts. Most foreign convicts were immigrants from European countries and were classified based on their place of origin (French, German, etc.). Despite opposition, in 1930, the U.S. Congress mandated that the Federal Bureau of Investigation (FBI) collect and report crime data. By the 1960s, the increase in crime recorded in the FBI's Uniform Crime Reports (UCR)—especially in urban areas—was used to justify the implementation of more punitive crime control policies. Today, there are several sources of data on the extent of crime and victimization (see Table 2.1). Most of the data available are funded and/or collected by federal agencies. The Bureau of Justice Statistics (BJS) is the primary statistical agency in the U.S. Department of Justice (DOJ). It provides data analysis tools and facilitates online data analyses for some crime and victimization data. It recently added access to the UCR Crime Trends tool for analyses of UCR crime data. Other DOJ agencies, such as the FBI, the Office of Juvenile Justice and Delinquency Prevention (OJJDP), and other federal agencies including the **Centers for Disease Control and Prevention** and Department of Education, provide useful crime, victimization, and justice statistical information.

Table 2.1

Sources of Crime and Victimization Statistics

Source	Sponsor	Inception	Methodology	Scope	Race Included	Online Analysis	Website
Behavioral Risk Factor Surveillance System (BRFSS)	CDC	1984	Annual survey	Yes	Yes, 2005 only	Yes	Yes
Crime in the United States (UCRs)	FBI	1930	Crimes reported to the police	• Crimes reported • Crimes cleared • Persons arrested • Law enforcement personnel	Yes	Yes	Yes
Indicators of School Crime and Safety	• BJS • National Center for Education Statistics (NCES) • Institute of Education Sciences (IES) • Both in DOE	1997	Annual survey	• Compendium of information on school crime and student safety from varying sources	Yes	No	Yes
National Crime Victimization Survey (NCVS)	Bureau of Justice Statistics (BJS)	1972	Interviews	• Victims • Offenders • Offenses	Yes	No	Yes
Sourcebook of Criminal Justice Statistics	BJS	1973	Compendium of statistics	• Criminal justice system • Public attitudes • Arrests • Judicial processing • Prisoners	Yes	No	Yes
Law Enforcement Management and Administrative Statistics (LEMAS)	BJS	1987	Surveys of police agencies	• Personnel expenditures • Operations • Equipment	Yes	No	Yes

(Continued)

(Continued)

Source	Sponsor	Inception	Methodology	Scope	Race Included	Online Analysis	Website
National Incident-Based Reporting System (NIBRS)	FBI	1988	Crime incidents	• Victims • Offenders • Offenses • Circumstances	Yes	Available from the Criminal Justice Archive of Criminal Justice Data	Yes
Hate Crime Statistics	FBI	1991	Crimes reported to the police	• Victims • Offender motivation • Location	Yes	No	Yes
Statistical Briefing Book	OJDP	1998	Juvenile delinquency	• Juvenile offenders • Victims • Juvenile justice system	Yes	Yes	Yes
Supplemental Homicide Reports (SHR)	FBI	1980	Homicides reported to the FBI	• Characteristics of homicide incidents	Yes	Available from the Criminal Justice Archive of Criminal Justice Data	No
Homicide Trends	BJS	2001	Secondary data analysis	• Trends	Yes	Available from the Criminal Justice Archive of Criminal Justice Data	Yes

The United States continues to include information on race and ethnicity in crime and victimization data (see Box 2.1). Although the information is useful for understanding patterns and trends, it also contributes to misperceptions about race and crime. The majority of both Americans and persons arrested are White, although some minorities comprise a larger proportion of persons arrested and victimized in comparison to their representation in the population. For example, in 2009 African Americans made up about 13% of the population in the United States. In that year they represented an estimated 28% of all persons arrested, 48.7% of persons arrested for murder, 55% of persons arrested for robbery, and 34% of persons arrested for motor vehicle theft (FBI, 2011b). Some of these arrest patterns persisted throughout the 20th century and into the 21st century. Of persons who are arrested, regardless of their racial categories, fewer are arrested for murder, rape, robbery, or aggravated assault, which are considered the most serious crimes against the person, than for property offenses, most notably larceny/theft.

BOX 2.1

Controversial Issue: Should Race Be Excluded From Crime Statistics?

The United States is one of the very few countries that includes racial categories in crime and victimization data. In 1992, a moratorium on the release of national race-crime statistics was issued by Canada's Justice Information Council (Knepper, 1996). In large part, this policy is based on the belief that race-crime statistics promote racial stereotypes. Despite this concern, in recent years, Canadian scholars and activists have been trying to change their policy (Owusu-Bempah & Millar, 2010). If changed, the Canadian policy would mirror that of the United States. Although the U.S. policy of recording race-crime statistics has been in place since the 1930s, Gabbidon and Higgins (2012) recently conducted a preliminary study on the level of public support for the current policy.

In 2010, using a sample of 758 randomly selected adults from Pennsylvania, Gabbidon and Higgins (2012) asked respondents two questions on race-crime statistics: (1) "Do you support law enforcement agencies' recording of arrest statistics by race?" and (2) "Please indicate your level of agreement with the following statement: The recording of arrest statistics by race promotes racial stereotypes." On the first question, the results showed that more than 50% of the sample did not support the recording of race-crime statistics. It was also revealed that Whites supported the policy more than non-Whites. On the second question, the results showed that nearly 60% of the sample felt that recording race-crime statistics promotes racial stereotypes. On this question, non-Whites were more likely than Whites to believe that recording race-crime statistics promotes stereotypes.

What is your view? Why do you think there are differences between Whites and non-Whites regarding the policy of recording race-crime statistics? Should the United States reassess its policy of collecting race-crime statistics? What are the advantages and disadvantages of collecting race-crime statistics?

The 2009 National Crime Victimization Survey (NCVS) findings indicate that Blacks, males, and persons under age 25 were more likely to be victims of violent crime, and Blacks and Hispanics have higher violent victimization rates than Whites (Truman & Rand, 2010). Most troubling is the fact that less than half of violent crime victimizations are reported to the police (Truman & Rand, 2010). Although the prospect of there being more crime and victimizations than we can ever measure or know is daunting, it must be remembered that the majority of Americans are neither arrested nor victimized, regardless of their race. In 2010, the estimated population of the United States (reported in the UCR) was 308,745,538, and the estimated number of persons arrested was only 13.1 million (FBI, 2011b). In that same year, "U.S. residents aged 12 or older only experienced an estimated 20 million violent and property victimizations" (Truman & Rand, 2010, p. 1). According to the BJS (2011b), "In 2009, for every 1,000 persons aged 12 or older, there occurred 1 rape or sexual assault, 2 robberies, 3 aggravated assaults and 11 simple assaults."

Is there a relationship between immigration, crime, and victimization? As discussed in Chapter 1, immigrants and their involvement in crime have been a concern since the 1800s, often resulting in restrictive immigration quotas. Today a considerable amount of attention is focused on crimes committed by and victimizations of undocumented/illegal immigrants. The Department of Homeland Security's controversial Secure Communities program has transformed the process of identifying and removing criminal aliens (see Chapter 4). Crime by illegal immigrants is difficult to analyze because traditional sources of crime and victimization statistics don't include them. The Morrison Institute for Public Policy (2010) identified several issues concerning "crimes by illegals" (in Arizona), including crimes committed by human smugglers and their clients, crimes related to drug trafficking, general crimes, and rivalry between Mexican drug cartels close to the Arizona border. Illegal border crossings and human trafficking are also associated with illegal immigrants. The Department of Homeland Security estimates that there are about 10.8 million illegal immigrants in America (U.S. Government Accountability Office, 2011). Using the FBI Integrated Automated Fingerprint Identification System (IAFIS), which includes fingerprint and physical characteristics, the Government Accountability Office (GAO) prepared a report for Congress titled *Criminal Alien Statistics* (2011) and estimated that 65% of the 249,000 criminal aliens in their study population were arrested at least once for either a civil or criminal immigration violation. Most (65%) were arrested for immigration violations followed by drug offenses (50%), and most were arrested in California, Texas, and Arizona (p. 22).

As the quote at the beginning of this chapter suggests, crime statistics can be misleading. Despite the fact that most Americans are not involved in crime, over time, both crime and the administration of justice have become racialized (Covington, 1995; Keith, 1996). Covington (1995) used the concept of racialized crime to describe the process of generalizing the traits, motives, or experiences of individual Black criminals to the whole race or communities of noncriminal Blacks. The concept also can be applied to other minorities. For example, the GAO study of criminal aliens mentioned above indicates that most are arrested for immigration violations, not for their involvement in the violent crime that tends to receive more media attention. Nevertheless, some might conclude that most illegal immigrants are involved in crime, especially in communities with large Latino populations, or that most immigrants are illegal, when in fact the majority have lawful immigration status. Although crime statistics were not initially designed to label certain groups of people as criminals, this is exactly what has occurred. The overrepresentation of some racial and ethnic minorities in arrest and victimization data, especially for violent crimes, has led to misperceptions about race and crime.

In this chapter, we present a brief overview of the history of crime and victimization statistics, some limitations of crime and victimization data, and analyses of data that provide information about race and crime. Here, we focus on two major sources of statistics: the UCR, compiled by the FBI and titled *Crime in the United States,* and the NCVS, an annual publication funded by the DOJ (BJS) and compiled by the U.S. Bureau of the Census, titled *Criminal Victimization.* The goal of the chapter is to assess arrest and victimization trends in the United States during the 20th and 21st centuries, to better understand what they do and do not tell us about race and crime. Finally, we summarize data from the FBI National Hate Crime Data Collection Program. At the outset, we acknowledge that there are variations by race, class, and gender that are often overlooked and difficult to assess with currently available crime and victimization data sources. First, an overview of the history of collecting crime and victimization data in our country is presented.

❖ History of Crime and Victimization Statistics in the United States

The history of crime statistics in the United States dates back to the 19th century. L. N. Robinson (1911) was one of the first to analyze crime statistics and noted,

> The purpose of criminal statistics is two-fold: (1) that one may judge of the nature and extent of criminality in a given geographical area, and (2) that one may determine the transformation, if any, which is occurring in these two phases. The results, when known, may give direction to many movements of one kind or another, but the purpose of the statistics is to furnish these two sets of data. Their application is another question. (pp. 27–28)

Some states started collecting crime data in the early 19th century. Several state legislatures mandated the collection of statistics on crime and criminals in two categories: judicial and prison statistics. Judicial statistics included information on persons appearing before the courts and their offenses. New York (1829) and Pennsylvania (1847) required clerks of the courts to submit transcripts or statements of convictions and/or criminal business. In 1832, Massachusetts mandated that the attorney general report his work and the work of the district attorneys to the legislature. In Maine (1839), county attorneys were required to report the number of persons prosecuted and their offenses to the attorney general, who also was required to submit a report to the governor. Twenty-five states legislated the collection of judicial criminal statistics between 1829 and 1905 (L. N. Robinson, 1911). State prison statistics were collected in two ways: Sheriff and prison officials sent information to either the secretary of state or a state board of charities and corrections. Massachusetts required reports as early as 1834; most other states mandated prison statistics later in the 1800s or early in the 20th century. Robinson described these statistics as less comprehensive than judicial statistics.

At the federal level, the collection of crime statistics was the responsibility of the U.S. Bureau of the Census during the 1800s. Beginning in 1850, the sixth census of

the population required U.S. Marshals to collect population statistics for free inhabitants of jails and penitentiaries. In addition to counting inmates, data were collected on
the sex, age, nativity, and color (of the native born) of convicted persons and prisoners
(L. N. Robinson, 1911). For the native born, the categories of Native, White, and Colored
were included. Knepper and Potter (1998) attributed distinctions between foreign-born
and native-born criminals to immigration in the last two decades of the 1800s. A shift
from nativity to biological conceptions of race in crime statistics paralleled developments in eugenics and criminal anthropology (Knepper, 1996; Knepper & Potter, 1998).
According to L. N. Robinson (1911), federal crime statistics really began with the 1880
census, when prisoner, judicial, and police statistics were collected and published for
the first time. Noted penologist Frederick H. Wines was given the responsibility of revis-
ing the crime statistics for the 1880 census. Since 1880, there have been several changes
in the collection of census crime statistics, but, for the most part, they continue to be
prison criminal statistics.

In 1870, Congress passed a law requiring the attorney general to report statistics on
crime annually, including crimes under federal and state laws. A year later, in 1871, the
organizing conference that created the National Police Association (now known as the
International Association of Chiefs of Police) called for "crime statistics for police use" (Maltz,
1977, p. 33). The 1880 and 1890 censuses collected police statistics, although they were not
reported.

By the 1880s, lynching, a form of social control, was a crude, cruel, and often ritualized
form of murder, especially in the South. Due to prevailing attitudes about both race and
crime, lynching was not always viewed as a crime, and lynchers were not always viewed
as criminals. There is no mention of lynching in the early historical analyses of crime
statistics (see e.g., Maltz, 1977; L. N. Robinson, 1911; Wolfgang, 1963). Data on lynchings
were collected by the *Chicago Tribune,* and in 1882, the newspaper began publishing the
number of persons lynched and the reasons why (Perloff, 2000). During the early 20th
century, Tuskegee Institute and the National Association for the Advancement of Colored
People (NAACP) also collected lynching data. Early lynching statistics only included Whites
and Negroes. Even though the historical record focused primarily on Negroes and Whites,
Latinos, Native Americans, and Asian Americans were victimized as well (Gonzales-Day,
2006). Mexicans were targeted in Arizona, California, New Mexico, and Texas (Delgado,
2009). Mexicans and Blacks were often lynched for "acting 'uppity,' taking away jobs, making advances toward a white woman, . . . with one exception, Mexicans were lynched for
acting 'too Mexican'—speaking Spanish too loudly or reminding Anglos too defiantly of
their Mexicanness" (Delgado, 2009, p. 299).

Between 1880 and 1891, it is estimated that 100 Negroes (the classification at the
time) were lynched each year (Perloff, 2000). Reported lynchings appeared to be most
frequent between 1884 and 1901 (Raper, 1933; Zangrando, 1980). In 1892, the largest number of lynchings (255) was reported, and in 1932, the lowest number (8) was
reported. Between 1889 and 1932, there were 3,745 lynchings reported; 2,954 were
Negroes, and 791 were Whites (Raper, 1933; see Table 2.2). Between 1882 and 1968,
there were 4,742 lynchings recorded, and 3,445 (73%) victims were Black (Perloff, 2000).
Delgado (2009) noted that even though there is very little information on Latino lynching, the rate of lynching for Blacks and Latinos was similar during and immediately after
Reconstruction. It remains unclear how lynchings were recorded in the major source of
crime data described next.

Table 2.2

Reported Lynchings, Whites and Negroes, 1889–1932

Year	Whites	Negroes	Total
1889	81	95	176
1890	37	90	127
1891	71	121	192
1892	100	155	255
1893	46	155	201
1894	56	134	190
1895	59	112	171
1896	51	80	131
1897	44	122	166
1898	25	108	133
1899	23	84	107
1900	8	107	115
1901	28	107	135
1902	11	86	97
1903	17	86	103
1904	4	83	87
1905	5	61	66
1906	8	65	73
1907	3	60	63
1908	7	93	100
1909	14	73	87
1910	9	65	74
1911	8	63	71

(Continued)

(Continued)

Year	Whites	Negroes	Total
1912	4	61	65
1913	1	50	51
1914	3	49	52
1915	13	54	67
1916	4	50	54
1917	2	36	38
1918	4	60	64
1919	7	76	83
1920	8	53	61
1921	5	59	64
1922	6	51	57
1923	4	29	33
1924	0	16	16
1925	0	17	17
1926	7	23	30
1927	0	16	16
1928	1	10	11
1929	3	7	10
1930	1	20	21
1931	1	12	13
1932	2	6	8
TOTAL	791	2,954	3,745

Note: The deaths from the race riots in Atlanta, Chicago, Tulsa, and other places are not classified as lynchings; neither are gang murders in Southern or Northern cities. As popularly defined, a chief distinction between a lynching and a gang murder is that whereas the latter is premeditated and carried out by a few people in conspired secrecy from constituted authorities, the former is usually spontaneous and carried out in public fashion with scores, hundreds, and not uncommonly thousands of eyewitnesses. Gang murderers—like other murderers—operate in secrecy to evade the law; lynchers operate in the open and publicly defy the law.

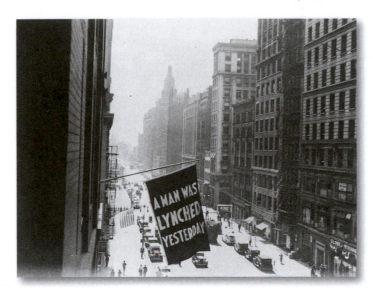

❖ The Uniform Crime Reporting Program

The history of the FBI's **Uniform Crime Reporting program** began in 1927, when a sub-committee of the International Association of Chiefs of Police (IACP) was charged with the task of studying uniform crime reporting. In 1930, the FBI began collecting data from police departments. At the time, there was considerable debate about what data should be collected, the responsible federal agency, and the reliability of the data (Maltz, 1977). Wolfgang (1963) noted that Warner (1929, 1931) was opposed to the federal government collecting statistics on crimes known to the police. Warner (1931), in a report on crime statistics for the National Commission on Law Observance and Enforcement (the Wickersham Commission), recommended that police crime statistics not be collected by the federal government. He believed that the UCRs would do more harm than good because they were both inaccurate and incomplete. By publishing crime statistics, the federal government would give credence to the UCRs, which, in turn, would influence public opinion and legislation.

Despite support for the U.S. Bureau of the Census to collect crime data, in 1930, the FBI was mandated by Congress to compile crime data collected by the police. Reports were issued monthly (1930–1931), quarterly (1932–1941), semi-annually with annual accumulations (1942–1957), and annually beginning in 1958. UCR contributors compile information on crimes reported, cleared, persons arrested, and law enforcement personnel, and they forward it to either a state UCR program or directly to the FBI. Seven offenses comprised what was known as the crime index—murder/nonnegligent manslaughter, forcible rape, robbery, aggravated assault, burglary, larceny/theft, and motor vehicle theft—until 1979, when arson was added. The UCR program's Supplementary Homicide Report (SHR) provides information about murder victims, offenders, and incidents.

During its history, several changes have occurred in the UCR program. In 1957, a Consultant Committee on Uniform Crime Reporting made 22 recommendations for changes, although only two were implemented, including changes in statistical presentation and revision in classification of the crime index (Wolfgang, 1963). In 1980, the UCR renamed arrest categories to include American Indian or Alaskan Native and Asian or Pacific Islander. During the 1980s, efforts began to modernize the UCR program, which culminated in implementation of the National Incident-Based Reporting System (NIBRS) in 1988. According to the FBI (1998), the NIBRS was created to enhance the quantity, quality, and timeliness of crime statistical data collected by the law enforcement community and to improve the methodology used for compiling, analyzing, auditing, and publishing the collected crime data.

NIBRS data are collected on eight index crimes and 38 other offenses, victims, offenders, and circumstances of crime incidents. Unlike the UCR, the NIBRS records each offense occurring, attempted and completed crimes, and weapons information for all violent offenses (Rantala & Edwards, 2000). It also includes information on multiple victims, offenders, and crimes that are part of the same incident. Today, only 19 states and all local agencies in only three states (Idaho, Iowa, and South Carolina) participate in the NIBRS. Thus, they are not representative of the nation as a whole (Finkelhor & Ormrod, 2004). Although informative, NIBRS data are weakened by the low participation of police agencies and most states.

The FBI Criminal Justice Information Services Division established a Data Providers' Advisory Policy Board (APB) in 1988 that, in 2004, approved discontinuing the use of the Crime Index and using a violent crime total and property crime total instead (FBI, 2010a). More recent changes mandated by federal legislation require that the FBI collect cargo theft data, human trafficking crime data, and more detailed hate crime statistics.

A year after President George H. W. Bush signed the Hate Crime Statistics Act into law in April, 1990, the FBI developed the National Hate Crime Data Collection Program (NHCDCP) and began reporting hate crime statistics in 1992 (Nolan, Akiyama, & Berhanu, 2002). Hate/bias crime statistics include information on victims, offenders, and incidents for eight index crimes, as well as simple assault, intimidation, and destruction/damage/vandalism. An incident is considered a **hate crime** whenever the facts indicate actions by an offender were motivated by bias against certain individuals or groups. In 2009, the Hate Crime Statistics Act of 1990 was amended to include gender, gender identity bias, and crimes committed by and directed against juveniles under the Matthew Shepard and James Byrd, Jr. Hate Crime Prevention Act. The number of police agencies participating in the NHCDCP has increased since 1991. In 2006, 12,620 agencies representing about 85.2% of the total U.S. population (FBI, 2007b) were participating. In 2009, 14,422 agencies were included and represented about 90.9% of the total U.S. population (FBI, 2010b). Hate/bias crime information is available in both the FBI UCR program and the NCVS.

Photo 2.2

FBI Criminal Justice Information Services Building, West Virginia

❖ Victimization Surveys

One of the earliest victimization surveys was conducted by the National Opinion Research Center for the President's Commission on Law Enforcement and the Administration of Justice in the 1960s. Letting citizens self-report their victimizations was viewed as another way to determine the extent of crime, especially crime that never came to the attention of the police. Today, the NCVS is the primary source of information on victims of nonfatal violent and property crimes in the United States. In 1972, the Law Enforcement Assistance Administration implemented the NCVS, originally known as the National Crime Survey. Since its inception, the U.S. Bureau of the Census has administered the NCVS. Initially, there were four surveys, a complex survey design, sampling, and estimating schemes. Criminal victimization reports have been issued annually since 1973 and are now prepared by BJS statisticians.

The early surveys included about 100,000 persons and 50,000 households in 26 cities. Information about victims, offenders, and reporting was collected from a representative sample of households. Interviews of persons 12 years old and over identifies rape, robbery, assault, personal and household larceny, burglary, and auto theft victimizations. The NCVS includes both attempted and completed crimes that "are of major concern to the general public and law enforcement authorities" (BJS, 1992, p. iii). Initially, businesses were included, but they were dropped, along with city surveys of individuals, in the 1970s (Mosher, Miethe, & Phillips, 2002). The NCVS includes data on homicide victims although it does not collect it. Historically, victimization data were more detailed than UCR arrest data and provided more information about the race, gender, and age of victims.

The NCVS also has undergone changes since its inception. In 1992, the name was changed after a redesign of the survey was implemented (Kindermann, Lynch, & Cantor, 1997). The Crime Survey Redesign Consortium recommended numerous changes in the crime survey to improve its accuracy (B. M. Taylor, 1989). The redesign specifically focused on improving the collection of data by expanding the capability of the survey to prompt recall by respondents. The Crime Victims with Disabilities Awareness Act of 1998 mandated the inclusion of victims with disabilities in the NCVS (Harrell & Rand, 2010). In 2000, questions were added to the NCVS to identify victims of hate crimes (Harlow, 2005).

Enhanced screening questions are believed to have improved recall of respondents about domestic violence, rape, and sexual attacks, which has led to higher estimates of some victimization rates (Kindermann et al., 1997). Approximately 87,000 households and 159,000 persons were interviewed in 2000 (Mosher et al., 2002). In 2006, 135,300 persons and 76,000 households were included, and the NCVS sample was redrawn to include households in the 2000 census, resulting in a sample of first-time interviews. Unlike in the past, first-time interviews that are not comparable to interviews completed in previous years are included in the 2006 report, due to insufficient funding (Rand & Catalano, 2007). In 2009, the NCVS included even fewer persons (68,665) and households (38,728) than in previous years (Truman & Rand, 2010). This NCVS limitation and others of both arrest and victimization data are discussed next.

❖ Limitations of Arrest and Victimization Data

Since the inception of the various sources of crime statistics, their problems have been acknowledged. One criticism of crime statistics is that they are unreliable because they cannot tell us how much crime takes place, how many persons were arrested, or how many crime victims there are. At most, arrest statistics are no more than "descriptions of the persons who, for a veritably endless array of reasons (many of which are beyond our knowledge) are subjected to arrest" (Geis, 1972, p. 65). As previously noted, there was opposition to the collection of police crime statistics early in the 20th century due, in part, to their limitations. Victimization surveys have several deficiencies as well (Mann, 1993; Mosher et al., 2011). Table 2.3 provides a summary of the limitations of arrest (police) statistics and victimization data. Despite improvements, each collection method still has problems, including definitions of racial categories; variations in reporting and recording; and utilization of population, crime, arrest, and victimization estimates. These limitations are briefly described next (for a comprehensive overview of these limitations, see Mosher et al., 2011).

Definitions of Racial Categories

Racial categories in the 2000 and 2010 census were guided by Directive No. 15, issued by the Office of Federal Statistical Policy and Standards in 1977. The 2000 and 2010 census expanded racial categories to reflect the diversity of multiracial Americans. Despite improvements in racial categories in the census and other federal statistical compilations, racial categories in crime and victimization statistics are still problematic. One problem is the classification of persons of Hispanic origin. Hispanics are classified as an ethnic group in federal statistics, but the category is not included in FBI UCR arrest statistics.

Table 2.3

Limitations of Arrest and Victimization Data

Issue	Arrest (Police) Statistics	Victimization Data
Arrest estimates	X	
Citizen reporting	X	X
Counting only the most serious crime	X	
Crime estimates	X	
Definition of crime categories	X	X
Definition of racial categories	X	X
Omission of offenses		X
Police recording	X	
Population estimates	X	X
Political manipulation	X	
Social construction of crime/criminals	X	X
Victimization estimates		X

Knepper (1996) noted that there is no scientific definition of race, that social categories of race are both simplistic and wrong, and that official racial categories are the result of legal definitions that date back to slavery. He stated, "Race is a political concept. . . . [It] represents a powerful means of reinforcing an ideology of distinct races that began during the colonial period and was cemented during Jim Crow" (p. 86). Knepper argued that contemporary race-coded statistics descended from an ancestry of scientific racism. He questioned how analyses using official statistics can provide objective findings if race cannot be objectively defined. As the quotation at the beginning of the chapter indicates, crime statistics can be misleading and perpetuate errors and myths about racial minorities (Geis, 1972).

Racial data first appeared in the UCR in 1933 and included three categories: Whites, Blacks, and Others. In 1934, the UCR included a Mexican category that was dropped in 1941. Initially, age, sex, and race of persons arrested were compiled from fingerprint cards submitted by police departments to the FBI. Since 1953, race has been taken from the reported arrest information. Arrests for Whites (foreign and native born), Negroes, Indians, Chinese, Japanese, Mexicans, and others were reported separately. Chinese and Japanese were counted separately until 1970, when the Asian American category was included (LaFree, 1995). Today, there are four racial categories: White, Black, American Indian and Alaskan Native, and Asian and Pacific Islander. According to the FBI UCR, it will expand race categories from four to five (to include Native Hawaiian; FBI, 2010a).

A Hispanic ethnic category was added in 1980, although it did not distinguish between Hispanic/Latino groups (Puerto Rican, Mexican, Cuban, etc.) and was discontinued after 1985. Since then, Hispanic/Latinos have been included in the White category. The FBI ethnic categories will change from Hispanic and Non-Hispanic to Hispanic or Latino Origin and Not of Hispanic or Latino Origin to conform to the Office of Management and Budget directive (FBI, 2010a). It's not clear whether this information will be provided in UCR arrest tables. Counting American Indians is also problematic because they are located in a variety of jurisdictions under numerous police agencies (Greenfield & Smith, 1999). The NCVS has included racial categories since its inception in 1973. Initially, victimizations for Blacks, Whites, and Others were reported. The "Other" category was used for Asian Pacific Islanders, American Indians, Aleut and Eskimos; Hispanics were omitted until 1977 and do not appear in *Criminal Victimization, 2006.* Despite efforts to develop and improve racial categories, they are fatally flawed for two reasons. First, they are unable to capture intraracial and intraethnic heterogeneity. As Georges-Abeyie (1989) correctly noted, there is no Black ethnic monolith. All Blacks are not the same; they have different cultural and ethnic backgrounds representing numerous countries and different social classes. Other racial categories also suffer from this limitation. Asian Americans, Latinos/Latinas, Native Americans, and Whites have varying backgrounds, experiences, and cultures that cannot be captured by counting them as if they were all the same. If the racial categories are in actuality meaningless, perhaps they are unnecessary. Second, how racial categories and ethnicity are determined is questionable and often inaccurate. In both the UCR and NCVS, discretionary determinations about race and ethnicity for both arrestees and victims occur. In the past, race was initially determined by the interviewer's observation, and respondents were asked about the racial/ethnic identity of the offender.

Variations in Reporting and Recording

Wolfgang (1963) noted the problems associated with efforts to obtain uniform reporting when police agencies participate and report voluntarily to the UCR program. Throughout the history of the UCR, some agencies have submitted incomplete reports or no reports. For various reasons, citizens do not report and police do not record all crimes. Likewise, and perhaps more germane, police selectively enforce the law, which contributes to variations by race. Variations in crime categories and counting only the most serious crimes are also especially problematic for the UCR. Underreporting is also common. For example, although Native American arrest rates appear to be low, an analysis of victimization trends showed much higher levels of Native American victimizations than expected (Greenfield & Smith, 1999). Recording and reporting discrepancies also affect the NCVS because the accuracy in reporting victimizations remains unknown.

Utilization of Population, Crime, Arrest, and Victimization Estimates

Estimations are an important part of the methodology and findings reported in both the UCR and NCVS. The UCR uses population estimates to calculate the crime and arrest rates. Inaccurate population estimates affect crime and arrest statistics. According to Mosher et al. (2011), these estimates are misleading because the census counts the population only every 10 years.

The NCVS relies on a sample of the population to estimate crime victimizations experienced by citizens. Their estimation procedures are important to understanding their utility. Although efforts are made to minimize differences between the sample population and the total population, there are biases related to recall and estimates of multiple victimizations (BJS, 1992). Due to NCVS methodological changes in 2006, estimates for that year were not comparable to pre- and post-2006 survey results.

Several problems have been identified that are particularly relevant to understanding racial victimizations. First, it is unclear how representative the samples are because they are based on census data that are known to undercount minorities. Second, survey estimates are based on sampling units that may not adequately capture all racial groups in the population. Third, for Asians and American Indians, the sample size is so small that it affects the reliability of the estimate (Rennison, 2001b).

Despite the limitations of the UCR and NCVS, scholars continue to rely on them to gauge the extent of crime and victimization. For decades, comparisons of White and Black arrestees and victims have been a major focus in the study of race and crime. These comparisons have resulted in misperceptions about race and crime, which is why it is important to understand not only the sources of crime data and their limitations, but also what arrest and victimization trends do and do not tell us about race/ethnicity and crime/victimization. To better understand the extent of crime and victimization, we examine arrest patterns over time (1933–2009), arrests for murder for 60 years (1950–2010), and recent victimization trends (2007–2009).

❖ Arrest Trends

The UCR provide crime and arrest data on four violent crimes against the person—murder (and nonnegligent manslaughter), forcible rape, robbery, and aggravated assault—and four property crimes: burglary, larceny/theft, motor vehicle theft, and arson, formerly known as Part I offenses. The FBI estimates that 1,246,248 violent crimes and 9,082,887 property crimes occurred in the United States in 2010 (FBI, 2011c). That year, there were an estimated 10,177,907 persons arrested, 429,166 for violent crimes and 1,288,295 for property crimes (FBI, 2011e). Historically, most persons arrested for violent offenses were arrested for aggravated assault. For decades, Blacks have been overrepresented in arrests for violent crimes and at various times have outnumbered Whites arrested for murder, robbery, and aggravated assault but not for forcible rape. More recent trends show Whites arrested more often than Blacks for aggravated assault and rape. Although there are fewer homicides reported than other violent personal crimes, they receive considerable attention. As previously mentioned, arrest data have been reported annually since 1933. Analyzing both historical and contemporary arrest data and trends provides a better temporal perspective than just looking at the past year, the past two years, the past five years, or the past 10 years.

A summary of arrests by race between 1933 and 2010 is presented in Table A.1 (see Appendix). In the early years (1933–1941), total arrests increased steadily, as did White and Black arrests; declined for Whites between 1942 and 1944; and declined for Blacks between 1942 and 1943. There was fluctuation in arrests of Mexicans, Indians, Chinese, Japanese, and "Other" races during this period. The downward trend in total arrests and arrests of Whites ended in 1945 and ended a year earlier for Blacks. Arrests continued to increase between 1945 and 1953, and there was a substantial increase in arrests in 1952, when total arrests were more than 1 million for the first time. By 1953, there were more than 1 million arrests of Whites, and by 1960, more than 1 million arrests of Blacks. Arrest data between 1950 and 1972 provide support for the concern about crime at that time. By 1970, the number of total arrests surpassed 6 million; by 1978, the number was 9 million, and it finally peaked in 1992 at almost 12 million arrests. Between 1994 and 2000, total arrests steadily decreased and fluctuated slightly from year to year for all racial categories. Between 2000 and 2009 total arrests continued to fluctuate, and between 2009 and 2010 there were decreases in arrests in all racial categories. Table A.2 (see Appendix) presents the total number of arrests and arrests for murder and nonnegligent manslaughter by race between 1950 and 2010. Since 1952, with a few exceptions (1950 and 1951, 1979–1981, 1984–1986, and 2003–2005), the number of Blacks arrested for murder/nonnegligent manslaughter has outnumbered Whites. Between 1952 and 1962, the number of Blacks and Whites arrested for murder tripled. Between 1963 and 1972, Black arrests for murder steadily increased and tripled from 2,948 to 8,347. Arrests for Whites doubled during this same period. There were fewer arrests of American Indians, Chinese, Japanese, and Others. Between 1976 and 1978, murder arrests increased and continued to fluctuate until 1994. Between 1994 and 2000, homicide arrests steadily decreased, although there was some fluctuation within racial categories. Between 2000 and 2006, the number of persons arrested for murder continued to fluctuate. Since 2007, arrests for murder have decreased and are much lower than reported arrests for murder during the 1970s, 1980s, and most of the 1990s. In 2009 there were 9,739 reported arrests for murder and in 2010 there were 8,641—considerably fewer than the number of arrests reported in the late 1960s through the late 1990s.

Snyder (2011) provides a comprehensive analysis of arrest rates by gender, age, and race from 1980 to 2009 for several violent and property crimes as well as weapons and drug violations. "Over the 30-year period the black arrest rate for murder averaged 7 times the white rate" (p. 3). The Black arrest rate fluctuated during the period and fell sharply between 1991 and 2009, while the White rate gradually declined. "The American Indian/Alaskan Native (AIAN) rate averaged twice the white arrest rate, while the Asian/Pacific Islander (API) rate averaged half the white rate" (p. 3).

Arrest trends for murder/nonnegligent manslaughter also can be analyzed by type of jurisdiction where the arrest occurred. As Schwartz (2010) states,

> Homicide is rare, but it is more common in some groups, places, or time periods than in others . . . Homicide offenders and victims tend to be concentrated more heavily in communities characterized by economic and social disadvantages. (p. 294)

Between 2006 and 2009, Blacks arrested for murder outnumbered Whites arrested in cities. In metropolitan and nonmetropolitan counties and suburban areas, the number of Whites arrested for murder outnumbered Blacks (see Table 2.4).

Although arrests for violent crimes are significant due to their seriousness, continuing to focus on them minimizes the importance of other arrest trends. Again, most Americans are not arrested for serious violent crimes; the data actually reveal that more Americans are arrested for other types of offenses. Table 2.5 shows the five offenses for which individuals were most likely to be arrested in 2010, by racial categories. These offenses include larceny/theft, drug abuse violations, driving under the influence, drunkenness, disorderly conduct, liquor law violations, and other assaults. Most Whites were arrested for driving under the influence, most Blacks were arrested for drug abuse violations, most American Indian/Alaskan Natives were arrested for other assaults, and most Asian or Pacific Islanders for driving under the influence. Whites outnumber Blacks arrested for drug abuse violations, and American Indian/Alaskan Natives outnumber Asian/Pacific Islanders arrested for driving under the influence.

❖ Victimization Trends

In the past, the BJS periodically published reports from the NCVS that provided more comprehensive information on victimization trends and analyses for racial groups (see, e.g., Greenfield & Smith, 1999; S. W. Perry, 2004; Harrell, 2007, 2009; Whitaker, 1990; Bastian, 1990; Rennison, 2001, 2002). More recent BJS publications provide limited data useful for race and ethnicity trend victimization analyses (see, e.g., Rand & Catalano, 2007; Truman & Rand, 2010), although recent reports on hate crime victims and crime against persons with disabilities do include information on race (Harlow, 2005; Harrell & Rand, 2010; Langton & Planty, 2011).

Figure 2.1 presents trends in violent victimization rates for blacks and whites between 1973 and 2007. Reported victimizations have decreased substantially during the past two decades. In 1973, there were an estimated 35,661,030 victimizations. Violent victimization rates (VVRs) fluctuate over time. Between 1986 and 1990, the VVR steadily increased to 31.7 per 1,000 persons. Personal theft victimization rates fluctuated between a low of 67.5 (1986) and a high of 97.3 (1977). During this period, Whites had higher victimization rates for simple assault, whereas Blacks had higher victimization rates for aggravated assault and robbery. Black females had a pattern of higher victimization rates for rape than did White females. Victimization levels and rates for larceny/theft with contact were higher for Blacks than Whites, and larceny/thefts without contact victimization were higher for Whites than Blacks. This pattern occurred regardless of gender. Rates of burglary incidents and motor vehicle thefts were much higher for Blacks and others than for Whites

Table 2.4

Reported Arrests for Murder by Race, 2006–2010, in Cities, Metropolitan Counties, Nonmetropolitan Counties, and Suburban Areas

	Total	White	Black	American Indian or Alaskan Native	Asian or Pacific Islander	Percentage White	Percentage Black	Percentage American Indian or Alaskan Native	Percentage Asian or Pacific Islander
2006									
City	7,210	2,999	4,054	65	92	41.6	56.2	0.9	1.3
Metropolitan county	1,969	1,195	747	16	11	60.7	37.9	0.8	0.6
Nonmetropolitan county	622	401	189	29	3	64.5	30.4	4.7	0.5
Suburban areas	3,073	1,775	1,254	26		18	57.8	40.8	0.8
2007									
City	7,505	3,151	4,201	66	87	42.0	56.0	0.9	1.2
Metropolitan county	1,944	1,213	713	6	12	62.4	36.7	0.3	0.6
Nonmetropolitan county	618	425	164	27	2	68.8	26.5	4.4	0.3
Suburban areas	3,093	1,761	1,293	17	22	56.9	41.8	0.5	0.7
2008									
City	7,392	3,215	4,022	62	93	43.5	54.4	0.8	1.3
Metropolitan county	1,864	1,128	718	9	9	60.5	38.5	0.5	0.5
Nonmetropolitan county	603	378	195	28	2	62.7	32.3	4.6	0.3
Suburban areas	2,960	1,718	1,210	13	19	58.0	40.9	0.4	0.6

(Continued)

(Continued)

	Total	White	Black	American Indian or Alaskan Native	Asian or Pacific Islander	Percentage White	Percentage Black	Percentage American Indian or Alaskan Native	Percentage Asian or Pacific Islander
2009									
City	7,149	3,112	3,896	65	76	43.5	54.5	0.9	1.1
Metropolitan county	1,840	1,121	694	8	17	60.9	37.7	0.4	0.9
Nonmetropolitan county	750	508	211	27	4	67.7	28.1	3.6	0.5
Suburban areas	2,903	1,683	1,184	12	24	58.0	40.8	0.4	0.8
2010									
City	6,350	2,832	3,406	46	66	44.6	53.6	0.7	1.0
Metropolitan county	1,655	997	636	11	11	60.2	38.4	0.7	0.7
Nonmetropolitan county	636	432	167	34	3	67.9	26.3	5.3	0.5
Suburban areas	2,675	1,560	1,075	18	22	58.3	40.2	0.7	0.8

Table 2.5

Five Most Frequent Arrest Offenses Within Racial Categories, 2010

White		Black		American Indian/Alaskan Native		Asian/Pacific Islander	
Driving under the influence	927,516	Drug abuse violations	404,609	Other assaults	14,848	Driving under the influence	16,338
Drug abuse violations	846,736	Other assaults	318,117	Larceny/theft	14,323	Larceny/theft	14,298
Larceny/theft	687,609	Larceny/theft	282,246	Liquor law violations	14,129	Other assaults	12,137
Other assaults	659,171	Disorderly conduct	162,521	Driving under the influence	13,980	Drug abuse violations	10,332
Drunkenness	362,396	Driving under the influence	124,467	Drug abuse violations	8,766	Liquor law violations	5,389

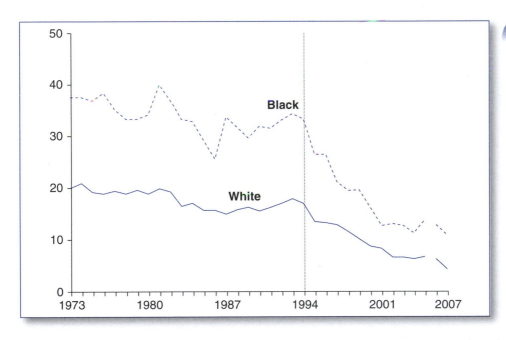

Figure 2.1

Violent Crime Rates by Race of Victim

Note: Adjusted victimization rate per 1,000 persons age 12 or older.

What are the most plausible explanations for decreases in violent victimization trends for both Blacks and Whites since 1994?

(Bastian, 1992). In 1993, the VVR was 69.3; in 2001 it was 29.7; in 2005 it was 28.6; and in 2009 the VVR was at the lowest rate ever, 16.9 per 1,000 population age 12 or older (Harrell, 2007).

American Indian violent victimizations between 1992 and 1996 were more than twice as high as the national rate. The aggravated assault rate was twice as high as that of Blacks and three times the national rate (Greenfield & Smith, 1999). Estimates of Hispanic victimizations between 1992 and 2000 fell from 63 to 28 per 1,000. Similar to violent victimization in other racial categories, simple assaults were common, and Hispanic males were victimized most often (Rennison, 2002). The Hispanic VVR fluctuated more between 1993 and 2000; the highest rate was reported in 1994 (61.6) and the lowest rate in 2002 (23.6).

An examination of violent victimizations in the 2000s shows that a decline that began in 1994 continued until 2002 (Rennison & Rand, 2003). In 2001, Americans experienced approximately 24.2 million victimizations, 18.3 million property victimizations, and 5.7 million violent victimizations; in 2005, an estimated 23 million violent and property victimizations occurred. Average annual violent victimizations between 2001 and 2005 indicate that Blacks have higher VVRs for rape/sexual assault and robbery, although American Indian/Alaska Natives have the highest VVR (56.8; Catalano, 2006). Between 2002 and 2006, Asians had the lowest VVR and were the least likely to be victims of serious violent crimes (Harrell, 2009). In 2006 there were an estimated 25 million violent and property crime victimizations of persons over the age of 12; approximately 19 million were property crime victims, and 6 million were violent crime victims. This was an increase over previous years. However, the methodology for the NCVS changed in 2006 (Rand & Catalano, 2007). Violent victimization trends between 2007 and 2009 are presented in Tables 2.6 and 2.7. The victimization patterns in 2009 are similar to previous years: higher VVR for males (18.4), Blacks (26.8), and youth aged 12 to 15 (36.8). Homicide victimizations are discussed next.

Homicide Victimizations

If you watch the nightly news you might conclude that homicide offenses occur quite often when in fact, compared to other offenses, they are rare. Homicide is one of the more accurately measured offenses (Schwartz, 2010). As previously stated, homicide victimizations are reported annually in the UCR Supplementary Homicide Reports and have been published in the NCVS reports as well. Table 2.8 presents the characteristics of homicide victims known to the police in 2009. Of the 13,636 victims, most were males. Although fewer females were victims, like males, they were more likely to be between the ages of 20 and 29. There were more White than Black homicide victims in 2009, and more White victims (654) than Black victims (639) under the age of 18.

Even though most victims of homicides are males, White females are more likely to be victims of intimate homicides. Black offenders are more likely than Whites to commit drug-related homicides, whereas Whites are more likely to commit murders in the workplace and have multiple victims (Fox & Zawitz, 2007).

Hate Crime Trends

The terms *hate* and *bias crimes* refer to offenses committed against individuals because of their race, religion, ethnicity, sexual orientation, or disability. The Civil Rights Division of the DOJ "enforces federal statutes prohibiting discrimination on the basis of race, color, sex, disability, religion, familial status and national origin" (DOJ, 2011). As previously mentioned, the Matthew Shepard and James Byrd, Jr. Hate Crimes Prevention Act enacted in October, 2009 broadened the scope of the original 1990 hate crime legislation. The first

Table 2.6

National Crime Victimization Rates and Percent Change in Rates, by Type of Crime, 2007–2009

Type of crime	Rates per 1,000 persons or households			Percent change[a]		
	2007	2008	2009	2007-2008	2007-2009	2008-2009
Violent crime[b]	20.7	19.3	17.1	−6.9%	−17.3%*	−11.2%*
Rape/sexual assault	1.0	0.8	0.5	−18.5	−50.0*	−38.7**
Robbery	2.4	2.2	2.1	−8.3	−12.0	−4.0
Assault	17.3	16.3	14.5	−6.0	−16.2*	−10.8*
Aggravated	3.4	3.3	3.2	−2.9	−5.6	−2.7
Simple	13.9	12.9	11.3	-6.8	−18.8*	−12.9*
Personal theft[c]	0.8	0.5	0.5	−30.1%*	−32.4%*	−3.3%
Property crime	146.5	134.7	127.4	8.1%*	−13.1%*	−5.5%*
Burglary	26.9	26.3	25.6	−2.2	−4.7	−2.6
Motor vehicle theft	8.2	6.6	6.0	−19.9*	−26.6*	−8.4
Theft	111.4	101.8	95.7	−8.6*	−14.1*	−6.0*
Population						
Person age 12 or older	250,344,870	252,242,520	254,105,610			
Households headed by persons age 12 or older	119,503,530	121,141,060	122,327,660			

Source: Truman and Rand (2010, Table 3, p. 3)

* Difference is significant at the 95% confidence level.

** Difference is significant at the 90% confidence level.

a. Not Hispanic or Latino. Percent change calculated based on unrounded estimates.

b. Based on 10 or fewer sample cases. Excludes murder because the NCVS is based on interviews with victims and therefore cannot measure murder.

c. Includes pocket picking, completed purse snatching, and attempted purse snatching.

Table 2.7

Rates of Violent Crime, by Gender, Race, Hispanic Origin, and Age of Victim, 2009

Demographic characteristics of victim	Population	Violent victimizations per 1,000 persons age 12 or older					
		Total	Rape/sexual assault	Robbery	Total assault	Aggravated assault	Simple assault
Gender							
Male	121,041,190	18.4	0.2^	2.7	15.6	4.3	11.3
Female	130,064,420	15.8	0.8	1.6	13.5	2.3	11.2
Race							
White	206,331,920	15.8	0.4	1.6	13.7	2.7	11.0
Black	31,046,560	26.8	1.2	5.6	19.9	6.8	13.0
Other race*	13,982,530	9.8	—^	0.5^	9.3	1.9^	7.4
Two or more races	2,744,600	42.1	—^	5.2^	36.9	9.3^	27.5
Hispanic origin							
Hispanic	35,375,280	18.1	0.5^	3.4	14.2	3.2	11.0
Non-Hispanic	218,238,010	17.0	0.5	1.9	14.6	3.3	11.3
Age							
12-15	16,230,240	36.8	0.9^	3.1	32.8	6 9	25.9
16-19	17,203,070	30.3	0.6^	5.2	24.6	5.3	19.3
20-24	20,620,150	28.1	0.8^	3.5	23.8	7.5	16.3
25-34	41,073,240	21.5	0.8^	2.8	17.9	4.5	13.4
35-49	64,323,190	16.1	0.4^	2.0	13.7	2.6	11.1
50-64	56,651,170	10.7	0.3^	1.1	9.3	1.9	7.5
65 or older	38,004,060	3.2	0.2^	0.4^	2.5	0.3^	2.2

Source: Truman and Rand (2010, Table 5, p. 5).

Note: Violent crimes measured by the National Crime Victimization Survey include rape, sexual assault, robbery, aggravated assault, and simple assault. Because the NCVS interviews persons about their victimizations, murder and manslaughter cannot be included.

— Rounds to less than 0.05 violent victimizations per 1,000 persons age 12 or older.

^ Based on 10 or fewer sample cases.

* Includes American Indians, Alaska Natives, Asians, Native Hawaiians, and other Pacific Islanders.

Table 2.8

Murders and Nonnegligent Manslaughters Known to Police (by sex, race, and age of victim, United States, 2009)

Age of victim	Total	Sex of victim			Race of victim			
		Male	Female	Unknown	White	Black	Other	Unknown
Total	13,636	10,496	3,122	18	6,568	6,556	360	152
Under 18 years[a]	1,348	913	435	0	654	639	44	11
Under 22 years[a]	3,304	2,603	701	0	1,381	1,813	79	31
18 years and older[a]	12,095	9,459	2,632	4	5,821	5,847	313	114
Infant (under 1 year)	193	102	91	0	106	72	9	6
1 to 4 years	298	158	140	0	159	129	9	1
5 to 8 years	72	34	38	0	40	27	4	1
9 to 12 years	71	36	35	0	43	23	5	0
13 to 16 years	400	319	81	0	190	199	9	2
17 to 19 years	1,246	1,068	178	0	476	738	22	10
20 to 24 years	2,426	2,081	344	1	931	1,407	64	24
25 to 29 years	1,941	1,605	335	1	789	1,097	39	16
30 to 34 years	1,534	1,216	318	0	645	845	25	19
35 to 39 years	1,205	950	255	0	573	583	40	9
40 to 44 years	1,006	734	271	1	543	419	34	10
45 to 49 years	926	642	284	0	559	337	23	7
50 to 54 years	701	519	181	1	423	242	27	9
55 to 59 years	455	309	146	0	286	144	21	4
60 to 64 years	312	216	96	0	210	88	11	3
65 to 69 years	227	152	75	0	165	57	4	1
70 to 74 years	134	85	49	0	104	26	1	3
75 years and older	296	146	150	0	233	53	10	0
Unknown	193	124	55	14	93	70	3	27

Note: These data were compiled by the Federal Bureau of Investigation through the Uniform Crime Reporting (UCR) Program. On a monthly basis, law enforcement agencies (police, sheriffs, and State police) report the number of offenses that become known to them in the following crime categories: murder and nonnegligent manslaughter, forcible rape, robbery, aggravated assault, burglary, larceny-theft, motor vehicle theft, and arson. A count of these crimes is taken from records of all complaints of crime received by law enforcement agencies from victims or other sources and/or from officers who discovered the offenses. Whenever complaints of crime are determined through investigation to be unfounded or false, they are eliminated from an agency's count (Source, About Crime in the U.S., Methodology). The Uniform Crime Reporting Program requests that supplementary information be transmitted to the FBI when a murder or nonnegligent manslaughter has been committed. The actual number of offenses presented in the tables displaying characteristics of murders and nonnegligent manslaughters known to the police may differ from figures in other tables that reflect data from only the initial report of the offense. For example, supplementary data were provided by contributing agencies for 13,636 of the estimated total of 15,241 murders and nonnegligent manslaughters in 2009 (Source, 2009, Violent Crime, Murder).

a. Does not include unknown ages.

person convicted for a violation of the 2009 Act was Sean Popejoy, 19 years old, a resident of Green Forest, Arkansas (see Box 2.2). Thomas E. Perez, Assistant Attorney General for the DOJ Civil Rights Division stated,

> It is unacceptable that violent acts of hate committed because of someone's race continue to occur in 2011, and the department will continue to use every available tool to identify and prosecute hate crime whenever and wherever they occur. (DOJ, 2011)

BOX 2.2

Washington—The Justice Department announced today the arrest of Sean Popejoy, 19, and Frankie Maybee, 20, both of Green Forest, Ark., on charges related to a racially motivated assault on five Hispanic men. A federal grand jury in the Western District of Arkansas returned an indictment on April 5, 2011, charging Popejoy and Maybee with federal hate crime charges and conspiracy to commit a federal hate crime.

According to the indictment, Popejoy and Maybee have been charged with one count of conspiracy and five counts of violating the Matthew Shepard and James Byrd, Jr. Hate Crimes Prevention Act, which was enacted in October, 2009. Specifically, the indictment alleges that on June 20, 2010, the defendants yelled anti-Latino epithets at the victims while at a gas station parking lot. When the victims drove away, the defendants chased after them in the defendants' truck. The defendants eventually caught up to the victims' car and repeatedly rammed their truck into the victims' car, causing the victims' car to go off the road, overturn, and ignite. All five of the victims were physically injured as a result of the defendants' actions.

If convicted, the defendants face maximum penalties of 10 years in prison on each of the civil rights charges.

This case is being investigated by the FBI's Fayetteville Division in cooperation with the Arkansas State Police Department and the Carroll County Sheriff's Office. The case is being prosecuted by U.S. Attorney Conner Eldridge and Assistant U.S. Attorney Kyra Jenner for the Western District of Arkansas and Trial Attorney Edward Chung of the Department of Justice's Civil Rights Division.

An indictment is merely an accusation, and the defendants are presumed innocent unless proven guilty.

What do you think should be the punishment for Popejoy and Maybee? Use the Internet to determine the punishment they actually received.

Hate crimes are "severely underreported" (Gerstenfeld, 2010, p. 263). In addition to underreporting by victims, there are other problems with hate crime data, including differences in how hate crimes are recorded by police agencies (Gerstenfeld, 2010, 2011). As previously mentioned, hate crime statistics are collected and reported annually by the FBI. The NCVS reports information on hate crime victims as well. Even though the rate of violent hate crime victimizations appears to be decreasing, most hate crime victimizations involve violence (Langton & Planty, 2011).

Hate crime is more likely than street crime to involve crimes against the person than crimes against property (B. Perry, 2002). In 2010, the most commonly reported offenses against persons were intimidation, simple assault, and aggravated assault. Although there were fewer crimes against property, destruction/damage/vandalism ranked second to intimidation in hate/bias crime incidents. Most hate crimes motivated by race occur at the victim's residence/home. Hate crime also is more likely to be interracial; the race of most known offenders is White (FBI, 2011f). In a study of hate crimes reported in the NIBRS, the BJS (Strom, 2001) found that younger offenders were responsible for most hate crimes.

According to the NCVS, race is perceived by victims as the primary offender motivation (Harlow, 2005; Langton & Planty, 2011). Anti-Black bias crimes continue to outnumber offenses against other races as well as bias crimes motivated by victims' religion, sexual orientation, ethnicity, or disability (FBI, 2011f). Table 2.9 presents offenses classified as "single-bias incidents" by race and ethnicity between 2006 and 2010. The total number of single-bias incidents fluctuated between 2006 and 2009, as did incidents occurring within racial categories. Anti-Hispanic single-bias incidents steadily increased between 2006 and 2007 and decreased in 2008 and 2009.

❖ Conclusion

Decades of comparisons made between Blacks and Whites as arrestees and victims have resulted in several misperceptions about race and crime. In fact, comparisons between racial categories reveal more similarities than differences. For more than 80 years, the UCR has been the primary source of crime statistics, and for more than 30 years, the NCVS has provided victimization data. Although the data provide information about race and crime, racial categories in each data set are problematic. The effect, if any, of jurisdictional differences in reporting from time to time and place to place also are difficult to determine. The limitations of these data sets have persisted since their inception. At best, we can conclude that Americans are arrested for a variety of offenses, including violent crimes, property crimes, alcohol-related offenses, and drug abuse violations. Fewer persons are arrested for violent personal crimes, although they tend to receive the most attention in the study of crime. With few exceptions over time, Blacks continue to be arrested for murder more often than any

Table 2.9

Hate/Bias Crime Incidents Reported

	2006	2007	2008	2009	2010
Total single-bias incidents	4,000	7,621	7,780	6,698	6,624
Single-bias race					
Anti-White	890	749	716	545	575
Anti-Black	2,640	2,658	2,876	2,284	2,201
Anti-American Indian or Alaskan Native	60	61	54	65	44
Anti-Asian American or Pacific Islander	181	188	137	126	150
Anti-multiple races	229	214	209	179	165
Ethnicity					
Anti-Hispanic	576	595	561	483	534
Anti-other ethnicity/national origin	408	412	333	294	313

other race, although reported murders and arrests have decreased (compared with earlier decades), and Black homicide victimizations are at their lowest levels. Martinez, Stowell, and Lee (2010) noted that lethal violence research doesn't contribute to our understanding of nonlethal violence and property crime, especially among immigrants.

Victimization surveys provide some support for patterns found in UCR arrest data: Theft victimizations are more likely to be reported than rapes, aggravated assaults, and robberies. Among violent victimizations, simple assaults are reported most often. Unfortunately, fixation on violent crimes has contributed to the racialization of crime; statistics are used to provide empirical support for the overrepresentation of most minorities as arrestees and victims. As a result, many Americans equate violent crime with minorities and downplay other patterns and trends. Support for this idea can be easily found by asking students enrolled in criminal justice courses a few questions about persons arrested before presenting the material. Invariably, they believe that more Blacks than Whites are arrested, especially for drug offenses and rape.

Despite what they do tell us, what these two sources of crime statistics do not tell us is just as important. Arguably, they really do not tell us much about race and crime because we have vague categories to describe race and Latinos/Latinas are still included in the White category for arrest data. The data do not tell us about police bias and how that affects arrests. Most important, crime statistics tell us either nothing (UCR) or little (NCVS) about class and crime. The extent of race and crime as reported in arrest and victimization data is useful, although not definitive. It is important to recognize offenses that are most frequently reported in arrest and victimization data and move away from our fixation on violent crimes.

Finally, although hate/bias crimes have occurred for several hundred years, the collection of hate crime statistics is rather recent. White violence such as lynching may not be a crime problem today, but assaults and intimidation against individuals based on their race and/or ethnicity are problems today. Unlike most reported victimizations, hate/bias crimes are often interracial. Blacks are more likely than any other group to be the victims of bias crimes, although violence against Latinos and persons of Middle Eastern descent is increasing. With the expansion of the focus of hate crime legislation, it remains to be seen whether or not "new" victims of hate crimes will vary by race and ethnicity.

Photo 2.3

Derrick Donchak and Brandon Piekarsky, high school football players in Shenandoah who beat, stomped, and punched Luis Ramirez in 2008 because he was Mexican. Ramirez later died.

Discussion Questions

1. Discuss the importance of crime and victimization data in the study of race and crime.

2. Discuss the definitional issues related to racial categories in crime and victimization data.

3. Do you think that recent crime and victimization trends are accurate?

4. Why do you think some minorities are disproportionately arrested and victimized?

5. Why is there less publicity about anti-Black hate crimes than about Black arrests and victimizations?

Internet Exercises

1. Visit the United States Department of Justice Office of Civil Rights webpage (http://www.justice.gov/crt/) and peruse the Cases and Matters section. Summarize the information for two cases in a jurisdiction in your state or in close proximity to where you reside.

2. At the Bureau of Justice Statistics website, use the UCR Data Tool (http://www.ucrdatatool.gov/) to build a table to analyze crime statistics for at least one violent crime and one property crime in a city and state of your choice.

3. Use the UCR Data Tool (http://www.ucrdatatool.gov) to examine crime statistics in several large police agencies.

Internet Sites

Bureau of Justice Statistics: http://www.ojp.usdoj.gov/bjs

Bureau of Justice Statistics, Homicide in the United States: http://www.ojp.gov/bjs/homicide/homtrnd.htm

Crime and Victim Statistics: http://www.ojp.usdoj.gov/bjs/cvict.htm

Federal Bureau of Investigation: http://www.fbi.gov

Theoretical Perspectives on Race and Crime

A wide variety of sociological, psychological, and biological theories have been proposed to explain the underlying causes of crime and its social, spatial, and temporal distribution. All of these theories are based on the assumptions that crime is accurately measured. But when variation in crime patterns and characteristics is partially attributable to unreliability in the measurement of crime, it is impossible to empirically validate the accuracy of competing criminological theories.

—Mosher, Miethe, and Hart (2011, p. 205)

Considering the historical and contemporary crime and victimization data and statistics presented in Chapter 2, the logical next question is, What explains the crime patterns of each race? Based on this question, we have formulated two goals for this chapter. First, we want to provide readers with a rudimentary overview of **theory**. Second, we want to provide readers with a summary of the numerous theories that have relevance for explaining race and crime. In addition to this, where available, we also discuss the results of tests of the theories reviewed. Last, we also document some of the shortcomings of each theory.

Decades ago, criminology textbooks devoted a chapter to race and crime (Gabbidon & Taylor Greene, 2001). Today most texts cover the topic, but only in a cursory way. In general, because of the additional focus on race and crime, scholars have written more specialized books, such as this one, to more comprehensively cover the subject. But even in these cases, many authors devote little time to reviewing specific theories related to race and crime (Walker, Spohn, & DeLone, 2012). In her 1993 tome on race and crime, *Unequal Justice: A Question of Color,* Mann provided one of the most comprehensive reviews of theories that have been applied to race and crime. In recent years, Gabbidon's (2010) *Criminological Perspectives on Race and Crime* considerably updated and expanded Mann's coverage and represents the first text solely devoted to examining how well criminological theories contextualize race and crime. We attempt to provide an overview of the vast number of major and lesser-known theories that have been applied to understanding racial patterns in crime and victimization. Before we begin, however, we review the fundamentals of theory, noting what theory is, distinguishing the various types of theories, and discussing the usefulness of having theory.

❖ What Is Theory?

According to Bohm and Vogel (2010), "A theory is an explanation" (p. 1). Some theory can be found in practically everything we do. When it comes to explaining crime, just about everyone has an opinion. All of these insights, however, might not qualify as *scientific* theory. Curran and Renzetti (2001) noted that a scientific theory is "a set of interconnected statements or propositions that explain how two or more events or factors are related to one another" (p. 2). Furthermore, scientific theories are usually logically sound and empirically testable (Curran & Renzetti, 2001).

Theories can be further categorized as macrotheories, microtheories, or bridging theories (Williams & McShane, 2010). Macrotheories focus on the social structure and are generally not concerned with individual behavior; conversely, microtheories look to explain crime by looking at groups, but in small numbers, or at the individual level (Williams & McShane, 2010). Bridging theories "tell us both *how social structure comes about and how people become criminals*" (Williams & McShane, 2010, p. 8). Many of the theories reviewed in this chapter fit some of these criteria, whereas others do not, but in our view, they nonetheless provide useful insights into race and crime. Thus, we discuss some nontraditional approaches that have not been folded into the mainstream of scientific criminological theory. It is important to note here that this chapter does not review every criminological theory. Our aim was to simply examine some of those that have been applied to the issue of race and crime. Others, such as rational choice theory, might also have some relevance, but they were left out because there is limited scholarship that makes the connection between the perspective and racial disparities in crime and justice.

Theories are valuable for a number of reasons. Curran and Renzetti (2001) provided an important summary of the usefulness of theory:

> Theories help bring order to our lives because they expand our knowledge of the world around us and suggest systematic solutions to problems we repeatedly confront. Without the generalizable knowledge provided by theories, we would have to solve the same problems over and over again, largely through trial and error. Theory, therefore, rather than being just a set of abstract ideas, is quite practical. It is *usable knowledge.* (p. 2)

There are several paradigms within criminological theory that are reviewed here. We review biological approaches that look to physical features and/or genetic inheritance to explain crime; other theories that have their foundations in the American social structure, social processes, or one's culture; and theories that have psychological foundations. Theorists have also sought to integrate some of these approaches (Agnew, 2004; Messner, Krohn, & Liska, 1989). As one might expect, many of these theories have been applied to explain race and crime. We begin with a review of biological explanations of crime.

❖ Biology, Race, and Crime

Early Developments in Biological Explanations

The linking of biology and crime has its roots in Europe. Reid (1957) wrote that "[in] the year 1843 a Spanish physician Soler was [the] first to [mention] the concept of the born criminal" (p. 772). It was also in Europe that phrenology, the study of the external shape of the head, was first popularized (Vold, Bernard, & Snipes, 1998). Darwin's *On the Origin of Species* (1859) and *Descent of Man* (1871) were also influential in this era. Once the ideas became accepted, **Cesare Lombroso**, a doctor in the Italian Army in the 19th century and the so-called father of criminology, began studying army personnel from the southern portions of Italy where, in addition to being considered inferior beings, the citizens were thought to be "lazy, incapable, criminal, and barbaric" (Vold et al., 1998, pp. 42–43).

In Lombroso's first major work, *Criminal Man* (1876/1911), he made clear the importance of race in explaining crime. He mentioned that some tribes in parts of India and Italy had high **crime rates** due to "ethnical causes" (p. 140). He added that "the frequency of homicide in Calabria, Sicily, and Sardinia is fundamentally due to African and Oriental elements" (p. 140). When Lombroso took on the task of explaining criminality among women, he again saw race as being an important contributor to crime. In his view, "Negro" women and "Red Indian" women were manly looking, which contributed to their criminality. His works were widely hailed and were translated into English, by which time the notion of biological determinism had already taken hold on American shores.

As in Lombroso's work, in the United States, racial and ethnic groups were the focus of ideas that inferior "stocks" were polluting society. The most virulent attacks were reserved for African Americans. Books such as Charles Carroll's (1900) *The Negro a Beast* spoke to the notion that African Americans were not human; they were more akin to apes. Relying heavily on biblical interpretations, Carroll sought to show why the White race was superior to the African American race. Around the same time, there was the thought that because of their genetic inferiority, African Americans would eventually die off (Hoffman, 1896). Although these notions were vigorously challenged here and abroad, such ideas dominated the late 19th- and early 20th-century literature and gave rise to the racist eugenics movement. However, as noted in Chapter 1, with increased immigration to the United States, these ideas were also applied to the unwelcome new arrivals (see Hooton, 1939a, 1939b). There were, however, continuing critics of this early work (Bonger, 1943; Merton & Ashley-Montagu, 1940).

Recent Developments in Biological Explanations

Crime and Human Nature

Because of the persistent criticism of the biological perspective, support for the ideology lay dormant until 1985, when Wilson and Herrnstein resurrected it with their publication of *Crime and Human Nature*. In their chapter on race and crime, Wilson and Herrnstein pointed to constitutional factors that may contribute to the overrepresentation of Blacks in crime; such constitutional factors "merely make a person somewhat more likely to display certain behavior; it does not make it inevitable" (p. 468). Wilson and Herrnstein next suggested that Black males tend to be more mesomorphic (muscular) than White males;

in addition, because they have higher scores on the Minnesota Multiphasic Personality Inventory (MMPI) than Whites, they are "less normal." Another constitutional factor mentioned by the authors is low **IQ**. This connection is discussed further in the next section of the chapter.

As with their predecessors, Wilson and Herrnstein (1985) have had their critics. Most notably, there were concerns about the clarity of concepts and other measurement issues. Another concern related to their exclusive use of the theory to explain crime in the streets, not "crimes in the suites" (Lilly, Cullen, & Ball, 2001, pp. 212–213). This obviously speaks to race and crime because it is clear that these conservative thinkers have more interest in explaining crimes associated with racial minorities than those overwhelmingly committed by middle- and upper-class Whites.

Intelligence, Race, and Crime

With the development and acceptance of intelligence tests, another linkage was developed: intelligence and crime (S. Gould, 1996). Much of the early literature suggested that criminals were of low intelligence or "feebleminded." This line of thinking was based on Richard Dugdale's 19th-century Jukes study, which chronicled the genealogy of a family that had experienced generations of immorality and criminality.

Building on the Jukes study, in the early 1900s, Henry H. Goddard studied the lineage of a family in New Jersey. Goddard found that one side of the family produced primarily descendants of superior intelligence, whereas the other side of the family produced offspring that were considered immoral, criminal, and alcoholics. Goddard's study was later found to be faulty because he had his assistant, Elizabeth S. Kite, conduct the research, and she failed to use an IQ test to determine feeblemindedness. Instead, she made her assessments based on physical appearance (Knepper, 2001). In addition, it was found that Goddard had altered some of the pictures in his books to make study participants look diabolical. The notion of a link between intelligence and crime had existed prior to the aforementioned studies, but the development of the IQ test gave proponents of the idea a tool with which to test their beliefs.

Because of a critical review of numerous studies on IQ and crime by Edwin Sutherland, as well as Simon Tulchin's (1939) classic *Intelligence and Crime*, intelligence-based theories disappeared from the criminological literature until the 1970s. At this time, two prominent criminologists, Hirschi and Hindelang (1977), conducted a review of the literature on intelligence and crime. On the issue of race, they wrote, "There can be no doubt that IQ is related to delinquency within race categories" (p. 575). From their research, they concluded that students with low intelligence had difficulty in school and, as a result, were more likely to engage in delinquency—ergo, given that Blacks have traditionally scored lower on IQ tests, they are likely to commit more crimes.

The debate lingered until Herrnstein and Murray (1994) published their controversial work, *The Bell Curve*. The book picked up where the debate left off. They suggested that low IQ contributed to a host of factors, including crime, poverty, illegitimacy, unemployment, welfare dependency, and others. How? Well, the authors present a few ways in which this connection materializes. First, they state that low IQ results in school failure, which tends to lead to crime. Second, they argue that low IQ leads to people being drawn to danger and having "an insensitivity to pain or social ostracism, and a host of derangements of various sorts" (p. 240). Combined, these factors, in their minds, were precursors for a criminal career. Finally, the authors suggest that those with low IQs would have a hard time following ethical principles. According to their theory,

> [people with low IQ might] find it harder to understand why robbing someone is wrong, find it harder to appreciate values of civil and cooperative social life, and are accordingly less inhibited from acting in ways that are hurtful to other people and to the community at large. (pp. 240–241)

Implicit in their thinking is that, because Blacks tend to have lower IQs, they are likely at greater risk for engaging in criminality.

Following the publication of *The Bell Curve*, the American Psychological Association convened a committee of scholars to assess the state of knowledge on IQ. The committee found that IQ does predict school performance and that there are unexplained racial differences in IQ. There were concerns expressed by the committee that IQ doesn't cover all dimensions of intelligence, such as creativity, wisdom, practical sense, and so on (Neisser et al., 1996). Critics of IQ tests continue to assert that if a lack of intelligence is associated with crime, then what explains the fact that persons with high IQs commit white-collar and political crime (M. Lanier & Henry, 1998)?

Long after the dust settled from the IQ debate inspired by *The Bell Curve*, biosocial criminology, with some of its lineage connected to the IQ and crime debate, emerged as a paradigm in the field. There are a few incarnations of the perspective. One incarnation is the r/K selection theory, which is based largely on evolutionary foundations. And recently, John Wright has integrated evolutionary and biosocial foundations to offer a perspective to explain offending among Blacks in particular. We review both theories below.

Contemporary Biosocial Criminology and Race

r/K Selection Theory

One of the more controversial criminological theories related to race in general and crime in particular is the r/K selection theory. Created by Harvard biologist E. O. Wilson to explain population growth and the decline in plants and animals, the theory has been adapted to humans by Rushton (1999), professor of psychology at Western Ontario University. This gene-based evolutionary theory links many of the differences among the races, including crime patterns, to migrations out of Africa.

Rushton (1999) agrees with the hypothesis that all humans came out of Africa. It is his contention, however, that there was a split of the population before humans left Africa and that this split is responsible for the current position of Blacks, Whites, and Asians. As he sees it, those who stayed in Africa (now referred to as Black people) were subjected to unpredictable droughts and deadly diseases, which caused them to die young. Those who migrated to Eurasia (now referred to as Whites and Asians) had to deal with other concerns, such as "gathering and storing food, providing shelter, making clothes, and raising children during the long winters" (p. 85). These tasks were more mentally demanding and, according to Rushton, required greater intelligence. Moreover, "They called for larger brains and slower growth rates. They permitted lower levels of sex hormones, resulting in less sexual potency and aggression and more family stability and longevity" (p. 85).

At the heart of the r/K selection theory are reproduction, climate, and intelligence. R-selected organisms are those that evolved to survive in less crowded, but unstable, environments. K-selected organisms have the ability to compete successfully for limited resources in a stable environment. Because Africans were faced with early death, they often had to bear more children to maintain their population, which left them unable to provide significant care for their offspring. Conversely, those falling under the K-strategy, Whites and Asians (Rushton acknowledges only three races: Negroid, Caucasoid, and Mongoloid), reproduced less and generally spent more time caring for their offspring.

Rushton's theory relates to race and crime in that aggression, impulsive behavior, low self-control, low intelligence, and lack of rule following are all associated with criminals and, according to Rushton, those who fall under the r-strategy, namely, Black people. To support his approach, Rushton has conducted cross-national studies that looked at race and crime (see Rushton, 1995; Rushton & Whitney, 2002). Other scholars have also adopted some of Rushton's ideas in the areas of crime (Ellis, 1997; Ellis & Walsh, 1997, 2000; Walsh, 2004; Walsh & Ellis, 2003; J. Wright, 2008) and skin color and intelligence (Lynn, 2002).

As with all theories, there have been several notable criticisms of the r/K selection theory. First, Rushton generally ignores sociological factors. Most of his cross-national comparisons point strictly to numbers, without taking into account variables such as socioeconomic status, discrimination, and other important sociological variables. Second, in the 21st century, there are few "pure" races, especially in the United States, where, as noted in Chapter 1, White sexual aggression against Black females during the slave era produced countless mixed-race offspring. Therefore, the rigorous adherence to the Black-White-Asian split is problematic. Finally, if Rushton's theory were true, what would explain White aggression as early colonizers and their current involvement in wars and violence across the globe? In contrast to Rushton's theory, Bradley (1978) argued that, as a result of migration to colder regions, since the beginning of humanity, Whites have been the global aggressors.

John Wright's Biosocial Thesis on Race and Offending

In recent years, the connection between biology and behavior has emerged as a more accepted area of study in criminology (Cullen, 2009). Contemporary adherents to this theory point to the influence of biological and social factors in criminal behavior (Walsh & Beaver, 2009; Wright & Boisvert, 2009). In particular, the researchers have called for the consideration of neuroscience and genetics in criminological research. Among the assertions by biosocial theorists is that race does matter in biosocial criminology (Walsh, 2004). For example, John Wright (2009), drawing on evolutionary and biological considerations, argues that there is an "inconvenient truth" pertaining to the existence of race and the evolutionary basis of race-based patterns of behavior. While acknowledging the potential role of past societal injustices in America, he points to the persistent pattern of high crime in Black communities in America and abroad as further evidence that something biological is likely a contributing factor.

Moving away from structural and racism-based explanations, Wright (2009) offers two reasons for race and problem behavior that "are highly couched in an evolutionary understanding of race differences and, as such, overlap with one another" (p. 147). He turns first to executive functions, which are "a range of brain-based activities housed in the frontal, prefrontal, and orbital frontal cortex. These abilities are highly heritable and provide humans with their unique abilities to plan, organize their lives, and control their emotions" (p. 147). Self-control and IQ are two key components of executive functions. Wright's argument here rests on the belief that those with low self-control will have difficulties throughout the life course, and this will be reflected in problems in education and employment. Although he believes these problems can befall all racial groups, he does add the caveat that "due to the distribution of low IQ and low self-control found in black populations, it is more often reflected in the lives of blacks" (p. 148). Wright next proffers that

> collective social behavior is an evolved ability and set the stage for the beginning of complex societies we see today . . . it entails individuals making a choice to sacrifice or risk something they value personally for the overall good. (p. 149)

Wright (2009) believes that in neighborhoods where most residents exhibit collective social behavior and enforce basic social norms, crime will be minimized. In his view, this is simply not the case in Black neighborhoods. Specifically, Wright closes his perspective with the following:

> In many black neighborhoods, but especially in inner cities and ghettos, there are too few individuals with the ability to act collectively and there are too many who violate basic social norms and laws. And the undeniable fact is that individual differences in IQ and other executive functions, which tend to cluster within neighborhoods by race, is intimately tied to the lack of collective social behavior, to the lack of social control . . . and to the violation of rudimentary norms of appropriate conduct. (p. 150)

Wright's (2009) theory doesn't explain within-race class differences. That is, if his theory is correct, then wouldn't all Black neighborhoods—not just "many"—exhibit the same levels of social norm and law violation? In other words, if all Blacks of all classes suffer from "deficits in executive functions," then it stands to reason that the same problems should be found among all groups in that population. If that is not the case, then the role of class is being underemphasized in favor of race. Furthermore, the lack of collective social behavior could be a product of cultural inclinations that are a product of past inaction on the part of criminal justice officials. As such, the observed unwillingness of Blacks to follow "rudimentary norms of appropriate conduct" might be simply an artifact of the longstanding "no snitch" cultural norm that is pervasive in many of the inner-city communities that appear to be the targets of Wright's theory. Also, since Blacks reside in the most depressed areas of inner cities, it stands to reason that they might turn to violating norms of appropriate conduct to survive.

In large part, biosocial criminologists have relied on data from The National Longitudinal Study of Adolescent Health (Add Health) to test ideas related to their suppositions. Though this stream of scholarship is fairly new, some findings have begun to emerge that partially support biosocial assertions regarding the intersection of race, gender, behavior, and alleles (Vaske, Beaver, Wright, Boisvert, & Schnupp, 2009; Vaske, Makarios, Boisvert, Beaver, & Wright, 2009). Notably, none of these findings support any of the evolutionary aspects of Rushton's (1999) or Wright's (2009) work. In addition, the authors have yet to show us how this work can be useful in reducing crime and averting future offending. In summary, many of the current biologically oriented theories either directly or indirectly point to some race and crime linkage. Nevertheless, for more than a century, opponents of such approaches have countered with alternative sociological perspectives, some of which are reviewed in the next section.

❖ Sociological Explanations

Early Sociological Explanations

Sociological explanations for crime in general have existed for nearly two centuries. Beginning with the early work of the cartographic school, led by Adolphe Quetelet, who some have said produced the first scientific work on crime (see Quetelet, 1833/1984), this approach looked to sociological factors to explain criminality (age, social class, poverty, education level, etc.). Quetelet was likely among the first to aver some relationship between race and crime when he divided French citizens into distinct races and offered explanations why each group was engaged in crime (Mosher et al., 2011). Several decades after the publication of Quetelet's work, as noted earlier, biological notions related to crime were being espoused in America. Numerous American scholars, however, challenged the biological approach using sociological analyses of crime problems. With the development of the first sociology department at the University of Chicago in 1892, and other such programs at universities across the United States, scholars saw this new discipline and a sociological approach as a means to solve some of the pressing issues particularly plaguing overcrowded northern cities.

In the late 1890s, Philadelphia was one of those cities looking for answers to its concerns regarding the burgeoning African American population. At the time, city officials sought out **W. E. B. Du Bois** to conduct a study of Philadelphia's notorious Seventh Ward. Du Bois (1899/1996) conducted a comprehensive review of the ward, outlining the conditions in the area and also pointing to several possible explanations for crime among African Americans. One of his explanations was as follows:

> Crime is a phenomenon of organized social life, and is the open rebellion of an individual against his social environment. Naturally then, if men are suddenly transported from one environment to another; the result is lack of harmony with the new conditions; lack of harmony with the new physical surroundings leading to disease and death or modification of physique; lack of harmony with social surroundings leading to crime. (p. 235)

He felt that the mass migration from the South to the North produced problems of adjustment for African Americans, who were previously familiar only with Southern life.

Du Bois's ideas were in line with the concept of **social disorganization**. Like Quetelet earlier, to explain criminality in the Seventh Ward, Du Bois pointed to issues related to age, unemployment, and poverty. Du Bois, however, added the sociological variable of discrimination, noting that Blacks were arrested for less cause than Whites, served longer sentences for similar crimes, and were subject to employment discrimination (Gabbidon, 2007; Taylor Greene & Gabbidon, 2000). Other early studies would echo similar sentiments on crime in the African American community (Grimke, 1915; K. Miller, 1908/1969; R. Wright, 1912/1969). Recently, Unnever and Gabbidon (2011) have offered an expansion of Du Bois's ideas and argued for the consideration of **racial discrimination** as a potential contributor to African American offending.

Social Disorganization

Northern cities, such as Chicago, were also experiencing the same social problems that Du Bois found in Philadelphia as a result of population booms caused by the mass immigration by racial and ethnic groups outlined in Chapter 1. With unparalleled philanthropic support from numerous foundations (Blumer, 1984), by the 1920s, the University of Chicago had put together a formidable cadre of scholars to investigate the social ills plaguing the city. Together, these scholars combined their ideas to formulate what is now known as the "Chicago School."

The leaders of the school were Robert Park and Ernest Burgess. They viewed the city as an environment that functioned much like other ecological environments: It was formed based on the principles of invasion, dominance, and succession. In short, one group moves in, battles the previous group until they dominate the area, after which, to continue the cycle, it is likely that another group will invade the area and pursue dominance. This ecological approach was believed to explain the conflict that occurred in emerging cities across the United States. Moreover, it was Burgess (1925) who had earlier conducted a study that produced the notion that towns and cities "expand radially from its central business district—on the map" (p. 50). From this, he and Park produced their now famous map of Chicago. The map divided the city into several concentric circles or "zones," as described by Park and Burgess. Of the numerous zones, Zone 2 is of most significance to the theory. This area was referred to as "the capital zone in transition" or "the slums," which, according to the theory, is where most of the crime should take place. As predicted by the theory, the farther one moves away from this zone, the more crime decreases (Shaw & McKay, 1942/1969).

In the tradition of Quetelet's earlier work, two researchers, Clifford Shaw and Henry D. McKay, who worked at the University of Chicago's Institute for Juvenile Research but were not faculty members, tested the theory by examining juvenile delinquency. To do so, they made use of 20 different types of maps. Each of the maps charted out different characteristics of Chicago's residents and delinquent youth. For example, there were maps that outlined neighborhood characteristics such as population fluctuations, percentage of families on welfare, monthly rents, percentage of foreign-born and Negro residents, and distribution of male delinquents (Shaw & McKay, 1942/1969). Their results were striking. As postulated by the theory, over several decades and with several changes in ethnic groups, Zone 2 had the most delinquency. Describing this dramatic finding, Shaw and McKay (1942/1969) wrote,

> the proportions of Germans, Irish, English-Scotch, and Scandinavians in the foreign-born population in 8 inner-city areas underwent, between 1884 and 1930, a decided decline (90.1 to 12.2 per cent); while the proportion of Italians, Poles, and Slavs increased . . . the 8 areas maintained, throughout these decades, approximately the same rates of delinquents relative to other areas. (pp. 150–151)

In the end, the scholars concluded that the crime in these areas was caused by social disorganization. Social disorganization refers to areas characterized by the following conditions: (a) fluctuating populations, (b) significant numbers of families on welfare, (c) families renting, (d) several ethnic groups in one area, (e) high truancy rates, (f) high infant mortality rates, (g) high levels of unemployment, (h) large numbers of condemned buildings, and (i) a higher percentage of foreign-born and Negro heads of families (Sampson & Groves, 1989; Shaw & McKay, 1942/1969).

During the late 1930s and early 1940s, a 1923 graduate of the "Chicago School," Norman Hayner, utilized social disorganization theory while investigating crime in diverse communities populated by Whites, Asian Americans, African Americans, and Native Americans (Hayner, 1933, 1938, 1942).Under the "Oriental crime" heading, Hayner (1938) compared the situation of the Japanese, Chinese, and Filipinos in the Pacific Northwest. Overall, he noted that each of the groups had little criminality in comparison with Whites. However, he decided to look at variations among the three Asian American populations. According to Hayner, the Japanese had low rates of crime and delinquency because of their closely integrated families, the efficiency and organization of the community, and the lack of acquaintance with American ways. The closely integrated families were characteristic of their home countries. The organization of the community reflected the concern of the community for their youth. At that time, they maintained language schools to keep youngsters busy after their regular school days. Community attitudes concerning crime were so strong that, according to Hayner's research, those caught engaging in crime would likely commit suicide before facing the community. Finally, some Japanese steered their youth away from American traditions because there was the belief that increasing Americanization would lead to increasing levels of crime and delinquency. In general, both of the other two groups had more crime than the Japanese, which was explained as a result of their either becoming too Americanized or having a gender imbalance (significantly more males than females), often due to earlier government immigration restrictions.

Turning to Native Americans, Hayner (1942) examined their conditions on three reservations in the Pacific Northwest. He sought to determine why these Native Americans had become engaged in more crime. The first of his explanations pointed to the increased mixing between Whites and Native Americans. In his words, "As the Indian becomes more like the White biologically and, as a result, associates more freely with him, his criminal behavior tends to approximate more closely the White patterns" (p. 605). Hayner also pointed to the social disorganization that occurred among Native Americans because of social isolation, concerns about sustenance, and, in other situations, "some Indians, pauperized by too much money [from successful suits against the government] or unwisely administered relief lack the incentive to work; others, including many boarding-school graduates, want to work but lack the opportunity" (p. 613).

Contemporary Social Disorganization Theory

Since these early articles, scholars have continued to explore the viability of social disorganization to explain crime, particularly in urban areas. Sampson (1987) found a connection between Black male joblessness and economic deprivation and violent crime. This connection was an indirect one mediated by family disruption (i.e., female-headed households). Another important article by Sampson and Groves (1989) expanded the theory and found considerable support for it. Building on this prior research and the important research of William Julius Wilson (1987), Sampson and Wilson (1995) posited a theory targeted at explaining race and crime with structural and cultural constructs:

> [Our] basic thesis is that macro social patterns of residential inequality give rise to the social isolation and ecological concentration of the truly disadvantaged, which in turn leads to structural barriers and cultural adaptations that undermine social organization and hence the control of crime. This thesis is grounded in what is actually an old idea in criminology that has been overlooked in the race and crime debate—the importance of communities. (p. 38)

The theory, which is referred to as the "racial invariance thesis," draws heavily on two of W. Wilson's (1987) concepts from *The Truly Disadvantaged*. The first, concentration effects, speaks to the fact that Whites and Blacks live in considerably different areas. In his research,

Wilson found that many African Americans live in areas where there are significant concentrations of poverty. Once neighborhoods reach this point, working-class and middle-class African Americans abandon them.

This removes important **social buffers** (role models) who show neighborhood kids that there are successful people who go to work, day in and day out. When all the "social buffers" have abandoned a community, Wilson (1987) suggested that the remaining individuals are in a state of *social isolation*, which he defined as "the lack of contact or of sustained interaction with individuals and institutions that represent mainstream society" (p. 60). The notion of social isolation adds the cultural component to the theory. By not being exposed to mainstream individuals and institutions, socially isolated people tend to develop their own norms within these isolated areas. In a series of articles, Lauren Krivo and Ruth Peterson of Ohio State University have tested some of the ideas of Wilson (1987) and Sampson and Wilson (1995) and have found considerable support for them (see Krivo & Peterson, 1996, 2000; Peterson & Krivo, 1993, 2005, 2010). Returning to the perspective, Sampson and Bean (2006) have called for a revision of the theory to account for concentrated immigration and culture, both of which have profound implications for communities (see Box 3.1).

BOX 3.1

"Culture of Poverty" Makes a Comeback

By Patricia Cohen

For more than 40 years, social scientists investigating the causes of poverty have tended to treat cultural explanations like Lord Voldemort: That Which Must Not Be Named.

The reticence was a legacy of the ugly battles that erupted after Daniel Patrick Moynihan, then an assistant labor secretary in the Johnson administration, introduced the idea of a "culture of poverty" to the public in a startling 1965 report. Although Moynihan didn't coin the phrase (that distinction belongs to the anthropologist Oscar Lewis), his description of the urban black family as caught in an inescapable "tangle of pathology" of unmarried mothers and welfare dependency was seen as attributing self-perpetuating moral deficiencies to black people, as if blaming them for their own misfortune.

Moynihan's analysis never lost its appeal to conservative thinkers, whose arguments ultimately succeeded when President Bill Clinton signed a bill in 1996 "ending welfare as we know it." But in the overwhelmingly liberal ranks of academic sociology and anthropology the word "culture" became a live grenade, and the idea that attitudes and behavior patterns kept people poor was shunned.

Now, after decades of silence, these scholars are speaking openly about you-know-what, conceding that culture and persistent poverty are enmeshed.

"We've finally reached the stage where people aren't afraid of being politically incorrect," said Douglas S. Massey, a sociologist at Princeton who has argued that Moynihan was unfairly maligned.

The old debate has shaped the new. Last month Princeton and the Brookings Institution released a collection of papers on unmarried parents, a subject, it noted, that became off-limits after the Moynihan report. At the recent annual meeting of the American Sociological Association, attendees discussed the resurgence of scholarship on culture. And in Washington last spring, social scientists participated in a Congressional briefing on culture and poverty linked to a special issue of *The Annals,* the journal of the American Academy of Political and Social Science.

"Culture is back on the poverty research agenda," the introduction declares, acknowledging that it should never have been removed.

The topic has generated interest on Capitol Hill because so much of the research intersects with policy debates. Views of the cultural roots of poverty "play important roles in shaping how lawmakers choose to address poverty issues," Representative Lynn Woolsey, Democrat of California, noted at the briefing.

This surge of academic research also comes as the percentage of Americans living in poverty hit a 15-year high: one in seven, or 44 million.

With these studies come many new and varied definitions of culture, but they all differ from the '60s-era model in these crucial respects: Today, social scientists are rejecting the notion of a monolithic and unchanging culture of poverty. And they attribute destructive attitudes and behavior not to inherent moral character but to sustained racism and isolation.

To Robert J. Sampson, a sociologist at Harvard, culture is best understood as "shared understandings."

"I study inequality, and the dominant focus is on structures of poverty," he said. But he added that the reason a neighborhood turns into a "poverty trap" is also related to a common perception of the way people in a community act and think. When people see graffiti and garbage, do they find it acceptable or see serious disorder? Do they respect the legal system or have a high level of "moral cynicism," believing that "laws were made to be broken"?

As part of a large research project in Chicago, Professor Sampson walked through different neighborhoods this summer, dropping stamped, addressed envelopes to see how many people would pick up an apparently lost letter and mail it, a sign that looking out for others is part of the community's culture.

In some neighborhoods, like Grand Boulevard, where the notorious Robert Taylor public housing projects once stood, almost no envelopes were mailed; in others researchers received more than half of the letters back. Income levels did not necessarily explain the difference, Professor Sampson said, but rather the community's cultural norms, the levels of moral cynicism and disorder.

The shared perception of a neighborhood—is it on the rise or stagnant?—does a better job of predicting a community's future than the actual level of poverty, he said.

William Julius Wilson, whose pioneering work boldly confronted ghetto life while focusing on economic explanations for persistent poverty, defines culture as the way "individuals in a community develop an understanding of how the world works and make decisions based on that understanding."

For some young black men, Professor Wilson, a Harvard sociologist, said, the world works like this: "If you don't develop a tough demeanor, you won't survive. If you have access to weapons, you get them, and if you get into a fight, you have to use them."

Top of Form

Seeking to recapture the topic from economists, sociologists have ventured into poor neighborhoods to delve deeper into the attitudes of residents. Their results have challenged some common assumptions, like the belief that poor mothers remain single because they don't value marriage.

In Philadelphia, for example, low-income mothers told the sociologists Kathryn Edin and Maria Kefalas that they thought marriage was profoundly important, even sacred, but doubted that their partners were "marriage material." Their results have prompted some lawmakers and poverty experts to conclude that programs that promote marriage without changing economic and social conditions are unlikely to work.

Mario Luis Small, a sociologist at the University of Chicago and an editor of *The Annals'* special issue, tried to figure out why some New York City mothers with children in day care developed networks of support while others did not. As he explained in his 2009 book, *Unanticipated Gains,* the answer did not depend on income or ethnicity, but rather the rules of the day-care institution. Centers that held frequent field trips, organized parents' associations and had pick-up and drop-off procedures created more opportunities for parents to connect.

Younger academics like Professor Small, 35, attributed the upswing in cultural explanations to a "new generation of scholars without the baggage of that debate."

(Continued)

(Continued)

Scholars like Professor Wilson, 74, who have tilled the field much longer, mentioned the development of more sophisticated data and analytical tools. He said he felt compelled to look more closely at culture after the publication of Charles Murray and Richard Herrnstein's controversial 1994 book, *The Bell Curve,* which attributed African-Americans' lower I.Q. scores to genetics.

The authors claimed to have taken family background into account, Professor Wilson said, but "they had not captured the cumulative effects of living in poor, racially segregated neighborhoods."

He added, "I realized we needed a comprehensive measure of the environment, that we must consider structural *and* cultural forces."

He mentioned a study by Professor Sampson, 54, that found that growing up in areas where violence limits socializing outside the family and where parents haven't attended college stunts verbal ability, lowering I.Q. scores by as much as six points, the equivalent of missing more than a year in school.

Changes outside campuses have made conversation about the cultural roots of poverty easier than it was in the '60s. Divorce, living together without marrying, and single motherhood are now commonplace. At the same time prominent African-Americans have begun to speak out on the subject. In 2004 the comedian Bill Cosby made headlines when he criticized poor blacks for "not parenting" and dropping out of school. President Obama, who was abandoned by his father, has repeatedly talked about "responsible fatherhood."

Conservatives also deserve credit, said Kay S. Hymowitz, a fellow at the conservative Manhattan Institute, for their sustained focus on family values and marriage even when cultural explanations were disparaged.

Still, worries about blaming the victim persist. Policy makers and the public still tend to view poverty through one of two competing lenses, Michèle Lamont, another editor of the special issue of *The Annals,* said: "Are the poor poor because they are lazy, or are the poor poor because they are a victim of the markets?"

So even now some sociologists avoid words like "values" and "morals" or reject the idea that, as *The Annals* put it, "a group's culture is more or less coherent." Watered-down definitions of culture, Ms. Hymowitz complained, reduce some of the new work to "sociological pablum."

"If anthropologists had come away from doing field work in New Guinea concluding 'everyone's different,' but sometimes people help each other out," she wrote in an e-mail, "there would be no field of anthropology—and no word *culture* for cultural sociologists to bend to their will."

Fuzzy definitions or not, culture is back. This prompted mock surprise from Rep. Woolsey at last spring's Congressional briefing: "What a concept. Values, norms, beliefs play very important roles in the way people meet the challenges of poverty."

How much do you think culture matters in society today?

Scholars have also applied social disorganization theory to diverse groups such as Native Americans and found partial or full support for the theory (Bachman, 1991; Lanier & Huff-Corzine, 2006). Besides Native Americans, Martinez (2003) and Lee and Martinez (2002) have found support for aspects of the perspective in Latino communities. Velez (2006) argues that there is a lower level of social disorganization in Latino communities. This speaks to the so-called "Latino Paradox" that finds that even though Latinos are exposed to the same social disadvantages as other groups, they tend not to exhibit the extreme adverse effects (e.g., extreme levels of crime). Velez outlines four characteristics for this difference. First, she notes that there are lower levels of concentrated disadvantage in such communities. This includes things such as male joblessness and female-headed households. Moreover, in contrast to conventional wisdom, she argues that the presence of more immigrants "provide protective mechanisms against crime" (p. 92). This supposition contradicts the longstanding immigration and crime perception held by the public (Higgins, Gabbidon, & Martin, 2010). And recent research has supported the notion that immigration does not increase crime but has actually contributed to a reduction of some crimes in Latino communities (Feldmeyer, 2009; Stowell, Messner, McGeever, & Raffalovich, 2009; Velez, 2009). Third, she indicates that Latino communities have better relations with economic officials, the police, and local politicians, all of whom are key "players" in all communities. Finally, she argues that Latinos tend to benefit from living in communities that are close to advantaged Whites. She provides data from Chicago that support her assertions (Velez, 2006).

Mass Incarceration and Social Disorganization

In the late 1990s, Dina Rose and Todd Clear (1998) articulated an expansion of social disorganization theory. Contrary to the punitive approach being heralded at the time, Rose and Clear posited that mass incarceration actually exacerbated social disorganization in the most depressed communities. According to their thesis, this happens for three reasons. First, it impacts the socioeconomic nature of the community. Second, because mass incarceration results in people leaving for prison and then being released from prison, it increases the mobility in certain communities. Finally, mass incarceration increases the heterogeneity of communities. This occurs because offenders who spend time in correctional institutions learn new antisocial behaviors that they bring back to their communities (for a recent articulation of the perspective, see Clear, 2007; see also Western, 2006; Western & Wildeman, 2009). Using data from Florida, they found support for their theory (Clear, Rose, & Ryder, 2001; Clear, Rose, Waring, & Scully, 2003).

❖ Collective Efficacy

In the 1990s, Sampson, Raudenbush, and Earls (1997) sought to determine why urban communities differ in their levels of crime. From their research, they concluded that crime was related to the amount of **collective efficacy** found in a particular community. They defined collective efficacy as "social cohesion among neighbors combined with their willingness to intervene on behalf of the common good" (p. 918). In short, in the communities where residents do not retreat behind their locked doors and actively look out for one another, there is a diminished likelihood that they will have many of the ills found in other urban areas. Since their work, other scholars have found some support for collective efficacy among African Americans (Simons, Gordon Simons, Burt, Brody, & Cutrona, 2005). Other research has suggested that the impact of collective efficacy is not as significant in communities as more official strategies such as community policing (Xu, Fiedler, & Flaming, 2005).

Both social disorganization and collective efficacy theories generally speak to high-crime urban areas. Because not all African Americans live in high-crime urban areas, some have wondered whether those in middle-class areas also encounter higher crime rates than those in similarly situated White areas. To investigate this question, Pattillo (1998) conducted participant observation and 28 in-depth interviews in one such area of Chicago. She found that "middle class Black areas tend to be nestled between areas that are less economically stable and have higher crime rates" (p. 751). In addition, many of the Black residents who make it to middle-class areas are "unstable" middle-class residents and struggle to maintain their status. In some instances, they cross over the line into crime to do so. Therefore, Pattillo also found that such residents were "given a degree of latitude to operate in the neighborhood" (p. 770). Based on the premise of social organization, which, along with being goal oriented, "stresses the importance of kin and neighborly ties for the social control of crime and disorder," Pattillo showed how these communities maintain order while allowing "the integration of licit and illicit networks both working toward common goals, with variant strategies" (p. 770). Recent research by Hassett-Walker (2009, 2010) has also investigated crime among the Black middle class and found that structural factors were not as significant a contributor to middle-class delinquency as peer influence.

There is both support for and persistent criticisms of social disorganization theory in the research literature. The most often-cited weakness of the social disorganization perspective is the so-called ecological fallacy. This refers to the fact that the perspective is usually tested at the aggregate level, but researchers still use the data to make assertions about individuals. The theory also does not explain how certain groups, such as Asians and Jewish communities, maintained low levels of crime and delinquency, although they lived in areas that might be categorized as socially disorganized (Lanier & Henry, 1998). Moreover, although there were high levels of delinquency in the study areas, the theory does not explain why, in general, most juveniles in these areas do not become delinquent.

❖ Culture Conflict Theory

Originally formulated by criminologist Thorsten Sellin in the late 1930s, culture conflict theory, according to Williams and McShane (2010), is heavily based on the work of Chicago School graduates Louis Wirth and Edwin Sutherland (who collaborated with Sellin). A central idea of the theory relates to the rules or norms within a culture. Sellin (1938) suggested that, over a period of time, certain behavior becomes accepted within a culture, so that "the violation of [it] arouses a group reaction. These rules or norms may be called *conduct norms*" (p. 28).

Sellin's (1938) theory states that all societies have conduct norms, which vary from one culture to the next and could result in violations in one society not being a violation of conduct norms in another. Within each society, those in power can control the definitions of conduct norms and hence determine what behaviors become crimes. This leads to the potential for culture conflict. In general, Sellin pointed to three ways that conflicts between various cultural codes arise: (a) when the codes clash on the border of contiguous cultural areas; (b) when, as may be the case with legal norms, the law of one cultural group is extended to cover the territory of another; or (c) when members of one cultural group migrate to another.

Summarizing these ideas, Sellin (1938) formulated two types of culture conflicts. Regarding the first type, called *primary conflicts*, he noted,

> [If] the immigrant's conduct norms are different from those of the American community and if these differences are not due to his economic status, but to his *cultural origin,* then we speak of a conflict of norms drawn from different cultural systems or areas. Such conflicts may be regarded as *primary* culture conflicts. (p. 104)

Sellin (1938) described *secondary conflicts* as "conflicts of norms which grow out of the process of social differentiation which characterize the evolution of our own culture"

(p. 105). As an example of the applicability of his perspective, Sellin used Native Americans as an illustrative population:

> We need only to recall the effect on the American Indian of the culture conflict induced by our policy of acculturation by guile and force. In this instance, it was not merely contact with the White man's culture, his religion, his business methods, and his liquor, which weakened tribal mores. In addition, the Indian became subject to the White man's law and this brought conflicts as well, as has always been the case when legal norms have been imposed upon a group previously ignorant of them. (p. 64)

Although the theory clearly has relevance for Native Americans and the various ethnic immigrants who were arriving in America during the early part of the 20th century, in recent years, it has not received much attention. One exception to this trend was a study by N. Lee (1995) that studied culture conflict and crime in Alaskan villages. Based on comparative data on eight Yupiit Nation villages and eight non-Yupiit villages, Lee explored the following proposition: "that colonization (invasion, dominance, and succession) results in conflict (disorder/crime) related to the imposition of laws (social control) associated with the dominant group" (p. 181). Essentially, Lee wanted to find out whether crime was less prevalent in villages that maintained their traditional values. Moreover, Lee was interested in finding out whether villages that enforce alcohol laws have a higher or lower number of alcohol-related incidents. On the first point, Lee found that "the rates for felonies and misdemeanors are lower in Nation villages with the exception of liquor violation, drunk in public, minor in possession, and protective custody" (p. 184). On the second point, the results were mixed; however, one thing was clear: The formal laws were "not keep[ing] the villagers from drinking or acting out while drunk" (p. 186). Overall, the study found support for culture conflict theory. Even with these positive results, criminologists have generally neglected the theory; they have, however, borrowed some ideas from the theory and formulated related theories, such as strain theory, subcultural theory, and conflict theory. We look at these theories in the following sections.

❖ Strain/Anomie Theory

In the same year as the publication of Sellin's work on culture conflict, another important theory was presented. The 1938 publication of Robert K. Merton's "Social Structure and Anomie" produced what is likely one of the most cited theories in criminology: strain or anomie theory. The theory was influenced by the classic work of Emile Durkheim, who first made use of the word *anomie* in a criminological sense. According to Akers (2000), "Durkheim (1951[1897]) used the term anomie to refer to a state of normlessness or lack of social regulation in modern society as one condition that promotes higher rates of suicide" (p. 143). Merton's (1938) work showed that in every society, there are "culturally defined goals, purposes, and interest" (p. 672). He also suggested that there are generally "acceptable modes of achieving these goals" (p. 673). Turning to American society, Merton recognized that "the extreme emphasis upon the accumulation of wealth as a symbol of success in our own society mitigates against the completely effective control of the institutionally regulated modes of acquiring a fortune" (p. 675). In short, in pursuit of the "American Dream," some people turn to alternative means to secure this cultural goal. When applying the theory to race and crime, Merton recognized the special case of African Americans:

> Certain elements of the Negro population have assimilated the dominant caste's values of pecuniary success and advancement, but they also recognize that social ascent is at present restricted to their own caste almost exclusively. The pressures upon the Negro which would otherwise derive from the structural inconsistencies we have noticed are hence not identical to those upon lower class Whites. (p. 680)

Merton (1938) understood that the strain experienced by African Americans was unlike any other in American society. Basically, no matter how much they sought to achieve the "American dream," they could never "legitimately" reach the status of Whites, so they maintained lower aspirations and were resigned to achieving a lower level of success and advancement. Such a situation likely contributed to a strain that resulted in some African Americans turning to crime.

Epps (1967) tested some of Merton's ideas regarding race and crime. Using a racially diverse sample (159 Whites, 111 African Americans, and 76 Asian Americans) of high school juniors from Seattle, Washington, Epps tested several hypotheses that looked at whether there were differences in delinquency and aspirations by race and class. He did find some differences between the occupational expectations and aspirations and the educational aspirations of the students. In all cases, Whites and Asian Americans had higher aspirations and expectations than did African Americans. No support, however, was found for any of the other hypotheses.

More than 30 years after Epps's research, Cernkovich, Giordano, and Rudolph (2000) tested whether African Americans still subscribe to the American Dream and whether this is related to their involvement in criminal behavior. Making use of longitudinal data involving African Americans and Whites from private households and an institutional sample (both from Toledo, Ohio), the authors found

> that African Americans maintain a very strong commitment to the American dream. Blacks report higher levels of commitment to economic success goals than do their White counterparts and indicate that they are prepared to work harder and sacrifice more to realize them. Even though the young Black adults in our study report low incomes and are more likely to be unemployed than are Whites, they continue to maintain a very strong commitment to the American dream. (pp. 158–159)

Their study, which also partially tested social control theory, found support for **strain theory**, but only in the case of Whites. That is, many of the variables used to test strain theory "were significant correlates of crime among . . . Whites in our sample but not among African Americans" (Cernkovich et al., 2000, p. 161), a finding that the authors could not explain, but curiously implied that the African American participants might not have been forthright with their answers—something that likely applied to all participants. McCluskey (2002) applied strain theory to Latinos and found that the theory was a weak predictor of delinquency. As a result, she argued for a culturally specific model that supports the notion that criminological research pertaining to Latinos needs to consider the unique nuances of their experience.

Limitations of Strain/Anomie Theory

Most of the criticisms of strain theory have been leveled at Merton's original formulation of the theory. Bohm (2001), for example, noted that anomie theories have a middle-class bias; they presume that lower class individuals commit crimes in an effort to reach middle-class status. As was seen by some of the research reviewed, this is not always the case. Another persistent criticism is that the theories do not explain white-collar and government crimes. Given that people at this level have already achieved middle-class status, why, then, do they engage in crime? Even in its various incarnations, the theory is generally silent on this issue.

Bohm (2001) also suggested that the theory suffers from overprediction. As he put it, "If strain is caused by the inability to achieve the American dream and is as widespread as Merton implies, then there ought to be much more crime than occurs" (p. 80). Because of the shortcomings of strain/anomie theory, Agnew (1992, 2006) developed a revised version of the theory.

❖ General Strain Theory

Robert Agnew, first in a pioneering *Criminology* article in 1992 and later in a book-length exposition (Agnew, 2006), renewed interest in strain theory by adding that the removal (or loss) of positive or introduction of negative stimuli into an environment can cause a strain that, as with blocked opportunities, can result in criminal behavior. As for the removal of positively valued stimuli, Agnew (1992) specifically pointed to the following: "loss of a boyfriend/girlfriend, the death of or serious illness of a friend, moving to a new school district, the divorce/separation of one's parents, suspension from school, and the presence of a variety of adverse conditions at work" (p. 57). Turning to the presentation of negative stimuli, Agnew pointed to the following: child abuse and neglect, criminal victimization, physical punishment, negative relations with parents, negative relations with peers, adverse or negative school experience, stressful life events, verbal threats and insults, physical pain, unpleasant odors, disgusting scenes, noise, heat, air pollution, personal space violations, and high density.

Building on these ideas, Jang and Johnson (2003) used the National Survey of Black Americans (composed of a sample of 2,107 African American adults) to test whether Agnew's theory holds true for African Americans. In addition to testing core tenets of Agnew's work, they sought to determine whether African American religiosity, an area in which research has consistently shown more commitment by African Americans than by other ethnic groups, has any impact on helping them cope when strain occurs. In contrast to the earlier research of Cernkovich et al. (2000), these authors found support for Agnew's modified version of strain theory, noting the following regarding the role of religiosity:

> We find that individuals who are religiously committed are less likely than those who are not to engage in deviant coping in reaction to personal problems because their religiosity buffers the effects of negative emotions on deviance as well as directly and indirectly (via outerdirected emotions) affects their coping strategies. (Jang & Johnson, 2003, p. 98)

Studies have continued to find support for the theory (Eitle & Turner, 2003; Rocque, 2008; Simons, Chen, Stewart, & Brody, 2003). In the Simons et al. (2003) research study, the authors found that experiencing discrimination was a significant predictor of delinquency. Eitle and Turner's (2003) work revealed that disparities in crime commission were largely attributable to African Americans' increased exposure to stressors. Most recently, Jang and Johnson (2005) found additional support for their earlier research on the benefit of religiosity when coping with strain (see also Jang & Lyons, 2006). In addition, some research has also shown that there are ethnic-specific strains that influence delinquency among Hispanics (Perez, Jennings, & Giver, 2008).

Kaufman, Rebellon, Thaxton, and Agnew (2008) have recently clarified how **general strain theory** can explain racial differences in criminal offending. In particular, they posit that "A GST explanation of racial differences in offending . . . implies that African-Americans experience disproportionate strain in the social environment and/or have fewer resources for coping with strain in conventional ways" (p. 424). Kaufman and his colleagues point to economic strains, family strains, community strains, and a host of other strains that Blacks are more likely to encounter (e.g., discrimination in all aspects of life). Their work has provided additional clarity for how general strain theory applies to African Americans. Despite these clarifications, at least one recent study has found only mixed support for the theory as applied to race and offending (Piquero & Sealock, 2010). We now turn our attention to subcultural theory.

❖ Subcultural Theory

In the 1950s, several theories were formulated that considered criminality to be tied to the development of subcultures among White middle-class youth. In *Delinquent Boys*, Albert Cohen (1955) argued that gang delinquency was associated with juveniles being unable to achieve status among their peers. When they were unable to meet established White middle-class standards, they established their own values, which generally involved activities and behaviors that were in conflict with middle-class values.

While examining a diverse, lower class area in Boston, Walter Miller (1958) also formulated a subcultural theory. Referred to as the "focal concerns" theory, Miller's thesis was based on three years of field research. His focal concerns were considered values to which lower class residents adhered. These included trouble, toughness, smartness, excitement, fate, and autonomy. *Trouble* referred to youth engaging in risk-taking activities. *Toughness* represented the notion that one was fearless and could "handle oneself" in a physical encounter. *Smartness* referred to street smarts, which are valued in lower class communities. *Excitement* is the pursuit of thrill seeking. *Fate* is the belief among lower class youth that their lives are controlled by things over which they have no control. *Autonomy* was the final focal concern and represents the resentment that lower class youth have regarding the control others have over their lives (Miller, 1958).

Two years after Miller's work, Cloward and Ohlin's (1960) *Delinquency and Opportunity* pointed to opportunity structure as the key to understanding gang activities. They suggested that when there are limited opportunities, youth join gangs with one of three orientations. Those who cannot find legitimate opportunities join criminal gangs whose aim is to make money through a variety of illegitimate avenues. If, however, there remain few illegitimate opportunities, the youth might join a "conflict" gang. Such gangs primarily engage in violent activities, doing whatever is necessary to maintain their status in the streets. Youth who end up in "retreatist" gangs are what Cloward and Ohlin refer to as "double failures." Because such youth did not make it in either legitimate or illegitimate opportunities, they retreat to drug usage.

The same year Miller published his theory, noted criminologist M. Wolfgang (1958) published *Patterns in Criminal Homicide*. This was significant because, as an outgrowth of this pioneering work, less than a decade later he, along with Franco Ferracuti, formulated the subculture of violence theory, which has been used to explain homicide, particularly in the African American community. We review this theory next.

The Subculture of Violence Theory

As reflected in Chapter 2, African Americans and Latinos are overrepresented in the violent crime categories. In the case of African Americans, this is nothing new. In the late 1950s, while studying homicides in Philadelphia, Wolfgang (1958) found high homicide rates among African Americans in Philadelphia. In addition, Wolfgang found interesting results related to sex differences, victim-offender relationships, weapons involved, and motives for the homicides. From this research and that of his colleague Franco Ferracuti, who had also conducted homicide research in Italy, Wolfgang and Ferracuti (1967) formulated the subculture of violence theory. Their theory, which draws from several other criminological theories, consists of seven propositions.

These propositions speak to a range of factors that encapsulate the subculture of violence. Some of these factors include the fact that those invested in the subculture of violence are not violent all the time. Although the subculture is found in all age segments of society, it is found most in those in the late-adolescence to middle-age categories. Because those vested in the subculture do not see violence as "illicit conduct," they have no feelings of guilt about their actions (Wolfgang & Ferracuti, 1967).

Several authors have either critiqued or tested the theory as it relates to race and the commission of violent crimes. Hawkins (1983) provided one of the earliest and most comprehensive critiques of the theory. In doing so, he also provided an alternative perspective. We begin with a summary of his critique; then we turn to a brief overview of his alternative theory. Hawkins pointed to the following five major weaknesses of the theory:

1. There is an extreme emphasis on mentalistic value orientations of individuals—orientations that in the aggregate are said to produce a subculture.

2. The theory lacks empirical grounding and, indeed, is put in question by some empirical findings.

3. Much of the theory has tended to underemphasize a variety of structural, situational, and institutional variables that affect interpersonal violence. For Blacks, these variables range from historical patterns developed during slavery to the immediate social context of an individual homicidal offense to the operation of the criminal justice system, past and present.

4. Subcultural theory underemphasizes the effects of the law on patterns of criminal homicide.

5. There are other plausible ways apart from the inculcation of values by which the economic, political, and social disadvantages of American Blacks may produce high rates of homicide. (pp. 414–415)

Hawkins' (1983) alternative theory provided three propositions that were meant to address the holes in the subculture of violence theory. Proposition 1 states, "American Criminal Law: Black life is cheap but White life is valuable" (p. 415). Here, Hawkins believes that, based on history, Black lives have taken on less value than White lives; as a result, African Americans can kill other African Americans without fear of being punished. In line with this argument, Hawkins expanded the work of G. Johnson (1941) and presented a hierarchy of homicide seriousness, interpolated between the least and most serious types of homicides (see Figures 3.1 and 3.2). Hawkins' (1983) second proposition states the following: "Past and present racial and social class differences in the administration of justice affect Black criminal violence" (p. 422). This proposition speaks to the lack of attention paid to prehomicide behaviors in the Black communities. Hawkins believes that, because various prehomicidal assaults in the African American community do not receive the attention they deserve, homicides that could be prevented are not. Such inattention is also a product of the poor relationship between African Americans and police agencies (Brunson, 2007; Jones-Brown, 2007; Rios, 2011; Stewart, 2007).

As a product of poor relations with the police, in some instances, response times are slower, and at some point, African Americans lose faith in the police and refuse to call on them for assistance in certain instances. Relatedly, once a homicide is committed and

Figure 3.1

Johnson's Hierarchy of Homicide Seriousness

Source: Johnson (1941).

Rating	Offense
Most Serious	Negro versus White, White versus White
Least Serious	Negro versus Negro, White versus Negro

Figure 3.2

Hawkins' Hierarchy of Homicide Seriousness

Source: Hawkins (1983, pp. 420–421).

Rating	Offense
Most Serious	Black kills White, in authority
	Black kills White, stranger
	White kills White, in authority
	Black kills White, friend, acquaintance
	Black kills White, intimate, family
	White kills White, friend, acquaintance
	White kills White, intimate, family
	Black kills Black, stranger
	Black kills Black, friend, acquaintance
	Black kills Black, intimate, family
	White kills Black, stranger
	White kills Black, friend, acquaintance
Least Serious	White kills Black, intimate, family

the police are called in, their lack of serious attention provides no deterrent effect to the community. The final proposition—that "economic deprivation creates a climate of power-lessness in which individual acts of violence are likely to take place" (p. 429)—speaks to the association between socioeconomic disadvantage and violence, a connection generally lack-ing in the subculture of violence theory, but that was incorporated into Sampson's (1985) test of Wolfgang and Ferracuti's (1967) version of the theory. Sampson tested the theory, looking at disaggregated homicide rates for 55 of the largest American cities. According to Sampson (1985), if the theory were correct, he would find that "Black offending rates should be related positively to percent of Black violent crimes, independent of other structural characteristics, particularly poverty and inequality" (p. 52). Using a variety of sophisticated methods, no support was found for the theory.

During the 1990s, the theory also was tested to determine its applicability to Black women. Mann (1990a) examined homicide data from six major cities and found Black women comprised 77% of female murderers. However, after taking all factors into consid-eration, she concluded, "These women are not part of a 'subculture of violence' but of a 'subculture of hopelessness.' Their fierce independence, their tendency to batter or to kill when battered and their almost insurmountable economic obstacles represent a constant struggle" (Mann, 1990a, p. 198). When Ray and Smith (1991) took up the subject the fol-lowing year, they noted that if there is a "subculture of violence" among African American females, there must also be one among White females who had identical offending patterns, primarily committing homicides against males of the same race with whom they have a close relationship.

During the mid-1990s, Harer and Steffensmeier (1996) did find support for the subcul-ture of violence theory. Their research made use of prison misconduct data and exam-ined the theory as applied to institutional violence. They found that Blacks were twice as likely to be found guilty of violent misconduct as were Whites, even after controlling for standard variables. Even so, they pointed out that the differences also could be attribut-able to racial discrimination in the disciplinary process, something their research did not take into consideration.

Cao, Adams, and Jensen (2000) tested the theory using General Social Survey (GSS) data from 1983 to 1991 (excluding 1985). Focusing on all core elements of the theory, the authors found that, in contrast to the theory, "Whites are found to be significantly more vocal than Blacks in expressing their support for the use of violence in defensive situations, with the effects of other factors held constant" (p. 54). Finally, the authors concluded with this:

> Based on our data and analyses, there is enough evidence to conclude that Blacks in the general U.S. population are no more likely than Whites to embrace values favor-able to violence. Our findings thus repudiate the idea that the causes of Black crime are rooted in unique aspects of Black culture. (p. 58)

They suggested that, given the limited support for the theory, for scholars to continue to promote it as an explanation for racial differences in violence implies that all African Americans are violent, something that is "unfair and potentially racist in nature" (Cao et al., 2000, p. 58). More recent results have been mixed, with some scholarship finding little sup-port for the perspective (Chilton, 2004; Pridemore & Freilich, 2006), and other research find-ing qualified support for the theory (Staff & Kreager, 2008).

Other criticisms also have been leveled at the theory. Covington (2003) noted that supporters of the theory "fail to explain how [the] Black subculture of violence came to be more combative than the White subculture of violence" (p. 258). Psychologists also have argued that Wolfgang and Ferracuti (1967) "ignore the psychological underpinnings of [the] subculture" (Poussaint; cited in Covington, 2003, p. 259).

The Code of the Streets

A recent subcultural theory approach that has some connections to several of the approaches previously reviewed is the **code of the streets** (Anderson, 1994, 1999). Based on his research in Philadelphia, Elijah Anderson, an urban ethnographer, published a highly acclaimed article, "The Code of the Streets," which focused on interpersonal violence in an impoverished Philadelphia neighborhood and how residents in the area adopted the "code of the streets" to survive. Anderson (1994) believes that "at the heart of the code is the issue of respect—loosely defined as being treated 'right,' or granted deference one deserves" (p. 82). In such an environment, something that has little meaning to one person might be interpreted as "dissing" by someone else and result in a confrontation that could lead to violence. Being able to defend oneself is also an important part of the code. Within such depressed neighborhoods, Anderson suggested, there are "decent" and "street" families. Decent families "tend to accept mainstream values more fully and attempt to instill them in their children" (pp. 82–83). Such families are also strict and teach their children to respect authority and act in a moral way. In addition, they are not seriously tied to the code.

In contrast, Anderson (1994) described "street families," who loosely supervise their children and, in many cases, are unable to cope with them. Unlike the decent families, "they believe in the code and judge themselves and others according to its values" (Anderson, 1994, p. 83). Consequently, their lives "are marked by disorganization" (p. 83). In such families, children learn early on that they must fend for themselves. This produces a cycle in which they also become vested in the code and take to the streets to prove their "manhood," which involves securing pretty women, being able to defend themselves, and being able to support themselves "by any means necessary."

Research conducted within the last decade has provided some support for Anderson's ideas focusing on Blacks (Baumer, Horney, Felson, & Lauritsen, 2003; Brezina, Agnew, Cullen, & Wright, 2004; Chilton, 2004; Stewart, Simons, & Conger, 2002; Stewart & Simons, 2006), Hispanics (Lopez, Roosa, Tein, & Dinh, 2004), and, more recently, young Black women (Brunson & Stewart, 2006; N. Jones, 2010). Other studies have also noted the role of rap music in the perpetuation of the code of the streets (Kubrin, 2005). In contrast to these positive findings, Stewart, Schreck, and Simons (2006) found limited support for the perspective. In line with the theory, they postulated that adhering to the code of the streets would reduce one's likelihood of being victimized. However, their research revealed the opposite: Adherents to the code of the streets reported *higher* levels of victimization (see also McGee, 1999; McGee, Barber, Joseph, Dudley, & Howell, 2005; Stewart, Schreck, & Brunson, 2008).

Besides the need for nationwide replications of the theory, there have been other concerns expressed about the viability of Anderson's ideas. Commenting on one of the life histories presented in Anderson's work, J. Miller (2001) wrote that, based on the way Anderson described the person's prison experience, it could be that the prison, not the streets, is the more powerful contributor to the development of the code of the streets. Elaborating on this point, he wrote,

> I do not feel that Professor Anderson gives enough weight to the influences of prison on the code of the streets. It is no accident that most of the known violent gangs in California developed in the institutions of the California Youth Authority or the California prisons. Leadership is confirmed by a stint in prison. The walk, the "pose," the language, the argot, the dress, the focus of one's eyes, and the studied indifference all bespeak prison. (p. 157)

Wacquant (2002) provided a more expansive critique of Anderson's work, pointing to the "loose and over-expansive definition of the code of the streets" (p. 1491). Another point of concern is that "there is considerable confusion as to the origins and vectors of the code of the streets" (p. 1491). Wacquant further observed,

> Because he starts from an overly monolithic vision of the ghetto and conflates folk with analytic concepts, Anderson cannot relate the *moral distinctions* he discovers in it to the internal *social stratification*. He thus boxes himself into a culturalist position with deeply disturbing political implications insofar as they render ghetto residents responsible for their own plight through their deviant values or role ineptness. (p. 1500)

Anderson took exception to Wacquant's (2002) critique and produced a rejoinder that suggested that Wacquant had misread his work and distorted its findings. Outside commentators on the debate have noted that both scholars had valid arguments (Wilson & Chaddha, 2009).

In general, a common shortcoming of subcultural theories is that they ignore criminality in the middle and upper classes (Hagan, 2002). In addition, as noted in the critiques of Hawkins (1983) and Cao and his colleagues (2000), tests of the theory (specifically the popular subculture of violence theory) have found minimal support. A final persistent criticism of subcultural theories is that, in most instances, they speak only to male criminality (Lilly et al., 2001).

One of the most popular theories used to explain racial differences in offending is conflict theory. Our discussion of the theory is presented next.

❖ Conflict Theory

Conflict theory likely represents the most popular theoretical framework used to explain race and crime. The theory, which has seeds in many of the ones previously discussed, has some of its origins in Germany. Specifically, the works of German scholars Karl Marx, George Simmel, and Max Weber have been credited with providing the impetus for the theory. According to Lilly, Cullen, and Ball (2011), "Theories that focus attention on struggles between individuals and/or groups in terms of power differentials fall into the general category of *conflict theory*" (p. 166). In short, when applying conflict theory to race and crime, one would look to whether the enforcement of laws and the distribution of punishment are done in a discriminatory manner. Although social class and gender also would be important to investigate, the way in which the White power structure administers justice would be of central concern to conflict theorists.

Conflict Theory, Race, and Crime

An early observer of race and crime, W. E. B. Du Bois studied under Weber and produced one of the earliest works to incorporate a conflict analysis (Gabbidon, 1999, 2007; Taylor Greene & Gabbidon, 2000). In 1901, he published an article on the convict-lease system (for more discussion on this system, see Chapter 8), which spoke to the conflict perspective. Du Bois (1901/2002) traced the history of the system whereby immediately after the passage of the Thirteenth Amendment, states leased convicts out to private landowners who no longer had the free labor of African American slaves.

Du Bois (1901/2002) wrote about how states strategically enacted various laws (referred to as the "Black codes") to snare Blacks into the criminal justice system so they could be returned to the labor force, which helped maintain the power and privileged status of Southern White landowners. In the article, Du Bois also rebutted the biological theorists of his day by declaring,

> Above all, we must remember that crime is not normal; that the appearance of crime among Southern Negroes is a symptom of wrong social conditions—of a stress of life greater than a large part of the community can bear. The Negro is not naturally criminal; he is usually patient and law-abiding. If slavery, the convict-lease system, the traffic in criminal labor, the lack of juvenile reformatories, together with the unfortunate discrimination and prejudice in other walks of life, have led to that sort of social protest and revolt we call crime, then we must look for remedy in the sane reform of these wrong social conditions, and not in intimidation, savagery, or legalized slavery of men. (p. 88)

By this time, as reviewed earlier, Du Bois had already made significant statements on crime, pointing to discrimination, segregation, lynching, and the attitudes of the courts as explanations for African American criminality (Gabbidon, 2001; Taylor Greene & Gabbidon, 2000). Other prominent scholars would find considerable support for Du Bois's ideas (Myrdal, 1944; Sellin, 1928, 1935; Work, 1900, 1913). In each case, the authors wrote of the discrimination and economic conditions that were contributing to African American involvement in the criminal justice system—matters that directly speak to conflict theory.

It would be some time, however, before the formal articulation of conflict theory (also referred to as "critical criminology") and a little longer before it incorporated race as a central component. The development of conflict theory over the last 40 years is often credited to the writings of Chambliss (1964, 1969), Turk (1969), and Quinney (1970). Much of these writings were class-based analyses that suggested that capitalism, class structure, and the manipulation of laws were significant contributors to crime, and, as such, changing the structure of society would go a long way toward eliminating crime.

In addition to these scholars, in his classic work *Crime and Privilege*, Krisberg (1975), while articulating a critical perspective (referred to then as "New Criminology"), clearly added the dimension of race to the theory by integrating the history of criminal justice practices used to control oppressed groups and also highlighting the prison writings of George Jackson, Angela Davis, and other high-profile African American prisoners of the early 1970s. Notably, building on the work of Blauner (1972), Krisberg (1975) devoted a whole section of the work to race privilege, which in recent years has been translated into the notion of "White privilege" (see McIntosh, 2002). This notion of White privilege within criminal justice translates into more focus on "crimes in the streets," as opposed to "crimes in the suites." This focus criminalizes the actions of other races and poor Whites while minimizing or looking past the crimes of Whites in power. Over the years, in several editions of his classic text *The Rich Get Richer, and the Poor Get Prison* (2004), Reiman has spoken of this in terms of white-collar crimes, environmental crimes, and other corporate crimes that kill thousands of people, who are primarily poor and American minorities, but rarely result in anyone being severely punished.

Hawkins (1987) further expanded the conflict model by examining it in terms of race, crime, and punishment. He emphasized the need to consider race discrimination in conflict theory. According to Hawkins, other considerations usually lacking in conflict theory included victim characteristics, region, and accounting for race-appropriate behaviors. Whereas the first two characteristics are self-explanatory, for the latter, Hawkins noted that anomalies found in some studies do not take into account behaviors that are generally committed by one race and that, when committed by another race, result in a punishment that seems out of line. Finally, Hawkins also suggested that too often conflict theorists do not consider the power threat approach of Blalock (1967). The approach, which some have called a "power threat version of conflict theory" (Ellis & Walsh, 2000, pp. 384–385), argues that once a majority population sees a minority group encroaching on spheres traditionally reserved for majority group members, they respond in a number of ways, including imposing additional social control (Hawkins, 1987). This usually comes in the form of increased investments in police forces. According to past and recent scholarship, there is support for the "power threat" thesis (see D'Alessio, Eitle, & Stolzenberg, 2005; Jackson, 1989; R. King, 2007; Sharp, 2006). Recent scholarship has also found support that Hispanics represent a new minority threat (Eitle & Taylor, 2008).

Around the same time of Hawkins's important research, Wilbanks (1987), a professor of criminal justice at Florida International University, published his controversial work, *The Myth of a Racist Criminal Justice System*. In contrast to conflict theorists, who argue that discrimination is a significant reason why minorities are overrepresented in the criminal justice system, Wilbanks argued that, although he believed there was some discrimination in the criminal justice system (using the analogy of having a few bad apples in a barrel), contrary to what was being espoused in much of the race and crime literature,

> I do not believe that *the system* is characterized by racial prejudice or discrimination against Blacks; that is, prejudice and discrimination are not "systematic." Individual cases appear to reflect racial prejudice and discrimination by the offender, the victim, the police, the prosecutor, the judge, or prison or parole officials. But conceding individual cases of bias is far different from conceding pervasive racial discrimination. (pp. 5–6)

Wilbanks' perspective became known as the "no discrimination thesis" (NDT).

BOX 3.2

Walker, Spohn, and DeLone's (1996) Discrimination-Disparity Continuum

Building on the "no discrimination thesis" (NDT) and "discrimination thesis" (DT) articulated by Wilbanks and Mann, Samuel Walker, Cassia Spohn, and Miriam DeLone created the "discrimination-disparity continuum," which was presented in the first edition of their book, *The Color of Justice* (1996). The continuum provides a useful framework for the NDT/DT debate. As they see it, discrimination in the criminal justice and juvenile justice systems can fall somewhere along their continuum (see Figure 3.3). At the one end of the continuum is systematic discrimination, whereby discrimination takes place "at all stages of the criminal justice system, at all times, and at all places" (Walker, Spohn, & DeLone, 2007, p. 19). At the other end of the continuum, there is pure justice, which suggests that there is no discrimination in the criminal justice system and the overrepresentation of minorities in the criminal justice system is likely a product of offending patterns. In between these poles, you have institutionalized discrimination, contextual discrimination, and individual acts of discrimination. Walker et al. (2007) defined institutional discrimination as "racial and ethnic disparities in outcomes that are the result of the application of racially neutral factors, such as prior criminal record, employment, and demeanor" (p. 19).

Figure 3.3   Discrimination-Disparity Continuum

Systematic Discrimination	Institutionalized Discrimination	Contextual Discrimination	Individual Acts of Discrimination	Pure Justice

Source: Walker, Spohn, & DeLone (2007).

Contextual discrimination is discrimination that occurs only in certain contexts. The examples presented by the authors include discrimination found in "certain regions, particular crimes, or special victim-offender relationships" (Walker et al., 2007, p. 19). Individual acts of discrimination occur when there are simply individuals within the criminal justice and juvenile justice systems—not whole agencies—engaged in discrimination.

After presenting their continuum, the authors surveyed the current race and crime literature and concluded that although the criminal justice and juvenile justice systems were once characterized by systematic discrimination, that is no longer the case. Their most recent review of the literature suggests that the two justice systems are now characterized by contextual discrimination (see Walker et al., 2007, p. 420).

Pick a topic related to race and crime (e.g., the death penalty, racial profiling) and find three refereed journal articles on the subject. After reviewing the articles, see whether, as a whole, you also find that contextual discrimination pervades your selected area of race and crime.

Wilbanks's (1987) book and its perspective initiated a series of debates between Wilbanks and Coramae Richey Mann. In contrast to Wilbanks's position, Mann (1990b) felt,

The racism in the criminal justice system has become institutionalized in the same way that it has in other organizational segments of the nation such as education, politics, religion, and the economic structure; and the barrel *is* rotten. (p. 16)

Mann's perspective became known as the "discrimination thesis" (DT). Although the debates became heated, the two had brought to the fore an issue that lay below the surface among criminologists for many years. In 1993, Mann responded with her contemporary classic *Unequal Justice: A Question of Color*. Although the debate cooled after the publication of her book, the level of discrimination in the criminal justice system continued to be a central focus of race and crime researchers (Walker et al., 2007). Moreover, although Wilbanks never produced the second edition he planned to write (Wilbanks, 1987, p. x), other scholars have continued in his tradition (see, e.g., Delisi & Regoli, 1999; DiLulio, 1996a; MacDonald, 2003, 2008).

Along with Hawkins's (1987) concern about the oversimplification of the theory, a few other shortcomings of conflict theory have been noted. Bohm (2001) noted that the perspective does not take into account individual differences. That is, not all people who are oppressed or discriminated against will respond the same way. Finally, some have suggested that, in some of its forms, the theory is not testable. A perspective related to conflict theory that has been applied to race and crime is the colonial model.

❖ The Colonial Model

The **colonial model** has its foundations in the work of psychiatrist and activist Frantz Fanon (Tatum, 1994). Although Fanon used the model to examine the relations between Blacks and Whites in colonial settings, Blauner (1969) and Staples (1975), leaning heavily on intellectuals of the Black power movement, such as Stokely Carmichael and Charles Hamilton, were among the first to substantively apply the theory to crime. Applying the perspective to the conditions of African Americans, Blauner (1969) provided the following definition of colonialism:

> Colonialism traditionally refers to the establishment of domination over a geographically external political unit, most of them inhabited by people of a different race and culture, where this domination is political and economic, and the colony exists subordinated and dependent on the mother country. Typically the colonizers exploit the land, the raw materials, the labor, and other resources of the colonized nation; in addition a formal recognition is given to the difference in power, autonomy, and political status, and various agencies are set up to maintain this subordination. (p. 395)

Blauner (1972) also generally applied the model to Native Americans. In the work *Gringo Justice*, Mirande (1987) reviewed the historical treatment of Mexican Americans by the criminal justice system and formulated a theory of "gringo justice," integrating the colonial model and conflict theory. Although African Americans were not colonized in the sense that Native Americans or Mexican Americans were, according to Tatum (1994), internal colonialism, which is "when foreign control of a state or territory is eliminated and the control and exploitation of subordinate groups passes to the dominant group within the newly created society" (p. 41), produces many of the same characteristics of the more traditional **colonization** process. Such characteristics include "a caste system based in racism, cultural imposition, cultural disintegration and recreation and members of the colonized being governed by representatives of the dominant power" (p. 41). Such characteristics within a society leave the colonized with feelings of alienation, which results in either crime and delinquency or the desire to assimilate or protest.

All articulations of the theory note the important role that agents of the criminal justice system (or "internal military agents," as they are called by Staples, 1975) play in maintaining order in a colonial society. In the words of Blauner (1969),

> The police are the most crucial institution maintaining the colonized status of Black Americans. . . . Police are key agents in the power equation as well as the drama of dehumanization. In the final analysis they do the dirty work for the larger system by restricting the striking back of Black rebels to skirmishes inside the ghetto, thus deflecting energies and attacks from the communities and institutions of the larger power structure. (pp. 404–405)

R. Austin (1983) was one of the first to empirically test the theory. Using violence rates before and after the decolonization of the Caribbean island of St. Vincent, he sought to determine whether crime rates declined following the removal of British colonial rule. Although he did find that crime rates declined after the end of colonial rule, this did not hold true when he examined data related to murder and manslaughter. Here, Austin noted that the increasing availability of guns might have played a role in this finding.

More than a decade ago, Tatum (2000) provided one of the more comprehensive tests of the theory. In her test of the theory, she formulated several propositions related to the model, including the connections among race, class, and oppression; how race and class are associated with the availability of social support; and issues related to alienation. Relying on survey data from African American, Mexican American, and White juniors and seniors at two high schools in a major southwestern urban area, she found limited support for the model.

The colonial model has applicability for racial groups who have been subjected to colonization (most notably, Native Americans, African Americans, and Mexican Americans). There have been mixed results when the theory has been tested, and there need to be more direct tests of it. Tatum (1994) also noted several additional concerns with the theory. First, as reflected in other structural models, she noted that two people can be exposed to the same oppression yet respond differently; in such instances, the model does not account for the different adaptations. Second, as with conflict theory, the model is difficult to test. Another weakness of the model is that it does not adequately address class issues (Tatum, 1994).

Criminologist Agozino (2003) also has considered colonialism in his groundbreaking work *Counter-Colonial Criminology: A Critique of Imperialist Reason*. In the work, he argued that "criminology is concentrated in former colonizing countries, and virtually absent in the former colonized countries, because criminology is a social science that served colonialism more directly than many other social sciences" (p. 1). More specifically, Agozino focused on

> how imperialism used criminological knowledge and how it can be seen as a criminological project—imprisonment with or without walls, a widening of the net of incarceration, and how the close kinship between the two fields of knowledge and power, criminology and imperialism, served both. (p. 6)

He also highlighted that the discipline of criminology originated "at the height of European colonialism" (p. 6). As a product of these origins, he noted that "criminology is dominated by scholars in former colonial centres of authority," which has led to what he considers "theoretical underdevelopment through the concealment of the bloody legacy of colonialist criminology" (p. 6). Although on the surface his ideas might seem controversial, it is clear that Agozino's work provides a critical new direction for race and crime theorists.

In general, however, the impact of colonialism on countries around the globe has been neglected too long by criminologists. Notably, scholars have begun to revisit the role of colonialism in crime and justice (see Bosworth & Flavin, 2007; Gabbidon, 2009; Hawkins, 2011; Saleh-Hanna, 2008).

❖ Integrated and Nontraditional Theories on Race and Crime

Integrated theories of crime and nontraditional theories of race and crime receive less attention in crime and justice textbooks. Integrated theories incorporate more than one theory to explain criminal behavior. Nontraditional theories tend to have nontraditional ideas behind them. They also tend to be controversial. The integrated and nontraditional theories discussed here include structural-cultural theory; the abortion, race and crime thesis; and critical race theory.

Structural-Cultural Theory

In the 1980s, Oliver (1984) proposed that, to explain Black male criminality, one needs to use an integrated theory combining structural conditions of African Americans and their cultural adaptations to such conditions. In one of his early articles, he explored Black males and their "tough guy image" or, as he called it, the "Black compulsive masculinity alternative." Oliver believes that because of racial oppression, Black males exhibit masculine behavior that places an overemphasis on "toughness, sexual conquest, manipulation, and thrill-seeking" (p. 199).

Oliver (1984) has argued that Black males act this way for two reasons. First, "lower-class Black males who adopt the compulsive masculinity alternative do so in order to mitigate low self-esteem and negative feelings which emerge as a consequence of their inability to enact the traditional masculine role" (p. 199). The second reason relates to the notion that males who adapt the masculine approach pass it on to other males. In later publications, Oliver (1989a, 1989b) applied his theory to sexual conquest and the adaptation of an Afrocentric perspective to ameliorate social problems in the African American community, and he also has examined violence among African Americans in barroom settings (Oliver, 1994). More recently, he has continued to refine his perspective (see Oliver, 2003, 2006).

One limitation of Oliver's perspective relates to the central role of low self-esteem. There has been some debate as to whether low self-esteem is really the central problem contributing to social problems among African Americans generally and African American males in particular (see Ross, 1992). Covington (2003) also has argued that Oliver's approach labels activities "race specific" that Whites also engage in. For example, many of the functions that bars serve for African Americans serve the same functions for Whites. Finally, Covington noted that in one of his studies, Oliver's "sample of African-American participants in violent transactions report that many of their fights seem to have been precipitated for non-race-specific reasons that apply equally well to violent Whites" (p. 266).

Abortion, Race, and Crime

In a highly controversial paper, Donohue and Levitt (2001) proposed that more than 50% of the crime drop in the 1990s could be attributed to the 1973 *Roe v. Wade* Supreme Court decision that legalized abortion. They pointed to three important factors that support this thesis. First, they noted that the decline in crime coincided with the landmark decision and the period when those who would have been born would have reached their peak years of criminal activity (ages 18–24). Second, they suggested that the states that legalized abortion three years before the *Roe v. Wade* decision experienced earlier crime drops than the remaining states. Finally, they pointed to the fact that states that have the highest abortion rates also have had the largest declines in crime.

At the core of the theory are two premises. First, abortion reduces the pool of individuals who would later engage in crime. Second, the theory relates to race and crime in that, according to this view, abortion is not random. According to their thesis, those likely to have abortions include unwed women, teenagers, and Blacks. As such, because of a host of challenges often faced by such parents, they would be less than ideal parents and would place their children "at risk" for criminal activity. Donohue and Levitt's thesis, which has been widely disseminated in the scholarly community as well as in Levitt and Dubner's (2005) best-selling book *Freakonomics*, has garnered significant attention.

Among scholars, there has been vigorous debate about the veracity of their thesis, with some scholars supporting the thesis (Barro, 1999), and other researchers (some of whom conducted re-analyses of Donohue and Levitt's data) having found little to no support for the thesis (Chamlin, Myer, Sanders, & Cochran, 2008; Foote & Goetz, 2006; Hay & Evans, 2006; Joyce, 2004a, 2004b; Lott & Whitley, 2007). More recently, scholars have tried to apply the abortion and crime thesis to England and Wales and found no support (Kahane, Paton, & Simmons, 2008). Some noted scholars, such as Al Blumstein, have suggested that, although creative, the thesis does not give enough "attention to other factors, such as the decline in crack cocaine street dealing, the booming economy, and the efforts of police to keep guns away from juveniles" ("Renowned Criminologist Eschews Alarmist Theories," 1999, p. B5). Overall, although Donohue and Levitt (2004, 2006) have vigorously defended their perspective, there has not been a major shift toward using their thesis to explain the significant crime dip of the 1990s.

Critical Race Theory

In addition to theories based on biological, sociological, or other traditional perspectives, critical race theory (CRT), which emanated from the critical legal studies movement during the 1970s (K. Russell, 1999) and closely aligns with radical criminology (Delgado & Stefancic, 2001, p. 113), represents another perspective that has proved useful for contextualizing race and crime. Founded by Derrick Bell, Richard Delgado, and other legal scholars, in recent years it also has become more widely known in social science circles. The perspective has two goals. The first is to understand how the law is used to maintain White supremacy and continue to oppress people of color. The second is countering or stopping the use of the law to maintain White supremacy (K. Russell, 1999). It is here that critical race theorists have expressed concern about laws (e.g., "three strikes and you're out") and practices (e.g., racial profiling, wrongful convictions) that directly impact racial and ethnic minorities.

In addition to the aforementioned goals, there are several tenets of the perspective. First, racism is ever present in American society and is, thus, a daily occurrence. The second tenet is referred to as "interest convergence," or the notion that Whites benefit (materially and in other ways) from racism, so they "have little incentive to eradicate it" (Delgado & Stefancic, 2001, p. 7). Third, critical race theorists believe race to be socially constructed, manufactured classifications. Here, critical race theorists are particularly concerned about the racialization of groups. Specifically, they express concern about "the ways the dominant society racializes different minority groups at different times, in response to shifting needs such as the labor market" (p. 8). Critical race theorists also believe that, because of their distinct histories and experiences, racial and ethnic minorities have a "unique voice of color" perspective to offer society.

There have been a few persistent criticisms of the theory. First, because much of the work is based on storytelling and personal narratives, which move away from "objective" or "value-free" analyses, some critics have concluded that the perspective is unscientific. Also, according to K. Russell (1999), some have argued that "CRT amounts to academic whining about women and minorities" (p. 183). Even with these criticisms, the perspective has become a standard legal theory, especially among women and minority legal scholars. In addition, criminologists have also started to use the theory as the foundation for studies in the discipline (Glauer, 2009; Longazel, Parker, & Sun, 2011; Ross, 2010).

❖ Conclusion

Just as there is little consensus among criminologists about the causes of crime (Cooper, Walsh, & Ellis, 2010; Ellis & Walsh, 1999), there is even more debate about which theory best explains racial patterns in crime and victimization. However, one thing is apparent from the coverage in this chapter—numerous theories have been applied to the question of race and crime (see Table 3.1). In the beginning, scholars turned to the biology of African Americans, Native Americans, and Asian Americans to answer this question; however, over the years, this has changed. The decline in popularity of the biological approach gave rise to the sociological approach. Beginning with scholars such as Du Bois, the sociological approach continues to be a mainstay of those interested in studying race and crime. Subcultural approaches seem to

Table 3.1

Theoretical Contexts of Race and Crime

Theory	Context
Biological	White superiority, genetic inferiority, low IQ, physical characteristics, evolutionary factors
Biosocial	Interaction of biological and environmental factors
Sociological	Social conditions, social structure, heterogeneity, mobility, mass migration, impact of mass incarceration on communities
Culture conflict	Cultural differences, violation of social norms within a community
Subcultural	Street culture, code of honor rooted in violence
Conflict	Racial discrimination in criminal justice
Colonial/counter-colonial	Role of imperialism, criminology's role in imperialism
Structural-cultural	Social structure, culture, and black masculinity
Legalized abortion	Unborn "at-risk" children
Critical race theory	Law maintains White supremacy

have also maintained their place in the race and crime literature. Conflict theory now represents one of the more popular theoretical frameworks when studying race and crime. In addition, scholars are beginning to reexamine the role of colonization in race, crime, and justice.

There are clearly limits to the utility of these various theories. Even with the increasing scholarship on race, crime, and gender (Gabbidon, 2010), there remains a dearth of knowledge as to minority female offending. It is also noteworthy that much of the existing theoretical research on race and crime is centered on African Americans (and males in particular). While it is obvious that the research on Latinos and crime is on the rise, scholars need to test the existing theories to determine their relevancy for other racial/ethnic groups.

Finally, with the return of the biological-sociological debate in the form of biosocial criminology, the discipline has come full circle. Moreover, with the discoveries tied to the Human Genome Project, scholars have become even more interested in the influence of genetics on human behavior and also in explaining racial disparities in offending. When one reviews the various theories, it seems safe to say that, although the research methodologies have become more sophisticated, many of the same ideas presented about race and crime 100 years ago remain popular today. Chapter 4 looks at the police and their historical and contemporary roles in handling race and crime.

Discussion Questions

1. Why are theoretical perspectives so critical for race and crime researchers?

2. How do biologically based theories explain racial differences in crime trends?

3. How do sociologically based theories explain racial differences in crime trends?

4. What is colonialism? How does it explain the disproportionate involvement of racial and ethnic minorities in certain criminal offenses?

5. In your view, which of the theories in the chapter best explains racial differences in offending?

Internet Exercises

1. Review the index offenses presented at http://www.fbi.gov/ucr/ucr.htm and discuss which of the theories presented in this chapter can provide an explanation for robbery trends by race.

2. Spend 30 minutes at the Eugenics Archives (http://www.eugenicsarchive.org/eugenics/) examining some of the history and materials related to the Eugenics Movement.

Internet Sites

Eugenics Archive: http://www.eugenicsarchive.org/eugenics/

W.E.B. Du Bois: http://www.pbs.org/wnet/jimcrow/stories_people_dubois.html

CHAPTER 4

Policing

*Police have historically enforced laws that are today widely regarded as viola-
tions of the human rights of racial and ethnic minorities. One may argue that
the people who drafted these laws were a product of a specific time in history;
however, such arguments are based on the assumption that human rights are
relative and cannot be applied across time and place. We reject this assumption.*

—Barlow & Barlow (2000, p. 53)

Police are on the front line of the criminal justice system. This means that a citizen's introduction to the administration of justice usually begins with contact with a police officer. Most Americans have positive attitudes toward the police, although minorities are less likely to view the police as favorably as Whites do. For example, in 2003, while 92% of Whites had either a great deal or some confidence in the police, only 80% of minorities and 73% of Blacks did (Maguire & Pastore, 2003). In 2011, 86% of respondents to the Gallup poll had a great deal/some confidence in the police, including 92% of Whites, 73% of minorities, and 74% of Blacks (Maguire, 2011a). Why has confidence in police not changed very much since 2003 for Whites and Blacks and decreased for minorities overall (from 80% to 73%)? Unfortunately, recurring incidents of police brutality, racial profiling, the use of **Tasers** and controversial efforts to control immigration continue to frame confidence in the police. In their book *Police in a Multicultural Society*, the authors of the opening quote note the long history of conflict between police and communities of racial and ethnic minorities (Barlow & Barlow, 2000). Yet as Russell-Brown (2004) noted, "the historically oppressive relationship between police and African-Americans is lost in contemporary discussions" (p. 66).

Today, police agencies are more diversified, professional, and technologically advanced than at any other time in our history. There are more minority, women, and educated officers. Many departments have a website, utilize computer mapping, and have access to the National DNA Index System and the Department of Homeland Security Law Enforcement Information Sharing Service (LEIS). The 9/11 terrorist attacks led to what Forst (2003) has described as the "Terrorist Era of Policing," characterized by increased federalism, loss of civil liberties, greater reliance on private security, and a propensity toward errors of justice. The 2001 USA PATRIOT Act (and its reauthorization in 2006 and 2011) was enacted to counter terrorism, although it is viewed by some as infringing on the rights of citizens. Today there is increased concern about privacy and due process for all Americans, as well as closer scrutiny of "new" minority groups, including Middle Easterners and Muslims, and those who are identified as belonging to groups perceived as threatening (although they may not be), such as Sikhs. Aside from shifting the focus to "new" minority groups, it is unclear how police relations with "traditional" minority groups will unfold during this era. Has the shift in focus to terrorism, terrorists, and homeland security improved or exacerbated the strained relationship between police and minority groups?

The goals of this chapter are to provide an overview of policing in America, present the history of race and policing minority groups in America, and examine several contemporary issues, including citizen satisfaction with the police, police deviance, immigration and policing, and community policing. This chapter focuses primarily on policing in municipal (local) police agencies for two reasons. First, police histories usually focus on cities like Boston, New York City, Philadelphia, Chicago, and Charleston, SC. Second, most police are employed at the local level in cities and counties. We forgo an extensive overview of policing that can be found in most law enforcement and criminal justice textbooks. Our overview describes major **components of the policing industry** in America and provides the most recent employment data for minorities. Our history of policing presents developments since the colonial era and relevant historical information on policing Native Americans, African Americans, Asian Americans, Latinos, and immigrant Whites. By examining the past, we are able to better understand the complexities of police and community relations today.

❖ Overview of Policing in America

Police are the most visible symbol of governmental authority in our country. There are numerous federal, local, and state agencies, which vary in size and are bureaucratic and quasi-military in structure. In addition, there are Native American (tribal) police agencies, special police agencies with limited jurisdiction (e.g., transit police), and private police. The roles and functions of police agencies are specified in federal and state **statutes** and local ordinances. In municipal agencies, the police role consists primarily of maintaining the social order, preventing and controlling crime, and enforcing the law. Police are responsible for social control, have a considerable amount of discretion (decisional latitude), and are authorized to use force in the performance of their duties. Public police agencies rely heavily on the citizenry and work closely with other local, state, and federal police agencies in task forces to address specific problems, including gangs, homeland security, immigration fraud, narcotics law enforcement, human trafficking, and terrorism.

Research on employment patterns and practices in police agencies tends to focus on large metropolitan agencies in which minorities have made substantial gains. In large cities, minority representation increased from 29.8% in 1990 to 38.1% in 2000. Hispanic representation increased the most (from 9.2% to 14.1%), followed by Blacks (18.4% to 20.1%; Reaves & Hickman, 2002b). At that time, minority officers outnumbered White officers in some agencies, although the ratio of minority police officers to minority group members in large cities had increased only slightly, from .59 in 1990 to .63 in 2000. This means that there were 63 minority officers for every 100 minority citizens. The ratio for Blacks increased to .74, for

Latinos to .56, and for other minorities to .37 (Reaves & Hickman, 2002b). Although many officers are employed in large cities, 63% of local police departments employ only between 2 and 24 sworn officers (Reaves & Hickman, 2002a). In 2000, minorities comprised 22.7% of local sworn police officers and 17.1% of sworn officers in sheriffs' departments (Hickman & Reaves, 2003; Reaves & Hickman, 2003). Minority representation in local police agencies between 1987 and 2007 is presented in Figure 4.1. Over time, the number of minorities in local agencies has continued to increase, although the percentage of minorities has remained about the same since 2003 (Reaves, 2010). The representation of women in policing has improved as well, although the representation of minority women in federal, state, and local agencies is not readily available (Langton, 2010).

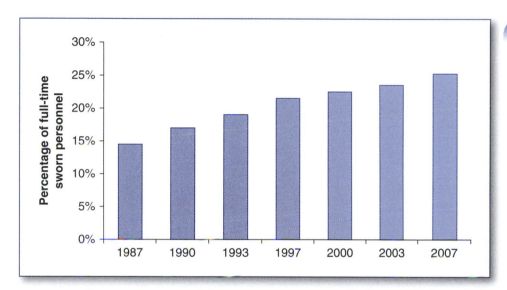

Figure 4.1

Minority Representation Among Local Police Officers, 1987–2007

Note: Includes Blacks or African Americans, Hispanics or Latinos, Asians, Native Hawaiians or other Pacific Islanders, American Indians, Alaska Natives, and persons identifying two or more races.

The most recent data available indicate that in 2007 there were an estimated 12,575 local police agencies that employed 463,000 full-time sworn personnel (Reaves, 2010, p. 6). Table 4.1 shows the race and ethnicity of full-time sworn personnel in police departments of varying sizes in 2007. Sometimes relying on percentages masks the actual representation of minorities in policing. For example, in 2000, 22.7% of the 440,000 sworn officers in local police agencies represent about 101,000 officers, and 17.1% of police in sheriffs' agencies represents almost 30,000 sworn officers (nationwide). Minority representation in smaller police departments as well as in state and federal agencies is still relatively low.

At the federal level, passage of the Homeland Security Act in 2002 created the **Department of Homeland Security** (DHS) in order to provide a more integrated approach to security in the United States. The legislation transferred all or part of 22 federal agencies to the DHS, making it the largest employer of federal law enforcement officers, and created the Transportation Security Administration (Reaves & Bauer, 2003). Prior to the creation of the DHS in 2002, the Department of Justice (DOJ) and Department of Transportation were the largest employers of federal officers with arrest and firearm authority. The Immigration and Naturalization Service had the largest minority percentage (46.75%), composed primarily

Table 4.1

Race and Ethnicity of Full-Time Sworn Personnel in Local Police Departments, by Size of Population Served, 2007

Population served	Percent of full-time sworn personnel who are—					
	White	Black/African American	Hispanic/ Latino	Asian/Pacific Islander	American Indian/ Alaska Native	Multi-race
All sizes	74.7%	11.9%	10.3%	2.0%	0.7%	0.3%
1,000,000 or more	56.0%	17.6%	22.9%	3.2%	0.3%	0.0%
500,000–999,999	60.6	24.1	9.3	4.1	0.4	1.6
250,000–499,999	69.5	16.5	11.2	2.0	0.6	0.1
100,000–249,999	73.7	13.4	9.1	2.6	0.9	0.3
50,000–99,999	83.6	7.0	7.5	1.4	0.3	0.3
25,000–49,999	88.2	5.0	5.1	0.9	0.6	0.2
10,000–24,999	87.5	5.6	5.1	0.6	1.0	0.2
2,500–9,999	87.9	5.1	4.4	0.6	1.8	0.1
Under 2,500	88.3	5.8	3.0	0.1	2.3	0.5

of Latinos (38.1%). Other DOJ agencies, including the Federal Bureau of Investigation (FBI; 16.8%), Drug Enforcement Administration (17.7%), and U.S. Marshals Service (17.6%), had lower minority representation.

The 2004 Census of Federal Law Enforcement Officers identified 105,000 full-time personnel authorized to arrest and carry firearms. The U.S. Customs and Border Protection (CBP) and U.S. Immigration and Customs Enforcement (ICE) employ more than 38,000 officers. Most federal officers are White males, and about one-third are members of a racial or ethnic minority group (see Figure 4.1; Reaves, 2006).

Changes in police hiring practices during the latter part of the 20th century contributed to current representation of minorities in policing, especially in local agencies. Despite considerable progress, minorities are still underrepresented in law enforcement. Efforts to make policing a more diverse profession often were met with resistance by police officers and the citizenry throughout American history.

❖ Historical Overview of Race and Policing

Historical accounts of the police often exclude the horrendous treatment of minorities by the police, and instead focus on the need for social control of these "threatening" groups. Facts about policing minorities and some White immigrants in earlier centuries are often omitted from criminal justice and law enforcement textbooks. It is impossible to separate the history of policing minority groups from the general history of the experiences of minorities in the United States, which were presented in Chapter 1. Similar to their treatment by most segments of our society, Native Americans, African Americans, Asian Americans, Latino/ Hispanic Americans, and some White immigrants were treated differently from the so-called law-abiding native Whites by the police. Here, we provide (a) a brief summary of the history of policing in America, beginning with the colonial period to the present; and (b) a discussion of the historical treatment of racial/ethnic groups by the police. It is important to remember that historical research on some groups is still limited and that policing practices varied considerably from one time to another and from one locale to another.

According to Walker and Katz (2002), "American policing is a product of its English heritage" (p. 24). During the colonial era, there were no formal police departments. Like their British counterparts, the colonists initially made policing the responsibility of every citizen and later utilized the sheriff, constable, and watch system (Uchida, 1997). During this time, there were regional differences in policing. For example, in some places, like Boston and New Amsterdam, NY, night watches were established, whereas in the South, slave patrols were more common. Over time, social disorder and crime increased so much, especially in Northern cities, that the early forms of policing proved ineffective and were gradually replaced with more formal police agencies patterned after the British model (Fogelson, 1977; Lane, 1967; Monkkonen, 1981; Richardson, 1970). Unlike the British police, American police agencies were decentralized, locally controlled, and influenced by politics.

"The history of American police during the nineteenth century is the history of separate forces in separate cities" (Emsley, 1983, p. 101). For example, White immigrants dominated police forces in some Northern cities, and slave patrollers in the South were usually poorer Whites. Slave patrols relied on a more military style of policing. The first African American police were "free men of color" who served in police organizations in New Orleans between 1805 and 1830. For the most part, they were responsible for slaves (W. Dulaney, 1996). D. Johnson (1981) mentioned that social tensions among immigrants, Blacks, and native Whites often resulted in conflicts and crime. Examples of these conflicts include verbal and physical abuse of abolitionists, race riots, labor strikes, and draft riots (Barlow & Barlow, 2000). Outside the urban areas, especially on the frontier, policing was characterized as vigilante in nature.

Although paid police forces that emerged in the 1800s were viewed as better than the night-and-day watches of the colonial era, social disorder and crime continued to be challenges. This led to the formation of private police, such as the Pinkerton Agency, and the reorganization of public police. Law enforcement textbooks allude to two important reform efforts. The first, during the late 1800s, attempted to reduce political control of the police. The next occurred during the early 20th century and focused on developing more professional police forces (McCamey, Scaramella, & Cox, 2003; Thurman, Zhao, & Giacomazzi, 2001; Walker & Katz, 2002). These reforms are important because the police were abusing their powers and resorting to unsavory practices such as corruption and the "third degree" (discussed later). Although the reform movement in the beginning of the 20th century was significant, much-needed personnel, policy, and training reforms did not occur until much later. During the 1960s, police were closely scrutinized following a great deal of civil unrest and several U.S. Supreme Court decisions, including *Mapp v. Ohio* (1961), *Escobedo v. Illinois* (1964), and *Miranda v. Arizona* (1966). Between 1970 and the present, policing has changed dramatically due to the convergence of several previously mentioned factors, including the hiring of minorities and women, technological developments, community policing, and the research revolution.

Kelling and Moore (1988) identified three eras in the history of policing often cited in many law enforcement textbooks: political (1840s to early 1900s), reform (1930s to 1960s), and community problem-solving (1970s to present). Williams and Murphy (1990) viewed Kelling and Moore's analysis as incomplete:

> The fact that the legal order not only countenanced but sustained slavery, segregation, and discrimination for most of our nation's history—and the fact that the police were bound to uphold that order—set a pattern for police behavior and attitudes toward minority communities that has persisted until the present day. . . . The existence of this pattern . . . meant that, while important changes were occurring in policing during our Nation's history, members of minority groups benefited less than others from these changes. (p. 2)

The following sections describe how the police (and other governmental officials) interacted with minority groups to uphold the legal and social order throughout American history.

Policing Native Americans

In the foreword to F. Cohen's (1971) classic book *Handbook of Federal Indian Law*, Robert L. Bennett and Frederick M. Hart described the complexities of understanding Indian law due to the numerous treaties, statutes, judicial decisions, and administrative rulings that emerged during the 1800s and 1900s. F. Cohen noted further that "Indian country" must be viewed temporally because federal and tribal law had changed over time. For example, although the Act of May 19, 1796 set the boundary between Indian country and the United States, by 1799, the boundary was changed to give federal courts jurisdiction over U.S. citizens who committed crimes against Indians. The Act of March 3, 1817 further extended federal law to prevent "White desperados" from escaping federal and state law (F. Cohen, 1971, p. 6). Indian country and/or territory were defined as "country within which Indian laws and customs and federal laws relating to Indians are generally applicable" (p. 5).

Following the Civil War, the United States minimized the political autonomy of tribal leaders and encouraged government representatives to deal with individual Indians and families (Tyler, 1973). As early as 1878, Congress established the U.S. Indian Police, which by 1881 was composed of 40 agencies, 162 officers, and 653 privates (Tyler, 1973). By the 1880s, the West was becoming rapidly developed and settled by Whites, which precipitated the demand for the acquisition of Indian land and resources. According to Tyler, there were chiefs of Indian police on the reservations who often mediated between White man's law and Indian custom. At the same time, the decimation of tribal leadership often resulted in the breakdown of social control. In 1887, the General Allotment or Dawes Act permitted tribal lands to be allotted to individual Indians, making them landowners and farmers. Although not applicable to all tribes initially, over time, the Dawes Act was extended to the Five Civilized Tribes in Indian Territory (Cherokees, Choctaws, Creeks, Chickasaws, and Seminoles) by the Curtis Act of 1898. By the turn of the century, the allotments were primarily an opportunity for the U.S. government and White settlers to secure both land and natural resources.

Interestingly, the FBI's first major homicide investigation involved Native Americans. During the 1800s, oil was discovered on the land of the Osage Indian tribe of Oklahoma. Beginning in the late 1800s, the reservations began yielding barrels of oil. By the early 1900s, the tribe was extremely wealthy considering that "in 1923 alone, the Osage Tribe received $27 million. In two decades, the Osage would receive more money from oil than all the old west gold rushes combined had yielded" (Hogan, 1998, p. 28). Eventually, this made them the target of elaborate schemes to defraud them of their wealth. After asking for assistance from the government, during the 1920s, the FBI infiltrated the tribe and uncovered a major scheme that involved intermarriage and murder. In the end, the FBI solved the case but had local officials make the arrests "since Special Agents of the FBI did not have the power of arrest (or the authority to carry firearms) at the time" (Hogan, 1998, p. 194).

On August 15, 1953, **Public Law 280** transferred federal responsibility for criminal and civil jurisdiction, including law enforcement duties, to six states (Alaska, California, Minnesota, Nebraska, Oregon, and Wisconsin) and made it optional for several other states to assert jurisdiction (Luna-Firebaugh, 2003; Tyler, 1973). Although P.L. 280 did not terminate tribal jurisdiction, it was the belief that states and sheriffs were now responsible for law enforcement. When it was widely recognized that states were not providing adequate policing services, some tribal governments sought to reestablish and strengthen tribal police services. In 1974, almost a century after the federal government first established police in Indian country, police protection on reservations was described as follows:

> On reservations where State laws apply, police activities are administered in the same manner as elsewhere. On reservations where State laws do not apply, tribal laws or Department of the Interior regulations are administered by personnel employed by the Bureau of Indian Affairs, or by personnel employed by the tribe, or by a combination of both. (Bureau of Indian Affairs, 1974, p. 27)

In February, 1973, a group of young Indians seized the village of Wounded Knee, South Dakota to protest conditions on the Pine Ridge reservation. Federal agents were called in to end the takeover, which lasted 71 days. Afterward, relations between the FBI and the American Indian Movement, a more radical American Indian rights group, continued to be tense. By 1976, the Bureau of Indian Affairs and/or tribes maintained law enforcement services on 126 reservations assigned to 61 Indian agencies. These agencies were responsible for around 200,000 square miles, 416,000 Indians, and numerous other non-Indians (Bureau of Indian Affairs, 1976).

In the 1990s, more than 56 million acres of land were owned and policed by tribal nations in the United States. "Indian country" includes reservations in 34 states, most of which are located west of the Mississippi River (Wakeling et al., 2001). The workload of officers in Indian police departments has increased as a result of several factors, including more reliance on the police (instead of traditional methods) and more crime and emergencies (Wakeling et al., 2001). Tribal police have responsibility for large land areas and often share criminal jurisdiction with federal and state agencies, "depending upon the particular offense, the offender, the victim and the offense location" (M. Hickman, 2003, p. 4). There are several administrative arrangements for policing Native Americans that include cross-deputization agreements with neighboring tribes, neighboring non-tribal authorities, and federal law enforcement agencies (Perry, 2005). According to the *Census of State and Local Law Enforcement Agencies, 2004*, there were 154 tribal police agencies with 2,490 sworn personnel (Reaves, 2007). In 2008 there were 178 law enforcement agencies, 157 general purpose police departments, and 21 agencies with special jurisdiction concerned with the enforcement of natural resources laws (Reaves, 2011). As previously mentioned, tribes have assumed responsibility and control of policing on many reservations. The typical department is small, and therefore there is considerably less police protection than in other urban and rural agencies.

Table 4.2 presents the 25 largest tribal law enforcement agencies in the United States, to illustrate the complexities of tribal law enforcement. The Navajo and Seminole police departments are the largest tribal agencies, but most tribal agencies have fewer than 50 full-time sworn personnel.

The Relocation Program of the Bureau of Indian Affairs transplanted Native Americans to cities in the early 1950s. By 1973, more than 100,000 Native Americans had relocated to urban areas, where they were faced with social, economic, and psychological challenges (Fixico, 2000). Historical research does not focus on either police-Indian relations in urban areas or crime among Indians who relocated, although considerable attention is devoted to the problem of alcohol-related crimes both on and off the reservation. More recent research has also been devoted to the nature of policing in Indian Country (Perry, 2009).

Policing African Americans

African Americans have posed a unique problem for America since their arrival as slaves in the 16th century. By the early 18th century, most of the early colonies regulated the movement and activities of free and enslaved Negroes by enacting special codes to totally control them. During the antebellum period, slaves were unprotected from crimes by slave owners, including murder, rape, assault, and battery (Kennedy, 1997). According to Dulaney (1996), by the mid-1700s, "patterrollers," or slave patrols, the first distinctively American police system, existed in every Southern colony. Slave patrols carried out numerous duties, including checking passes of slaves leaving plantations, routinely searching slave quarters for stolen property, and administering whippings (Websdale, 2001). Relatedly, slave revolts were of increasing concern and, along with slavery, mandated a brutal policing mechanism to both protect Whites and dehumanize Blacks (T. Jones, 1977).

During the 1800s, in the North and South, both before and after Emancipation, free Blacks were treated like slaves. Their movements were regulated: They were prohibited from entering several states and had to be employed to remain in states; in Virginia, an emancipated slave had to leave the state within 12 months or forfeit his freedom (Taylor Greene & Gabbidon, 2000). Kennedy (1997) describes the unwillingness of Southern Whites to recognize Blacks' rights to protection and the failure of local authorities to restrain or punish violence against them.

African Americans were excluded from policing in most cities until the mid-1800s. Black police did serve in Washington, D.C. as early as 1861 (Kuykendall & Burns, 1980). The first wave of Black police officers in the United States appeared during Reconstruction. Several cities in the North and South employed Blacks, including Chicago; Philadelphia; Columbia and Charleston, South Carolina; and several cities in Mississippi and Texas. However, by the 1890s, most Blacks had been eliminated from police agencies in the South (Dulaney, 1996). At the same time, lynching was a serious problem. Some police participated in lynchings or silently supported attacks against African Americans by White mobs (Russell-Brown, 2004).

Table 4.2

The 25 Largest Tribally Operated Law Enforcement Agencies, by the Number of Full-Time Sworn Personnel, 2008

Name and location of agency	Number of full-time sworn personnel	BIA service population. 2005	Full-time sworn personnel per 1,000 residents	Reservation land area (square miles)	Full-time sworn personnel per 25 square miles
Navajo Police Department (AZ, NM, UT)	393	192,067	2.0	22,174	0.4
Seminole Police Department (FL)	144	3,165	45.5	141	25.5
Salt River Police Department (AZ)	125	7,313	17.1	81	38.6
Gila River Indian Community Police Department (AZ)	93	14,966	6.2	584	4.0
Tohono O'odham Police Department (AZ)	66	26,673	2.5	4,453	0.4
Choctaw Police Department (MS)	50	8,313	6.0	25	50.0
Oglala Sioux Tribe Department of Public Safety (SD)	49	43,146	1.1	3,159	0.4
Cherokee Indian Police Department (NC)	45	13,562	3.3	83	13.6
Muscogee (Creek) Nation LighthorseTribal Police (OK)	39	55,817	0.7	4,648	0.2
Miccosukee Police Department (FL)	36	589	61.1	128	7.0
Poarch Creek Tribal Police Department (AL)	33	1,567	21.1	0.4	—
Cherokee Nation Marshal Service (OK)	32	197,684	0.2	6,702	0.1
Choctaw Nation Tribal Police Department (OK)	32	99,371	0.3	10,613	0.1
Colville Tribal Police Department (WA)	32	5,052	6.3	2,117	0.4
Saginaw Chippewa Tribal Police Department (MI)	30	1,799	16.7	218	3.4
Tulalip Tribal Police Services (WA)	30	2,369	10.5	35	21.4
Warm Springs Tribal Police Department (OR)	30	4,079	7.4	1,011	0.7
White Mountain Apache Police Department (AZ)	30	12,213	2.5	2,628	0.3
Isleta Police Department (NM)	29	3,980	7.3	331	2.2
Yakama Nation Tribal Police Department (WA)	28	16,815	1.7	2,153	0.3
Pascua Yaqui Tribal Police Department (AZ)	27	14,787	1.8	2	—
PuyallupTribal Police Department (WA)	27	24,016	1.1	29	23.3
Rosebud Sioux Tribal Police Department (SD)	27	22,293	1.2	1,388	0.5
Red Lake Tribal Police Department (MN)	26	10,338	2.5	880	0.7
Oneida Indian Nation Police (NY)	25	650	38.5	0.1	—

Note: Land area data are from the U.S. Census Bureau and include reservation land only.

— Reservation land area is less than 25 square miles.

A similar problem occurred in numerous cities during race riots in the 19th and early 20th centuries. Race riots were clashes between Black and White citizens, in which the police were often accused of indifference, brutality, and leaving the scene. With few exceptions, police did not protect Blacks from these attacks on their persons and property, and sometimes they even participated in these events. Police officers played a pivotal role in race riots in East St. Louis (1917), Chicago (1919), Tulsa (1921), Detroit (1943), and Washington, D.C. (1919). In the 20th century, efforts were made to protect Blacks in some instances, and federal troops were sometimes called in to assist in restoring order (Grimshaw, 1969).

In 1938, Gunnar Myrdal undertook a comprehensive study of the Negro in the United States. His findings are reported in *An American Dilemma*, where he states,

> The average Southern policeman is a promoted poor White with a legal sanction to use a weapon. His social heritage has taught him to despise the Negroes, and he has had little education which could have changed him. . . . The result is that probably no group of Whites in America have a lower opinion of the Negro people and are more fixed in their views than Southern policemen. (Myrdal, 1944, pp. 540–541)

There were approximately 50 Black policemen by 1940. At the time, three-fourths of the Black population lived in the South. Alabama, Georgia, Louisiana, Mississippi, and South Carolina, the states with the largest Black populations, had no Black policemen (Rudwick, 1960). Substantial gains were made by Blacks in law enforcement as a result of the civil rights movement of the 1960s, although it would take numerous court battles to integrate police departments, and the problems of underprotection and police violence persisted. Since the 1970s, there has been an increase in the number of Black police officers and police administrators. Black police organizations and police leaders have been instrumental in calling attention to police use of deadly force, brutality, and racial profiling, issues of concern to Black Americans (Taylor Greene, 2004). Nevertheless, the ratio of Black officers to Black citizens is still low, even in larger cities. It is important to note that employment gains by Blacks in law enforcement have caused some citizens to complain that their treatment by Black officers often is just as problematic as the historical treatment by White officers.

Policing Asian Americans

As discussed in Chapter 1, many Chinese immigrated to the United States as laborers. In 1876, there were 151,000 Chinese in the United States, and 116,000 were in the state of California. Like others, many Chinese immigrated to California in search of gold, although they were also known to serve as cooks, laundrymen, and servants (Norton, 2004). Early laborers were indentured servants who financed their passage by agreeing to work for merchant creditors (Courtwright, 2001). Around 1880, El Paso, Texas became a point of entry for Chinese laborers from Mexico after the United States made entry for Chinese workers illegal. Often referred to as "coolies," the Chinese were involved in laying tracks for the Southern Pacific Railroad or remained in El Paso after completing railroad tracks that originated in the West (Dickey, 2004; Institute of Texan Cultures, 1998).

The fact that many Chinese immigrants were illegal did not seem to matter as much as their opium smoking and **opium dens**. Opium smoking was common among Chinese immigrants and confined to them between 1850 and 1870. Soon after, opium and opium dens gained popularity with the underworld of gamblers, prostitutes, and other criminals (Courtwright, 2001). In 1883, several dens were operating in El Paso and were frequented by members of both the lower and upper classes. Many believe that the opium dens were eventually targeted by the police and other governmental officials because of concerns that Whites were mixing with Chinese, viewed by some as "polluting" (Institute of Texan Cultures, 1998). In the 1870s and 1880s, federal, municipal, and state governments passed laws that penalized opium smoking. According to Courtwright (2001), "Dens patronized by Whites were the most likely to be raided" (p. 77). By 1909, federal legislation banned the importation of opium for smoking by stipulating that it could be imported only for medicinal purposes.

After the anti-opium smoking legislation, imports decreased and coincided with a decrease in the size of the Chinese population that was also related to more restrictive immigration policies. During most of the 20th century, Asian Americans were more likely to remain in cultural enclaves and less likely to be involved in crime in their communities. Thus, although Asian gangs in California and other jurisdictions are still involved in drug distribution (heroin, ice), prostitution, and other illegal activities, the fact that most Asian Americans are insulated from police attention is due, at least in part, to their cultural values, ethnic isolation, and language barriers. More recent Southeast Asian immigrants and some second-generation Asian Americans target other Asian immigrants, Asian Americans, and businesses (http://www.asian-nation.org/gangs.shtml). These individuals, often belonging to gangs, are more likely to come to the attention of police today.

Policing Latinos

Research on the experiences of Mexican Americans in the Southwest and Los Angeles is more readily available than studies of the historical experiences with the police of other Latino groups such as Puerto Ricans, Dominicans, and Colombians. Trujillo (1974/1995) described how American capitalists who colonized the Southwest during the 1850s and 1860s created a cheap labor force and perpetuated an atmosphere of violence against Chicano immigrants. He maintained that repression of Chicanos by the police, military, and vigilantes led to the formation of protective guerilla units and bandits that are misrepresented in American history. Brutality against Mexican Americans included lynchings and murders. The number of brutal incidents in California and Texas prompted the Mexican ambassador to formally protest the mistreatment of Mexicans in 1912 (Kanellos, 1977). According to Chabrán and Chabrán (1996), Latino migrant workers in the Southwest received the harshest treatment. Because many of them were illegal immigrants, they were minimally protected by the American legal system.

In the 1931 Wickersham Commission Report on Crime and the Foreign Born, three chapters specifically address the Mexican American immigrant. The focus is primarily on arrests, although there is some information on discriminatory treatment by the police. For example, P. Taylor (1931) found several individuals who noted how the police in Chicago and Gary, Indiana were more likely to arrest Mexican Americans than Poles for drunkenness.

By the 1940s, police-Chicano relations in Los Angeles, where many Mexican Americans resided, had deteriorated to what Escobar (1999) described as extreme hostility and suspicion toward each other. Chicano youth were viewed as a social threat. On June 3, 1943, several sailors stated that they were attacked by a group of Mexicans, which marked the beginning of what is referred to as the "**zoot suit riots**" or "sailor riots." The sailors retaliated by going to East Los Angeles and attacking Mexican Americans, especially those wearing zoot suits. The riots continued until June 7, when the navy finally put an end to the wanton attacks by declaring Los Angeles off limits to military personnel. The police and sheriff arrested several sailors, although none were charged with crimes. In contrast, hundreds of Chicano youth were arrested without cause (Suavecito Apparel Co., 2004).

During the latter part of the 20th century, Latinos, like African Americans, continued to have strained relations with the police. The problems of illegal immigration, human smuggling, and drug smuggling, especially in the southwest region of the country, have increased the amount of contact between Latinos and state, local, and federal police agencies. Although the representation of Latinos in local police agencies increased from 4.5% in 1987 to 10.3% in 2007 (Reaves, 2010), relations between police and the Latino community are still best characterized as strained. Since 2001 the DHS has implemented several immigration enforcement strategies, including the Secure Communities Program, in an effort to identify and remove criminal aliens (DHS, 2009). In 2010, DHS apprehended 517,000 foreign nationals, of whom more than 80% were natives of Mexico. The majority of aliens removed were also from Mexico, followed by Guatemala, Honduras, and El Salvador nationals (DHS, 2011).

Policing White Immigrants

Throughout American history, the majority of immigrants have been of European descent. During the 1800s, immigration increased considerably as waves of Germans, Irish, and the "new immigrants" (Italians, Poles, Greeks, Portuguese, Jews, and others) arrived in the United States. These new immigrants were viewed less favorably than those who had arrived prior to 1850. This was due, at least in part, to beliefs that "incoming migrants from eastern and

Photo 4.1

A group of Hispanic men stand chained together on their way to court in June, 1943.

central Europe brought many negative social characteristics often attributable to their race," a term used rather carelessly to refer to nationality and/or culture (Graham, 2004, p. 25). By the late 1800s, immigration was seen by Progressive Era reformers as a threat to democracy, social order, and American identity (Graham, 2004). Poverty, illiteracy, unemployment, and underemployment in the ethnic ghettos meant that various types of criminal enterprises were common, including gambling, prostitution, theft, and con men (Fogelson, 1977).

The police experiences of White immigrants were drastically different from those of Native Americans, African Americans, Asian Americans, and Latinos. First, it was easier for foreign-born Whites to gradually blend into American society. Second, many White immigrants were able to secure jobs as police officers. Third, White immigrants often were assisted by the police in their transition to life in a new country. As early as the 1850s, the Boston police provided firewood and other necessities to Irish immigrants. Decades later, one function of the Boston police department was to distribute free soup in station houses, especially during the winter (Lane, 1967). Police also assisted parents looking for lost children (Monkkonen, 1981) and accommodated overnight lodgers (Lane, 1967; Monkkonen, 1981).

By the turn of the 20th century, tension between upper- and middle-class native-born and foreign-born Whites often resulted in more aggressive policing that emphasized law enforcement more than service. In some cities, policing of White immigrants depended on whether the police were controlled by political machines friendly to either immigrants or Progressive Era reformers seeking to restrict the immorality of immigrants (Brown & Warner, 1992). Ironically, because policemen were recruited from the lower and lower middle classes, they "had little or no inclination to impose the morality of the upper middle and upper classes on the ethnic ghettos" (Fogelson, 1977, p. 38). Later in the 20th century, serial killers, including Theodore Bundy, David Berkowitz, and John Wayne Gacy; White supremacists Randy Weaver and the Ruby Ridge incident; and domestic terrorists Timothy McVeigh and Terry Nichols, who bombed the Alfred P. Murrah Federal Building in Oklahoma City, were key factors in the development of criminal profiles and revisions to training and policy, especially at the federal level.

It is easy to lose sight of the fact that, throughout history, most persons who have been arrested (i.e., have had contact with the police) have been White. Historically, interactions between the police and Whites were less controversial than encounters between police and minority groups. Compared with early periods in American history, policing minorities has gradually improved as a result of the civil rights movement, federal legislation, affirmative action policies, human rights advocates, community policing, minority political empowerment, minority ascendancy in police organizations, policing research, and increased media attention focusing on police behaviors. Despite improved **police-community relations**, there are several contemporary issues regarding race and policing, which are discussed next.

❖ Contemporary Issues in Race and Policing

As noted at the beginning of the chapter, the majority of Americans view the police favorably. Nevertheless, there is still variation in citizen satisfaction with the police, and several problematic police behaviors continue to capture the attention of all Americans. For example, minorities continue to be disproportionately the victims of racial profiling, use of force, and conducted-energy devices (CEDs, i.e., Tasers). It is also unclear how recent developments in the application of technology to policing impact minorities. These issues are discussed next.

Citizen Satisfaction With Police

Police need the cooperation of the citizenry to effectively perform their duties. Citizens who are dissatisfied with the police and are distrustful are less likely to partner with them to prevent and control crime. They also are unlikely to aspire to law enforcement careers (Ross, 2001). Race is one of the strongest predictors of attitudes toward the police (Weitzer, 1999). Efforts to gauge public opinion about the police measure several related concepts, including perceptions of satisfaction, confidence, and citizens' preferences. Citizen satisfaction research assesses perceptions about different aspects of policing, including community policing (Skogan, Steiner, DuBois, Gudell, & Fagan, 2002; S. Smith, Steadman, Minton, & Townsend, 1999; Wilder, 2003), police misconduct (Sigelman, Welch, Bledsoe, & Combs, 1997; Weitzer, 1999), racial profiling (Higgins, Gabbidon, & Jordan, 2008; Weitzer & Tuch, 2002), and complaint procedures (Walker, 2001).

During the 1960s, when the National Opinion Research Center conducted a national survey for the President's Commission on Law Enforcement and the Administration of Justice, they found that 67% of the general public responded that their police did an "excellent" or "good" job, and 77% responded that police did a "pretty good" to "very good" job of protecting people in their neighborhoods. Non-Whites (primarily Blacks) gave a rating of "very good" half as often as Whites and a "not so good" rating twice as often. Blacks were also more likely to view the police as discourteous (President's Commission on Law Enforcement and the Administration of Justice, 1967). In 1979, according to the National Crime Survey, whereas 54% of White victims of crime evaluated their local police as "good," only 25% of Blacks and 19.2% of Hispanic victims did (Carter, 1983).

The Gallup Organization also collects public opinion data. Citizens are queried on several topics, including their confidence in the criminal justice system, the police, honesty and ethical standards of the police, and perceptions of when it is acceptable for police to strike a citizen. The findings appear annually in the *Sourcebook of Criminal Justice Statistics*. Since 1998, the majority of survey respondents report a great deal/quite a lot of satisfaction with the police. In 2000, the Gallup Poll Social Audit found that Black Americans' general perception of fair treatment decreased to 36%, down from 49% in 1997 and lower than ratings of fairness in the 1960s, which ranged from 41% to 44% (Newport & Ludwig, 2000). More troubling is the fact that 55% to 64% of Blacks believe they are not treated as fairly as Whites by police (Newport & Ludwig, 2000). Table 4.3 presents trends between 2002 and 2011 in the percentage of respondents agreeing with the statement that they have a great deal/quite a lot of confidence in the police. During the 10-year period, the majority of Whites continued to have the most confidence in the police, although in 2011 it was much lower than in 2004. The confidence of Blacks increased in 2011 to 43%, although it is still much lower than in 2005 when it was at its highest level in the decade. Although not disaggregated by race, confidence in the police by political affiliation varies considerably (see Table 4.3).

In addition to public opinion polls, there is a considerable amount of research on citizen satisfaction with police in the context of their experience with police and neighborhood conditions (quality of life; Reisig & Parks, 2001; Wilder, 2003), quality of police service (Skogan, 2005), neighborhood context (Schafer, Huebner, & Bynum, 2003), and police preferences (Nation, 2011). Direct and indirect contact with the police have been found to impact citizen satisfaction with the police differently, as do perceptions of crime, fear of crime, and neighborhood conditions. Some researchers have explored the intersection of race and class and found that both factors are important (Weitzer, 1999; Weitzer & Tuch, 2002). Weitzer (1999)

Table 4.3

Reported Confidence in the Police by Demographic Characteristic, United States, 2002–2011

Question: "I am going to read you a list of institutions in American society. Please tell me how much confidence you, yourself, have in each one—a great deal, quite a lot . . . : the police?"

| | Great Deal/Quite a Lot | | | | | | | | | |
	2002	2003	2004	2005	2006	2007	2008	2009	2010	2011
National	59%	61%	64%	63%	58%	54%	58%	59%	59%	56%
Sex										
Male	61	60	64	65	58	58	66	59	59	55
Female	57	61	64	61	58	51	50	59	61	58
Race										
White	63	65	70	66	63	60	62	63	62	61
Non-White[a]	43	43	43	53	40	32	47	51	52	45
Black	31	43	41	49	28	22	36	38	35	43
Age										
18 to 29 years	56	61	61	52	55	55	61	50	52	56
30 to 49 years	55	59	62	66	60	56	58	60	58	52
50 to 64 years	60	63	65	63	57	50	57	63	65	61
50 years and older	64	64	68	64	59	52	57	64	64	NR
65 years and older	69	66	71	66	62	56	56	65	64	64
Education										
College post grad	62	67	66	72	65	59	65	66	66	65
College graduate	69	70	72	70	64	57	64	69	74	61

(Continued)

(Continued)

	2002	2003	2004	2005	2006	2007	2008	2009	2010	2011
Great Deal/Quite a Lot										
Some college	56	64	61	61	59	58	65	57	60	56
No college	56	53	64	59	53	48	47	55	52	53
Income										
$75,000 and over	68	70	69	72	65	59	66	70	66	59
$50,000 and over	65	68	70	63	69	51	65	65	67	62
$30,000 to $49,999	58	64	60	64	58	55	59	52	55	51
$20,000 to $29,999	51	48	57	48	45	44	42	52	57	65
Under $20,000	49	49	60	53	47	51	47	50	49	43
Community										
Urban area	53	59	60	61	55	52	NR	NR	NR	NR
Suburban area	60	64	64	66	62	59	NR	NR	NR	NR
Rural area	60	55	69	61	56	47	NR	NR	NR	NR
Region										
East	63	58	62	61	62	52	64	60	61	64
Midwest	56	62	68	64	58	59	56	62	60	64
South	53	64	63	65	58	53	51	60	56	52
West	64	57	65	62	56	53	62	58	64	49
Politics										
Republican	73	70	79	78	68	70	74	71	69	69
Democrat	51	58	59	60	54	44	52	53	54	57
Independent	52	55	55	52	55	52	51	56	58	48

a. Includes Black respondents.

NR = not reported.

found that perceptions of the extent of police misconduct were inversely related to neighborhood class and that middle-class Blacks experienced more suspicion and mistreatment outside their own neighborhoods. The lack of satisfaction and trust in the police does not bode well for citizens either working with the police or entering the law enforcement profession. One explanation posits that racial variations in citizen preferences for policing influence citizens' attitudes toward and satisfaction with the police (Nation, 2011). Another explanation for minorities' (especially Blacks') lower opinions and levels of trust of the police is related to their overrepresentation as victims of varying forms of police deviance (Weitzer, Tuch, & Skogan, 2008).

Police Deviance

Police deviance is a broad term used to refer to "police officer activities that are inconsistent with the officer's official authority, organizational authority, values, and standards of ethical conduct" (Barker & Carter, 1991, p. 4). Use of excessive force (including both police homicides and police brutality), corruption, perjury, sex, sleeping and drinking on duty, discrimination, and failure to enforce the law are examples of police deviance (Barker & Carter, 1991). Police deviance has been known to exist since the 1800s (see, e.g., Fogelson, 1977; Richardson, 1970; Sherman, 1974). When President Herbert Hoover appointed a commission to investigate the shortcomings of the administration of justice, the third degree, a mostly secret and illegal practice, was a common form of police deviance. The *Report on Lawlessness in Law Enforcement* stated,

> After reviewing the evidence obtainable the authors of the report reach the conclusion that the third degree—that is, the use of physical brutality, or other forms of cruelty, to obtain involuntary confessions or admissions—is widespread. (National Commission on Law Observance and Enforcement, 1931b, p. 4)

Deviant police practices continued to receive considerable attention throughout the 20th century. During the civil unrest of the 1960s, following several questionable police homicides during the 1970s and 1980s, and after the Rodney King beating in 1991, police abuse of their authority precipitated research and legislative changes. Another egregious incident of police deviance occurred in 1999 in Tulia, Texas, when 46 people (the majority of whom were Black) were arrested by Officer Tom Coleman and charged with being cocaine dealers. Many of them went to prison and later were pardoned by Governor Rick Perry after an appellate judge accused Coleman of lying, falsifying evidence, and racism (Drug Policy Alliance, 2008). A similar incident occurred in Hearne, Texas in 2000 when 27 were arrested (Frontline, 2004).

Police deviance is an inevitable outcome of the right to use force that Americans grant police. We entrust the police with the ability to use their power legitimately and want to hold them accountable when they do not. In 2001, more than a dozen police departments, including Cincinnati, New York City, Detroit, New Orleans, and Tulsa, were under investigation by the DOJ Office of Civil Rights (OCR), to determine whether they engaged in a pattern and/or practice of either racial discrimination or brutality (Roane, 2001). Recent investigations include departments in Miami, FL; Warren, OH; Alabaster, AL; and Franklinton, LA. In 2010, the OCR was investigating 17 police departments across the country and monitoring five settlements regarding four police agencies (DOJ, 2010). On May 15, 2010, the OCR opened an investigation of the New Orleans Police Department (NOPD) and on March 17, 2011 released its findings that the NOPD has engaged in patterns of misconduct that violate the Constitution and federal law (see Box 4.1). The OCR also provides technical assistance to police agencies in an effort to remedy complaints of police misconduct and discrimination.

BOX 4.1

Excerpts From a Letter to Mayor Landrieu From Thomas E. Perez, Assistant Attorney General, Immediately Following the US DOJ OCR Investigation of the NOPD

Dear Mayor Landrieu:

We are writing to report the findings of the Civil Rights Division's investigation of the New Orleans Police Department ("NOPD") pursuant to the Violent Crime Control and Law Enforcement Act of 1994, 42U.S.C. § 14141, the Omnibus Crime Control and Safe Streets Act of 1968,42 U.S.C. § 3789d, and Title VI of the Civil Rights Act of 1964,42 U.S.C. § 2000d. These laws give the United States Department of Justice ("DOJ") authority to seek declaratory or equitable relief to remedy patterns or practices of conduct by law enforcement officers that deprive individuals of rights, privileges, or immunities secured by the Constitution or laws of the United States. These laws also give DOJ the authority to seek the withdrawal of federal funding from police departments that discriminate on the basis of race, color, religion, sex or national origin.

Our investigation has been thorough, wide ranging, and independent. We have conducted a top to bottom review of the Department, and have examined a wide range of policies, practices, and issues. Civil pattern or practice investigations have a different focus and legal standard from criminal investigations and our investigation was kept separate from ongoing federal criminal prosecutions of NOPD officers. During this investigation, in addition to retaining police practices experts specifically for this project, we have consulted with experts within the Department of Justice, including the Office of Justice Programs, the Office on Violence Against Women, the Office of Community Oriented Policing Services, the Office on Juvenile Justice and Delinquency Prevention, and the Access to Justice Initiative.

We received the complete cooperation of the City and the Police Department during the course of our investigation. In addition, we could not have completed our investigation without the contributions of the many community members and groups who met with us on weekends and on evenings until late into the night to ensure that we had as full a picture of New Orleans and its Police Department as possible. The Community Relations Service of the Department of Justice facilitated many of these meetings, further enabling community members to voice their concerns and proposals. We also appreciate the involvement of rank and file police officers and the police union.

Throughout our investigation, Superintendent Ronal Serpas has been working to improve policing in New Orleans to make it more effective and accountable. We find that City and NOPD leadership understand that smart, constitutional policing is directly tied to crime prevention and the restoration of public confidence in NOPD. The City and Department recognize that they must provide officers with the policies, training, supervision, and facilities necessary to consistently police with effectiveness, integrity and professionalism—and hold officers accountable when they do not.

City and Department leadership, as well as others in NOPD, have also acknowledged that for NOPD's policing efforts to be successful, all segments of New Orleans' racially, ethnically, and socio-economically diverse community must feel they are in partnership with the police in keeping their neighborhoods safe.

Achieving this culture shift will require the Department to engage and protect all of the City's communities, to treat them with dignity, and to work diligently to prevent and solve the problems that cause crime in their neighborhoods. This fundamental reform will require the collaborative efforts of the entire criminal justice system, including the District Attorney's Office, Public Defender's Office, Courts, Sheriffs Department and Juvenile Justice System. We are hopeful that the findings and recommendations in this letter will assist this critically important effort.

The challenges confronting the New Orleans Police Department are serious, systemic, wide-ranging, and deeply rooted. We find reasonable cause to believe that there are the following patterns or practices of unconstitutional conduct and/or violations of federal law:

- Use of excessive force;
- Unconstitutional stops, searches, and arrests;
- Biased policing:

  o Racial, ethnic and LGBT discrimination;
  o National origin discrimination—systemic failure to provide effective policing services to persons with limited English proficiency; and
  o Gender-biased policing—systemic failure to investigate sexual assaults and domestic violence.

We find further that a number of long-standing and entrenched practices within NOPD cause or contribute to the patterns or practices of unconstitutional conduct that we observed. These practices include:

- Failed systems for officer recruitment, promotion and evaluation;
- Inadequate training;
- Inadequate supervision;
- Ineffective systems of complaint intake, investigation and adjudication;
- A failed Paid Detail system;
- Failure to engage in community-oriented policing;
- Inadequate officer assistance and support services; and
- Lack of sufficient community oversight.

As devastating as Hurricane Katrina was, our investigation has revealed that these serious deficiencies existed long before the storm. We provide recommendations not only to improve the relationship between NOPD and the broader New Orleans community, but also to ensure that the City and NOPD give their officers the support they need to be safer and more effective each day.

Why do you think these police practices in New Orleans persisted for so long without intervention by the police department leadership or the mayor?

Goldkamp (1982) identified two perspectives that help us to understand why minorities are overrepresented as victims of police use of force. Belief Perspective I points to differential law enforcement and the possible effects of prejudice and discrimination. Belief Perspective II posits that minorities are involved in crimes that increase their likelihood of victimization by the police. The OCR findings in the investigation of the NOPD and numerous other agencies lend some support for Belief Perspective I. The National Organization of Black Law Enforcement Executives (NOBLE) offers some support for Belief Perspective I as well. They believe that justice is a system of people influenced by biases and stereotypes that are often incorporated into police decision making and actions. They have noted that the use of excessive force, brutality, and shootings of unarmed minority suspects and undercover officers are "symptoms and manifestations of biased-based policing" (NOBLE, 2001, p. 4). Another explanation of how discrimination manifests itself in police behavior is referred to as "reasonable racism." Kennedy (1997) explained,

> Most courts . . . have authorized police to use race in making decisions to question, stop, or detain persons so long as doing so is reasonably related to efficient law enforcement and not deployed for purposes of racial harassment. (p. 141)

> More troubling is the fact that "reasonable" racial discrimination continues to be viewed as "a practical aspect of good law enforcement." (p. 141)

He went on to state,

> Reasonableness, then, is not a definite, arithmetic objective quality that is independent of aims and values. It is a concept that is considerably more subtle, complex, malleable, and mysterious than the simplistic model of human decision making relied upon by those who accept at face value the "reasonableness" and "rationality" of conduct that not only expresses controversial moral and political judgments but that also expresses deep seated, perhaps unconscious, affections, fears, and aversions. (pp. 144–145)

Police discrimination is not as blatant and overt today. For example, police use of deadly force is no longer as extensive as it was before the U.S. Supreme Court decision in *Tennessee v. Garner* (1985), which found shooting of fleeing felons unconstitutional. Ironically, the police officer and victim in that case were both Black. Before the Court ruled in the *Garner* decision, researchers and practitioners were questioning the disproportionate number of minorities shot and killed by the police (see, e.g., Fyfe, 1981, 1982; Sherman, 1980; Takagi, 1974). In 1989, the U.S. Supreme Court addressed the issue of reasonable force by police officers in *Graham v. Connor* and concluded that the perspective of a reasonable officer, as well as the facts and circumstances, must be considered (Novak, 2009; Terrill, 2009). More recently, the impact of an officer's perceptual distortions during police shootings and how such distortions might relate to "reasonableness" has garnered attention in the research (Engel & Smith, 2009; Klinger & Brunson, 2009).

Goldkamp's Belief Perspective II has some support as well. The disproportionate involvement of minorities (especially Blacks) in arrests for violent crimes, as discussed in Chapter 2, leads to more contact with the police. The Death in Custody Reporting Act of 2000 mandates that all states collect and report data on arrest-related deaths. The first reported findings provide some support for Belief Perspective II; between 2003 and 2005, 2,002 deaths were reported. Of these, 1,095 arrest-related homicides were by police officers, and 75% involved arrests for a violent crime. In 80% of the homicides, a weapon was used by the arrestee. Relatedly, 16 of the 24 CED-related deaths were of persons arrested for violent crimes (Mumola, 2007).

An examination of police officers feloniously killed in the line of duty might be considered as support for Belief Perspective II. In 2006, 48 officers were killed; 12 died during arrest situations, 10 were ambushed, 8 were responding to disturbance calls, and 8 were killed during traffic pursuits or stops. Thirty-eight of the officers killed were White, 5 were Black, 1 was American Indian/Alaskan Native, and 1 was Asian/Pacific Islander. Among the

55 alleged assailants, 29 were Black and 25 were White (FBI, 2006c). In 2010, 162 officers were killed, many in incidents that involved more than one officer (MSNBC, 2011).

Opponents of Goldkamp's second perspective argue that many victims of police use of excessive force are not engaged in violent criminal acts when they are beaten or killed by police. Before Rodney King refused to stop his car, was he involved in a violent crime? In New York City, several controversial incidents of police use of deadly force were not preceded by a violent crime, including those involving Abner Louima (savagely sodomized and beaten in 1997), Amadou Diallo (a Guinean immigrant shot and killed by New York City police in 1999), and Sean Bell (killed by police after leaving a Queens strip club in 2007). Russell-Brown (2004) has succinctly noted,

> There is no evidence that the level of police assaults against Blacks increases and decreases on the basis of the rate of Black offending. Further, according to this reasoning, the majority of Blacks are required to pay the debt incurred by the small percentage of the group who are offenders. (p. 60)

Earlier in this chapter, some historical evidence of police brutality was provided (Myrdal, 1944; National Commission on Law Observance and Enforcement, 1931b). The International Association of Chiefs of Police has been developing a use-of-force database since the 1990s, although it is not representative of either police agencies or the population. Since 1995, 564 agencies have submitted data, and in 2001, about 225 agencies provided data (International Association of Chiefs of Police, 2003). If the limited data available are accurate, police brutality is rare, involves few officers, and occurs most often during arrests (Adams, 1999; International Association of Chiefs of Police, 2003). It is estimated that only 1%, or approximately 446,000 police-citizen encounters, involved either the threat or use of force (Adams, 1999). Between 1999 and 2000, the most common form of force was physical, followed by chemical and firearm force (International Association of Chiefs of Police, 2003). Most officers who did use force were White, and about 53% of victims were minorities.

Citizen Complaints About Police Use of Force (Hickman, 2006) provides data from large state and local agencies collected in 2002. More than 26,000 complaints were received, most of them in large agencies. Only 8% of the complaints were sustained and warranted disciplinary action. It was estimated that the rate of police use of excessive force is about 1 incident per 200 full-time sworn officers. Like crime and victimization statistics presented in Chapter 2, this data source has methodological problems related to reporting and participation by agencies. One problem is the inclusion of only large state and local agencies. Another is the collection of data by police agencies. The most recent Police-Public Contact Survey (discussed below) found that an estimated 776,000 people—about 1.9% of the 40 million U.S. residents who had contact with police during 2008—reported police use of force or threat of force. Although there were fewer such incidents than in 2002 and 2005, in 2008 males, Blacks, and younger persons were more likely to have had contact with police that resulted in the use of force (Eith & Durose, 2011, p. 11).

Interestingly, police officers' attitudes toward treatment of minority and poor citizens also vary by race. Weisburd, Greenspan, Hamilton, Williams, and Bryand (2000) reported considerable variation in White, Black, and other minority officers' perceptions of treatment of Whites versus Blacks and use of physical force. Forty-seven percent of Black officers felt that police officers treat Whites better, compared with 11.2% of Whites and 21% of other minority officers. Forty-eight percent of Black officers felt that police are more likely to use physical force against Blacks and other minorities than against Whites, compared with 4.5% of Whites and 10% of other minorities. In a study in the Commonwealth of Virginia, Ioimo, Tears, Meadows, Becton, and Charles (2007) found that 21% of police officers believed officers practice biased policing, 15% reported witnessing such behaviors, and many believed it was a serious or somewhat serious issue.

Biased policing and the historical pattern of police discrimination against minorities may help us to understand the contemporary practice referred to as "racial profiling." Police officers often use characteristics of a crime or group of crimes to develop a criminal profile (Harris, 2002). **Racial profiling** refers to "any action that results in the heightened racial scrutiny of minorities—justified or not" (Russell-Brown, 2004, pp. 98–99). This definition recognizes racial discrimination by store clerks, governmental officials, and police. In recent years, profiling has become a subspecialty within policing and has produced countless articles and books on the topic (Rice & White, 2010; Weitzer & Tuch, 2006; Withrow, 2006). Profiling on the highways and in the streets is much more dangerous because it is based on beliefs about those who might commit crimes (predictive), rather than those who have committed them (descriptive) and is less formal (based on empirical support) and more informal (based on personal experiences; Harris, 2002). During the 1990s, "**driving while Black/ brown**" (DWB) was the most visible form of racial profiling, although other forms exist, including "walking and shopping while Black" (Gabbidon, 2003; Gabbidon, Craig, Okafo, Marzette, & Peterson, 2008; Gabbidon & Higgins, 2007; Higgins & Gabbidon, 2008; Jordan, Gabbidon, & Higgins, 2009; Russell, 2002) and **profiling in airports**. Public opinion polls about racial profiling indicate that most Americans believe it exists (Higgins, Gabbidon, & Vito, 2010; McMahon, Garner, Davis, & Kraus, 2002).

Fredrickson and Siljander (2002) argued that racial profiling does not exist because race is just one of several factors considered in the process of police profiling. Rather, they posited that criminal profiling may sometimes be racially biased and discriminatory. Harris (2002) credited lawyers in the New Jersey case of *State v. Soto* (1996) with demonstrating that at least in New Jersey, criminal profiling had become racial profiling.

The drug courier profile is an earlier version of what is now referred to as "racial profiling during traffic stops." It remains unclear whether DWB traffic stops are driven by honest efforts to control drug trafficking, or are the result of biased and racist beliefs about minority involvement in the drug trade, or are a more sinister and less recognized opportunity for police to seize drug assets. In 1996, in their controversial *Whren v. United States* decision, the U.S. Supreme Court exacerbated the DWB problem by granting police officers the power to stop persons suspected of drug crimes under the pretext of probable cause for a traffic violation. Whren and Brown, two Black males, argued that the police officers were racist, and that if they had been White, the traffic stop would not have occurred. Cooper (2001/2002) pointed out that the more troubling aspect of the *Whren* decision was the Court's ruling that a police officer's state of mind is irrelevant if probable cause for his or her action exists. For many observers, by ignoring the importance of an officer's racial prejudices, *Whren* opened the door to racial profiling during traffic stops (Russell, 2002). Since *Whren*, the Supreme Court has granted police even greater powers over drivers and passengers (American Civil Liberties Union, 1999).

Statewide studies and other racial profiling/traffic stop research provide overwhelming support for the overrepresentation of Blacks and Latinos in traffic stops (Durose, Smith, & Langan, 2007; Greenleaf, Skogan, & Lurigio, 2008; Growette Bostaph, 2008; Harris, 2002; Racial Profiling Data Collection Resource Center at Northeastern University, 2003; Warren,

Tomsakovic-Devey, Smith, Zingraff, & Mason, 2006). In a survey of African American police officers in the Milwaukee Police Department, Barlow and Barlow (2002) found that 69% of their respondents felt they had been victims of racial profiling. A more recent analysis of this data confirmed that young Black and Hispanic males are at greater risk of coercive action by police (Engel & Calnon, 2004).

In October, 2011, BJS released a special report titled *Contacts Between Police and the Public, 2008* (Eith & Durose, 2011) that provides further evidence for the overrepresentation of Blacks among drivers who are stopped and searched. The report estimates that face-to-face contact with police decreased from 2002–2008, and the majority of contacts continue to occur during traffic stops. Even though traffic stop contacts increased for males, females, Whites, and Hispanics, Black drivers were about three times as likely as White drivers, and about two times as likely as Hispanic drivers, to be searched during a traffic stop (p. 1).

Table 4.4 provides the most recent demographic characteristics of contact with police reported in 2002 and 2008. Interestingly, Hispanics' contact with police during traffic stops has increased considerably.

Are traffic stops used as a pretext for curtailing illegal immigration? Increased attention has been placed on immigration and policing, discussed next.

Immigration and Policing

The CBP and ICE are responsible for the enforcement of immigration law within the DHS (DHS, 2011). Policing immigrants is not a new issue. What is new is the approach of the DHS Immigration and Customs Enforcement's *Secure Communities: A Comprehensive Plan to Identify and Remove Criminal Aliens* (Secure Communities) that was implemented in 2009 (see Box 4.2). Even before this controversial plan was implemented, some states enacted legislation requiring state and local law enforcement officers to act as federal immigration agents ("Minnesota Advocates for Human Rights," 2008). Activists and police agencies have taken varying positions on the role of state and local officials in immigration law enforcement, which some believe is the responsibility of the federal government. Nevertheless, immigration status checks have become routine during traffic stops nationwide. At issue is whether an aggressive strategy of verifying residency during traffic stops results in racial profiling of immigrants (S. Williams, 2007; Young, 2007). An article in the *St. Louis Post-Dispatch* highlighted the arrests of 52 illegal immigrants during routine traffic stops in the first five weeks of Missouri Governor Blunt's get-tough policy.

The Secure Communities (S-Comm) program was envisioned as an effort to improve public safety that would include technological advances and cooperation with local and state law enforcement agencies (LEAs). It is designed as a multi-faceted and multi-agency effort that requires stakeholders in federal agencies as well as tribal LEAs to work with ICE and other LEAs to apprehend and remove criminal aliens. More than 100 localities entered into Memorandums of Agreement with ICE to participate in S-Comm, as it is sometimes referred to, since its implementation.

In spite of support for S-Comm, opposition to the program is increasing. In May, 2011, Illinois Governor Pat Quinn withdrew from the program after discovering that many deportees had never been convicted of any crime (La Mala, 2011). Many police leaders and police officers in several states have voiced concerns about the program as well. In July, 2011, the National Latino Peace Officers Association sent a letter to S-Comm task force members

Table 4.4

Number of U.S. Residents Age 16 or Older Who Had Contact With Police, by Demographic Characteristics and Reason for Contact, 2002 and 2008

Demographic characteristic	Driver during traffic stop				Resident reported crime/problem to police			
	Number (in thousands)		Difference in contacts, 2002–2008		Number (in thousands)		Difference in contacts, 2002–2008	
	2002	2008	Number (in thousands)	Percent change	2002	2008	Number (in thousands)	Percent change
Total	16,783	17,663	880	5.2%	11,960	8,345	−3,615	−30.2%
Sex								
Male	10,210	10,330	119	1.2%	5,232	3,665	−1,567	−29.9%
Female	6,573	7,333	760	11.6	6,727	4,679	−2,048	−30.4
Race/Hispanic origin								
White[a]	12,842	12,933	91	0.7%	9,202	6,379	−2,823	−30.7%
Black/African American[a]	1,852	1,845	−8	−0.4	1,347	713	−634	−47.1
Hispanic/Latino	1,596	2,038	442	27.7	1,072	837	−234	−21.9
Other[a,b]	493	710	217	44.0	339	314	−25	−7.4
Two or more races[a]	~	137	~	~	~	102	~	~
Age								
16–17	487	331	−156	-32.1%	292	182	−110	−37.6%
18–24	3,874	3,547	−327	−8.5	1,449	1,122	−327	−22.6
25–34	3,765	4,122	357	9.5	2,466	1,597	−869	−35.2
35–44	3,714	3,620	−94	−2.5	3,050	1,665	−1,385	−45.4
45–54	2,712	3,042	330	12.2	2,457	1,792	−665	−27.1
55–64	1,459	1,978	520	35.6	1,142	1,209	68	5.9
65 or older	773	1,024	251	32.5	1,104	777	−327	−29.6

Note: Data are based on residents whose most recent contact with police in 2002 or 2008 occurred as the result of being a driver in a traffic stop or reporting a crime or problem.

-Not applicable. The 2002 PPCS did not separately identify persons of two or more races.

[a]Excludes persons of Hispanic origin.

[b]Includes American Indians, Alaska Natives, Asians, Native Hawaiians, and other Pacific Islanders.

expressing concern about how the program has eroded police-community relations "as the federal government and some state legislatures sought to expand police roles in immigration enforcement" (Holub, 2011, p. 1). A major concern of citizens and police is that S-Comm is eroding progress made in building better police-community relations through community policing initiatives, discussed next.

BOX 4.2

Executive Summary

Secure Communities: A Comprehensive Plan to Identify and Remove Criminal Aliens (Secure Communities) is working with ICE senior leadership and offices, as well as the broader law enforcement community, to better identify criminal aliens, prioritize enforcement actions on those posing the greatest threat to public safety, and transform the entire criminal alien enforcement process. Through improved technology, continual data analysis, and timely information sharing with a broad range of law enforcement agency (LEA) partners, we are helping to protect communities across the country. This document outlines our goals, objectives, and our strategic approach to accomplishing them.

Mission

The Secure Communities program seeks to improve public safety by implementing a comprehensive, integrated approach to identify and remove criminal aliens from the United States. We coordinate with the Office of the Assistant Secretary and other ICE offices to implement all ICE planning, operational, technical, and fiscal activities devoted to transforming, modernizing, and optimizing the criminal alien enforcement process.

Goals and Objectives

1. *IDENTIFY* criminal aliens through modernized information sharing
    1.1. Biometric Identification—Deploy a biometric identification system nationally
    1.2. Integrated Record Check—Conduct integrated DHS/DOJ record checks on all arrested and incarcerated persons, and on criminals previously released from custody
    1.3. Timely Response—Provide results of record checks to law enforcement agency partners promptly
2. *PRIORITIZE* enforcement actions to ensure apprehension and removal of dangerous criminal aliens
    2.1. Threat-Based Approach—Prioritize criminal aliens for enforcement action based on their threat to public safety
    2.2. Removal—Prioritize removal efforts on highest-threat category of removable criminal aliens
3. *TRANSFORM* criminal alien enforcement processes and systems to achieve lasting results
    3.1. Process Efficiency—Reduce time spent in ICE custody by criminal aliens
    3.2. Optimize Capacity—Optimize ICE capacity for bed space, transportation, and staffing
    3.3. Strengthen Capabilities—Strengthen analytical, planning and performance management capabilities to increase accountability and transparency

How do you think this plan impacts police-community relations in Latino communities?

Community Policing

Community policing (COP) has been utilized for more than two decades in numerous jurisdictions in the United States and abroad. It was touted as having benefits over the traditional policing strategy because it is a proactive approach that provides opportunities for citizens and police to work together to solve problems of crime and disorder. Many Black police administrators, including Lee P. Brown, Hubert Williams, Rueben Greenberg, and other members of NOBLE, were early proponents of COP. In the 1980s, Brown and Williams were among the first in a cadre of progressive chiefs of police to successfully implement foot patrol programs in an effort to reduce the fear of crime in Houston, Texas, and Newark, New Jersey, respectively. COP was attractive to many progressive police administrators because it could be tailored to fit the needs of a particular neighborhood or jurisdiction. Other administrators and police officers resisted COP because it required a completely different police role; crime control was replaced with addressing not only crime, but also problems of disorder.

COP received a major impetus when the Crime Control Act of 1994 made federal funds available for hiring COP officers. At the time, although many agencies had adopted COP programs, most others were not convinced of its utility. During the past decade, research on COP addressing numerous topics and varying methodologies, including descriptive studies of implementation, organizational issues, evaluative studies, and analyses of citizen and officer perceptions of COP, informs us about its progress and obstacles. Today, most COP programs have a problem-solving component that originated in problem-oriented policing (POP).

POP, as conceived by Goldstein (1979), differs from (early) COP programs in that it is a reactive approach that initially did not require citizen input. According to Piquero and Piquero (2001), POP requires that the underlying causes of repeated calls for service be identified and addressed. POP uses a process known as scanning, analysis, response, and assessment (SARA) to identify and respond to problems (Dempsey, 1999). Early and more recent problem-solving strategies often target public housing developments and other high-crime neighborhoods (Braga et al., 1999; Greene, Piquero, Collins, & Kane, 1999; Mazerolle & Terrill, 1997). More recently, the Indianapolis Directed Patrol Experiment and the Boston Gun Project have used POP approaches.

COP has had varied responses in different places, and the verdict is still out as to whether it improves police-community relations. Some municipal agencies have excelled at adopting a philosophy of COP that is emphasized in their organizations' mission statements and values, although they have had more limited success in gaining support from minority groups. Kusow, Wilson, and Martin (1997) noted that citizen satisfaction with the police, as well as community trust and confidence, are prerequisites to successful COP programs. COP initiatives in minority and immigrant communities have improved relationships between police and citizens in many locales. After 9/11, federal, state, and local policing priorities shifted to homeland security and terrorism. As a result, funding for COP programs, research, and evaluation was drastically reduced. Many police leaders believe that the new emphases, including immigration enforcement, have eroded some of the progress made in COP programs. Even though relationships built with citizens by utilizing COP strategies can be helpful in detecting threats to the homeland, citizens might be more reluctant to cooperate with police. It remains to be seen whether or not COP initiatives and Secure Communities can coexist.

❖ Conclusion

Race and policing is an important topic in the study of crime. This chapter provided a brief overview of policing and traced its history, paying specific attention to policing racial and ethnic groups. Several contemporary issues, including citizen satisfaction with the police, police deviance, immigration and policing, and community policing were examined. The quality of policing has improved dramatically during the past 200 years. Countless individuals and organizations have labored to ensure that citizens are provided with police who understand their role to protect and serve. New recruits receive more training and are better educated than ever before. Officers who successfully complete the police academy are more representative of minorities in their communities. The changing face of police officers did not occur overnight and was initially resisted by the police establishment. Today, there is still a need for affirmative action at all levels of government, and racial conflict within police departments as well as between police and the citizenry continues.

Despite progress, citizen confidence in the police, especially among minorities, hasn't improved very much. And police deviance and misconduct are ongoing problems in policing. Cases of police brutality and racial profiling continue to occur and thus contribute to lower confidence and less trust in the police by Blacks, other minorities, and some Whites. Recent efforts to curtail illegal immigration have led to more allegations of racial profiling during traffic stops. The data collected on racial profiling attest to differential treatment of minorities (Blacks and Hispanics). Although police brutality and use of excessive force incidents are thought to be rare, there is still no reliable data set. The DHS Secure Communities program implemented in 2009 is very controversial and viewed by some as having a negative impact of policing, especially in minority communities. Community policing strategies that have helped improve police and minority group relations in some jurisdictions are undermined in Latino communities as a result of initiatives like the Secure Communities program.

Discussion Questions

1. Do you think public confidence in the police has improved among minorities in the past decade?

2. Why do you think minorities are often involved in brutality and use of force incidents?

3. Do you think racial profiling is still a problem in the United States?

4. Does the DHS Secure Communities initiative help or hinder confidence in the police?

5. Has the era of community policing ended as we progress to more threat-based policing?

Internet Exercises

1. Visit the National Institute of Justice Predictive Policing Symposium webpage (http://www.nij.gov/topics/law-enforcement/strategies/predictive-policing/symposium/welcome.htm). How do you think predictive policing will impact minorities?

2. Review the Annual report on Immigration Enforcement Actions: 2010 prepared by the Office of Immigration Statistics (http://www.dhs.gov/files/statistics/publications/immigration-enforcement-actions-2010.shtm). Do you think the data support the belief of some that Latino criminal aliens are targeted?

Internet Sites

Department of Homeland Security: http://www.dhs.gov/index.shtm

Sourcebook of Criminal Justice Statistics: http://www.albany.edu/sourcebook/

USA PATRIOT Act: http://www.justice.gov/archive/ll/highlights.htm

CHAPTER 5

Courts

My experience in the criminal court is that the colored defendant, even in bail-able cases, is unable to give bail. He has to stay in jail, and therefore his case is very quickly disposed of by the prosecutor. Defendants locked up are usually tried first. The colored man is more apt to be out of work than the White man, and that is a possible reason for the large number of arrests of Negroes. His sphere is very limited, and if there is any let up in the industry that is involved in that sphere, he is a victim. I have often wondered if you could change the skin of a thousand White men in the city of Chicago and handicap them the way the colored man is handicapped today, how many of those White men in ten years' time would be law-abiding citizens.

—Judge Kickham Scanlan
(cited in Chicago Commission on Race
Relations, 1922, p. 356)

As one of the key components of the criminal justice process, the courts represent an entity in which nationally billions of dollars are spent each year. Moreover, according to the Bureau of Justice Statistics, in 2006, these courts dealt with more than 1.1 million adults who were convicted of felonies (Rosenmerkel, Durose, & Farole, 2009), most of whom were handled in state courts. Furthermore, 38% of those convicted in state courts were Black (Rosenmerkel et al., 2009). Given these statistics, prior to and following Judge Scanlan's telling comments, the question of the courts and their treatment of persons of color piqued scholarly interest. It is also important to note here the central role that class and social status play in the justice received in the courts (see Box 5.1).

BOX 5.1

Lindsay Lohan's Release Prompts Questions About Preferential Treatment

By Andrew Blankstein and Richard Winton

Los Angeles—Lindsay Lohan's journey to jail Friday on a 30-day hold—only to be released hours later—has raised new questions about whether the actress is being treated differently than other inmates.

On Friday morning, Beverly Hills Judge Elden Fox ordered Lohan jailed without bail until a hearing Oct. 22 on whether Lohan should be incarcerated for using drugs in violation of her probation on a drunken-driving conviction.

It also appeared to be an effective way to skirt Los Angeles County's early release policy and keep Lohan incarcerated for a month. The 24-year-old actress has twice received jail sentences but both times served less time than ordered because of overcrowding at the women's jail. Most female inmates serve a quarter of their sentence.

But Lohan's attorney, Shawn Chapman Holley, immediately challenged the legality of holding her client without bail based on a probation violation for a misdemeanor. On Friday afternoon, another judge granted Lohan $300,000 (U.S.) bail, and she was able to leave jail.

Attorney Mark Geragos said it was not unusual for a judge to deny bail on a probation violation and set a date for a hearing in the time it might take to serve a full jail sentence.

"More and more judges are doing this very thing to ensure the sheriff doesn't release the person early," Geragos said.

Veteran defense attorney Glen Jonas said the judge's actions effectively side-stepped the early-release process, which covers inmates sentenced to jail time but not to inmates awaiting sentencing.

"Judge Fox guaranteed Ms. Lohan will not receive early release by setting the hearing a month out with no bail. Judge Fox is fed up. Ms. Lohan is being treated like a drug addict on probation instead of a celebrity" with a drug issue, Jonas said.

But others said Fox was treating Lohan differently than other defendants.

"She neither presents a danger to the community nor is she a flight risk," said L.A. defense attorney Mike Cavalluzzi. "Those are the primary criteria for either denying bail or setting an appropriate amount of bail, especially given that this is a misdemeanor."

The star of *Freaky Friday* and *Mean Girls* was processed out of the Century Regional Detention Facility about 11:40 p.m. Friday after posting $300,000 bail. She was whisked out of a back door and driven to an undisclosed location.

But in posting bail, Lohan must agree to conditions including wearing a SCRAM alcohol and drug detection device, refraining from being in areas where alcohol or drugs are being consumed, and being subject to immediate search by law enforcement.

Do you believe celebrities receive preferential treatment in the criminal justice system? Explain.

Considering the significance of the courts in the race and crime discourse, our objectives for this chapter are threefold. First, we provide an overview of how the American courts operate. This is followed by a brief historical overview of race and the American courts. Last, we examine some contemporary issues related to race and the courts. Our primary focus here is on the various aspects of the court process and whether discrimination (on the basis of race or gender) remains a problem. In addition, we examine drug courts, which, over

Photo 5.1

Lindsay Lohan in court. U.S. actress Lindsay Lohan (L) looks over at her attorney Shawn Chapman Holley (R) during court proceedings at the Beverly Hills Courthouse for her probation status hearing in Beverly Hills, California, USA, 06 July 2010. Lohan was charged with violating her probation when her alcohol detection device went off at a MTV Movie Awards after party. The hearing relates to her August 2007 no contest pleas to two counts each of drunk driving and being under the influence of cocaine, along with a reckless driving charge.

the past decade, have served as a way to handle the overflow of drug cases. Because racial minorities are frequently diverted to drug courts, after reviewing drug courts' structure and philosophy, we examine some recent evaluations.

❖ Overview of American Courts: Actors and Processes

Like so many other facets of American life, the American court system owes much to the English justice system (Chapin, 1983). In general, as American society gained its independence, the courts became more complex with the development of the federal court system and the Supreme Court (Shelden, 2001). Today, because of these early changes, the U.S. court system is referred to as a "**dual-court system**." There are both state and federal courts, each with trial courts at the lowest level and appellate courts at the top of the hierarchy. The federal court system starts with U.S. magistrate courts, "who hear minor offenses and conduct preliminary hearings" (Shelden & Brown, 2003, p. 196). U.S. District Courts are trial courts that hear both civil and criminal cases. Positioned above the U.S. District Courts is the U.S. Court of Appeals, which is the final step before reaching the U.S. Supreme Court. The Supreme Court represents the highest court in the land and has the final say on matters that make it to that level. The American court system (both state and federal) involves several actors and processes. Over time, some of these actors and processes have come under scrutiny for a variety of reasons, including race- and class-related concerns (Reiman, 2007). As for actors, the court is generally composed of three main figures: the judge, the prosecutor, and the defense attorney. Although the system is theoretically based on the ancient system of "trial by combat," in practice, it has been suggested that these main figures are part of the "courtroom workgroup" who actually work together to resolve matters brought before the court (Neubauer, 2002).

Photo 5.2

The U.S. Supreme Court Justices, 2010. Back row (left to right): Sonia Sotomayor, Stephen G. Breyer, Samuel A. Alito, and Elena Kagan. Front row (left to right): Clarence Thomas, Antonin Scalia, Chief Justice John G. Roberts, Anthony Kennedy, and Ruth Bader Ginsburg.

There are several processes involved when one is navigating through the court system. First, there is a pretrial process, where the decision is made whether to move forward with a particular case. If the case is moved forward, the question of pretrial detention and **bail** is decided next. Other processes in the court system include the preliminary hearing, grand jury proceedings, and the arraignment, at which a defendant first enters his or her plea. Although **plea bargaining** determines the outcome in most cases, if the case happens to go to trial, there are other processes that move the case along. Once the decision to go to trial is made, unless the case is going to be decided solely by a judge (referred to as a "bench trial"), the next process would be jury selection. Following the completion of jury selection, the trial begins. If the defendant is found guilty, the sentencing phase begins (this phase is discussed in detail in Chapter 6).

A Note on the Philosophy, Operation, and Structure of Native American Courts

Because of the unique history and worldview of Native Americans, much of the previous dialogue on American courts does not apply to Native American courts. Consequently, we provide a brief overview of the extent, philosophy, operation, and structure of their court system. Recent figures reveal that there are more than 200 courts in Native American jurisdictions. These courts have "approximately 200 judges, 153 prosecutors and 20 peacemakers. Nearly half of all tribes rely on state courts for judicial services due to a lack of resources and shortage of personnel" (J. Smith, 2009, p. 574). J. Smith (2009) noted that there are three fundamental differences between Native American courts and American courts. First, Native American courts have limited jurisdiction:

> Tribal courts only have jurisdiction when (a) both the offender and victim are Native Americans, (b) the crime occurs on the reservation, and (c) the punishment does not result in longer than a year imprisonment or exceed $5,000 in fines. (p. 574)

Second, because Native American tribes are considered sovereign nations, they are not bound by the Constitution. Finally, the American and Tribal Courts operate under two distinct philosophies. The philosophy of tribal courts certainly follows a different paradigm than Anglo-American justice systems (see Table 5.1). Tarver et al. (2002) noted that the indigenous justice paradigm follows an approach that includes spirituality and oral customs, which are not welcome in non-Native American courts.

As was mentioned in Chapter 4, after the enactment of Public Law 280 in 1953, the jurisdiction for criminal and civil cases on tribal lands in several states was turned over to local and state governments (Tarver et al., 2002). Other jurisdictions were also impacted by this new law, which "gave to state and local police the enforcement authority in Indian communities, and cases would be adjudicated in state courts" (p. 88). The complexity of jurisdictional issues on tribal land is illuminated by Table 5.2.

Although almost no research examines whether there are American Indians who are discriminated against in their own court system, it remains important to provide an overview of how their courts operate. To do this, we focus on the courts of the Navajo, the second largest American Indian tribe (U.S. Census Bureau, 1995). Tso (1996) noted that over the years, Navajo courts have been structured like Anglo courts. There are several judicial districts; as is seen in Table 5.2, the jurisdiction is based on the parties involved (i.e., Indian or non-Indian). In general, however, district courts are courts of general civil jurisdiction and of limited criminal jurisdiction. Civil jurisdiction extends to all persons residing within the Navajo Nation or who cause an act to occur within the nation. The limitations of criminal jurisdiction are determined by the nature of the offense, the penalty to be imposed, where the crime occurred, and the status and residency of the individual charged with an offense (Tso, 1996).

There are also children's courts within each district. These courts hear "all matters concerning children except for custody, child support and visitation disputes arising from divorce proceedings, and probate matters" (Tso, 1996, p. 172). The Navajo also have a Supreme Court and Peacemaker Courts. The Navajo Nation Supreme Court "hears appeals from final lower court decisions and from certain final administrative orders" (Tso, 1996, p. 173). Peacemaker Courts rely on mediation to resolve some lesser matters.

Table 5.1

Comparison of American and Indigenous (Native) Justice Paradigms

American Justice Paradigm	Indigenous (Native) Justice Paradigm
Vertical power structure	Vertical power structure
Communication is rehearsed	Communication is fluid
Written statutory law derived from rules and procedures	Oral customary law learned as a way of life
Separation of church and state	The spiritual realm is invoked in ceremonies and with prayer
Time-oriented process	No time limits on the process

Table 5.2

Indian Country Jurisdiction in Criminal Cases

Suspect	Victim	Jurisdiction
Indian	Indian	Misdemeanor: Tribal jurisdiction Felony: Federal jurisdiction No state jurisdiction No federal jurisdiction for misdemeanors
Indian	Non-Indian	Misdemeanor: Tribal jurisdiction Felony: Federal jurisdiction No state jurisdiction
Non-Indian	Indian	Misdemeanor: Federal jurisdiction Felony: Federal jurisdiction Normally not state jurisdiction (the U.S. Attorney may elect to defer prosecution to the state) No tribal jurisdiction
Non-Indian	Non-Indian	Misdemeanor: State jurisdiction Felony: State jurisdiction Normally U.S. Attorney will decline prosecution No tribal jurisdiction
Indian	Victimless	Misdemeanor: Tribal jurisdiction Felony: Federal jurisdiction
Non-Indian	Victimless	Misdemeanor: Usually state jurisdiction Felony: Usually state jurisdiction Normally U.S. Attorney will decline prosecution

Judiciary selections are screened by the Judiciary Committee of the Navajo Tribal Council. Using the Navajo Tribal Code as its basis for selection, the committee selects those who are most qualified. In Navajo courts, where the Navajo Tribal Code prevails, people can represent themselves; however, only members of the Navajo Bar Association can represent others in the courts. These include actual lawyers who have attended law school and those who have followed nontraditional pathways (i.e., passing a certified Navajo Bar Training Course or having served as a legal apprentice). More than a decade ago, the Navajo Nation Council revamped the Navajo Nation Criminal Code to reflect more indigenous practices. Shortly after the revision, the Honorable Robert Yazzie, Chief Justice of the Navajo Nation, reflected on the changes. Box 5.2 presents his reflections.

BOX 5.2

Navajo Justice

This year, the Navajo Nation quit jailing people for dozens of offenses that used to land people behind bars. Now tribal courts are turning to peacemakers.

by The Honorable Robert Yazzie Chief Justice of the Navajo Nation

In January 2000, the Navajo Nation Council decided to revamp the Navajo Nation Criminal Code. The Council eliminated jail time and fines for 79 offenses, required the use of peacemaking in criminal cases, and required that the courts see to the rights of victims. The Council also incorporated the traditional concept of *nalyeeh* into the criminal code. Nalyeeh refers to the process of confronting someone who hurts others with a demand that they talk out the action and the hurt it caused so that something positive will come of it.

This decision represents a serious challenge to the courts of the Navajo Nation, whose jurisdiction includes tribal members in Arizona, New Mexico, and Utah. Navajo Nation judges had gotten used to the western revolving-door approach to wrongdoings—jailing, probation, new charges, revocation of probation, and the rest of it. Those hurt by crime were left out—the $1,000 restitution orders did not address the trauma caused by the crimes. But the Navajos now realize that the prison approach to crime does not work.

The western criminal justice system assumes that the problem is the actor, and imprisonment is primarily designed to work on convicted defendants. In contrast, traditional Navajo justice deals with people's actions. Western adjudication is a search for what happened and who did it; Navajo peacemaking is about the effects of what happened. Who got hurt? What do they feel about it? What can be done to repair the harm? The Navajo Nation courts get close to 28,000 criminal cases each year. The largest categories of crime are assaults and batteries (most often among family members), other crimes against family members, driving while intoxicated and other alcohol-related crimes, and disorderly conduct. The judges have few sentencing options because there is jail space for only 220 people at any one time. Instead, the Navajo justice system is turning to peacemakers.

In Navajo peacemaking, offenders are brought in to a session involving the person accused of an offense and the person who suffered from it, along with the "tag-along" victims of the crime, namely the relatives of the accused and of the person hurt by the accused. (I am hesitant to use the term victim, because we know that in many situations such as fighting within the family, the roles and accompanying labels are not that simple.)

The sessions are moderated by a community leader called a "peacemaker." The action is put on the table. People talk about what happened and how they feel about it.

A harmful act is "something that gets in the way of living your life," and Navajo peacemaking deals with such an act by identifying it, talking about it, and devising a plan to deal with it.

One factor especially leaps out that is part of Navajo traditional knowledge. Navajos know post-traumatic stress disorder as *nayee,* or "monster." What is the essence of the cycle of violence, in which children who are abused or neglected become offenders themselves? *Nayee.* Antisocial personality disorder? *Nayee.*

Peacemaking is based upon family therapy. As Philmer Bluehouse and James Zion of the Navajo peacemaker system have said, peacemaking is a ceremony that uses traditional practices now being "discovered" by the western world to kill or weaken "monsters." The act is the focus of peacemaking; you get it out, put it on the table, and look at it. The process is much the same as the ceremonial practice of turning abstract monsters into something tangible and concrete before you, and then dealing with them.

Traditional Navajo law requires families to take responsibility for their family members. It is not a coerced responsibility, but one that comes from the respect and love people should have for their relatives. In peacemaking, the relatives of those who hurt someone else come forward to help with restitution and to watch over their relative to be sure he or she does not offend again.

(Continued)

(Continued)

Rewriting the Script

Donald Nathanson, a psychiatrist in the restorative justice movement, tells us that the key to violence control is "affect modulation." He says that as we grow from childhood, we learn scripts—ways of responding to things that frighten or anger us. These scripts follow what he calls the "compass of shame," relying on withdrawal, avoidance, "hurting self," "hurting other," or some combination of these. If the script is an intense one, we see withdrawal into alcohol, avoidance by becoming a street person, literally hurting others, and hurting self in drug-dependence, suicide, and other self-destructive behaviors.

Those kinds of scripts are familiar. Harmful scripts cannot be addressed using suppression tactics. They are best addressed by showing people the harmful effects of their conduct and the fact there are better ways of dealing with the things that frighten or challenge them. Navajo peacemaking speaks precisely to "the compass of shame" by subduing harmful scripts and teaching people how to avoid hurting others.

In Navajo thinking, thought is the inner form of speech, and speech is the inner form of action. It's a simple enough concept—as you think, so will you speak, and as you speak, so will you do.

If your action is fueled by alcohol or drugs, it is going to hurt others. What does someone who hurts others think or reflect about that? In the western system, there is nothing other than ineffective punishment to compel someone who hurts another to reflect on what he or she has done. There is nothing to make people face their actions and their effects. There is little to involve those who get hurt, including the tag-along victims—spouses, children, and relatives.

We say you should start your day with prayer and by seeking inspiration, and take that inner thinking and turn it into a plan. The plan then becomes action, following on what you thought, planned, and spoke. At the end of the day, you reflect on what you did so that you can do better tomorrow. That is the good way.

A Symbol of Healed Relations

Some are surprised to learn that in traditional Navajo justice, restitution for a wrongdoing can be symbolic. It can be a piece of jewelry or some other item of little nominal value but great symbolic value. Horses are prized highly by Navajos, and they are a form of restitution for serious sexual insults.

How does symbolic restitution help someone who is hurt? Navajos are more interested in what the restitution means than its value. Does the item used for restitution say, "I'm sorry"? Does it say, "I honor your worth and dignity with this thing that we Navajos prize"? Does it say, "Let this be a symbol and something tangible to remind us that we have talked this hurt out and entered into good relations with each other"?

We know that peacemaking works. It has proven successful in problem areas such as driving while intoxicated, delinquency, family violence, and alcohol-related crime. It allows families to be involved in helping their relatives (whether they were the ones doing the hurting or the ones who got hurt), and it helps everyone look at the monster of the action and its effects.

Can Navajo peacemaking prevent harm in addition to dealing with crimes after they happen? About 25 percent of all Navajos are children nine and under—a huge youth cohort. If we know that a child who is abused or neglected is more likely to enter the cycle of violence, doesn't it make sense to put resources in place for children? Peacemaking supplements child protection programs to help both children and parents. Philmer Bluehouse left the Judicial Branch recently to take Navajo peacemaking into the schools, where he can reach out to the children who are hurt.

The Peacemaking Challenge

The Navajo Nation Council exercised a great deal of courage and foresight in declaring the system broken and making traditional Navajo justice the preferred criminal justice method.

Will this new approach work? It poses difficult logistical problems. There are now approximately 250 peacemakers; how can the Navajo Nation courts recruit and train enough peacemakers to handle 28,000 criminal cases a year?

If you can't build new prisons and fill them, what do you do? You leave the process of putting serious offenders in prison to the federal government under the Major Crimes Act (which punishes felonies committed in Indian Country), and you direct the Navajo Nation justice system to focus upon traditional Navajo justice.

This is a bold experiment, but if it works, it may offer lessons to an America that is beginning to recognize that you can't lock up a major portion of the population (usually people of color).

Perhaps there are other ways to deal with crime; the answers may lie in dealing with actions, not actors, allowing people to face and solve their own problems, using peacemaking for crime prevention by getting at the nayee early on, and rewriting old scripts.

We Navajos knew about all that stuff traditionally, and it is time for us to remember.

Do you believe the American court system can be improved by adopting the same philosophy as the Navajo Justice System?

The irony of the Navajo justice system is that, with the emerging acceptance of the philosophy of restorative justice, American courts are trying to operate more like Native American courts. This is especially true of juvenile justice systems in some states (such as Pennsylvania), where the guiding philosophy is now restorative justice. We now turn to a historical overview of race and the courts.

❖ Historical Overview of Race and the Courts in America

Native Americans

It is widely accepted that America had its beginnings long before Europeans began arriving in colonial America, and the record shows that the Native Americans who were here had already created their own norms and ways of handling deviants. As Friedman (1993) noted, once Europeans began to come en masse, there was a "clash of legal cultures" (p. 20). In many instances, this clash resulted in the conqueror Europeans imparting their system onto Native Americans and African Americans, who also began to arrive en masse after the slave trade began. Due to the smallness of 142 communities in colonial America, these early court procedures were more informal, which, as noted before, owed much to the English system. In fact, the courts were also places where community members looked for social drama (Friedman, 1993).

Early on, both Native Americans and African Americans had similarly low status in American society. As such, other than being a means of social control, the courts were generally not concerned about their lives. In Massachusetts, for example, the courts treated Native Americans with indifference (Higginbotham, 1978). For example, according to Higginbotham (1978), "The general court of the colony enforced the English right to take the Indians' 'unimproved' land in 1633" (p. 69). This action was followed by the courts treating Native Americans more harshly (Higginbotham, 1978). During this period, it was not unusual for the Massachusetts courts to use the punishment of either enslavement or banishment for Native Americans (Higginbotham, 1978). On occasion, however, magistrates were concerned about uprisings that could occur if Native Americans felt they were being mistreated by the courts. Because of this concern, on occasion, "The magistrates involved other Indians, either as viewers of the trial and punishment or ideally as witnesses of the accused" (Chapin, 1983, p. 117).

As noted by J. Smith (2009), formal court systems in Native American communities have been around since the 1880s. At that time, the Court of Indian Offenses was established by the Department of the Interior and the Bureau of Indian Affairs. These courts were created to handle minor offenses (J. Smith, 2009). In the 1930s, tribal courts were enacted in concert with the Indian Reorganization Act. Such courts were established with the intention of having Native Americans "enact their own laws and establish their own court system to reflect those laws" (J. Smith, 2009, p. 574). Notably, more than 50% of tribes have such courts today.

Whether the courts were a place where justice prevailed for Native Americans is subject to debate. In Chapter 6, we look a bit more closely at early sentencing patterns, shedding some light on this topic. For now, we turn our attention to a brief historical overview of African Americans and the courts.

African Americans

Much of the early race-related legislation, which guided the courts, was directed at Blacks (Higginbotham, 1978). However, some legislation did target White ethnic group members. An example of such early legislation was Act VI, which was passed by the Virginia legislature in the 1600s and "required Irish servants arriving in the colony without indentures to serve longer terms than their English counterparts" (Higginbotham, 1978, p. 33). As one reviews the early literature, it becomes apparent that legislation contributed to the inequities observed in the courts. Given these connections, it is also apparent that politics played a key role in how the courts ruled. Therefore, even after the Revolutionary War and the subsequent ratification of the Constitution, Southern states still had a vested interest in controlling African American slave labor. Legal scholar Randall Kennedy (1997) wrote,

> In terms of substantive criminal law and in terms of punishment, slaves were . . . prohibited from testifying or contradicting Whites in court. Moreover, in some jurisdictions, such as Virginia, South Carolina, and Louisiana, slaves were tried before special tribunals—slave courts—designed to render quick, rough justice. (p. 77)

For those who did not go before slave courts, "plantation justice" prevailed solely under the discretion of the master or overseer (Friedman, 1993). To refer to plantation justice as being brutal is an understatement. Even minor events resulted in serious punishments. Friedman (1993) provided an example of how one slave, Eugene, was disciplined:

> William Byrd of Westover, Virginia, recorded the following in a dry, matter-of-fact tone in his diary: On November 30, 1709, Eugene, a house hand, "was whipped for pissing in bed." On December 3, Eugene repeated this offense, "for which I made him drink a pint of piss." On December 16, "Eugene was whipped for doing nothing yesterday." Three years later, on December 18, 1712, "found Eugene asleep instead of being at work, for which I beat him severely." (p. 53)

Byrd's actions were sanctioned by slave codes, which, several decades earlier, had made it a minor offense for a master to kill a slave in colonial Virginia (Higginbotham, 1978).

With the abolition of slavery in Northern states and the arrival of emancipation in 1863, it was anticipated that justice would prevail more often for African Americans. At least in the South, such conventional wisdom did not prevail. As is further discussed in Chapter 6, the courts became a cog in the operation of the convict-lease system, which, as was noted in Chapter 1, allowed states to lease out convicts to Southern landowners.

Using familiar tactics, legislators enacted laws to snare African Americans. The courts were eager participants and ensured that an ample labor supply flowed to Southern landowners (Sellin, 1976). When these "legal" measures failed to produce the desired outcome, Southerners resorted to trickery and violence (Friedman, 1993). Such actions led many African Americans to lose faith in both the political and justice systems (Du Bois, 1901/2002).

Well into the 20th century, little changed regarding the treatment of African Americans and the courts. Higginbotham (1996) provided a classic review of how courts were bastions of racism. By the very nature of the segregated practices that prevailed in courtrooms, one could presume that the courts were places where White supremacy prevailed and African Americans received little justice. Providing reviews of cases where there were segregated courtroom seating, cafeterias, and restrooms, Higginbotham noted how such discriminating practices reminiscent of "Apartheid" stood in the way of African Americans receiving equal standing in court. Of equal concern was the practice of referring to African Americans by their first names while addressing Whites by their last names and using their appropriate titles (e.g., Mr. or Mrs.). Again, such forms of disrespect produced an air of inequality, which translated into African Americans being at a disadvantage in courts.

During the 1960s and 1970s, there were national inquiries into civil disorders (riots) and also the state of racism in the criminal justice system. One such inquiry looking at the courts was prepared by the National Minority Advisory Council on Criminal Justice (1979), which was created in 1976. The report, "Racism in the Criminal Courts," surveyed the literature to determine the prevalence of racism in the courts. Drawing on the literature and public hearings in 13 cities, the report noted particular concerns with the paucity of minority judges at both the federal and state levels. Many of the other concerns expressed with the courts remain with us today (see section below on "Contemporary Issues in Race and the Courts"). For example, the council expressed concerns about unfairness in the bail process, the potentially discriminatory use of **peremptory challenges** in jury selection, the quality of public defense, and prosecutorial misconduct in the plea-bargaining process.

Latinos

The early literature on Latinos and the courts is quite sparse, and much of that early literature discussed Mexicans and immigration concerns. Another central focus of the literature is Mexicans' experience with the criminal justice system in the western and midwestern United States. The 1931 Wickersham Commission report, *Crime and the Foreign Born*, noted a common problem when dealing with persons, such as Mexicans, who did not speak English:

> With the best intentions in the world, an investigating officer, a prosecutor, or a court will have the greatest difficulty in getting at the exact truth and all the facts in the case when the accused is a non-English-speaking immigrant. (National Commission on Law Observance and Enforcement, 1931a, p. 173)

The report also noted that in California, Mexican defendants were abused by bail bonds-men, loan sharks, and "shyster lawyers" (p. 175). The report also mentioned that Los Angeles had an excellent **public defender system** in the 1920s, which "very frequently appear[ed] on behalf of the foreign born, especially the penniless Mexican" (p. 175).

Paul Warnshuis (1931), as part of the Wickersham Commission report, conducted a study of how Mexicans were faring with criminal justice agencies in Illinois. Besides the notion that Mexicans were often arrested on flimsy charges, an overriding theme in the report is that Mexicans were at a serious disadvantage in the court process because of language concerns. In many instances, interpreters, although needed, were not used, which resulted in the swift conviction of Mexicans. In some instances, judges simply ruled on the evidence and, if convinced of the defendants' guilt, proceeded without hearing testimony (Warnshuis, 1931). As one can imagine, the courts were a place where, for Mexicans, justice was not always received.

During the 1940s, the "Sleepy Lagoon Case" became the high-profile case that brought the issue of Latinos and the courts to the fore. The case revolved around the murder of Jose Diaz. Following the murder, 22 Mexicans were arrested, whereas another 17 were convicted (the convictions were overturned two years later). According to most reports, the trial was unfair. The media played a large role in this by creating a moral panic. Friedman (1993) wrote that the media spewed headlines calling for concern about the "zoot-suit gangsters" and "pachuco killers." One representative from law enforcement stated the following to the grand jury:

> Mexicans [have] a "biological" tendency to violence. They were the descendants of "tribes of Indians" who were given over to "human sacrifice," in which bodies were "opened by stone knives and their hearts torn out while still beating." Mexicans had "total disregard for human life"; the Mexican, in a fight, will always use a knife; he feels "a desire . . . to kill." (Friedman, 1993, p. 382)

Outrageous statements such as these colored the way in which society viewed Mexicans. A year after the Sleepy Lagoon case, the city of Los Angeles exploded with the "zoot suit riots." The riots ignited after rumors spread that a Mexican had killed a serviceman, and the city broke out into four days of rioting. During this time, "service-men and off-duty policemen chased, beat, and stripped 'zoot-suiters'" (Friedman, 1993, p. 382). As for the courts, little is ever mentioned of them punishing those who attacked the Mexicans.

In later years, the National Minority Advisory Council on Criminal Justice (1979) would also express concern about the treatment of Hispanics in the courts. As in the case of African Americans, they expressed concern about the treatment of Hispanics throughout the court system. Particularly disturbing to the council was the lack of Hispanics in significant judiciary roles. The report also noted that nearly 50 years after the Wickersham report, language remained a problem, commenting,

> Non-English speaking minorities have special problems of access to courts, to legal counsel and representation because of language and the failure of the courts and priorities of resources to have trained, impartial translators at every stage of courts and trial related proceedings. (p. 63)

Asian Americans

As was mentioned in Chapter 1, when Asians began arriving in the United States, they were primarily located on the West Coast. Like other immigrants, they were despised by many. Friedman (1993) described some of the more gruesome early incidents:

> In 1871, a mob in Los Angeles killed nineteen Chinese. In the 1880s, riots in Rock Springs, Wyoming, left twenty-eight Chinese dead; Whites in Tacoma, Washington, put the torch to the Chinatown in that city; and there were outrages in Oregon, Colorado, and Nevada. (p. 98)

Eventually, as in the case of other minorities, legislation in concert with the courts was used to deal with Asian Americans. But in the case of Asian Americans, the aim of such actions was to remove them from the country. Friedman (1993) put it best, writing, "The goal of anti-Chinese policy was not suppression but expulsion. . . . The keystone of Asian policy was immigration law, exclusion, and deportation" (p. 100).

Although our focus now turns to contemporary issues in race and the courts, the unfortunate reality is that many of the same issues from our historical overview are still with us. One would have anticipated that problems related to racial bias in the courts would have been resolved, but, from the literature we review next, we can see that this is not always the case.

❖ Contemporary Issues in Race and the Courts

Many of the contemporary issues pertaining to race and the courts are related to whether there is either race or gender discrimination in the various court processes (Walker et al., 2012). Drug courts have also emerged as an institution that has provided some hope in stemming the tide of drug addiction and its residual effects. Given the heavy presence of racial minorities circulating through drug courts, we examine the structure, philosophy, and effectiveness of these specialized courts. We begin with a review of the literature that examines whether race or gender has been found to have an influence on each respective court process. Our first review examines the role of race and gender during the bail and pretrial processes.

Bail and the Pretrial Process

Although bail is not guaranteed by the Constitution, the **Eighth Amendment** does state that when given, it should not be "excessive." Since the creation of this amendment, various **pretrial release** options have been used. During the early 1950s and 1960s, the Vera Institute of New York conducted studies on bail practices in Philadelphia and New York. The early study in Philadelphia found that "18% of persons jailed pending trial because they could not afford bail were acquitted, whereas 48% of persons released on bail were acquitted" (Anderson & Newman, 1998, p. 215). In the 1960s, the Vera Institute created the Manhattan Bail Project, which was meant to see whether those released on their own recognizance (ROR) absconded any more often than those released on monetary bail. The project convincingly showed that "the rate of return for ROR releases was consistently equal to or better than the rate for those on monetary bail" (Anderson & Newman, 1998, p. 215). Mann (1993) has noted that many of the defendants in the pioneering Manhattan Bail Project were minorities, the majority of whom did return for trial. Even with these findings, during the Reagan presidency, the Bail Reform Act of 1984 provided judges more discretion as to who can be given pretrial release. In general, judges can hold defendants in jail if they consider them either a risk for flight or if they pose a danger to the community. Because of risk concerns, the courts consider a variety of factors when making the decision to grant pretrial release on bail. In fact, some states, such as New York, have bail statutes that require judges to consider risk factors such as the nature of the offense, prior record, previous record in appearing when required in court, employment status, community ties, and the weight of the evidence against a defendant.

There are generally three broad categories of pretrial release: nonfinancial release, financial release, and emergency release (Cohen & Reaves, 2007; see Table 5.3). Nonfinancial release means the accused is released without having to provide any monetary collateral. This typically comes in the form of ROR or citation releases, which are typically

Table 5.3

Types of Pretrial Release Used in State Courts

Type of release	Defendant	Financial liability for failure to appear	Liable party
Financial			
Surety bond	Pays fee (usually 10% of bail amount) plus collateral if required, to commercial bail agent.	Full bail amount	Bail agent
Deposit bond	Posts deposit (usually 10% of bail amount) with court, which is usually refunded at successful completion of case.	Full bail amount	Defendant
Full cash bond	Posts full bail amount with court.	Full bail amount	Defendant
Property bond	Posts property title as collateral with court.	Full bail amount	Defendant
Non-financial			
Release on recognizance (ROR)	Signs written agreement to appear in court (includes citation releases by law enforcement).	None	N/A
Conditional (supervised) release	Agrees to comply with specific conditions such as regular reporting or drug use monitoring.	None	N/A
Unsecured bond	Has a bail amount set, but no payment is required to secure release.	Full bail amount	Defendant
Emergency release	Released as part of a court order to relieve jail crowding.	None	N/A

administered by law enforcement. Other such releases include conditional releases that involve having to either contact or report to some official to ensure compliance with the conditions of release (e.g., drug treatment). Under this type of release, a third party can also be entrusted to ensure the return of the accused. The final release is referred to as an "emergency release" and occurs when, due to jail crowding, the defendant is given pretrial release under generally nonstringent release conditions.

Cohen and Reaves (2007) provide some recent figures on pretrial releases of felony defendants in state courts. Their report notes that between 1990 and 2004, more than 60% of felony defendants were released prior to a final decision. They note that 1998 was a turning point when financial releases became more prevalent than nonfinancial releases. Defendants who were not released prior to the final disposition were most often unable to post bail (5 out of 6) or denied bail (1 out of 6). In terms of offenses, defendants charged with more serious offenses were less likely to receive pretrial release. Table 5.4 highlights the type and number of pretrial releases. Surety bond and ROR represent the most frequent types of pretrial releases.

Table 5.4

Type of Pretrial Release or Detention for State Court Felony Defendants in the 75 Largest Counties, 1990–2004

Detention-release outcome	State court felony defendants in the 75 largest counties	
	Number	Percent
Total	424,252	100%
Released before case disposition	264,604	62%
Financial conditions	125,650	30%
Surety bond	86,107	20
Deposit bond	23,168	6
Full cash bond	12,348	3
Property bond	4,027	1
Non-financial conditions	136,153	32%
Personal recognizance	85,330	20
Conditional release	32,882	8
Unsecured bond	17,941	4
Emergency release	2,801	1%
Detained until case disposition	159,647	38%
Held on bail	132,572	32
Denied bail	27,075	6

Note: Counts based on weighted data representing 8 months (the month of May from each even-numbered year). Detail may not add to total because of rounding.

Turning to the race and gender of those encountering the pretrial process, Cohen and Reaves (2007) found that females (74%) were more likely than males (60%) to be granted pretrial release. Also, as shown in Table 5.5, Whites (68%) were more likely to be released than Blacks (62%) and Hispanics (55%). Of particular significance to the pretrial process is pretrial misconduct, or whether the defendant fails to appear, is rearrested, or is a fugitive after a year. Table 5.6 highlights the nuances of pretrial misconduct. It shows that males have higher rates of misconduct than females and Blacks and Hispanics have higher misconduct rates than Whites. Although these figures provide a preliminary overview of the workings of the pretrial process across the country, scholars have investigated the complexities of the influence of a host of factors (including race and gender) on pretrial. In the next section, we review some of the recent studies in this area.

Table 5.5

State Court Felony Defendants in the 75 Largest Counties Released Prior to Case Disposition, 1990–2004

Variable	Percent released	Predicted probability of release
Most serious arrest charge		
Murder	19%	11%**
Rape	53	44**
Robbery	44	36**
Assault	64	59*
Burglary	49	49**
Motor vehicle theft	49	50**
Larceny/theft	68	66
Forgery	72	67
Fraud	82	76**
Drug sales (reference)	63	63
Other drug (non-sales)	68	70*
Weapons	67	65
Driving-related	73	76**
Age at arrest		
Under 21 (reference)	68%	64%
21–29	62	63

Variable	Percent released	Predicted probability of release
30–39	59	60**
40 or older	62	60**
Gender		
Male (reference)	60%	60%
Female	74	69**
Race/Hispanic origin		
White non-Hispanic (reference)	68%	66%
Black non-Hispanic	62	64
Other non-Hispanic	65	63*
Hispanic, any race	55	51**
Criminal justice status at arrest		
No active status (reference)	70%	67%
Released on pending case	61	63
On probation	43	49**
On parole	26	37**
Prior arrest and court appearance		
No prior arrests (reference)	79%	65%
Prior arrest record without FTA	59	62*
Prior arrest record with FTA	50	58*
Most serious prior conviction		
No prior convictions (reference)	77%	70%
Misdemeanor	63	64**
Felony	46	51**

Note: Logistic regression (predicted probability) results exclude the year 1990 because of missing data. Asterisks indicate category differed from the reference category at one of the following significance levels: * ≤ .05, ** ≤ .01. Not all variables in the model are shown.

Table 5.6

State Court Felony Defendants in the 75 Largest Counties Charged With Pretrial Misconduct, 1990–2004

Variable	Number of defendants	Percent of released defendants charged with pretrial misconduct			
		Any type	Rearrest	Failure to appear	Fugitive
Type of pretrial release					
Release on recognizance	80,865	34%	17%	26%	8%
Surety bond	78,023	29	16	18	3
Conditional release	31,162	32	15	22	6
Deposit bond	20,993	30	14	22	7
Unsecured bond	17,001	36	14	30	10
Full cash bond	11,190	30	15	20	7
Property bond	3,649	27	17	14	4
Emergency release	2,656	52	17	45	10
Most serious arrest charge					
Murder	741	19%	12%	9%	1%
Rape	3,481	18	9	10	2
Robbery	12,947	35	21	21	6
Assault	32,931	23	12	14	4
Burglary	18,377	37	19	25	6
Larceny/theft	26,667	33	16	25	7
Motor vehicle theft	6,415	39	20	29	7
Forgery	8,374	33	15	24	7
Fraud	9,094	21	8	15	5
Drug trafficking	47,182	39	21	27	8
Other drug	50,547	37	18	29	8
Weapons	8,574	27	13	17	5
Driving-related	8,148	28	14	18	5

Variable	Number of defendants	Percent of released defendants charged with pretrial misconduct			
		Any type	Rearrest	Failure to appear	Fugitive
Age at arrest					
20 or younger	55,505	33%	20%	21%	5%
21–29	90,768	34	17	24	7
30–39	71,049	33	16	24	7
40 or older	44,701	28	13	20	6
Gender					
Male	211,396	34%	18%	23%	6%
Female	52,291	28	12	21	6
Race/Hispanic origin					
Black, non-Hispanic	96,348	36%	19%	25%	7%
White, non-Hispanic	64,571	28	14	19	4
Hispanic, any race	49,544	34	17	25	8
Other, non-Hispanic	5,165	23	13	14	3
Criminal justice status at arrest					
On parole	6,012	47%	25%	32%	7%
On probation	25,765	44	26	30	6
Released pending prior case	25,955	48	30	30	7
No active status	167,227	27	12	19	6
Prior arrests and FTA history					
Prior arrest record with FTA	59,468	49%	27%	35%	8%
Prior arrest record, no FTA	75,806	30	17	18	5
No prior arrests	85,366	23	8	18	7
Most serious prior conviction					
Felony	75,187	43%	25%	28%	6%
Misdemeanor	44,989	34	19	23	5
No prior convictions	129,975	27	12	19	7

❖ Scholarship on Race/Ethnicity, Bail, and Pretrial Release

In the last decade, there has been at least one comprehensive review of the existing scholarly literature that concluded that Whites receive more leniency than non-Whites in the bail and pretrial process (Free, 2002). Since the early 2000s, scholars have continued to investigate the influence of race and gender in the bail and pretrial process. Researchers who examine this question seek to determine whether legal or extra-legal factors play a role in the outcomes of the decisions related to bail, pretrial release, and sentencing (discussed in Chapter 6). Legal factors are factors that are specifically related to the criminal justice system, such as serious-ness of offense, prior convictions, and type of attorney (public or private). Examples of extra-legal factors, or those elements of a case that are unrelated or extraneous to the criminal justice system, include race/ethnicity, age, gender, employment status, marital status, and educational level.

The research produced during the 2000s sought to correct some of the problems present in earlier research, such as the lumping of Hispanics in with Whites that is believed to mask the punitiveness toward Hispanics and contribute to the nonsignificant findings between Blacks and Whites in pretrial research. In addition, earlier studies did not "distinguish and analyze separately pretrial release decisions as compared to pre-trial release outcomes. . . . The decisions are the preventative [sic] detention decision, the financial/nonfinancial release decision, the bail amount decision, and the ability to pay decision" (Demuth & Steffensmeier, 2004, p. 224). These decisions clearly impact the prospects for release. But by researching the two stages separately, one can deter-mine whether groups are being differentially impacted during the decision or outcome part of the pretrial process. With these caveats in mind, Demuth and Steffensmeier examined four years of data concerning felons charged in state courts in the 75 most populous counties. Their results showed that females received more favorable pretrial decisions (e.g., nonfinancial release, lower bail amounts) than males, and Black and Hispanic defendants received less favorable treatment than White defendants. In par-ticular, "Black and Hispanic defendants were more likely to receive pretrial decisions that discouraged pretrial release (e.g., financial release options, higher bail amounts) than White defendants, and they were less likely to gain pretrial release than White defendants" (pp. 237–238). Although White females had the most favorable decisions (no pretrial detention), White males also received particularly favorable decisions that the authors felt was a product of their

> greater ability to make bail. Relative to similarly situated gender and race-ethnic sub-groups, white defendants of both sexes apparently have greater financial capital or resources either in terms of their personal bankroll/resources, their access to family or social networks willing to pay, or their greater access to bail bondsmen for pur-poses of making bail. (p. 238)

The last decade has seen a limited stream of scholarship on bail and pretrial release. This research includes a handful of studies that examine race/ethnicity, bail, and the pretrial pro-cess. Some of these studies continue to support the findings of Demuth and Steffensmeier (2004), but emphasize that Hispanics receive the least favorable pretrial decisions.

Turner and Johnson (2005), for example, found that, among a sample of more than 800 felony defendants in Nebraska, "Hispanic defendants charged with bailable offenses were found to receive higher bail amounts than other similarly situated African American and White defendants" (p. 49). Schlesinger (2005), using a national sample of 36,709 felony defendants, found that "both Blacks and Latinos receive less beneficial pretrial release decisions and outcomes than Whites" (pp. 185–186).

Recent studies have also found that extra-legal factors matter in the bail and pretrial process. Freiburger and Hilinski (2010) studied the role of race, gender, and age on the pretrial process. Focusing on one urban county in Michigan, they found support for the findings of Demuth and Steffensmeier (2004). More specifically, they found that

> A strong race effect was found prior to entering the economic variables into the model, with Black defendants less likely to be released pretrial than Whites. Once these variables were included, however, race was no longer significant. . . . Therefore, it appears that Black defendants are more likely to be detained because they do not have the financial means necessary to secure release. (Freiburger & Hilinski, 2010, p. 330)

The authors point to the fact that inequalities in the larger society might be contributing to the disadvantages Blacks face in the pretrial release process. Other findings were that Black females (of all age groups) were least likely to be detained and that legal factors were less relevant for females than males. For the latter finding, the authors surmise that judges believe males who commit a serious offense pose a greater risk to society than similarly situated females (p. 330). A recent study by Wooldredge (2012) considered the role of race in the pretrial process in a large trial court in Ohio. The findings revealed that young Black males (18–29) were less likely to receive ROR than all other defendants. This finding also held true for African Americans eligible for bond. In particular, Wooldredge noted that "African American males were also assigned significantly higher bond amounts relative to white males, although the additional age breakdown created a wider gap in the average bond amounts" (p. 63). Additional support for the findings related to race has also been supported in the work of Lee and Ruiz (2011).

Taken together, the past and more recent research suggest that there are a variety of nuances related to understanding whether extra-legal factors such as race and gender influence the bail and pretrial process. Even so, the most recent scholarship makes clear that, at some level, race/ethnicity, gender, class, and age are all factors that must be considered in an effort to determine whether this early stage of the criminal justice system is characterized by bias.

Legal Counsel

As a result of the blatant racism in the previously discussed Scottsboro case, since 1932, the U.S. Supreme Court has mandated that indigent defendants in capital cases have the right to adequate counsel (see *Powell v. Alabama*, 1932). Four decades later, in *Gideon v. Wainwright* (1963), the Court ruled that all felony defendants have a right to counsel, a ruling that was expanded in 1972 when the Court mandated that counsel be provided for defendants in misdemeanor cases if there was the possibility of incarceration (see *Argersinger v. Hamlin*, 1972).

To meet these Supreme Court mandates, states created several legal defense systems. Many states have adopted a public defender system in which, as with a district attorney, the local or state government hires a full-time attorney to provide legal counsel for indigent defendants. In other cases, defendants are assigned counsel from a list of private attorneys who are selected on a case-by-case basis by a judge. Another option is the use of contract attorneys. These people are also private attorneys who are contracted to provide legal representation to indigent defendants (DeFrances & Litras, 2000). In the following section, we review some recent national governmental studies that examine the operation of these systems.

Defense Counsel

Most indigent offenders (82%) are represented by public defenders (DeFrances & Litras, 2000). A 2007 survey of public defender offices found nearly 1,000 such offices in 49 states. These offices handled more than 5.5 million cases and had more than 15,000 attorneys (4,000 at the state level and 11,000 at the county level) and nearly 10,000 full-time staff members (investigators, paralegals, and administrative staff). The total expense for public defense services was $2.3 billion (Langton & Farole, 2009). Table 5.7 lists the criteria used to determine eligibility for public defense services, by system (state or county).

The public defense systems clearly show signs of strain, with the average state public defense system receiving "82 felony (non-capital) cases, 217 misdemeanor cases, and two appeals cases per full-time equivalent litigating attorney" (Langton & Farole, 2009, p. 2; see also Farole & Langton, 2010). County public defense systems have somewhat lighter loads, with 100 felony (non-capital) cases and 146 misdemeanor cases per attorney at any given time. Langton and Farole (2010) also note that nearly 70% of the 22 states that have statewide public defense systems did not have the requisite number of attorneys to meet caseload guidelines.

Considering the investment in public defense systems, one wonders how defendants fare with the use of public defenders. Several studies have examined whether defendants represented by public defenders receive more or less favorable outcomes than similarly situated defendants who are represented by assigned counsel or private attorneys. On the whole, the literature has found that type of representation is not significant (Hanson & Ostrom, 1998; Hartley, Ventura Miller, & Spohn, 2010; Spohn & Holleran, 2000; Williams, 2002). The most recent comprehensive analysis of legal representation using data from the 75 most populous

Table 5.7

State and County Public Defense Systems Most Commonly Used Criteria for Determining Indigence

State Criteria for Indigence	County-Level Criteria for Indigence
• Income level • Defendant's receipt of public assistance • Sworn defendant's application • Defendant's debt level	• Income level • Sworn defendant's application • Judge's discretion • Defendant's residence in a public institution • Defendant's debt level

counties in the United States during 2004 and 2006 also found no significant differences in the outcome of cases handled by public defenders and private attorneys. Cohen (2011) did, however, find that defendants represented through assigned counsel programs received less favorable outcomes (conviction, imprisonment, and sentence length).

Despite Cohen's (2011) recent findings, there has been some evidence to support the notion that public defender offices might be at a disadvantage in carrying out their duties. A study of Pennsylvania's public defense systems provided a snapshot of the functioning of the system. The survey revealed some troubling findings. First, only the Philadelphia office provided any formalized training to their new public defenders. Even with this training, the public defenders were then thrust into positions where they were overworked and underpaid (Pennsylvania Supreme Court, 2003). They generally also had fewer resources than the district attorney's office. These findings were repeated when comparing them with the data from the other Pennsylvania jurisdictions. Most troubling was that "most court-appointed lawyers and many public defenders do not make use of investigators, and therefore do not conduct independent investigations of cases" (p. 185). Because of the paucity of resources, one jurisdiction pointed out "that a case that might require a psychologist or forensic expert might exhaust the whole budget" (p. 185). A study published shortly after the release of the Pennsylvania study provides a glimpse of the potential result of inferior public defense systems. Hoffman, Rubin, and Shepherd (2005) found that defendants represented by public defenders in Denver received more severe sentences than those represented by private attorneys.

In July 2011, the Justice Policy Institute released the report *System Overload: The Costs of Under-Resourcing Public Defense.* The report provided a variety of stunning figures regarding the sparse resources devoted to public defense. In 2008, for example, there were nearly $104 billion spent on policing, $74.1 billion spent on corrections, and $5.3 billion spent on public defense. Even more revealing was the data presented in the report from Tennessee that provided a comparison of the annual spending on public defense and prosecution. In 2005, Tennessee spent between $130 to $139 million on prosecution and a paltry $56.4 million on public defense (K. Taylor, 2011, p. 9).

In support of the previously reviewed Pennsylvania Supreme Court's findings nearly a decade earlier, K. Taylor (2011) outlined the sparse resources being devoted to the public defense office across the county. In the report, the situation in Cumberland County, New Jersey is provided as an example. In that jurisdiction, it was revealed that

> public defenders . . . handle about 90 percent of all criminal cases, but there are twice as many lawyers and more than seven times as many investigators working on criminal cases in the prosecutor's office than the public defender's office. (p. 9)

The report also outlines five primary ways in which poor public defense can increase incarceration: unnecessary pretrial detention, increased pressure to plead guilty, wrongful convictions and other errors, excessive and inappropriate sentences that fail to take into account the unique circumstances of the case, and increased barriers to successful reentry into the community. Each of these points speaks to the wide-ranging impact that poor public defense can have on whether defendants end up in prison, for how long, and whether they can make it once they are released. The report concludes with the suggestion that public defense systems should adopt the American Bar Association's (ABA) minimum standards for public defense (see Box 5.3).

BOX 5.3

Ten Principles of a Public Defense Delivery System

1. The public defense function, including the selection, funding, and payment of defense counsel, is independent.

2. Where the caseload is sufficiently high, the public defense delivery system consists of both a defender office and the active participation of the private bar.

3. Clients are screened for eligibility, and defense counsel is assigned and notified of appointment, as soon as feasible after clients' arrest, detention, or request for counsel.

4. Defense counsel is provided sufficient time and a confidential space within which to meet with the client.

5. Defense counsel's workload is controlled to permit the rendering of quality representation.

6. Defense counsel's ability, training, and experience match the complexity of the case.

7. The same attorney continuously represents the client until completion of the case.

8. There is parity between defense counsel and the prosecution with respect to resources, and defense counsel is included as an equal partner in the justice system.

9. Defense counsel is provided with and required to attend continuing legal education.

10. Defense counsel is supervised and systematically reviewed for quality and efficiency according to nationally and locally adopted standards.

The Justice Policy Institute also provided additional recommendations. First, public defense systems should integrate a holistic and community-based approach to public defense. In short, they should also consider the root causes of justice system involvement as a way to prevent future encounters with the justice system. Second, better data should be collected and there should be more evaluations of the impact of public defense systems on society and the criminal justice system. Third, the Institute recommended that both the public defenders and the community be involved in the policymaking process. Finally, the Institute called on the collaboration of policymakers, researchers, and advocates to seek out additional voices from those who have used public defense services to help better understand the nuances of how the system operates (K. Taylor, 2011, p. 34).

Even though the empirical literature suggests that defendants (of all racial/ethnic backgrounds) have minimal disadvantage when represented by public defenders, there is still a heavy reliance on plea bargaining. We provide a brief overview of the plea-bargaining process and the potential influence of race.

Plea Bargaining

Before actually proceeding to the trial phase, in any given year, an estimated 96% of convictions are reconciled through a guilty plea in the plea-bargaining process (Reaves, 2001). Early in American history, however, plea bargaining was frowned on by justice system officials and, as a result, comprised a small percentage of how cases were resolved. Only since the 20th century have courts accepted it as an important part of the criminal justice process (Shelden & Brown, 2003). Predictably, a process involving no real oversight and such broad discretion has come under scrutiny because of concerns related to race and class.

An example of how racial bias can influence the plea-bargaining process can be seen in a comprehensive study of California criminal cases conducted by the *San Jose Mercury News* in 1991. Using a computer analysis of nearly 700,000 criminal cases from 1981 to 1990, the study found,

> At virtually every stage of pretrial plea bargaining Whites were more successful than minorities. All else being equal, Whites did better than African-Americans and Hispanics at getting charges dropped, getting cases dismissed, avoiding harsher punishment, avoiding extra charges, and having their records wiped clean. (Donzinger, 1996, p. 112)

In addition, the study found that, although one-third of Whites who started out with felony charges had their charges reduced to misdemeanors, African Americans and Hispanics received this benefit only 25% of the time (Donzinger, 1996). Seeking to explain some of these results, one California judge stated that there was no conspiracy among judges to produce such outcomes. When put to a public defender, he explained the disparities this way:

> If a White person can put together a halfway plausible excuse, people will bend over backward to accommodate that person. It's a feeling, "You've got a nice person screwing up," as opposed to the feeling that "this minority person is on track and eventually they're going to end up in state prison." It's an unfortunate racial stereotype that pervades the system. It's an unconscious thing. (p. 113)

More recent scholarship has continued to study whether extra-legal factors such as race, class, or gender matter in the plea-bargaining process. O'Neill Shermer and Johnson (2010) studied the role of plea-bargaining in U.S. Federal District Courts. The authors found that males were less likely than females to receive charge reductions through the plea-bargaining process. Other findings of note include the following: Young minority youth were not less likely than other similarly situated offenders to receive charge reductions, and "older white males, young white females and young and old Hispanic females are significantly more likely to receive charge reductions, but these effects are driven by gender rather than by race/ethnicity" (p. 413). The authors also noted that offense matters in the plea-bargaining process, with property offenders being twice as likely to receive a charge reduction as violent offenders. The researchers also note that immigration offenses were among the offenses least likely to receive charge reductions. Further, offenders who accepted responsibility for their offense also received a significant charge reduction. Finally, the authors found that "male offenders were especially unlikely to be given charge reductions for drug and violent crimes and black and Hispanic offenders were disadvantaged in charging decisions for weapons offenses" (p. 421). Hence, while some extra-legal factors did appear to matter, O'Neill Shermer and Johnson conclude that "despite public concern, widespread prejudices do not seem to dominate prosecutorial decision-making at the federal level" (p. 424).

In the rare event that a case is not resolved during the plea-bargaining process, the next stage of the process requires preparation for a jury trial. Jury selection begins this phase of the process.

Jury Selection

Once it is decided that a case is going to trial, the case is decided by either a jury or a judge in a bench trial (where a judge alone is responsible for the determination of guilt or innocence). In the event of a jury trial, the jury selection process begins with a *venire*, or the selection of a jury pool. This provides the court with a list of persons from which to select the jury members. The Constitution requires that citizens be tried before a jury of their peers. Those in the legal profession generally agree that this should translate into juries being representative of the community in which the defendant resides. In the jury selection process, however, race and gender concerns have continued to pervade the process. The Scottsboro case discussed in Chapter 1 was an example of how racial bias in jury selection resulted in all-White juries trying African Americans because of long-standing discrimination in the courts. Although times have changed, in some jurisdictions, when minorities are underrepresented on juries in their own communities, questions have been raised and radical action has been taken, with some judges delaying trials until juries have acceptable diversity (Mandak, 2003). But in other instances, the courts have refused to intervene. Results from a study commissioned by the Pennsylvania Supreme Court (2003) on racial and gender bias have provided some examples of how issues related to race and gender influence the makeup of jury pools.

To investigate ethnic and gender bias in jury selection in Pennsylvania, researchers sent surveys to every county in the state to assess the various practices. More than 80% of the 67 counties returned the surveys (Pennsylvania Supreme Court, 2003). Once the surveys were tabulated, it was revealed that there were a variety of barriers to minorities and women participating in jury service. For minorities, these barriers included receiving fewer summonses for jury duty, transportation issues, child-care issues, and employer issues. Minorities, more so than others, have transportation difficulties that result in them being unable to serve on juries. Often, they are also impeded from serving on juries because they are unable to secure appropriate child care. In some instances, employers of hourly wage employees are unsupportive of jury service. The second part of the study, which looked in depth at four of Pennsylvania's largest counties (Allegheny, Lehigh, Montgomery, and Philadelphia), found that "African Americans were under-represented in juror yield in all four counties; Latinos were under-represented in juror yield in three of the counties; and Asian Americans were under-represented in juror yield in Philadelphia County" (p. 70).

In addition to surveys, the committee charged with completing the study also heard public testimony. When they queried one Pittsburgh attorney on the state of affairs concerning the racial composition of juries, he responded,

> In all of the cases which I have tried on behalf of African American plaintiffs in the past five years, a grand total of one African American was involved in the deliberations that determined the outcome of the case. Indeed, in most of the cases, the only African American in the courtroom was my client. (Pennsylvania Supreme Court, 2003, p. 74)

Turning to the underrepresentation of women on juries, the report revealed some of the interconnections between race and gender. Women were generally the ones responsible for child care; therefore, they were often unable to serve on juries. The committee also noted that women had difficulty reaching the courthouse, a concern shared by non-Whites. In certain situations, women, like men, were unable to serve on juries due to economic hardships. A final gender-related concern was "[the finding of] evidence that the interpersonal dynamics within the jury room can operate to the detriment of female jurors" (Pennsylvania Supreme Court, 2003, p. 106). More specifically, "Women in Pennsylvania were less likely than men to be chosen as presiding jurors" (p. 106).

Once the jury pool is formed, the opportunity for race and gender bias does not end there. There have been concerns with the subsequent **voir dire** process, during which jurors are screened for their fitness to serve on a particular case.

Voir Dire

Considering the difficulty in locating non-White jurors, it would seem that once the final juror selection process begins, non-White jurors would not be the targets for removal. To the surprise of some, this is not the case. Both the defense and prosecution often use their peremptory challenges to remove jurors based, in large part, on their race. In general, peremptory challenges can be used to remove jurors without cause. This was challenged in the 1965 case of *Swain v. Alabama*. In the case, Robert Swain, a Black teenager, was convicted of raping a White teenager (Cole, 1999). During the case, the prosecution "struck all six prospective Black jurors," and after investigation, it was revealed "that no Black had ever served on a trial jury in Talladega County, Alabama," despite the fact that Blacks made up 25% of the county population (p. 119). Based on this information, the conviction was challenged, and the Supreme Court decided to hear the case. However, the Supreme Court found no problem with striking the prospective Black jurors, indicating among other things that, "in the quest for an impartial and qualified jury, Negro and White, Protestants and Catholic, are alike subject to being challenged without cause" (p. 119). But according to the 1986 Supreme Court decision in ***Batson v. Kentucky***, race or gender must not be the deciding factor. It is notable that, six years later, in *Hernandez v. New York* (1991), the Supreme Court ruled

> that a criminal defendant's Fourteenth Amendment rights to equal protection were not violated when a prosecutor exercised a peremptory challenge excluding potential Latino/a jurors who understood Spanish on the basis that they might not accept the court interpreter's version as the final arbiter in the case. The defendant had argued that the elimination of potential Latino/a jurors violated his right to a trial by his peers in violation of his constitutional rights. (cited in Morin, 2005, p. 78)

In the eyes of the Supreme Court, the prosecutor's reason for the removal of Latino/a jurors was "race neutral" (Morin, 2005, p. 78).

Prior to the *Batson* decision, studies of jurisdictions in Texas and Georgia found that peremptory challenges were used to strike 90% of Black jurors (Cole, 1999). In fact, in large cities such as Philadelphia, district attorneys were given clear instructions to strike non-White jurors. A now infamous training tape by one Philadelphia assistant district attorney declared,

> Young Black women are very bad. There's an antagonism. I guess maybe they're downtrodden in two respects. They are women and they're Black . . . so they somehow want to take it out on somebody, and you don't want it to be you. (p. 118)

Scholars have also noted that, in certain instances, defense attorneys follow similar practices (Cole, 1999).

Since the *Batson* decision, prosecutors have turned to deception to strike non-White jurors. According to Cole (1999), prosecutors are masking their race-based actions by using neutral explanations to remove jurors. In some instances, for example,

> Courts have accepted explanations that the juror was too old, too young, was employed as a teacher or unemployed, or practiced a certain religion. They have accepted unverifiable explanations based on demeanor: the juror did not make eye contact or made too much eye contact, appeared inattentive or headstrong, nervous or too casual, grimaced or smiled. And they have accepted explanations that might often be correlated to race: the juror lacked education, was single or poor, lived or worked in the same neighborhood as the defendant or a witness, or had previously been involved with the criminal justice system. (pp. 120–121)

Gabbidon, Kowal, Jordan, Roberts, and Vincenzi (2008) confirmed these findings after reviewing five years' worth of litigation in which plaintiffs sued because they felt allegedly race-neutral peremptory challenges were race-based. Based on an analysis of 283 cases from the U.S. Court of Appeals, the researchers found that Blacks were the ones most likely to be removed from juries. The explanations used to justify their removal include questionable body language, questionable mannerisms, medical issues, child-care issues, limited life experiences, and unemployment. The courts accepted these explanations, considering that 79% of the appellants lost their cases (Gabbidon et al., 2008). For those who actually won their appeal, there was an extremely high burden of proof. However, at the heart of winning was being able to show some inconsistency on the part of the attorney who made the removals. As an example, Gabbidon et al. noted that in one instance, the prosecutor struck a juror "because he was concerned that she did not seem to understand or respond appropriately to certain *dire* questions" (p. 64). But after further review, "the courts ruled against the prosecutor because they found that the prosecutor declined to strike white jurors whose answers were far more inappropriate or unresponsive" (p. 64).

Sommers and Norton (2007) conducted an experiment using 90 undergraduate college students, 81 advanced law students (second and third year), and 28 practicing attorneys to determine several things, including (a) to what extent does race affect jury selection judgments, and (b) if decision makers fail to report the influence of race on jury selection judgments, how do they justify their decisions? On the first point, the authors found that "across three samples, this investigation provides clear empirical evidence that a prospective juror's race can influence peremptory challenge use and that self-report justifications are unlikely to be useful for identifying this influence" (p. 269). Furthermore, the researchers reported that when justifying their reason for removing Black jurors, the respondents used a race-neutral explanation. Thus, as Sommers and Norton (2007) aptly note, "The practical implications of these findings are clear: even when attorneys consider race during jury selection, there is little reason to believe that judicial questioning will produce information useful for identifying the bias" (p. 269).

Considering the frequent removal of racial and ethnic minorities from jury pools, one wonders how jurors perceive the jury selection process. McGuffee, Garland, and Eigenberg (2007) explored this question based on a survey sent to Tennessee residents summoned for jury service. In general, most of the 138 respondents felt that most jury verdicts are correct (92%) and "that juries try hard to do the right thing" (p. 456).

Fewer respondents reported that they felt the system was fair (83%). As for questions related to race and the jury system, the authors found that

> About half the respondents (52%) agreed that it is important for African-Americans to have African-Americans on the jury in order to get a fair trial. Similarly one-half of the respondents (49%) reported that if you are African American you want other African-Americans on the jury to get a fair trial. (p. 457)

Other findings showed that the respondents were less likely to feel that having Whites on the jury was critical for Whites to receive a fair trial. Also, a little more than 25% of the respondents felt that African Americans were "more likely to be dismissed from jury duty than are whites. Furthermore, about one-fifth (18%) of the respondents believed that whites are more apt to convict than minorities." In terms of fairness in decision making, "only 7% of the respondents believe that whites are fairer than minorities in jury decisions" (McGuffee et al., 2007, p. 457). It is also important to note that most of the respondents (57%) felt that race had nothing to do with jury selection or jury verdicts (68%).

Even with these generally positive sentiments from admittedly a limited sample of jurors, prosecutors and defense attorneys still resort to peremptory challenges to remove racial and ethnic minorities from jury pools. Recently the Equal Justice Initiative published a monograph, *Illegal Racial Discrimination in Jury Selection: A Continuing Legacy* (see Stevenson, 2010). The report confirms the findings from the empirical research regarding the exclusion of racial minorities from juries. In fact, the Supreme Court of Mississippi is quoted in the report as saying "racially motivated jury selection is still prevalent twenty years after *Batson* was handed down" (p. 24). In response to the disappointing findings, the Initiative proposed 14 recommendations to help remedy the problem (see Box 5.4). Concerns regarding **jury nullification** likely lie at the heart of the practice. We review jury nullification and the fears surrounding it in the next section.

BOX 5.4

Equal Justice Initiative: Recommendations to Reduce Bias in the Jury Selection Process

1. Dedicated and thorough enforcement of anti-discrimination laws designed to prevent racially biased jury selection must be undertaken by courts, judges, and lawyers involved in criminal and civil trials, especially in serious criminal cases and capital cases.

2. The rule banning racially discriminatory use of peremptory strikes announced in *Batson v. Kentucky* should be applied retroactively to death row prisoners and others with lengthy sentences whose convictions or death sentences are the product of illegal, racially biased jury selection but whose claims have not been reviewed because they were tried before 1986.

3. To protect the credibility and integrity of criminal trials, claims of illegal racial discrimination in the selection of juries should be reviewed by courts on the merits and exempted from procedural bars or technical defaults that shield and insulate from remedy racially biased conduct.

(Continued)

(Continued)

4. Prosecutors who are found to have engaged in racially biased jury selection should be held accountable and should be disqualified from participation in the retrial of any person wrongly convicted as a result of discriminatory jury selection. Prosecutors who repeatedly exclude people of color from jury service should be subject to fines, penalties, suspension, and other consequences to deter this practice.

5. The Justice Department and federal prosecutors should enforce 18 U.S.C. §243, which prohibits racial discrimination in jury selection, by pursuing actions against district attorney's offices with a history of racially biased selection practices.

6. States should provide remedies to people called for jury service who are illegally excluded on the basis of race, particularly jurors who are wrongly denigrated by state officials. States should implement strategies to disincentivize discriminatory conduct by state prosecutors and judges, who should enforce rather than violate anti-discrimination laws.

7. Community groups, civil and human rights organizations, and concerned citizens should attend court proceedings and monitor the conduct of local officials with regard to jury selection practices in an effort to eliminate racially biased jury selection.

8. Community groups, civil and human rights organizations, and concerned citizens should question their local district attorneys about policies and practices relating to jury selection in criminal trials, secure officials' commitment to enforcing anti-discrimination laws, and request regular reporting by prosecutors on the use of peremptory strikes.

9. States should strengthen policies and procedures to ensure that racial minorities, women, and other cognizable groups are fully represented in the jury pools from which jurors are selected. States and local administrators should supplement source lists for jury pools or utilize computer models that weight groups appropriately. Full representation of all cognizable groups throughout the United States easily can be achieved in the next five years.

10. Reviewing courts should abandon absolute disparity as a measure of underrepresentation of minority groups and utilize more accurate measures, such as comparative disparity, to prevent the insulation from remedy of unfair underrepresentation.

11. State and local justice systems should provide support and assistance to ensure that low-income residents, sole caregivers for children or other dependents, and others who are frequently excluded from jury service because of their economic, employment, or family status have an opportunity to serve.

12. Court administrators, state and national bar organizations, and other state policymakers should require reports on the representativeness of juries in serious felony and capital cases to ensure compliance with state and federal laws barring racial discrimination in jury selection.

13. The criminal defense bar should receive greater support, training, and assistance in ensuring that state officials do not exclude people of color from serving on juries on the basis of race, given the unique and critically important role defense attorneys play in protecting against racially biased jury selection.

14. Greater racial diversity must be achieved within the judiciary, district attorney's offices, the defense bar, and law enforcement to promote and strengthen the commitment to ensuring that all citizens have equal opportunities for jury service.

Jury Nullification

Given the numerous measures being taken in some jurisdictions to diversify jury pools, one would think that keeping non-Whites on the jury would be a high priority. On the contrary, as discussed in the previous section on peremptory challenges, prosecutors and defense attorneys alike often eliminate jurors based on race if they believe it will help them secure a victory. The underlying premise is surely a lack of trust, particularly of non-White jurors. Why else would someone not want non-Whites on juries? The concern relates to the practice of jury nullification. According to Walker et al. (2007),

> Jury nullification . . . occurs when a juror believes that the evidence presented at trial establishes the defendant's guilt, but nonetheless votes to acquit. The juror's decision may be motivated either by a belief that the law under which the defendant is being prosecuted is unfair or by an application of the law to a particular defendant. (p. 223)

In the past two decades, there has been increasing debate on this practice. In 1995, Paul Butler, a professor of law at George Washington University, published a seminal and controversial article on the utility of African Americans engaging in jury nullification. Since Professor Butler published his controversial article, he has continued to refine his perspective (Butler, 2009). During the beginning of his tenure as a federal prosecutor, Butler (1995) wrote that "we would lose many of our cases, despite having persuaded a jury beyond a reasonable doubt that the defendant was guilty. We would lose because some Black jurors would refuse to convict Black defendants who they knew were guilty" (p. 678). After considering the concept, Butler used two case studies to show how the practice can send a message to society regarding injustices. The first case study reviewed the case of *United States v. Barry* (1991). After a long and expensive federal investigation, Marion Barry, the former mayor of Washington, D.C., was observed on videotape in a sting operation smoking crack cocaine. Two prominent and controversial African American leaders, Reverend George Stallings and Minister Louis Farrakhan, were provided with passes by Barry to attend the trial. However, in both cases, they were denied access because the presiding judge felt they might influence juror sentiment. The American Civil Liberties Union (ACLU) took up the cases and argued that they both had a right to attend the trial. In the end, the trial court conceded and let the two attend the trial; however, they were given "special rules" that had to be followed (Butler, 1995). Although Barry was clearly guilty, at the end of the trial, he was found guilty of only 1 of 14 charges.

The second case study involved John T. Harvey III, a prominent Washington, D.C. attorney. During a trial in the early 1990s, Harvey's attire became the subject of controversy while he was representing a client. Along with a traditional suit, Harvey wore a stole made of *Kente* cloth, which has roots in African culture. During the pretrial process, a judge warned him about wearing the cloth. Apparently, the judge felt that wearing the cloth would "send a hidden message to jurors" (Butler, 1995, p. 685). Given his convictions on the matter, the judge offered Harvey three options: "He could refrain from wearing the *Kente* cloth; he could withdraw from the case; or he could agree to try the case before the judge, without a jury" (p. 685). After considerable wrangling, Harvey was allowed to wear the *Kente* cloth. The judge even suggested that Harvey be charged for the time devoted to the *Kente* cloth issue. Eventually, "Harvey's client is tried before an all-Black jury and is acquitted" (p. 686).

On the whole, Butler (1995) advocated the use of jury nullification to fight against unfair practices, which are outlined in his two case studies, as well as unjust laws, such as the controversial crack cocaine laws, which annually send a disproportionate number of people of color to jail and prison. In Butler's (1995) words

> The Black community is better off when some nonviolent lawbreakers remain in the community rather than go to prison. The decision as to what kind of conduct by African-Americans ought to be punished is better made by African-Americans themselves, based on the costs and benefits to their community, than by the traditional criminal justice process, which is controlled by White lawmakers and White law enforcers. Legally, the doctrine of jury nullification gives the power to make this decision to [African-American jurors who sit in judgment of] African-American defendants. (p. 679)

Although acknowledging some merits of Butler's arguments, Krauss and Schulman (1997) see the general concern of Black juror nullification as being based on anecdotal evidence. In their analysis, the discussion comes down to the following equation: "Black defendant + Black jurors + non-conviction = miscarriage of justice" (p. 60). As they see it, those who believe in this equation ignore the fact that, in some of these cases, "Black jurors are being condemned for doing exactly what jurors are supposed to do: demanding that the prosecution prove its case beyond a reasonable doubt" (p. 60). Furthermore, they view the continuing outrage over jury nullification as a response to an article published in the *Wall Street Journal* shortly after the conclusion of the O. J. Simpson trial in 1995. The article provided figures showing that nationwide there was an overall acquittal rate of 17%, whereas in jurisdictions such as the Bronx, New York, and Washington, D.C., the acquittal rates were 47.6% and 28.7%, respectively. The authors countered these figures, showing that the acquittal rate nationally was closer to 28% (p. 62). Subsequently, contrary to the notion of jury nullification, the authors noted that the Bronx rate was likely a result of "(1) jurors doing their jobs well, [and] (2) prosecutors who are not doing their jobs well" (p. 63).

Krauss and Schulman (1997) also noted that there is the belief that only White jurors can be color blind. They responded that it is impossible to have a color-blind jury because race is the first thing that people see in others. Another important point discussed by the authors relates to police testimony. Although in many instances the testimony of police officers is believed without challenge, the authors pointed out that, because of their historically negative experiences with police officers, persons of color give equal weight to police testimony and that of other witnesses, even when they differ (pp. 70–71).

❖ Drug Courts

Drug courts are a fairly recent initiative. Dade County, Florida is credited with starting the first one in 1989 (Goldkamp & Weiland, 1993). Since then, partly as a result of Title V of the Violent Crime Control and Law Enforcement Act of 1994, which awarded federal monies to drug court programs (U.S. General Accounting Office [GAO], 1997), the number of drug courts has risen to more than 2,500 (National Drug Control Strategy, 2011). Figure 5.1 shows the tremendous growth in drug courts. These courts surfaced when drug-related cases began to overwhelm traditional courts, which was largely due to the wide-scale

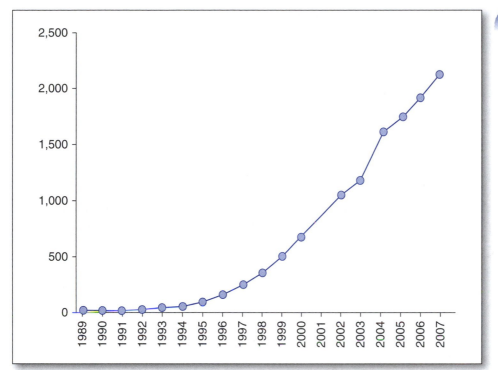

Figure 5.1
The Number
of Drug Courts
Continues
to Increase
Nationwide
(1989–2007)

use of mandatory minimum drug sentences (Fox & Huddleston, 2003). This sentencing approach had a disparate impact on minorities (see Chapter 6), and consequently a large share of those diverted to drug courts have been minorities (Fielding, Tye, Ogawa, Imam, & Long, 2002). Before we discuss the effectiveness of drug courts, we review the structure and philosophy of the courts.

Structure and Philosophy of Drug Courts

Court Structure

Drug courts (also referred to as "drug treatment courts") attempt to provide "a bridge between criminal justice and health services" (Wenzel, Longshore, Turner, & Ridgely, 2001, p. 241). This bridge results in a combination of court oversight and therapeutic services and the use of "an intense regimen of drug treatment, case management, drug testing, and supervision, while reporting to regularly scheduled status hearings before a judge" (Fox & Huddleston, 2003, p. 13). The judge, the prosecutor, defense attorney, treatment provider, law enforcement officer, probation officer, case manager, and program coordinator are part of the "drug court team" (p. 13).

Based on a report commissioned by the U.S. Department of Justice and the National Association of Drug Court Professionals, there are 10 key components of drug courts (Fox & Huddleston, 2003). To receive federal funding, drug courts must adhere to the following components. First, they must use a multidisciplinary process to address the needs of persons who are diverted to the court. Second, the courts are also seen as nonadversarial. Going against the traditional philosophy of courts, all parties work together to ensure that the participant has the best chance of success. Early identification is the third component of drug courts. Here, the courts try to get to prospective participants as early in the criminal justice process as possible. The fourth component of the court is to offer a "continuum of treatment and rehabilitation services" (p. 16). This acknowledges the diverse needs of those who come under the purview of the court. Regular alcohol and drug testing is another key component. Such random testing, which should be observed by a program official, is essential to ensure participants have not had relapses.

The sixth key component of the court is to have regular meetings to discuss the progress of participants. Philosophically, these meetings should not take on a punitive tone (Fox & Huddleston, 2003). In line with the sixth component, the seventh requires that there should be ongoing interaction with the judge. Evaluation is the eighth essential component of a drug court. Using goals and objectives as a starting point, each court should periodically measure its effectiveness. The ninth component requires that team members seek out additional education or training to stay abreast of current drug court practices. The final key component of drug courts is developing community partnerships. Drug courts are encouraged to make links to "enhance program effectiveness and general local support" (p. 17).

Court Philosophy

In short, the underlying philosophy of the court is that persons with drug addictions need treatment rather than prison sentences. That is, because some of the problems that result from drug abuse are related to criminal justice, drug courts seek to address the addiction problem through treatment services in the hopes of producing the following positive outcomes: a reduction in drug use, less criminal activity, lower recidivism, better health, better social and family functioning, better educational/vocational status, and residential stability (Fischer, 2003; Wenzel et al., 2001). Taking into consideration the unique approach and philosophy of drug courts, the next section looks at how effective they have been.

Effectiveness of Drug Courts

After more than 20 years in existence, drug courts have been the focus of a considerable number of evaluations. In 1997, the GAO reviewed 20 studies that evaluated the effectiveness of drug courts. The GAO noted the serious shortcomings in many of the evaluations that had been done up to that point. In general, the report found mixed results. Some programs recorded relapse rates from 7% to 80%, with some programs reporting recidivism rates ranging from 0% to 58%. In addition, completion rates were mixed, ranging from 1% to 70%, with an average of 43%. A review of studies conducted for drug courts in California, Florida, and Delaware found that Hispanics and African Americans were less likely to complete the programs. In Nevada, however, researchers reported "no difference in the termination rates between ethnic groups and between male and female participants" (p. 77).

Los Angeles County started its first drug court in 1994. By June, 2001, there were "11 pre-plea drug court programs . . . operating in 11 of Los Angeles County's 24 judicial districts" (Fielding et al., 2002, p. 218). Like others around the country, the court "provide[s] a treatment alternative to prosecution for non-violent felony drug offenders" (p. 218). To measure the effectiveness of the drug court, the researchers used a quasi-experimental design with three sample groups. The first group included those who participated in the drug court program. The second group participated in another diversion program, whereas the third group was composed of felony defendants who went to trial. The study aimed to investigate the program completion and recidivism rates of the groups. Most of the persons in the three groups were male and minorities, with an average age in the low 30s. When Fielding et al. (2002) examined recidivism among the three groups, they found that

> Drug court participants were less likely to be re-arrested than drug diversion participants or felony defendants. However, results differ by risk strata. Low risk study participants' re-arrest rates did not differ significantly from those of the diversion sample. However, for those classified at medium or high risk, the re-arrest rate for drug court participants was significantly below those of the diversion and/or felony defendant groups. (pp. 221–222)

Moreover, the time to rearrest was longer for those who participated in drug courts than those who were in the other groups. This held true for time to new drug arrests. On the whole, drug court graduates fared better than those in the other groups. A final area of interest to the researchers was cost. The cost for drug court ranged from nearly $4,000 to nearly $9,000. Yet the alternatives to drug courts—prison ($16,500) and residential treatment centers ($13,000)—were considerably more expensive.

Other studies have also found the courts to be effective in reducing recidivism (Gottfredson, Najaka, & Kearley, 2003; Johnson Listwan, Sundt, Holsinger, & Latessa, 2003; Mitchell, Wilson, Eggers, & MacKenzie, 2012), improving the participants' job prospects and self-image (Creswell & Deschenes, 2001), and reducing costs (Carey, Finigan, Crumpton, & Waller, 2006). More recent research has examined how effective drug courts are outside urban settings. Thus, although most of the evaluations have been of urban-based drug courts, little has been done to determine whether the success of the courts is transferrable to nonmetropolitan areas. Galloway and Drapella (2006) examined the effectiveness of drug courts in such an area. Their results suggest that the success of the courts is not limited to urban areas. Their study of a drug court in a small nonmetropolitan area revealed lower recidivism among drug court participants even after controlling for age, race, gender, and other key variables.

Still other research has examined the effectiveness of family treatment drug courts (FTDCs), which are designed to get drug-addicted parents the treatment they need "to be reunited with their children" (Green, Furrer, Worcel, Burrus, & Finighan, 2007, p. 44). In such instances, the courts often work in conjunction with the child welfare system. Green et al. conducted an assessment of FTDCs at multiple sites using a quasi-experimental approach. The research revealed that

> Participants in FTDCs entered treatment more quickly, stayed in treatment longer, and were more likely to successfully complete treatment, even when controlling for a host of risk factors. Moreover, FTDC participants were more likely to be reunited with their children, and children were placed in permanent living situations more quickly compared to those in the comparison groups. (p. 56)

Although some of the earlier research on drug courts found mixed results (J. Anderson, 2001; Bavon, 2001; Cooper, 2003; Fischer, 2003; Harrell, 2003; Johnson Listwan et al., 2003), recent studies on drug courts have yielded positive results (Marlowe, 2011; Rossman, Roman, Zweig, Rempel, & Lindquist, 2011). That is, in most studies, drug court participants are faring better than those in comparison groups. Even when the outcomes are quite similar, the cost of the drug court is far lower than the alternative. In addition, offenders who are supervised through drug courts are able to improve family relationships and continue to make a living. As a result, in the 2011 National Drug Control Strategy, drug courts are lauded as "a proven method for addressing substance-abusing offenders" (p. 45).

❖ Conclusion

This chapter examined race and the American court system. From the earliest period of American history, race/ethnicity and class have played a role in the operation of American courts. More recent research has shown race effects during every aspect of the court process. However, unlike in the past when the discrimination was blatant, some of the bias is now masked, such as in the jury selection process and the use of peremptory challenges to remove racial/ethnic groups from jury pools. It is clear from the research in this area that both defense and prosecutors do not trust racial/ethnic minorities to make reasoned decisions when serving on juries. This mistrust leads to actions that deny minority defendants the opportunity to have minorities (their peers) serve on their juries.

Finally, drug courts were discussed as a way to reduce the prison population, while also giving drug-addicted offenders the treatment they need. We reviewed their structure, philosophy, and promise for dealing with some of the addiction problems. Although the results of early evaluative studies were mixed, more recently the initiative has shown considerable promise for diverting racial minorities and other drug-addicted offenders out of regular courts. Closely tied to the courts is the sentencing process. Chapter 6 looks at how racial minorities fare in the sentencing phase of the court process.

Discussion Questions

1. Explain how race, class, gender, or celebrity status can play a role in the American court system.

2. How do Native American courts differ in philosophy from non-Native American courts?

3. Discuss why the discrimination thesis (DT) and the no-discrimination thesis (NDT) are critical considerations in the American court process.

4. Explain how peremptory challenges can be misused in the American court system.

5. What program characteristics make drug courts so promising?

Internet Exercises

1. Visit http://www.jurybox.org and read the statements from significant American figures concerning jury nullification. Do any of their thoughts sway your feelings on jury nullification? Take a look at the other links and see whether you agree with the suggestions for improving the jury system.

2. Visit the Equal Justice Initiative Website (http://www.eji.org/eji/) and read their full report on "Illegal Racial Discrimination in Jury Selection: A Continuing Legacy."

Internet Sites

National Center for State Courts: http://www.ncsconline.org/

U.S. Supreme Court: http://www.supremecourtus.gov/

National Drug Court Institute: http://www.ndci.org

CHAPTER 6

Sentencing

The social responsibility for crime is so widely recognized that when the criminal is arrested, the first desire of decent modern society is to reform him, and not to avenge itself on him. Penal servitude is being recognized only as it protects society and improves the criminal, and not because it makes him suffer as his victim suffered.

—Du Bois (1920, p. 173)

Sentencing represents the stage of the criminal justice process when, following conviction, a defendant is given a sanction for committing his or her offense. Sanctions that are regularly used because they are not in violation of the Eighth Amendment's cruel and unusual punishment clause include fines (which cannot be excessive); being placed on **probation**, given an intermediate sanction (something in between probation and incarceration), and/or incarceration; and the death penalty. Such a process has considerable potential for discrimination and errors. It is important to consider, however, that, like the laws that send the criminal justice process in motion, state and federal legislatures are primarily responsible for determining the appropriate sentence for each offense. Although the legislature has a significant role to play in the creation of sentences, in many instances, judges also have considerable discretion in the sentencing process. Therefore, a variety of legislative enactments (e.g., sentencing guidelines) have been created to "equalize" or reduce the disparities in the sentencing process, yet sentences still can be influenced appreciably by judicial discretion. Because of this, over the years, the actions of the judiciary have been scrutinized more closely by citizens and social scientists alike.

In this chapter, we examine the following three areas related to sentencing: (a) sentencing philosophies, (b) historical overview of race and sentencing, and (c) contemporary issues in race and sentencing. The first section reviews the various sentencing philosophies (also called justifications) that influence the direction of sentencing policies. Such philosophies generally shift based on political leanings, which are also discussed. Our historical overview provides some early examples of patterns in race and sentencing. Finally, the last segment of the chapter explores contemporary race and sentencing issues.

❖ Sentencing Philosophies

Punishment is meted out in the sentencing phase of the criminal justice process. According to van den Haag (1975), "'punishment' is a depravation, or suffering, imposed by law" (p. 8). Drawing on the works of English philosopher H. L. A. Hart, Cassia Spohn (2009), a leading scholar in the area of sentencing, wrote that there are five necessary elements of punishment: It must (a) involve pain or other consequences normally considered unpleasant, (b) be enacted for an offense against legal rules, (c) be imposed on an actual or supposed offender for his offense, (d) be intentionally administered by human beings other than the offender, and (e) be imposed and administered by an authority constituted by a legal system against which the offense was committed.

Spohn (2009) added that some scholars feel that, in addition to the five elements outlined by Hart, there must also be an appropriate justification for the punishment. These justifications amount to what are generally referred to as "philosophies of punishment" or "sentencing philosophies." Generally speaking, there are four different sentencing philosophies: (a) justice/retribution, (b) incapacitation, (c) deterrence, and (d) treatment/rehabilitation. According to van den Haag (1975), "Justice [or retribution] is done by distributing punishments to offenders according to what is deserved by their offenses as specified by law" (p. 25). Incapacitation suggests that as long as offenders are detained, society is protected from them. Deterrence operates under the premise that the public will be affected by seeing others punished (van den Haag, 1975). There are two forms of deterrence: specific and general. Specific deterrence operates under the notion that when you punish someone, he or she will be deterred from further criminal activity. General deterrence suggests that when you punish someone, the larger society is deterred from committing crimes (van den Haag, 1975). Making the offender better is the overriding aim of the treatment or **rehabilitation** philosophy. In some instances, each of these might be present in a sentence; however, one will typically predominate (Anderson & Newman, 1998). Predictably, each of these philosophies is tied to politics. We discuss this connection next.

Sentencing and Politics

Sentencing philosophies are germane to any discussion of punishment because such considerations tend to drive the nature of what happens at the "back end" of the system (i.e., corrections). Thus, depending on the prevailing philosophy, sentences could be longer and harsher, or, conversely, sentences could be lighter and more treatment oriented. Each of these two possibilities has consequences for society as a whole. For example, when sentences are longer, jails and prisons often reach or exceed their capacity; government officials justify such expensive policies by pointing to cases in which people who were released early went out and committed new crimes. However, when sentences are lighter and more treatment oriented, government officials argue that a shorter sentence under the rehabilitation approach is cheaper and more effective. Therefore, more often than not, politics at the local, state, and federal levels dictate the prevailing philosophy (Beckett & Sasson, 2000; Hagan, 2010; Scheingold, 1984).

A good example of this is the formulation of the crime control and due process models of criminal justice decision making constructed by Herbert Packer (1968) in the late 1960s, which 20 years later was refined by Samuel Walker (1989). In both formulations, there are those who adhere to a more conservative approach when handling crime control, and, on the other side, there are those who adhere to a more liberal approach. In short, those who adhere to the conservative approach take a more hard-line stance on crime and are generally supportive of sentencing philosophies that are both punitive and deterrent in orientation. Adherents to the liberal philosophy lean more toward the rehabilitation/treatment approach. They tend to believe that people can be "cured" or, at the least, made better through a variety of treatments. Therefore, they generally recommend shorter jail or prison sentences combined with appropriate treatment. Such thinking reigned during the 1960s, when some literature actually pointed to the counterproductiveness of punishment (see, e.g., Menninger, 1966). However, during the punitive decades of the 1980s and 1990s, some liberals, particularly those in inner cities, were influenced by the conservatism that swept the country. This saw some people calling for "personal responsibility" and more punitive sanctions for those engaging in urban violence.

The liberal and conservative approaches have predominated for the last 40 years. As is widely acknowledged, the rehabilitation approach was dealt a near fatal blow in the 1970s by the increasing crime rate and the controversial Martinson (1974) report, which reviewed numerous treatment-oriented approaches and suggested that few were having their desired outcome. In the end, Martinson's study was interpreted as saying when it comes to rehabilitation, "nothing works." Such a dismal forecast set in motion a movement toward the conservative philosophy, which most would agree remains the predominant approach.

❖ Historical Overview of Race and Sentencing

Punishment in Colonial America

A good place to begin a historical overview of race and sentencing is colonial America. This era provides us with a sense of the punishments that were rendered in the early years of the colony. Moreover, a review of court records and other documents also provides us with some indication as to racial/ethnic disparities in sentencing.

As has been previously noted, much of the law in colonial America was based on English practices. The remainder of the laws that were created originated from the colonists or the Bible (Chapin, 1983). The colonists took biblical influence one step further by having some cases actually handled by religious congregations. In general, it is thought that summary proceedings administered by judges were the primary way many cases were handled. For those who desired a trial by jury, Chapin wrote, "A defendant could have a jury in almost any kind of case if he asked and paid for it" (p. 41). It is obvious from this practice that class bias was present from the earliest colonial times and was also present when administering punishments.

One of the first things the colonists did when they began to construct their justice system was to do away with the excessive use of the death penalty, which prevailed in England. Many of the more brutal sentences were reserved for servants and "lesser men." One such servant was Richard Barnes, whose offense, aggravated contempt, resulted in him having "his arms broken and his tongue bored through and [he] was forced to crawl through a guard of forty men who kicked him" (Chapin, 1983, p. 50). Certainly, the colonists did execute people and were fond of corporal punishment and other public displays. Some people were whipped in public (see Photo 6.1), but class lines again prevailed because those who

Photo 6.1
Gordon, a free slave in Baton Rouge, Louisiana, displays his whip-scarred back on April 2, 1863. He later became a corporal in the Union Army.

were considered "gentlemen" could substitute some other satisfaction (likely money) to fulfill their sentences. According to Chapin, however, "The most common punishment was a fine payable in money or tobacco" (p. 51). As they are today, the punishments were incremental. For example, "A convicted burglar or robber in Connecticut and Massachusetts was branded on the forehead with the letter 'B' for a first offense, branded and whipped for a second, and executed as incorrigible for a third conviction" (p. 49). This example also suggests that, although the moniker might be new, three-strikes laws are not.

Early Colonial Cases

The colonists were clearly sensitive to economic issues, which, along with their xenophobia, translated into unfairness in the justice system. One way to examine this unfairness is to review early cases and their sentencing patterns. To get a glimpse of the justice that pre-vailed for African Americans in early America, some scholars have turned to Helen Tunnicliff Catterall's (1926/1968) four-volume work, *Judicial Cases Concerning American Slavery and the Negro,* which provides brief summaries of early relevant cases (see also Higginbotham, 1978; Russell, 1998). Four cases decided in colonial Virginia that have received considerable attention by legal scholars seeking to see how race impacted on sentences in early America are *Re Davis, Re Sweat, Re Negro John Punch,* and *Re Negro Emmanuel.*

The summary from the 1630 trial of *Re Davis* reads,

Hugh Davis to be soundly whipt before an assembly of negroes and others for abusing himself to the dishonor of God and shame of Christianity by defiling his body in lying with a negro, which fault he is to acknowledge next sabbath day. (Catterall, 1926/1968, p. 77)

Here, one could interpret the transcript as saying that Davis was White and he had violated the law by sleeping with a Black woman. His obvious sentence was penance on the next Sabbath day. But the mere suggestion that he defiled his body by sleeping with the woman suggests notions of superiority and inferiority. As noted earlier by Higginbotham (1978), religion also played a key role in maintaining African Americans and other undesirables in their "place." A decade later, *Re Sweat* (1640) also spoke to the criminal liaisons between White men and Black females, but in this case, where a child resulted, the penalties were distinctly different. The case summary reads,

> Whereas Robert Sweat hath begotten with child a negro woman servant belonging unto Lieutenant Sheppard, the court hath therefore ordered that the said negro woman shall be whipt at the whipping post and the said Sweat shall tomorrow in the forenoon do public penance for his offense at James city church in the time of divine service according to the laws of England in that case provided. (Catterall, 1926/1968, p. 78)

Here, Sweat was given part of the punishment as Davis in the prior case; however, the whipping was reserved for the Black woman. Although the punishments were obviously disparate, the sentence was likely even more stinging for the Black woman considering that, given the time period, it is likely that the relationship was not consensual. Thus, there is the possibility that a convicted rapist did penance while the victim was whipped for being raped. Such contradictions or inequities were also present in other trials.

In *Re Negro Punch*, the case record stated the following:

> Whereas Hugh Gwyn hath . . . Brought back from Maryland three servants formerly run away . . . the court doth therefore order that the said three servants shall receive the punishment of whipping and to have thirty stripes apiece one called Victor, a Dutchman, and other a Scotchman called James Gregory, shall first serve out their times with their master according to their Indentures, and one whole year apiece after the time of their service is Expired . . . and after that service . . . to serve the colony for three whole years apiece, and that the third being a negro named John Punch shall serve his said master or his assigns for the time of his natural Life here or elsewhere. (Catterall, 1926/1968, p. 78)

In this case, the punishments rendered suggest that the two White servants received less punishment than the Black servant. The two Whites received extended indentures and service to the colony, with the Dutchman also receiving a whipping. Yet the Black servant received *lifetime* servitude. Another case that shows the early disparities in sentencing is *Re Negro Emmanuel*.

In *Re Negro Emmanuel*, a plot to run away was foiled. Again, the summary of the case is illuminating:

> Complaint . . . by Capt. Wm. Pierce, Esqr. That six of his servants and a negro of Mr. Reginolds has plotted to run away unto the Dutch plantation . . . and did assay to put the same in Execution. They "had . . . taken the skiff of . . . Pierce . . . and corn, powder and shot and guns . . . which said persons sailed down . . . to Elizabeth river where they were taken . . . order that . . . Emmanuel the Negro to receive thirty [lashes] and to be burnt in the cheek with the letter R, and to work in shakle one year or more as his master shall see cause. (Catterall, 1926/1968, p. 77)

Except for Emmanuel, each of the conspirators received additional service to the colony, with one White conspirator also being branded and whipped. Although Emmanuel received no additional service, which some have suggested was an indication that he was already in lifetime servitude (Higginbotham, 1978), he was whipped, branded with "R" (presumably so everyone would know he had previously run away), and made to wear shackles for a year.

Scores of related cases existed in the colonial era. Based on an analysis of these cases, Catterall (1926/1968) noted that a hierarchy of social precedence developed (see Figure 6.1).

1. White indentured servants

2. White servants without indentures

3. Christian Black servants

4. Indian servants

5. Mulatto servants (Black or Indian)

6. Indian slaves

7. Black slaves

Figure 6.1

Catterall's Hierarchy of Social Precedence

Source: Catterall (1926/1968, pp. 53–54).

According to her analysis, at the top of the hierarchy were White indentured servants, whereas at the bottom of the hierarchy were Black slaves. Based on the case studies presented, one can confidently assume that justice in the courts was distributed in line with this hierarchy.

To further investigate these early disparities in case outcomes, we turn to one of the more diverse colonies, New York. From the late 1600s through the 1700s, New York was the gateway for an influx of racial and ethnic groups. Therefore, looking at data from this colony provides a more expansive picture than the cases presented by Catterall.

Crime and Justice in Colonial New York

Greenberg (1976) provided data on more than 5,000 cases that were prosecuted in New York from 1691 to 1776. Of these cases, nearly 75% involved persons of English background, most of whom were males. As seen in Table 6.1, the remaining persons were of a variety of racial and ethnic backgrounds. What stands out most in the figures is that both the Dutch and slaves had sizeable populations but were underrepresented in the criminal cases.

In the case of the Dutch, Greenberg (1976) surmised that, given that in some estimates they were nearly 50% of the population of the colony, they were likely misidentified and undercounted in the case figures. The discrepancy related to slaves was explained differently. Because they were constantly under the threat of being brutally punished, they were less likely to engage in criminal activity. Furthermore, as noted previously, virtually every aspect of slave life was controlled, which naturally resulted in fewer offenses. Greenberg (1976) also pointed out,

> [Another] factor that accounts for the apparently small volume of slave crime is that prosecutions for what was probably the most common and, from the master's point of view, the most costly of slave crimes—running away—appear very infrequently in the records, since slave runaways were seldom captured. (p. 45)

Table 6.1

Ethnic Distribution of Criminal Cases in Colonial New York, 1691–1776

Ethnic Group	Number Accused	Percentage of All Accusations
English	3,889	73.4
Dutch	693	13.1
Jewish	44	0.8
Other Whites	252	4.8
Slaves	353	6.7
Free Blacks	35	0.7
Indians	31	0.6
Total	5,297	100

Before looking at the case outcomes, it is important to review the distribution of crimes by ethnic group (see Table 6.2). The review resulted in no unusual patterns except that the English and Blacks predominated in thefts. Explaining the large number of Blacks involved in theft, Greenberg (1976) wrote,

Table 6.2

Ethnic Distribution of Major Categories of Crime in New York, 1691–1776

Crime	English	Dutch	Jews	Whites	Blacks	Indians	N
Crimes of violence*	871	156	27	65	18	3	1,140
Thefts	585	30	4	19	86	3	727
Contempt of authority	221	79	1	10	1	0	312
Crimes by public officials	137	47	0	15	0	0	199
Disorderly houses	163	17	0	10	3	0	193
Violations of public order	795	135	6	48	7	6	997
Crimes against masters**	3	0	0	0	217	8	228

* Against persons, not resulting in death.

** By servants or slaves.

Prosecutions for theft were almost twice as frequent among Blacks as in the defendant population at large. This figure is a function both of the "real" position of Blacks in the eighteenth century and prevailing ideas *about* Blacks. On the one hand, slaves stole because they were deprived, and on the other, they were deprived because people believed them inherently sinful. (p. 61)

Conviction patterns also speak to how ethnic and racial groups were treated in this early period. Here, as noted in Table 6.3, although slaves represented 6.7% of the accusations, they represented nearly 10% of all convictions (Greenberg, 1976). Tables 6.3 and 6.4 illustrates that slaves had higher conviction rates than other ethnic or racial groups, with an overall conviction rate of 68.6%. American Indians had the next highest conviction rate (51.6%). Given their status within colonial America, for obvious reasons, slaves would not have been expected to receive the same consideration as other racial or ethnic groups. Their higher conviction rates speak to their low status in American society.

Closely related to conviction trends are sentencing dispositions. Although Greenberg's (1976) analysis does not provide sentences by ethnic or racial group, he does note that the nature of punishments changed in the mid-1750s. In particular, he observed that whereas before 1750, most thefts resulted in whippings and few executions, after 1750, the number of whippings for theft dropped, whereas the use of branding and the number of executions increased dramatically. Although Greenberg did not make the connection, this change in sentencing practices could have been a response to the increasing number of racial or ethnic minorities who were engaging in theft to survive. Although the first two sections of our historical overview presented information on early cases from two distinct colonies, we now review some early national figures on race and sentencing.

Early National Sentencing Statistics

Following the Revolutionary War, in terms of treatment, little changed for racial or ethnic minorities. Although it was a major development when the new government created federal courts, including the Supreme Court, criminal justice remained a place where race and class bias persisted (Shelden, 2001). The development of these courts only provided new mechanisms to reinforce the race and class bias in state judiciaries (Shelden, 2001). Accurate sentencing trends from the 18th and 19th centuries are difficult to ascertain because there were no national statistics until the 1880 census (Cahalan & Parsons, 1986, p. 31). Taken from penitentiaries, the data in that first report revealed that "99% [of the offenders] were reported to be under sentence at the time of the survey . . . and 88% had sentences listed over 1 year" (Cahalan & Parsons, 1986, p. 31). In jails, "about 55% of the inmates were under sentence and of these only 8% had sentences of 1 year or longer" (p. 31).

The 1890 census provided even more detailed information of the characteristics of offenders, noting the ethnicity of those who were sentenced. At that time, the most severe average sentence was for crimes against the person, at 7.8 years (Cahalan & Parsons, 1986; see Table 6.5). Table 6.6 shows the average sentences by race, nativity, and gender. The figures show that Chinese received the longest average sentences (6.58 years), followed by Indians (5.64 years). When looking for the female group with the longest average sentence, Negroes were highest (2.8 years), with persons of Chinese origin closely

Table 6.3

Patterns of Judgment for Ethnic Groups in New York, 1691–1776

Ethnic Group	Number Accused	Percentage of All Accusations	Number Convicted	Percentage Convicted of Those Accused	Percentage of All Convictions	Number Acquitted	Percentage Acquitted of Those Accused	Percentage of All Acquittals
English	3,889	73.4	1,809	46.5	71.3	542	13.9	68.0
Dutch	693	13.1	329	47.5	13.0	118	17.0	14.0
Jews	44	0.8	14	31.8	0.6	16	36.4	2.0
Other Whites	252	4.8	115	45.6	4.5	48	19.0	6.0
Slaves	353	6.7	242	68.6	9.5	59	16.7	7.4
Free Blacks	35	0.7	13	37.0	0.5	6	17.1	0.8
Indians	31	0.6	16	51.6	0.6	8	25.8	1.0

Table 6.4

Conviction Patterns for Slaves in Colonial America, 1691–1776

Crimes by Slaves	Number of Accusations	Number of Convictions	Percentage Convicted of Those Accused	Percent of All Convictions Against Slaves
Thefts	69	38	55.1	15.7
Crimes against masters	214	149	69.6	61.6
Crimes against morality (all Sabbath breach)	32	32	100.0	13.2
Crimes of violence not resulting in death	16	13	81.3	5.4
Total (these crimes)	331	232	71.0	95.9
Total (all cases involving slaves)	353	242	68.6	100.0

Table 6.5

Average Sentence in Years, by Gender and Offense, 1890

Offense Against	Male	Female
Government	2.76	1.75
Society	.79	.67
Person	7.8	6.99
Property	3.9	2.29
On high seas	2.75[a]	
Other	4.67	.8

a. Not separately enumerated.

behind (2.54 years; Cahalan & Parsons, 1986). Although the data do not speak to offense trends by specific racial group, they do show that, from the earliest records available, disparities by race were present.

How far have we come in race and sentencing? Before answering this question, we examine how politics and the "get tough" philosophy have impacted sentencing over the last 30 years. The last section of the chapter takes a deeper look at contemporary issues related to race and sentencing.

Table 6.6

Average Sentence in Years, by Gender and Nativity and Race, 1890

Color, Nativity, Race	Male	Female
White	3.66	1.12
Native	3.79	1.51
Parents native	4.25	1.76
One parent foreign	3.66	1.08
Parents foreign	3.10	1.08
Unknown	2.47	1.28
Colored	5.04	2.79
Negroes	5.01	2.80
Chinese	6.58	2.54
Indians	5.64	.2

The 1980s to 2000s: The Changing Nature of Sentencing Practices

Coinciding with the 1980 election of President Ronald Reagan was the largest number of homicides in U.S. history. That year, according to the FBI's Uniform Crime Reports, there were 23,040 homicides. Pointing to this unprecedented level of violent crime, to reduce these figures, President Reagan championed a conservative and more punitive approach (Hagan, 2010). Following the lead of the federal government, most states moved away from sentencing policies that were generally more indeterminate in nature, which had allowed for minimum and maximum sentences and gave discretion to release offenders when they were thought to be rehabilitated. Observers from all sides felt such a sentencing approach was unfair and in too many instances resulted in bias against poor people and racial minorities. Nevertheless, over time, the public also bought into the punitive approach.

A 1995 national opinion survey on crime and justice of more than 1,000 randomly selected U.S. citizens revealed that when asked whether the government should focus on rehabilitation or punishing and putting away violent offenders, nearly 60% responded "punish," whereas only 27% said "rehabilitate" (Gerber & Engelhardt-Greer, 1996). There were, however, significant differences by race. Nearly half of the Black respondents (46%) indicated that rehabilitation should be the focus, with Hispanics (38%) also being more receptive to rehabilitation than Whites (23%) (Gerber & Engelhardt-Greer, 1996).

In line with national sentiment, states created "get tough" approaches such as determinate sentencing, sentencing guidelines that included mandatory minimum statutes, three-strikes-and-you're-out legislation, and truth-in-sentencing laws (Spohn, 2009). In addition to being more punitive, proponents of these approaches suggested that such policies also reduced judicial discretion, which some felt contributed to leniency in some instances and racial disparities in other instances. One of the first alternative sentencing approaches enacted by states was determinate sentencing.

In contrast to indeterminate sentencing, this approach required states to create "a presumptive range of confinement for various categories of offenses. The judge imposed a fixed number of years from within this range, and the offender would serve this term minus time off for good behavior" (Spohn, 2009, p. 231). In the few states that did enact this form of sentencing, the results were mixed; therefore, most states lost interest in the approach (Spohn, 2009).

One of the most popular sentencing approaches adapted during the 1970s was presumptive sentencing guidelines. Such guidelines based sentencing decisions on the various aspects of the crime and the offender history. According to Spohn (2009), there are several common aspects of this approach. First, there is generally some sentencing commission or committee that makes the recommendations for the guidelines. Second, the guidelines take into consideration "the severity of the offense and the seriousness of the offender's prior criminal record" (Spohn, 2009, p. 234). Finally, although this approach allows for some judicial discretion, judges who deviate from the specified sentence must justify their rationale. An often-cited example of this approach is the Minnesota Sentencing Guidelines (see Figure 6.2).

Following the lead of states, the federal government created its own guidelines. Once the Federal Sentencing Guidelines were enacted in 1984, federal parole was eliminated (Hickey, 1998). Moreover, during this process, in 1987, the U.S. Sentencing Commission was created. Spohn (2009) noted that the commission was created "to develop and implement presumptive sentencing guidelines designed to achieve 'honesty,' 'uniformity,' and 'proportionality' in sentencing" (p. 239).

Mandatory minimum sentences were created in the 1970s and 1980s in response to concerns about drug dealing and violent crimes involving guns. Such sentences stated a minimum penalty for a particular offense, and in some instances there were mandatory penalties for using a gun in the commission of a crime. Generally, the proscribed minimums were fairly harsh and provided little, if any, room for judicial discretion in sentencing. Prosecutors generally have the leeway to charge the offender with an offense that carries a particular sentence. As a result, under such an approach, prosecutors determine the nature of one's sentence (Spohn, 2009).

Popularized in the 1990s by the states of Washington and California, three-strikes-and-you're-out legislation caught on, as evidenced by the fact that "as of 2004, 23 states and the federal government had adopted some variation of the three-strikes-you're-out laws" (Spohn, 2009, p. 264). Although from state to state there were different versions of the legislation, the common theme was, like a batter in a baseball game, when an offender committed his or her third "strike" (felony offense), he or she was "out" (sentenced to 25 years to life or some other draconian sentence).

Another sentencing innovation was the Truth in Sentencing Act of 1997. Clearly falling under the incapacitation philosophy, the Act "awarded funds to states that kept their offenders—particularly those serving time for violent offenses—in prison for at least 85% of their sentences" (Blumstein, 2002, p. 461). It was anticipated that such a policy would have serious implications for preventing serious crimes and also for the size of correctional populations. It is notable that although crime did decrease during the 1990s, whether this sentencing strategy produced the reductions has been subject to debate (Blumstein & Wallman, 2005). Each of the aforementioned sentencing approaches, in varying magnitudes, contributed to

Figure 6.2

The Minnesota Sentencing Guidelines Grid

1. One year and 1 day.

2. M.S. § 244.09 requires the Sentencing Guidelines to provide a range of 15% downward and 20% upward from the presumptive sentence. However, because the statutory maximum sentence for these offenses is no more than 40 years, the range is capped at that number.

Presumptive Sentence Lengths in Months

Italicized numbers within the grid denote the range within which a judge may sentence without the sentence being deemed a departure. Offenders with non-imprisonment felony sentences are subject to jail time according to law.

SEVERITY LEVEL OF CONVICTION OFFENSE (Common offenses listed in italics)		CRIMINAL HISTORY SCORE						
		0	1	2	3	4	5	6 or more
Murder, 2nd Degree (intentional murder; drive-by-shootings)	XI	306 *261-367*	326 *278-391*	346 *295-415*	366 *312-439*	386 *329-463*	406 *346-480[2]*	426 *363-480[2]*
Murder, 3rd Degree Murder, 2nd Degree (unintentional murder)	X	150 *128-180*	165 *141-198*	180 *153-216*	195 *166-234*	210 *179-252*	225 *192-270*	240 *204-288*
Assault, 1st Degree Controlled Substance Crime, 1st Degree	IX	86 *74-103*	98 *84-117*	110 *94-132*	122 *104-146*	134 *114-160*	146 *125-175*	158 *135-189*
Aggravated Robbery, 1st Degree Controlled Substance Crime, 2nd Degree	VIII	48 *41-57*	58 *50-69*	68 *58-81*	78 *67-93*	88 *75-105*	98 *84-117*	108 *92-129*
Felony DWI	VII	36	42	48	54 *46-64*	60 *51-72*	66 *57-79*	72 *62-86*
Assault, 2nd Degree Felon in Possession of a Firearm	VI	21	27	33	39 *34-46*	45 *39-54*	51 *44-61*	57 *49-68*
Residential Burglary Simple Robbery	V	18	23	28	33 *29-39*	38 *33-45*	43 *37-51*	48 *41-57*
Nonresidential Burglary	IV	12[1]	15	18	21	24 *21-28*	27 *23-32*	30 *26-36*
Theft Crimes (Over $2,500)	III	12[1]	13	15	17	19 *17-22*	21 *18-25*	23 *20-27*
Theft Crimes ($2,500 or less) Check Forgery ($200-$2,500)	II	12[1]	12[1]	13	15	17	19	21 *18-25*
Sale of Simulated Controlled Substance	I	12[1]	12[1]	12[1]	13	15	17	19 *17-22*

☐ Presumptive commitment to state imprisonment. First Degree Murder is excluded from the guidelines by law and continues to have a mandatory life sentence. See section II.E. Mandatory Sentences for policy regarding those sentences controlled by law.

☐ Presumptive stayed sentence; at the discretion of the judge, up to a year in jail and/or other non-jail sanctions can be imposed as conditions of probation. However, certain offenses in this section of the grid always carry a presumptive commitment to state prison. See sections II.C. Presumptive Sentence and II.E. Mandatory Sentences.

an increasing number of persons being incarcerated (see Chapter 8). In fact, many of those who bore the brunt of such policies were poor persons and racial minorities. Another set of legislative enactments from the 1980s through the 2000s, which influenced the nature of sentencing, targeted the "**War on Drugs**."

The "War on Drugs"

Declaring a "War on Drugs" in the late 1980s was also a major contributor to the increase in punitive sentencing policies during the last 20 years. Beginning with Ronald Reagan and taking shape under George H. W. Bush, the White House Office of National Drug Control Policy, which was officially established under the Anti-Drug Abuse Act of 1988 and extended under the Violent Crime Control and Law Enforcement Act of 1994, was created to "establish policies, priorities, and objectives for the Nation's drug control program" (Office of National Drug Control Policy, n.d.). In line with its purpose, "The goals of the program are to reduce illicit drug use, manufacturing, and trafficking, drug-related crime and violence, and drug-related health consequences" (Office of National Drug Control Policy, n.d.). In some ways, the role of the director (also referred to as the "drug czar") is symbolic in that that person is the face of drug control for each president. Although the director drafts and promotes the annual *National Drug Control Strategy* (2011) report, he or she does not actually carry out the activities proposed to meet its goals. Nevertheless, because the director is a component of the Executive Office of the President, he or she does "[advise] the President regarding changes in the organization, management, budgeting, and personnel of Federal Agencies that could affect the Nation's anti-drug efforts; and regarding Federal agency compliance with their obligations under the Strategy" (Office of National Drug Control Policy, n.d.).

With such an influential role, the director can push either punitive or treatment-oriented drug-control strategies. However, given that the position is an appointed one, it is likely that the director will simply follow the party line on most issues. Again, as in the sentencing strategies discussed in the previous section, the party line on such issues in the 1980s and early 1990s was punitive in orientation. Even with the election of President Bill Clinton (a Democrat) and the appointment of Lee P. Brown as director, who championed rehabilitative and education-oriented initiatives, such punitive approaches had become so institutionalized that during Clinton's administration one of the most punitive crime bills in history was enacted. During the 2000s, the collateral consequences of two decades of the punitive ideology had actually brought the system back to rehabilitation. Why? Because states finally realized that they could not afford to maintain the correctional building programs of the 1980s and 1990s. As such, states were increasingly looking for ways to divert or release non-violent drug offenders—an option that was not on the table during the height of the "War on Drugs." We return to this issue later in the chapter.

❖ Contemporary Issues in Race and Sentencing

We begin our discussion of contemporary issues with a review of current sentencing patterns at the state and federal levels. Following this initial discussion, we examine race and sentencing scholarship, as well as the role of judges in **sentencing disparities**.

Felony Convictions in State Courts

In 2006, more than 1.1 million adults were convicted of a felony in state courts; nearly 70% of them were sentenced to either jail (28%) or prison (41%), with the remainder being sentenced to probation (Rosenmerkel et al., 2009). In 2006, the average sentence was 4 years and 11 months. For those who committed murder and nonnegligent manslaughter, the average was 20 years. In line with the arrest statistics presented in Chapter 2, most persons convicted for felony offenses were Whites; however, Blacks were overrepresented in nearly every category (see Table 6.7). In 2006, for example, Blacks, who make up 12% of the population, represented 38% of those persons convicted of a felony in state courts and 39% of convicted felons who committed a violent crime. Other races (American Indians, Alaska Natives, Asian and Pacific Islanders) represented 2% of all felony convictions and the same percentage of convictions for violent crime ((Rosenmerkel et al., 2009). Table 6.8 provides a glimpse of the different sentences being received by Blacks and Whites for certain offenses.

Table 6.7

Gender and Race of Persons Convicted of Felonies in State Courts, by Offense, 2006

| Most serious conviction offense | Total | Gender | | Race | | |
		Male	Female	White	Black	Other[a]
All offenses	100 %	83	17	60	38	2
Violent offenses	100 %	89	11	58	39	3
Murder/nonnegligent manslaughter	100 %	90	10	46	51	3
Sexual assault	100 %	97	3	74	24	3
Rape	100 %	96	4	70	28	2
Other sexual assault[b]	100 %	97	3	77	21	2
Robbery	100 %	91	9	42	57	1
Aggravated assault	100 %	86	14	59	39	3
Other violent[c]	100 %	88	12	69	28	3
Property offenses	100 %	75	25	65	33	3
Burglary	100 %	90	10	66	32	2
Larceny	100 %	75	25	64	34	2
Motor vehicle theft	100 %	86	14	70	26	5
Fraud/forgery[d]	100 %	59	41	66	32	2

Most serious conviction offense	Percent of convicted felons					
	Total	Gender		Race		
		Male	Female	White	Black	Other[a]
Drug offenses	100 %	82	18	55	44	1
Possession	100 %	80	20	62	36	2
Trafficking	100 %	83	17	50	49	1
Weapon offenses	100 %	95	5	43	55	2
Other specified offenses[e]	100 %	87	13	67	30	3

Note: Data on gender were reported for 86% of convicted felons and data on race for 74%. Detail may not sum to total because of rounding. Racial categories include persons of Latino or Hispanic origin.

a. Includes American Indians, Alaska Natives, Asians, Native Hawaiians, and other Pacific Islanders.

b. Includes offenses such as statutory rape and incest with a minor.

c. Includes offenses such as negligent manslaughter and kidnapping.

d. Includes embezzlement.

e. Comprises nonviolent offenses such as vandalism and receiving stolen property.

Table 6.8

Type of Felony Sentences Imposed in State Courts, by Offense and Race of Felons, 2006

Most serious conviction offense	Percent of felons sentenced to—					
	Total	Incarceration			Nonincarceration	
		Total	Prison	Jail	Total	Probation	Other
White							
All offenses	100 %	66	37	29	34	29	4
Violent offenses	100 %	74	52	23	26	22	3
Murder/nonnegligent manslaughter	100 %	93	92	2	7	4	3
Sexual assault[a]	100 %	81	64	16	19	16	4
Robbery	100 %	83	70	14	17	15	2
Aggravated assault	100 %	69	40	29	31	27	3
Other violent[b]	100 %	68	40	28	32	27	4
Property offenses	100 %	65	36	29	35	30	5
Burglary	100 %	71	46	25	29	25	4
Larceny	100 %	66	32	34	34	30	4
Fraud/forgery[c]	100 %	59	31	27	41	35	6

(Continued)

(Continued)

Most serious conviction offense	Total	Percent of felons sentenced to—					
		Incarceration			Nonincarceration		
		Total	Prison	Jail	Total	Probation	Other
Drug offenses	100 %	61	31	30	39	34	5
Possession	100 %	63	28	35	37	33	4
Trafficking	100 %	59	33	26	41	35	6
Weapon offenses	100 %	73	45	28	27	23	4
Other specified offenses[d]	100 %	69	34	35	31	27	4
Black							
All offenses	100 %	72	45	27	28	25	4
Violent offenses	100 %	78	58	20	22	19	3
Murder/nonnegligent manslaughter	100 %	95	93	2	5	3	2
Sexual assault[a]	100 %	80	65	15	20	16	4
Robbery	100 %	86	71	14	14	12	2
Aggravated assault	100 %	72	46	26	28	23	4
Other violent[b]	100 %	68	37	31	32	28	4
Property offenses	100 %	69	41	28	31	27	4
Burglary	100 %	78	57	20	22	20	3
Larceny	100 %	69	36	33	31	28	3
Fraud/forgery[c]	100 %	60	30	30	40	35	5
Drug offenses	100 %	70	43	27	30	25	4
Possession	100 %	71	38	33	29	24	5
Trafficking	100 %	70	46	25	30	26	4
Weapon offenses	100 %	73	45	28	27	25	2
Other specified offenses[d]	100 %	70	38	31	30	27	3

Note: For persons receiving a combination of sentences, the sentence designation came from the most severe penalty imposed—prison being the most severe, followed by jail, probation, and then other sentences, such as a fine, community service, or treatment. Prison includes death sentences. In this table, *probation* is defined as straight probation. Details may not sum to total because of rounding. Racial categories include persons of Latino or Hispanic origin.

a. Includes rape.

b. Includes offenses such as negligent manslaughter and kidnapping.

c. Includes embezzlement.

d. Comprises nonviolent offenses such as vandalism and receiving stolen property.

Convictions in Federal Courts

In addition to state-level data, there are also data on offenders convicted in federal court. In fiscal year 2010, the **United States Sentencing Commission** reported more than 83,000 convictions for offenses at the federal level (see Table 6.9). The average sentence for federal offenders is 44.3 months or 3.7 years. At the federal level, those offenders convicted of homicide serve approximately 23 years, or roughly 3 more years than murderers convicted in state courts. Table 6.10 provides information on the number of convictions in the assorted offense categories, as well as the race/ethnicity of the offenders. Here we see that Blacks—and especially Hispanics—are overrepresented as offenders in the federal system. Strikingly, the Black (20.7%), Hispanic (48.1%), and Other (3.6%) categories represent 72% of the offenders in the federal system. A cursory examination of the data suggests that these numbers are being driven by offenses related to drug trafficking, firearm violations, and immigration offenses. Unquestionably, as we have highlighted in other chapters, immigration is a major concern. This is borne out by the immigration figures presented in Table 6.10, in which Hispanics represented 87.1% of the offenders—a figure that amounted to a whopping 21,009 offenders, or approximately 25% of the total number of federal offenders.

Table 6.9

Average Sentence Length in Each Primary Offense Category, Fiscal Year 2010

Primary Offense	Mean Months	Median Months	N
TOTAL	44.3	21.0	83,919
Murder	276.1	251.0	66
Manslaughter	72.6	44.0	64
Kidnapping/hostage taking	162.7	144.0	39
Sexual Abuse	108.6	96.0	384
Assault	37.6	24.0	631
Robbery	76.8	62.0	1,081
Arson	78.6	60.0	75
Drugs: Trafficking	74.9	60.0	23,503
Drugs: Communication facility	34.3	32.0	512
Drugs: Simple possession	3.4	3.0	1,024

(Continued)

(Continued)

Primary Offense	Mean Months	Median Months	N
Firearms	85.0	57.0	7,984
Burglary/breaking and entering	16.7	13.5	36
Auto Theft	51.0	24.0	91
Larceny	7.6	0.0	1,617
Fraud	23.2	10.0	8,065
Embezzlement	7.8	3.0	434
Forgery/counterfeiting	14.4	12.0	880
Bribery	19.7	12.0	224
Tax	16.3	12.0	665
Money laundering	30.6	15.0	806
Racketeering/extortion	76.7	44.0	675
Gambling/lottery	6.0	5.0	76
Civil rights	22.5	12.0	61
Immigration	16.8	10.0	28,496
Child pornography	118.0	80.0	1,886
Prison offenses	15.4	12.0	424
Administration of justice offenses	18.1	12.0	1,157
Environmental/wildlife	3.0	0.0	188
National defense	53.5	34.0	69
Antitrust	7.4	8.0	16
Food and drug	10.3	0.0	84
Other miscellaneous offenses	10.4	0.0	2,606

Note: Of the 83,946 cases, 27 were excluded due to missing or indeterminable sentencing information. Sentences of probation only are included in this table as zero months of imprisonment. In addition, the information presented in this table includes time of confinement as described in USSG §5C1.1.

Table 6.10

Race of Offenders in Each Primary Offense Category, Fiscal Year 2010

Primary Offense	Total	White		Black		Hispanic		Other	
		N	%	N	%	N	%	N	%
Total	75,378	20,796	27.6	15,613	20.7	36,293	48.1	2,676	3.6
Murder	65	18	27.7	8	12.3	7	10.8	32	49.2
Manslaughter	64	1	1.6	4	6.3	8	12.5	51	79.7
Kidnapping/Hostage Taking	38	7	18.4	6	15.8	23	60.5	2	5.3
Sexual Abuse	383	171	44.6	40	10.4	31	8.1	141	36.8
Assault	550	151	27.5	109	19.8	78	14.2	212	38.5
Robbery	1,075	479	44.6	428	39.8	130	12.1	38	3.5
Arson	75	44	58.7	10	13.3	6	8.0	15	20.0
Drugs: Trafficking	23,382	6,087	26.0	6,169	26.4	10,378	44.4	748	3.2
Drugs: Communication Facility	508	124	24.4	191	37.6	173	34.1	20	3.9
Drugs: Simple Possession	282	147	52.1	57	20.2	67	23.8	11	3.9
Firearms	7,917	2,293	29.0	3,961	50.0	1,449	18.3	214	2.7
Burglary/breaking and entering	34	4	11.8	4	11.8	2	5.9	24	70.6
Auto Theft	91	46	50.5	17	18.7	26	28.6	2	2.2
Larceny	1,321	659	49.9	422	31.9	156	11.8	84	6.4
Fraud	6,820	3,200	46.9	2,074	30.4	1,190	17.4	356	5.2

(Continued)

(Continued)

Primary Offense	Total	White		Black		Hispanic		Other	
		N	%	N	%	N	%	N	%
Embezzlement	404	239	59.2	84	20.8	36	8.9	45	11.1
Forgery/Counterfeiting	868	388	44.7	324	37.3	137	15.8	19	2.2
Bribery	220	107	48.6	56	25.5	38	17.3	19	8.6
Tax	655	435	66.4	95	14.5	72	11.0	53	8.1
Money Laundering	779	283	36.3	114	14.6	307	39.4	75	9.6
Racketeering/Extortion	664	220	33.1	198	29.8	207	31.2	39	5.9
Gambling/Lottery	75	58	77.3	7	9.3	5	6.7	5	6.7
Civil Rights	58	39	67.2	10	17.2	9	15.5	0	0.0
Immigration	24,124	2,500	10.4	463	1.9	21,009	87.1	152	0.6
Child Pornography	1,878	1,665	88.7	59	3.1	118	6.3	36	1.9
Prison Offenses	392	102	26.0	122	31.1	129	32.9	39	9.9
Administration of Justice Offenses	1,097	471	42.9	271	24.7	265	24.2	90	8.2
Environmental/Wildlife	124	95	76.6	5	4.0	8	6.5	16	12.9
National Defense	67	22	32.8	5	7.5	28	41.8	12	17.9
Antitrust	13	11	84.6	0	0.0	0	0.0	2	15.4
Food and Drug	67	48	71.6	1	1.5	8	11.9	10	14.9
Other Miscellaneous Offenses	1,288	682	53.0	299	23.2	193	15.0	114	8.9

Note: Of the 83,946 cases, 8,568 were excluded due to missing race.

Given the large numbers of Blacks and Hispanics convicted of felony offenses in either state or federal courts, the next question is whether there are racial disparities in sentencing. In recent years, there has been an explosion of literature investigating this question. We review some of these studies next.

Scholarship on Race and Sentencing

In the past two decades, there have been numerous studies examining the relationship between race and sentencing. To provide context for these studies, we review several comprehensive studies that provide baseline summaries on the topic up to 2002 (Chiricos & Crawford, 1995; O. Mitchell, 2005; Pratt, 1998; Spohn, 2000; Zatz, 1987). Following a review of these studies, more recent studies are examined.

Zatz's Four Waves of Race and Sentencing Research

Separating sentencing research into four waves, Zatz (1987) provided a summary of the diverse research on race and sentencing. During Wave I (1930s to mid-1960s), the literature "showed clear and consistent bias against non-Whites in sentencing" (p. 71). Most of the early research suggested that Blacks and foreigners received biased sentences in the courts. A noted concern of this early research was its lack of methodological sophistication. On this point, Zatz wrote, "These studies were flawed by a number of serious methodological problems. The most damning flaw was the lack of controls for legally relevant factors, especially prior record" (p. 72).

Wave II (late 1960s to 1970s) followed on the heels of the successful civil rights movement. During this period, studies began to emerge that indicated that discrimination in sentencing had subsided. Moreover, more sophisticated studies began to suggest "that minorities were overrepresented in the criminal justice system and prisons because of their greater proportional involvement in crime, and not because of any bias in the system" (Zatz, 1987, p. 73). Studies were also beginning to show that race might have a "cumulative effect" by indirectly impacting minority offenders through other variables. In addition, "extralegal attributes of the offender could *interact* with other factors to influence decision making" (p. 73).

In Wave III (studies conducted in the 1970s and 1980s), the Wave II studies that suggested discrimination had subsided were reanalyzed and produced different results. Previously unaccounted for in earlier studies, Zatz (1987) noted that, "depending on the degree of victimization and the relative social harm perceived, minority members were treated more harshly in some situations and Whites in others" (p. 74). In addition, Zatz pointed to selection bias and specification error as two other common problems with earlier research. Here, she was concerned that some people were dropped out of study samples too early in the process, which can invalidate the results of studies. With specification error, in some instances, researchers were not considering interaction effects. Such effects highlight when

race/ethnicity can operate *indirectly* through its effect on other factors. It can interact with other variables to affect sentencing. That is, the impact of other variables (e.g., prior record, type of offense) could differ, depending on the defendant's race/ethnicity. (p. 75)

Another important type of indirect effect is referred to as "cumulative disadvantage." Here, race/ethnicity has a small effect on the initial stages of the process; however, "as the person moves through the system, these add up to substantial, and often statistically significant, disparities in processing and outcomes for different social groups" (Zatz, 1987, p. 76).

At the time of the publication of her article, Zatz (1987) indicated that Wave IV (data from the late 1970s to 1980s, conducted in the 1980s) was underway and substantive issues were emerging. Determinate sentencing was beginning to garner significant attention. Researchers were beginning to investigate the outcomes produced by this sentencing strategy.

Race and Sentencing Research in the 1990s

Eight years after the publication of Zatz's article, Chiricos and Crawford (1995) provided an updated summary of the literature on race and sentencing. Their review centered on whether African Americans were "more often sentenced to prison upon conviction" (p. 281). Moreover, they also wanted to see whether region (particularly the South), the percentage of Black population as a whole or percentage of Black population that is urban, and unemployment were influential in sentencing outcomes. To investigate the influence of these factors, Chiricos and Crawford examined 38 studies published over a 16-year period (1975–1991). In terms of the effect of region, most studies, even after controlling for prior record and crime seriousness, showed that Blacks were more likely to be incarcerated than Whites. Furthermore, Chiricos and Crawford found that "in no instance is the incarceration of White defendants significantly more likely in the south" (p. 297).

When reviewing the results of studies that examined the percentage of Blacks in the population, Chiricos and Crawford (1995) noted that "it is clear that Black defendants are disadvantaged much more often when the Black population exceeds the national average than when it does not" (p. 298). Relatedly, when they reviewed the influence of percentage of Black defendants who are urban, their results paralleled those of their regional comparison. As Chiricos and Crawford noted, "The disadvantage to Black defendants, as measured by significant positive results, is approximately twice as great in places where they are *less* concentrated in urban areas than in places where they are *more* concentrated" (p. 299). In their final area of focus, unemployment, Chiricos and Crawford found that "the disadvantage of Black defendants is more consistently demonstrated for places with higher levels of unemployment" (p. 299).

Picking up where Chiricos and Crawford (1995) left off, Pratt (1998) conducted a meta-analysis of the race and sentencing research. His analysis included race and sentencing studies published in social science journals from 1974 to 1996. In contrast to the earlier summaries of the extant race and sentencing literature, he found that "the severity of the offense is the only significant variable related to length of sentence. . . . Neither race nor prior criminal record variables were found to be significant" (p. 517). Pratt did note that one explanation for this finding was the way in which race was operationalized in some studies. As an example, he notes that it matters whether studies use the Black/White or White/Non-White categories. More specifically, he found that "When the race variable takes the form of a White/non-White classification scheme, the likelihood of finding a significant race effect on sentence length is greater than for either of the two other racial classification schemes" (p. 518).

Race and Sentencing Research in the 2000s

Two years after Pratt's work, Spohn (2000) examined 40 methodologically sophisticated studies on race and sentencing (32 on state sentencing and 8 on federal sentencing). In her review, she noted two considerable limitations. First, most of the studies reviewed centered on Black and White defendants; few of them explored beyond this racial dichotomy. In addition, although she reviewed 32 state-level studies, only 13 states were represented. Concluding her review of these studies, Spohn wrote,

> Considered together . . . race and ethnicity do play an important role in contemporary sentencing decisions. Black and Hispanic offenders sentenced in State and Federal courts face significantly greater odds of incarceration than similarly situated White offenders. In some jurisdictions, they also may receive longer sentences or differential benefits from guideline departures than their White counterparts. (p. 458)

More specifically, the studies revealed interaction effects between race/ethnicity and several legally irrelevant offender characteristics. Studies reviewed by Spohn (2000) showed that "Racial minorities are sentenced more harshly than Whites if they (1) are young and male, (2) are unemployed, (3) are male and unemployed, (4) are young, male, and unemployed, (5) have lower incomes, and (6) have less education" (p. 462).

Spohn (2000) also found that, in several studies, when looking at the interaction between the offenders' race and process-related factors, "Racial minorities are sentenced more harshly than Whites if they (1) are detained in jail prior to trial, (2) are represented by a public defender rather than a private attorney, (3) are convicted at trial rather than by plea, and (4) have more serious prior criminal records" (p. 462). Other studies looking at the interaction between offender race and victim race revealed that "racial minorities who victimize Whites are sentenced more harshly than other race of offender/race of victim combinations" (p. 463). Finally, Spohn's review found studies that showed interaction effects between offender race and type of crime: "Racial minorities are sentenced more harshly than Whites if they are (1) convicted of less serious crimes, or (2) convicted of drug offenses or more serious drug offenses" (p. 463).

Following Spohn's (2000) comprehensive review, researchers continued to examine the question of race and sentencing (Engen et al., 2003; B. Johnson, 2003; Steffensmeier & Britt, 2001; Steffensmeier & Demuth, 2000, 2001; Ulmer & Johnson, 2004), and, unfortunately, they continued to find that race and ethnicity matters in the sentencing process. For example, an increasing finding in studies of both state (Steffensmeier & Demuth, 2001) and federal (Steffensmeier & Demuth, 2000) courts is that Hispanics are receiving the harshest sentences. In addition, studies are beginning to look at more contextual factors, noting that African Americans and Hispanics tend to be sentenced more harshly in areas where they are the majority populations (Ulmer & Johnson, 2004).

In the mid-2000s, a meta-analysis by Mitchell (2005) again sought to determine whether race matters in a large selection of empirical studies. Mitchell's analysis included both published and unpublished studies (e.g., dissertations). In all, he whittled down 331 studies to 71 that met his rigorous criteria for inclusion in the meta-analysis. In contrast to Pratt's earlier work, Mitchell (2005) found that "even after taking into account offense seriousness and prior criminal history, African-Americans were punished more harshly than whites" (p. 456). He did note, however, that

> the observed differences between whites and African-Americans generally were small, suggesting that discrimination in the sentencing stage is not the primary cause of overrepresentation of African-Americans in U.S. correctional facilities. The size of unwarranted sentencing disparities grows considerably, however, when contrasts examined drug offenses, imprisonment decisions, discretionary sentencing decisions, and recently collected Federal data. (p. 462)

Although some of the recent research has continued to find that Blacks and Hispanics are more likely to be prosecuted (Crow & Johnson, 2008) and treated more harshly (Brennan & Spohn, 2008; Spohn & Brennan, 2011) than Whites, other recent research (examining federal sentencing data) has found that Blacks had longer sentences than Whites, but Hispanic sentences were not significantly longer than those received by Whites (Feldmeyer & Ulmer, 2011). Feldmeyer and Ulmer also found that "district percentages of Blacks and Hispanics make no difference in terms of the average district sentence lengths of *all* defendants" (p. 254).

Another recent study by Johnson and Betsinger (2009) explored whether Asian Americans were sentenced any differently than other racial ethnic minorities in federal courts. In other words, they studied whether the positive "model minority" stereotype influences sentencing outcomes. Using data from the U.S. Sentencing Commission, the authors found that punishments were race graded, in that "Black and Hispanic offenders typically receive more severe outcomes than their similarly situated white counterparts, whereas Asian offenders do not" (p. 1076). In particular, young Asian offenders did not receive as severe sentences as young Black and Hispanic males—especially in terms of incarceration decisions. The researchers also found that citizenship status worked against Blacks and Hispanics, as compared to Asians. Taken together, the research supported the "model minority" thesis in that Asians were treated more leniently than not only Blacks and Hispanics, but Whites as well.

Given the breadth and contradictions of the race and sentencing literature, we now look at a few other important areas. Our specific areas of foci include sentencing disparities related to race and misdemeanor sentencing, the "War on Drugs," and the impact of minority judges in reducing sentencing disparities. To determine the extent of racial disparities in sentencing, we turn to studies that have considered the role of race/ethnicity and misdemeanor sentencing.

Race and Misdemeanor Sentencing

Although much of the research reviewed earlier focused on felony defendants, studies have examined race and misdemeanor. Munoz and McMorris (2002) reviewed more than 8,000 misdemeanor cases in Nebraska to determine whether racial/ethnic bias was present. Their analysis found that, in line with studies focusing on felony sentencing,

> Non-Whites in comparison to Whites were charged with more serious misdemeanors and more total number of offenses. Latinos experienced unfavorable outcomes

in comparison to Whites, but not to the extent Native Americans did. In addition to having the highest average total number of offenses, Native Americans were most likely to find themselves charged with alcohol/drug, property, and assault-related offenses. (p. 254)

Mirroring felony studies, legal variables such as prior record and seriousness of the offense were the best predictors of sentence severity. Extralegal factors such as race and gender were also contributors to the observed disparities (see also Munoz, McMorris, & DeLisi, 2005; Munoz & Freng, 2008).

Leiber and Blowers (2003) tested whether, in the case of misdemeanor offenses, African Americans were punished more severely than Whites. With a sample of more than 1,700 defendants, they examined the influence of extralegal variables (race, age) and legal variables (crime type, weapons use, property loss, and prior arrest). The findings of Leiber and Blowers revealed that "race does not have a direct effect on the conviction and incarceration decisions" (p. 477). They contextualized their findings by noting that the race effect was indirect. That is, in their study, the race effect was masked through the procedural variables of case status and continuance. On this finding they wrote,

> The prioritizing of a case and not having a continuance increase the chances of being convicted and incarcerated. Because African Americans are more likely to have their case classified as a priority and not have a continuance, they have a greater probability than Whites to be convicted and incarcerated. (p. 477)

Brennan (2006) examined a sample of female misdemeanants from New York City courts to determine whether there were any racial/ethnic disparities in sentencing. By restricting her sample to females, she was able to take a more critical look at outcomes among females. Her study of nearly 700 Black, Hispanic, and White females revealed that race/ethnicity did not directly affect sentencing outcomes. The study did, however, find that

> class discrimination resulted in indirect racial discrimination. Both Black and Hispanic women were less likely to be high school graduates than White women. They were also less likely to be employed. Ultimately, both limited educational attainment and unemployment indirectly increased the chances that Black and Hispanic women serve jail terms. (p. 89)

Golub, Johnson, and Dunlap (2007) examined whether misdemeanor marijuana arrests during the height of the "quality of life" policing initiative in New York City discriminated against Blacks and Hispanics. In particular, the authors investigated "marijuana in public view" arrests in New York City from 1980 to 2003. Their analysis found that Blacks and Hispanics were overrepresented in the marijuana in public view arrests. The disparities persisted as the authors analyzed several additional aspect of the data. Specifically, Blacks and Hispanics were more likely than Whites to be detained, and they were also two times more likely to be convicted of marijuana in public view offenses than Whites (p. 149). Golub et al. concluded that Blacks and Hispanics were punished more severely than Whites.

Each of these studies reviewed in this section provides evidence (either direct or indirect) that racial disparities in sentencing are not limited to felony cases. The "War on Drugs" has also been suggested as a substantial contributor to racial disparities in criminal justice. This is discussed next.

Sentencing Disparities and the "War on Drugs"

As noted earlier in the chapter, the "War on Drugs" rang in a new era of punitive sanctions. Unfortunately, as has been noted by several researchers, minorities have been impacted most by the war (Donzinger, 1996; J. Miller, 1996; Mitchell, 2009; Tonry, 1995). On the federal level alone, Tonry (1995) noted that, in 1980, drug offenders represented 22% of the admissions to institutions, but by 1989, this had risen to 39%, and by 1990, this had risen to 42%. Strikingly, by 1992, 58% of federal inmates were drug offenders (Tonry, 1995). At the state level, Shelden and Brown (2003) noted that, "between 1980 and 1992, sentences on drug charges increased by more than 1,000%" (p. 252). They continued by noting that when taking race into consideration, "The number of African Americans sentenced to prison on drug charges increased by over 90%, almost three times greater than White offenders" (p. 252). Shelden and Brown also pointed to figures that show that, during the 10-year period of 1985 to 1995, "the number of African American inmates sentenced for drug offenses increased by 700%" (p. 252). Reflecting on the striking figures related to race and the War on Drugs, Tonry (2011) recently had the following to say:

> So there it is. When all the relevant data are pulled together, it is clear that black people bear most of the brunt of the War on Drugs. It is also clear that racial disparities among people imprisoned for drug offenses arise primarily from racial profiling by police, deliberate police policies to focus drug law enforcement on inner-city drug markets, and deliberate legislative decisions to attach the longest prison sentences to drug offenses for which blacks are disproportionately arrested. I have purposely not used the word racism to this point, but it is difficult not to wonder. (p. 75)

During the mid-1980s to mid-1990s, crack cocaine became a significant concern for the government, which led to the formulation of differential mandatory minimum penalties. For example, someone with 500 grams of powder cocaine would receive a mandatory minimum sentence of 5 years, whereas someone with 5 grams of crack cocaine would receive the same 5-year mandatory minimum penalty. For those caught with 50 grams of crack cocaine, the mandatory minimum penalty was 10 years, whereas those caught with 5,000 grams of powder cocaine also received a 10-year mandatory minimum sentence. Unfortunately, although minorities are overrepresented in the use of crack cocaine, the majority of those who use crack cocaine are White, yet most of those serving time under these federal policies are African Americans and Hispanics (Russell-Brown, 2004).

Tracing the origin of this much-maligned 100-to-1 crack cocaine-to-powder cocaine sentencing differential, Russell (1998) suggested that the sudden death of University of Maryland basketball star Len Bias contributed to this "moral panic" or unsupported fear about crack cocaine (Brownstein, 1996; Jenkins, 1994). Because Bias's death was initially linked to crack cocaine, a cheaper form of cocaine, many public officials felt that this was a sign that crack would devastate the Black community.

It is important to note that, in the ensuing legislative debates, according to Kennedy (1997), Black legislators such as Charles Rangel and Major Owens argued vociferously for their legislative colleagues to move quickly in drafting legislation to head off a potential epidemic in the African American community. Although Kennedy noted that the legislators didn't call for the differential penalties that ensued, "Eleven of the twenty-one Blacks who were then members of the House of Representatives voted in favor of the law which created the 100–1 crack-powder differential" (p. 370).

Many observers would agree the early efforts to stave off an impending epidemic were noble, but others have argued that because of these actions, an "incarceration epidemic" ensued (Mauer, 1999; Radosh, 2008; Tonry, 1995). Moreover, once it became clear that the sentencing differential was leading to massive incarceration disparities, in 1995 and 1997, the government had two opportunities to rectify the situation. But according to Russell (1998), Congress overwhelmingly voted against taking such action, although it was recommended by the U.S. Sentencing Commission. To the surprise of many in the African American community, President Clinton did not follow the recommendations of the Commission. In response to this inaction, prisoners at several federal correctional facilities rioted (Russell, 1998). Congress returned to the matter in 2002, when the Senate held hearings on the federal cocaine policy (see U.S. Senate, 2002). In preparation for this congressional hearing, in 2002, the U.S. Sentencing Commission produced the report, *Cocaine and Federal Sentencing Policy.*

The Commission based its report on empirical analyses of federal cocaine offenders sentenced in 1995 and 2000, a survey of state cocaine sentencing policies, public opinion, and public hearings. From these sources, the Commission reported the following four major findings: (a) current penalties exaggerate the relative harmlessness of crack cocaine, (b) current penalties sweep too broadly and apply most often to lower level offenders, (c) current quantity-based penalties overstate the seriousness of most crack cocaine offenses and fail to provide adequate proportionality, and (d) current penalties' severity impact mostly minorities (U.S. Sentencing Commission, 2002, pp. v–viii).

With the first finding, the Commission recognized that the form of cocaine is irrelevant; either crack or powder cocaine "produces the same physiological and psychotropic effects" (U.S. Sentencing Commission, 2002, p. v). In addition, speaking to the short-lived, unsuccessful, and, some believe, racism-based attempt of some states (e.g., South Carolina and Kentucky) to prosecute mothers (who happened to be overwhelmingly Black) who used drugs during pregnancy (Kennedy, 1997; Russell-Brown, 2004), the Commission noted that "the negative effects of prenatal crack cocaine exposure are identical to the negative effects of prenatal powder cocaine exposure and are significantly less severe than previously believed" (U.S. Sentencing Commission, 2002, pp. v–vi). Equally important, the Commission added that "the negative effects from prenatal cocaine exposure are similar to those associated with prenatal tobacco exposure and less severe than the negative effects of prenatal alcohol exposure" (p. vi).

Under the second finding, the Commission noted that more than a quarter of the federal crack cocaine offenses involved small quantities (less than 25 grams). In contrast, "Only 2.7% of federal powder cocaine offenses involved less than 25 grams of the drug, perhaps because the statutory minimum penalties would not apply to such a small quantity of powder cocaine" (U.S. Sentencing Commission, 2002, p. vi). If what the Commission surmised is true, then those dealing in powder cocaine actually have the law on their side. To further illustrate the nature of the sentencing disparity in practice, the Commission provided the following figures:

Defendants convicted of trafficking less than 25 grams of powder cocaine received an average sentence of 13.6 months, just over one year. In contrast, defendants convicted of trafficking an equivalent amount of crack received an average sentence of 64.8 months, over five years. (p. vi)

The third finding by the Commission argued that the crack cocaine–violence link was unsupported by the empirical evidence. As they reported, "In 2000 . . . three-quarters of federal crack cocaine offenders had no personal weapon involvement, and only 2.3% discharged a weapon" (U.S. Sentencing Commission, 2002, p. vii). In the Commission's view, the penalty "sweeps too broadly" and does not acknowledge that, although some crack cocaine offenders do engage in violence, the majority do not. The final finding discussed by the Commission was that minorities were hit hardest by the current cocaine penalties. They noted that, in 2000, 85% of those impacted by the crack cocaine penalties were Black, whereas only 31% of those impacted by the powder cocaine laws were Black.

Taking their findings into consideration, the Commission provided three recommendations. First, they recommended "increas[ing] the five-year mandatory minimum threshold quantity for crack cocaine offenses to at least 25 grams and the ten-year threshold quantity to at least 250 grams (and repeal the mandatory minimum for simple possession of crack cocaine)" (U.S. Sentencing Commission, 2002, p. viii). Second, rather than having a blanket mandatory minimum sentence, they recommended providing sentencing enhancements based on the nature of the offense. Such enhancements would take into consideration whether a weapon was used, bodily injury occurred, the person was a repeat offender, and so on. Finally, the Commission recommended maintaining the current powder cocaine thresholds, but also incorporating the said sentencing enhancements.

Five years later, the Commission returned to the topic with another report, *Cocaine and Federal Sentencing Policy* (2007). The Commission returned to similar themes from the 2002 report, noting the continuing "universal criticism from representatives of the Judiciary, criminal justice practitioners, academics, and community interest groups" (p. 2). In addition, the report noted that the major conclusions from the 2002 report remained valid. During 2007, however, the Commission had the benefit of two Supreme Court cases that provided additional impetus to change the disparity. The cases of *Blakely v. Washington* (2004) and *United States v. Booker* (2005) both involved issues related to sentencing. In the *Blakely* case, the Court ruled that judges could not enhance penalties based on facts outside of those noted by the jury and the offender. In doing so, they violated one's Sixth Amendment rights to a jury trial. In the *Booker* case, the Court affirmed this decision. Thus, when mandatory sentences are in place and they go against a jury's findings, the judge can view such mandatory penalties as being advisory. Consequently, the draconian mandatory crack cocaine sentences can be seen as advisory, and, with these decisions, judicial discretion was permissible. In December 2007, the Supreme Court ruled in the case of *Kimbrough v. United States* that mandatory crack penalties were advisory in nature and judges could take into account the crack and powder cocaine disparities when sentencing. Given all these significant cases and the longstanding efforts of numerous entities, the Commission's recommended changes were partially adopted and made "sentences for crack offenses between two and five times longer than sentences for equal amounts of powder" (*Kimbrough v. United States,* 2007). In recent years, Blacks and Hispanics have continued to bear the brunt of the federal cocaine convictions (see Table 6.11) and lengthy sentences (see Table 6.12).

Not until August, 2010, however, was there a legislative change in the crack cocaine and powder cocaine sentencing disparity. At that time, President Barack Obama signed

Table 6.11

Race of Drug Offenders for Each Drug Type, Fiscal Year 2010

Drug Type	Total	White		Black		Hispanic		Other	
		N	%	*N*	%	*N*	%	*N*	%
Total	24,319	6,194	25.5	6,721	27.6	10,648	43.8	756	3.1
Powder Cocaine	5,708	959	16.8	1,532	26.8	3,124	54.7	93	1.6
Crack Cocaine	4,887	359	7.3	3,838	78.5	638	13.1	52	1.1
Heroin	1,625	262	16.1	449	27.6	898	55.3	16	1.0
Marijuana	6,328	1,552	24.5	484	7.6	4,078	64.4	214	3.4
Methamphetamine	4,303	2,243	52.1	102	2.4	1,784	41.5	174	4.0
Other	1,468	819	55.8	316	21.5	126	8.6	207	14.1

Note: Of the 83,946 cases, 24,713 were sentenced under USSG Chapter Two, Part D (Drugs). Of these, 24,366 cases were sentenced under §§D1.1 (Drug Trafficking), 2D1.2 (Protected Locations), 2D1.5 (Continuing Criminal Enterprise), 2D1.6 (Use of a Communication Facility), 2D1.8 (Rent/Manage Drug Establishment), or 2D2.1 (Simple Possession). Of these 24,366 cases, 47 were excluded due to missing information on offender's race.

Table 6.12

Average Length of Imprisonment in Each Type of Drug, Fiscal Year 2010

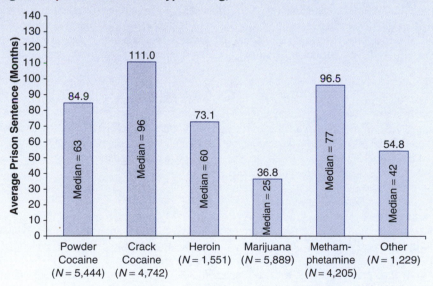

Note: Of the 83,946 cases, 9,039 had missing guideline application information. Of the remaining 74,907 cases, 24,713 were sentenced under USSG Chapter Two, Part D. Of these, 24,366 cases were sentenced under §§D1.1, 2D1.2, 2D1.5, 2D1.6, 2D1.8, or 2D1.1 as in the previous table. Additionally, 1,294 with zero months prison ordered were excluded. Of the remaining 23,072 cases, 12 were missing sentence information.

the Fair Sentencing Act of 2010, which included the provision that the sentencing disparity between the two forms of cocaine be reduced from 100 to 1 to 18 to 1. Since the passage of the Act, numerous offenders have now become eligible for retroactive sentence reductions (see Box 6.1).

BOX 6.1

Crack Offenders Eligible for Early Release

People already in prison will benefit from change in sentencing rules

By Jessica Gresko

Washington—Thousands of federal prisoners locked up for offenses involving crack cocaine will be eligible for early release after a vote Thursday by the U.S. Sentencing Commission.

Congress passed a law last year substantially lowering recommended sentences for people convicted of crack cocaine crimes, ranging from possession to trafficking. The idea was to fix a longstanding disparity in punishments for crack and powder cocaine crimes, but the new, lower recommended sentences didn't automatically apply to offenders already in prison. On Thursday the six-member sentencing commission unanimously decided that offenders locked up for crack offenses before the new law took effect should also benefit.

"I believe that the commission has no choice but to make this right," said Ketanji Brown Jackson, a vice chair of the commission. "I say justice demands this result."

The commission's decision is final unless Congress decides to intervene by the end of October, though that is considered unlikely.

According to the commission's own research, approximately 12,000 of the roughly 200,000 people incarcerated in federal prisons nationwide will be eligible to have their sentences reduced because of Thursday's vote. The average sentence reduction is expected to be approximately three years, though a judge will have to approve any lower sentence. Individuals convicted under state law and in state prisons will not be affected. The **Bureau of Prisons** estimates that over the first five years the change will save $200 million.

In its ruling Thursday the commission took a broad view of who should benefit from lower recommended sentences, though various groups had urged the commission to act more narrowly. A group of 15 Republican lawmakers from the House and Senate wrote to the commission saying the Fair Sentencing Act passed by Congress last year was not intended to benefit any past offenders. And U.S. Attorney General Eric Holder took the position that prisoners who used weapons during their crimes or who have significant criminal histories should not be eligible for reduced sentences. That would have cut in half the number of prisoners eligible for early release from 12,000 to approximately 6,000.

Prisoners eligible for a reduction can begin petitioning judges for a revised sentence beginning in November, assuming Congress does not act.

The reductions would not be automatic. A lawyer, the overwhelming majority of them public defenders, would file paperwork in court for the prisoner seeking a reduction, and the reduction would have to be approved by a judge. Prisoners would not necessarily have to appear in court, but prosecutors would also weigh in.

Courts have had prior experience with the process. In 2007 approximately 16,000 crack offenders had their sentences reduced after another action by the Sentencing Commission.

Do you support the retroactive reductions in sentences for crack offenders? Please explain your opinion.

Photo 6.2

President Obama Signs the Fair Sentencing Act. U.S. President Barack Obama (C) signs the Fair Sentencing Act in the Oval Office of the White House, in Washington DC, USA, 03 August 2010. Also in the picture (L-R) Attorney General Eric Holder, Democratic Senator Patrick Leahy of Vermont, Democratic Representative Bobby Scott of Virginia, Democratic Senator Dick Durbin of Illinois, Republican Senator Jeff Sessions of Alabama, Republican Senator Orrin Hatch of Utah and Democratic Representative Sheila Jackson-Lee of Texas.

Throughout the last 30 years, some citizens (particularly racial and ethnic minorities) have often questioned the neutrality of judges when racial disparities are revealed. As such, a consistent theme in policy considerations related to the judiciary is the assumption that if there were more minority judges, the courts would be run more equitably. Drawing on the scholarly literature, we investigate this supposition next.

Minority Judges

More than 150 years ago, Robert Morris became the first African American to be appointed as a judge (Washington, 1994). Less than 20 years later, during the Reconstruction period, another milestone was reached when Jonathan Jasper Wright was elected to the Supreme Court of South Carolina in 1872 (Washington, 1994). Since these early breakthroughs, few minorities have served as judges. Although this could be a product of the fact that in 2010 Blacks and Hispanics combined represented less than 8% of American lawyers (U.S. Bureau of Labor Statistics, 2010), proactive measures have resulted in some increases in minority judicial appointments.

Looking at judicial appointments to the U.S. District Courts since the early 1960s, one does notice a considerable improvement in diversity, but only during the tenure of four presidents (Carter, Clinton, the second Bush, and Obama) were there substantial gains (see Table 6.13). During the Carter era, nearly 14% of the appointments were African American, and nearly 7% were Hispanic (Maguire, 2011b). During this span, significant gains were also made for women. In the Johnson era, only 1.6% of the appointees were women, while during the current presidency of Barack H. Obama, nearly 55% of the appointments are women. During the period reviewed, President Barack H. Obama also had the highest average rating for his appointees: 75% of them were rated by the American Bar Association to be "exceptionally qualified" or "well qualified." This figure was followed by George W. Bush's presidency at 70% (Maguire, 2011b). It is also notable that during Bush's presidency, the percentage of Latino appointees to the U.S. District Courts was higher than at any other point in history, and during the Obama presidency a quarter of the appointments were Black.

Turning to judicial appointments for the U.S. Court of Appeals (see Table 6.14), the Clinton and Obama presidencies stand out. During Clinton's presidency, nearly 33% of his appointments were females, and nearly 25% were racial minorities (13.1% Black, 11.5% Hispanic; Maguire, 2011c). Contrary to some concerns about minority judicial appointments, nearly 79% of Clinton's judicial appointments were rated as either "exceptionally well qualified" or "well qualified" by the American Bar Association, a figure that was unsurpassed during all the presidential administrations since the early 1960s. Although Obama has only selected a small number of judges to the U.S. Court of Appeals, his appointment trend has been a favorable one for women and racial/ethnic minorities. Since taking office in 2009, 33% of his appointees to the U.S. Court of Appeals have been women, with minorities comprising more than 50% of the appointments (33.3% Blacks, 13.3% Hispanic, and 6.7% Asian). If these appointment trends continue throughout his presidency, Obama will likely hold the record for the most diverse judicial appointments of any president.

Two things stand out from these data. First, Asian Americans and Native Americans are minimally represented in the appointment figures. The absence of qualified Native American judges could be a product of many of them serving in such positions on reservations. In the case of Asian Americans, although their population figures are low, by now there are surely an ample number of potential nominees. It is promising that 11.4% of President Obama's appointments to the U.S. District Courts and 6.7% of his appointments to the U.S. Court of Appeals were Asian Americans (see Tables 6.13 and 6.14). Nevertheless, for minorities who have made it to the judiciary, are there differences between their decisions and those of White judges? We explore this question next.

Do Minority Judges Make a Difference?

Most people are familiar with the instant classic *Black Robes, White Justice* by New York State Judge Bruce Wright (1987). Judge Wright's poignant criticism of the justice system served as a much-needed case study of how, in his experience, race operated in the courts. Since the publication of his work, several observers have investigated the impact of minority judges, such as Wright, to see whether they are bringing balance to the bench. In essence, because many minority judges have experienced racism along the way, some observers believe they will be more sensitive to the plight of minorities who come before them. Other observers believe that because of the nature of the judicial role, minority or female judges are more apt to conform to the norm so they can fit in (Spohn, 2009).

Reviewing the literature on the subject, Spohn (2009) noted that there were few differences between the sentences dispensed by Black, Hispanic, and White justices. In fact, in some instances, both Black and White judges sentenced Black defendants more harshly than White defendants. Spohn suggested that minority judges could be more sensitive to the justice given to Black *victims,* as opposed to being sensitive to the plight of Black offenders. Yet others contend that at times Black judges hand down longer sentences because they sit on the bench in high-crime areas (see Muhlhausen, 2004). Worse yet, minority judges might

Table 6.13

Characteristics of Presidential Appointees to U.S. District Court Judgeships by Presidential Administration, 1963–2010[a]

	President Johnson's appointees 1963–68 (N = 122)	President Nixon's appointees 1969–74 (N = 179)	President Ford's appointees 1974–76 (N = 52)	President Carter's appointees 1977–80 (N = 202)	President Reagan's appointees 1981–88 (N = 290)	President George H.W. Bush's appointees 1989–92 (N = 148)	President Clinton's appointees 1993–2000 (N = 305)	President George W. Bush's appointees 2001–2008 (N = 261)	President Obama's appointees 2009–2010 (N = 44)
Sex									
Male	98.4%	99.4%	98.1%	85.6%	91.7%	80.4%	71.5%	79.3%	45.5%
Female	1.6	0.6	1.9	14.4	8.3	19.6	28.5	20.7	54.5
Race, ethnicity									
White	93.4	95.5	88.5	78.2	92.4	89.2	75.1	81.6	59.1
Black	4.1	3.4	5.8	13.9	2.1	6.8	17.4	6.9	25.0
Hispanic	2.5	1.1	1.9	6.9	4.8	4.0	5.9	10.0	4.5
Asian	0	0	3.9	0.5	0.7	0	1.3	1.5	11.4
Native American	NA	NA	NA	0.5	0	0	0.3	0	0
Education, undergraduate									
Public-supported	38.5	41.3	48.1	55.9	37.9	46.0	44.3	47.1	45.5
Private (not Ivy League)	31.1	38.5	34.6	34.2	48.6	39.9	42.0	45.2	40.9
Ivy League	16.4	19.6	17.3	9.9	13.4	14.2	13.8	7.7	13.6
None indicated	13.9	0.6	0	0	0	0	0	0	0
Education, law school									
Public-supported	40.2	41.9	44.2	52.0	44.8	52.7	39.7	49.0	45.5

(Continued)

(Continued)

	President Johnson's appointees 1963-68 (N=122)	President Nixon's appointees 1969-74 (N=179)	President Ford's appointees 1974-76 (N=52)	President Carter's appointees 1977-80 (N=202)	President Reagan's appointees 1981-88 (N=290)	President George H.W. Bush's appointees 1989-92 (N=148)	President Clinton's appointees 1993-2000 (N=305)	President George W. Bush's appointees 2001-2008 (N=261)	President Obama's appointees 2009-2010 (N=44)
Private (not Ivy League)	36.9	36.9	38.5	31.2	43.4	33.1	40.7	39.1	31.8
Ivy League	21.3	21.2	17.3	16.8	11.7	14.2	19.7	11.9	22.7
Occupation at nomination or appointment									
Politics or government	21.3	10.6	21.2	5.0	13.4	10.8	11.5	13.4	11.4
Judiciary	31.1	28.5	34.6	44.6	36.9	41.9	48.2	48.3	52.3
Law firm, large	2.4	11.2	9.6	13.9	17.9	25.7	16.1	18.8	13.6
Law firm, medium	18.9	27.9	25.0	19.3	19.0	14.9	13.4	10.0	13.6
Law firm, small	23.0	19.0	9.6	13.9	10.0	4.7	8.2	6.1	4.5
Professor	3.3	2.8	0	3.0	2.1	0.7	1.6	1.1	2.3
Other	0	0	0	0.5	0.7	1.4	1.0	2.3	2.3
Occupational experience[b]									
Judicial	34.4	35.2	42.3	54.0	46.2	46.6	52.1	52.1	54.5
Prosecutorial	45.9	41.9	50.0	38.1	44.1	39.2	41.3	47.1	47.7
Other	33.6	36.3	30.8	31.2	28.6	31.8	28.9	24.9	29.5
Political party									
Democrat	94.3	7.3	21.2	91.1	4.8	6.1	87.5	8.0	88.6

	President Johnson's appointees 1963-68 (N = 122)	President Nixon's appointees 1969-74 (N = 179)	President Ford's appointees 1974-76 (N = 52)	President Carter's appointees 1977-80 (N = 202)	President Reagan's appointees 1981-88 (N = 290)	President George H.W. Bush's appointees 1989-92 (N = 148)	President Clinton's appointees 1993-2000 (N = 305)	President George W. Bush's appointees 2001-2008 (N = 261)	President Obama's appointees 2009-2010 (N = 44)
Republican	5.7	92.7	78.8	4.5	91.7	88.5	6.2	83.1	0
Independent or none	0	0	0	4.5	3.4	5.4	5.9	8.8	11.4
Other	NA	NA	NA	0	0	0	0.3	0	0
American Bar Association rating									
Exceptionally well/well qualified	48.4	45.3	46.1	51.0	53.5	57.4	59.0	70.1	75.0
Qualified	49.2	54.8	53.8	47.5	46.6	42.6	40.0	28.4	25.0
Not qualified	2.5	0	0	1.5	0	0	1.0	1.5	0

Note: These data were compiled from a variety of sources. Primarily used were questionnaires completed by judicial nominees for the U.S. Senate Judiciary Committee, transcripts of the confirmation hearings conducted by the Committee, and personal interviews. Other sources of demographic and background data included newspaper articles and various resources online or on the Internet.

Law firms are categorized according to the number of partners/associates: 25 or more associates for a large firm, 5 to 24 associates for a medium firm, and 4 or less for a small firm. The American Bar Association's (ABA) ratings are assigned to candidates after investigation and evaluation by the ABA's Standing Committee on Federal Judiciary, which considers prospective Federal judicial nominees only upon referral by the U.S. Attorney General or at the request of the U.S. Senate. The ABA's Committee evaluation is directed primarily to professional qualifications—competence, integrity, and judicial temperament. Factors including intellectual capacity, judgment, writing and analytical ability, industry, knowledge of the law, and professional experience are assessed. Prior to President George H.W. Bush's administration, the ABA's Standing Committee on Federal Judiciary utilized four ratings: exceptionally well qualified, well qualified, qualified, and not qualified. Starting with that administration, the ABA Standing Committee on Federal Judiciary dropped its "exceptionally well qualified" rating and "well qualified" became the highest rating. Nominees who previously would have been rated "exceptionally well qualified" and nominees who would have been rated "well qualified" now receive the same rating. The "exceptionally well qualified" and "well qualified" categories have been combined for all administrations' appointees, and therefore figures prior to President George H.W. Bush's administration may differ from previous editions of *Sourcebook.* Some data have been revised by the Source and may differ from previous editions of *Sourcebook.*

a. Percents may not add to 100 because of rounding.

b. Percents will add to more than 100 because some appointees have had more than one type of previous experience.

Table 6.14

Characteristics of Presidential Appointees to U.S. Court of Appeals Judgeships by Presidential Administration, 1963–2010[a]

	President Johnson's appointees 1963-68[b] (N = 40)	President Nixon's appointees 1969-74 (N = 45)	President Ford's appointees 1974-76 (N = 12)	President Carter's appointees 1977-80 (N = 56)	President Reagan's appointees 1981-88 (N = 78)	President George H.W. Bush's appointees 1989-92 (N = 37)	President Clinton's appointees 1993-2000 (N = 61)	President George W. Bush's appointees 2001-2008 (N = 59)	President Obama's appointees 2009-2010 (N = 15)
Sex									
Male	97.5%	100%	100%	80.4%	94.9%	81.1%	67.2%	74.6%	66.7%
Female	2.5	0	0	19.6	5.1	18.9	32.8	25.4	33.3
Race, ethnicity									
White	95.0	97.8	100	78.6	97.4	89.2	73.8	84.7	46.7
Black	5.0	0	0	16.1	1.3	5.4	13.1	10.2	33.3
Hispanic	0	0	0	3.6	1.3	5.4	11.5	5.1	13.3
Asian	0	2.2	0	1.8	0	0	1.6	0	6.7
Education, undergraduate									
Public-supported	32.5	40.0	50.0	30.4	24.4	29.7	44.3	35.6	13.3
Private (not Ivy League)	40.0	35.6	41.7	51.8	51.3	59.5	34.4	47.4	33.3
Ivy League	17.5	20.0	8.3	17.9	24.4	10.8	21.3	17.9	53.3
None indicated	10.0	4.4	0	0	0	0	0	0	0
Education, law school									
Public-supported	40.0	37.8	50.0	39.3	41.0	32.4	39.3	39.0	20.0
Private (not Ivy League)	32.5	26.7	25.0	19.6	35.9	37.8	31.1	35.6	53.3
Ivy League	27.5	35.6	25.0	41.1	23.1	29.7	29.5	25.4	26.7

	President Johnson's appointees 1963-68[b] (N=40)	President Nixon's appointees 1969-74 (N=45)	President Ford's appointees 1974-76 (N=12)	President Carter's appointees 1977-80 (N=56)	President Reagan's appointees 1981-88 (N=78)	President George H.W. Bush's appointees 1989-92 (N=37)	President Clinton's appointees 1993-2000 (N=61)	President George W. Bush's appointees 2001-2008 (N=59)	President Obama's appointees 2009-2010 (N=15)
Occupation at nomination or appointment									
Politics or government	10.0	4.4	8.3	5.4	6.4	10.8	6.6	18.6	6.7
Judiciary	57.5	53.3	75.0	46.4	55.1	59.5	52.5	49.1	80.0
Law firm, large	5.0	4.4	8.3	10.7	14.1	16.2	18.0	11.9	0
Law firm, medium	17.5	22.2	8.3	16.1	9.0	10.8	13.1	6.8	6.7
Law firm, small	7.5	6.7	0	5.4	1.3	0	1.6	3.4	0
Professor	2.5	2.2	0	14.3	12.8	2.7	8.2	6.8	6.7
Other	0	6.7	0	1.8	1.3	0	0	3.4	0
Occupational experience[c]									
Judicial	65.0	57.8	75.0	53.6	60.3	62.2	59.0	61.0	80.0
Prosecutorial	47.5	46.7	25.0	30.4	28.2	29.7	37.7	33.9	73.3
Other	20.0	17.8	25.0	39.3	34.6	32.4	29.5	25.4	6.7
Political party									
Democrat	95.0	6.7	8.3	82.1	0	2.7	85.2	6.8	93.3
Republican	5.0	93.3	91.7	7.1	96.2	89.2	6.6	91.5	0

(Continued)

(Continued)

	President Johnson's appointees 1963-68[b] (N = 40)	President Nixon's appointees 1969-74 (N = 45)	President Ford's appointees 1974-76 (N = 12)	President Carter's appointees 1977-80 (N = 56)	President Reagan's appointees 1981-88 (N = 78)	President George H.W. Bush's appointees 1989-92 (N = 37)	President Clinton's appointees 1993-2000 (N = 61)	President George W. Bush's appointees 2001-2008 (N = 59)	President Obama's appointees 2009-2010 (N = 15)
Independent or none	0	0	0	10.7	2.6	8.1	8.2	1.7	6.7
Other	0	0	0	0	1.3	0	0	0	0
American Bar Association rating									
Exceptionally well/ well qualified	75.0	73.3	58.3	75.0	59.0	64.9	78.7	71.2	66.7
Qualified	20.0	26.7	33.3	25.0	41.0	35.1	21.3	28.8	33.3
Not qualified	2.5	0	8.3	0	0	0	0	0	0

Note: These data were compiled from a variety of sources. Primarily used were questionnaires completed by judicial nominees for the U.S. Senate Judiciary Committee, transcripts of the confirmation hearings conducted by the Committee, and personal interviews. Other sources of demographic or background data included newspaper articles and various resources online or on the Internet.

Law firms are categorized according to the number of partners/associates: 25 or more associates for a large firm, 5 to 24 associates for a medium firm, and 4 or less for a small firm.

The American Bar Association's (ABA) ratings are assigned to candidates after investigation and evaluation by the ABA's Standing Committee on Federal Judiciary, which considers prospective Federal judicial nominees only upon referral by the U.S. Attorney General or at the request of the U.S. Senate. The ABA's Committee evaluation is directed primarily to professional qualifications—competence, integrity, and judicial temperament. Factors including intellectual capacity, judgment, writing and analytical ability, industry, knowledge of the law, and professional experience are assessed. Prior to President George H.W. Bush's administration, the ABA's Standing Committee on Federal Judiciary utilized four ratings: exceptionally well qualified, well qualified, qualified, and not qualified. Starting with that administration, the ABA Standing Committee on Federal Judiciary dropped its "exceptionally well qualified" rating and "well qualified" became the highest rating. Nominees who previously would have been rated "exceptionally well qualified" and nominees who would have been rated "well qualified" now receive the same rating. The "exceptionally well qualified" and "well qualified" categories have been combined for all administrations' appointees, and therefore figures prior to President George H.W. Bush's administration may differ from previous editions of *Sourcebook*. Some data have been revised by the Source and may differ from previous editions of *Sourcebook*.

a. Percents may not add to 100 because of rounding.

b. No ABA rating was requested for one Johnson appointee.

c. Percents will add to more than 100 because some appointees have had more than one type of previous experience.

buy into the idea that minorities are more dangerous than Whites. One thing is clear from Spohn's (2009) review: The current body of macrolevel studies does not provide definitive answers to this question.

Could it be that we expect too much from minority judges? In line with this question, the late Judge A. Leon Higginbotham noted,

> No Black judge should work solely on racial matters. I think that would be a profoundly inappropriate abstention, and I would further argue that there is no special role that a Black jurist should play. (cited in Washington, 1994, p. 4)

Reviewing the decision of Supreme Court Justice Clarence Thomas in the case of *Hudson v. McMillian* (1992), in which a Black prisoner was assaulted by two prison guards while he was shackled at the hands and feet, Higginbotham added,

> A Black judge, like all judges, has to decide matters on the basis of the record. But you would hope that a Black judge could never be as blind to the consequences of sanctioning violence and racism against Blacks by state officials as Clarence Thomas was in the *Hudson* case. (cited in Washington, 1994, p. 5)

So, barring exceptional cases, according to one of the leading African American jurists of the 20th century, we should not expect anything different from minority judges; irrespective of race, the facts should dictate case outcomes.

Although this debate will likely rage on in scholarly and other circles ad infinitum, the larger issue likely relates to opportunity. Whether a minority or female judge rules in accordance with Whites is, in some ways, beside the point. The more central issue is that qualified minority and female attorneys should be afforded equal opportunities to serve in these important roles. Although it could be that in modern times race discrimination continues to be a factor in not appointing more minority attorneys, such a trend could also be tied to politics. That is, which political party is in office might be an equally strong explanation of why some minorities are selected for the judiciary while others are not.

❖ Conclusion

This chapter reviewed race-related issues in the sentencing phase of the criminal justice process. After a historical review of early cases that illustrated sentencing patterns, it was shown that race and class disparities have always existed in the American justice system. Following a review of the American sentencing process and its various philosophies, we noted that during the 1990s more punitive philosophies prevailed. As such, numerous "get tough" approaches were devised to deal with offenders. Most notably, mandatory minimum, three-strikes-and-you're-out, and truth-in-sentencing policies swelled prison populations with minorities and poor persons. The "War on Drugs" also contributed to the sway toward punitive policies with the passage of the 1986 and 1988 Anti-Drug Abuse Acts, which also contributed to the infamous disparities between penalties for crack cocaine and powder cocaine and further pronounced the racial disparities in sentencing outcomes. It was promising to note that, after two decades of draconian sentencing, policymakers accepted recommendations by the U.S. Sentencing Commission, which resulted in thousands of unfairly sentenced crack cocaine offenders being eligible for early release.

Next, we reviewed the extant scholarship on race and sentencing. This review showed the numerous characteristics that predict whether minorities will be sentenced more harshly than Whites. Some of these characteristics include being young, male, poor, and unemployed; being detained prior to trial; and victimizing Whites. In contrast to the harsh treatment of Blacks and Hispanics during sentencing, some recent research has shown that Asians receive leniency in the sentencing process. Turning to the judiciary, we also examined the discretion wielded by judges and investigated the conventional wisdom that by having more minority judges, the scales of justice would be more balanced. Contrary to this thinking, however, it was found that the sentences administered by minority judges are in line with those of White judges. In fact, in some instances, for a variety of reasons, minority judges' sentences are actually longer than those set by Whites. We concluded that the most important concern is that qualified minority judges should be afforded equal opportunities to serve in the judiciary.

Discussion Questions

1. Discuss the sentencing disparities found in colonial America.

2. Discuss the sentencing trends from the 1980s through the 2000s.

3. What was the significance of the "War on Drugs" for racial and ethnic minorities?

4. Discuss Zatz's (1987) four waves of sentencing research.

5. Explain the trends regarding racial/ethnic minorities and judicial appointments.

Internet Exercises

1. Go to http://www.whitehousedrugpolicy.gov and examine how much of the most recent *National Drug Control Strategy Report* focuses on drug treatment or law enforcement.

2. Listen to the following podcast by scholar John McWhorter and see whether you agree with his suggestion to end the War on Drugs: http://www.cato.org/multime dia/daily-podcast/race-relations-war-drugs

3. Visit the Families Against Mandatory Minimums (FAMM) website (http://www .famm.org/) and read some of the profiles on injustice.

Internet Sites

Sentencing Project: http://www.sentencingproject.org

U.S. Sentencing Commission: http://www.ussc.gov

National Drug Control Strategy: http://www.whitehousedrugpolicy.gov

The Death Penalty

The history of American Indian executions is clearly nestled within a sociopolitical context of genocidal colonialism calculated to dispossess American Indians of their Indianism by removing them from their sacred tribal territories, disrupting their traditional cultures, and continuing their marginalized status in the U.S. society today.

—David V. Baker (2007, pp. 316–317)

O ver the years, there has been considerable debate about the merits of the death penalty as a form of punishment. Although some debates have centered on whether it is cruel and unusual punishment, a considerable portion of the debate has centered on who receives the death penalty. Racial minorities remain overrepresented among those who are sentenced to death and those who, in the end, are executed. This chapter begins with a review of several significant Supreme Court decisions, followed by a historical overview of race and the death penalty. The chapter also reviews the following related areas: current death penalty statistics, recent scholarship on race and the death penalty, public opinion and the death penalty, the Capital Jury Project, wrongful convictions, the death penalty moratorium movement, and judicial overrides in death penalty sentencing.

❖ Significant Death Penalty Cases

The Peach State and the Foundational Death Penalty Cases

The continued use of the death penalty in America can be credited to a series of Supreme Court cases in the 1970s involving the state of Georgia that reaffirmed its constitutionality. The cases also provided guidance for the application of the death penalty. The first of these was the 1972 decision in ***Furman v. Georgia***. The case centered on a 25-year-old

Black man (William Henry Furman) with an IQ of 65 who was charged with killing a 30-year-old White man (Bohm, 2007). Furman's lawyers argued that because of the lack of instructions given to jury members about deciding which cases warrant the death penalty and which ones do not, the way the death penalty was being administered violated Furman's Fourteenth Amendment right to due process and was also a violation of the Eighth Amendment, which protects citizens against cruel and unusual punishment. In a decision in which the nine justices each wrote a separate opinion, the majority agreed that the death penalty was being administered in an arbitrary and capricious manner. That is, there was little uniformity across states as to who should receive the death penalty and under what circumstances. Those in the majority also pointed out that the death penalty had been applied in a discriminatory manner. Concurring with the majority decision, Justice Douglas wrote,

> It is cruel and unusual punishment to apply the death penalty selectively to minorities whose numbers are few, who are outcasts of society, and who are unpopular, but whom society is willing to see suffer though it would not countenance general application of the same penalty across the boards. (*Furman v. Georgia,* 1972, p. 1)

Given some of these considerations, in the end, Furman's sentence was commuted to life in prison (he was paroled in 1985). As Baker (2003) noted,

> The aftermath of *Furman* saw the Court vacate 120 cases immediately before it and some 645 other cases involving death row inmates. The decision rendered defective the death penalty statutes of thirty-nine states, the District of Columbia, and the federal government. (p. 180)

The *Furman* decision, however, would stand only four years. In the 1976 case of **Gregg v. Georgia**, the Court indicated that states that used **guided discretion** statutes removed concerns regarding previous procedures that were considered to be arbitrary and capricious. According to Bohm (1999), such statutes

> set standards for juries and judges when deciding whether to impose the death penalty. The guided discretion statutes struck a reasonable balance between giving the jury some discretion and allowing it to consider the defendant's background and character and circumstances of the crime. (p. 25)

The year following the *Gregg* decision, the Court provided states with further guidance on the application of the death penalty. Specifically, in **Coker v. Georgia** (1977), the Court ruled that sentencing rapists to death was cruel and unusual punishment. Considering that between 1930 and the 1970s, 405 Black men were executed in the South for the crime of rape, whereas only 48 Whites were executed for the same offense during this period (Holden-Smith, 1996), it is perplexing that the Court skirted around the racial dynamics of the historical use of executions for rapists. With about 90% of such death sentences being given to Blacks (who presumably had raped White women), it appears that this punishment was historically reserved for Blacks.

In June of the same year as the *Coker* decision, the court also ruled in *Eberheart v. Georgia* (1977) that kidnappings not resulting in death cannot be punished with the death penalty. A decade later, the 1987 decision in **McCleskey v. Kemp** represents another important Supreme Court case, which challenged the constitutionality of the death penalty based on racial discrimination in its application.

McCleskey v. Kemp

Warren McCleskey, a Black man, was convicted of the 1978 shooting of a White police officer during an armed robbery. Once caught, tried, and convicted following Georgia's death penalty statute, the jury found beyond a reasonable doubt that the murder had occurred with one of their statutorily defined aggravating circumstances. In this case, however, there were two aggravating circumstances. First, McCleskey had committed the murder during an armed robbery, and second, the victim was a police officer. In the course of his appeals, McCleskey claimed that Georgia's death penalty process was being administered in a racially discriminatory manner, which violated his Eighth and Fourteenth Amendment rights. As evidence of this discrimination, McCleskey's defense showed that

> even after taking account of numerous nonracial variables, defendants charged with killing Whites were 4.3 times more likely to receive a death sentence in Georgia as defendants charged with killing Blacks, and that Black defendants were 1.1 times as likely to receive a death sentence as other defendants. (*McCleskey v. Kemp*, 1987, p. 1)

After working its way through the courts, the case finally made its way to the Supreme Court in 1986. In an opinion written by Justice Powell and joined by four other justices (Rehnquist, White, O'Connor, and Scalia), the majority held

> the statistical evidence was insufficient to support an inference that any of the decision makers in the accused's case acted with discriminatory purpose in violation of the equal protection clause of the Fourteenth Amendment, since (a) the accused offered no evidence of racial bias specific to his own case, and (b) the statistical evidence alone was not clear enough to prove discrimination in any one case; (2) the study was insufficient to prove that the state violated the equal protection clause by adopting the capital punishment statute and allowing it to remain in force despite its allegedly discriminatory application; and (3) the study was insufficient to prove that the state's capital punishment system was arbitrary and capricious in application and that therefore the accused's death sentence was excessive in violation of the Eighth Amendment. (*McCleskey v. Kemp*, 1987, pp. 1–2)

Conversely, the dissenting justices in the case (Brennan, Marshall, Stevens, and Blackmun) provided a host of contrasting points. First, as noted in previous cases, justices Brennan and Marshall reiterated that the death penalty was cruel and unusual and therefore violated the Eighth and the Fourteenth Amendments. Furthermore, in their eyes, the statistical evidence was valid and showed that there was "an intolerable risk that racial prejudice influenced his particular sentence" (*McCleskey v. Kemp*, 1987, p. 2). In his dissenting opinion, Justice Blackmun, who was joined by justices Marshall and Stevens, suggested that the statistical data showed

> (1) The accused was a member of a group that was singled out for different treatment, (2) the difference in treatment was substantial in degree, and (3) Georgia's process for seeking the death penalty was susceptible to abuse in the form of racial discrimination. (*McCleskey v. Kemp*, 1987, p. 2)

The study that was debated by the majority has come to be known as the "Baldus study" (see Baldus, Woodworth, & Pulaski, 1990). Leading up to the *McCleskey* case, Baldus et al. had conducted two important death penalty studies: the procedural reform study and the charging and sentencing study. The first study was designed to

> compare how Georgia sentenced defendants convicted of murder at trial, before and after the statutory reforms prompted by *Furman v. Georgia*, and to assess the extent to which those reforms affected the levels of arbitrariness and discrimination observed in its sentencing decisions. (p. 42)

For the second study, Baldus and his colleagues (1990) were hired by the NAACP Legal Defense Fund to conduct the study "with the expectation that the results might be used to challenge the constitutionality of Georgia's death sentencing system as it has been applied since *Gregg v. Georgia* (1976)" (p. 44). In the end, the second study was the one considered but rejected in the *McCleskey* decision. Using a sophisticated methodological design, which controlled for hundreds of variables, the Baldus study remains the standard when examining race and the death penalty. Probably the most discussed and important finding from the study was the strong race-of-the-victim effect, which showed that Black offenders in Georgia who victimized Whites were considerably more likely to receive death sentences than White persons who victimized Blacks. In fact, looking at this dynamic nationally over a 370-year period (1608–1978), only 30 Whites in the United States have been executed for killing African Americans (Radelet, 1989).

It has been suggested that had the Supreme Court ruled in McCleskey's favor, it would have opened "a Pandora's box of litigation" (Kennedy, 1997, p. 333). In short, ruling in McCleskey's favor would have, as Justice Powell stated, "throw[n] into serious question the principles that underlie our entire criminal justice system" (cited in Kennedy, 1997, p. 333). Moreover, he noted that such a decision would produce similar claims "from other members of other groups alleging bias" (p. 333). Nonetheless, the fact remains that those who support the death penalty outnumber those who oppose it. Even so, given the historical and contemporary racial disparities in who receives the death penalty, in 1988, Congressman John Conyers introduced the Racial Justice Act, which prohibits executions if there is a pattern of racial discrimination in death sentences at the state and federal levels. Although the bill was defeated several times, in 1998, Kentucky became the first state to enact a Racial Justice Act. Since then, North Carolina also enacted a Racial Justice Act in 2009 (see Boxes 7.1 and 7.2). As noted in Box 7.2, as of 2011, the Act was being attacked by Republican legislators who were attempting to repeal it. In December 2011, North Carolina Governor Bev Perdue vetoed a bill aimed at repealing the Act.

BOX 7.1

North Carolina Racial Justice Act

General Assembly of North Carolina

Session 2009

Senate Bill 461

Ratified Bill

An Act to prohibit seeking or imposing the death penalty on the basis of race; to establish a process by which relevant evidence may be used to establish that race was a significant factor in seeking or imposing the death penalty within the county, the prosecutorial district, the judicial division, or the State, to identify types of evidence that may be considered by the court when considering whether race was a basis for seeking or imposing the death penalty, including statistical evidence, and to authorize the defendant to raise this claim at the pretrial conference or in postconviction proceedings; to provide that the defendant has the burden of proving that race was a significant factor in seeking or imposing the death penalty and to provide that the State may offer evidence to rebut the claims or evidence of the defendant and in doing so to use statistical evidence as well as any other evidence the Court deems relevant and material; to provide that if race is found to be a significant factor in the imposition of the death penalty, the death sentence shall be vacated and the defendant resentenced to life imprisonment without the possibility of parole; to provide that this Act is effective when it becomes law and applies retroactively, that motions under this Act for those currently under a death sentence shall be filed within one year of the effective date of this Act, and that motions for those whose death sentence is imposed on or after the effective date of this Act shall be filed as provided in this Act.

BOX 7.2

Fayetteville Man's Death Row Hearing Is First Under the Racial Justice Act

By Paul Woolverton and Gregory Phillips, Fayetteville Observer *staff writers*

A death row inmate from Fayetteville is set to be the first in North Carolina to argue to a judge that his sentence should be converted to life without parole under the controversial Racial Justice Act.

Marcus Reymond Robinson, convicted in 1994 of killing a teenager during a robbery, will present statistics to a Cumberland County Superior Court judge in an effort to show an ongoing record of racism in decisions that lead to death sentences.

The Racial Justice Act of 2009 says that a death row inmate who has evidence that his sentence was racially motivated can seek to have it converted to life in prison. Nearly everyone on death row in North Carolina—151 out of 158 convicts—is pursuing Racial Justice Act claims. Robinson is the first to have a hearing date set before a judge, according to the nonprofit Center for Death Penalty Litigation, which is representing him.

Robinson's lawyers will argue that he got the death penalty partly because he is a black man who killed a white victim. They will say that follows a pattern in Cumberland County, along with how juries are picked and in which cases prosecutors decide to seek capital punishment.

(Continued)

(Continued)

Prosecutors have filed motions arguing that the statistics are incomplete and that Robinson raised no claim of discrimination during or after his trial.

Gregory Weeks, a senior resident Superior Court judge, is scheduled to hear the arguments Sept. 6.

Gerda Stein, a spokeswoman for the Center for Death Penalty Litigation, said many judges have been wary of hearing Racial Justice Act cases because it's possible the Republican-controlled legislature could repeal the law next year. Weeks just happens to be the first judge to schedule a hearing, she said.

Robinson was convicted for the 1991 robbery and murder of 17-year-old Eric Tornblom. The teen was on his way home from work when he met Robinson and Roderick Sylvester Williams Jr. at a convenience store. Williams talked the victim into giving the pair a ride. They then used a sawed-off shotgun to force Tornblom to drive to a field between Legion and Camden roads, where they made him lie on the ground and shot him in the face. They stole his car and $27.

Williams is serving a life sentence for the murder and robbery.

Robinson was set to die in January 2007, but all executions in the state were postponed indefinitely while the courts sorted out other controversies about North Carolina's execution procedures.

Race Factor

In Robinson's motion, his lawyers say that prosecutors offered evidence that Robinson told someone he was going to "kill himself a whitey," and that made race a factor in the case.

His lawyers will point to statistics to say that prosecutors in North Carolina reject minorities for juries in capital cases at twice the rate that they reject whites. The lawyers also say "individuals who kill whites are punished much more harshly than those who kill blacks or other racial minorities," according to their court paperwork.

In Robinson's case, the prosecutors rejected half the potential jurors who were black but only 15 percent of potential jurors who were other races, the motion says.

Ultimately, Robinson's jury had nine whites, one American Indian and two blacks, plus two white alternates.

"Moreover, racial minority defendants accused of capital crimes in Cumberland County face significantly higher odds of receiving a death sentence than white defendants," the lawyers say in their motion.

They cite several studies that examined the death penalty in North Carolina and locally. They say these studies show racism permeates the system in deciding who gets sentenced to death.

One study found that between 1990 and 2009 in North Carolina, a defendant who killed a white person was 2.6 times more likely to be sentenced to death than if there were no white victims in the crime, the motion says.

The lawyers also say that in death penalty–eligible murder cases since 1990, if at least one victim was white, Cumberland County prosecutors pursued the death sentence at more than triple the rate than for cases in which no victims were white.

And defendants were 3.4 times more likely to be sentenced to death if the victim was white, the motion says.

Prosecutors disagree with the validity of the statistics cited. Their motion claims Robinson's lawyers used numbers from two studies, one of which is incomplete with its own creators admitting in an affidavit the results were "initial findings."

The prosecutors' motion argues they have not been given the opportunity to scrutinize the statistical analyses and raw data from either study.

The Racial Justice Act passed the legislature when it was controlled by Democrats. Most Democrats favored the law, while Republicans voted against it.

Republicans in control of the General Assembly this year advanced legislation to repeal the act, but the bill is not expected to be considered until at least May 2012.

Note: The North Carolina Legislature did vote to repeal the Act in 2011; however, the bill failed by one vote. It is anticipated that there will be another attempt to repeal the Act in 2012.

Do you agree with the premise of racial justice acts? Explain your view.

After reviewing these significant cases, one is left to wonder whether or not race has always mattered in the application of the death penalty. We examine this question in the next section.

❖ Historical Overview of Race and the Death Penalty

As with other sentences, the death penalty followed colonists from their homeland, where English law provided for so many offenses resulting in death that it was referred to as the "**bloody code**." In a pioneering article on the death penalty as it relates to Native Americans, Baker (2007) notes that besides the well-known early genocidal actions of Europeans, since their arrival there have been at least 450 formal executions of Native Americans. The 1639 execution of Nepauduct was the first execution of a Native American. Moreover, during the 17th century, there were 157 executions of Native Americans (Baker, 2007).

Besides the execution of Native Americans, Banner (2002) noted that the colony had numerous death penalty statutes that were solely applied to Blacks. There were a variety of such statutes, beginning in New York in 1712. However, it is in the South where many of these statutes prevailed. Because of the greater number of slaves in the South, there was considerable concern that they might rebel; therefore, as a means of deterrence, there were wide-ranging capital statutes. For example, "In 1740 South Carolina imposed the death penalty on slaves and free Blacks for burning or destroying any grain, commodities, or manufactured goods; on slaves for enticing other slaves to run away; and on slaves maiming or bruising Whites" (Banner, 2002, pp. 8–9). Other statutes made it punishable by death for slaves to administer medicine (to guard against poisoning); "strike Whites twice, or once if a bruise resulted"; or burn a house (Banner, 2002, p. 9; see Box 7.3). It is noteworthy that Black female slaves were not spared the death penalty, unlike White women, who rarely received the death penalty. Baker (2008) noted that the first recorded execution of a Black woman was in 1681 when Maria, a slave, was executed for arson and murder. After this initial execution, 58 more slave women were executed before 1790, with another 126 being executed prior to the Civil War (Baker, 2008).

BOX 7.3

Slave-Era Capital Crimes and Slave Owner Compensation in Virginia, 1774–1864

One little known fact from the slave era relates to slave owners being compensated for capitally sentenced slaves. Thus, whenever slaves committed an executable offense, the state had a set fee that was given to slave owners. Why? Phillips (1915) asserted that "to promote the suppression of crime, various colonies and states provided by law that the owners of slaves capitally sentenced should be compensated by the public at appraised valuations" (p. 336). Using Virginia as his study site, Phillips noted that the first such vouchers were distributed in the 1770s. Besides serving as a window into crimes committed by slaves, the practice also

(Continued)

(Continued)

showed how critical the loss of a slave was for Southern landowners. In terms of the records, though incomplete, they provide a look at 1,117 out of 1,418 capital crimes committed by slaves from the 1700s to the 1860s. An analysis of the crimes reveals that murder represented the largest share of the offenses (347). Of these, Phillips extracted a bit more context from the state records:

Murder of the master, 56; of overseer, 7; of the white man, 98; of mistress, 11; of other white woman, 13; of master's child, 2; of other white child, 7; of free negro man, 7; of slave man, 59; of slave woman, 14; of slave child, 12 (all of which were murders by slave women of their own children); of persons not described, 60. Of the murderers 307 were men and 39 were women. (p. 337)

The remaining convictions are summarized in Table 7.1. While Phillips noted that most of the crimes were typical of the era, he did note a few unusual punishments. In one case, after one slave killed another, the offending slave "had his head cut off and stuck on a pole at the forks of the road" (p. 338). In another instance, a slave stole a silver spoon from his owner's kitchen and was put to death.

Table 7.1

The Capital Crimes of Slaves in Virginia: 1774–1864

Crime	Number of Offenses
Murder	346
Rape/attempted rape	105[a]
Poisoning	55[b] (40 men and 15 women)
Administering medicine to Whites	2[c]
Assault/attempted murder	111[d]
Insurrection/conspiracy	91
Arson	90
Burglary	257
Highway robbery	15
Horse theft	20
Other theft	24
Forgery	2

a. According to records, all of these appear to have been of White women.

b. These were mostly targeted at Whites.

c. One of these persons was pardoned and transported away from the colony.

d. Only two of these crimes involved Black victims.

As shown in Figure 7.1, the compensation for the lives of the capitally sentenced slaves fluctuated from the 1700s to the 1800s. The rates fluctuated from a low of less than $300 in the 1700s to a high of $4,000 in 1864. Although a host of economic factors likely accounted for these fluctuations, the reality is that the state continuously provided some compensation to slave owners for their losses attributable to slaves sentenced to death.

Figure 7.1 Compensation for Capitally Sentenced Slaves, 1700s–1860s

Source: Phillips (1915, pp. 336–340).

In general, a few critical things stand out from the Virginia data. First, the state was so wedded to the economics of the slave system that it felt a need to compensate slave owners for the loss of their "property." Second, the data reveal the wide range of offenses for which slaves were executed. It is likely that executing slaves for so many offenses was used as a tool to control the slave population. Third, it is plausible that many of the property crimes were committed by slaves in response to the deprivation inherent in the slave system, and personal crimes may have been a way for slaves to fight back against the brutal system of slavery.

Do you think reparations should be paid to the descendants of slaves? Explain your opinion.

The obvious undercurrent with early death penalty statutes was that landowners were intent on controlling the slave population by fear and state-sanctioned brutality. As Banner (2002) noted, colonial officials "streamlined" the process by cutting out juries and using local justices of the peace to ensure the "justice" was rapid. As one can imagine, although a host of capital offenses also applied to Whites, the processes that prevailed in the slave era resulted in disparities. Looking at one state, North Carolina, the record shows that "at least one hundred slaves were executed in the quarter-century between 1748 and 1772, well more than the number of Whites executed during the colony's entire history, spanning a century" (p. 9).

Predictably, such disparities persisted well into the 19th century. Not until 1880, however, were there national statistics on capital punishment (Cahalan & Parsons, 1986). In that first report, there were 80 people listed as "present under the sentence of death" (p. 9).

These early reports provided information on the number of state-sanctioned executions, as well as those that were considered illegal (lynchings). Tables 7.2 and 7.3 highlight two important trends. First, Table 7.2 reveals that, from 1890 to 1984, 5,726 persons were executed, of which 54% (2,915) were non-Whites (Cahalan & Parsons, 1986). Furthermore, Table 7.3 shows that of the 4,736 illegal lynchings that occurred between the 1880s and the 1960s, nearly 73% (3,442) were of Blacks (Cahalan & Parsons, 1986). Given this early history, scholars have continued to research race and the death penalty. Our review of the death penalty continues with a review of current statistics at both the state and federal levels.

❖ Current Statistics on the Death Penalty

State Death Penalty Statistics

Using the year following the *Gregg* decision as a reference point, from 1977 to 2009, there were 1,188 inmates executed (Snell, 2010). Table 7.4 shows the racial breakdown by year of those who were executed. The figures reveal that approximately 57% of those executed since 1977 were White and about 35% have been Black. A review of data on the time spent on death row between sentencing and December, 2009 reveals that Hispanics averaged 133 months and both Blacks and Whites averaged 155 months. Strikingly, the following five states accounted for nearly two-thirds of the executions since 1977: Texas (447), Virginia (105), Oklahoma (91), Florida (68), and Missouri (67; Snell, 2010). Table 7.5 shows that there were 3,173 persons under a death sentence at the end of 2009. In addition, 98% of those persons were male, with more than 90% of them having a high school diploma/GED or less. More than half of them had never been married (54.7%). Of those under sentence of death, 41.5% were Blacks and 56.1% were Whites. Hispanics accounted for 13.5% of those prisoners under death sentence, whereas all other races accounted for 2.4%. There were 58 females under sentence of death in 2009. More than two-thirds (40) of them were White, 25.8% (15) were Black, and the remaining women were categorized as "Other races" (Snell, 2010). In 2009, 52 persons were executed. Of these, 31 were White (Hispanics were included under this classification) and 21 were Black. On average, these persons had been serving a death sentence for 14 years.

Table 7.6 provides additional information on death sentenced inmates. In particular, the criminal histories of the offenders are highlighted. Most of the offenders sentenced to death had prior convictions, but fewer than 10% had a prior conviction for homicide. This held true across race/ethnicity. Also, approximately 60% of the offenders had no charge pending at the time of the offense. Nonetheless, slightly more than 25% of them were on probation or **parole** when they committed the offense that resulted in a death sentence. A recent survey of states found that the death penalty remains an option in 34 states. Despite this, very few executions are actually carried out. This is clearly illustrated by Table 7.7, which shows the sharp decrease in the number of persons executed since 1930, in comparison to the number of executions since the *Gregg* decision.

Federal Death Penalty Statistics

Largely as a result of the increasing number of death penalty statutes passed during times of heightened concern regarding drug-related activity, throughout the 1980s and 1990s there

Table 7.2

Executions per Decade Under Civil Authority and Illegal Lynchings: 1890–1984

	1890s[a]	1900s	1910s	1920s	1930s	1940s	1950s	1960s	1970s	1980–1984	Total
Total under state authority	155	289	636	1,038	1,523	1,177	684	192	3	29	5,726
Race											
Number non-White	70	157	286	481	745	706	361	99	1	9	2,915
Percent non-White	55	62	47	49	52	63	56	52	33	31	54
Race unknown	(27)	(37)	(26)	(51)	(79)	(55)	(32)	(1)	(0)	(0)	(308)
Offense											
Murder	155	281	570	961	1,383	980	564	152	3	29	5,078
Rape	0	5	40	69	112	172	91	28	0	0	518
Other	0	3	26	8	28	23	19	8	0	0	115
Offense unknown	(0)	(0)	(0)	(0)	(0)	(2)	(9)	(4)	(0)	(0)	(15)
Total under local authority	1,060	901	406	131	147	110	35	0	0	0	2,790
Total under civil authority (state and local)	1,215	1,190	1,042	1,169	1,670	1,287	719	192	3	29	8,516
Illegal lynchings	1,540	895	621	315	130	33	8	1	—[b]	—[b]	3,543
Total per decade (legal and illegal)	2,755	1,995	1,663	1,484	1,800	1,292	721	192	3	29	12,059

a. The earliest recorded execution under state authority was in 1864. Between 1864 and 1890, 57 persons were reported executed under state authority.

b. No lynchings were reported after 1962.

Table 7.3

Illegal Lynchings by Race and Offense by Decade: 1880–1962

	1880s[a]	1890s	1900s	1910s	1920s	1930s	1940s	1950s	1960s[b]	Total
Total	1,203	1,540	895	621	315	130	33	8	1	4,736
Race										
Number Blacks	534	1,111	791	568	281	119	31	6	1	3,442
Percentage Blacks	44	72	89	91	89	92	94	75	100	
Offense Reportedly Causing Lynchings										
Homicide	537	606	372	278	100	39	5	0	0	1,937
Felonious assault	4	37	56	51	40	14	2	1	0	205
Rape	259	317	154	88	70	22	0	1	0	911
Attempted rape	9	75	99	56	22	21	6	0	0	288
Robbery and theft	58	87	33	38	6	6	4	0	0	232
Insults to White persons	4	10	11	31	17	8	2	1	0	85
All other causes	331	408	160	79	60	20	14	5	1	1,078

a. Statistics for 1880s are for 1882 through 1889.

b. Statistics for 1960s are for 1960, 1961, and 1962; no lynchings recorded after 1962.

Table 7.4

Number of Inmates Executed, by Race and Hispanic Origin, 1977–2009

Year of execution	Number executed				
	All executions	White[a]	Black[a]	Hispanic	All other races[a,b]
Total	1,188	672	411	91	14
1977	1	1	0	0	0
1979	2	2	0	0	0
1981	1	1	0	0	0
1982	2	1	1	0	0
1983	5	4	1	0	0
1984	21	13	8	0	0
1985	18	9	7	2	0
1986	18	9	7	2	0
1987	25	11	11	3	0
1988	11	6	5	0	0
1989	16	6	8	2	0
1990	23	16	7	0	0
1991	14	6	7	1	0
1992	31	17	11	2	1
1993	38	19	14	4	1
1994	31	19	11	1	0
1995	56	31	22	2	1
1996	45	29	14	2	0
1997	74	41	26	5	2
1998	68	40	18	8	2
1999	98	53	33	9	3
2000	85	43	35	6	1
2001	66	45	17	3	1
2002	71	47	18	6	0

(Continued)

(Continued)

	Number executed				
Year of execution	All executions	White[a]	Black[a]	Hispanic	All other races[a,b]
2003	65	41	20	3	1
2004	59	36	19	3	1
2005	60	38	19	3	0
2006	53	25	20	8	0
2007	42	22	14	6	0
2008	37	17	17	3	0
2009	52	24	21	7	0

Note: In 1972, the U.S. Supreme Court invalidated capital punishment statutes in several states (*Furman v. Georgia*, 408 U.S. 238 [1972]), effecting a moratorium on executions. Executions resumed in 1977, when the Supreme Court found that revisions to several state statutes had effectively addressed the issues previously held unconstitutional (*Gregg v. Georgia*, 428 U.S. 153 [1976] and its companion cases).

a. Excludes persons of Hispanic/Latino origin.

b. Includes American Indians, Alaska Natives, Asians, Native Hawaiians, and other Pacific Islanders.

Table 7.5

Demographic Characteristics of Prisoners Under Sentence of Death, 2009

	Prisoners under sentence of death, 2009		
Characteristic	Yearend	Admissions	Removals
Total inmates	3,173	112	149
Sex			
Male	98.1 %	98.2 %	100 %
Female	1.9	1.8	0
Race[a]			
White	56.1 %	58.0 %	53.7 %
Black	41.5	37.5	45.6
All other races[b]	2.4	4.5	0.7
Hispanic origin			
Hispanic	13.5 %	19.4 %	12.4 %
Non-Hispanic	86.5	80.6	87.6
Number unknown	396	19	12

Characteristic	Prisoners under sentence of death, 2009		
	Yearend	Admissions	Removals
Age			
20–24	1.2 %	11.6 %	0 %
25–29	5.5	14.3	4.7
30–34	12.3	18.8	7.4
35–39	16.8	19.6	16.1
40–44	17.0	5.4	12.1
45–49	17.9	16.1	19.5
50–54	13.3	5.4	19.5
55–59	7.8	4.5	5.4
60–64	5.6	3.6	10.7
65 or older	2.6	0.9	4.7
Mean age	44	38	47
Median age	44	36	47
Education			
8th grade or less	13.5 %	8.1 %	10.5 %
9th-11th grade	36.0	38.4	49.2
High school graduate/GED	41.5	47.7	29.0
Any college	9.0	5.8	11.3
Median	12th	12th	11th
Number unknown[c]	532	26	25
Marital status			
Married	21.9 %	17.0 %	25.0 %
Divorced/separated	20.5	33.0	21.3
Widowed	2.8	1.1	4.4
Never married	54.7	48.9	49.3
Number unknown	376	18	13

Note: Calculations are based on those cases for which data were reported. Detail may not add to total due to rounding.

a. Includes persons of Hispanic/Latino origin.

b. At year end 2009, inmates in "all other races" consisted of 26 American Indians, 36 Asians, and 14 self-identified Hispanics. During 2009, 1 Asian and 4 self-identified Hispanic inmates were admitted, and 1 American Indian was removed.

c. Due to a large number of cases with missing data on the education variable, users are advised to use caution when interpreting the distribution on this variable.

Table 7.6

Criminal History Profile of Prisoners Under Sentence of Death, by Race and Hispanic Origin, 2009

	Percent of prisoners under sentence of death[a]			
	All[b]	White[c]	Black[c]	Hispanic
U.S. total	100 %	100 %	100 %	100 %
Prior felony convictions				
Yes	65.7 %	62.1 %	71.4 %	61.8 %
No	34.3	37.9	28.6	34.3
Number unknown	257			
Prior homicide convictions				
Yes	8.6 %	8.8 %	9.0 %	6.7 %
No	91.4	91.2	91.0	93.3
Number unknown	56			
Legal status at time of capital offense				
Charges pending	7.7 %	8.6 %	7.6 %	5.0 %
Probation	10.5	9.1	11.7	11.4
Parole	15.2	12.9	16.5	19.2
On escape	1.5	2.0	0.9	1.5
Incarcerated	4.1	4.5	3.9	3.5
Other status	0.5	0.4	0.5	0.6
None	60.6	62.5	58.9	58.9
Number unknown	347			

a. Percentages are based on those offenders for whom data were reported. Detail may not add to total because of rounding.

b. Includes American Indians, Alaska Natives, Asians, Native Hawaiians, and other Pacific Islanders.

c. Excludes persons of Hispanic/Latino origin.

was increased attention on the federal death penalty. In March, 1994, the House Judiciary Subcommittee on Civil and Constitutional Rights produced a report looking at racial disparities in federal death penalty prosecutions over a six-year period (1988–1994). Out of concern that the federal death penalty provisions in the 1988 Anti–Drug Abuse Act were contributing to this, the committee examined the existing prosecution data. What they found was troubling. When looking at data on those who had been prosecuted under the so-called

Table 7.7

Number of Persons Executed, by Jurisdiction, 1930–2009

Jurisdiction	Number executed	
	Since 1930	Since 1977
U.S. total	5,047	1,188
Texas	744	447
Georgia	412	46
New York	329	0
North Carolina	306	43
California	305	13
Florida	238	68
Ohio	205	33
South Carolina	204	42
Virginia	197	105
Alabama	179	44
Mississippi	164	10
Louisiana	160	27
Pennsylvania	155	3
Oklahoma	151	91
Arkansas	145	27
Missouri	129	67
Kentucky	106	3
Illinois	102	12
Tennessee	99	6
New Jersey	74	0
Maryland	73	5
Arizona	61	23
Indiana	61	20
Washington	51	4

(Continued)

(Continued)

Jurisdiction	Number executed	
	Since 1930	Since 1977
Colorado	48	1
Nevada	41	12
District of Columbia	40	0
West Virginia	40	0
Federal system	36	3
Massachusetts	27	0
Delaware	26	14
Connecticut	22	1
Oregon	21	2
Utah	19	6
Iowa	18	0
Kansas	15	0
Montana	9	3
New Mexico	9	1
Wyoming	8	1
Nebraska	7	3
Idaho	4	1
Vermont	4	0
South Dakota	2	1
New Hampshire	1	0

Note: Statistics on executions under civil authority have been collected by the federal government annually since 1930. These data exclude 160 executions carried out by military authorities between 1930 and 1961.

drug kingpin law, "Twenty-nine [78%] of the defendants have been Black and 4 have been Hispanic. All ten of the defendants approved by Attorney General Janet Reno for capital prosecution have been Black" (Subcommittee on Civil and Constitutional Rights, 1994, p. 3). The report also noted that, although Whites had traditionally been the ones executed under federal law (85% between 1930 and 1972), the new drug kingpin laws were causing a dramatic change in this trend—so dramatic, in fact, that the report called for remedial action (p. 4).

In January, 1995, a policy was adopted whereby a death penalty "protocol" was instituted. This policy resulted in a process in which "United States Attorneys are required to submit for review all cases in which a defendant is charged with a capital-eligible offense, regardless of whether the United States Attorney actually desires to seek the death penalty in that case" (U.S. Department of Justice, 2000, p. 2). During this process, some of the cases are withdrawn, whereas others are dismissed (some or all charges). Five years after the passage of this protocol, the Department of Justice conducted an analysis of the federal death penalty system (U.S. Department of Justice, 2000). The report began by showing that overall the use of the death penalty at the federal level pales in comparison to its use at the state level. It also showed that, between 1930 and 1999, the federal government executed 33 defendants, and up until the report was written, no one had been executed since 1963 (Timothy McVeigh and two other federal inmates have been executed since 2001). At the end of 2010, there were 58 persons with pending federal death sentences. Of these, 26 (45%) were Black, 23 (40%) were White, 8 were Latino (14%), and 1 (1%) was Native American (Death Penalty Information Center, 2011).

Even with the small numbers of persons being passed through the federal system, there were still concerns about the obvious disparities. Prior to the institution of the "protocol" procedure, between 1988 and 1994, of those being considered for the federal death penalty, 75% (39) were Black and 10% (5) were Hispanic. Once the procedures changed, out of 682 defendants reviewed between 1995 and 2000, 48% (324) were Black, 29% (195) were Hispanic, and 4% were "Other" (U.S. Department of Justice, 2000). Although 682 cases were submitted for review, only in 183 cases did the U.S. Attorneys recommend seeking the death penalty. Blacks accounted for 44% of those persons, Whites represented 26%, Hispanics represented 21%, and Other represented 8% (U.S. Department of Justice, 2000). Combined, cases involving Blacks (49%) and Hispanics (31%) accounted for 80% of the cases in which U.S. Attorneys recommended against seeking the death penalty (U.S. Department of Justice, 2000).

The U.S. Department of Justice (2000) reported that 74% (500) of the cases were intraracial (i.e., race of offender and victim were the same). U.S. Attorneys recommended the death penalty in 24% of cases where homicides were intraracial. For homicides that were interracial, U.S. Attorneys sought the death penalty in 35% of the cases (U.S. Department of Justice, 2000). In addition, in the majority of the cases where the death penalty was sought, there was only one victim (77%). Of the cases involving multiple victims (157), Blacks represented 54% (84) of these defendants, whereas Hispanics represented 27% (42) and Whites represented 17% (26; U.S. Department of Justice, 2000).

Because the death penalty continues to be used as a punishment, scholars have sought to contextualize its application. The next section reviews some of the recent scholarship on race and the death penalty.

❖ Scholarship on Race and the Death Penalty

For decades, scholars have considered a variety of issues related to the death penalty, including whether race matters when death sentences are administered (Garfinkel, 1949). Because of the expansive nature of the literature, our emphasis here is on a brief overview of select areas of death penalty research.

Nearly four decades ago, Wolfgang and Riedel (1973) concluded that, after controlling for numerous factors, racial discrimination was likely the reason that Blacks received the death penalty more often than Whites. Since this pioneering research, numerous studies have been done that focus on racial disparities in the administration of the death penalty. With the development of more sophisticated methodological approaches, researchers have confirmed that discrimination permeates the initial charging and sentencing phases of capital cases (Bowers & Pierce, 1980; Paternoster, 1983). Yet, as noted earlier in the chapter, it was the Baldus study that most potently brought to the fore the issue of the race-of-victim effects (Baldus et al., 1990; see also GAO, 1990).

During the 2000s, researchers have continued to study and find race-of-victim effects and other race/ethnicity-related aspects of the death penalty (for a cogent review of post 1990s research, see Baldus & Woodworth, 2003). Stauffer, Smith, Cochran, Fogel, and Bjerragaard (2006) investigated whether the race-of-victim effect applies to situations involving not only White female victims, but females in general. Their research built on the work of M. Williams and Holcomb (2004), who found that the death penalty was more likely in cases involving White female victims. Based on data from more than 950 North Carolina capital cases, Stauffer et al. (2006) did not find any significant differences between cases involving Black and White female victims. Hence, they argued that there was a general "gender [effect] versus a racial effect in sentencing outcomes" (p. 110). Explaining this result, the authors wrote: "We may likely find that female victim cases are disproportionately selected for capital prosecution in North Carolina because they fit the profile (such as it is) of a murder that evokes a particularly severe criminal justice reaction" (p. 110). The authors also note other aggravating factors, such as females are generally perceived as being vulnerable, and their murders often involve other acts that might provoke an additional level of outrage (e.g., rape).

Not all the recent literature has supported the race-of-victim effect. In fact, Berk, Li, and Hickman (2005) disputed some of the earlier findings of Paternoster and Brame's (2003) research examining racial disparities in the application of the death penalty in Maryland that revealed significant race-of-victim effects. In their re-analysis of the Paternoster and Brame data using a new analytical approach, the race-of-victim effect was less pronounced; Berk and his colleagues concluded that there was no definitive support for the findings from the Maryland data. Paternoster and Brame (2008) responded to the re-analysis with another paper, which included new analyses that affirmed their earlier findings. This stalemate suggests that, in this and other instances, the selected analysis procedure might have an influence on the results reported. Berk and his colleagues have certainly opened up questions on the nature of the analyses used in most studies that examine race and the death penalty. Interestingly, other recent studies on race and the death penalty in Tennessee (Scheb, Lyons, & Wagers, 2008) and Texas (Petrie & Coverdill, 2010) have found that race of the victim was not significant in death sentences for racial minorities even when controlling for the standard legal and extralegal factors. Despite these findings, which as with all state-level studies are limited in their generalizability, the bulk of the studies on race and the death penalty continue to find Blacks receiving the death sentence more often when they kill Whites (for a cogent recent summary, see Kavanaugh-Earl, Cochran, Smith, Fogel, & Bjerregard, 2008; Pierce & Radelet, 2011).

Hispanics and the Death Penalty

Although much of the existing death penalty research has centered on Black and White experiences, little research has solely examined how Hispanics fare regarding capital cases. To fill this gap in the literature, C. Lee (2007) analyzed death penalty data from San Joaquin County, California. More specifically, using data from 128 death penalty cases from 1977 through 1986, she sought to determine whether Hispanics were treated more like Blacks or Whites in death penalty cases. Lee's diverse sample included defendants with the following racial characteristics: 34% White, 33% Hispanic, 25% African American, and 7% Asian American. The results from her analysis were rather telling. First, cases involving White victims "netted the most death-eligible charges" (p. 21). Next, the study showed that "A death-eligible charge was never levied against Asian American defendants" (p. 21). Turning to race-of-victim effects, C. Lee noted the following: "In a case where the victim was Hispanic or African American, the defendant was less likely to be charged with a capital homicide than if the victim was White or Asian" (p. 21). Furthermore, as found in the study by Stauffer and her colleagues, there was a strong gender effect. Here, it was revealed that "Defendants in male victim cases were *forty-three times* [emphasis added] less likely to face a death-eligible charge than those accused of killing a woman" (p. 22). To explain this effect, C. Lee turned to similar explanations postulated by Stauffer et al. (2006; e.g., vulnerability, additional offenses involved). Lee's results point to a clear need to move beyond the Black/White emphasis in death penalty research.

We turn our attention to the substitution thesis, which has, over the years, emerged as a way of contextualizing the racial disparities in the use of the death penalty in the United States.

Substitution Thesis/Zimring Analysis

One important area of research related to race and the death penalty has been the notion that, following the reduction in illegal lynchings, states "substituted" state-sanctioned executions for lynchings (Ogletree & Sarat, 2006; Tolnay & Beck, 1995; Vandiver, 2006). Referred to as the "substitution thesis," scholars have found support for this supposition (see J. Clarke, 1998; Tolnay & Beck, 1995; Vandiver, 2006). Zimring (2003) has also made a strong case for this perspective. In his death penalty research, Zimring has noted that, of all the industrialized nations, America remains one of the few that use the death penalty. He noted that, within the last 50 years, European nations such as Italy (1944), West Germany (1949), Austria (1950), Britain (1969), Portugal (1976), Spain (1978), and France (1981) have all abolished the death penalty (Zimring, 2003). Given this trend, he wonders why America has not abolished the death penalty. To answer the question, he turned to an analysis of executions by region, noting similarities between the current patterns in the use of the death penalty and historical lynching trends.

These data show that, from 1889 to 1918, lynchings were predominantly carried out in the South (88%). When one looks at the executions during the same period, again, the South predominated, producing 56% of the executions. During this early period, the North accounted for nearly 23%. Turning to the modern era of the death penalty (1977–2000), Zimring noted the similarities to the lynching patterns of earlier times (see Figure 7.2).

During the current period, 81% of the executions were in the South, with the Midwest (10%) and the West (8%) carrying out nearly all of the remaining executions. After considering these striking similarities, Zimring (2003) surmised that the South has a "culture of punishment." Of this culture, he wrote,

Figure 7.2

Regional Percentage Distributions of Lynchings and Executions

Source: Zimring (2003, p. 94).

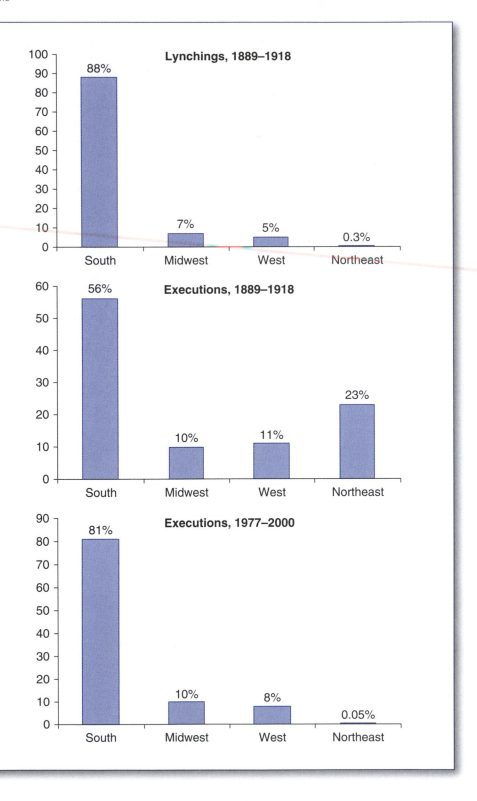

The Southern inclination towards high levels of punishment cannot be separated from the vigilante tradition itself. Rather than two separate traditions, the values and practices associated with extensive uses of the plantation prison, high levels of corporal and capital punishment, and those associated with lynchings and vigilante nostalgia overlap extensively with each other and with racial repression. Racism, vigilantism, and high levels of punishment were concurrent conditions in the South when high levels of punishment came to characterize the region. (p. 116)

On the racial dynamics of this culture, he opined,

It is likely that the long tradition of viewing punishments as a community rather than state institutions and the coercive White supremacist context in which such punishments took place were defining elements of the Southern propensity to punish. . . . The larger willingness to punish was a function of the particular targets and the particular context of punishment. (pp. 116–117)

Zimring's (2003) arguments are provocative and provide an important analysis that shows the parallels between illegal lynchings and state-sanctioned executions, which some have considered modern-day lynchings (J. Jackson & Jackson, 1996). Because of analyses such as Zimring's, there continues to be considerable debate about the application of the death penalty.

Over the years, public opinion researchers have measured public sentiment on the use of the death penalty. Next, we review some recent public opinion poll data on the death penalty.

❖ Public Opinion and the Death Penalty

According to Bohm (2007), public opinion on the death penalty is important for the following five reasons. First, strong public support for the death penalty is the likely reason that it is still used as a punishment in the United States. Consequently, politicians will continue to support the death penalty as long as support from the public remains high. Second, because the public wants the death penalty, Bohm believes that prosecutors are willing to appease them by seeking the death penalty in cases in which other penalties might be more suitable. Third, feeling the pressure from public sentiment, judges, like prosecutors, might feel undue pressure to impose death sentences (Bohm, 2007). Fourth, governors are also swayed by public opinion in their decisions to commute sentences. If public support for the death penalty is strong, few governors are willing to risk political disfavor by going against such sentiment. Finally, because state supreme courts and the U.S. Supreme Court consider public sentiment in their decisions regarding whether the death penalty is cruel and unusual punishment, the results of public opinion polls take on an added measure of significance.

Beginning in 1936, the Gallup poll began an annual tradition of asking Americans their opinions related to the death penalty. That early poll showed that 61% of those polled were in favor of the death penalty (Bohm, 1991). Since then, such polls have been annually conducted by several American polling organizations. Over time, support for the death penalty has ranged from a low of 42% in 1966 to a high of 80% in 1994 (Bohm, 1991). Over the 50-year period between 1936 and 1986, public support for the death penalty has averaged about 59% (Bohm, 1991). Recent polls continue to indicate strong support for the death penalty, with overall support at 64% in 2010 (Newport, 2010). In some instances, even when given the option of choosing between the death sentence and life in prison without the possibility of parole, a large share of Americans (49%) remain supportive of the death penalty (Newport, 2010). In fact, nearly half of the American population (48%) believes that the death penalty is not imposed often enough, with 26% believing that it is imposed in the right number of cases. Less than 20% of Americans believe that the death penalty is used too often (Newport, 2010). Although most Americans also believe that the death penalty is applied fairly (60%), many (73%) believe that someone who was innocent was executed within the last five years; even so, only if there were "quite a substantial number of innocent people" convicted of murder would a slim majority (51%) of Americans oppose the death penalty (Harris Poll, 2004).

Even with the continuing high level of support for the death penalty, the differences in levels of support for the death penalty have been attributed to a variety of characteristics, including race, political party affiliation, region, education level, occupation, religion, and gender (Longmire, 1996). Such differences have remained constant over time. Racial differences in support for the death penalty have also been consistent.

Race and Support for the Death Penalty

During the 1970s, there was a consistent trend in support for the death penalty; however, Black support was considerably less than White support (Longmire, 1996). Reviewing General Social Survey (GSS) data from 1974 to 1994, Arthur (1998) found that, in 1974, only 40% of Blacks supported the death penalty. He noted that, during the 1980s, this trend began to change, with Black support for the death penalty peaking in 1989 at 59%. During the mid-1990s, Black support dipped a little to 57%. Characteristics such as age, income, education, marital status, and political affiliation all had an impact on whether Blacks supported the death penalty.

According to Arthur (1998), "Blacks whose income exceeded $40,000 were found to be more approving of the death penalty than Blacks earning $10,000 or less" (p. 165). Thus, Blacks in the middle and upper classes were more supportive of the death penalty. Moreover, Blacks who were married and conservative showed strong support for the death penalty. Although as a whole more educated Blacks supported the death penalty (high school diploma and above), out of this educated group, those with only high school diplomas had the strongest support for the death penalty (Arthur, 1998). As for regional considerations, "Blacks who live in large metropolitan districts and suburbs are more likely than those who live in 'other urban' and rural places to favor the death penalty for murder" (p. 165). Another study looking at the geographic variation in attitudes about capital punishment also noted the significance of political affiliation, percentage of Blacks in the population, and areas with higher levels of homicides in predicting higher levels of support for the death penalty (Baumer, Messner, & Rosenfeld, 2003).

Reviewing data from the 1995 National Opinion Survey on Crime and Justice, Longmire (1996) provided a more expansive view of death penalty opinions, which included the opinions of Hispanics. The 1995 survey data revealed that Whites were most strongly in support of the death penalty (77%), followed by Hispanics (52%) and Blacks (40%; Longmire, 1996). In line with other public opinion studies, there were also differences found by location of the respondents, with the strongest support [coming] from those who resided in rural areas (82%), and the strongest opposition [coming] from those residing in urban areas (25%). Urban residents also reported the lowest levels of support for the death penalty (58%) and the highest levels of uncertainty (17%). (p. 99)

So what accounts for the racial differences in support for the death penalty? Barkan and Cohn (1994) explored the notion that racial prejudice might play a role. Using 1990 GSS data, they examined questions that might speak to prejudice, such as whether Whites strongly favor or strongly oppose "living in a neighborhood where half your neighbors were Black" and "having a close relative or family member marry a Black person" (p. 203). Based on questions on the survey, they constructed a racial stereotyping scale out of questions that were meant to measure "the degree to which they thought Blacks were lazy, unintelligent, desirous of living off welfare, unpatriotic, violent, and poor" (p. 203). Barkan and Cohn's results showed that "many White people are both prejudiced against Blacks and are more likely to support the death penalty" (p. 206).

Bobo and Johnson's (2004) study on attitudes toward the death penalty found that more than 80% of Whites and slightly more than 50% of Black respondents favored the death penalty. Such support was not mediated when the researchers introduced respondents to concerns regarding bias in the administration of criminal justice. There was, however, an effect when respondents were told that if someone murdered a White person he was more likely to receive the death penalty than if he murdered a Black person. This caveat significantly reduced Black support for the death penalty, whereas White support was not significantly impacted. When Bobo and Johnson posed a hypothetical question involving executing innocent people on death row, there were only slight changes in the views of Whites and Blacks toward support for the death penalty.

Analyzing 14 years' worth of GSS data, spanning from the 1970s to 2002, related to attitudes toward the death penalty, Unnever and Cullen (2007) also reported that African Americans were significantly more likely than Whites to oppose the death penalty. Their research also found that "respondents with more years of education, who resided in the central city, and often attended church were significantly less likely to support the death penalty, and males and Americans who feared being victimized were significantly more likely to support the death penalty" (pp. 140–141). Income was also a significant variable in determining support for the death penalty. Here, respondents with higher incomes were more likely to support the death penalty. In general, this study, like other recent ones, found considerable support for the "racial divide" in public opinion on the death penalty (see also Cochran & Chamlin, 2006).

Scholars have found that White racism accounts for a percentage of the racial divide in support for the death penalty (Unnever & Cullen, 2007). Hurwitz and Peffley (2010) also found that White racism was a factor in White support for the death penalty. They conducted an experiment that asked a sample of respondents for their views about the death penalty, and to measure the influence of certain factors on the level of support for the punishment, they informed the respondents that "some" people believe that it is administered in a discriminatory fashion. This caveat caused "African Americans . . . to become even more oppositional to the penalty, while, shockingly, a nontrivial number of Whites became *more* supportive once informed that the punishment is administered disproportionately to Blacks" (p. 473). Another consideration related to the death penalty public opinion research is called the **Marshall hypotheses**.

The Marshall Hypotheses

Drawing on the statements of the late Supreme Court Justice Thurgood Marshall in *Furman v. Georgia*, researchers have presented hypotheses derived from his suggestions that (a) "American citizens know almost nothing about capital punishment," and (b) "[people] fully informed as to the purposes of the penalty and its liabilities, would find the penalty shocking, unjust, and unacceptable." Marshall qualified his second supposition by noting that this would not be the case if someone adhered to the retributive sentencing philosophy.

On the whole, scholars have found support for Marshall's first hypothesis—that the public is uninformed about the death penalty (Bohm, Clark, & Aveni, 1991; Lambert & Clarke, 2001). However, Lambert and Clarke (2001) noted that "of the five studies that directly attempt to test Marshall's second hypothesis, three found small decreases in support for the death penalty after subjects were presented with information concerning capital punishment" (p. 218). Guided by this past research, Lambert and Clarke conducted a study to determine whether reading an essay would influence college students' views on the death penalty.

To do so, Lambert and Clarke (2001) created three different essays. The first essay spoke to the major reasons for punishing criminals. The second essay presented empirical research on "the deterrence effect of the death penalty" (p. 222). The third essay discussed the "possibility and frequency of sentencing the innocent to death" (p. 222). Making use of a self-administered survey design, more than 700 students were randomly given surveys with one of these essays in it. The first section of the survey asked questions regarding the students' initial knowledge and attitudes toward the death penalty (serving as a pretest); the authors wanted to see whether their views changed depending on their exposure to one of the essays. Thus, following their review of the essay, students were again queried about their views on the death penalty. Although their research did show support for Marshall's second hypothesis, that an informed citizen would not support the death penalty, Lambert

Photo 7.1

A gathering of exonerated death row inmates (2002)

and Clarke wrote, "The type of information is critical. Although those who read the deterrence essay stated that their view of the death penalty had changed, only the innocence essay group had a statistically significant reduction in support for capital punishment" (p. 227). Although those who had read the essays on convicting innocent people showed statistically significant changes in their views, the authors did note that the change was slight. A recent re-analysis of their data continued to support the Marshall hypotheses (Lambert, Camp, Clarke, & Jiang, 2011).

Cochran and Chamlin (2005) used a pretest/posttest design to determine whether students' views on the death penalty would be influenced by exposure to materials presented in a course on the death penalty. The authors did find mixed support for the supposition "that death penalty attitudes and beliefs were inversely associated with student's level of knowledge" (p. 582). The researchers also found that exposure to knowledge about the death penalty decreased the level of support for capital punishment and increased students' support for life without parole as an alternative to capital punishment (see also Cochran, Sanders, & Chamlin, 2006).

A. Mitchell (2006) also examined whether Marshall's suppositions could be supported using a pretest/posttest approach with a seminar course as the experimental stimulus. An interesting finding from his research was that White and Hispanic views were minimally impacted by taking the seminar. In contrast, following exposure to the materials in the seminar, Blacks' opposition to the death penalty significantly increased (A. Mitchell, 2006). A. Mitchell attributed this finding to the legacy of Blacks being disproportionately sentenced to the death penalty. When comparing the experimental group to a control group that did not take the seminar, the study did find that the seminar increased the participants' knowledge of the death penalty.

Because of the importance of the Capital Jury Project, wrongful convictions, the death penalty moratorium movement, and judicial overrides in death penalty sentencing, we conclude the chapter with brief discussions of these topics.

❖ Contemporary Issues in Race and the Death Penalty

Capital Jury Project

Funded by the National Science Foundation in 1991, the Capital Jury Project (CJP) was originally founded to investigate the following research objectives:

> (1) to systematically describe jurors' exercise of capital sentencing discretion;
> (2) to assess the extent of arbitrariness in jurors' exercise of capital discretion; and
> (3) to evaluate the efficacy of the principal forms of capital statutes in controlling arbitrariness in capital sentencing. (University at Albany, School of Criminal Justice, 2011)

In addition, the CJP has secured additional funds to investigate "the role played by jurors' race in making the life or death sentencing decision" (University at Albany, School of Criminal Justice, 2011). To date, nearly 1,200 jurors from 353 capital trials in 14 states have been interviewed. Drawn from a combination of structured and unstructured questions, the interviews conducted for the project typically lasted from three to four hours.

The project has already yielded some general findings and also some related to race and capital juror decision making (Bowers, Sandys, & Steiner, 1998; Bowers, Steiner, & Sandys, 2001; Fleury-Steiner & Argothy, 2004). As an example, Fleury-Steiner and Argothy (2004) considered what happens in Latino capital cases. Making use of 35 juror narratives from 14 cases involving Latino capital defendants from Texas and California, the authors illuminated the racialized perceptions that jurors had of Latinos. Such racialized views manifested themselves in narratives that included the concepts of "colorblindness," "ethnic threat," and "ethnic deceit" (p. 74). With the concept of colorblindness, it is commonly thought that there is a general denial that racism exists in American society. As such, in capital cases involving Latinos, it impacts "the ways jurors evaluate witnesses, deliberate with other jurors, and justify their decisions to impose the death penalty" (p. 75). The concept of ethnic threat centers on the notion that Latinos are prone to violence and, as a result, the "belief in 'dangerous hombres' may *itself* play a role in capital sentencing jurors' decision to impose the death penalty" (p. 77). The notion of ethnic deceit relates to the belief that Latinos will do anything to enter the United States. As such, they simply cannot be trusted. Thus, Fleury-Steiner and Argothy believe that "racial deceit may be activated at various points in the trial process, including when a Latino defendant who happens not to speak English testifies" (p. 79).

Summarizing some of the major findings from the CJP, Fleury-Steiner (2009) writes that jurors were found to "have their minds made up on punishment before the sentencing phase of the trial had begun" (p. 91). Thus, jurors are neglecting the Supreme Court mandate to consider aggravating and mitigating factors in the capital sentencing process. Jurors also "[do] not believe that a life sentence actually means that the defendant will remain in prison the rest of his or her life" (p. 92). In short, because they cling to the belief that the offender might eventually be released, rather than risk the offender being released and harming someone else, they sentence the person to death. As for race, the results revealed that the possibility of being convicted was higher when there were fewer non-Whites on the jury. Even more disturbing was the finding that, in cases involving Black offenders and White victims, "a strong majority of White jurors as compared to Black jurors are more likely to be predisposed to the death sentence even before the sentencing trial begins" (p. 92). Finally, jurors were less likely to consider mitigating circumstances in cases involving Black offenders and White victims. In an earlier study, Brewer (2004) also weighed in on this general finding and provided additional context. Using a subset of the CJP data, he found that "only when Black jurors are faced with killing an out-group member, White victim, that they become significantly more receptive to mitigation than their White colleagues on the jury" (p. 542).

Taken together, the CJP has provided findings that align with the thoughts of some notable jurists (see Higginbotham, 1996) as well as yield new insights into capital jurors and their decision-making process. Whereas in the past researchers conducted simulations involving nonjurors to study jury decision making, the CJP has provided key insights into how *actual* jurors weigh in on capital cases. Such insights might hold the key to changing misperceptions that too often influence jury decision making. An obvious reason that this project is so critical relates to the potential for misguided verdicts and sentencing practices, which, in their worst manifestation, can result in wrongful convictions. We review various aspects of wrongful convictions in the next section.

❖ Wrongful Convictions

Concerns regarding innocent people being convicted are not new. Early on, both American (Borchard, 1932) and British (Brandon & Davies, 1973) scholars investigated this issue. Generally, however, most American citizens understand that, given the nature of our justice system, at times the guilty will go free and at other times innocent people will be sent to jail or prison. Therefore, when it comes to criminal justice, we generally adhere to a utilitarian philosophy. That is, because the system works for most citizens, we can tolerate it when a small number of citizens are wrongfully convicted. Essentially, this is the price we are willing to pay to maintain our adversarial "trial by combat" justice system. Although such a philosophy might be acceptable if the stakes were low, that is not the case with the American justice system. Considering that the United States still maintains the death penalty, to some, adhering to such a system leaves us open to executing innocent people. In fact, pioneering research in this area suggests that the United States has already executed hundreds of innocent people (Radelet, Bedau, & Putnam, 1992).

Numerous authors have elucidated the major contributors to wrongful convictions (Bedau, 2009; Castelle & Loftus, 2002; Christianson, 2004; S. Cohen, 2003; Gould & Leo, 2010; Harmon, 2001, 2004; Huff, 2004; Huff, Rattner, & Sagarin, 1996; Leo, 2002; Martin, 2002; Smith & Hattery, 2011; Zalman, 2011; Zimmerman, 2002). Of these, the most consistent contributors are (a) eyewitness error, (b) police misconduct, (c) prosecutorial misconduct, (d) plea bargaining, (e) community pressure for conviction, (f) inadequacy of counsel, (g) false confessions, (h) mistaken identity, (i) fabrication of evidence, (j) having a criminal record, (k) misinformation from criminal informants, and (l) race. Most of these contributors are self-explanatory; therefore, given the focus of this book, we concentrate on the role of race in wrongful conviction cases.

Bedau and Radelet (1987) were among the first to discuss race as a factor in wrongful conviction cases: Of the 350 capital cases they reviewed, 40% involved instances in which Blacks were wrongly accused. Huff et al. (1996) have also noted that historically there have been disproportionate numbers of Blacks and Hispanics among those wrongly convicted. He and his coauthors alluded to the fact that many of the early instances of wrongful convictions involving minorities were likely a result of being tried by racist prosecutors, who also had all-White, prejudiced juries on their sides.

According to Parker, Dewees, and Radelet (2002), the 40% figure generally holds true across studies. One exception to this is the research done by Barry Scheck and Peter Neufeld, in which their **Innocence Project** (housed at Cardozo Law School at Yeshiva University in New York) has found that, of those exonerated by the use of DNA, 57% have been Black (Parker et al., 2002). Parker et al. also surmised that, based on past criminal justice practices, "Among those wrongly convicted of felonies, Black defendants are significantly less likely than White defendants to be vindicated" (p. 118).

Another contribution of the Parker et al. (2002) paper is that it attempts to link theoretical explanation to the disproportionate representation of minorities among the wrongly convicted. Among their individual explanations, they pointed to racism, stereotyping, and Blacks being easy targets for a variety of reasons, including their lack of access to resources. As for structural explanations, Parker et al. relied on the conflict-oriented (see Chapter 3) power threat hypothesis; according to this perspective, "Because Blacks are perceived as a threat to Whites, they face higher conviction rates, even wrongfully as Whites respond to this perceived threat" (p. 125). The authors also noted that urban disadvantage might play a role in minorities being overrepresented in instances of wrongful convictions. As they opined,

> The racial patterns in cases of wrongful conviction, particularly the finding that Blacks are more likely to be erroneously convicted, are crystallized under these conditions. That is, these conditions—residential segregation, concentrated poverty, joblessness, and other forms of concentrated disadvantage—reinforce racial disparities in the treatment of minorities in the criminal justice system, including racial bias in convictions of the innocent. (p. 126)

In a recent book that builds on past scholarship on race and wrongful convictions, Free and Ruesink (2012) analyzed more than 300 cases (from 1970 to 2008) in which African American males have been wrongfully convicted. Their research showed that the three states with the highest number of wrongful convictions of African Americans were Texas, Illinois, and Ohio. More than half the cases involved instances in which the African Americans were wrongly convicted of murder or attempted murder. Other significant offenses that were represented among the cases included rape, sexual assault, drug offenses, and robbery. The authors also found that in more than 90% of the rape and sexual assault cases there were witness errors that often involved cross-race identification issues. Other factors in the wrongful conviction included forensic errors, police and prosecutorial misconduct, and questionable informants (Free & Ruesink, 2012). This important work will hopefully lead to additional empirical research on race and wrongful convictions. In particular, we note the dearth of information on race, sex, and wrongful convictions.

High Profile Wrongful Conviction Cases

Central Park Jogger Case

Although there are numerous case studies that highlight the racial tenor of wrongful conviction cases, we make note of a few. First, the "Central Park Jogger" case represents a classic example in which many of the contributors to wrongful convictions, especially race, played roles in the unfortunate outcomes (Burns, 2011). In April, 1989, a White, 28-year-old investment banker was seriously injured when, according to the original reports, she was allegedly brutally attacked and raped by several Harlem teenagers. That night, 40 teenagers from Harlem were alleged to have engaged in "randomly molesting, robbing, and assaulting strangers who were jogging or bicycling through the Upper East Side of the park" (S. Cohen, 2003, p. 255). Following the incident, as S. Cohen noted, "The term *'wilding'* [was] introduced to the vernacular of oppression" (p. 255). Eventually, five Black youth between the ages of 15 and 17 were charged with the offense. Reviewing the facts of the case, S. Cohen wrote,

> The only physical evidence the police had were hairs on the clothing of one of the boys that were said to be consistent with the hair of the jogger. But all five youths would soon be offering detectives what passed for confessions of guilt. The videotaped statements were the backbone of the prosecutor's case. (p. 256)

All of the youth were eventually convicted of all or some of the charges. A year later, however, it was found that "semen found in the victim did not come from any of the five youths convicted of the crime" (S. Cohen, 2003, p. 257). However, not until 2002, when a convicted rapist admitted to a New York correctional officer that he had committed the offense, did anyone pay any additional attention to the fate of the youth. Although the youth were eventually released and *partially* exonerated (some officials continued to insist some of the youth participated in the crime), the racial element of the case cannot be overstated. One of the most disturbing elements of this case was that, although officials centered on the five innocent youth and looked past the obvious inconsistencies in their confessions and the overall weak evidence, the real rapist, Matias Reyes, went on "raping, assaulting, and tormenting" women (p. 259). In fact, in the weeks following the arrest of the five youth, he also murdered a pregnant woman (S. Cohen, 2003). In the end, had the racial elements of the case not overtaken the fears of Whites, it is likely that the evidence in the case would have led them to conduct a more thorough investigation, which would have surely exonerated the youth shortly after their arrest.

Duke Lacrosse Case

The second case took place in March, 2006. At that time, several White Duke University lacrosse players were arrested on charges of raping a Black stripper who was invited to perform at a college party. After the party, the stripper provided the sordid details of the incident, which was later proved to be a hoax. Nevertheless, during the incident, racial tensions at Duke and around the country were divided on the issue. Because of the furor over the incident, the prosecutor, Michael Nifong, vigorously pursued the case, which, in the end, revealed the innocence of the Duke students. At the conclusion of the case, Nifong was disbarred for his misconduct in the case and also faced the additional charge of criminal contempt of court for lying to a judge about the details of the case (Beard, 2007). The youth and their families have also filed a $30 million federal civil rights lawsuit against the city of Durham that is still pending. In contrast to the Central Park Jogger case, some observers suggest that the economic status of the Duke students played a key role in securing their freedom (see Box 7.4).

BOX 7.4

The Duke Lacrosse Scandal Revisited: Five Years Later

On April 18, 2011, Crystal Mangum was indicted for murder in the stabbing death of her boyfriend Reginald Daye. This case wasn't Mangum's first brush with the law. In 2010, she was convicted of a misdemeanor for setting fire to her house while her three children were inside.

But in Mangum's most famous—or should I say, infamous—interaction with the criminal justice system, she claimed to be the "victim."

Mangum, who is black, accused three white lacrosse players from Duke University of raping her at an off-campus party in March 2006, a fact that's noted in nearly every article on her current legal predicament.

The charges against the players were eventually dropped in April 2007 after an investigation by the North Carolina Attorney General's Office uncovered prosecutorial misconduct and a lack of evidence to support Mangum's accusations.

Mike Nifong, the district attorney responsible for the case, resigned and was disbarred. However, Mangum was never charged over the false accusations.

(Continued)

(Continued)

During the 13 months the case was active, the national media ran full tilt with the story. It was covered in newspapers such as the *New York Times* and *Los Angeles Times;* magazines such as *Newsweek* and *Rolling Stone;* blogs and cable news. Even the venerable *60 Minutes* did several segments on it.

The consensus now seems to be that much of this coverage represented a rush to judgment of the players and was unfair and unprofessional. (But at least one journalist, Andrew Cohen of the *Washington Post*, thought the coverage was slanted in favor of the players.)

I won't rehash all of the mistakes various media entities made in covering what's often simply referred to as the Duke lacrosse scandal. (The *American Journalism Review* did a wonderful job of reviewing and analyzing the media feeding frenzy that descended on Duke and the accused players.) But the missteps broadly occurred in two areas: the initial framing of the case and the response to the dropping of the charges.

Everything takes place in a context, which is relevant to understanding the true nature of events. Crime is no different. For example, a man who robbed a store to fund his drug habit is guilty of the same crime as a man who lost his job and so robbed the same store to feed his family.

But because the context of each of these crimes is very different, the media will appropriately cover each differently.

In the case of the Duke lacrosse scandal, the accusations were quickly framed in the context of race, sex and class—three wild, rich white men attending an elite university were accused of preying on a poor black woman. A story as old as time, right?

In this case, it wasn't actually true.

However, this hook was so attractive and played into so many public beliefs and stereotypes that many journalists forgot about the presumption of innocence, failed to objectively evaluate the "facts," and just ran with that angle.

Even as it became clear that there were serious problems with the prosecution's case—for example, there was no DNA evidence tying any of the Duke players to Mangum, and the other stripper who was with her at the party called the rape claim "a crock"—many reporters refused to let go of the assumption that the players were guilty.

And once the charges were officially dropped, they reported it with a lot less enthusiasm than their coverage of the original accusations—if they covered it at all.

There were some exceptions. For example, *New York Times* Op-Ed columnist David Brooks, who'd originally condemned the Duke players, later called the case a "witch hunt" and concluded that "maybe the saddest part of the whole reaction is not the rush to judgment at the start, but the unwillingness by so many to face the truth now that the more complicated reality has emerged."

One journalist went even further and issued an apology to the Duke players.

Ruth Sheehan of the *Raleigh News & Observer* had been an outspoken critic of the players, condemning them for their initial silence in the face of the charges and calling for the firing of the lacrosse team's coach. She'd written 14 columns on the case.

But after the charges were dropped, her final column on it began, "Members of the men's Duke lacrosse team: I am sorry." Sheehan went on to acknowledge her errors and promised to do better in the future.

Where did the media go wrong?

In large part, journalists got caught up in the public outrage over Mangum's claims. So reporters blindly trusted the information from the prosecutor's office without objectively analyzing it. In contrast, they dismissed information and claims from the defense attorneys.

And they relied on and played into stereotypes.

What *should* journalists have done in covering that case? In the *American Journalism Review's* piece on media coverage of the Duke scandal, Rachel Smolkin correctly asserts that reporters should have stayed true to journalism's most basic tenets: "Be fair; stick to the facts; question authorities; don't assume; pay attention to alternative explanations."

Robin L. Barton, a legal journalist based in Brooklyn, NY, is a former assistant district attorney in the Manhattan District Attorney's Office and a regular blogger for The Crime Report. She welcomes readers' comments.

Do you believe the media can influence the way prosecutors pursue cases? Why or Why not?

The Jena 6 Case

Not long after the Duke case, in late 2006, the Jena 6 case reached the national spotlight. In the small town of Jena, Louisiana, a Black student asked one of his high school teachers for permission to sit under a tree that was believed to be reserved for White students. After receiving permission to sit under the tree, and doing so, the following day there were three nooses hanging from the tree. The details remain murky after this. It has been suggested that six Black youths (Robert Bailey, Carwin Jones, Bryant Purvis, Theodore Shaw, Jesse Beard, and Mychal Bell [the Jena 6]) got into an altercation with two White youths who were believed to have placed the nooses on the tree. During the altercation, one of the White youths, Justin Barker, was injured; as a result, the Black youths were charged with attempted second-degree murder and conspiracy (Sims, 2009). As one of the Black youths, Mychal Bell, moved through the justice system, there was increasing outrage concerning the case. Observers wondered why such serious charges were being levied against the Black youths while nothing had happened to the White youths. This disparity in treatment led to nationwide protests, as well as a significant protest march in Jena that was attended by tens of thousands of protesters, including national civil rights leaders. In the wake of these protests, the District Attorney, Reed Walters, reduced the charges against the youths. In addition, it was later ruled that some of the youths should have been tried as juveniles; thus, their cases were moved to the juvenile court. It is likely that without national attention the Black youths would have been the victims of a rogue district attorney who overcharged them while neglecting to file any charges against the White youths. Again, such a case had the potential to lead to youths being wrongly prosecuted.

All three cases highlighted here illustrate the problems related to the "rush to judgment" that often takes place when high-profile cases involving race occur. However, this approach often results in both mistakes and unethical cover-ups that can often lead to misguided prosecutions or, in the worst-case scenarios, wrongful convictions. Because of the high-profile nature of wrongful conviction cases in which persons on death row have been exonerated, scholars have continued to call for an increased emphasis on wrongful convictions in the discipline (Leo, 2005), as well as continuing to investigate the nature and scope of wrongful convictions (see Denov & Campbell, 2005; Ramsey & Frank, 2007; Zalman, 2006, 2011).

Addressing Wrongful Convictions in the 21st Century

It is notable that C. Ronald Huff devoted his 2001 American Society of Criminology presidential address to the topic of wrongful conviction and public policy (Huff, 2002). Although he repeated many of the previously discussed facts and figures, his address laid out several important policy considerations aimed at reducing the number of persons wrongfully convicted. First, Huff recommended that those wrongly convicted should be adequately compensated and also provided the appropriate social services to deal with the trauma and reintegration. Second, he suggested replacing the death penalty with sentences of 20 years, 30 years, or life imprisonment without parole. Third, he advocated granting prisoners access to DNA tests. In line with this policy suggestion, the Innocence Protection Act of 2003, if enacted, would require DNA tests when federal inmates claim they are innocent. Fourth, Huff suggested ensuring that qualified expert witnesses be used to minimize misidentification, which is a major contributor to wrongful convictions. Fifth, legal counsel should be present when any identification procedure is used. Sixth, police interrogations of suspects should be taped. Seventh, criminal justice officials who engage in unethical, unprofessional, or illegal activity should be removed and prosecuted. Finally, Huff recommended that individual states and the federal government establish innocence commissions to handle these situations.

There can be no doubt that instituting Huff's proposed policies would go a long way toward reducing the number of wrongful convictions in general. In recent years, states have responded to public concern about wrongful convictions. Norris (2011) recently assessed the compensation statutes for the wrongly convicted across the United States. Using the Innocence Project's compensation provision as the model standard, he compared how well states' policies stacked up. The Innocence Project recommends $50,000 minimum for each year spent in prison plus $25,000 for time spent on parole or probation. The model policy also recommends other types of compensation such as mental and physical services, child support payments, and so on. None of the 27 states that have such statutes included all the provisions recommended in the model policy. Notably, only four states matched the $50,000 annual compensation recommendation. After scoring the states on the comprehensiveness of their statutes, Texas emerged as a leader. In particular, Texas provides $80,000 per year compensation and also provides vocational training and tuition and fees at a state university or college (p. 16). Medical and support services are also available for one year, and the Texas statute was also the only one to pay child support for exonerees.

It is apparent that some states have taken heed of the concerns surrounding wrongful convictions and, in response, have enacted moratoriums on the death penalty. We briefly review this movement next.

Death Penalty Moratorium Movement

Because of the increasing recognition that errors were being made in capital cases, states have begun to consider moratoriums on executions. Governor George Ryan of Illinois (a nominee for the Nobel Peace Prize) was the first governor to take such drastic action. When asked why he felt a need to enact such a policy, he noted,

> We have now freed more people than we have put to death under our system—13 people have been exonerated and 12 have been put to death. . . . There is a flaw in the system, without question, and it needs to be studied. ("Illinois Suspends Death Penalty," 2000)

Like Illinois, other states such as Nebraska and Pennsylvania have considered such action ("Illinois Suspends Death Penalty," 2000; "Pennsylvania Panel Advises Death Penalty Moratorium," 2003), but it has not passed muster with the legislatures of these states. In 2002, former Maryland governor Parris Glendening issued a moratorium, only to have his successor, governor Robert Ehrlich, lift it shortly after he was sworn in the next year. Citizens in some states have formed groups, such as New Jerseyans for a Death Penalty Moratorium (see http://www.njmoratorium.org), that are aimed at pressuring state governments to enact moratoriums in order to study the fairness of the death penalty. Although the movement is clearly picking up momentum, few other states that currently use the death penalty have gone as far as Illinois did without turning back. A 2003 poll sheds some light on why more states have not followed Illinois's lead. A January, 2003 ABC/*Washington Post* national poll of 1,133 citizens found that when asked, "Would you support or oppose it if the governor in your state changed the sentence of every death row inmate to life in prison instead?" only 39% supported such a policy, whereas the majority (58%) did not (ABC/*Washington Post* Poll, 2003). Such figures indicate that death penalty opponents have considerable work to do in order to increase the number of moratoriums nationwide. It is notable, however, that as a result of the efforts of the New Jerseyans for a Death Penalty Moratorium, in December, 2007, the New Jersey legislature approved legislation to abolish the death penalty in the state (Hester & Feeney, 2007). In 2009, New Mexico also abolished the death penalty, becoming the 15th state to do so; and in 2011, Illinois became the 16th state to abolish the death penalty.

Judicial Overrides in Death Penalty Sentencing

One of the more recent "hot button" contemporary death penalty issues is the use of judicial override in capital cases, particularly in Alabama (see Box 7.5). A recent report by the Equal Justice Initiative has brought this issue front and center in Alabama. Alabama is one of the few states that allow judges to override the sentence recommended by the jury in death penalty cases. The override can involve the changing of a life without parole sentence to a death sentence or, alternatively, it can reduce a death sentence to life without parole. Currently, only three states allow judicial overrides (Alabama, Florida, and Delaware). Yet only in Alabama is the practice regularly used. Data from the Equal Justice Initiative show that in Delaware the override has been primarily used by judges to override death sentences and impose life sentences. In Florida, the practice hasn't been used in more than a decade.

BOX 7.5

Overriding the Jury in Capital Cases

By Adam Liptak

Washington—Alabama allows judges to reject sentencing decisions from capital juries, which sounds like a sensible idea. You might want a mature and dispassionate jurist standing between a wounded community's impulse toward vengeance and a defendant at risk of execution.

"If you didn't have something like that," said Judge Ferrill D. McRae, who spent 40 years on the bench in Mobile before he retired in 2006, "a jury with no experience in other cases would be making the ultimate decision based on nothing. The judge has seen many, many cases, not just one."

Judge McRae, chatting on the phone the other day, recalled having breakfast with Justice Thurgood Marshall at an American Bar Association meeting not long after the Supreme Court reinstated the death penalty in 1976.

Justice Marshall was a fierce opponent of the death penalty. But, according to Judge McRae, the justice also saw the wisdom of the override system. "He thought it was better that someone who had seen more than one case was making the decision," Judge McRae said.

What Justice Marshall probably did not anticipate, though, was that judges in Alabama would not use their power for mercy—that they would, in fact, be even tougher than juries. Since 1976, according to a new report, Alabama judges have rejected sentencing recommendations from capital juries 107 times. In 98 of those cases, or 92 percent of them, judges imposed the death penalty after juries had called for a life sentence.

(Continued)

(Continued)

More than 20 percent of the people on death row in Alabama are there because of such overrides, according to the report from the Equal Justice Initiative, a nonprofit law firm that represents poor people and prisoners. The overrides in Alabama contributed to the highest per capita death sentencing rate in the nation, far outstripping Texas.

Judge McRae himself ordered six defendants executed notwithstanding jury verdicts calling for life sentences, more than any other judge in Alabama in the modern history of capital punishment. But he never rejected a jury's recommendation of death.

Judge McRae said he had tried to determine, in the words of an Alabama law, whether the crime in question was "especially heinous, atrocious or cruel." Having seen a lot of cases helped him make that decision, he said. "Juries don't know," he said, "what is 'especially heinous, atrocious or cruel.'"

Alabama judges have justified their decisions to override in favor of death on other grounds as well. Judge Dale Segrest, who retired in 2001, said he had rejected one jury's recommendation that a white defendant's life be spared on the ground of racial equality. "If I had not imposed the death sentence, I would have sentenced three black people to death and no white people," he said at a sentencing hearing in 2000.

Judge Charles C. Partin, who sat in Bay Minette, said the defendant before him was probably not mentally disabled, a factor that may have figured in the jury's life verdict. "The sociological literature suggests that Gypsies intentionally test low on standard I.Q. tests," he wrote in a 1990 sentencing order.

Florida and Delaware also allow overrides, but they are subject to strict standards. No one has been sentenced to death in Florida as a result of a judicial override since 1999, and no one is on death row in Delaware as a consequence of an override. The most recent override in favor of death in Alabama was in March.

Judges in Delaware are appointed and generally use their authority to reject death sentences. Alabama judges are elected, often running on tough-on-crime platforms. Overrides are more common in election years.

"Not surprisingly, given the political pressures they face, judges are far more likely than juries to impose the death penalty," Justice John Paul Stevens wrote in a 1995 dissent from a decision that upheld Alabama's capital sentencing system. Much has changed in sentencing law since then, and it is not clear that the system would survive a new look from the Supreme Court.

One thing that is clear is that Justice Marshall, whatever he said at breakfast, was appalled by how things turned out in Alabama. "It approaches the most literal sense of the word 'arbitrary,'" he wrote in a 1988 dissent, "to put one to death in the face of a contrary jury determination where it is accepted that the jury had indeed responsibly carried out its task."

Alabama jurors are not notably squeamish about the death penalty, and those opposed to it are automatically excluded from service. Deliberations can be agonizing, former jurors say, adding that they would expect their recommendations to count.

William Davis, who served on a capital jury that voted for a life sentence, said he did not see the point of the exercise after a judge dismissed the jury's unanimous recommendation as "not helpful."

"If the judge is going to overrule the jury," he said in a court hearing in Montgomery last year, "then you don't need a jury. The jury don't serve a purpose."

Do you believe judges should be able to override jury sentencing decisions in capital cases? Why or why not?

In contrast to Delaware and Florida, judicial overrides in Alabama are a common practice in death penalty cases. Judges in Alabama consistently override jury verdicts in death penalty cases. In fact, "more than 20% of the people currently sentenced to death in Alabama were condemned by a judge after the jury voted for life" (Stevenson, 2011, p. 8). To date, 92% of the overrides have involved the changing of life sentences to death sentences. It is believed that because judges in Alabama are elected they take tough stances by overriding jury sentencing decisions that might appear lenient. The Equal Justice Initiative has gone further by outlining the following potential reasons for the heavy use of overrides in Alabama: "The data suggests that override in Alabama is heavily influenced by arbitrary factors such as the timing of judicial elections, the politics of the county where the accused is prosecuted, and the outsized enthusiasm of certain judges for overriding jury life verdicts" (p. 8). While there has been at least one legal challenge to the practice, the courts have found that it is not unconstitutional for Alabama judges to use overrides.

The racial dynamics of the judicial overrides have also been noted. As with other death penalty research, race appears to play a role in the judicial overrides in Alabama. In particular, it has been found that "African Americans in Alabama constitute 26% of the total population, but more than half of the overrides in Alabama have imposed the death penalty on African Americans" (Stevenson, 2011, p. 18). In addition, the Alabama data reveal that "While just 6% of all the murders in Alabama involve black defendants and white victims, in 31% of Alabama override cases, the trial judge condemned a person of color to a death sentence for killing someone white" (p. 18). It is apparent from the existing data that the practice of judicial overrides, even with the requirement that judges explain their decisions, has the potential to produce racial disparities.

To stem the concerns related to judicial overrides, in 2007 the Alabama legislature considered a bill that would disallow their use; the bill failed. Others have suggested that electing judges is part of the problem and should be eliminated because decision making might be tied to concerns about re-election (Serwer, 2011). In general, judicial overrides in death penalty cases is a problem that is only now receiving national attention, but it clearly has been a concern in Alabama for some time. The national spotlight on the issues will certainly cause Alabama to reconsider its policy and, more generally, cause the nation to think about the way in which judges are selected.

❖ Conclusion

This chapter reviewed several aspects of race and the death penalty. Our historical overview showed that the death penalty has been applied in a discriminatory fashion since colonial times. Sadly, recent state and federal death penalty figures do not show much promise for resolving this issue in the immediate future. After reviewing several significant Supreme Court cases on the death penalty, we reviewed public opinion on the subject. Although support has remained strong, it has varied based on characteristics such as race, class, area of residence, education level, political party affiliation, and religion.

We concluded the chapter by focusing on the Capital Jury Project, wrongful convictions, the death penalty moratorium movement, and judicial overrides in death penalty cases. These areas are clearly intertwined in the search for justice. Moreover, this literature has shown that the criminal justice system is not infallible. In fact, several hundred people have been wrongly convicted of capital offenses in the United States, and some of these persons have actually been executed. Scholars have suggested a variety of reasons for these errors, all of which should be the focus of policymakers to ensure that the justice system works. Because of the furor over wrongful convictions involving death sentences, several states have discussed or instituted moratoriums on executions, with states like Illinois commuting death row inmates' sentences to life without parole.

In Chapter 8, we turn our attention to corrections and the race-related issues that plague the so-called back end of the criminal justice system.

Discussion Questions

1. What was the nature of capital punishment during the colonial era?

2. Describe the significance of *Gregg v. Georgia* and *McCleskey v. Kemp*.

3. Discuss two significant findings regarding public opinion polls on the death penalty.

4. Explain the significance of the Capital Jury Project.

5. What are five of the most significant contributors to wrongful convictions?

Internet Exercises

1. Go to the Web site http://www.deathpenaltyinfo.org, and select the link for the list of exonerees from death row since 1973. Using the data provided, summarize the overall racial trends and also the average time between conviction and exoneration.

2. Visit the website for the National Coalition to Abolish the Death Penalty (http://www.ncadp.org/) and see whether the arguments presented concerning the abolishment of the death penalty are convincing.

3. Visit the website for the Center for Wrongful Convictions (http://www.law.northwestern.edu/cwc/) and read the stories of at least three persons who were wrongly convicted. See whether there are any common threads among the stories.

Internet Sites

Capital Jury Project: http://www.cjp.neu.edu

Death Penalty Information Center: http://www.deathpenaltyinfo.org

The Innocence Project: http://www.innocenceproject.com

CHAPTER 8

Corrections

In many prisons, one feels as if there is an invisible sign on the front door that reads: Only Blacks and Hispanics Need Apply.

—National Trust for the Development of African American Men (cited in Petersilia, 2003, p. 26)

O nce offenders are convicted and sentenced, the courts generally turn them over to correctional officials. Correctional departments typically oversee inmates sentenced to probation, jail, and prison. Another key component of the criminal justice system, **corrections** represents one of the most costly expenditures of the system. Billions of dollars are spent each year to carry out this difficult function. To reduce such expenditures, over the last several decades, more nontraditional approaches, such as community-based initiatives, have expanded the umbrella of corrections (see Clear & Dammer, 2003). Even with the adoption of more innovative initiatives, prison overcrowding has continued to plague correctional systems throughout the United States. In fact, there has been an increasing concern in society about the expense of corrections. This is illustrated by Figure 8.1, which highlights the ratio of corrections spending to higher education spending in 2007. The Pew Center on the States' illuminating report, *One in 100: Behind Bars in America 2008*, presents figures showing the staggering financial investment being made in corrections at the expense of other important state institutions, such as higher education (see also the recent NAACP report, *Misplaced Priorities: Over Incarcerate, Under Educate*, 2011).

Along with financial concerns, the correctional system has also remained an arena in which race-related concerns have persisted. Considering that, in 2009, 54% of sentenced prisoners in state and federal facilities in the United States were Black and Hispanic (West, Sabol, & Greenman, 2010), questions have arisen about social justice. In line with Goldkamp's (1982) belief perspectives presented in Chapter 4, one question of critical concern is whether disparities in corrections are based on discrimination or whether they exist because minorities commit more serious offenses and should expect to be overrepresented in prison populations (Delisi & Regoli, 1999; MacDonald, 2008; Mann, 1993; Wilbanks, 1987). As noted next, this chapter aims to explore this and other related questions.

Figure 8.1

Ratio of Corrections to Higher Education Spending in 2007. While states don't necessarily choose between higher education and corrections, a dollar spent in one area is unavailable for another.

Source: Reanalysis of data presented in the National Association of State Budget Officers, "State Expenditure Report" series

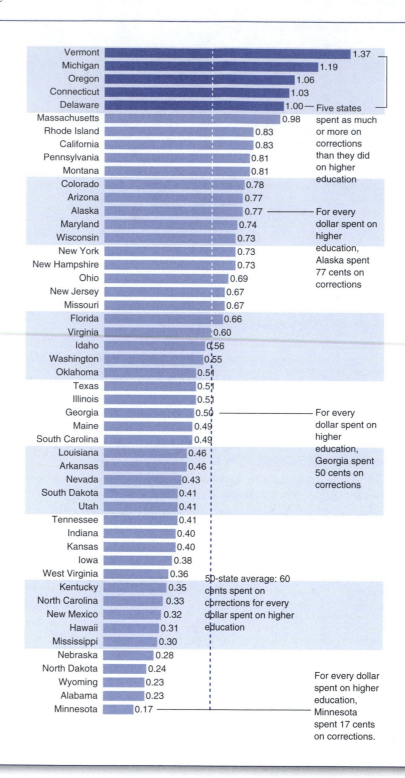

State	Ratio
Vermont	1.37
Michigan	1.19
Oregon	1.06
Connecticut	1.03
Delaware	1.00
Massachusetts	0.98
Rhode Island	0.83
California	0.83
Pennsylvania	0.81
Montana	0.81
Colorado	0.78
Arizona	0.77
Alaska	0.77
Maryland	0.74
Wisconsin	0.73
New York	0.73
New Hampshire	0.73
Ohio	0.69
New Jersey	0.67
Missouri	0.67
Florida	0.66
Virginia	0.60
Idaho	0.56
Washington	0.55
Oklahoma	0.51
Texas	0.51
Illinois	0.51
Georgia	0.50
Maine	0.49
South Carolina	0.49
Louisiana	0.46
Arkansas	0.46
Nevada	0.43
South Dakota	0.41
Utah	0.41
Tennessee	0.41
Indiana	0.40
Kansas	0.40
Iowa	0.38
West Virginia	0.36
Kentucky	0.35
North Carolina	0.33
New Mexico	0.32
Hawaii	0.31
Mississippi	0.30
Nebraska	0.28
North Dakota	0.24
Wyoming	0.23
Alabama	0.23
Minnesota	0.17

Five states spent as much or more on corrections than they did on higher education

For every dollar spent on higher education, Alaska spent 77 cents on corrections

For every dollar spent on higher education, Georgia spent 50 cents on corrections

50-state average: 60 cents spent on corrections for every dollar spent on higher education

For every dollar spent on higher education, Minnesota spent 17 cents on corrections.

The purpose of this chapter is to provide an overview of corrections and the race-related issues that are connected to its operation. Our coverage of corrections begins with a brief overview of the structure, function, and public opinion pertaining to corrections in America. A brief historical overview of race and American corrections is presented next. We then review the current state of corrections in America. The chapter concludes by focusing on several contemporary issues in corrections. Specifically, our focus here is reviewing explanations for disparities in correctional populations, **prisoner reentry** into the community, and felony disenfranchisement.

❖ Overview of American Corrections

Often referred to as the "back end" of the criminal justice system, corrections is generally the place where the system ends. Although there is the perception that *corrections* is synonymous with incarceration, more than 70% of those persons in the corrections phase of the criminal justice system are actually being supervised in the community (Glaze & Bonczar, 2010). Clear and Cole (2000) suggested that "the central purpose of corrections is to carry out the criminal sentence" (p. 7). Furthermore, describing the scope of American corrections, they wrote that "corrections . . . encompasses . . . the variety of programs, services, facilities, and organizations responsible for managing people accused or convicted of criminal offenses" (p. 8). Within this description, they are distinguishing between the various correctional options. We discuss these options in turn.

American corrections include a continuum of sanctions that range from being incarcerated in a jail or prison facility to being sentenced to a fine or restitution (Clear & Cole, 2000). Depending on the nature of their offenses, those who are incarcerated are placed in minimum-, medium-, or maximum-security prisons. Nationwide, there are also approximately 57 "supermax" prisons in 40 states (Mears & Watson, 2006). According to Clear and Cole (2003), "These institutions are designed to hold the most disruptive, violent, and incorrigible prisoners" (p. 252). Persons who are awaiting trial and are unable to secure bail are held in jails. In addition, persons who are sentenced to a year or less are typically housed in jails. Because of overcrowding, however, some jurisdictions have turned to housing more serious offenders in jails (Allen, Simonsen, & Latessa, 2004). Other sanctions falling under the corrections umbrella include fines, community service, drug and alcohol treatment, probation, home confinement, and **intensive probation** supervision. Each of these sanctions provides nonincarcerative options for offenders. Such options are also attractive to corrections officials because they are considerably cheaper than incarcerating offenders.

All of these various correctional options have also resulted in considerable employment opportunities. For example, in 1983, there were 146,000 correctional workers (U.S. Census Bureau, 2003); however, by 2010, there were 465,000 correctional officers. Blacks (22%) and Hispanics (13.3%) were beneficiaries of this growth. Females also took advantage of this growth, representing more than a quarter (26.1%) of those employed as correctional officers (U.S. Census Bureau, 2011d, p. 394).

As with sentencing philosophies, public opinion and politics play important roles in the way the correctional system operates. Given the importance of public opinion research, we review public opinion on corrections for the last four decades.

Public Opinion on Corrections

Because of the various "get tough" laws that were legislated in the 1980s and 1990s, jails and prisons have become considerably overcrowded (Alexander, 2010). This overcrowding coincided with the decline in support for rehabilitation. For example, during the early 1970s, 76% of Americans were in support of rehabilitation (Flanagan, 1996). By 1980, however, only a little more than 50% of the public supported such an approach. Summarizing the public opinion literature from 1968 to 1982, Flanagan (1996) wrote, "The proportion of Americans selecting rehabilitation as the main emphasis of prisons declined 40%; the proportion selecting punishment rose 171%, and the proportion of protection of society rose 166%" (p. 79). Even with the support for this punitive approach being strong nationally, there remain considerable differences in opinion by race and gender.

In the 1995 National Opinion Survey on Crime and Justice (NOSCJ), respondents were asked whether violent offenders could be rehabilitated and what portion of them (most, some, only a few, or none of them). Responses varied by race, with 26% of Blacks feeling that most of such offenders could be rehabilitated; only 17% of Hispanics and 13% of Whites felt this way (Flanagan, 1996). Females were also less optimistic than Blacks; 17% of them felt that way (Flanagan, 1996). Turning to prison programs (e.g., prisoners learning trades, literacy programs), there was a high level of support among all racial groups for such programs (Flanagan, 1996). One area of difference was that more Whites (79%) than Blacks (52%) were opposed to giving parole violators another chance if they had previously failed on parole. Hispanics fell in the middle: 65% of them were against giving offenders another chance (Flanagan, 1996).

The final area investigated by the NOSCJ related to corrections had to do with acceptable alternatives to prison and solutions to overcrowding. Here, the focus was on determining whether the public favored or opposed various strategies to reduce prison overcrowding. Except for raising taxes to build more prisons, Blacks had stronger support for all the proposals to reduce prison overcrowding than did other racial groups. There were also significant differences by gender. A national *Parade Magazine* poll conducted in June, 2001 found that, to reduce prison overcrowding, Americans still leaned heavily on increasing more community-oriented sanctions, especially for nonviolent offenders. Less than half (42%) of the respondents endorsed "building more prisons" to alleviate prison crowding (*Parade Magazine* Poll, 2002).

A 2002 national ABC News Poll also provided insights into the public's views on how to handle certain offenders. The poll found that when asked whether someone convicted of using drugs should go to jail or receive treatment, 89% responded "treatment." Only after multiple convictions for using drugs was the majority of the public (66%) in favor of jailing drug addicts (ABC News Poll, 2002). A 2009 national poll by Rasmussen Reports also found support for rehabilitation. When asked "To fight crime, what is more important—funding programs for the rehabilitation of criminals, hiring more police or building more prisons?" respondents from across the nation placed rehabilitation (34%) just below hiring more police (42%). Building more prisons was only endorsed by 12% of the respondents (Rasmussen Reports, 2009).

Overall, the public remains committed to the punitive sentencing strategies, with one poll finding that 98% supported giving repeat offenders longer sentences for committing violent crimes (*Parade Magazine* Poll, 2002). The ABC News Poll confirmed this sentiment, finding that 82% of the public supported three-strikes-and-you're-out policies, which obviously has serious implications for corrections (ABC News Poll, 2002). The majority of the public (76%), however, was not supportive of such a policy for nonviolent offenders who had committed their third offense (ABC News Poll, 2002).

Because of budget shortfalls across the country, the handling of nonviolent offenders by correctional departments has become a major issue. In California, for example, when former Governor Arnold Schwarzenegger proposed the release of 22,000 nonviolent offenders to ease state spending on prison and correction, there was sizeable support within a state that had previously championed the three-strikes-and-you're-out policies. More specifically, a statewide poll found that nearly half the population was in favor of the governor's proposal. As expected, the support varied by political affiliation, with Democratic support at 55%, whereas Republican support was nearly 20 points lower at 37% (Public Policy Institute of California, 2008).

On the whole, racial minorities have been the ones disproportionately affected by what some have called America's "imprisonment binge" (Alexander, 2010; J. Austin & Irwin, 2001; Baadsager, Sims, Baer, & Chambliss, 2000; Clear, 2007; Tonry, 2011; Western, 2006). This was borne out by a national poll of African Americans revealing that 19% of African Americans had an immediate family member incarcerated in either a prison or juvenile detention facility (National Urban League Poll, 2001).

A recent study by Unnever (2008) examined public opinion as to why African Americans were disproportionately imprisoned. In general, African Americans and Whites had differing views. African Americans, more so than Whites, felt that police bias (71% vs. 37%) and unfair courts (67% vs. 28%) were big reasons why African Americans were disproportionately incarcerated. Another big difference in opinion was with denial of jobs. African Americans were much more likely than Whites to see this as a big reason (59% vs. 37%). Both African Americans and Whites felt that poverty was a big reason (67% vs. 63%) for the disproportionate incarceration of African Americans. Unnever (2008) noted that a big reason for the "racial divide" in opinions has to do with personal experience:

> The more African Americans report that they have encountered racial discrimination the more likely they are to attribute the disproportionately high rates of imprisonment among black males to structural disadvantages such as bad schools and a lack of job opportunities and to racial discrimination within the criminal justice system. (Unnever, 2008, pp. 531–532)

Has race always mattered in corrections? The next section looks into this question by providing a historical overview of race and corrections.

❖ Historical Overview of Race and Corrections

Because of the uneven nature of the historical scholarship and statistics on groups other than African Americans, chronicling the history of race and corrections is a considerable challenge. However, even with these limitations, we attempt to provide some insight into how race has historically intersected with American corrections. We begin our discussion with a brief overview of the history of race and corrections.

Early History of Race and Corrections

American corrections had its origins in the European workhouses, which were places where vagrants and other minor offenders were sent (Langbein, 1976). According to Shelden (2001), the first such institution to house offenders opened in Amsterdam in 1596. Referred to as the *Rasphaus*, the purpose of this facility was to "discipline the inmates into accepting a regimen analogous to an 'ideal factory,' in which the norms required for capitalist accumulation were ingrained in the code of discipline" (Shank, 1978; cited in Shelden, 2001). Shelden proposed that these facilities were more appropriately called "poorhouses," which were essentially modeled to support the need for industrial workers. As a result, "When released from these workhouses, the inmates would theoretically willingly adapt to the regimentation of the factory and other forms of labor under the new capitalist system" (Shelden, 2001, p. 155).

Over time, England developed three types of facilities: (a) jail, (b) house of corrections, and (c) workhouse (Collins, 1997). By the founding of colonial America in the early 17th century, some of these facilities made their way to America. Similar to today, in colonial times, jail and prisons were expensive to build and maintain (Chapin, 1983). As a result, most offenders were rarely sentenced to prison, with fines, corporal punishments (e.g., whippings), and banishment serving as the most common punishments (Chapin, 1983; Shelden, 2001). Chapin (1983) noted that "jails were used most commonly to hold persons accused of serious crimes before trial and to detain convicted persons until they could pay fines or make restitution" (p. 52).

Because of economic considerations, it was rare to find slaves, Native Americans, or indentured servants incarcerated. On this subject, Collins (1997) wrote,

> Jailing of slaves was not profitable for the slave owners, so very few slaves were ever incarcerated for an extended period of time. Instead, prior to the Civil War, Black slaves would be imprisoned in plantation-built jails and punished for crimes committed (for example, running away, stealing, assaulting an overseer, or disobeying an order) by the slave master who had unlimited power, including deadly force. (p. 6)

To legitimize their actions, slave masters created "Negro courts," which meted out punishments (Sellin, 1976).

In 1790, legislation was passed to create an institution in which solitary confinement and hard labor were required (Clear & Cole, 2000). In response to the legislation, the Quakers restructured the **Walnut Street Jail** (which began to receive prisoners in 1776) to fit the required specifications. At that moment, the Walnut Street Jail became America's first prison (Shelden, 2001). Reviewing the early prison records (1795–1826), McIntyre (1992) noted that the free African American population in Philadelphia ranged from 4.6% in 1790 to 9.4% in 1810. When she looked at prisoner statistics in the Walnut Street Jail, McIntyre found,

> Throughout the period from 1795 to 1826 in Philadelphia City and County, Blacks comprised 35% with "Mulattoes" equaling an additional 9%. This 44% reflected an inmate population for African Americans more than 13 times greater than the state's and nearly 5 times greater than the city's total African American population. (pp. 170–171)

Race and Corrections in the 1800s

As one might expect, soon the Walnut Street facility became overcrowded. To alleviate this overcrowding, as happens today, the legislature approved the construction of two prisons: Western Penitentiary (1826) and Eastern Penitentiary (1829). As a prelude of things to come, Clear and Cole (2000) noted that Prisoner Number 1, who arrived at the Eastern Penitentiary (near Philadelphia) on October 25, 1829, was "Charles Williams, an 18-year-old African American from Delaware County, Pennsylvania . . . serving a two-year sentence for larceny" (p. 35). Inmate records from 1829 to 1841 show that a steady stream of African Americans followed Williams into Eastern Penitentiary. An inspector's report of the records revealed that there were 1,353 prisoners from 1829 to 1841, "with a breakdown of 846 White inmates (823 males and 23 females) and 508 Black inmates (456 males and 52 females). The Black men represented 37.5% of all males, and the Black women equaled 66% of the females" (McIntyre, 1992, p. 171).

Other states had similar trends in relation to the racial composition of early correctional facilities. For example, from 1812 to 1832, the Maryland state prison in Baltimore "held 45% African American males and 68% African American females for a 51% overall Black inmate population" (McIntyre, 1992, p. 172). Over a 10-month period, from 1832 to 1833, records show that in Richmond, Virginia, on average 28% of the inmates were African American. Although African American men represented 22% of this number, African American women represented 100% of the female inmates (McIntyre, 1992).

Strikingly, according to these statistics, White women did not commit any crimes requiring incarceration during this period. A more likely explanation is that "the chivalry factor" was in effect for White women, but not Black women. That is, Southerners might have done all they could to protect White women from entering prisons, but such a consideration was not given to Black women.

So how did early observers of the system explain these disparities? When Beaumont and Tocqueville (1833/1964) visited the United States in the early 1800s to examine the feasibility of applying the American penitentiary system to France, they provided some early commentary on these disparities. Examining the trends in crime across the country, Beaumont and Tocqueville wrote, "In order to establish well-founded points of comparison between the various states, it would be necessary to deduct from the population of each the foreigners, and to compare only the crimes committed by the settled population" (p. 93). Even after doing this, Beaumont and Tocqueville (1833/1964) noted that Maryland had a high crime rate, which was, as they put it,

> explained by a cause peculiar to the southern states—the colored race. In general it has been observed, that in those states in which there exists one Negro to thirty Whites, the prisons contain one Negro to four White persons. (p. 93)

In their view, "The states which have many Negroes must therefore produce more crimes" (p. 93). Beaumont and Tocqueville (1833/1964) speculated that crime was high not just in Southern states, but, more specifically, those states that manumitted slaves. On this point, they opined,

> We should deceive ourselves greatly were we to believe that the crimes of the Negroes are avoided by giving them liberty; experience proves, on the contrary, that

in the south the number of criminals increases with that of manumitted persons; thus, for the very reason that slavery draws nearer to its ruin, the number of freed persons will increase for a long time in the south, and with it the number of criminals. (p. 93)

Without much more said, such statements could have been interpreted as arguing for the continued enslavement of Blacks. In addition, Christianson (1998) has aptly wondered why the two men did not see slavery as being criminogenic.

The mid-1800s brought African Americans closer to their eventual emancipation. However, as noted in Chapter 1, following their emancipation in 1863 and the passage of the Thirteenth Amendment in 1865, Southern landowners were devastated. Sellin (1976) noted that, following the passage of the Thirteenth Amendment,

The penal laws of the southern states became applicable to all offenders regardless of race. This was a distressing prospect for states which had created industrial penitentiaries for offenders from the master class and now faced the rapidly growing criminality of poor, unskilled, bewildered ex-slaves cast into a freedom for which few of them were prepared. (p. 145)

Sellin added that, although Blacks were legally free, Southern landowners "did not change their opinions on the status of Blacks in a society dominated by Whites" (p. 145). Because of Whites' "reluctance to labor," they created a system to maintain an able-bodied labor force (Sellin, 1976). Taking advantage of the language in the Thirteenth Amendment, which allowed slavery and involuntary servitude as punishment for certain crimes, Southern landowners created the convict lease system, which

Reintroduce[d] a species of slavery for Negro criminals and lower-class Whites. They were to be forced to do work which would more than compensate the state for their keep. The sole aim of the convict lease system was financial profit of the lessees who exploited the labor of the prisoners to the fullest, and to the government which sold the convicts to the lessees. (Sellin, 1976, p. 146)

Southern states invested in the system because it was profitable while also keeping taxes down (Oshinsky, 1996). To make the system work, the change in the racial composition of prison populations was dramatic. Oshinsky (1996) wrote,

In Alabama and Arkansas, Texas and Virginia, Florida and Georgia, North and South Carolina, Louisiana and Mississippi, the convict populations were overwhelmingly Black. Of South Carolina's 431 state prisoners in 1880, only 25 were White; of Georgia's 1,200 state prisoners in that year, almost 1,100 were Negro. (p. 63)

Furthermore, in Georgia, "Between 1870 and 1910, the convict population grew ten times faster than the general one. Prisoners became younger and Blacker, and the length of their sentences soared" (Oshinsky, 1996, p. 63). Records from Georgia prisons in the late 1800s showed that Blacks were serving sentences twice as long as Whites, with 50% of the inmates serving sentences of more than 10 years (Oshinsky, 1996).

Myers (1998) has shown the full extent of the racial dimension of punishment in Georgia. Looking at the Georgia system from 1870 to 1940, she chronicled the ups and downs of the convict lease system, as well as the use of other punishments (e.g., chain gangs) to provide services to the state (e.g., public roads projects). She noted that the trends in punishments were often dictated by economic factors such as depressions and recessions (Myers, 1998).

During the 1800s, race also intersected with gender in corrections. For a long time, women prisoners were housed in the same facilities as men (Young & Reviere, 2006). Because of overcrowding issues and scandals such as women prisoners becoming impregnated, during this time, several states built reformatories for women (Collins, 1997; LeFlouria, 2011). Although White women were initially housed in these facilities, Black women were later housed in segregated cottages. Prison officials justified their actions with ridiculous rationales, such as "a peculiar attraction has been found to exist between 'colored' and White women in confinement which intensifies much danger, always present in an institution, of homosexual involvement" (Lekkerkerker, 1931, cited in Collins, 1997, p. 10). Some officials, such as Katherine Bemet Davis, the first female corrections commissioner of New York City, refused to segregate female prisoners. More significant segregation took place in the housing of Black women in penitentiaries, whereas White women were housed in treatment-oriented reformatories. This segregation reduced the chance that Black women would be successful on their release from prison (Collins, 1997).

Early National Prison Statistics

The earliest national statistics on corrections were recorded in 1850, when the national census on prisons took a one-day count and recorded 6,737 prisoners. By 1860, there were an additional 13,000 prisoners, with records indicating 19,086 prisoners. Dramatic increases would occur over the next several decades: 1870 (32,901), 1880 (30,659), 1890 (45,233), and 1904 (57,070; Cahalan & Parsons, 1986). Tracking the trends by race and ethnicity, Table 8.1 shows that not only did state and federal prison populations increase, but the percentage of Blacks incarcerated also increased, from 31% in 1923 to 37% in 1960 (Cahalan & Parsons, 1986).

Figures from the 1931 Wickersham Commission Report show that in 1926, native-born Whites represented 68% of those in federal and state prisons. The racial breakdown for the remainder of the inmates was 8% foreign-born White, 21% Negro, and 3% Other (Indian, Mexican, Chinese, Japanese, and all other races; National Commission on Law Observance and Enforcement, 1931a). During this same period, Black females were also considerably represented in the nation's prisons. Russell-Brown (2004) presented figures that show that, from 1926 to 1946, the percentage of Black female prisoners fluctuated from a low of 21% to a high of 40% of the female inmates.

In the decades between the Reconstruction period and 1960, although much changed in terms of overall advancements for racial minorities, much stayed the same, with Blacks continuing to be overrepresented in state and federal correctional institutions. However, the 1960s saw the civil rights movement, the increasing visibility of Black Muslims, and the Black Power movement influenced both Black prisoners and various segments of the Black community.

Table 8.1

Characteristics of Persons in State and Federal Prisons, Institutional Population Census Data, 1910–1980

Year	Number of Prisons	Inmates Present	Percentage						
			Female	Foreign-Born	White	Black	Other Races	Spanish Origin[a]	Juvenile (under 18)
1910	61	67,871	4	—[b]	—[b]	—[b]	—[b]	—[b]	—[b]
1923	64	80,935	4	12	68	31	1	—[b]	2.0
1933[b]	117	137,997	3	(5)	(74)	(23)	(3)	—[b]	(3.9)
1950[c]	158	178,065	4	3	65	34	1	—[b]	2.9
1960[d]	1,072	226,344	4	1	61	37	2	—[b]	2.3
1970[e]	633	198,831	3	—[b]	58	41	—[b]	7	2.2
1980[f]	2,560[g]	302,377	5	3	47	44	—[b]	10	—[b]

a. Persons of Spanish origin may be of any race.

b. Not available or not obtained.

c. Except for the 3% female prison population, which is calculated on the basis of inmates present (137,997), details are calculated on the basis of prisoners received from courts (62,801) according to available data.

d. 1940 is excluded because juvenile facilities were not separated from state and federal. However, only those over 14 were enumerated. Detail data in 1950 were calculated on 3½% sample with an estimated base of 181,080 for total prison population; the complete count is 178,065.

e. Data based on 25% sample.

f. Data based on 20% sample.

g. Counted each budget unit as individual facility.

Photo 8.1
Two chain gang prisoners in Georgia (1937)

Black Muslims, the Black Panther Party, Political Prisoners, and the Prisoners' Rights Movement

Although each of the above movements can be credited with bringing to the fore issues related to police brutality, they each played a role in the evolution of corrections in the 1960s and 1970s as well. Prior to this period, Black inmates essentially accepted their status without any resistance (Reasons, Conley, & Debro, 2002). Reasons et al. (2002) noted that, although Blacks were exposed to inhumane conditions, they did not protest because "(1) the courts had a hands-off policy with respect to penal conditions and issues, and (2) the institutions were located primarily in rural areas and thus functioned in relative isolation, and the guards were all White" (p. 271). Discussing the importance of the mass migration from the South to northern and western states among African Americans, Reasons et al. wrote, "This demographic shift made racial segregation more difficult and expensive to maintain in all institutions, including penal institutions" (p. 271). Another contributor to change was the fact that leaders from the civil rights movement (e.g., Martin Luther King, Jr., Ralph Abernathy, and Medgar Evers), Black Panther movement (e.g., Stokely Carmichael, H. Rap Brown, Huey Newton, and Angela Davis), and Black Muslim movement (most notably, Malcolm X) were all incarcerated at some point and spoke out about their experiences (Reasons et al., 2002). It was, however, the Black Muslim and Black Panther movements that had the greatest influence on correctional systems.

According to Conley and Debro (2002), the Black Muslim (also known as the "Nation of Islam") movement in California prisons can be traced to San Quentin in the late 1950s. On the one hand, the movement was popular among Black inmates because, along with preaching racial pride, instituting strict discipline, and pushing for economic self-sufficiency, the group preached that Whites were evil and the cause of the current plight of African Americans (Reasons et al., 2002). On the other hand, correctional officials saw the movement as both a threat and "management problem," so they took steps to suppress the movement using a variety of strategies, including dispersing the members. Even with these strategies, the Black Muslims continued to challenge correctional policies in court.

Beginning with the 1962 case of *Fulwood v. Clemmer*, courts began to recognize the Black Muslim religion. Furthermore, this decision sparked the prisoners' rights movement, which resulted in thousands of lawsuits being filed by inmates. Some of these lawsuits resulted in substantive changes in the way correctional institutions were run. For example, in *Battle v. Anderson* (1974), following an earlier loss in the courts to maintain the right to read literature that was considered inflammatory, the courts reinforced inmates' First Amendment rights and provided that "prison officials had the burden of proving to the court that the publications *Elijah Muhammad Speaks* and *The Message to the Black Man in America* present[ed] a threat to security, discipline, and order within the institution" (Palmer, 2010, p. 86). A related case, *Northern v. Nelson* (1970), ruled that Black Muslims should have access to religious literature. Other cases challenged the request of Black Muslims to be served a pork-free diet (*Young v. Robinson*, 1981), the right to correspond with their religious leaders (*Desmond v. Blackwell*, 1964), and the right to free access to ministers (*Jones v. Willingham*, 1965). The efforts of Black Muslims to challenge correctional officials represents a monumental contribution to prisoners' rights.

One could argue that the early concerns expressed by correctional officials were somewhat exaggerated, but it also is likely that some of the disturbances caused by Black Muslims were instigated by prison officials (Conley & Debro, 2002). In recent years, the group has continued to be involved in correctional settings through the Nation of Islam Prison Reform Ministry, which has received several awards (Gabbidon, 2004).

During the 1960s and 1970s, the Black Panther Party also impacted corrections through its nationwide efforts to steer Black youth away from the criminal justice system. But it was the party's influence on several high-profile inmates that highlighted the abuses in correctional facilities. Inmates such as George Jackson typified the inmates who adhered to the "Black power" philosophy of the Black Panther Party. These inmates were often considered **political prisoners** or individuals who, based on their political, social, or environmental beliefs, are brought within the jurisdiction of the criminal justice system, with most of them eventually being incarcerated. Historically, the term *railroaded* was used to describe the swift and unfair manner in which political prisoners are handled. According to Aptheker (1971), some inmates become political prisoners while they are incarcerated. In particular, she writes that, "as soon as they give expression to their political views they become victims of politically inspired actions against them by the prison administration and the parole boards" (p. 47). Because of George Jackson's activism in prison, he represents one of the most notable political prisoners in American correctional history. Jackson's story began when he was 18 years old and

[He] was accused of stealing $70 from a gas station in Los Angeles. Though there was evidence of his innocence, his court-appointed lawyer maintained that because Jackson had a record (two previous instances of petty crime), he should plead guilty in exchange for a light sentence in the county jail. He did, and received an indeterminate sentence of one to life. Jackson spent the next ten years in Soledad Prison, seven and a half of them in solitary confinement. (G. Jackson, 1970, p. ix)

Jackson's case became a cause célèbre and was brought to even more prominence with his critically acclaimed work *Soledad Brother: The Prison Letters of George Jackson*. The year after his book was published, Jackson was shot, on August 21, 1971, allegedly trying to escape. Jackson's influence was so wide, even among prisoners in other states, that the next day at Attica prison in New York,

> Inmates . . . graphically demonstrated their reaction to the shooting of Jackson. Instead of the usual banter and conversation of inmates coming out of their cells to line up for the march to breakfast, officers on many companies were greeted by somber inmates who moved silently out of their cells and lined up in rows of twos with a Black man at the head of each row; many of them wore Black armbands. (New York State Special Commission on Attica, 1972, pp. 139–140)

A few weeks later, Attica erupted in a riot that lasted four days, with 43 people killed and 80 wounded. Most of the dead (39 people) and all of the wounded were the result of the state police operation to take back the institution. Referring to that infamous assault, the preface to the report investigating the riot noted, "With the exception of the Indian massacres in the late 19th century, the State Police assault which ended the four-day prison uprising was the bloodiest one-day encounter between Americans since the Civil War" (New York State Special Commission on Attica, 1972, p. xi). In 2000, more than 25 years after the riot, former inmates and families of those inmates killed received a settlement of $12 million. However, the families of the employees of Attica never received any compensation. In an effort to remedy this, former New York Governor George Pataki appointed a task force to look into the claims of former correctional employees (Public Report of the Forgotten Victims of Attica, 2003).

The Attica riot rang in an era in which more scholars began to examine correctional institutions. What they found were highly segregated institutions with increasing Black and Hispanic populations (L. Carroll, 1974; Davidson, 1974). Each of these populations was struggling for control, which increased the level of violence within institutions. Coupled with the inhumane treatment and emerging overcrowding, the prisons throughout the country were susceptible to "rage riots," which, unlike the political riots of the late 1960s and early 1970s, were "very spontaneous and expressive, as most of the violence was directed at fellow inmates, rather than prison officials or the 'system' itself. Often they were the result of racial conflicts, especially between rival gangs" (Shelden & Brown, 2003, p. 304).

Prison Gangs

Prevalence and Racial/Ethnic Backgrounds of Prison Gangs

One of the earliest prison gangs was the "Gypsy Jokers" in Washington State prisons, where gangs have been present since the 1950s (Fleisher & Decker, 2001). Some researchers have estimated that the population of prison gang members ranges from 15,000 (Trulson, Marquart, & Kawuncha, 2006) to somewhere between 50,000 and 100,000 (Fleisher & Decker, 2001), while other researchers have estimated that 13% of the jail population, 12% to 17% of the prison population, and 9% of the federal prison population are gang members (Pyrooz, Decker, & Fleisher, 2011). Over time, the gangs have formed along racial/ethnic lines, which, with the burgeoning prison population, has perpetuated conflict within institutions. Some of the more infamous gangs include the Mexican Mafia (*La Eme*), the Black Guerilla Family, the Aryan Brotherhood, *Nuestra Familia* ("our family"), and the Texas Syndicate (Fleisher & Decker, 2001). The Mexican Mafia was the first prison gang with nationwide ties, whereas the Black Guerilla Family had its origins in the larger Black Panther movement and was politically oriented, having Marxist-Leninist leanings (Fleisher & Decker, 2001). The Aryan Brotherhood, a White supremacist gang, was started in 1967 "by inmates who wanted to oppose the racial threat of Black and Hispanic and/or counter the organization and activities of Black and Hispanic gangs" (Fleisher & Decker, 2001, p. 4). *Nuestra Familia* is a Hispanic prison gang that formed to provide protection against the Mexican Mafia. The Texas Syndicate is primarily composed of Mexicans/Hispanics.

Race and Prison Gang Activity

Other well-known street gangs such as the Crips and the Bloods have also been found in correctional institutions around the country. Table 8.2 provides a comparison of the characteristics of prison gangs and street gangs. Each of the various racial/ethnic gangs and the new ones that continue to emerge has caused its share of problems within correctional

Table 8.2

A Comparison of Prison and Street Gangs

Variable	Prison gang	Street gang
Race	Single race or ethnicity	Mostly single race or ethnicity
Age	Concentrated in mid-20s, with members into 30s-40s	Average age in upper teens
Organizational structure*	Hierarchical	Situational/hierarchical
Sources of violence	Symbolic and instrumental; core activity	Symbolic; core activity
Offending style**	Entrepreneurial	Cafeteria style
Visibility of behavior	Covert	Overt
Drug trafficking	Major activity; organized, collective	Varies; mostly individualistic
Loyalty to gang	Absolute	Weak bonds
Key to membership	Unqualified fidelity, abide by gang rules; willingness to engage in violence	Real or perceived fidelity; hanging out; abide by street rules
Key psychological attribute***	Oppositional, intimidation, control, manipulation	Oppositional, intimidation, camaraderie

* *Situational* refers to structural flexibility from loose to more rigid.

** *Entrepreneurial activity* refers to specific types of profit-generating activity. *Cafeteria-style activity* refers to a range of profit-generating and nonprofit activities.

*** *Oppositional* refers to attitudes toward correctional supervision in the case of prison gangs. For street gangs, it reflects a generalized opposition to authority.

institutions. Some have argued that a considerable amount of the violence and drugs in prisons are attributable to prison gangs (G. M. Camp & Camp, 1985; Fleisher & Decker, 2001; Gaes, Wallace, Gilman, Klein-Saffran, & Suppa, 2002; Huebner, 2003; Varano, Huebner, & Bynum, 2011).

Griffin and Hepburn (2006) examined the notion that prison gangs impact on violence in prisons. In their study of a diverse sample of more than 2,000 Arizona inmates, they found support for this belief, reporting that: "Inmates with no gang affiliation were significantly less likely than those with either street gang affiliation or prison gang affiliation to have been guilty of violent misconduct in the first 3 years of confinement" (p. 434). The authors also found that

> assault misconduct was significantly more likely to occur among younger inmates and among White inmates. Compared to White inmates, African American inmates, Mexican American inmates, and inmates who were Mexican Nationals were significantly less likely to be guilty of a major misconduct for assault. Native American inmates, in contrast, were no more or less likely than White inmates to commit assault. (p. 436)

Sorenson, Cunningham, Vigen, and Woods (2011) studied serious assaults on prison staff in Texas during 14 months in 2007 and 2008 and found that nearly half the assaults were of White correctional officers (48.2%), followed by assaults on Hispanic (36.5%), and Black officers (14.1%). The attacks were largely on male correctional officers (76.7%). The researchers found that although Blacks represented slightly less than 40% of the inmates, they were involved in nearly 70% of the assaults. Black and White inmates were heavily involved in interracial assaults, while Hispanics were as likely to victimize other Hispanics as they were those outside their group. In their models, the authors found that "Black inmates and gang members were each three times more likely to be among the assaulters as the controls" (Sorenson et al., 2011, p. 148).

Given the security issues raised by the presence of prison gangs, correctional officials have had to use intelligence and other strategies to control institutions (Carlson, 2001; Scott, 2001). One strategy that had been used previously in California was to segregate offenders by race. However, in the Supreme Court case *Johnson v. California* (2005), it was ruled that such practices were unconstitutional. Prisons use other measures such as segregating gangs into separate units, using prison informants, isolating gang leaders, locking down institutions, prosecuting gang members who engage in crime, interfering with gang communications, and scrutinizing gang offenses (Pyrooz et al., 2011). Unfortunately, there has been limited research evaluating these measures. Winterdyk and Ruddell (2010) recently took up this challenge by sending surveys to 37 correctional systems (incarcerating 1.19 million inmates) representing public and private correctional facilities across the United States to determine the effectiveness of some prison gang suppression measures. Table 8.3 provides a summary of the effectiveness of the various gang management strategies (also referred to as security threat group strategies, or STG) being used in prisons across the country. As seen in the table, segregation/isolation, specialized housing units, and restrictions on privileges are perceived to be the most effective strategies. This important study hopefully represents the first of many that will assess the measures being used to suppress violent and disruptive prison gangs. The next section reviews the current state of corrections.

Table 8.3

Effectiveness of STG Management Strategies

Programs or Responses	Percent			
	Very Effective	Somewhat Effective	Not Effective	Not Applicable
Segregation/isolation	75	18.8	0	6.3
Specialized housing units	50	18.8	0	31.3
Restrictions on privileges				
Visits	64.7	17.6	5.9	11.8
Program participation	29.4	58.8	5.9	5.9
Commissary/canteen	31.3	25.0	6.3	37.5
Participation in employment	31.3	18.8	12.5	37.5
Access to community	25	12.5	12.5	50.0
Access to communication	42.9	21.4	0	35.7
Loss of good-time credits	31.3	18.8	0	50.0
Delay parole eligibility	37.5	12.5	0	50.0
Control release destination	26.7	13.3	0	60.0
Increase of security rating/classification	41.2	23.5	0	35.3
Gang-free prisons	6.7	20.0	0	73.3

❖ Contemporary State of Corrections

In 2009, there were nearly 2.3 million people incarcerated in the United States (Glaze, 2010). The incarceration rate in 2009 was 502 persons per 100,000 persons in the U.S. population (West et al., 2010). Table 8.4 shows the massive increase in the incarceration rate from 1980 to 2009. The figures for persons under **community supervision** are equally dramatic. In 2009, there were 5,064,975 adults under community supervision, including probation and parole (Glaze & Bonczar, 2010).

The breakdown of these increases by most serious offense is also illuminating. Although there were increases in incarceration for violent, property, drug, and public order offenses, the trends for drug offenses and public order offenses are most dramatic. In 1980, there were 19,000 persons incarcerated for drug offenses. Twenty-six years later, in 2006, there were 264,300 people incarcerated for drug offenses (Bureau of Justice Statistics, 2003; West et al., 2010).

Reviewing the trends by race/ethnicity, Blacks had the highest incarceration rates at 3,119 per 100,000 in 2009. Hispanics/Latinos followed Blacks with an incarceration rate of 1,193 per 100,000, and Whites had the lowest rate at 487 per 100,000 (West et al., 2010). It is important to note, however, that data from 2000 and 2009 actually reveal a reduction of the number of Blacks among sentenced state and federal prisoners (see Table 8.5). Even so, it is equally important to note that Black men comprised the largest share of inmates in state or federal prisons (563,500 prisoners). Whites were second (479,000 prisoners), followed by Hispanic males (303,500; West et al., 2010). Turning to the state of incarcerated women, the data also show that "One in 703 black females was imprisoned, compared to about 1 in 1,987 white females and 1 in 1,356 Hispanic females" (p. 9). Incarceration rates for Black women dropped from 205 per 100,000 in 2000 to 142 per 100,000. Although this remained the highest rate among women, it was notable that the rates increased for Hispanic women from 60 (in 2000) per 100,000 to 74 per 100,000 (2009) and White women from 34 per 100,000 (2000) to 50 per 100,000 in 2009 (West et al., 2010). In actual numbers, in 2009, there were more White women incarcerated (51,200) in state and federal prisons than Black women (28,200) and Hispanic women (17,500; West et al., 2010).

❖ Jails

Table 8.6 shows the significant increases in jail populations from 2000 to 2010. During this period, the number of Whites in jails increased from 260,500 in 2000 to 331,600 in 2010, whereas the number of Blacks increased from 256,300 to 283,200. Over the same period, the number of Hispanics held in jails increased from 94,100 in 1990 to 118,100 in 2009 (Minton, 2011a). In 2010, the racial composition of jails was as follows: 44.3% White, 37.3% Black, and 15.8% Hispanic (Minton, 2011a).

There are also separate jail facilities in Indian country (see Table 8.7). According to Minton (2011b), in 2009, there were 2,176 inmates in 80 jails located in Indian country. Of the inmates incarcerated in these facilities, 37% were being held for violent offenses (domestic violence, assault, and rape or sexual assault), 11% for DWI/DUI, and 5% for drug law violations. Overall, these facilities were operating at 75.3% of their capacity.

Table 8.4

Number of Sentenced Inmates Incarcerated Under State and Federal Jurisdiction per 100,000, 1980–2009

Year	Incarcerated Population per 100,000
1980	139
1981	154
1982	171
1983	179
1984	188
1985	202
1986	217
1987	231
1988	247
1989	276
1990	297
1991	313
1992	332
1993	359
1994	389
1995	411
1996	427
1997	444
1998	461
1999	476
2000	478
2001	470
2002	476
2003	482
2004	486
2005	491
2006	501
2007	506
2008	504
2009	502

Table 8.5

Estimated Number of Sentenced Prisoners Under State or Federal Jurisdiction, by Sex, by Race, and Hispanic Origin, December 31, 2000–2009

Year	Male				Female			
	Total[a]	White[b]	Black[b]	Hispanic	Total[a]	White[b]	Black[b]	Hispanic
2000	1,237,500	436,500	572,900	206,900	83,700	34,500	37,400	10,000
2001	1,259,500	449,200	585,800	199,700	85,000	36,200	36,400	10,200
2002	1,291,300	436,800	586,700	235,000	89,000	35,400	36,000	15,000
2003	1,316,500	454,300	586,300	251,900	92300	39,100	35,000	16,200
2004	1,337,700	449,300	551,300	260,600	96,100	42,500	32,100	15,000
2005	1,362,500	459,700	547,200	279,000	98,600	45,800	29,900	15,900
2006	1,399,100	478,000	534,200	290,500	103,100	49,100	28,600	17,500
2007	1,427,300	471,400	556,900	301,200	105,500	50,500	29,300	17,600
2008	1,434,800	477,500	562,800	295,800	105,300	50,700	29,100	17,300
2009	1,443,500	479,000	563,500	303,500	105,200	51,200	28,200	17,500

Note: Totals based on prisoners with a sentence of more than 1 year. All estimates include persons under age 18.

a. Includes American Indians, Alaska Natives, Asians, Native Hawaiians, other Pacific Islanders, and persons identifying two or more races.

b. Excludes persons of Hispanic or Latino origin.

Table 8.6

Number of Inmates in Local Jails, by Characteristics, Midyear 2000 and 2005–2010

Characteristic	2000	2005	2006	2007	2008[a]	2009[a]	2010
Total	621,149	747,329	765,819	780,174	785,333	767,434	748,728
Sex							
Male	550,162	652,958	666,819	679,654	685,862	673,728	656,360
Female	70,987	94,571	99,000	100,520	99,670	93,706	92,368
Adults	613,534	740,770	759,717	773,341	777,829	760,216	741,168
Male	543,120	646,807	661,164	673,346	678,457	667,039	649,284
Female	70,414	93,963	98,552	99,995	99,172	93,176	91,384
Juveniles[b]	7,615	6,759	6,102	6,833	7,703	7,218	7,560
Held as adults[c]	6,126	5,750	4,835	5,649	6,410	5,846	5,647
Held as juveniles	1,489	1,009	1,268	1,184	1,294	1,373	1,912
Race/Hispanic origin[d]							
White[e]	260,500	331,000	336,500	338,200	333,300	326,400	331,600
Black/African American[e]	256,300	290,500	295,900	301,700	308,000	300,500	283,200
Hispanic/Latino	94,100	111,900	119,200	125,500	128,500	124,000	118,100
Other[e,f]	10,200	13,000	13,500	13,900	14,000	14,800	15,000
Two or more races[e]	NC	1,000	700	800	1,300	1,800	800

Note: Detail may not sum to total due to rounding.

NC = not collected.

a. Based on revised data from selected jail jurisdictions for the number of inmates confined at midyear 2008 and 2009.

b. Juveniles are persons under the age of 18 at midyear.

c. Includes juveniles who were tried or awaiting trial as adults.

d. Estimates are based on reported data adjusted for nonresponse.

e. Excludes persons of Hispanic or Latino origin.

f. Includes American Indians, Alaska Natives, Asians, Native Hawaiians, and other Pacific Islanders.

Table 8.7

Number of Inmates Confined in Indian Country Jails, by Demographic Characteristics, Conviction Status, and Offense, Midyear 2002, 2004, and 2007–2009

Characteristic	Number of Inmates held at midyear[a]						Percent of inmates held at midyear					
	2000	2002	2004	2007	2008	2009	2000	2002	2004	2007	2008	2009
Total	1,775	2,006	1,745	1,996	2,135	2,176	100%	100%	100%	100%	100%	100%
Sex												
Male	1,421	1,618	1,346	1,582	1,678	1,754	80%	81%	77%	79%	79%	81%
Female	354	388	398	414	457	422	20	19	23	21	21	19
Age group/sex												
Adults	1,498	1,699	1,546	1,743	1,882	1,919	84%	85%	89%	87%	88%	88%
Male	1,214	1,399	1,222	1,415	1,498	1,571	68	70	70	71	70	72
Female	284	300	324	328	384	348	16	15	19	16	18	16
Juveniles	277	307	198	253	253	257	16	15	11	13	12	12
Male	207	219	124	167	180	183	12	11	7	8	8	8
Female	70	88	74	86	73	74	4	4	4	4	3	3
Conviction status												
Convicted	1,072	1,120	966	1,116	1,340	1,496	61%	57%	58%	59%	63%	69%
Unconvicted	689	857	697	763	776	680	39	43	42	41	37	31
Type of offense												
Domestic violence	NC	291	257	362	307	252	NC	15%	18%	20%	15%	12%

Characteristic	Number of inmates held at midyear[a]						Percent of inmates held at midyear					
	2000	2002	2004	2007	2008	2009	2000	2002	2004	2007	2008	2009
Assault	NC	NC	190	233	308	299	NC	NC	13	13	15	15
Rape or sexual assault	NC	NC	34	45	42	42	NC	NC	2	2	2	2
Other violence	NC	NC	79	108	177	168	NC	NC	6	6	9	8
DWI/DUI[b]	274	226	195	137	184	229	17	11	14	8	9	11
Drug law violation	133	126	104	132	104	107	8	6	7	7	5	5
Other	NC	NC	569	804	954	955	NC	NC	40	44	46	47
Offense not reported	NC	NC	317	175	59	124	NR	NR	NR	NR	NR	NR

Note: Detailed characteristics may not be equal to the total number of confined inmates because of incomplete data. See Appendix Tables 1–3 in *Jails in Indian Country, 2009*, NCJ 232223, BJS Web, February 2011, for a list of all facilities and inmate characteristics.

a. Midyear count is the number of inmates held on the last weekday in June.

b. Includes driving while intoxicated and driving while under the influence of drugs or alcohol.

NC = not collected; NR = not reported.

Probation and Parole

In 2009, there were 5,018,855 men and women being supervised on probation or parole. Reviewing racial and ethnic data from 2009 for those on probation reveals that Whites comprised 55% of those on probation, with Blacks representing 30%, Hispanics 13%, and Asians and American Indians representing 1% (Glaze & Bonczar, 2010). Of those on parole in 2009, Whites represented 41%, Blacks 39%, Hispanics 18%, 1% Asians, and 1% American Indian/Alaskan Native (Glaze & Bonczar, 2010). At the federal level, in 2009, there were 10,872 Whites on probation and 35,921 on parole; 5,962 Blacks on probation and 39,163 on parole; 3,797 Hispanics on probation and 22,140 on parole; 897 Asians on probation and 2,538 on parole; and 585 American Indian/Alaskan Native on probation and 2,008 on parole (Glaze & Bonczar, 2010).

Taken together, these figures lead some to speculate about the causes of the considerable growth of American corrections. In Box 8.1, two leading figures in the **mass incarceration** dialogue tackle some of the most persistent myths pertaining to incarceration. As the figures presented in this chapter reveal, Blacks and Hispanics are overrepresented in nearly all areas of corrections. Whether this is a product of discrimination has been an ongoing question during the last two decades (Mann, 1993; MacDonald, 2003, 2008; Morgan & Smith, 2008; Walker et al., 2012; Wilbanks, 1987). Along with this question, race-related topics surface when considering correctional systems in America. In the next section, we begin with a review of the most salient scholarship that has been used to explain the disparities reviewed here. Furthermore, we look at several other contemporary issues related to race and corrections: prisoner reentry and felony disenfranchisement.

BOX 8.1

Five Myths About Americans in Prison

By Marc Mauer and David Cole

No country on Earth imprisons more people per capita than the United States. But for America, mass incarceration has proved a losing proposition. The Supreme Court recently found California's overcrowded prisons unconstitutional, and state legislators want to cut the vast amounts of public money spent on prison warehousing.

Why are so many Americans in prison, and which ones can be safely released? Let's address some common misunderstandings about our incarceration problem.

1. Crime has fallen because incarceration has risen.

U.S. crime rates are the lowest in 40 years, but it's not clear how much of this drop is a result of locking up more people.

In Canada, for example, violent crime declined in the 1990s almost as much as it did in the United States. Yet, Canada's prison population dropped during this time, and its per capita incarceration rate is about one-seventh that of the United States. Moreover, while U.S. incarceration rates have steadily risen for four decades, our crime rate has fluctuated—rising through the 1970s, falling and then rising in the 1980s, and falling since 1993.

Harvard University sociologist Bruce Western believes that increased incarceration accounts for only about 10 percent of the drop in crime rates; William Spelman, a professor of public affairs at the University of Texas, puts the figure at about 25 percent. Even if the higher figure is accurate, three-quarters of the crime decline had nothing to do with imprisonment. Other causes include changes in drug markets, policing strategies and community initiatives to reshape behavior.

2. The prison population is rising because more people are being sentenced to prison.

In the 1980s and early 1990s, the number of people sent to prison grew mainly because of the war on drugs. The number of drug offenders sentenced to state prisons increased by more than 300 percent from 1985 to 1995.

Since then, however, longer prison terms more than new prison sentences have fueled the prison population expansion. These are a result of mandatory sentencing measures such as "three strikes" laws and limits on parole release. Today, 140,000 prisoners, or one of 11 inmates, are incarcerated for life, many with no chance of parole.

Longer stays in prison offer diminishing returns for public safety. As prisoners age, the likelihood that they will commit crimes drops, but the cost of their imprisonment rises, primarily because of increased medical care. Harsher sentences also offer little deterrence: When people consider committing crimes, they may think about whether they will be caught, but probably not about how harshly they will be punished. In 1999, the Institute of Criminology at Cambridge University reviewed studies of deterrence and sentencing and found no basis "for inferring that increasing the severity of sentences generally is capable of enhancing deterrent effects."

3. Helping prisoners rejoin society will substantially reduce the prison population.

Ninety-five percent of American prisoners will return home someday. While reentry programs can aid reintegration into the community, they do little to reduce our reliance on incarceration. Prison appears to make inmates as likely to commit crime as not; about half of released inmates return to prison within three years. Congress appropriated only $83 million for reentry in fiscal year 2011, or less than $120 per released prisoner. Even with additional state funds, one is not likely to overcome a lifetime of low educational attainment, substance abuse and/or mental health disabilities with this meager commitment.

Investing in prevention and treatment instead of imprisonment is more likely to shrink the prison population. The Washington State Institute for Public Policy, for example, found that home-based supervision of juvenile offenders produced $28 in taxpayer benefits for every dollar invested.

4. There's a link between race and crime.

Yes, African Americans and Latinos disproportionately commit certain crimes. But in a 1996 study of crime rates in Columbus, Ohio, criminologists from Ohio State University concluded that socioeconomic disadvantages "explain the overwhelming portion of the difference in crime."

Nowhere are racial disparities in criminal justice more evident than in drug law enforcement. In 2003, black men were nearly 12 times more likely to be sent to prison for a drug offense than white men. Yet, national household surveys show that whites and African Americans use and sell drugs at roughly the same rates. African Americans, who are 12 percent of the population and about 14 percent of drug users, make up 34 percent of those arrested for drug offenses and 45 percent of those serving time for such offenses in state prisons. Why?

In large measure, because police find drugs where they look for them. Inner-city, open-air drug markets are easier to bust than those that operate out of suburban basements, and numerous studies show that minorities are stopped by police more often than whites. For example, a Center for Constitutional Rights study found that 87 percent of the 575,000 people stopped by the police in New York City in 2009 were African American or Latino.

5. Racial disparities in incarceration reflect police and judges' racial prejudice.

Shocking instances of racism still come to light in the justice system. But racist cops and courts are not the primary reason for racial disparities in incarceration.

(Continued)

(Continued)

Consider increased penalties for drug offenses in school zones. Though not racially motivated, these laws disproportionately affect minorities, who more often live in densely populated urban areas with many nearby schools. In New Jersey, for example, 96 percent of people incarcerated under such laws in 2005 were African American or Latino. Judges didn't necessarily want to sentence these defendants to more prison time than those convicted outside school zones, but under the law, they had to.

Where we spend money also contributes to the problem. The Violent Crime Control and Law Enforcement Act of 1994 appropriated $9.7 billion for prisons and $13.6 billion for law enforcement, but only $6.1 billion for crime prevention. Politicians eager to be seen as tough on crime too often find ways to fund new prison cells, even though they know that minorities will predominantly fill them. This isn't the fault of racist individuals. It's the fault of a system that fails to take the promise of equality seriously.

The United States imprisons a larger proportion of its population than Russia or Belarus. Our incarceration rate is eight times that of France. These tragic statistics force us to ask: Would the American public accept these rates if incarceration were distributed more equally across race and class?

Do you believe that there would be less acceptance of the current rates of incarceration if they "were distributed more equally across race and class"?

❖ Contemporary Issues in Race and Corrections

Explaining Racial Disparities in Corrections

Blumstein's Pioneering Work

During the early 1980s, scholars began to examine in earnest the racial disparities in corrections (see, e.g., Christianson, 1981; Petersilia, 1983). It is, however, the work of Blumstein (1982) that is most used as the benchmark study for explaining racial disproportionality in prisons. In Blumstein's state-level study, he investigated the role of discrimination in Black overrepresentation in prisons. Taking into account arrest patterns of Blacks and Whites, Blumstein found "that 80% of the actual racial disproportionality in incarceration rates is accounted for by differential involvement in arrest" (pp. 1267–1268). Although he noted that this explains the majority of the racial differences in incarceration, Blumstein also noted that if the unexplained 20% (which at the time translated to 10,500 prisoners) of overrepresentation of Blacks in prison "were attributable to discrimination, that would be a distressing level of discrimination" (p. 1268). It is important to note that, although Blumstein's work has become one of the benchmark studies in this area, his analysis is based on arrest statistics, which, as noted in Chapter 2, have serious limitations.

Pointing to other possible explanations for the disproportionality, Blumstein (1982) suggested that although Blacks are more involved in the most serious types of offenses, they may also be involved in the more serious "versions *within* each of the offense types (e.g., *stranger-stranger* homicides, in the *armed* robberies, etc.)" (p. 1268). Furthermore, he pointed to the possibility that Black offenders might accumulate longer criminal records. Noting the complexity of various extraneous factors that could impact on the accuracy of studies like his, Blumstein pointed to research that showed that, in some instances, "Discrimination in the criminal justice system might work in the opposite direction, resulting in Black offenders receiving more favorable treatment than White offenders" (p. 1269). More specifically, using rape cases as an example, he wrote,

> Because less certain and less severe punishment results when the victim is Black, and because the victims of Black offenders more often are Black, this could result in Black defendants being treated less severely than White defendants. Thus, this act of discrimination against Black *victims* could result in discrimination in favor of Black *offenders*. (p. 1269)

Blumstein also suggested that regional issues, educational issues, and socioeconomic factors could all play roles in explaining the unexplained 20%. He noted, however,

> Even after taking into account all factors that are at least arguably legitimate and that could explain the racial disproportionality in prison, it would certainly not be surprising to find a residual effect that is explainable only as racial discrimination. (Blumstein, 1982, p. 1270)

Following the publication of Blumstein's work, other scholars sought to test some of his findings. Focusing on arrest and prison admissions data for three years in North Carolina, Hawkins (1986) found that from 1978 to 1979, 30% of the prison disproportionality was explained by arrest patterns.

For the subsequent two years, Hawkins (1986) noted that the figures increased to 40% and 42%. In line with Blumstein's earlier supposition for certain crimes, Hawkins's research showed that Blacks received more favorable sentences than Whites. Specifically, Hawkins found that "fewer Blacks than White assault offenders received prison sentences. Fewer Blacks than Whites also received prison terms for larceny and armed robbery" (p. 260). These findings were in line with Hawkins's earlier work noting that, in certain contexts, Black life was devaluated and resulted in justice officials minimizing Black-on-Black offenses, which manifested itself in less serious punishments for such offenses (Hawkins, 1983).

Using state-level arrest and prison data for 39 states (with a 1% or greater Black population), Hawkins and Hardy (1989) found some variation across states. For example, their study revealed,

> In nine states the level of arrest explains only 40% or less of Black-White imprisonment rate differences. On the other hand, for six other states the level of arrests explains more than 80%. Thus, even allowing for some discrepancy due to differences in data sources, Blumstein's figure of 80% would not seem to be a good approximation for all states. (Hawkins & Hardy, 1989, p. 79)

Racial Disparities Scholarship

The 1990s found more researchers concentrating on disparities in corrections. At the beginning of the decade, two nonprofit organizations, the Sentencing Project and the National Center on Institutions and Alternatives (NCIA), released reports that highlighted the control rates for African Americans. Russell-Brown (2004) noted that such rates "refer to the percentage of a population that is under the jurisdiction of the criminal justice system—on probation, parole, in jail, or in prison. It provides a snapshot of a group's overall involvement in the justice system" (pp. 123–124).

In 1990, the Sentencing Project released a report that showed that "almost one in four African American males in the age group of 20–29 was under some form of criminal justice supervision" (Mauer, 1990). In April 1992, J. G. Miller (1992a) of the NCIA reported,

> On an average day in 1991, 21,800 (42%) of Washington, D.C.'s 53,375 African American males ages 18 through 35 were either in jail or prison, on probation or parole, out on bond awaiting disposition of criminal charges or being sought on an arrest warrant. (p. 1)

Five months later, J. G. Miller (1992b) returned to the subject, reporting that "of the 60,715 African American males age 18–35 in Baltimore, 56% were under criminal justice supervision on any given day in 1991" (p. 1). Updating their report in 1995, the Sentencing Project found things had worsened since 1990, reporting that "nearly one in three (32.2%) of African American males in the age group 20–29—827,440—is under criminal justice supervision on any given day—in prison, or jail, on probation or parole" (Mauer & Huling, 1995). An update of the NCIA's reports also noted that things had worsened in Washington, D.C. (Lotke, 1998).

During the release of these important reports, Blumstein (1993) also returned to the task of seeking to explain some of these disparities. Blumstein noted that the situation had marginally worsened, with 24% of the disproportionality of Blacks in prison not being explained by offending patterns. More specifically, he wrote,

> The bulk of the disproportionality is a consequence of the differential involvement in the most serious kinds of crime like homicide and robbery, where the ratio of arrests is between five and ten to one. For these crimes, the race ratio in prison is still very close to that at arrest. (Blumstein, 1993, p. 6)

However, there was a disparity related to less serious offenses (i.e., drug offenses). To explain these disparities, Blumstein (1993) surmised that, because of the increased level of discretion in less serious offenses, factors such as discrimination could be contributing to the disparity.

The early 1990s also saw concerns being expressed about the increasing expenditures on prisons and the decreasing spending on education (Chambliss, 1991). Sometime during the decade, prisons became "hot commodities"; unlike in prior years, communities, especially in rural areas hit hard by economic downturns, saw them as desirable for their overall economic impact (Lotke, 1996). Some states, like Florida, created brochures to promote the economic impact of prisons for prospective communities. Residents were told that a 1,100-person rated capacity prison could produce $25 million annually in revenue and create 350 jobs (Lotke, 1996). Downtrodden rural communities bit on the carrot, which is reflected by the fact that 5% of the increase in rural populations between 1980 and 1990 was attributed to prisons (Lotke, 1996).

Huling (2002) noted that, prior to 1990, 36% of prisons were built in nonmetropolitan areas. Furthermore, according to her figures, "Between 1990 and 1999, 245 prisons were built in rural and small town communities—with a prison opening somewhere in rural America every fifteen days" (p. 198). Noting that the economic impact is often overstated, she pointed to the "hidden" costs, such as increasing cost for local court and police services and the fact that some industries might be discouraged from investing in an area where a prison was located. Another unanticipated consequence of placing prisons in rural areas is the prevalence of racism in many rural communities. Such racism is a problem for guards and inmates. Huling (2002) provided an illustration of such problems:

> In at least six states, guards have appeared in mock Klan attire in recent years. Guards have also been accused of race-based threats, beatings and shootings in ten states. Lawsuits have been filed in at least thirteen states by Black guards alleging racist harassment or violence from White colleagues. (pp. 208–209)

In Washington State, a rural institution (Clallam Bay Correctional Center) had only 4 Black officers out of 326 correctional officers. The Black officers eventually filed a lawsuit (which was settled out of court for $250,000), claiming,

> Black officers were denied promotions, subject to threats and racial epithets like "coon," and the minority prisoners were harassed and set up for beatings. Some White guards had taken to calling Martin Luther King, Jr., Day "Happy Nigger Day" and a handful of guards openly bragged about associations with hate groups such as the Ku Klux Klan. (Huling, 2002, p. 209)

The late 1990s and early 2000s saw scholars seeking to explain disparities in corrections with radical critiques that referred to the "**prison-industrial complex**." Writers such as Parenti (1999) and Dyer (2000) have argued that government and citizens were profiting from the mass incarceration of principally African Americans and Hispanics. Private prison companies such as Corrections Corporation of America and the GEO Group, Inc. were in some cases found unknowingly in the retirement portfolios of many Americans (Dyer, 2000). As such, society was "investing" in prisons, which obviously relied on an ample supply of prisoners to keep the prison boom going (Dyer, 2000; Hallett, 2006; Price, 2006). Other writers of the period stressed the rebirth of the convict lease system in the form of the modern-day use of cheap prison labor by private companies partnering with state corrections departments (Davis, 1997, 2000, 2003). Scholars of this genre believe that because of the continuing need for bodies to keep the prison-industrial complex going, disparities in corrections will likely persist. Today, there remains a continuing reliance on privatization. In fact, **private prisons** housed 7% of the incarcerated adults in state and federal prisons in 2007 (Sigler, 2010). In addition, 35 states (and Washington, DC) have private prisons. The federal government has 11.5% of their inmates housed in private prisons, while "at the end of 2007, Immigration and Customs Enforcement housed about 38% of its detainees in privately managed facilities" (Sigler, 2010, p. 150).

In response to the growing prison-industrial complex that has become a global problem (see Sudbury, 2005), the critical resistance movement was forged after a national conference in 1998 (see http://www.criticalresistance.org). The aim of the movement is to dismantle the prison-industrial complex "by challenging the belief that policing, surveillance, imprisonment, and similar forms of control make . . . communities [of color] safe." To date, the movement has sued the California Department of Corrections to prevent it from building a new maximum-security prison. In addition, several regional chapters have been formed, and the organization has focused on educating communities about the prison-industrial complex. In September, 2008, the organization held its 10th anniversary conference in Oakland, California.

In the 2000s, scholars have continued to examine disparities (Crutchfield, 2004; Fernandez & Bowman, 2004; Mauer, 2004, 2006; Sorenson, Hope, & Stemen, 2003; Western, 2006), but there has been more of an emphasis on the consequences of mass incarceration on communities in general and minority communities in particular (see Alexander, 2010; Clear, 2007; Loury, 2008; Wacquant, 2000, 2001, 2011). Disparities in prisons create what some call "**collateral consequences**" or byproducts of the decision to incarcerate so many minority offenders. Two additional concerns related to corrections are prisoner reentry and felony disenfranchisement. We discuss prisoner reentry concerns first.

Prisoner Reentry Concerns

Reentry is a critical concern because one recent report placed the **recidivism** rate (as measured by three-year return to prison rate) across the United States at approximately 40% (The Pew Center on the States, 2011). Thus, because of the mass incarceration that took place in the 1980s and 1990s, America has more offenders being released and likely to be recidivists than ever before (Glaze & Bonczar, 2010; Petersilia, 2003; Travis, 2005). Moreover, because sentences were extended and 16 states eliminated parole (Hughes, James Wilson, & Beck, 2001), more prisoners than ever before have spent and continue to spend extended periods of time incarcerated. Glaze and Bonczar (2010) indicated that, at the end of 2009, there were 819,308 persons on parole (see Table 8.8). In addition to those on parole, thousands of persons "max out," or complete their entire sentences and leave prison without any supervision. Considering that a large share of those persons sentenced to jails and prisons are minorities, it is only logical that the majority of those coming home will also be minorities. Unfortunately, in 2006, "about 4 in 10 parolees exited supervision because they were returned to incarceration for a new offense or a technical violation" (Glaze & Bonczar, 2007, p. 7). Such figures speak to the need to explore prisoner reentry issues.

Petersilia (2003) defined *prisoner reentry* as "all activities and programming conducted to prepare ex-convicts to return safely to the community and to live as law-abiding citizens" (p. 3). According to Petersilia (2002), the key factors that contribute to failure on both probation and parole (which has been eliminated at the federal level and in some states) include the following:

> Conviction crime (property offenders have higher rates), prior criminal record (the more convictions the higher the recidivism), employment (unemployment is associated with higher recidivism), age (younger offenders have higher rates), family composition (persons living with spouse or children have lower rates) and drug use (heroin addicts have the highest recidivism rates). (p. 491)

Because minorities are more likely to fit some of these characteristics, they are at even higher risk for reentry problems (Pager, 2007a, 2007b). Employment and maintaining family ties are especially big concerns for minorities (Bushway, Stoll, & Weiman, 2007; Visher, 2007; Western & Wildeman, 2009). To address these issues, in 2003, the federal government passed the Serious and Violent Offender Reentry Initiative (Lattimore, 2007). This Act, which allocated $100 million for grants, focuses on "employment-based programming for inmates" (p. 88). Moreover, the Marriage and Incarceration Act was enacted to address

Table 8.8

Percentage and Estimated Number of Parolees Who Exited Supervision, by Type of Exit, 2006–2009

Type of exit	2006	2007	2008	2009
Total	100%	100%	100%	100%
Completion	45%	46%	49%	51%
Incarcerated	38	38	36	34
With new sentence	11	10	9	9
With revocation	26	27	25	24
Other/unknown	2	1	1	1
Absconder	11	11	11	9
Other unsatisfactory[a]	2	2	2	2
Transferred to another state	1	1	1	1
Death	1	1	1	1
Other[b]	3	2	1	3
Estimated number	532,200	543,600	574,000	579,100

Note: Detail may not sum to total because of rounding. Distributions are based on parolees for which type of exit was known. See "Methodology" in *Probation and Parole in the United States, 2008*, BJS Web, 8 December 2009, for a discussion about changes in estimating parole exits from 2000–2008.

a. Includes parolees discharged from supervision who failed to meet all conditions of supervision, had their parole sentence rescinded, or had their parole sentence revoked but were not returned to incarceration because their sentence was immediately reinstated, and other types of unsatisfactory exits; includes some early terminations and expirations of sentence.

b. Includes parolees who were deported or transferred to the jurisdiction of Immigration and Customs Enforcement (ICE), had their sentence terminated by the court through an appeal, were transferred to another state through an interstate compact agreement or discharged to probation supervision, and other types of exits.

"family programming for adult male inmates" (p. 88). Even with these initiatives, because of the bias against ex-cons, some have turned to creative measures to get their foot in the door of employers. In his highly acclaimed work *When Work Disappears*, W. J. Wilson (1996) noted the stereotypical views of employers in the Chicago region. When he asked employers about their perceptions of inner-city workers (especially young Black males), many of the 197 participating firms referred to them as "uneducated," "uncooperative," and "dishonest" (p. 111). Such perceptions have obvious implications for ex-cons. Building on the work of Wilson, Pager (2007b) sought to determine the impact of race and criminal histories on employment in entry-level jobs. Her experimental study of Milwaukee-area businesses found that Whites with criminal records had a better chance at employment than Blacks without criminal records. Such findings can only continue the cycle of recidivism among Blacks.

As for maintaining family ties, concerns about Black inmates and their families are not new (Swan, 1977). However, given the overrepresentation of Blacks and Hispanics among those who are incarcerated and eventually come home, it is important to note the consequences of fractured families. Studies have shown that "imprisonment and parole affects family stability and childhood development" (Petersilia, 2002, p. 494). Incarcerated and paroled inmates have increased chances of separation and divorce, which in the long run can impact their children. Petersilia (2002) wrote, "Children of incarcerated and released parents often suffer confusion, sadness, and social stigma; and these feelings often result in school-related difficulties, low self-esteem, aggressive behavior, and general emotional dysfunction" (p. 494). More disturbingly, "Children of incarcerated parents are five times more likely to serve time in prison than are children whose parents are not incarcerated" (p. 494). Employment also intersects with family concerns in that, among other things, being unemployed raises the risk that there will be violence in the home of a recently released offender (Petersilia, 2002). Recent scholarship has continued to confirm some of these problems associated with families coping with the incarceration of a loved one (see Braman, 2002; Richie, 2002).

With a change in tone at the state and federal levels regarding crime and criminals, there has been considerable effort to address the reentry problem (Travis, 2007; Visher, 2007). One way to combat reentry concerns is through the development of **reentry courts**. Jeremy Travis developed this concept in 1999. The idea moves the role of reentry to the judicial branch of government. Based largely on the concept of drug courts, reentry courts require that a parolee and the parole officer work with the courts to formulate a reentry plan. Each month parolees are required to provide evidence of their progress. Travis (2005) argues that the court can be effective because

> the judges are able to marshal community resources, and wield both "carrots" and "sticks" in their efforts to promote successful reintegration. The carrots are services, positive reinforcement, family and community support, and a forum for the acknowledgement of success. The sticks are enhanced levels of supervision (such as curfews, more intensive drug treatment, or more frequent drug testing), and ultimately short periods of incarceration, typically measured in days rather than months. (p. 59)

The reentry court model is still new, with pilot sites in Delaware, Florida, Iowa, Kentucky, New York, Ohio, and West Virginia (E. Miller, 2007). These courts, drawing on Travis's model, are based on four core components: a reentry transition plan, a range of supportive services, regular appearances for oversight of the plan, and accountability to victims or communities (E. Miller, 2007). To date, E. Miller (2007) has identified three major challenges faced by reentry courts: health, employment, and housing. As for health, E. Miller notes that inmates are typically troubled by numerous ailments, and this is yet another challenge reentry courts need to consider (see Box 8.2). As for employment, it goes without saying that this represents an essential key to the successful reentry of formerly incarcerated people. Programs such as the Center for Employment Opportunities (CEO) in New York could serve as models for other communities struggling with this issue. The nonprofit organization "provides immediate, paid employment for people coming home with criminal records, followed by placement in a permanent job and job retention services" (Tarlow & Nelson, 2007, p. 138). Their program includes a few days of job-readiness instruction, after which there are two months of paid transitional work, followed by permanent employment largely in the private sector. Because of various legislative mandates, securing housing can be quite a challenge during the reentry process. As such, it might actually require changes to current policies to open more options for ex-inmates (E. Miller, 2007).

BOX 8.2

Black Men Survive Longer in Prison Than Out: Study

By Genevra Pittman

New York (Reuters Health)—Black men are half as likely to die at any given time if they're in prison than if they aren't, suggests a new study of North Carolina inmates.

The black prisoners seemed to be especially protected against alcohol- and drug-related deaths, as well as lethal accidents and certain chronic diseases.

But that pattern didn't hold for white men, who on the whole were slightly more likely to die in prison than outside, according to findings published in Annals of Epidemiology.

Researchers say it's not the first time a study has found lower death rates among certain groups of inmates—particularly disadvantaged people, who might get protection against violent injuries and murder.

"Ironically, prisons are often the only provider of medical care accessible by these underserved and vulnerable Americans," said Hung-En Sung of the John Jay College of Criminal Justice in New York.

"Typically, prison-based care is more comprehensive than what inmates have received prior to their admission," Sung, who wasn't involved in the new study, told Reuters Health by email.

The new study involved about 100,000 men between age 20 and 79 who were held in North Carolina prisons at some point between 1995 and 2005. Sixty percent of those men were black.

Researchers linked prison and state health records to determine which of the inmates died, and of what causes, during their prison stay. Then they compared those figures with expected deaths in men of the same age and race in the general population.

Less than one percent of men died during incarceration, and there was no difference between black and white inmates. But outside prison walls, blacks have a higher rate of death at any given age than whites.

"What's very sad about this is that if we are able to all of a sudden equalize or diminish these health inequalities that you see by race inside a place like prison, it should also be that in places like a poor neighborhood we should be able to diminish these sort of inequities," said Evelyn Patterson, who studies correctional facilities at Vanderbilt University in Nashville, Tennessee.

"If it can be done (in prison), then certainly it can happen outside of prison," Patterson, who wasn't linked to the new work, told Reuters Health.

As in the general population, cancer and heart and blood vessel diseases were the most common cause of death among inmates—accounting for more than half of deaths.

White prisoners died of cardiovascular diseases as often as expected and died of cancer slightly more often than non-prisoners.

Black inmates, by contrast, were between 30 and 40 percent less likely to die of those causes than those who weren't incarcerated. They were also less likely to die of diabetes, alcohol- and drug-related causes, airway diseases, accidents, suicide and murder than black men not in prison.

All told, their risk of death at any age was only half that of men living in the community.

(Continued)

(Continued)

For white men, the overall death rate was slightly higher—by about 12 percent—than in the general population, with some of that attributed to higher rates of death from infection, including HIV and hepatitis. When the researchers broke prisoners up by age, death rates were only higher for white prisoners age 50 and older.

"For some populations, being in prison likely provides benefits in regards to access to healthcare and life expectancy," said study author Dr. David Rosen, from the University of North Carolina at Chapel Hill.

But, he added in an email, "it's important to remember that there are many possible negative consequences of imprisonment—for example, broken relationships, loss of employment opportunities, and greater entrenchment in criminal activity—that are not reflected in our study findings but nevertheless have an important influence on prisoners' lives and their overall health."

For Rosen, one of the main messages from the study is the need to make the world outside of prison walls safer, and to make sure people living there have adequate access to healthcare.

Do you think that the health care prisoners receive in the institution should be available to them upon release? Explain your answer.

Faith-based reentry programs also have flourished and worked in conjunction with reentry courts (Herz & Walsh, 2004). As with other faith-based initiatives, faith-based reentry programs are eligible for federal funds. In general, faith-based initiatives range from "faith-saturated" to those that have no apparent faith component (Mears, 2007). Whatever role such programs fall under, they "cannot expend funds for inherently religious activities such as worship, religious instruction or proselytization" (p. 30). It is also critical to note that, to date, little substantive research has examined the effectiveness of these programs. Consequently, there is little evidence that faith-based reentry programs are more effective than other reentry programs (Mears, 2007).

Although many reentry issues concern all inmates, as noted earlier, minorities are particularly hard hit with such concerns. Until these issues are addressed in a serious way, the cycle of recidivism will continue to pervade minority communities. A promising development occurred when former President George W. Bush announced in his 2004 State of the Union address that he was planning to implement a $300 million mentoring program to help ex-felons entering the job market (Kroeger, 2004). As part of this commitment, the Second Chances Act that was passed in 2008 has numerous provisions for reentry, including monies for jurisdictions to start reentry courts. Given the magnitude of the reentry problem, however, this was only a start.

In fact, the U.S. Department of Justice now has a Reentry Initiative (http://www.ojp.usdoj.gov/reentry/learn.html) that seeks to address many of the issues that offenders face during reentry. The initiative is a collaborative initiative with the U.S. Departments of Education, Health and Human Services, Housing and Urban Development, and Labor. In January, 2011, the first Reentry Council was held with Attorney General Eric Holder. The U.S. Department of Justice's website points to the council's threefold mission: "to make communities safer by reducing recidivism and victimization; to assist those returning from prison and jail in becoming productive, taxpaying citizens; and to save taxpayer dollars by lowering the direct and collateral cost of incarceration." Although the initiative is new, it appears to address many of the key issues related to reentry.

Another collateral consequence of being convicted of a felony is the loss of the right to vote. In recent years, felon disenfranchisement has become a major focus of scholars and community activists. In the next section, we review the history, current state, and implications of this practice.

Felon Disenfranchisement

Being able to vote is a fundamental right in a democracy. Nevertheless, beginning in ancient times, taking away a criminal offender's right to vote "was thought to offer both retribution and a deterrent to future offending" (Behrens, Uggen, & Manza, 2003, p. 562). Although such laws may seem "race neutral," recent research has challenged these notions (Behrens et al., 2003; Fellner & Mauer, 1998; Manza & Uggen, 2006; Preuhs, 2001; Shapiro, 1997; Uggen & Manza, 2002; Uggen, Manza, & Behrens, 2003). The United States' adoption of the practice dates to the colonial era. Initially, only a few offenses resulted in disenfranchisement. But according to Behrens et al. (2003), "Many states enacted felon disenfranchisement provisions in the aftermath of the Civil War. Such laws diluted the voting strength of newly enfranchised racial minority groups, particularly in the Deep South but in the North as well" (p. 563). Since these early times, the prevalence of such laws has grown. For example, "Whereas 35% of states had a broad felon disenfranchisement law in 1850, fully 96% had such a law by 2002, when only Maine and Vermont had yet to restrict felon voting rights" (p. 564).

Behrens et al. (2003) sought to determine whether the composition of prison populations is associated with the enactment of state felony disenfranchisement laws from 1850 to 2002. Their results showed,

> The racial composition of state prisons is firmly associated with the adoption of state felon disenfranchisement laws. States with greater non-White prison populations have been more likely to ban convicted felons from voting than states with proportionately fewer non-Whites in the criminal justice system. (p. 596)

Such findings suggest an effort to minimize the impact of the votes of felons.

A study by Uggen and Manza (2002) investigated the potential impact of felony disenfranchisement on past elections. Noting that the disenfranchised population represents 2.3% of the electorate, Uggen and Manza controlled for turnout and voter choice, which estimates the level at which felons would have participated in the election process and their party preferences. Their estimates revealed that, "On average . . . about 35% of disenfranchised felons would have turned out to vote in presidential elections, and that about 24% would have participated in Senate elections during nonpresidential election years" (p. 786). Estimates for political party preference showed,

> Democratic candidates would have received about 7 of every 10 votes cast by the felons and ex-felons in 14 of the last 15 U.S. Senate election years. By removing those Democratic preferences from the pool of eligible voters, felon disenfranchisement has provided a small but very clear advantage to Republican candidates in every presidential and senatorial election from 1972 to 2000. (pp. 786–787)

When Uggen and Manza (2002) examined the impact of these figures on senatorial elections from 1978 to 2000, they found "7 outcomes that may have been reversed if not for the disenfranchisement of felons and ex-felons" (p. 789). Although seven outcomes might not seem substantial, they noted that this could have resulted in the Democrats controlling the Senate during the 1990s, which could have impacted on the nature of the punishment policies during the decade. Finally, when examining the 2000 presidential election, Uggen and Manza found that, without the restrictions on felons and ex-offenders, Al Gore would have won the popular election by 1 million votes, as opposed to 500,000, and, more important, "If disenfranchised felons in Florida had been permitted to vote, Democrat Gore would certainly have carried the state, and the election" (p. 792).

Given the implications of felony disenfranchisement, one wonders how the public feels about the practice. Manza, Brooks, and Uggen (2004) investigated this question in a national poll. More specifically, they were interested in finding out whether the public supported the enfranchisement of offenders and whether this support was contingent on "the level of supervision or the specific nature of the crime" (Manza et al., 2004). Their poll showed that the majority of the public was willing to enfranchise probationers (68%); however, with a slight change in the phrasing of the question, which included the word *prison*, the support slipped to 60%. The aversion to supporting enfranchisement for those imprisoned was also seen with a direct question on the matter, which showed only 31% of the respondents supporting such a policy. Eighty percent of the public supported enfranchising ex-felons. But when the ex-felon category was disaggregated by offense, in some cases, the support was lower, with 63% supporting enfranchisement for white-collar offenders and 66% supporting enfranchisement for violent offenders (Manza et al., 2004). The lowest level of support was found for enfranchising sex offenders (52%).

There have been considerable changes in felony disenfranchisement laws across the nation because of the hard work of scholars and activists. Their efforts led to considerable public exposure and debate on the topic. This led to legislatures across the country revisiting their felon disenfranchisement laws. According to Porter (2010), since 1997, 23 states have revised their policies. In Porter's assessment of the changes, she highlights the following:

- Nine states either repealed or amended lifetime disenfranchisement laws.
- Two states expanded voting rights to persons under community supervision (probation and parole).
- Eight states eased the restoration process for persons seeking to have their right to vote restored after completing their sentence.
- Three states improved data and information sharing. (Porter, 2010, p. 1)

Because of these changes, Porter (2010) estimates that 800,000 persons "have regained their right to vote" (p. 2). Despite these promising developments, there remain more than five million people who have lost the right to vote as a result of a felony conviction—a large number of whom are racial/ethnic minorities (Porter, 2010; see Box 8.3). Given this reality, it is likely that scholars and activists will continue to apply pressure to those who can continue to change the landscape regarding felon disenfranchisement laws. In fact, emerging articles from well-known advocates are making strong arguments for allowing inmates to vote while incarcerated (Mauer, 2011).

BOX 8.3

I Am a Criminal and So Are You

By Michelle Alexander, Special to CNN

Editor's note: America's 300 million-plus people are declaring their identity in the 2010 Census this year. This piece is part of a special series on CNN.com in which people describe how they see their own identity. Michelle Alexander is the author of *The New Jim Crow: Mass Incarceration in the Age of Colorblindness* (The New Press, 2010). She is the former director of the Racial Justice Project of the ACLU of Northern California and of the Civil Rights Clinic at Stanford Law School. She holds a joint appointment with the Kirwan Institute for the Study of Race and Ethnicity and the Moritz College of Law at The Ohio State University.

Who Am I? How Do I Identify?

Lately, I've been telling people that I'm a criminal. This shocks most people, since I don't "look like" one. I'm a fairly clean-cut, light-skinned black woman with fancy degrees from Vanderbilt University and Stanford Law School. I'm a law professor and I once clerked for a U.S. Supreme Court Justice—not the sort of thing you'd expect a criminal to do.

What'd you get convicted of? people ask. Nothing, I say. Well, then why do you say you're a criminal? Because I am a criminal, I say, just like you.

This is where the conversation gets interesting. Most of my acquaintances don't think of themselves as criminals. No matter what their color, age or gender, most of the people in my neighborhood and in my workplace seem to think criminals exist somewhere else—in ghettos, mainly.

They have an unspoken, but deeply rooted identity as "law-abiding citizens." I ask them, "Haven't you ever committed a crime?" Oddly, people often seem perplexed by this question. What do you mean? they say. I mean, haven't you ever smoked pot, didn't you ever drink underage, don't you sometimes speed on the freeway, haven't you gotten behind the wheel after having a couple of drinks? Haven't you broken the law?

Well, yeah, they say, but I'm not a criminal. Oh, really? What are you, then? As I see it, you're just somebody who hasn't been caught. You're still a criminal, no better than many of those who've been branded felons for life.

Perhaps there should be a box on the census form that says "I'm a criminal." Everyone who has ever committed a crime would be required to check it. If everyone were forced to acknowledge their own criminality, maybe we, as a nation, would second-guess our apparent zeal for denying full citizenship to those branded felons.

In this country, we force millions of people—who are largely black and brown—into a permanent second-class status, simply because they once committed a crime. Once labeled a felon, you are ushered into a parallel social universe. You can be denied the right to vote, automatically excluded from juries and legally discriminated against in employment, housing, access to education and public benefits—forms of discrimination that we supposedly left behind.

This kind of stigma, discrimination and social exclusion may befall you for no reason other than you were once caught with drugs.

I doubt Barack Obama thinks of himself as a criminal, though he should. He has admitted to using illegal drugs during his college years—lots, in fact. What if he thought of himself as a criminal? What if he identified that way? Would it lead him to feel a bit more compassion for those who are branded drug felons for life, unable to find work or housing, and deemed ineligible even for food stamps?

(Continued)

(Continued)

Maybe if Obama thought of himself as a criminal he wouldn't have just endorsed spending even more money on prisons at a time when scarce resources would be much better spent on education or health care, or just about anything else.

I am a criminal. Coming to terms with this aspect of my identity has helped me to see more clearly—with blinders off—the ways in which I have been encouraged not to feel any connection to "them," those labeled criminals. I see now that "they" are me, and I am them.

Do you agree with Professor Alexander's perspective? Explain your view.

❖ Conclusion

This chapter began by examining the structure of American corrections. The review showed that the correctional system in America includes both community-based and incarceration options. Furthermore, a historical overview of race and corrections showed that race, class, and gender have always had a place in American corrections. Currently, Black and Hispanic prisoners represent a large share of the incarcerated population in the United States. Furthermore, with hundreds of thousands of prisoners annually returning to their communities in the United States, prisoner reentry has become a major concern in recent years. One innovative approach that has been used to handle this issue is reentry courts, which are based on the drug courts model. Although new, it is hoped that these courts will help stem the tide of recidivism among recently released inmates. Another promising development is that prison populations are declining. Fiscal crises in many states have resulted in reduced inmate populations. In fact, The Sentencing Project recently released a report that found that 24 states had reduced their prison populations during 2009 (Porter, 2011). In addition, several states are either closing or considering the closure of correctional facilities. These closures will reduce the number of prison beds across the nation by nearly 14,000 (Porter, 2011).

Our review of the extent and implications of felony disenfranchisement in the United States showed that Blacks and Hispanics have been disproportionately impacted by such laws. In fact, although public support is generally in favor of enfranchising most ex-cons, only two states have no restrictions on voting rights related to felony convictions. The exemplary efforts of scholars and activists have produced progressive policy changes across the nation regarding felon disenfranchisement.

Although much of our discussion in the first seven chapters has pertained to the adult criminal justice system, in Chapter 9, we turn our attention to the juvenile justice system. Operating under a separate philosophy, the juvenile justice system has also had to deal with the overrepresentation of racial minorities. Chapter 9 reviews some of the issues related to this phenomenon.

Discussion Questions

1. Discuss two historical trends related to race and corrections.

2. What is the significance of Blumstein's work related to explaining disparities in corrections?

3. How has felon disenfranchisement impacted American politics?

4. What are reentry courts?

5. Define "political prisoner."

Internet Exercises

1. Look at the data provided on the publications page of the Federal Bureau of Prisons Web site: http://www.bop.gov. Examine the statistical trends by race and note whether any patterns have developed during the years provided. What do you believe explains the trend(s) revealed?

2. Visit the Pew Center on the States website and review the report *One in 100: Behind Bars in America 2008* (http://www.pewcenteronthestates.org/report_detail.aspx?id=35904). Compare the incarceration situation in your state with a neighboring state.

Internet Sites

National Institute of Corrections: http://nicic.gov/

National Reentry Resource Center: http://www.nationalreentryresourcecenter.org/audiences/community-faith-based

U.S. Department of Justice Reentry Initiative: http://www.ojp.usdoj.gov/reentry/learn.html

Juvenile Justice

Thus, there is evidence to suggest that processing decisions in many state and local juvenile justice systems may not be racially neutral. Race effects may occur at various decision points, they may be direct or indirect, and they may accumulate as youths are processed through the system.

— Pope and Feyerherm (1990, p. 331)

The quotation above appears in a review of 46 studies on race effects in juvenile justice processing that was funded by the federal **Office of Juvenile Justice and Delinquency Prevention** (OJJDP) more than two decades ago. The most visible outcome of race effects is **disproportionate minority contact** (formerly confinement; DMC), a term used to refer to the proportion of juvenile minorities in contact with the juvenile justice system exceeding their proportion of the general population (Devine, Coolbaugh, & Jenkins, 1998). According to Models for Change (2011),

> Youth of color are overrepresented at nearly every point of contact with the juvenile justice system—and the finding is disturbingly persistent over time. Youth of color are more likely to be incarcerated and to serve more time than white youth, even when they are charged with the same category of offense. Whether these often-stark differences are the result of biases in decision making, social or economic differences that are merely correlated with race and ethnicity, or more complex structural factors, they are unacceptable in a democratic society. (p. 1)

This ongoing challenge for juvenile justice is discussed in more detail later in this chapter.

Most textbooks on juvenile delinquency and juvenile justice provide only a cursory discussion of race (Taylor Greene, Gabbidon, & Ebersole, 2001), and focus primarily on statistics, police arrest decisions, gangs, and, more recently, DMC. The history of discrimination and segregation in juvenile facilities since their inception in the 1800s is often omitted, as is the important role played by minority communities in protecting their youth from involvement in crime. Historical and contemporary information on race and juvenile justice often focuses on White and Black youth (Adams & Addie, 2010; Brunson & Weitzer, 2009;

Frey, 1981; Mennel, 1973; Pisciotta, 1983; Vaughn, Wallace, Davis, Fernandes, & Howard, 2008; Ward, 2001; Wines, 1903, cited in Pisciotta, 1983; Young, 1993). Contemporary research on juvenile delinquents and juvenile justice does include other minorities as well as Whites and Blacks. Research on Latinos/as (Cintron, 2005; Cuellar & Curry, 2007; Dillon, Robbins, Szapocznik, & Pantin, 2008; Flexon, Greenleaf, & Lurigio, 2010; Gallegos-Castillo & Patino, 2006; McCluskey, 2002; McCluskey, Krohn, Lizotte, & Rodriguez, 2002; McCluskey & Tovar, 2003; McGee et al., 2005; Miller, Barnes, & Hartley, 2011; Peguero & Shekarkhar, 2011; Shekarkhar & Gibson, 2011; Vega & Gil, 1998), Native Americans (Mmari, Blum, & Teufel-Shone, 2010), and Asian Americans (Guerrero et al., 2010; Wolf & Hartney, 2005) is also more readily available than in the past. Numerous government documents and edited volumes that focus on minority youth, delinquency, and justice are also available (see, e.g., Hawkins & Kempf-Leonard, 2005; Leonard, Pope, & Feyerherm, 1995; Parsons-Pollard, 2011; Penn, Taylor Greene, & Gabbidon, 2006). The purpose of this chapter is to explore race effects in juvenile justice. It begins with a brief overview of juvenile justice in the United States, a historical overview of race and juvenile justice, examines race and the extent of juvenile crime and victimization, and discusses several contemporary issues, including DMC, minority female delinquency, juvenile hate crimes, life without parole, and delinquency prevention.

❖ Overview of Juvenile Justice

Many students are surprised to learn that the concepts of juvenile delinquency and juvenile justice are of recent origin. Prior to the 19th century, youth were the primary responsibility of their families and communities. Those who could not be controlled were punished like adults or sent to live with other families, usually as apprentices to learn a skill or trade. During the 1800s, separate facilities for youth in trouble were established. These early institutions included asylums, orphanages, houses of refuge, and reformatories.

Later in the century, in 1899, the first **juvenile court** opened in Cook County (Chicago), Illinois. Today, the phrase *juvenile justice system* is used to refer to the agencies and processes responsible for the prevention and control of juvenile delinquency. In fact, according to the National Center for Juvenile Justice (2004), there are actually 51 separate juvenile justice systems in the United States. Figure 9.1 presents an overview of case flow through a contemporary juvenile justice system. Like the criminal justice system, the juvenile system includes law enforcement, courts, and corrections, and both systems have discretionary decision making power at several stages. The systems intersect because some juveniles are tried in criminal courts, detained in jails, and sentenced to adult prisons. Like adults, juveniles can be detained without bail before their trials (adjudicatory hearing), have procedural safeguards, have the right to an appeal (in some states), and can be placed on probation. In addition to these similarities, there are many differences between the two systems, including more parental involvement in the juvenile system, different terminology, and the fact that juveniles do not have a constitutional right to a jury trial (Siegel, 2002). Today teen (youth) courts and juvenile drug courts have been established in many jurisdictions.

The most important stages of the juvenile justice process are referrals (usually by police), **intake**, **adjudication**, and **disposition**. Juveniles may be diverted from the process at any stage by police, probation officers, and judges. For example, a juvenile referred to the court for a minor offense can be diverted from the process and/or detained by an intake/probation

Figure 9.1

Juvenile Justice
System Structure
and Processes

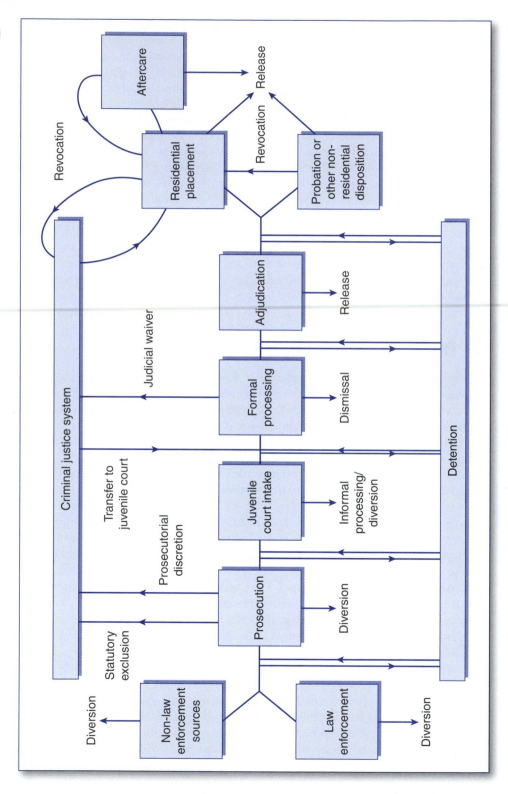

officer. A juvenile accused of a more serious crime, like rape, is less likely to be diverted. Rather, he could be formally petitioned to appear in juvenile court or transferred (waived) to adult court. If the juvenile accused of rape is adjudicated as a delinquent (in juvenile court), several dispositions are available, including (intensive) probation, restitution, community service, and secure confinement. If the juvenile accused of committing a rape is waived to adult court, there also are several possible outcomes, including either plea negotiations or a trial, and if found guilty, the sentencing alternatives are similar to dispositions available in juvenile court. Unlike youth tried in juvenile court, those waived to adult court who are found guilty and sentenced to confinement will go to prison.

Another unique characteristic of the juvenile justice system is the jurisdiction of the juvenile court over delinquent youth, status offenders, and youth who are dependent, neglected, and abused. Juvenile delinquency is described by Greenwald (1993) as a "euphemism for behavioral problems of children and youth that reach beyond mere non-conformity and existed since earliest man" (p. 735). In the early 19th century, it encompassed any illegal behavior by a minor who fell under a statutory age limit and was labeled a serious social problem (Clement, 1993). In most states, juveniles include youth who are under the age of 18. Delinquent acts include both criminal and status offenses. Unlike adults, juveniles can be apprehended for offenses due solely to their status as children or adolescents. Curfew violations, underage drinking, incorrigibility, and running away are examples of status offenses. In some states, these juveniles are referred to as either "children" or "persons in need of supervision."

The juvenile justice system today is quite different from a century ago. Initially, the goal of the early courts was to rehabilitate youth and act in the best interest of the child. In the 1960s, a fundamental shift away from the idea of rehabilitation began to occur (Urban, St. Cyr, & Decker, 2003). Several scholars have observed a gradual transition to what is now a more accountability-driven and punitive system (Benekos & Merlo, 2008; Feld, 1999; Hinton, Sims, Adams, & West, 2007; Urban et al., 2003; Ward, 2001; Ward & Kupchik, 2009). Today, the competing goals of rehabilitation and punishment have resulted in a system that places the personal, social, and educational needs of juvenile delinquents second to the need to punish them (Urban et al., 2003). Bernard and Kurlycheck (2010) identified the cycle of juvenile justice as being driven by three ideas: Crime is exceptionally high, the present policies make the problem worse, and changing the policies will reduce juvenile crime. According to the authors, the cycle of juvenile justice continues because the social conditions that foster juvenile delinquency are never adequately addressed. How did we go from a system that focused primarily on the best interest of the child to one that emphasizes punishment? When and why did we return to policies that blur the distinction between juveniles and adults? The following section provides some answers to these questions.

❖ Historical Overview of Race and Juvenile Justice

Children and youth have always misbehaved, and there have always been varying attitudes and practices toward what has come to be known as juvenile delinquency. Clement (1993) noted that, in colonial America, Southerners were more tolerant of misbehavior than were colonists in Massachusetts, Pennsylvania, and New York. More specifically, Southerners tolerated troublesome White males, but slave owners did not tolerate misbehavior of young (or adult) slaves. In the North, as the population in cities rapidly increased due primarily to urbanization, industrialization, and immigration, there was growing concern about youth crime. During the 1700s, the problem of youth misbehavior common to all children began to be referred to as the "crimes and conditions of poor children" (Mennel, 1973, p. xxvi). By the 1800s, concerned citizens referred to as "**child savers**" coalesced to protect children and youth and work on their behalf. Early in the century, these individuals and their organizations were instrumental in establishing separate facilities for youth; later in the century, they were instrumental in the creation of the first juvenile court. From the beginning of the movement to salvage youth, Black children were excluded and treated differently. Pisciotta (1983) concluded that, "Historians have been particularly negligent in not explicating the dynamics of racism and sexism in juvenile reformatories and courts" (p. 256).

As early as 1819, a group of individuals concerned about pauperism and the plight of youth in New York City formed the Society for the Prevention of Pauperism, which later became known as the Society for the Reformation of Juvenile Delinquents. On January 1, 1825, this organization opened the New York House of Refuge; Boston and Philadelphia soon followed suit, opening **houses of refuge** prior to the 1830s. Most youth in the early houses of refuge were not committing crimes, but rather were impoverished, neglected, and homeless adolescent White males. There was a considerable amount of prejudice in these early facilities toward immigrants, especially Irish youth, girls, and Black delinquents. The New York and Boston houses of refuge admitted Whites and Blacks, although they were segregated. In 1849, Philadelphia opened a separate house of refuge for "colored juvenile delinquents" (Frey, 1981; Mennel, 1973). Interestingly, all Black children born in Pennsylvania after 1780 were free, even though prejudice and separation of the races were the norm well into the 20th century. Though segregated, the houses of refuge in Philadelphia sought to maintain social control over poor and delinquent youth and to instill in them a basic education, the desire to work, and a moral foundation (Frey, 1981). Early houses maintained a practice of placing youth in apprenticeships or on rural farms. Because White girls and boys were preferred, Black youth stayed in the houses for longer periods of time (Ward, 2001).

Unlike Northern states, most Southern states moved slowly to open separate facilities for youth. Young (1993) noted "that the house of refuge established in Maryland in 1840 and opened in 1855 was restricted to White children due to the slave status of Black children" (p. 557). In Kentucky, the Louisville House of Refuge established in 1854 was for White children only (Young, 1994). Black youth were excluded from most facilities or treated quite differently. Managers believed that placing White and Black children together would be degrading to the White children (Mennel, 1973). Before and after the Civil War, in both the North and the South, Black youth were more likely to be sent to adult jails and prisons than to juvenile facilities. In Maryland, the children of free Blacks were perceived as a threat (as were their parents) and could be either sold or bound out if their parents could not provide for them (Young, 1993).

By the 1850s, houses of refuge that had opened earlier in the century were criticized and eventually replaced with **reformatories**. Massachusetts opened its reform school for boys in 1847 and for girls in 1856. These institutions differed from houses of refuge in several ways. First, smaller buildings that were maintained by the occupants were utilized. Second, there was a greater emphasis on education. By 1890, most states outside the South had reform schools for boys and girls (Mennel, 1973).

Like the houses of refuge, the early reformatories excluded Blacks and instead sent them to adult jails and prisons. There is little information about the treatment of Black youth in adult facilities. We do know that the convict lease system in jails and prisons in the South was difficult for all prisoners (Du Bois, 1901/2002; LeFlouria, 2011; Oshinsky, 1996; Woodward, 1971; Work, 1939). As noted in earlier chapters, many Southern states used the convict lease system as both a means of generating revenue to maintain their penal institutions and for profit. Punishment was excessive, death rates were high, sexual assaults and rapes were ignored, and oversight was rare (Colvin, 1997). Black youth outnumbered other juveniles in these facilities (Ward, 2001) and were subjected to the most brutal form of punishment. It was not until 1873 that one of the first separate reformatories for "colored boys" opened in Baltimore (Ward, 2001; Young, 1993). It would take several decades for other reformatories to open for Black youth. Virginia opened its first industrial home for "wayward colored girls" in 1915 and a facility for "wayward boys" in 1920 (Young, 1994). These segregated and often inferior reformatories were due, in large part, to the efforts of the child savers.

The Child Savers

As previously mentioned, child savers were concerned with the plight of poor, vagrant, and neglected children (Siegel, 2002). These activists were middle- and upper-class females, criminal justice practitioners, and various organizations that were primarily interested in saving White children, who usually came from immigrant families struggling with the transition to life in a new country. Most of the White child savers were not concerned about Negro children, who faced challenges similar to, if not worse than, immigrant youth. Although Platt (1969) and Shelden and Osborne (1989) questioned the benevolence of the child savers and posited that they were motivated by self-interest, they do not address how child savers overlooked Negro youth and the role of **Black child savers** (Ward, 2001). Frederick H. Wines, a leader in the National Conference of Charities and Correction and the National Prison Association in the late 1800s and early 1900s believed that "crime and delinquency among blacks was an 'insoluble problem'," and "because of their inherent biological, mental, and moral primitiveness . . . neither punishment or rehabilitation would work" (Wines in Pisciotta, 1983).

Youth facilities were originally opened to separate delinquents from adults and the poor conditions found in prisons. It also was believed that youth were malleable and could be "saved" from the harmful effects of poverty and harsh living conditions. Unlike White youth, Black youth often were placed in adult facilities, evidence of what Ward (2001) referred to as "historical racial inequality" in juvenile justice. In addition, ideas of Black childhood varied between the races: Whites viewed Black childhood as developmentally limited, whereas Blacks viewed their development as critical to the future of the race (Ward, 2001).

Since the late 1800s, historically Black colleges and universities were in the vanguard of efforts to improve their race and instrumental in calling attention to Black youth. As early as 1899, at the Hampton Negro Conference, the issues of the need for clubs for girls and the dangers faced by girls migrating to the North were discussed. Early in the 20th century, African American women who attended these institutions were prepared to be teachers, although it did not take long for them to realize that they would also need to become involved in community programs. For example, at the 1907 Hampton Conference, several women joined together to form the Virginia State Federation of Colored Women's Clubs. These women were at the forefront of the Black child savers who emerged in response to the unfair and prejudicial handling of Black youth. Like White child savers, the early Black child savers were initially women of a higher social class. However, they existed in a distinctly racially segregated community where the meaning of class was quite different. Although they held status and power in their own communities, Black child savers faced a greater challenge: a racialized justice system that was unwilling to invest in the rehabilitation of Black youth. They had to both challenge racial disparities and develop resources to finance facilities on their own (Ward, 2001).

Ward (2001) described at least three different types of Black child savers: early, reform oriented, and organizations. The early child savers were forced to work on the periphery of the justice system. The Federation of Colored Women's Clubs was at the forefront of the early Black child savers movement. These groups of women were active across the country, especially in the South, and were instrumental in creating the first reformatories for female and male Negro juveniles (Neverdon-Morton, 1989). The next group of Black child savers was more reform oriented and focused more directly on working as practitioners not only in juvenile justice, but in other agencies as well. They emerged early in the 20th century, when "African Americans were beginning to move from the periphery of juvenile justice, as community-based providers, toward its administrative center" (Ward, 2001, p. 164). These child savers were "African American participants in juvenile justice administration who aimed to affect outcomes in the legal processing of Black delinquents especially, though not exclusively" (p. 120). The National Association for the Advancement of Colored People (NAACP) provides an example of the third type of Black child savers. The organization devoted a tremendous amount of time and resources to the plight of Black youth in the justice system in the early part of the 20th century. Ward (2001) did not idealize the Black child savers in light of their incredible obstacles, although he does conclude that they probably did "improve the circumstances of Black juvenile delinquents" (p. 186). In addition, Black and White child savers coalesced in some places.

Juvenile Courts

One of the most important developments in the history of juvenile justice was the creation of the juvenile court. The juvenile court was viewed as a progressive idea that recognized the special needs of children not only in juvenile facilities, but in court as well. As previously stated, the primary goal of the first juvenile courts was rehabilitation and to act in the best interest of the child. There have always been two competing views of early juvenile courts; one viewed them as a "symbol of society's concern for its young" and another as oppressive and "dedicated to controlling the indigent and powerless" (Bortner, 1984, pp. 2–3). By the mid-1930s, most states had legislated some form of juvenile courts. Racial segregation in the juvenile courts (and reformatories) continued well into the 20th century. Ward and Kupchik (2009) note that the U.S. Supreme Court ruling against the "separate but equal" doctrine in the 1954 *Brown v. Board of Education* decision was one of the earliest efforts to hold juvenile justice systems accountable to all youth.

By the 1960s, juvenile courts were criticized for lacking procedural safeguards, insufficient training of judges and staff, and failing to control juvenile crime. During this decade U.S. Supreme Court rulings guaranteed juveniles in the system some procedural safeguards in two landmark decisions (*Kent v. United States* and *In re Gault*). There were important decisions in the 1970s as well (*In re Winship* and *Schall v. Martin*) even though juvenile courts nationwide continued to shift away from an emphasis on the welfare and rehabilitation of youth to an even more punitive "second-rate criminal court for young offenders" (Feld, 1999, p. 5). According to Ward and Kupchik (2009),

> A two-stage and limited philosophical displacement of the rehabilitative ideal occurred, beginning with discourse and policy focused on system accountability reforms in the 1950s, 1960s, and 1970s, followed by juvenile accountability reform efforts since the 1980s that mirror the punitive tenor of broader juvenile justice and criminal justice policy reform. (p. 101)

Although we know quite a bit about the development of juvenile courts, little information is available about the treatment of Black and minority youth in these courts during the early 20th century. Platt (1969, 1977, 2009) mentioned that the first juvenile court had one "colored" volunteer social worker. Frazier (1939, 1949) provided some information on Negro youth appearing before the children's court in the District of Columbia; Nashville, Tennessee; New York City; and other locales in the early 20th century, although he did not address race effects (Frazier emphasized community and family factors). In light of segregation and treatment in the early facilities, it is doubtful that Negro youth fared much better in juvenile courts. The Black child savers and other professionals may have played an important role in early juvenile courts in some locales, but there were not enough of them. Although they aimed to work in the best interest of the child, they could change neither the structural and economic conditions nor the stereotypical attitudes of other (White) justice professionals. Differential treatment of Black youth was tolerated and accepted, and practitioners were aware of the overrepresentation of Black and other minority youth well into the 20th century. Feld (1999) argued that, since its inception, one of the most important functions of the juvenile court was to control ethnic and racial minorities:

> The Progressives created the juvenile court to assimilate, integrate, and control the children of the eastern European immigrants pouring into cities of the East and Midwest at the turn of the century. In postindustrial American cities today, juvenile courts function to maintain social control of minority youths, predominantly young Black males. (p. 5)

Legislative changes to transfer laws have been one of the more punitive strategies designed to control juvenile crime since the 1980s. Judicial, legislative and prosecutorial waivers (sometimes known as transfers and/or certifications) facilitate trying youth as adults. In some states reverse waivers permit criminal courts to send cases back to juvenile court and utilize a juvenile disposition (Brooks & Willingham, 2009; Jordan & Myers, 2007). Between 1985 and 2007, Black youth were more likely to be waived to adult court regardless of the type of offense (person, property, drugs, public order). During the 1990s, Black youth were twice as likely as White youth to be waived for offenses against the person and more than three times as likely to be waived for drug offenses (Adams & Addie, 2010). In 2007, Black and White youth had similar likelihoods of waiver, although Black youth were still more likely to be waived for offenses against the person and drug crimes than White youth (p. 4). During the past two decades, the hybrid mix of rehabilitation, punishment, system accountability, and juvenile accountability has resulted in the implementation of numerous conflicting policies and programs to prevent and control juvenile delinquency.

Boot camps, mentoring programs, family therapy, teen (youth) courts, juvenile drug courts, trying juveniles as adults, mandatory sentences, and longer sentences are common. Some of the more punitive approaches were a reaction to increases in juvenile involvement in violent crime that occurred in the 1980s and early 1990s. This issue is discussed in more detail next.

❖ Juvenile Crime and Victimization

For decades, juvenile involvement in crime as perpetrators and victims has received considerable attention. Part of the concern is related to the disproportionate number of youth, especially Black and other minority youth, who are arrested and confined. Howell (2003) argued that one of the most damaging myths about juvenile crime and violence was the prediction about the emergence of a new breed of juvenile offenders, ostensibly labeled *superpredators* (DiLulio, 1995, 1996b). Implicit in the notion of the superpredator was the demonization of Black and Hispanic youth; these and other chronic offenders were projected as contributing to a youth violence epidemic in our country in the coming years (Blumstein, 1996). Although there were both increases and decreases in the number of juvenile arrests after these dire predictions, there was a "moral panic over juvenile delinquency" that resulted in more punitive measures and "a crisis of overload in the juvenile justice system" (Howell, 2003, p. 24). In fact, although the number of juveniles arrested for violent crime is still a problem, there has been a substantial decrease since 1994.

Chapter 2 provided an overview of several sources of crime and victimization data, including the FBI Uniform Crime Reports (UCR), National Incident Based Reporting System (NIBRS), and Hate Crime Statistics, as well as the Bureau of Justice Statistics (BJS) National Crime Victimization Survey (NCVS), which provide information on juveniles. In 1999 the OJJDP made its **Statistical Briefing Book** (SBB) available online (http://www.ojjdp.gov/ojstatbb/default.asp) to enable users to access information about juvenile delinquents, victims, juvenile court statistics, and data on youth in residential confinement. SBB data analysis tools and national data sets are useful for understanding race and juvenile justice. Chapter 2 also addressed the strengths and limitations of available data. Some of these limitations are important for understanding juvenile crime and victimization. First, Hispanics are included as "Whites" in FBI arrest data. Second, because FBI data are aggregated, we cannot examine arrests by age, race, and gender simultaneously. Third, UCR arrest data are based on estimates, and secondary analyses of UCR juvenile arrests vary considerably from the UCR estimates (see, e.g., Snyder, 1997, 2000, 2003).

NCVS data are also problematic. First, the NCVS excludes youth under 12 years of age. Second, NCVS data were disaggregated by race, age, and gender in the past, but not in more recent publications. Third, although the NCVS does include information on Hispanic victims, it is aggregated as well. There are other sources of juvenile crime and victimization data such as the Monitoring the Future survey, the National Adolescent Survey, National Survey on Drug Use and Health (formerly the National Household Survey on Drug Abuse), and the Youth Risk Behavior Surveillance System. Juvenile court and confinement data are informative, but dated. For example, Snyder and Sickmund's (2008) *Juvenile Offenders and Victims: 2006 National Report* (the most recent compilation available) includes data for 2003 and earlier. The most recent juvenile residential facility census includes 2008 information (Hockenberry, Sickmund, & Sladky, 2011). Despite these limitations, the available data do help us understand patterns and trends in juvenile participation in crime as arrestees, victims, and those who are processed in the juvenile justice system.

During the early 1980s, juvenile arrest rates fluctuated (Feld, 1999). Although juvenile arrests increased in the early 1990s, they have leveled off since then. Table 9.1 provides juvenile arrest estimates between 2001 and 2009. According to the UCR, in 2001, an estimated 1.5 million juveniles were arrested. In 2002, the number of juveniles arrested increased 0.5% for the first time in several years to 1,624,192 (FBI, 2002). After 2003, juvenile arrests increased between 2004 and 2007. Between 2008 and 2009 estimated juvenile arrests decreased to the lowest levels in the decade (FBI, 2003, 2004, 2005, 2006a, 2007a, 2008a, 2009a, 2010a). The majority of juveniles arrested in 2009 were either White (65.9%) or Black (31.3%); American Indians or Alaskan Natives and Asian or Pacific Islanders represented 1.2% and 1.6% of juvenile arrestees, respectively (FBI, 2010a; see Table 9.2).

The majority of arrestees are males, although the number of female arrestees has increased in recent years. For example, in 1980, only 20% of juveniles arrested were females (Snyder & Sickmund, 2008). According to the OJJDP Statistical Briefing Book, "The juvenile arrest rate for all crimes increased for both females and males between 1983 and 1997—the increase was greater for females than for males during this period." According to the UCR, in 2006, 18.9% and in 2009, 17% of juvenile arrestees were females (FBI, 2007, 2010a).

In 2009, juveniles under the age of 15 made up 3.8% of total arrests. Juveniles under 18 years of age accounted for 14.1% of total arrests, including 14.9% of those arrested for violent crime, 24.4% of those arrested for property crime, 44.3% of persons arrested for arson, and 33.6% of juvenile arrests for vandalism (FBI, 2010a). Most juveniles arrested for violent and property crimes, regardless of age, race, and gender, are arrested for larceny/theft (excluding the "all other offenses" category). Blacks outnumbered Whites and others arrested for murder, robbery, prostitution (and commercial vice), gambling, and suspicion. Black juveniles accounted for 51.6% of arrests for violent crime, whereas White juveniles accounted for 63.9% of juveniles arrested for property crime. After larceny-theft, and excluding the category of "all other offenses," more juveniles were arrested for other assaults, disorderly conduct, and drug abuse violations. Among American Indians or Alaskan Natives, more juveniles were arrested for larceny-theft and liquor law violations, whereas Asians or Pacific Islanders were more likely to be arrested for larceny-theft and other assaults (FBI, 2010a; see Table 9.2).

Youth involvement in violent crimes as both victims and offenders is of concern to families, child advocates, and juvenile justice practitioners and communities. According to the National Center for Injury Prevention and Control (2010), an agency in the Centers for Disease Control and Prevention, homicide was the

Table 9.1

Juvenile Arrest Estimates, 2001–2009

Year	Arrests	Total Arrests (%)
2001	1,558,496	16.7
2002	1,624,192	16.5
2003	1,563,149	16.2
2004	1,578,893	15.8
2005	1,582,068	15.3
2006	1,626,523	15.5
2007	1,649,977	15.4
2008	1,623,083	15.2
2009	1,515,586	14.1

Table 9.2

Juvenile Arrests by Race, 2009

	Arrests Under 18					Percentage Distribution[1]				
	Total	White	Black	American Indian or Alaskan Native	Asian or Pacific Islander	Total	White	Black	American Indian or Alaskan Native	Asian or Pacific Islander
Total	1,508,550	993,428	472,929	18,766	23,427	100.0	65.9	31.3	1.2	1.6
Murder and nonnegligent manslaughter	941	380	546	8	7	100.0	40.4	58.0	0.9	0.7
Forcible rape	2,368	1,501	818	19	30	100.0	63.4	34.5	0.8	1.3
Robbery	25,226	7,854	16,968	112	292	100.0	31.1	67.3	0.4	1.2
Aggravated assault	39,341	21,790	16,694	394	463	100.0	55.4	42.4	1.0	1.2
Burglary	59,237	36,073	22,082	511	571	100.0	60.9	37.3	0.9	1.0
Larceny-theft	253,467	164,701	80,670	3,148	4,948	100.0	65.0	31.8	1.2	2.0
Motor vehicle theft	15,664	8,452	6,765	234	213	100.0	54.0	43.2	1.5	1.4
Arson	4,203	3,222	865	56	60	100.0	76.7	20.6	1.3	1.4
Violent crime[2]	67,876	31,525	35,026	533	792	100.0	46.4	51.6	0.8	1.2
Property crime[2]	332,571	212,448	110,382	3,949	5,792	100.0	63.9	33.2	1.2	1.7
Other assaults	172,000	100,872	67,420	1,849	1,859	100.0	58.6	39.2	1.1	1.1
Forgery and counterfeiting	1,687	1,120	543	9	15	100.0	66.4	32.2	0.5	0.9
Fraud	4,980	3,083	1,793	55	49	100.0	61.9	36.0	1.1	1.0
Embezzlement	481	307	160	1	13	100.0	63.8	33.3	0.2	2.7
Stolen property; buying, receiving, possessing	14,831	8,104	6,461	117	149	100.0	54.6	43.6	0.8	1.0
Vandalism	71,158	55,801	13,683	845	829	100.0	78.4	19.2	1.2	1.2

	Arrests Under 18					Percentage Distribution[1]				
	Total	White	Black	American Indian or Alaskan Native	Asian or Pacific Islander	Total	White	Black	American Indian or Alaskan Native	Asian or Pacific Islander
Weapons; carrying, possessing, etc.	26,666	16,190	9,938	210	328	100.0	60.7	37.3	0.8	1.2
Prostitution and commercialized vice	1,072	426	626	4	16	100.0	39.7	58.4	0.4	1.5
Sex offenses (except forcible rape and prostitution)	10,494	7,468	2,788	89	149	100.0	71.2	26.6	0.8	1.4
Drug abuse violations	134,207	97,232	34,295	1,212	1,468	100.0	72.4	25.6	0.9	1.1
Gambling	1,395	95	1,293	0	7	100.0	6.8	92.7	0.0	0.5
Offenses against the family and children	3,576	2,642	870	48	16	100.0	73.9	24.3	1.3	0.4
Driving under the influence	10,629	9,774	541	191	123	100.0	92.0	5.1	1.8	1.2
Liquor laws	87,811	78,540	5,439	2,704	1,128	100.0	89.4	6.2	3.1	1.3
Drunkenness	11,067	9,799	966	210	92	100.0	88.5	8.7	1.9	0.8
Disorderly conduct	133,674	75,946	55,295	1,362	1,071	100.0	56.8	41.4	1.0	0.8
Vagrancy	2,151	1,539	588	9	15	100.0	71.5	27.3	0.4	0.7
All other offenses (except traffic)	256,855	177,661	71,845	2,844	4,505	100.0	69.2	28.0	1.1	1.8
Suspicion	175	74	100	0	1	100.0	42.3	57.1	0.0	0.6
Curfew and loitering law violations	89,578	54,439	33,207	872	1,060	100.0	60.8	37.1	1.0	1.2
Runaways	73,616	48,343	19,670	1,653	3,950	100.0	65.7	26.7	2.2	5.4

1. Because of rounding, the percentages may not add to 100.0.

2. Violent crimes are offenses of murder and nonnegligent manslaughter, forcible rape, robbery, and aggravated assault. Property crimes are offenses of burglary, larceny-theft, motor vehicle theft, and arson.

fourth leading cause of death for children aged 1 to 11 and second cause of death for youth aged 12 to 17. Many Americans mistakenly believe that minority youth are involved in more violent crime than is actually the case due, at least in part, to how serious crimes are highlighted by the news media (Dorfman & Schiraldi, 2001) and because of their disproportionate involvement in some violent crimes. Between 2000 and 2005, there were 9,312 juvenile murder victims, many of them very young. During this period, the number of victims fluctuated, steadily decreasing between 2003 and 2005 for the youngest victims and trending upward between 2004 and 2005 for all age groups except 0- to 5-year-olds (OJJDP, 2008). In 2008, juveniles represented about 10% of murder victims and most were White (see Box 9.1). Data on juvenile victims of nonfatal crimes are reported in victimization studies discussed next.

BOX 9.1

Violent Crime Victimization

Q: Does juvenile homicide victimization vary by race?
A: Black youth accounted for about 16% of the juvenile population between 1980 and 2008 but were the victims in 47% of juvenile homicides during the 29-year period.

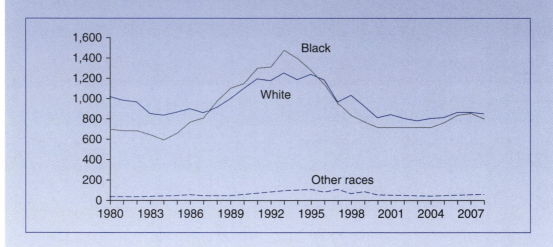

In the early 1980s, the homicide rate for black juveniles was 4 times the rate for white juveniles. This disparity increased so that by 1993 the black rate was 6 times the white rate. The relatively greater decline in black juvenile homicides between 1993 and 2002 (down 52%, compared with a 36% decline for whites) dropped the disparity in black-to-white homicide rates back to 4-to-1, before increasing slightly in the 2003 through 2008 period.

About half (49%) of juvenile murder victims in 2008 were white, 47% were black, and 3% were either American Indian or Asian.

Which theoretical explanation presented in Chapter 3 helps you understand the high homicide rate for Black juveniles?

The NCVS includes reported violent victimizations (rape, sexual assault, robbery, aggravated assault, and simple assault) and property victimizations (attempted and completed theft, household burglary, and motor vehicle theft). According to the NCVS, in 1995, the Black juvenile victimization rate for 12- to 15-year-olds was higher (120.4) than the White juvenile victimization rate (106.8) for crimes of violence, although the victimization rate for 16- to 19-year-olds was higher for Whites (110.5) than Blacks (100.0) (Klaus & Maston, 2000). When gender is included, victimization rates are higher for 12- to 15-year-olds and 16- to 19-year-old White males, compared with Black males, although Black female rates for both age groups were much greater than White female victimization rates (Klaus & Maston, 2000). According to the 2005 NCVS, youth between the ages of 12 and 15 had high rates of violent crime victimizations between 2002 to 2003 (48.1) and 2004 to 2005 (46.9), and there was a slight decrease (−2.5%) in victimization rates. In the 16- to 19-year-old category, violent victimizations fell from 55.6 to 45.09 between 2002–2003 and 2004–2005, a 19% decrease (Catalano, 2006). In 2009, youth between the ages of 12 and 15 had higher violent crime rates than youth in the 16- to 19-year-old category. Older youth (16–19) had higher rates than younger youth (12–15) for robbery (5.2, 3.1 respectively). Younger victims in the 12–15 age group had higher simple assault rates than persons between the ages of 16–19 and persons age 20 and older (Truman & Rand, 2010). According to Snyder and Sickmund (2008) important facts about juvenile victimizations include the following:

- Violent victimization is related to individual, family, and community characteristics (p. 30).
- A youth's risk of being a violent crime victim is most likely due to family and community characteristics, not race (p. 30).
- Juveniles are as likely to be victims of suicide as they are to be victims of homicide (p. 25).
- More than half of all victims of child maltreatment were White (p. 54).

Some juvenile crime and victimization is the result of youth in gangs. Youth gang members are involved in a disproportionate amount of serious and violent crime (Thornberry, 1998; Thornberry, Huizinga, & Loeber, 2004). Youth gang activity fluctuates and varies from time to time and place to place. Youth are far more likely to be violently victimized while in a gang than when they are not (Peterson, Taylor, & Esbensen, 2004). Unlike in the past, contemporary gangs that emerged in the past two decades have different characteristics that include mixed racial/ethnic members, more female members, more all-female gangs, and more involvement of Hispanic/Latino youth and White youth in certain communities (NYGC, 2008). Gang-related homicides are more likely to occur in large cities and suburban counties (Egley & Howell, 2011).

Some street gangs are involved in illegal drug sales and distribution. We can't say for sure how many youth who participate in street gangs either use or sell drugs, but drug use and sales appear to increase after joining a gang (Egley & Howell, 2011). Estimates of drug use among American youth are discussed next.

Juvenile drug behavior is often correlated with delinquency, although the nature of the relationship is unclear. Information about juvenile drug use is not included in the NCVS and is collected in other surveys such as the Monitoring the Future Series, the National Survey on Drug Use and Health, and the Youth Risk Behavior Surveillance System. Juvenile justice data on juveniles arrested for drug offenses are also available. Substance abuse appears to be widespread among American youth; in 2006, 46.8% of high school seniors reported trying an illicit drug by the time they graduated, and 35.9% had used an illicit drug in the past year (Johnston, O'Malley, Bachman, & Schulenberg, 2007). Finding from the 2010 Monitoring the Future Survey indicate that marijuana use continued to rise for 8th, 10th, and 12th graders, and the perceived risk of marijuana use has declined. "Nearly one in sixteen high school seniors today is a current daily, or near-daily, marijuana user" (Johnston, O'Malley, Bachman, & Schulenberg, 2011a, p. 5). One of the surprising findings from the annual Monitoring the Future Surveys is the subgroup differences for Whites, African Americans, and Hispanics. African Americans have lower percentages of marijuana use than do Whites and Hispanics. However, marijuana use among Hispanic 12th graders declined from 2000–2007, making them more similar to African Americans (Johnston, O'Malley, Bachman, & Schulenberg, 2011b).

Most youthful offenders are involved with drugs or alcohol at an early age, and their involvement "increases the likelihood of chronic contact with the juvenile justice system" (Belenko, Sprott, & Petersen, 2004, p. 4). Drug and alcohol use are more common among juvenile offenders than among non-offender students (Belenko et al., 2004). UCR estimates of arrests of juveniles for drug abuse violations by race between 2001 and 2009 are presented in Table 9.3. In 2001, there were an estimated 113,695 juvenile arrests for drug abuse violations, compared with an estimated 143,267 arrests in 2006 and 134,207 in 2009 (FBI, 2002, 2007a, 2010a). Most juvenile arrestees for drug abuse violations are White. The number of White and Black juveniles arrested has declined since 2007, while arrests for American Indian or Alaskan Native and Asian or Pacific Islanders saw more fluctuation.

Table 9.3

Juvenile Arrests by Race for Drug Abuse Violations, 2001–2009

Year	Total Arrests	White	Black	American Indian or Alaskan Native	Asian or Pacific Islanders
2001	113,695	77,744	33,947	892	1,112
2002	133,494	97,766	33,208	1,152	1,368
2003	137,052	98,849	35,638	1,225	1,340
2004	138,110	98,485	37,257	1,193	1,175
2005	139,776	96,207	41,076	1,301	1,192
2006	143,267	97,800	43,080	1,126	1,261
2007	146,785	101,152	43,343	1,295	995
2008	137,495	97,257	37,806	1,146	1,286
2009	134,207	97,232	34,295	1,212	1,468

❖ Youth in the Juvenile Justice System

Similar to patterns in FBI arrest data, most delinquency cases referred to juvenile court involve males, and most youth are referred for property offenses. In 2007 there were an estimated 1,666,100 delinquency cases in United States courts with juvenile jurisdiction. Property offenses comprised 36% of delinquency cases, a smaller proportion compared to 1985 when they comprised 61%. Offenses against the person (homicide, robbery, rape, and aggravated assault) accounted for 25% of all delinquency cases. Most of these cases were for either simple assault (274,900), larceny-theft (255,000), or obstruction of justice—a public order offense (214,700; Puzzanchera, Adams, & Sickmund, 2010). Delinquency cases involving females and person offense caseloads for females increased from 20% to 30% between 1985 and 2007 (Puzzanchera et al., 2010). Between 1997 and 2007, delinquency caseloads decreased for White, American Indian, and Asian youth and increased slightly for Black youth (p. 18).

In 2007, less than 1% of petitioned delinquency cases were waived to adult court. The decline in cases waived is thought to be the result of (1) declines in juvenile involvement in violent crimes and (2) expansion of nonjudicial transfer laws (Adams & Addie, 2010). The offense profile and characteristics of cases waived to adult criminal courts are presented in Table 9.4. When we take into consideration that many of the youth who are transferred to adult court are waived for property, drug, public order, and person offenses, the overrepresentation of Black and other minority youth in juvenile justice case processing is less clear.

Table 9.4

The offense profile and characteristics of cases judicially waived to criminal court have changed considerably.

Offense/demographic	1985	1994	2007
Total cases waived	7,200	13,100	8,500
Most serious offense			
Person	33%	42%	48%
Property	53	37	27
Drugs	5	12	13
Public order	9	9	11
Gender			
Male	95%	95%	90%
Female	5	5	10
Age at referral			
15 or younger	7%	13%	12%
16 or older	93	87	88

(Continued)

(Continued)

Offense/demographic	1985	1994	2007
Race/ethnicity			
White	59%	53%	59%
Black	40	44	37
Other	1	3	4

Note: Data for 1994 are presented because it is the peak year for the number of cases judicially waived to criminal court. Detail may not add to 100% because of rounding.

Most juveniles who are adjudicated delinquent are placed on probation; fewer are placed in secure confinement. Minority youth also are overrepresented in juvenile residential facilities placement. According to the most recent data, 29% of youth adjudicated delinquent for person offenses were placed in a residential facility in 2007 (Hockenberry, 2010). Black juveniles outnumber all others in residential facilities for all offenses except "other property" (see Table 9.5). The overrepresentation of Black youth might seem to make sense in that Black youth are disproportionately arrested for violent crimes against the person. However, as stated earlier, fewer juveniles are arrested for violent crimes, and most youth arrested overall are White. Several scholars have called attention to this issue, focusing primarily on the disproportionate number of minorities in confinement mentioned at the beginning of the chapter and presented in the next section.

❖ Contemporary Issues in Race and Juvenile Justice

Disproportionate Minority Confinement

Broadly speaking, DMC refers to the problem of overrepresentation of minority youth at different stages in the juvenile justice system (Snyder & Sickmund, 2008). As noted earlier, the concept of DMC has been expanded to include disproportionate contact as well as confinement. DMC exists in most states, at all decision points; is greater for African Americans than Hispanics; and is often greater in states with smaller minority populations (Leiber, 2002). DMC research has yielded varying results (for a recent summary, see Leiber & Rodriguez, 2011); in the earlier studies, some found no effects, whereas others found either direct and/or indirect race effects during intake (Leiber & Mack, 2003), detention (Wordes, Bynum, & Corley, 1994), probation (Bridges & Steen, 1998), confinement (Bridges, Conley, Engen, & Price-Spratlen, 1995), and in the child welfare system (Lau et al., 2003). More recent research has sought to identify effective strategies for reducing DMC (Cabaniss, Frabutt, Kendrick, & Arbuckle, 2007; Hsia, Bridges, & McHale, 2004; Short & Sharp, 2005) and examine DMC in the context of race and gender (Carr, Hudson, Hanks, & Hunt, 2008; Guevara, Herz, & Spohn, 2006; Leiber & Mack, 2003),

Table 9.5

Offense Profile by Race/Ethnicity for United States, 2007

Most Serious Offense	Total	Race/Ethnicity					
		White	Black	Hispanic	American Indian	Asian	Other
Total	86,927	29,534	35,447	18,056	1,577	1,035	1,278
Delinquency	83,515	27,858	34,301	17,750	1,437	1,016	1,153
Person	31,159	9,487	13,809	6,550	470	414	429
Violent Crime Index*	21,702	5,967	10,047	4,818	281	300	289
Other person	9,457	3,520	3,762	1,732	189	114	140
Property	21,082	8,018	8,000	4,100	369	272	323
Property Crime Index**	17,159	6,584	6,646	3,128	306	232	263
Other property	3,923	1,434	1,354	972	63	40	60
Drug	7,106	2,291	3,231	1,319	110	61	94
Public order	11,027	3,570	4,447	2,538	208	117	147
Technical violation	13,141	4,492	4,814	3,243	280	152	160
Status offense	3,412	1,676	1,146	306	140	19	125

Source: Sickmund, M., Sladky, T. J., & Kang, W. (2011). *Census of juveniles in residential placement databook.* Online (http://www.ojjdp.gov/ojstatbb/ezacjrp/). Data source: Author's analysis of OJJDP's Census of Juveniles in Residential Placement 1997, 1999, 2001, 2003, 2006, and 2007 (machine-readable data files).

Note: U.S. total includes 1,466 juvenile offenders in private facilities for whom State of offense was not reported and 124 juvenile offenders in tribal facilities. The "Hispanic" category includes persons of Latin American or other Spanish culture or origin regardless of race. These persons are not included in the other race/ethnicity categories.

*Includes criminal homicide, violent sexual assault, robbery, and aggravated assault.

**Includes burglary, theft, auto theft, and arson.

at multiple stages instead of just one (Guevara et al., 2006), and inclusive of Blacks, Latinos/as, and American Indians (Rodriguez, 2007).

Why is the proportion of juvenile minorities (especially African Americans, Native Americans, and Hispanics) at several stages in juvenile justice greater than their proportion of the general population? There are several plausible explanations. First, juvenile justice has always been a racialized system (Ward, 2001). Feld (1999) cited race and the macrostructural transformation of cities as two societal-level factors important for understanding juvenile justice policies and practices. More specifically, Feld was referring to the racial segregation in urban areas and the deindustrialization of cities that has occurred during the last few decades. Feld agreed with Sampson and Wilson's (1995) structural/cultural approach, which takes into consideration a community's structural disorganization, cultural isolation, and the concentration effects of poverty that foster criminal involvement (see Chapter 3). Feld (1999) stated, "As African Americans became urban Americans and the public attributed increases in crime primarily to urban Black youth, race and crime intersected to produce more punitive juvenile justice policies" (p. 6). Another explanation is that within a racialized system, police and other justice practitioners hold stereotypical views of minority youth that often result in differential treatment. Finally, minority youth's disproportionate involvement in violent crimes warrants stiffer penalties.

Even if discrimination and more punitive policies directed at Black and other minority youth account for some of the overrepresentation, their involvement in delinquency in some communities is also a factor. For some youth, delinquency and crime are accepted behaviors. Explanations for acceptance of and involvement in delinquency include alienation, reactions to discrimination, and "the street" factor. According to the colonial model (see Chapter 3), some youth turn to crime in response to their alienation (Tatum, 1994). Others are reacting to their perceptions of inequality, oppression, and discrimination (S. Johnson, 1996; Vega & Gil, 1998). There is often a belief that crime and delinquency are acceptable because of the lack of access to legitimate means of economic gain that many attribute to racism. Relatedly, the "street factor" often requires involvement in crime to prove one's toughness; violence is viewed favorably, often as a way of gaining status (E. Anderson, 1999), and is therefore more likely to be tolerated and perpetuated. S. Johnson (1996) coined the term *subcultural backlash* to refer to empathy for involvement in criminal behavior by members of an oppressed group.

The U.S. Congress formally addressed DMC in 1988 by amending the Juvenile Justice and Delinquency Prevention (JJDP) Act of 1974. Any state receiving federal funding through formula grants was required to determine whether DMC existed and, if necessary, address the problem. In 1991, OJJDP began to assist states in addressing DMC issues (Devine et al., 1998). Congress made DMC a core requirement of the JJDP Act in 1992, which mandated compliance as a condition of funding. OJJDP developed an equation for determining the extent of minority overrepresentation, known as the "DMC index." The DMC index is a ratio of the percentage of the confined minority juvenile population divided by the percentage of minority juveniles in the general population. According to Leiber (2002), OJJDP has adopted a tentative approach to DMC in light of the politics of race, crime, racial bias, state resistance, and other practical considerations. Leiber stated, "OJJDP has adopted a judicious approach to implementation of DMC, which appears to follow the 'spirit' of the mandate and attempts to make inroads—'to get something done' rather than accomplishing 'nothing at all'" (p. 16). OJJDP has developed a problem-solving process and provides technical assistance to the states.

The DMC problem-solving process usually involves several activities, which include assigning organizational responsibility, identifying the extent to which DMC exists, assessing the reasons for DMC if it exists, developing an intervention plan, evaluating the effectiveness of strategies to address DMC, and monitoring DMC trends over time (Devine et al., 1998). Unfortunately, there are several challenges to reducing DMC that include lack of resources, inadequate information systems, development of intervention strategies, and transition from planning (state) to implementation (local).

In a follow-up study to the Pope and Feyerherm (1990) review of the research literature discussed at the beginning of this chapter, Pope, Lovell, and Hsia (2002) reviewed DMC studies published between 1989 and 2001 and concluded, "The majority of studies continue to provide evidence of race effects, direct or indirect, at certain stages of juvenile justice processing and in certain jurisdictions" (p. 6). Relatedly, Ward (2001) noted,

> Despite these efforts among researchers and policy makers, nearly a decade later the DMC problem is only more entrenched, and its significance amplified in the wake of a retributive turn in the philosophy and organization of juvenile justice administration. . . . The limited impact of research and policy in this area extends in part from conceptual and empirical problems which have characterized efforts to understand and address the race-effect in juvenile justice. (p. 2)

Ward (2001) identified the following problems:

- Conceptualization of race as a category of social meaning and organization is ahistorical and theoretically narrow. (p. 2)
- Race [is] measured as an individual case-level characteristic. (p. 2)
- There has been virtually no effort to determine how race may operate at broader cultural and structural levels to affect outcomes in the administration of juvenile justice. (p. 2)
- DMC mandates assume that the existence of disparity can be summarily determined by whether or not minority youth are overrepresented among juveniles confined in institutions. This approach overlooks disparities in the types of institutions to which juveniles are committed as well as differential practices in the handling of juveniles within a given institution. (p. 3)
- Policies derived from a proportional measure of racial inequality in juvenile justice may therefore oversimplify the processes and forms through which race operates to produce categories of difference and structures of opportunity in juvenile justice administration. (p. 3)
- There is little empirical evidence to support the assumption that a decision maker's racial background is related to their orientation. (p. 3)
- Inability of the DMC index score to capture important qualitative manifestations of inequality in juvenile confinement, which may be masked by low levels of disproportionality. (p. 28)
- The DMC Index measure severely homogenizes the practice and experience of confinement, ignoring important social-contextual factors which differentiate the meaning of institutionalization in juvenile justice, and its relevance to racial inequality. (p. 29)

The JJDP Act of 2002 modified previous DMC provisions that focused solely on confinement to include contact, emphasizing the overrepresentation of minority youth at all points in the justice process. Additionally, states that fail to address DMC may forfeit 20% of their federal funding (OJJDP, 2004). After nearly three decades of DMC research and reform efforts, "although some progress is evident, there are no agreed-on strategies nor even complete accord on how best to explain the inequities" (Kempf-Leonard, 2007, p. 82). Some progress has been made in identifying effective strategies for reducing DMC that include data review and decision-point mapping, cultural competency training, increasing community-based detention alternatives, reducing decision-making subjectivity, reducing barriers to family involvement, and developing state leadership to legislate system-level changes (Cabaniss et al., 2007). The *2008 Annual Report* of the Federal Advisory Committee on Juvenile Justice provided a report card on national compliance with core protections of the JJDP act and concluded that DMC is the most complicated and the one with which the States have made the least progress. Most states and territories are in compliance with the DMC requirement for reporting data but many have not moved beyond data collection. DMC appears to stem from complicated social, economic, political, and even behavioral determinants. In the justice arena, some of the key challenges include a lack of urgency to address this issue, difficulty in collecting data, bias, lack of research about **best practices**, and failure to involve education systems (Davis, 2008, p. xv).

The Future of DMC

Future efforts to reduce DMC will require federal, state, and local officials to continue to recognize the importance of this problem for youth, families, communities, and juvenile justice. It requires a cadre of persons with a background in addressing DMC. One example is the W. Haywood Burns Institute, which assists communities in developing strategies to reduce the number of minority youth in detention (J. Bell, 2005). During this decade, several methodological issues important in DMC research have been identified. First, the limitations of the DMC Index are now more readily known. OJJDP has developed the DMC Relative Rate Index (RRI) to measure disparity at varying decision points (Snyder & Sickmund, 2008). The RRI is designed to "quantify the nature of the decisions at each decision point for each racial group and then compare these decisions" (p. 190). The information can be presented in an RRI matrix that might be useful for understanding disparity within jurisdictions, although it does not explain disparities. Second, DMC research is more comprehensive, focusing on multistages instead of one stage (Guevara et al., 2006). Third, DMC researchers also recognize that defining one's racial/ethnic status is more complex than knowing one's skin color and that culture, class, and country of origin also are important (Kempf-Leonard, 2007). Fourth, DMC research has expanded to include both race and gender (Carr et al., 2008; Guevara et al., 2006; Leiber & Mack, 2003). Future research will more directly address the issues presented earlier, as well as examine the treatment of mixed race youth in juvenile justice.

As Pope and Feyerherm (1990) noted, the DMC problem and race effects will not end until structural and economic factors that contribute to youth involvement in delinquency are recognized and addressed. It also is important to prevent delinquency and address the problem of youth with favorable attitudes about delinquency. In its *2010 Annual Report,* the Federal Advisory Committee recommended that the President and Congress amend federal legislation to address the needs of crossover youth, defined as those who "are known to both the child welfare system and the juvenile justice system" and are also referred to as "dual jurisdiction cases" (p. 3). Since there is disproportionality of minority youth in both systems, the committee recommended that they integrate their efforts and collaborate to "identify and develop resources and programs for crossover youth" (Gardell, 2010, p. 8).

Minority Female Delinquency

Girls' delinquency is not a new phenomenon, although it receives much more attention today than in the past. This is due, at least in part, to an increase in female arrests and court referrals for serious crimes. Arrests for two offenses, aggravated assaults and other assaults, increased more for both males and females than other violent crimes during the 1980s and early 1990s (Chesney-Lind & Shelden, 2004). It is important to keep in mind that violent crimes are a small portion of youth arrests, that they have declined in recent years, and that more males than females are arrested for these offenses. For example, in 2006, 40 females and 724 males under age 18 were arrested for murder (FBI, 2006a). According to Chesney-Lind and Shelden (2004), patterns of female juvenile arrests have not changed much during the past 25 years: "Females have typically been arrested for the following offenses: running away, larceny-theft, liquor law violations, curfew violations, disorderly conduct, other assaults, and the catch all category 'all other offenses'" (p. 18). Although patterns of female arrests have not changed much over time, the proportion of females referred to juvenile court for delinquency cases increased from 19% in 1989 to 24% in 1998. Those referred for offenses against the person increased from 20% in 1989 to 28% by 1998 (Puzzanchera, Stahl, Finnegan, Tierney, & Snyder, 2003a). Female person offense cases increased 22% between 1994 and 2004. In 2004, females accounted for 17% of delinquency, 20% of drug violation, 17% of property, 18% of public order, and 30% of person offense cases in juvenile courts (Stahl, 2008a). Females comprised 44% of petitioned status offense cases, primarily for running away (62%; Stahl, 2008b).

Interestingly, although the extent of female delinquency is less than male delinquency, patterns of behavior and risk factors for both groups are quite similar. For example, poverty, family problems, academic failure, dropping out of school, and substance abuse are risk factors for both sexes (Chesney-Lind & Shelden, 2004; Deschenes & Esbensen, 1999; Howell, 2003). Unlike males, female delinquents experience more physical and sexual abuse; experience pregnancy and adolescent motherhood; have lower self-esteem; and have family and school relationship issues that require programs that focus on their unique risk factors as well as those they share with males (American Bar Association and National Bar Association, 2001; Hubbard & Pratt, 2002). For years, researchers have considered whether females are treated differently in the juvenile justice system (see Chesney-Lind & Shelden, 2004). Carr et al. (2008) used a gendered organization framework to examine official responses to delinquency in two single-sex minimum-security residential programs and a coed aftercare program in an Alabama county. They concluded that "the girls' treatment facility confined more girls for less serious offenses than the boys' program" (p. 39).

Are minority female youth more delinquent than White females? This question is extremely difficult to answer because there is no specific data set that addresses this issue. Taylor, Biafora, Warheit, and Gil (1997) studied family factors and deviance in adolescent girls in Miami public schools. They found that 37.5% of the respondents engaged in serious delinquency, and Black respondents participated in more delinquent behaviors. They also reported that family factors influenced girls' delinquency differently in Hispanic, African American, and White non-Hispanic families. In a study of minority girls, Walker-Barnes, Arrue, and Mason (1998) found that friends were perceived to be a greater risk factor for gang involvement than family, neighborhood, and self. In a study of girls' sexual development in the inner city, Dunlap, Golub, and Johnson (2003) found that many girls were compelled to have sex by the age of 13, which often resulted in various forms of independent sexual behavior, such as prostitution and teen pregnancy.

According to Chesney-Lind and Shelden (2004), both Black and White girls are more likely to be arrested for traditional female offenses, like running away and prostitution. They cite a study by Snyder and Sickmund (1999) that reported higher alcohol consumption, cigarette smoking, and marijuana use among White and Hispanic females and higher percentages of assaults and sex for Black females. The number of girls in gangs is believed to be increasing (see Box 9.1). Deschenes and Esbensen (1999) found that most participants in their study were not gang members. Among those who were, Hispanic and the "Other" category of females were more likely to be gang members than were African American and White females. Girls in gangs were more likely to engage in violent behavior and to be victims of violent crime. Chesney-Lind and Shelden (2004) concluded that, although there are differences between Black and White girls' offending, they are not as pronounced as some might expect.

We do know that, according to the most recent data available, minority females comprise a disproportionate share of females in residential placement (American Bar Association and the National Bar Association, 2001; OJJDP, 2004; Snyder & Sickmund, 2008). A few studies have examined race and gender effects on juvenile justice decision making (Guevara et al., 2006; Leiber & Mack, 2003). Utilizing data from case files in two midwestern juvenile courts collected between 1990 and 1994, Guevara et al. (2006) reported that White females were more likely to receive out-of-home placements than non-White females. They concluded that non-White females were either treated no differently or more leniently than White females. In 2001, the American Bar Association and the National Bar Association issued a historic report on girls and juvenile justice. The report notes that, over the past two decades, the number of girls in the system has increased, and the system is not prepared to meet their special needs. Delinquent girls' experiences are believed to require different interventions than those usually found in community and institutional settings. There is now a focus on providing **gender-specific programs** that take into consideration the experiences and risks that girls face. Bloom, Owen, Deschenes, and Rosenbaum (2002) made several policy and program recommendations that focus on the needs of girls and young women for the state of California and policymakers in other states. Absent from their recommendations, and what is not known, is whether implementing gender-specific programs will take racial and ethnic differences into account.

Juveniles, Race, and Life Without Parole Sentences

Throughout U.S. history, there have been 12 known cases in which juveniles were executed for crimes committed before the age of 14. The first juvenile executed in the United States was Thomas Graunger, executed in Plymouth, Massachusetts for committing the crime of bestiality when he was 16 years old, in 1642. In 1885, James Arcene, a Cherokee, was hanged for a robbery and murder that occurred in 1872; he claimed that he was 10 years old when the crime was committed (Hakins, 2004). Since World War II, the youngest known person to be executed in the United States was George Stinney, a 14-year-old African American boy who was executed in South Carolina in 1944 for murdering two White girls, aged 8 and 11. Since 1976, 22 men have been executed for crimes committed as juveniles. Three were executed in Texas in 2002, and one was executed in Oklahoma in 2003.

Should juveniles be executed? Between 1982 and 2005 the United States Supreme Court decided several landmark cases related to the constitutionality of executing juveniles (*Eddings v. Oklahoma,* 1982; *Thompson v. Oklahoma,* 1988; *Stanford v. Kentucky,* 1989; *Wilkins v. Missouri,* 1989; *Atkins v. Virginia,* 2002; and *Roper v. Simmons,* 2005). *Roper v. Simmons* (2005) required that the Supreme Court decide whether a lower court can reject a standard set by the Supreme Court and whether the death penalty for a 17-year-old offender violated the Eighth Amendment. In a 5–4 decision, the Supreme Court ruled that executing juveniles is unconstitutional. As a result, the death sentence of Christopher Simmons and other juveniles were invalid. The close decision in this case is indicative of the lack of consensus on this issue.

Prior to the *Simmons* decision, all juvenile offenders under sentence of death were males, and most committed their offenses at the age of 17. Forty-eight offenders (65%) were minorities—1 American Indian, 2 Asians, 30 Blacks, and 15 Latinos—and 25 were Whites (Streib, 2004). According to the National Coalition to Abolish the Death Penalty (2004), two of three children sent to death row were people of color, and two of three people executed for crimes they committed as children have been African American.

Although the era of executing juveniles in the United States is over as a result of the Supreme Court decision in *Simmons,* there are many juveniles serving life sentences for crimes committed when they were under the age of 18. The Equal Justice Initiative (2007) refers to this as "death in prison sentences" (p. 3). In 2008, there were 2,225 juveniles sentenced to life without parole, which according to Kubiak and Allen (2011) is the most severe sanction available. In 2010, the Supreme Court ruled in *Graham v. Florida* that it is unconstitutional to sentence juveniles who haven't committed a homicide to life without parole. At that time, 37 states, the District of Columbia, and the federal government allowed life without parole for juvenile non-homicide offenses, six did not allow it, and seven allowed it for juveniles who committed homicide (National Conference of State Legislatures, 2010). In most states, mandatory sentencing policies determine sentencing decisions. Juveniles as young as 12 can be tried as adults in most states, although 14 states do not set a minimum age (Kubiak & Allen, 2011). In *Graham v. Florida,* the Court ruled that

[There] is no penological justification for this sentencing practice . . . that life without parole for juvenile non-homicide offenders accomplishes none of the traditional goals of penal sanctions—retribution, deterrence, incapacitation, and rehabilitation. (National Conference of State Legislatures, 2010, p. 1)

The Equal Justice Initiative (2007) identified 73 individuals sentenced to die in prison for crimes they committed when they were either 13 or 14 (p. 20); 49% were Black, 9.6% were Latino, 30% were White, and there was one Native American and one Asian American. "All of the children condemned to death in prison for non-homicide offenses are children of color. All but one of the children sentenced to life without parole for offenses committed at age 13 are children of color" (p. 21). In addition to the discriminatory manner in which life sentences appear to be imposed, they are contrary to international human rights law, such as the International Covenant on Civil and Political Rights and the United Nations Convention Against Torture and Other Cruel, Inhuman or Degrading Treatment or Punishment, both ratified by the United States (The Campaign for Fair Sentencing of Youth, 2009). There is limited research available on public opinion about life without parole sentences for juveniles (Kubiak & Allen, 2011).

Delinquency Prevention

According to the OJJDP website, the mission of OJJDP is to "provide national leadership, coordination, and resources to prevent and respond to juvenile delinquency and victimization."

The federal government has provided billions of dollars to state and local governments to assist them in their efforts to prevent crime (Sherman, 1997). In 2010, the Congressional Budget Office (CBO) estimated that the Senate version of the Juvenile Justice and Delinquency Prevention Reauthorization Act of 2009 (S. 678) would cost about $4.8 billion over the 2011–2015 period (CBO, 2010). Yet the amount spent on prevention programs pales in comparison to what is spent on punishment and placement of youth in secure confinement. According to Taylor Greene and Penn (2005), the pendulum might be shifting from punishment to prevention in juvenile justice due, at least in part, to the high cost of "get tough" policies that do not necessarily work. Howell (2003) identified several juvenile justice programs and strategies that do not work, including drug abuse resistance education, zero-tolerance policies, shock incarceration, and incarceration of juveniles in adult prisons. Although we know more about what does not work today, we still do not know enough about what does work. Lipsey, Howell, Kelly, Chapman, and Carver (2010) found that

> the juvenile justice supervisory apparatus of probation and court monitoring, group homes, correctional facilities, and the like has, at best, only modest favorable effects on subsequent recidivism. (p. 12)

More than a decade ago, Sherman et al. (1997) conducted a study of factors that relate to juvenile crime and the effect of prevention programs on youth violence. The study was in response to a mandate from Congress to the attorney general to evaluate the effectiveness of crime prevention programs. Sherman (1997) concluded that, although some programs work, some do not, and others are promising, there is a need to identify what works in areas of concentrated poverty where homicides are rampant. It is also important to know what works in delinquency prevention in any community where there is a heightened problem of fear, violence, and victimization. Numerous delinquency programs have emerged in the past several decades, and many of them target minority youth and are funded by OJJDP. OJJDP's Model Program Guide (MPG) provides a compendium of evidence-based prevention and intervention programs. The prevention section emphasizes a shift from reactive to proactive delinquency prevention, referred to as the "public health model of crime prevention."

The Center for the Study and Prevention of Violence has been identifying and evaluating violence prevention efforts since 1996. It selects "Blueprint Model Programs" based on several criteria for effectiveness, including evidence of a deterrent effect with a strong research design, sustained effect, and replication elsewhere (Center for the Study and Prevention of Violence, 2011). "Promising Programs" are required to meet only the first criteria. Currently, there are 11 Blueprint Model Programs and 17 Promising Programs. The Blueprint Model Programs include Big Brothers/Big Sisters of America (mentoring), Multisystemic Therapy, Olweus Bullying Prevention Program, Project Towards No Drug Abuse, and Life Skills Training (Center for the Study and Prevention of Violence, 2011).

Howell (2003) offered the "comprehensive strategy framework" for integrating the delinquency prevention and juvenile justice fields. The key components of this strategy are prevention, effective early intervention with at-risk children and families, and graduated sanctions for youth in the juvenile justice system. The comprehensive strategy is research based and flexible, and it has been implemented in several jurisdictions. It utilizes a developmental prevention approach that focuses on risk and protective factors in the family, school, peer group, community, and the individual. More recently, Lipsey et al. (2010), focusing primarily on intervention, point to the importance of evidence-based practices for reducing recidivism that take into consideration risk level of the juvenile, behavior change through personal development, as well as other factors.

Are any of the strategies mentioned earlier effective for minority youth who are locked into urban and rural environments plagued by poverty and disorder? Will they counter the pressures and temptations of drugs and delinquency? Do they take into consideration the pressures placed on some youth to engage in delinquent behaviors in order to survive in their neighborhoods? Do they acknowledge the relationship between violence and victimization? These and other questions about delinquency prevention programs for minority youth remain unanswered.

Taylor Greene and Penn (2005) noted that identifying programs that work for minority youth is difficult. First, just because programs like the Blueprint Models, for example, have proved effective based on their deterrent effects, research design, sustained effects, and replication does not necessarily mean that they work for minority youth. If we could determine that more than 50% of the study samples of effective programs are minority youth, then we could believe that they are effective with these youth. One Blueprint Model Program that probably works with minority youth is the Boys & Girls Clubs of America mentoring programs because this organization has traditionally serviced minorities in communities with concentrated effects of social disorganization and poverty.

Culturally specific programs such as the "rites of passage" programs that emerged decades ago have not been adequately evaluated. These programs provide training and rites-of-passage ceremonies for males and females and are used in both community and institutional settings (Taylor Greene & Penn, 2005). "Afrocentric prevention programs" emphasize traditional African values, including collectiveness and spirituality. Most culturally specific programs utilize a developmental approach and focus on encouraging youth to lead positive lifestyles. Many culturally relevant programs are locally funded and grassroots efforts that do not follow youth who complete their programs into adulthood. Although some specifically target delinquency prevention, others do not. Relatedly, there are few evaluations of culturally specific programs. Two studies of a community treatment program for juvenile felons in Cincinnati, Ohio found little support for the Afrocentric program (see King, Holmes, Henderson, & Latessa, 2001; Wooldredge, Hartman, Latessa, & Holmes, 1994). Some support has been found for drug prevention programs that are culturally specific and focus on Afrocentric values (Belgrave, Townsend, Cherry, & Cunningham, 1997), Native American culture (Van Stelle, Allen, & Moberg, 1998), and Asian American culture (Zane, Aoki, Ho, Huang, & Jang, 1998).

Understanding the relationship between violence and victimization is also important to developing effective prevention programs for minority youth. Youth who witness violence in their homes and in their communities are more vulnerable to involvement in delinquency. For some, the behavior is viewed as acceptable, and for others, it is required in order to have what E. Anderson (1999) described as "juice" or status. McGee (2003) and McGee and Baker (2002) found that direct victimization as a measure of exposure to violence was a predictor of problem behaviors. Victimization was linked to both internalizing and externalizing behaviors. McGee (2003) suggested that violence prevention programs must take into consideration the specific needs of students exposed to danger and the importance of developing problem- and emotion-focused coping strategies. Relatedly, programs that emphasize resilience also are important.

Klofas, Hipple, and McGarrell (2010) in *The New Criminal Justice* emphasize the importance of cooperation and collaborative problem solving across agencies (police, prosecutors, probation, etc.) in one locale. The Boston Gun Project implemented in the 1990s to target gun crimes and gun-related death of youths was one of the earliest efforts that included coordination and cooperation across justice agencies in one jurisdiction. Payne and Button (2009) point to the importance of involving all stakeholders in planning and implementing youth violence prevention plans. Policy makers should involve businesses, community members, and youth in an "empowered approach" to prevent youth violence (p. 530).

❖ Conclusion

This chapter traced the historical legacy of race in the juvenile justice system. It also presented information on the extent of juvenile crime and victimization and juveniles in the juvenile system. The issue of DMC was examined to shed light on the ongoing problem of minority youth in the system. When considered historically, it is not surprising that this problem exists, and it is likely to continue, if not worsen, unless society addresses the social conditions that foster delinquency and the racial attitudes that still taint the treatment of minority youth in the system. It was noted that Feld (1999) described social and demographic changes in the 1970s that produced macrostructural conditions that resulted in escalating youth violence in the 1980s. By the 1990s, the panic over violent juvenile crime adversely impacted urban Black males, who unfortunately were the perpetrators of the most violent of crimes: murder (Feld, 1999). The hybrid mix of rehabilitation and punishment that evolved in juvenile justice has had both positive and negative results. On the positive side, prevention has reemerged as a cost-effective approach to delinquency, and juvenile homicides and other violent crimes have decreased. However, the punitive era in juvenile justice has proved to be quite costly and not necessarily effective. More troubling is that DMC has only improved slightly.

Three other contemporary issues were also presented in this chapter: female delinquency, juveniles and life without parole sentences, and delinquency prevention. It is easy to lose sight of the fact that most of the more than 72 million juveniles in our country are not delinquent, regardless of their race, class, and gender. Parents, teachers, other individuals, and numerous community organizations are dedicated to the development of American youth. It makes much better sense to invest in education, health, and delinquency prevention than it does to invest in correctional institutions. This will require the identification of prevention programs that work, can be replicated, and are adequately funded. Research on the effectiveness of culturally relevant programs targeting minority youth also must receive more attention.

Discussion Questions

1. How relevant is the historical treatment of minority youth in juvenile justice to the DMC issue today?

2. Do you think programs for delinquent youth should vary by race/ethnicity?

3. Do you think minority females are delinquent for different reasons than minority males?

4. Is life without parole sentencing for juveniles "cruel and unusual"?

5. Does juvenile victimization in the home or the community lead to delinquency or future criminality?

Internet Exercises

1. Use the OJJDP Statistical Briefing Book Easy Access to the Census of Juveniles in Residential Placement: 1997–2007 State Comparisons tab to compare sex of juveniles in confinement by state and race and ethnicity of residents by state (http://www.ojjdp .gov/ojstatbb/ezacjrp/asp/State_Comparison.asp?topic=Offense_Race&year=2007).

2. Visit the National Conference of State Legislatures (http://www.ncsl.org/documents/ cj/jlwopchart.pdf) to examine life without parole laws for juveniles in the region of the country where you reside. Compare the laws and the number of juveniles sentenced to life without parole in at least two states.

Internet Sites

Office of Juvenile Justice and Delinquency Prevention Web page and Statistical Briefing Book: http://ojjdp.ncjrs.org, http://ojjdp.ncjrs.org/ojstatbb/index.html.

OJJDP Disproportionate Minority Contact Webpage: http://www.ojjdp.gov/dmc/index.html

OJJDP Girl's Delinquency: http://www.ojjdp.gov/programs/girlsdelinquency.html

National Youth Gang Center: http://www.iir.com/nygc/

Conclusion

Our examination of race and crime used a historical approach, providing overviews of components of the criminal justice system (police, courts, corrections, and juvenile justice) and examining numerous contemporary issues. Throughout the book, we presented and reviewed historical and contemporary research, relevant data, and both legal and sociohistorical factors that are important to understanding race and crime. In addition to the ongoing debate about the real meaning of the concepts of race and crime, our historical approach found that, unfortunately, little has changed over the past two centuries. Even so, a few things do stand out.

First, as we noted in Chapter 1, concerns regarding race/ethnicity are not new. They have existed since the founding of America. Beginning with the overstated "criminal aggression" of Native Americans, "superpredator" concerns expressed concerning African American and Latino youth in the 1990s, and more recently the treatment of Latino immigrants and criminal aliens, history continues to show that there have always been groups that have garnered special attention and were viewed as a social threat, even though it was not always warranted. Over time, numerous White ethnic immigrants and some Latinos have been able to assimilate into "Whiteness" and escape such continued scrutiny. Although some Blacks have "passed" as Whites, they have never received as much attention. Changes in the classification of race and ethnicity in the 2000 Census of the Population shed light on citizens who classify themselves as "mixed" instead of the other traditional racial categories. How we define race has implications for the study of race and crime because it is not clear how mixed races fit into cultural notions about race. In the past, individuals known to be of mixed heritage or foreign born and those with any characteristics that differed from the (White) nativists were not viewed the same as Whites. Today, the distinctions are less clear, especially for those who appear to be White. Race and ethnicity continue to maintain either a cultural or subcultural context, often based on physical characteristics.

Second, in most instances, legislation was enacted to respond to the perceived criminality of racial groups. Early legislation such as the slave codes, Black codes, the Indian Removal Act, and Chinese Exclusion Act was direct and clearly targeted specific groups. Later, legislation that purported to be race neutral (e.g., death penalty and drug statutes) continued to differentially impact racial minorities. Even legislation designed to alleviate differential treatment of minority groups was underenforced (e.g., Anti-Lynching Bills and Civil Rights Acts). The role of the law cannot be overstated. It is clear that, since the founding of America, there have been laws that were either explicitly or implicitly designed to harm certain racial/ethnic groups. More often than not, the "beneficiaries" of such laws have been racial/ethnic minorities. A recent example of this is the Department of Homeland Security's Immigration and Customs Enforcement Secure Communities program, developed to identify and deport criminal aliens through information sharing with state and local police agencies. Concerns about Secure Communities include racial profiling of Latinos and the lack of procedural safeguards. Although racial and ethnic minorities have been overrepresented in many criminal justice indices, legal and socioeconomic factors have undoubtedly contributed to this finding. We are left with no definitive evidence as to why elevated levels of crime have persisted in minority communities. And it is unclear why, even though crime, especially violent crime, in these communities has decreased substantially, incarceration rates remain high. Our review of the seemingly endless theoretical perspectives on the subject pointed to a variety of potential explanations, but more research still needs to be done.

Our final thoughts relate to prospects for the future of both the study of race and crime and the plight of those in the criminal and juvenile justice systems. We are encouraged about the increased attention that race and crime has received in the discipline during the past two decades. At this point in our history, it is difficult to know whether this trend will continue without thoroughly examining indicators such as integration in scholarly research and textbooks and the number of minority and majority scholars in the field who are involved in such research. Despite the increased attention, there is still so much we do not know. The study of race and crime requires more attention to historical, methodological, and theoretical issues.

Historical research is necessary to better understand the present. There continue to be gaps in information about race and crime for certain groups and during certain periods. One example of this is research on lynching and other minority groups including Latinos, Native Americans, and Asian Americans. Future historical research must include a more comprehensive analysis of the role of politics, and the ideologies of politicians and political parties, in order to better understand the political context of race and crime that goes beyond descriptive facts about legislation, case law, and key players in the administration of justice during different time periods. Researchers have examined race, crime, politics, and policy, although more information is needed to better understand how racist sentiments are connected to anticrime sentiments, often making crime a symbol for racism (see Alexander, 2010; Marion & Oliver, 2006; Tonry, 1995, 2011).

An analysis of legislative initiatives and crime and justice priorities during President Obama's administration is also important. For the first time in American history, Eric Holder, a Black person, serves as Attorney General. Does race matter? There have been some notable accomplishments during this administration, including revised hate crime legislation and the reduction of crack/powder cocaine sentencing disparities. The federal, state, and local Healthy Youth initiatives could also reduce youth exposure to violence and prevent delinquency. These accomplishments and initiatives either directly or indirectly affect racial/ethnic minorities. In the future, theoretical research must recognize diversity not only within racial categories, but also between individuals. Explanations of race and crime should continue to contextualize race and ethnic disparities, as well as recognize that, although there is no general theory of race and crime, some theoretical concepts are more generalizable than others (such as class and labeling) and that a more global perspective can be instructive (Gabbidon, 2010). Theories of race and crime that are based on data collection and statistics must acknowledge the limitations of data and strive to improve them. One necessary change is a distinction between Whites and Latinos in the FBI UCR arrest data (Steffensmeier, Feldmeyer, Harris, & Ulmer, 2011). A discussion about whether crime statistics should continue to be reported and recorded by race is essential. In light of the historical legacy of segregation and discrimination in justice agencies, it seems that recording racial categories is important, although some consistency from one source to another is required. Recent changes in the reporting of juvenile justice data by race/ethnicity make it easier to understand DMC at all stages. At the same time, the BJS has reduced the collection and dissemination of statistical data and removed race and ethnicity details in many publications. The online data analysis tools are useful for descriptive analyses but more disaggregated information is needed. As the primary source of most justice data, BJS should continue to report race and ethnicity information in their reports and publications.

Overall, we are not optimistic about the overrepresentation of racial minorities (primarily African Americans, Latinos, and, more recently, Native Americans) in the arrest, delinquency, victimization, and correctional figures. Unfortunately, more of the same also equates to more minority youth in the so-called "school-to-prison pipeline" who are taken into custody and more minorities being placed on death row, being wrongly accused, and incarcerated (and in the worst-case scenarios, executed) and as a consequence of such trends, in the coming years, more likely to be disenfranchised. Yet, there has been some progress, including the reduction of the crack/cocaine sentencing disparity, more attention being paid to wrongful convictions, the change in disenfranchisement laws in some states, the abolition of the death penalty for juveniles, recognition of the challenge of prisoner reentry, efforts to reduce DMC, efforts to reduce racial profiling at traffic stops, and recognition of the importance of prevention. A shift to evidence-based research is also promising, especially as it relates to reducing juvenile recidivism. At the same time, there are still challenges, including the profiling of Latinos/as in efforts to curb illegal immigration, continued injustice in the treatment of juveniles where racial issues might be more hidden, the school-to-prison pipeline, juveniles with life imprisonment sentences, juvenile involvement in hate crimes, and failure to seek alternatives to incarceration that will be less harmful to individuals, families, and communities. Further, drawing on our historical observations of racial and ethnic groups, we have noted that educational achievement holds a central place in changing the course of most minority involvement in crime.

If our dire forecast for the future is to change, a few things need to happen in this decade. First, racial minorities must continue to look beyond governmental institutions to provide the impetus for change. By now it should be clear that the government offers no panacea and that such expectations are unrealistic. More recognition of the contributions of practitioners, advocates, and community entities should be identified and included in the study of race and crime. Second, those legislators interested in tackling race and crime might want to heed the advice of Herbert Packer when seeking to determine what should be against the law. In his classic work, *The Limits of the Criminal Sanction* (1968), which is known for its delineation of the crime control and the due process models of justice, Packer also lays out the following criteria that serve as guidelines for determining what should be against the law:

1. the conduct is prominent in most people's view of socially threatening behavior, and is not condoned by any significant segment of society;

2. subjecting it to the criminal sanction is not inconsistent with the [societal] goals of punishment;

3. suppressing it will not inhibit socially desirable conduct;

4. it may be dealt with through even-handed and nondiscriminatory enforcement;

5. controlling [the conduct] through the criminal process will not expose that process to severe qualitative or quantitative strain; and

6. no reasonable alternatives to the criminal sanction exist for dealing with the behavior. (p. 298)

If legislators followed most of Packer's guidelines, it would go a long way toward ending the centuries-old trend of criminal justice legislation unfairly impacting racial minorities.

Third, legislators need to be open to more thoughtful approaches to investigating and handling certain offenses. For example, since September 11, 2001, police agencies across the country are devoting more attention to preventing terrorism. Many American law enforcement agencies have adopted the British model for preventing terrorism that advocates increased public surveillance (Klinger & Grossman, 2002). Although most Americans are willing to give up some rights in the interest of protecting the country from terrorism, the dangers of the abuse of powers are of concern, particularly to American minorities. The focus on homeland security during the current era must not diminish the importance of police and the citizenry working together to solve problems of crime and disorder. Relatedly, manpower and financial resources that have been diverted to fighting terrorism and homeland security could have a negative impact on both street crimes and progress made in the last decade in the extent of reported crime (see Lehrer, 2007).

Finally, there must be acknowledgment of the failure of both research and policy to ameliorate the historical and socioeconomic conditions that have contributed to the nexus of race, crime, and the administration of justice. Legislators must understand that the development of a nation's youth is an important component of national security. It is more fiscally sound to invest in the welfare of children, youth, and young adults than to ignore the adverse socioeconomic, biological, and psychological conditions that often lead to criminality. The cost of incarceration that does not work (for most offenders) is much more than the cost of investing in developmental prevention. If there is any hope for reducing the disproportionate involvement in crime by minorities in this century, legislation that adequately funds prevention research and requires evidence-based programs is critical. Recent efforts including the new criminal justice and predictive policing should be assessed to determine how they impact youth and whether or not they contribute to long-term crime and delinquency prevention.

Appendix

Table A.1

Arrests by Race, 1933–2010

Year	Total	White	Negro	Mexican	Indian	Chinese	Japanese	Other	Unknown
1933	312,360	236,125	76,224		1,233	1,040	176	7,813	11
1934	343,582	247,753	80,618	10,418	1,699	971	164		
1935	392,251	284,236	91,171	11,820	2,592	1,057	243	2,190	
1936	461,589	333,922	104,998	16,456	2,787	1,120	228	2,312	
1937	520,153	383,306	113,524	16,897	2,651	837	238	2,291	
1938	554,376	411,679	120,863	16,028	3,029	942	330	2,080	
1939	576,920	427,158	126,001	17,638	3,647	1,032	440	1,822	
1940	609,013	439,695	138,746	23,184	3,624	775	570	2,269	
1941	630,568	452,275	148,119	23,127	4,688	731	431	2,078	
1942	585,988	431,908	146,737	21,559	5,438	499	102	1,493	
1943	490,764	358,254	125,339	18,384	6,084	554	135	1,132	
1944	488,979	351,609	129,322	17,817	5,820	544	81	1,275	
1945	543,852	390,315	145,571	20,062	5,700	432	140	1,521	
1946	645,431	78,211	59,172	19,793	6,040	423	154	1,776	
1947	734,041	536,695	187,781	20,330	6,846	653	309	2,948	
1948	759,698	557,125	191,921		6,881	743	302	2,844	
1949	792,029	582,447	198,596		7,334	842	285	3,060	
1950	793,671	576,422	205,576		8,953	862	233	3,212	
1951	831,288	598,722	218,823		17,908	223	119	3,695	
1952	1,110,675	808,357	281,442		32,084	407	144	2,626	
1953	1,791,160	1,270,466	481,095		33,212	363	194	6,964	
1954	1,688,555	1,206,110	439,762		38,032	256	253	8,914	
1955	1,861,764	1,310,481	510,228					4,514	

(Continued)

317

(Continued)

Year	Total	White	Negro	Mexican	Indian	Chinese	Japanese	Other	Unknown
1956	2,070,794	1,390,944	634,022		40,554	236	114	4,924	
1957	2,068,677	1,405,967	616,028		37,715	267	273	8,427	
1958	2,340,004	1,583,070	696,209		43,126	1,252	296	16,051	
1959	2,612,704	1,742,399	788,799		56,555	1,486	3,000	20,465	
1960	3,498,926	2,320,635	1,064,814		71,662	2,066	5,570	34,179	
1961	3,608,317	2,424,631	1,073,491		79,716	1,725	3,428	25,326	
1962	3,923,465	2,602,011	1,195,796		86,027	2,003	3,116	34,512	
1963	4,259,463	2,943,148	1,186,870		101,253	1,817	2,640	23,735	
1964	4,381,419	3,053,818	1,194,377		99,195	1,097	2,488	30,444	
1965	4,743,123	3,235,386	1,347,994		113,398	1,293	2,970	42,082	
1966	4,797,741	3,329,475	1,315,796		108,489	1,482	3,626	38,873	
1967	5,265,302	3,630,787	1,462,556		121,398	1,726	3,490	45,345	
1968	5,349,450	3,700,012	1,471,730		119,265	1,666	4,186	52,591	
1969	5,576,705	3,842,895	1,558,740		115,645	1,426	3,613	54,386	
1970	6,257,104	4,373,157	1,688,389		130,981	2,582	3,882	58,113	
1971	6,626,085	4,623,891	1,791,474		138,677	3,274	3,832	64,937	
1972	6,706,950	4,664,220	1,847,566		130,375	4,234	1,821	58,734	
1973	6,248,286	4,458,567	1,636,237		110,433	3,049	2,134	37,866	
1974	5,853,060	4,112,443	1,561,781		86,725	4,033	4,827	83,251	
1975	7,671,230	5,538,890	1,935,422		115,554	4,629	5,817	70,918	
1976	7,383,960	5,336,889	1,870,206		104,797	2,998	3,925	65,145	
1977	8,972,109	6,428,993	2,308,429		108,520	5,999	5,240	114,928	
1978	9,687,995	6,792,934	2,562,454		105,881	8,212	5,802	212,712	
1979	9,467,502	6,849,179	2,342,664		102,392	6,089	7,668	159,510	

Year	Total	White	Black	American Indian/ Alaskan Native	Asian/Pacific Islander
1980	9,683,672	7,145,763	2,375,204	109,480	53,225
1981	10,264,187	7,482,012	2,619,463	104,261	58,451
1982	10,000,078	7,070,374	2,777,145	91,845	60,714
1983	10,247,859	7,291,129	2,796,038	93,736	66,956
1984	8,890,662	6,528,686	2,216,299	89,873	55,804
1985	10,239,478	7,337,681	2,721,144	111,459	69,194
1986	10,335,942	7,370,777	2,788,934	106,926	69,305
1987	10,750,309	7,386,639	3,168,129	116,916	78,625
1988	10,067,447	6,903,070	2,977,266	105,050	82,061
1989	11,224,528	7,559,138	3,459,177	113,777	92,436
1990	11,151,368	7,712,339	3,224,060	122,586	92,383
1991	10,516,399	7,251,862	3,049,299	115,345	99,893
1992	11,876,204	8,030,171	3,598,259	130,770	117,004
1993	11,741,751	7,855,287	3,647,174	126,017	113,273
1994	11,846,833	7,894,414	3,705,713	126,503	120,203
1995	11,386,627	7,607,522	3,523,409	129,843	125,853
1996	11,072,832	7,404,170	3,400,338	139,290	129,034
1997	10,516,707	7,061,803	3,201,014	132,734	121,156
1998	10,225,920	6,957,337	3,033,710	122,879	111,994
1999	9,100,050	6,283,294	2,600,510	113,705	102,541
2000	9,068,977	6,324,006	2,528,368	112,192	104,411
2001	9,306,587	6,465,887	2,617,669	119,281	103,750
2002	9,797,385	6,923,390	2,633,632	130,636	109,727
2003	9,529,469	6,723,093	2,570,770	125,438	110,168
2004	9,940,671	7,042,510	2,660,770	130,545	106,846
2005	10,189,691	7,117,040	2,830,778	135,877	105,996
2006	10,437,620	7,270,214	2,924,724	130,589	112,093
2007	10,656,710	7,426,278	3,003,060	142,969	84,403
2008	10,662,206	7,382,063	3,015,905	142,908	121,330
2009	10,690,561	7,389,208	3,027,153	150,544	123,656
2010	10,117,907	7,006,154	2,846,862	145,612	119,279

Table A.2

Total Arrests and Arrests for Murders by Race, 1950–2010

Year	Total Arrests	Murders	White	Negro	Indian	Chinese	Japanese	Other
1950	793,671	6,336	3,372	2,889	36	2	2	35
1951	831,288	6,522	3,407	3,029	46	7	4	29
1952	1,110,675	1,288	444	829	—	—	—	15
1953	1,791,160	2,199	883	1,306	5	—	—	5
1954	1,688,555	1,706	630	1,064	9	1	—	2
1955	1,861,764	2,073	807	1,241	17	2	1	5
1956	2,070,794	2,028	683	1,336	2	4	1	2
1957	2,068,677	2,007	761	1,225	4	1	1	15
1958	2,340,004	2,303	840	1,427	8	2	2	24
1959	2,612,704	2,610	975	1,596	13	2	1	23
1960	3,498,926	4,120	1,536	2,511	29	4	4	36
1961	3,608,317	3,694	1,493	2,154	18	4	2	23
1962	3,923,465	4,404	1,672	2,665	24	1	1	41
1963	4,259,463	5,338	2,288	2,948	53	1	3	45
1964	4,381,419	5,442	2,310	3,041	44	1	3	43
1965	4,743,123	6,509	2,675	3,704	46	3	5	76
1966	4,797,741	7,114	2,911	4,068	66	1	4	64
1967	5,265,302	8,218	3,200	4,883	49	2	9	75
1968	5,349,450	9,458	3,536	5,699	93	2	2	126
1969	5,576,705	10,412	3,743	6,444	63	3	5	154
1970	6,257,104	11,847	4,503	7,097	76	6	—	165
1971	6,626,085	13,302	4,716	8,276	88	7	4	211
1972	6,706,950	13,806	5,145	8,347	110	14	4	186
1973	6,248,286	12,913	5,236	7,478	118	18	3	60
1974	5,853,060	12,464	4,897	7,122	104	25	6	310

Year	Total Arrests	Murders	White	Negro	Indian	Chinese	Japanese	Other
1975	7,671,230	15,173	6,581	8,257	143	18	11	163
1976	7,383,960	12,875	5,792	6,886	100	6	4	87
1977	8,972,109	17,122	7,866	8,731	155	16	7	347
1978	9,687,995	18,698	8,703	9,243	153	16	10	573
1979	9,467,502	18,238	9,010	8,693	155	16	8	356
1980	7,663,682	16,987	8,533	8,199	136	119		
1981	10,264,187	20,404	10,129	9,998	133	144		
1982	10,000,078	18,475	9,008	9,174	141	152		
1983	10,247,859	18,027	8,836	8,935	114	142		
1984	8,890,662	13,656	7,339	6,133	91	93		
1985	10,239,478	15,612	7,817	7,562	109	124		
1986	10,355,942	15,953	8,028	7,659	146	120		
1987	10,750,309	16,678	7,642	8,746	131	159		
1988	10,067,447	16,090	7,243	8,603	99	145		
1989	11,224,528	17,944	7,567	10,118	120	139		
1990	11,151,368	18,190	7,942	9,952	132	164		
1991	10,516,399	18,096	7,861	9,924	143	168		
1992	11,876,204	19,463	8,466	10,728	107	162		
1993	11,741,751	20,243	8,243	11,656	131	213		
1994	11,846,833	18,475	7,705	10,420	126	224		
1995	11,386,627	16,691	7,245	9,074	134	238		
1996	11,072,832	14,439	6,176	7,928	119	216		
1997	10,516,707	12,759	5,345	7,194	94	126		
1998	10,225,920	12,318	5,478	6,580	139	121		
1999	9,100,050	9,716	4,460	5,029	105	122		
2000	9,068,977	8,683	4,231	4,238	87	127		

(Continued)

(Continued)

Year	Total Arrests	Murders	White	Negro	Indian	Chinese	Japanese	Other
2001	9,306,587	9,416	4,561	4,585	122	148		
2002	9,797,385	10,099	4,814	5,047	115	123		
2003	9,529,469	9,063	4,454	4,395	101	113		
2004	9,940,671	9,983	4,935	4,760	122	166		
2005	10,189,691	10,083	4,955	4,898	109	121		
2006	10,437,620	9,801	4,595	4,990	110	106		
2007	10,656,710	10,067	4,789	5,078	99	101		
2008	10,662,206	9,859	4,721	4,935	99	104		
2009	10,690,561	9,739	4,741	4,801	100	97		
2010	10,177,907	8,641	4,261	4,209	91	80		

Glossary

Adjudication: The process of disposing of (or settling) a juvenile or criminal matter.

Arrest rates: Refers to the number of arrests per 100,000 persons for all persons 18 years or older. These arrest rates are reported by police agencies to the FBI and are reported annually in the *Uniform Crime Reports*.

Assimilation: The merging of cultural traits from previously distinct cultural groups.

Bail: Money, property, or other security offered in exchange for the release from custody of an arrested person and to guarantee the person's appearance at trial. Bail is forfeited if the accused does not appear in court.

Batson v. Kentucky: Batson, a Black man in Kentucky, was convicted by an all-White jury of second-degree burglary. The prosecutor used all of his peremptory challenges to exclude the few prospective Black jurors from the jury pool. In the 1986 landmark case, the U.S. Supreme Court decided that peremptory challenges could not be used for a racially discriminatory purpose. Thus, creating an all-White jury by deliberately eliminating all prospective Black candidates was discriminatory. The Supreme Court ruled in favor of Batson.

Best practices: A best practice is a technique, method, or process that is believed to be most effective at delivering a particular outcome given the same conditions or circumstances.

Black child savers: The child savers were civic actors who led social movements during the late 19th and 20th centuries to establish and develop the juvenile justice system and other child welfare reform in the United States and elsewhere. The Black child savers were those Black civic actors who were effective in reconfiguring prevailing color lines of juvenile social control, not by making race insignificant, but by pushing Black youth and community stakeholders into child welfare networks of juvenile social control—uplifting the deliberative radical democracy of American juvenile justice.

Black codes: Laws which were enacted shortly after the Civil War in the ex-confederate states to restrict the liberties of the newly freed slaves to ensure an ample supply of cheap agricultural labor and to maintain White economic prosperity in the South.

Bloody code: The name given to the English legal system from the late 17th century to the early 19th century. It was known as the *bloody code* because of the huge numbers of crimes for which the death penalty could be imposed. At that time, the attitudes of the wealthy men who made the law were unsympathetic. They felt that people who committed crimes were sinful, lazy, or greedy and deserved little mercy. Since the rich made the laws, they made laws that protected their interests. Any act that threatened their wealth, property, or sense of law and order was criminalized and made punishable by death.

Bracero Program: Created in 1942 by an executive order and lasting for more than 22 years, the program allowed Mexican nationals to take temporary agricultural work in the United States. More than 4.5 million Mexican nationals were legally contracted for work in the United States. Mexican peasants, desperate for cash work, were willing to take jobs at wages scorned by most Americans. The Braceros' presence had a significant effect on the business of farming and the culture of the United States.

Bureau of Justice Statistics (BJS): The branch of the Office of Justice Programs (OJP) within the U.S. Department of Justice that promotes the collection and analysis of crime data in the states and territories.

Bureau of Prisons: Established in 1930, the Bureau consists of 115 institutions, 6 regional offices, a Central Office (headquarters), 2 staff training centers, and 28 community corrections offices. The Bureau protects public safety by ensuring that Federal offenders serve their sentences of imprisonment in facilities that are safe, humane, cost-efficient, and appropriately secure. The Bureau helps reduce the potential for future criminal activity by encouraging inmates to participate in a range of programs that have been proven to reduce recidivism.

Centers for Disease Control and Prevention: A research and funding arm of the Public Health Service, U.S. Department of Health and Human Services. The CDC, as it is known, oversees an ambitious research agenda on myriad health problems, including homicide, suicide, and intentional injuries. It is also the sponsor of the periodic *Youth Risk Behavior Survey*, a survey of U.S. high school students about their recent experiences with sexual activity and high-risk behaviors.

Cesare Lombroso: An Italian doctor, often referred to as the "father of criminology," who took a scientific approach to studying crime during the end of the 19th century. His influence spread not only throughout Europe, but to the United States and other countries as well. His theory was based on the idea of atavism, in which he deemed that criminals were an evolutionary throwback to an earlier stage in human evolution. His theory led to his classification of criminals in categories such as born criminals, criminaloids, and insane criminals, as well as to research on female offenders.

Child savers: Civic actors during the 19th and 20th centuries who led to the establishment and development of autonomous juvenile justice systems and other welfare reforms in the United States and elsewhere.

Chinese Exclusion Act of 1882: The first major and the only federal legislation that banned immigrants explicitly based on a specific nationality. The Act excluded Chinese laborers and those employed in mining from entering the country for 10 years under penalty of imprisonment and deportation.

Code of the streets: A theory developed by Yale University professor Elijah Anderson that presents an explanation for high rates of violence among African American adolescents. Anderson contends that economic disadvantage, separation from mainstream society, and racial discrimination encountered by some African American adolescents may lead to antisocial attitudes and to violent behavior.

Coker v. Georgia: Coker was convicted of raping a woman and was sentenced to death. In this 1977 landmark case, the United States Supreme Court overturned his death sentence, saying that death sentences are inappropriate punishments for rapes in which the life of the rape victim is not taken as well.

Collateral consequences: Unintended or unknown consequences certain offenders face for committing a crime, in addition to the penalties included in the criminal sentence. An example is the loss of voting rights for a convicted felon.

Collective efficacy: The tendency of members of a neighborhood or community to look out for one another's interests, including serving as surrogate parents.

Colonial model: A theory used to explain racial disparities in arrests and imprisonment. It builds upon the early writings of Frantz Fanon, who examined the relations between majority and minority groups in colonial settings. In an effort to explain high rates of crime and violence among Blacks, some criminologists have used the colonial model to analyze the psychological impact on those living in a society where the colonizer (often Whites) creates a race- and caste-based society based on racism. The colonial system, which devalues and discredits the culture and traditions of the colonized, leaves the colonized in a psychological state that results in self-hate and destructive behaviors such as crime (mostly intraracial).

Colonization: Occurs when one group forcibly takes over the country of another group. During this process, those who are colonized are then forced to adhere to the norms of the colonizer.

Community policing: A philosophy of policing that emphasizes identifying and solving a wide range of community problems that are thought to lead to crime and social disorder. In community-oriented policing, often simply termed *community policing,* the beat officer and community residents work together to exchange information, promote safety, and improve the overall quality of life in the neighborhood.

Community supervision: The spectrum of sentencing alternatives that permit the convicted offender to remain in the community as opposed to serving time in a remote correctional facility. Community supervision includes community-based correctional facilities, halfway houses, day reporting centers, probation, and parole.

Components of the policing industry: Refers to local police, state police, federal police, special jurisdiction police, and tribal police agencies that have law enforcement functions.

Conflict theory: A theoretical perspective in criminology that holds that opposing political, social, or other forces in society are responsible for a variety of social ills, including crime and delinquency.

Convict-lease system: After the Civil War, Southern states leased prison inmates to private companies that used them as forced laborers. This system of enforced labor ran from 1865 to 1920.

Corrections: The component of the criminal justice system concerned with the imprisonment, control, and rehabilitation of convicted offenders. Corrections include the administration and study of prisons, community-based sanctions, parole, probation, and less intrusive alternatives.

Crime rates: A ratio of the number of crimes per number of residents in a population, standardized by multiplying by 100,000. Violent crime rates, property crime rates, and arrest rates are used to analyze patterns and trends.

Crime statistics: Statistical data compiled by the police and the courts and routinely published by governments as indices of the extent of crime.

Death penalty: Punishment for a crime that results in the execution of the defendant.

Department of Homeland Security: Created in 2002 to prevent terrorist attacks within the United States, to reduce vulnerability to terrorism, and to minimize the impact from and assist in the recovery from terrorist attacks.

Disposition: The conclusion of juvenile court proceedings, often with an adjudication in a juvenile case. A disposition is similar to the imposition of a sentence in a criminal case.

Disproportionate minority contact: The overrepresentation of minority youth in the various stages of the juvenile justice system.

Driving while Black/Brown: Coined in the 1990s, this is an expression used to describe the practice by law enforcement officers of targeting Black and other minority motorists for traffic stops when there is no violation of the law.

Dual-court system: Refers to the judicial branch of American government consisting of both state and federal courts.

Eighth Amendment: The Amendment to the United States Constitution, also a part of the Bill of Rights, which prohibits the federal government from imposing excessive bail, excessive fines, or cruel and unusual punishments.

Ethnicity: Refers to a group of people who identify with each other through a common heritage, consisting of a common language, a common culture (often including a shared religion), and a tradition of common ancestry.

Furman v. Georgia: In this landmark case, Furman, a Black man, was accused of murder. Despite evidence at his trial that he was mentally deficient, he was convicted of murder and sentenced to death. He appealed his sentence on the grounds that his Fourteenth Amendment rights were violated. At the time of this case, disproportionately more Black murderers were being given the death sentence than White murderers. In 1972, the United States Supreme Court set aside Furman's death penalty, saying that the death penalty was administered in a racially discriminatory way in Georgia. In addition, the Court stated

this constituted cruel and unusual punishment. The case led to a moratorium on capital punishment in the United States until 1976.

Gender-specific programs: Programs for at-risk and delinquent girls that meet needs given their age and development. Gender-specific programs address such issues as teenage pregnancy, eating disorders, body self-image, and sexually transmitted diseases.

General strain theory: Robert Agnew's revision of the strain theory extended Robert Merton's anomie theory that was based on the general idea that economic strains are the primary contributor to crime. Agnew's theory also refers to the strains caused by the removal of positive stimuli (e.g., loss of a spouse, girlfriend/boyfriend) or the introduction of noxious stimuli (e.g., child abuse, criminal victimization), which can also contribute to criminal behavior.

Gregg v. Georgia: Gregg was convicted of robberies and murders in Atlanta, Georgia. This landmark case put an end to the moratorium set in *Furman v. Georgia* in 1972. The Supreme Court decision in *Gregg* rejected the legal argument that capital punishment, in and of itself, constituted "cruel and unusual punishment" and thus violated the Eighth Amendment of the U.S. Constitution. *Gregg* led to new death penalty statutes. Some state legislatures reformed their death penalty statutes to deal with the problem of undue jury discretion identified in *Furman* by mandating capital punishment for all persons convicted of first degree murder. In addition, the newly accepted provisions required two-stage trials in all death penalty cases, in which guilt or innocence would be determined in the first stage and the penalty would be assessed in the second stage.

Guided discretion: A term adopted from the landmark U.S. Supreme Court case *Gregg v. Georgia* that refers to the two-stage death penalty trial process. Under this approach,

if a defendant was convicted of first degree murder or another death-eligible offense, the prosecutor could ask the court to conduct a second "penalty stage" of the trial. After this second proceeding, the jury could impose the death sentence only if it found that the prosecution had proven a statutorily specified "aggravating circumstance," such as that the murder was committed for financial gain.

Hate crime: A criminal offense motivated by hatred of a specific race, ethnicity, religion, or sexual orientation. In many states, hate crimes are codified as offenses distinguished from the core offenses, such as assault, vandalism, and intimidation. In addition, hate crimes newly qualify for enhanced sentencing.

Houses of refuge: Facilities for juveniles opened in the 1800s as the result of increased juvenile presence on the streets after an influx of immigrant families entering the United States in the late 1700s and early 1800s. Although houses of refuge existed presumably to protect potentially criminal youth from being easily influenced by the negative aspects of society, some critics argue that the use of houses of refuge was discriminatory, affecting only poor White immigrants while excluding Blacks.

Innocence Project: The Innocence Project uses DNA testing to establish the innocence of wrongfully convicted offenders. It was founded by civil rights attorneys Peter J. Neufeld and Barry C. Scheck in 1992 at the Benjamin N. Cardoza School of Law, located at Yeshiva University in New York City.

Intake: The point at which a youth formally becomes involved in the juvenile justice process.

Intensive probation: A form of probation that involves an extra measure of supervision and control by the probation officer, often used for chronic and other high-risk offenders who pose a great probability of reoffending.

IQ: An intelligence quotient (IQ) is a purported measure of an individual's general intellectual ability. Over the past century, there have been repeated attempts to link low intelligence with propensity to commit criminal acts and frequent claims that some supposed racial groups have lower intelligence than others. Critics have rejected such claims as racist pseudoscience.

Jury nullification: The disregard by a jury of the evidence presented and the rendering of its verdict based on other criteria.

Juvenile court: A court of law, sometimes a subdivision of a common pleas court or domestic relations court, that has jurisdiction over matters pertaining to the delinquency and unruliness of persons who have not yet attained adulthood.

Juvenile justice system: Refers to the agencies and processes designed to meet the needs of delinquent and dependent youth.

Lynching: The practice of illegally taking the life of another by hanging, generally accomplished by a mob and often motivated by racial or ethnic hatred. Now infrequent, lynching in the United States is associated with White supremacists and their targeting of Blacks.

Manumission: The formal act of freeing a slave from slavery.

Marshall hypotheses: A series of conjectures by Supreme Court Justice Thurgood Marshall in *Furman v. Georgia* regarding the value of opinion poll data on public sentiments about capital punishment. Because the results of such polls can be of great importance to the U.S. Supreme Court's assessment of the constitutionality of various statutes and policies and practices, the validity of these data is especially important. The Marshall hypotheses are as follows: (1) Americans know almost nothing about the death penalty, and (2) those citizens who were fully informed about the purposes of the penalty and its liabilities would find the penalty shocking, unjust, and unacceptable.

Mass incarceration: The punitive sentencing practices of the 1980s to 2000s that resulted in the hyper-incarceration of offenders, especially Blacks and Hispanics.

McCleskey v. Kemp: McCleskey, a Black man, was convicted and sentenced to death for murdering a police officer during a grocery store robbery in 1978. Introducing into evidence that statistically more Black criminals receive the death penalty than White criminals and claiming that such disproportion is unconstitutional, McCleskey appealed. In 1987, the United States Supreme Court rejected the appeal, claiming Georgia's death penalty was not arbitrary and capricious, nor was it being applied in a discriminatory manner, regardless of the statistical evidence to the contrary.

Minority: Refers to a socially subordinate ethnic group (understood in terms of language, nationality, religion, and/or culture). Other minority groups include people with disabilities, "economic minorities" (working poor or unemployed), "age minorities" (who are younger or older than a typical working age), and sexual minorities. Members of minority groups are prone to differential treatment in the communities in which they live. This discrimination may be directly based on an individual's perceived membership in a minority group, without consideration of that individual's personal achievement. It may also occur indirectly, due to social structures that are not equally accessible to all.

Model minority: Used in social sciences to describe a racial minority group that has excelled in the United States despite prejudice and discrimination. This stereotype has become synonymous with the Asian American population.

National Crime Victimization Survey (NCVS): A survey of citizens 12 years of age and older conducted by the U.S. Bureau of the Census for the Bureau of Justice Statistics. The NCVS measures the respondents' experiences as victims of rape, robbery, assault, burglary, larceny, and motor vehicle theft.

National Incident-Based Reporting System (NIBRS): The crime reporting system designed to replace the *Uniform Crime Report*. NIBRS collects detailed data on the offender, time, place, and other aspects of the incident for each criminal offense reported by police agencies in participating agencies.

Office of Juvenile Justice and Delinquency Prevention (OJJDP): A branch of the U.S. Department of Justice's Office of Justice Programs. OJJDP is charged with promoting a variety of programs to reduce juvenile delinquency and to improve the administration of juvenile justice. Authorized by the Juvenile Justice and Delinquency Prevention Act of 1974, the OJJDP administers discretionary and formula grant programs and provides technical assistance to state and local governments.

Opium dens: Establishments where opium was sold and smoked, prevalent in many parts of the world in the 19th century, most notably China, Southeast Asia, North America, and France. Opium smoking began in North America with the first migration of the Chinese laborers who were addicted from the British expansionist policy of trade in opium. The first opium dens in the United States were located in the Chinese community.

Parole: The conditional release under supervision of a convict prior to the expiration of the sentence. Parole is generally granted by a parole board. Upon release on parole, the offender reports to a parole officer, who ensures compliance with specified conditions.

People of color: A term primarily used in the United States to refer to non-Whites. The term has been used to replace the term *minority*.

Peremptory challenges: The right during voir dire to challenge the seating of jurors without citing a specific cause.

Plea bargaining: The process and result of an agreement between a prosecuting attorney and defense counsel to reduce the seriousness or number of charges in a criminal case in return for a guilty plea.

Police-community relations: Efforts to create a positive relationship between police and citizens that developed in the late 1960s and 1970s.

Political prisoners: Prisoners who have been prosecuted and incarcerated because of their political beliefs.

Prejudice: When someone fosters a negative attitude toward a particular racial/ethnic group. This is usually in the form of acerbic stereotypes that often result in people making unfavorable generalizations about an entire group.

Pretrial release: The practice of conditionally releasing criminal defendants prior to trial without formal posting of bail. Those who participate in pretrial release generally must have stable residence and employment as well as other ties to the community that suggest they are likely to appear for trial.

Prisoner reentry: The return of offenders, probationers, parolees, and those released from jails to their community. Prisoner reentry involves the use of programs targeted at promoting the effective reintegration of offenders back to communities upon release from prison and jail. These programs are intended to assist offenders in acquiring the life skills needed to succeed in the community and become law-abiding citizens. These programs include prerelease programs, drug rehabilitation and vocational training, and work programs.

Prison-industrial complex: The industries that depend on the existence of prisons, including construction companies, food service companies, and other industries that are required to support the operation of prisons.

Private prisons: Correctional institutions that are either run or owned by private corporations.

Probation: The suspension of a sentence of a convicted offender and granting of freedom for a period of time under specified conditions. Probation is generally granted in lieu of confinement.

Profiling in airports: A term that became popular after the events of September 11, 2001. It refers to the targeting for a more intrusive inspection by airport security officials of Arabs, people of Middle Eastern descent, or those who appear to be Muslim. This practice has also been referred to as *flying while Arab*.

Public defender system: A federal, state, or local criminal justice agency that provides legal counsel for criminal defendants who have been accused or convicted of a crime or crimes and are too poor to hire a private attorney. Public defenders are attorneys paid as salaried government employees. The public defender system began in Los Angeles County in 1914 and has since become the most typical method of representing indigent defendants in court.

Public Law 280: A federal statute enacted by Congress in 1953 that enabled states to assume criminal, as well as civil, jurisdiction in matters involving American Indians as litigants on reservation land.

Race: Refers to the classification of humans into populations or groups based on various factors such as culture, language, social practice, or heritable characteristics.

Racial discrimination: The act of withholding or preventing someone from receiving social benefits, facilities, services, or opportunities on the basis of race, color, or national origin.

Racial profiling: Any police-initiated action that relies on the race, ethnicity, or national origin of an individual rather than the behavior of an individual or information that leads the police to a particular individual who has been identified as being, or having been engaged in, criminal activity.

Recidivism: Reoffending after an offender has been released from probation or corrections. The term includes re-arrest during terms of probation and arrest for technical violations/conditions of supervision.

Reentry courts: One of the problem-solving courts that have emerged since the 1990s. These courts are focused on ensuring that recently released offenders make a successful transition back to the community.

Reformatories: State correctional facilities intended to rehabilitate youthful or otherwise nonserious offenders. Reformatories were first used in the 1800s. Reformatories were originally intended to reform and educate young offenders rather than punish them.

Rehabilitation: A rationale for punishment that emphasizes correcting offender behavior through treatment. The goal of rehabilitation is to change behavior. Punishments that are in accordance with this theory are community service, probation orders, and any form of punishment that entails any form of guidance and aftercare toward the offender.

Relocation centers: Camps in the U.S. in which Japanese and Japanese Americans were interned during World War II. The U.S. internment camps were overcrowded and provided poor living conditions.

Sentencing disparities: Differences in sentences that include cases

with similarly situated offenders. Sentencing disparities can be the result of legislative differences between jurisdictions or judicial or prosecutorial discretion.

Slave patrols: Organized groups that regularly patrolled both rural and urban areas of the Southern United States to enforce restrictions that White colonists placed upon enslaved African Americans during the 18th and 19th centuries. Slave patrols were responsible for apprehending runaways, breaking up unsanctioned gatherings and celebrations of enslaved people, as well as other functions.

Social buffers: A term used to refer to working class and middle class role models in areas where there are significant concentrations of poverty. These individuals provide examples of success and serve as social buffers until they abandon these communities. Without these social buffers, residents of these communities become socially isolated and lack exposure to mainstream individuals.

Social disorganization: Social disorganization theory argues that crime and delinquency rates are a direct result of heterogeneous, transitional, and poverty-stricken neighborhoods. Neighborhoods characterized by social disorganization also include some of the following factors: large numbers of families on welfare, large numbers of condemned buildings, large numbers of renters, and high truancy rates.

Statistical Briefing Book (SBB): An online tool that enables users to access information via OJJDP's website to learn more about juvenile crime and victimization and about youth involved in the juvenile justice system. Developed for OJJDP by the National Center for Juvenile Justice, SBB provides timely and reliable statistical answers to the most frequently asked questions from policy makers, the media, and the general public. In addition, the data analysis and dissemination tools available through the SBB give users quick and easy access to detailed statistics on a variety of juvenile justice topics.

Statutes: Laws formulated by a legislative body that governs a particular jurisdiction and that are aimed at requiring or prohibiting something.

Strain theory: A theoretical perspective in criminology that is often tied to Robert Merton. The theory proposes that in every society there are culturally prescribed goals (e.g., American Dream) and institutionally accepted means (e.g., education, work) to achieve them. When citizens aspire to the societal goals but are unable to achieve them through institutionally approved means, a strain occurs that can lead them to commit crime and to engage in other illicit and harmful behaviors (e.g., drug abuse, alcoholism).

Tasers: Electronic weapons that work by discharging high-voltage electrodes attached to long wires that, when they penetrate human flesh, render the individual temporarily immobile. Originally designed as a less-than-lethal weapon for police personnel.

Theory: A set of statements or principles devised to explain a group of facts or phenomena. A theory that has been repeatedly tested or is widely accepted can be used to make predictions about natural phenomena.

Truly disadvantaged: Refers to a segment of the American population often referred to as the *underclass* or the *ghetto underclass*, predominately Black, who often live in disorganized inner cities and urban areas characterized by poverty, family instability, unemployment, a poor educational system, and crime.

Uniform Crime Reporting program: A crime statistics program of the Federal Bureau of Investigation. The UCR has been the national reporting system since the 1930s. UCR collects summary-based information from law enforcement agencies on offenses reported and arrests made as well as more detailed data on homicides.

United States Sentencing Commission: An independent agency of the judicial branch of the federal government. It has the following three purposes: (1) to establish policy, procedure, and sentencing practices related to the punishment of federal crimes; (2) to advise Congress regarding the creation of crime policies; and (3) to research, analyze, and distribute information on federal crimes and sentencing issues.

Victimization data: Information collected from persons that provides their perceptions about their involvement in crime as a victim. The National Crime Victimization Survey (NCVS) is the primary source of victimization data. The data collected include type of crime; relationship between victim and offender; characteristics of the offender, including the use of weapons, drugs, and alcohol; type of property lost; whether the crime was reported to the police and reasons for reporting or not reporting. Basic demographic information, such as age, race, gender, and income, is also collected to enable analysis of crime by various subpopulations.

Victimization rates: A percentage calculated using victimization data obtained from the victims themselves to measure the existence of actual, rather than reported, crimes.

Voir dire: The process of selecting jurors prior to the commencement of a criminal trial. During the voir dire, prospective jurors are questioned by both the prosecutor and the defense attorney to learn about their backgrounds and possible biases.

Walnut Street Jail: An early prison in Philadelphia that emphasized solitary confinement.

War on Drugs: Term used to describe the attempt by the federal and state authorities to control the supply and distribution of illegal drugs. The War on Drugs has drawn criticism for its emphasis on supply reduction, likened by many to Prohibition, which failed in its efforts to stem the flow of alcohol.

W.E.B. Du Bois: Considered by some to be one of the first major sociological criminologists. William Edward Burghardt Du Bois was also an American civil rights activist, leader, Pan-Africanist, sociologist, educator, historian, writer, editor, poet, and scholar. Du Bois's life and work were an inseparable mixture of scholarship, protest activity, and polemics. All of his efforts were geared toward gaining equal treatment for Black people and toward marshaling and presenting evidence to refute the myths of racial inferiority. Du Bois was among the founders of the National Association for the Advancement of Colored People (NAACP) in 1910 and was founder and editor of the NAACP's journal *The Crisis*.

White ethnic: A term used in the United States to refer to Whites who are typically of European origin. The term *White ethnic* almost always carried the connotation of being blue-collar and referred to White immigrants and their descendants from southern and eastern Europe. In the early 20th century, many White ethnics claimed to have been placed in a low socioeconomic level due to discrimination and ethnic stereotypes by the White Anglo-Saxon Protestant, commonly referred to as WASP, elite.

White immigrants: Refers to British, German, Italian, Irish, French, Spanish, and other White ethnic groups that came to the United States as early as the 1500s. Most early White immigrants, including Jewish immigrants, came from European countries.

Wrongful convictions: A conviction in court of an accused person who, in fact, did not commit the alleged offense.

Zoot Suit Riots: A term used to describe a series of conflicts that occurred in Los Angeles, California in the summer of 1943 between servicemen and Mexican American youths. Zoot suits were outfits popular among Mexican American youth at the time of the riots.

Credits and Sources

Chapter 1. Overview of Race and Crime

Figure 1.1: Shane, S. (1999, April 4). Genetic research increasingly finds "race" a null concept. *Baltimore Sun*, pp. 1A, 6A. Copyright 1999 by Baltimore Sun Company. Reproduced with permission of Baltimore Sun Company in the format Textbook via Copyright Clearance Center.

Figure 1.2: U.S. Census Bureau, 2010 Census questionnaire.

Table 1.1: U.S. Census Bureau, *Census 2000 Redistricting Data (Public Law 24-171) Summary File*, Tables PL1 and PL2, and *2010 Census Redistricting Data (Public Law 24-171) Summary File*, Tables P1 and P2.

Table 1.2: U.S. Census Bureau, *Census 2000 Summary File 1* and *Census 2010 Summary File 1.*

Table 1.3: U.S. Census Bureau, Department of Labor Statistics. Education Statistics: Table 225, http://www.census.gov/compendia/statab/2011/tables/11s0225.pdf; Unemployment Statistics: http://www.bls.gov/cps/cpsrace2009.pdf; Median Per Capita Income, Individuals Below Poverty Statistics: http://www.census.gov/prod/2010pubs/p60-238.pdf

Table 1.4: Higginbotham, A. L., & Jacobs, A. F. (1992). The law as an enemy: The legitimization of racial powerlessness through the Colonial and Antebellum criminal laws of Virginia. *North Carolina Law Review, 70,* 969–1070. As presented in Russell (1998, p. 16).

Box 1.1: Higginbotham, A. L. (1996). *Shades of freedom: Racial politics and the presumptions of the American legal process* (pp. 195-196). Oxford, UK: Oxford University Press.

Figure 1.3: Adapted from Cox, O. C. (1945). Lynching and the status quo. *Journal of Negro Education, 14,* 576–588. *Journal of Negro Education* by Howard University. Copyright 1945. Reproduced with permission of *Journal of Negro Education* in the format Textbook via Copyright Clearance Center.

Box 1.2: From CNN, March 4, 2011 © 2011 CNN. All rights reserved. Used by permission and protected by the copyright laws of the United States. The printing, copying, redistribution, or retransmission of this content without express written permission is prohibited.

Box 1.3: Alabama sets nation's toughest immigration law. Reuters, Thursday June 9, 2011 (http://www.reuters.com/article/2011/06/09/us-immigration-alabama-idUS-TRE7584C920110609). Edited by Colleen Jenkins and Greg McCune. All rights reserved. Republication or redistribution of Thomson Reuters content, including by framing or similar means, is expressly prohibited without the prior written consent of Thomson Reuters. Thomson Reuters and its logo are registered trademarks or trademarks of the Thomson Reuters group of companies around the world. © Thomson Reuters 2011. Thomson Reuters journalists are subject to an Editorial Handbook which requires fair presentation and disclosure of relevant interests.

Box 1.4: Reprinted with permission from New America Media (http://newamericamedia.org/).

Table 1.5: U.S. Census Bureau. Profile of General Population and Housing Characteristics: 2010—2010 Demographic Profile Data.

Photo 1.1: Corbis.

Table 1.6: Adapted from Feagin and Booher Feagin (2012) and Sowell (1981).

Chapter 2. Extent of Crime and Victimization

Table 2.1: Created by Shaun L. Gabbidon and Helen Taylor Green.

Box 2.1: Created by Shaun L. Gabbidon and Helen Taylor Green.

Table 2.2: Data secured from *The Negro Year Book* (1931–1932, p. 293) and from materials subsequently secured from the Department of Records and Research, Tuskegee Institute (Raper, 1933, see Appendix C, pp. 448–480).

Photo 2.1: Library of Congress, Prints and Photographs Division, reproduction number LC-USZ62-33793.

Photo 2.2: http://www.fbi.gov/about-us/cjis

Table 2.3: Created by Shaun L. Gabbidon and Helen Taylor Green.

Table 2.4: FBI, *Crime in the United States* (2007-2010, Tables 49, 55, 61, 67).

Table 2.5: FBI, Department of Justice. *Crime in the United States* (2010, Table 43).

Figure 2.1: National Crime Victimization Survey.

Table 2.6: National Crime Victimization Survey. Truman and Rand (2010, Table 3, p. 3).

Table 2.7: National Crime Victimization Survey. Truman and Rand (2010, Table 5, p. 5).

Table 2.8: U.S. Department of Justice, Federal Bureau of Investigation, *Crime in the United States, 2009,* Expanded Homicide Data Table 2 [Online]. Available: http://www2 .fbi.gov/ucr/cius2009/offenses/ expanded_information/data/shrt able_02.html [Oct. 14, 2010]. Table adapted by SOURCEBOOK staff.

Box 2.2: National Crime Victimization Survey (www.fbi.gov/littlerock/ press-releases/2011/lr040811.htm).

Table 2.9: Federal Bureau of Investigation, *Hate Crime Statistics,* Table 1, 2006–2010 (2007-2011).

Photo 2.3: AP File Photo, © Associated Press.

Chapter 3. Theoretical Perspectives on Race and Crime

Box 3.1: "Culture of Poverty" Makes a Comeback ; Patricia Cohen; October 17, 2010 (http://www.nytimes. com/2010/10/18/us/18poverty.html?_ r=2&pagewanted=1). From *The New York Times,* October 17, 2010 © 2010, *The New York Times.* All rights reserved. Used by permission and protected by the copyright laws of the United States. The printing, copying, redistribution, or retransmission of the material without express written permission is prohibited.

Figure 3.1: Hawkins, D. F. (1983). Black and White homicide differentials: Alternatives to an inadequate theory. *Criminal Justice and Behavior, 10,* 407–440. From Johnson (1941).

Figure 3.2: Hawkins, D. F. (1983). Black and White homicide differentials: Alternatives to an inadequate theory. *Criminal Justice and Behavior, 10,* 407–440.

*Box 3.*2: Written by S. Gabbidon. In Walker, S., Spohn, C., & DeLone, M. (2012). *The color of justice: Race,*

ethnicity, and crime in America (5th ed.). Belmont, CA: Cengage/ Wadsworth.

Figure 3.3: Walker, S., Spohn, C., & DeLone, M. (2012). *The color of justice: Race, ethnicity, and crime in America* (5th ed.). Belmont, CA: Cengage/Wadsworth. © 2007 Wadsworth, a part of Cengage Learning, Inc. Reproduced by permission. www.cengage.com/permissions

Table 3.1: Created by Shaun L. Gabbidon and Helen Taylor Green.

Chapter 4. Policing

Figure 4.1: Minority Representation Among Local Police Officers, 1987-2007. Brian A. Reaves, Ph.D., BJS Statistician U.S. Department of Justice. Office of Justice Programs. Bureau of Justice Statistics 2010. Local Police Departments, 2007, Figure 9.

Table 4.1: Minority Representation Among Local Police Officers, 1987-2007. Brian A. Reaves, Ph.D., BJS Statistician U.S. Department of Justice. Office of Justice Programs. Bureau of Justice Statistics 2010. Local Police Departments, 2007, Table 9.

Table 4.2: Tribal Law Enforcement Agency 2008, by Brian A. Reaves, Ph.D., BJS Statistician. U.S. Department of Justice, Office of Justice Programs. Bureau of Justice Statistics. Table 2.2, p. 3.

Photo 4.1: Corbis.

Table 4.3: Constructed from *Sourcebook of Criminal Justice Statistics,* 2002-2011, Table 2.2.

Box 4.1: U.S. Department of Justice, OCR (www.Justice.gov/crt/about/spl/ nop_letter_espanol.pdf).

Table 4.4: Eith and Durose (2011).

Box 4.2: U.S. Immigration and Customs Enforcement, Homeland Security (http://www.ice.gov/doclib/ foia/secure_communities/secure communitiesstrategicplan09.pdf).

Chapter 5. Courts

Box 5.1: http://www.toronto.com/ article/671993--lindsay-lohan-s-release-prompts-questions-about-pref erential-treatment

Photo 5.1: © DAVID MCNEW/POOL/ epa/Corbis.

Photo 5.2: Wikipedia (http:// en.wikipedia.org/wiki/File:Supreme_ Court_US_2010.jpg)

Table 5.1: Tarver, Marsha; Walker, Steve; Wallace, Harvey; Multicultural Issues in the Criminal Justice System, 1st. Copyright © 2002. Printed and electronically reproduced by permission of Pearson Education, Inc., Upper Saddle River, New Jersey.

Table 5.2: Tarver, Marsha; Walker, Steve; Wallace, Harvey; Multicultural Issues in the Criminal Justice System, 1st. Copyright © 2002. Printed and electronically reproduced by permission of Pearson Education, Inc., Upper Saddle River, New Jersey.

Box 5.2: Navajo Justice, by The Honorable Robert Yazzie, Chief Justice of the Navajo Nation. Retrieved from www.yesmagazine. org/issues/is-it-time-to-close-the-prisons/navajo-justice

Table 5.3: Pretrial Release of Felony Defendants in State Courts (Cohen & Reaves, 2007). Bureau of Justice Statistics.

Table 5.4: Pretrial Release of Felony Defendants in State Courts (Cohen & Reaves, 2007). Bureau of Justice Statistics.

Table 5.5: Pretrial Release of Felony Defendants in State Courts (Cohen & Reaves, 2007). Bureau of Justice Statistics.

Table 5.6: Pretrial Release of Felony Defendants in State Courts (Cohen & Reaves, 2007). Bureau of Justice Statistics.

Table 5.7: Langton and Farole (2009). Public Defender Offices, 2007—Statistical Tables. Bureau of Justice Statistics.

Box 5.3: Illegal Racial Discrimination in Jury Selection: A Continuing Legacy. Equal Justice Initiative (http://www .eji.org/eji/). Reprinted with permission of the Equal Justice Initiative.

Figure 5.1: National Drug Court Institute (January 2008).

Chapter 6. Sentencing

Photo 6.1: © Corbis.

Figure 6.1: H. Catterall (1926/1968). *Judicial cases concerning American slavery and the Negro* (Vol. 1). New York: Negro University Press.

Table 6.1: Reprinted from Crime and Law Enforcement in the Colony of New York, 1691-1776, by Douglas Greenberg. Copyright 1976 by Cornell University. Used by permission of the publisher, Cornell University Press.

Table 6.2: Reprinted from Crime and Law Enforcement in the Colony of New York, 1691-1776, by Douglas Greenberg. Copyright 1976 by Cornell University. Used by permission of the publisher, Cornell University Press.

Table 6.3: Reprinted from Crime and Law Enforcement in the Colony of New York, 1691-1776, by Douglas Greenberg. Copyright 1976 by Cornell University. Used by permission of the publisher, Cornell University Press.

Table 6.4: Reprinted from Crime and Law Enforcement in the Colony of New York, 1691-1776, by Douglas Greenberg. Copyright 1976 by Cornell University. Used by permission of the publisher, Cornell University Press.

Table 6.5: Cahalan, M., & Parsons, L. (1986). *Historical corrections in the United States, 1850–1984.* Washington, DC: Bureau of Justice Statistics.

Table 6.6: Cahalan, M., & Parsons, L. (1986). *Historical corrections in the United States, 1850–1984.* Washington, DC: Bureau of Justice Statistics.

Figure 6.2: Minnesota Sentencing Guidelines Commission: Sentencing

Practices, Annual Summary Statistics for Felony Offenders Sentenced in 2006.

Table 6.7: Rosenmerkel, S., Durose, M., & Farole, D. (2009). *Felony sentences in state courts, 2006: Statistical tables* (NCJ 226846). Washington, DC: Bureau of Justice Statistics.

Table 6.8: Rosenmerkel, S., Durose, M., & Farole, D. (2009). *Felony sentences in state courts, 2006: Statistical tables* (NCJ 226846). Washington, DC: Bureau of Justice Statistics.

Table 6.9: U.S. Sentencing Commission, 2010 Datafile, USSCFY10.

Table 6.10: U.S. Sentencing Commission.

Table 6.11: U.S. Sentencing Commission, 2010 Datafile, USSCFY10.

Table 6.12: U.S. Sentencing Commission, 2010 Datafile, USSCFY10.

Box 6.1: "Crack Offenders Eligible for Early Release." By Jessica Gresko, Associated Press 6/30/2011. Used with permission of The Associated Press Copyright © 2011. All rights reserved.

Photo 6.2: © Michael Reynolds—POOL/epa/Corbis.

Table 6.13: Sourcebook of Criminal Justice Statistics Online http:/ www.albany.edu/sourcebook/ pdf/t1822008.pdf. Sources of data for *Sourcebook* table: Sheldon Goldman, "Reagan's Judicial Legacy: Completing the Puzzle and Summing Up," *Judicature* 72 (April-May 1989), pp. 321, 322, Table 2; and Sheldon Goldman et al., "W. Bush's Judicial Legacy: Mission Accomplished," *Judicature* 92 (May-June 2009), p. 279. Table adapted by Sourcebook staff.

Table 6.14: Sourcebook of Criminal Justice Statistics Online http:/www .albany.edu/sourcebook/pdf/ t1812008.pdf. Sources of data for *Sourcebook* table: Sheldon Goldman, "Reagan's Judicial Legacy: Completing

the Puzzle and Summing Up," *Judicature* 72 (April-May 1989), pp. 324, 325, Table 4; and Sheldon Goldman et al., "W. Bush's Judicial Legacy: Mission Accomplished," *Judicature* 92 (May-June 2009), p. 284. Table adapted by Sourcebook staff.

Chapter 7. The Death Penalty

Box 7.1: General Assembly of North Carolina, North Carolina Legislature.

Box 7.2: Paul Woolverton and Gregory Phillips. *Fayetteville Observer.* Published July 25, 2011 (http://www .fayobserver.com/articles/2011/07/22 /1110294?sac=Home).

Box 7.3: Phillips, U. B. (1915). Slave crime in Virginia. *American Historical Review, 20,* 336-340.

Table 7.1: Phillips, U. B. (1915). Slave crime in Virginia. *American Historical Review, 20,* 336-340.

Figure 7.1: Phillips, U. B. (1915). Slave crime in Virginia. *American Historical Review, 20,* 336-340.

Table 7.2: Adapted from Cahalan, M., & Parsons, L. (1986). *Historical corrections in the United States, 1850–1984.* Washington, DC: Bureau of Justice Statistics. P. 10. *State authority:* Data for 1890–1980 tabulated from listings compiled by Negley K. Teeters and Charles J. Zibulka, 1864 to 1967, and revised by M. Watt Espy Jr. Listing published in Bowers, William; Pierce, Glen; and McDevitt, John, *Legal Homicide: Death as Punishment in America 1964–1982.* Boston: Northwestern University Press, 1984.

Local authority: Data taken from Table 2.3 in Bowers, William; Pierce, Glen; and McDevitt, John, *Legal Homicide: Death as Punishment in America 1964–1982.* Boston: Northwestern University Press, 1984. Sources for table include: Yearly Meeting of Friends, 1919, pgs. 57–58, for 1890–1917; Bedau, *The Death Penalty in America.* New York, Anchor Press, 1967, pg. 35, for 1918–1920; Barnes, J. E., and

Teeters, N. K., *New Horizons in Criminology.* Englewood Cliffs, *Journal of Delinquency* 1:6, 1950, pg. 7, for 1927–1919. NPS and BJS Bulletins after 1930.

Illegal lynchings: Table published in Bureau of the Census, *Historical Statistics of the United States From Colonial Times to 1957,* and compiled by Department of Records and Research, Tuskegee Institute, Alabama, printed in Ploski, Harry, and Williams, James; *The Negro Almanac: A Reference Work on the Afro-American,* 4th ed. New York: Wiley, 1983. Updated included to Census Bureau table, 1960, pg. 218.

1980–1984: Data taken from U.S. Department of Justice, Bureau of Justice Statistics; Washington D.C. Bureau of Justice Statistics Bulletin; Capital Punishment 1984; pg. 7.

Table 7.3: Cahalan, M., & Parsons, L. (1986). *Historical corrections in the United States, 1850–1984.* Washington, DC: Bureau of Justice Statistics. P. 11. Tabulations based on data compiled by Department of Records and Research, Tuskegee Institute, Alabama. Taken from Ploski, Harry, and Williams, James; *The Negro Almanac: A Reference Work on the Afro-American*, 4th edition. New York: Wiley, 1983.

Table 7.4: Snell, T. (2010). *Capital Punishment, 2009: Statistical Tables.* Bureau of Justice Statistics.

Table 7.5: Snell, T. (2010). *Capital Punishment, 2009: Statistical Tables.* Bureau of Justice Statistics.

Table 7.6: Snell, T. (2010). *Capital Punishment, 2009: Statistical Tables.* Bureau of Justice Statistics.

Table 7.7: Snell, T. (2010). *Capital Punishment, 2009: Statistical Tables.* Bureau of Justice Statistics.

Figure 7.2: From Zimring, F. *The Contradictions of American Capital Punishment* (2004), p. 94. Published by Oxford University Press. Originally adapted from Espy, M. Watt, and John

Ortiz Smylka. 1988. *Executions in the United States, 1680-1987: The Espy File.* Inter-university Consortium for Political and Social Research Study No. 8451. ETS. No. 14. National Association for the Advancement of Colored People. 1919. *Thirty Years of Lynching in the United States, 1889-1918.* New York: Arnos Press. United States Census Bureau 1900, 2000, 2002. United States Census Data. Death Penalty Information Center. 2002. Available at http://www.death penaltyinfo.org

Photo 7.1: Reuters/Scott Olson/Landov.

Box 7.4: Robin L. Barton (http://www.thecrimereport.org/viewpoints/2011-05-the-duke-lacrosse-scandal-revisited-five-years-later). This story originally appeared in *The Crime Report* (www.thecrimereport.org), America's most comprehensive criminal justice news service.

Box 7.5: Adam Liptak, Overriding the Jury in Capital Cases (http://www.nytimes.com/2011/07/12/us/12bar.html).

Chapter 8. Corrections

Figure 8.1: The Pew Center on the States. (2008). *One in 100: Behind Bars in America 2008.* Retrieved at http://www.pewcenteronthestates.org/report_detail.aspx?id=35904. Original data from National Association of State Budget Offices, State Expenditure Report series.

Table 8.1: Cahalan, M., & Parsons, L. (1986). *Historical corrections in the United States, 1850–1984.* Washington, DC: Bureau of Justice Statistics.

Photo 8.1: Bettmann/Corbis.

Table 8.2: Pyrooz, D.C., Decker, S.H., & Fleisher, M. (2011). From the street to prison, from the prison to the street: Understanding and responding to prison gangs. *Journal of Aggression, Conflict and Peace*

Research, 3, 12-24. © Emerald Group Publishing Limited, all rights reserved.

Table 8.3: Table 2, p. 733, in Winterdyk, J., & Ruddell, R. (2010). Managing prison gangs: Results from survey of U.S. prison systems. *Journal of Criminal Justice, 38,* 730-736.

Table 8.4: West, H.C., Sabol, W.J., & Greenman, S.J. (2010). *Prisoners in 2009.* Washington, DC: Bureau of Justice Statistics.

Table 8.5: West, H.C., Sabol, W.J., & Greenman, S.J. (2010). *Prisoners in 2009.* Washington, DC: Bureau of Justice Statistics.

Table 8.6: Minton, T.D. (2011). *Jail inmates at midyear 2010-statistical tables.* Washington, DC: Bureau of Justice Statistics.

Table 8.7: Minton, T.D. (2011). *Selected findings: Jails in Indian country, 2009.* Washington, DC: Bureau of Justice Statistics.

Box 8.1: Marc Mauer and David Cole, *Washington Post* (http://www.washingtonpost.com/opinions/five-myths-about-incarceration/2011/06/13/AGfIWvYH_story_1.html). Copyright © 2011 Washington Post.

Table 8.8: Glaze, L.E., Bonczar, T.B. (2009). *Probation and parole in the United States, 2009.* Washington, DC: Bureau of Justice Statistics.

Box 8.2: Genevra Pittman, Reuters (http://www.reuters.com/article/2011/07/14/us-prison-blacks-idUSTRE76D71920110714).

Box 8.3: Michelle Alexander, Special to CNN. I'm a criminal and so are you, May 19, 2010 (http://articles.cnn.com/2010-05-18/opinion/alexander.who.am.i_1_law-abiding-felons-criminal?_s=PM:OPINION).

Chapter 9. Juvenile Justice

Figure 9.1: Office of Juvenile Justice and Delinquency Prevention. *Statistical Briefing Book, 2011.*

Table 9.1: Federal Bureau of Investigation (2002–2010, Table 38).

Table 9.2: Federal Bureau of Investigation (2010, Table 43).

Box 9.1: Federal Bureau of Investigation. Supplementary Homicide Reports for the years 1980–2008 (machine-readable data files). Washington, D.C.: FBI. http://www.ojjdp.gov/ojstatbb/victims/qa02310.asp?qaDate=2008. Released on December 21, 2010. Adapted from Puzzanchera, C. and Kang, W. (2010). *Easy Access to the FBI's Supplementary Homicide Reports: 1980-2008.* Available online at: http://ojjdp.gov/ojstatbb/ezashr/. Data source: Federal Bureau of Investigation. *Supplementary Homicide Reports* for the years 1980–2008 [machine-readable data files]. Washington, D.C.: FBI.

Table 9.3: Federal Bureau of Investigation, UCR (2002–2010, Table 43).

Table 9.4: Adams, B., & Addie, S. (2010). *Delinquency cases waived to criminal court, 2007.* U.S. Department of Justice. Office of Juvenile Justice and Delinquency Prevention. Retrieved on July 30, 2011 from https://www.ncjrs.gov/pdf-files1/ojjdp/230167.pdf

Table 9.5: Author's analysis of OJJDP's Census of Juveniles in Residential Placement 1997, 1999, 2001, 2003, 2006, and 2007 (machine-readable data files).

Appendix

Table A.1: FBI, Crime in the United States, 1933–2010, Table 43.

Table A.2: FBI, Crime in the United States, 1950–2010, Table 43.

References

Abbott, E. (Ed.). (1931). *Crime and the foreign born* (National Commission on Law Observance and Enforcement, Report No. 10). Washington, DC: Government Printing Office.

ABC News Poll. (2002, March 7). Retrieved March 17, 2004, from the Polling the Nations database at http://www.orspub.com/

ABC/*Washington Post* Poll. (2003). Retrieved March 2, 2003, from Polling the Nations database at http://www.orspub.com/

Adams, B., & Addie, S. (2010). *Delinquency cases waived to criminal court, 2007*. Retrieved on July 30, 2011, from https://www.ncjrs.gov/pdffiles1/ojjdp/230167.pdf

Adams, K. (1999). What we know about police use of force. In *Use of force by police: Overview of national and local data* (NCJ 176330, pp. 1–14). Washington, DC: U.S. Department of Justice, Office of Justice Programs.

Agnew, R. (1992). Foundation for a general strain theory of crime and delinquency. *Criminology, 30,* 47–87.

Agnew, R. (2004). *Why do criminals offend? A general theory of crime and delinquency.* Los Angeles: Roxbury.

Agnew, R. (2006). *Pressured into crime: An overview of general strain theory.* Los Angeles: Roxbury.

Agozino, B. (2003). *Counter-colonial criminology: A critique of imperialist reason.* London: Pluto Press.

Akers, R. L. (2000). *Criminological theories: Introduction, evaluation, and application.* Los Angeles: Roxbury.

Alexander, M. (2010). *The new Jim Crow: Mass incarceration in the age of colorblindness.* New York: The New Press.

Allen, H. E., Simonsen, C. E., & Latessa, E. J. (2004). *Corrections in America: An introduction.* Upper Saddle River, NJ: Prentice Hall.

Allen, T. W. (1994). *The invention of the White race: Vol. 1. Racial oppression and social control.* New York: Verso.

American Bar Association and the National Bar Association. (2001). *Justice by gender.* Washington, DC: Author.

American Civil Liberties Union. (1999). *Driving while Black: Racial profiling on our nation's highways.* New York: Author.

Anderson, C. (1994). *Black labor, White wealth.* Edgewood, MD: Duncan & Duncan.

Anderson, E. A. (1994, May). The code of the streets. *Atlantic Monthly,* pp. 81–94.

Anderson, E. A. (1999). *The code of the streets: Decency, violence, and the moral life of the inner city.* New York: Norton.

Anderson, J. (2001). What to do about "much ado" about drug courts? *International Journal of Drug Policy, 12,* 469–475.

Anderson, P. R., & Newman, D. J. (1998). *Introduction to criminal justice* (6th ed.). New York: McGraw-Hill.

Aptheker, B. (1971). The social functions of the prisons in the United States. In A. Y. Davis (Ed.), *If they come in the morning* (pp. 39–48). New Rochelle, NY: Third Press.

Aptheker, H. (1993). *American Negro slave revolts.* New York:

International. (Original work published 1943)

Arab American Institute. (2011). *The AAI Foundation.* Retrieved from http://www.aaiusa.org

Argersinger v. Hamlin, 407 U.S. 25 (1972).

Arthur, J. A. (1998). Proximate correlates of Blacks, support for capital punishment. *Journal of Crime and Justice, 21,* 159–172.

Atkins v. Virginia, 536 U.S. 304 (2002).

Austin, J., & Irwin, J. (2001). *It's about time: America's imprisonment binge* (3rd ed.). Belmont, CA: Wadsworth.

Austin, R. (1983). The colonial model, subcultural theory, and intragroup violence. *Journal of Criminal Justice, 11,* 93–104.

Baadsager, P., Sims, B., Baer, J., & Chambliss, W. J. (2000). The overrepresentation of minorities in America's imprisonment binge. *Corrections Management Quarterly, 4,* 1–7.

Bachman, R. (1991). An analysis of American Indian homicide: A test of social disorganization and economic deprivation at the reservation county level. *Journal of Research in Crime and Delinquency, 28,* 456–471.

Baker, D. V. (2003). The racist application of capital punishment to African Americans. In M. Free (Ed.), *Racial issues in criminal justice: The case of African Americans* (pp. 177–201). Westport, CT: Greenwood.

Baker, D. V. (2007). American Indian executions in historical context. *Criminal Justice Studies, 20,* 315–373.

Baker, D. V. (2008). Black female executions in historical context.

Criminal Justice Review, 33, 64–88.

Baker, E. (2002). Flying while Arab: Racial profiling and air travel security. *Journal of Air Law and Commerce, 67,* 1375–1405.

Baldus, D. C., & Woodworth, G. (2003). Race discrimination and the death penalty: An empirical and legal overview. In J. Acker, R. Bohm, & C. S. Lanier (Eds.), *America's experiment with capital punishment* (2nd ed., pp. 501–551). Durham, NC: Carolina Academic Press.

Baldus, D. C., Woodworth, G., & Pulaski, C. A. (1990). *Equal justice and the death penalty: A legal and empirical analysis.* Boston: Northeastern University Press.

Banner, S. (2002). *The death penalty: An American history.* Cambridge, MA: Harvard University Press.

Barak, G., Flavin, J., & Leighton, P. (2010). *Class, race, gender, and crime* (3rd ed.). New York: Rowman & Littlefield.

Barkan, S. F., & Cohn, S. F. (1994). Racial prejudice and support for the death penalty by Whites. *Journal of Research in Crime and Delinquency, 31,* 202–209.

Barker, T., & Carter, D. (1991). *Police deviance* (2nd ed.). Cincinnati, OH: Anderson.

Barlow, D. E., & Barlow, M. H. (2000). *Police in a multicultural society.* Prospect Heights, IL: Waveland Press.

Barlow, D. E., & Barlow, M. H. (2002). Racial profiling: A survey of African American police officers. *Police Quarterly, 5,* 334–358.

Barro, R. J. (1999, September 27). Does abortion lower the crime rate? *Business Week,* p. 30.

Bastian, L. (1990). *Hispanic victims.* Washington, DC: U.S. Department of Justice, Bureau of Justice Statistics.

Bastian, L. (1992). *Criminal victimization in the United States: 1973–1990 trends.* Washington, DC: U.S. Department of Justice, Office of Justice Programs.

Batson v. Kentucky, 476 U.S. 79, 108 (1986).

Battle v. Anderson, 376 F. Supp. 402 (1974).

Baumer, E., Horney, J., Felson, R., & Lauritsen, J. (2003). Neighborhood disadvantage and the nature of violence. *Criminology, 41,* 39–71.

Baumer, E., Messner, S., & Rosenfeld, R. (2003). Explaining spatial variation in support for capital punishment: A multilevel analysis. *American Journal of Sociology, 108,* 844–875.

Bavon, A. (2001). The effect of the Tarrant County drug court project on recidivism. *Evaluation and Program Planning, 24,* 13–22.

Beard, A. (2007). *Judge finds Duke prosecutor in contempt.* Retrieved March 8, 2008, from http://www.abcnews.go.com/sports

Beaumont, G., & Tocqueville, A. (1964). *On the penitentiary system in the United States and its application in France.* Carbondale: Southern Illinois University Press. (Original work published 1833)

Beck, E. M., & Tolnay, S. E. (1995). Violence toward African Americans in the era of the White lynch mob. In D. F. Hawkins (Ed.), *Ethnicity, race, and crime: Perspectives across time and place* (pp. 121–144). Albany: State University of New York Press.

Beckett, K., & Sasson, T. (2000). *The politics of injustice.* Thousand Oaks, CA: Pine Forge Press.

Bedau, H. A. (2009). Racism, wrongful convictions and the death penalty. *Tennessee Law Review, 76,* 615–624.

Bedau, H. A., & Radelet, M. L. (1987). Miscarriage of justice in potentially capital cases. *Stanford Law Review, 40,* 21–179.

Behrens, A., Uggen, C., & Manza, J. (2003). Ballot manipulation and the "menace of Negro domination": Racial threat and felon disenfranchisement in the United States, 1850–2002. *American Journal of Sociology, 109,* 559–605.

Belenko, S., Sprott, J. B., & Petersen, C. (2004). Drug and alcohol involvement among minority and female juvenile offenders: Treatment and policy issues. *Criminal Justice Policy Review, 15,* 3–36.

Belgrave, F. Z., Townsend, T. G., Cherry, V. R., & Cunningham, D. M. (1997). The influence of an Africentric worldview and demographic variables on drug knowledge, attitudes, and use among African American youth. *Journal of Community Psychology, 25,* 421–433.

Bell, D. (1960). *The end of ideology.* Glencoe, IL: Free Press.

Bell, J. (2005). Solvable problem: Reducing the disproportionality of youths of color in juvenile detention facilities. *Corrections Today, 67,* 80–83.

Benekos, P. J., & Merlo, A. V. (2008). Juvenile justice: The legacy of punitive policy. *Youth Violence and Juvenile Justice, 6*(1), 28–46.

Berk, R., Li, A., & Hickman, L. J. (2005) Statistical difficulties in determining the role of race in capital cases: A re-analysis of data from the state of Maryland. *Journal of Quantitative Criminology, 21,* 365–390.

Bernard, T. J., & Kurlycheck, M. C. (2010). *The cycle of juvenile justice* (2nd ed.). New York: Oxford University Press.

Blakely v. Washington, 542 U.S. 296 (2004).

Blalock, H. M. (1967). *Toward a theory of minority group relations.* New York: Wiley.

Blankstein, A., & Winton, R. (2010, September 25). Lindsay Lohan's release prompts questions about preferential treatment. *Toronto.com.* Retrieved from http://www.toronto.com

Blauner, R. (1969). Internal colonialism and ghetto revolt. *Social Problems, 16,* 393–408.

Blauner, R. (1972). *Racial oppression in America.* New York: Harper & Row.

Bloom, B., Owen, B., Deschenes, E. P., & Rosenbaum, J. (2002). Moving toward justice for female juvenile offenders in the new millennium. *Journal of Contemporary Criminal Justice, 18,* 37–56.

Blumer, M. (1984). *The Chicago school of sociology: Institutionalization, diversity, and the rise of sociological research.* Chicago: University of Chicago Press.

Blumstein, A. (1982). On the racial disproportionality of the United States' prison populations. *Journal of Criminal Law & Criminology, 73,* 1259–1281.

Blumstein, A. (1993). Racial disproportionality of U.S. prison populations revisited. *University of Colorado Law Review, 63.* Retrieved August 25, 2002, from Lexis-Nexis database.

Blumstein, A. (1996). *Youth violence, guns, and the illicit drug markets* (Research preview). Washington, DC: National Institute of Justice.

Blumstein, A. (2002). Prisons: A policy challenge. In J. Q. Wilson & J. Petersilia (Eds.), *Crime: Public policies for crime control* (pp. 451–483). Oakland, CA: Institute for Contemporary Studies.

Blumstein, A., & Wallman, J. (Eds.). (2005). *The crime drop in America* (2nd ed.). New York: Cambridge University Press.

Bobo, L. D., & Johnson, D. (2004). A taste for punishment: Black and White Americans' views on the death penalty and the war on drugs. *Du Bois Review, 1,* 151–180.

Bohm, R. M. (1991). American death penalty opinion, 1936–1986: A critical examination of Gallup polls. In R. M. Bohm (Ed.), *The death penalty in America: Current research* (pp. 113–145). Cincinnati, OH: Anderson.

Bohm, R. M. (1999). *Deathquest: An introduction to the theory and practice of capital punishment.* Cincinnati, OH: Anderson.

Bohm, R. M. (2001). *A primer on crime and delinquency theory* (2nd ed.). Belmont, CA: Wadsworth/ Thomson Learning.

Bohm, R. M. (2007). *Death Quest III: An introduction to the theory and practice of capital punishment in the United States* (3rd ed.). Cincinnati, OH: Anderson.

Bohm, R. M., Clark, L., & Aveni, A. (1991). Knowledge and death penalty opinion: A test of the Marshall hypotheses. *Journal of Research in Crime and Delinquency, 28,* 360–387.

Bohm, R. M., & Vogel, B. L. (2010). *A primer on crime and delinquency theory.* Belmont, CA: Cengage/Wadsworth.

Bonger, W. A. (1943). *Race and crime.* New York: Columbia University Press.

Borchard, E. M. (1932). *Convicting the innocent: Sixty-five actual errors of criminal justice.* Garden City, NY: Doubleday.

Bortner, M. A. (1984). *Inside a juvenile court: The tarnished ideal of individualized justice.* New York: New York University Press.

Bosworth, M., & Flavin, L. (Eds.). (2007). *Race, gender, & punishment: From colonialism to the war on terror.* New Brunswick, NJ: Rutgers University Press.

Bowers, W. J., & Pierce, G. (1980). Arbitrariness and discrimination under post-Furman capital statutes. *Crime & Delinquency, 26,* 563–572.

Bowers, W. J., Sandys, M. R., & Steiner, B. D. (1998). Juror predispositions: Guilt-trial experience, and premature decision making. *Cornell Law Review, 83,* 1476–1556.

Bowers, W. J., Steiner, B. D., & Sandys, M. R. (2001). Death sentencing in Black and White: An empirical analysis of the role of jurors' race and jury composition. *The University of Pennsylvania Journal of Constitutional Law, 3,* 171–274.

Bradley, M. (1978). *The iceman inheritance: Prehistoric sources of Western man's racism, sexism, and aggression.* New York: Kayode.

Braga, A. A., Weisburd, D. L., Waring, E. J., Mazerolle, L. G., Spelman, W., & Gajewski, F. (1999). Problem-oriented policing in violent crime places: A randomized controlled experiment. *Criminology, 37,* 541–580.

Braman, D. (2002). Families and incarceration. In M. Mauer & M. Chesney-Lind (Eds.), *Invisible punishment: The collateral consequences of mass imprisonment* (pp. 117–135). New York: New Press.

Brandon, R., & Davies, C. (1973). *Wrongful imprisonment: Mistaken convictions and their consequences.* London: Archon Books.

Brennan, P. K. (2006). Sentencing female misdemeanants: An examination of the direct and indirect effects of race/ethnicity. *Justice Quarterly, 23,* 60–95.

Brennan, P. K., & Spohn, C. (2008). Race/ethnicity and sentencing outcomes among drug offenders in North Carolina. *Journal of Contemporary Criminal Justice, 24,* 371–398.

Brewer, T. W. (2004). Race and jurors' receptivity to mitigation in capital cases: The effect of jurors', defendants', and victims' race in combination. *Law and Human Behavior, 28,* 529–545.

Brezina, T., Agnew, R., Cullen, F. T., & Wright, J. P. (2004). The code of the street: A quantitative assessment of Elijah Anderson's subculture of violence thesis and its contribution to youth violence research. *Youth Violence and Juvenile Justice, 2,* 303–328.

Bridges, G. S., Conley, D., Engen, R. L., & Price-Spratlen, T. (1995). Social contexts of punishment: Effects of crime and community social structure on racial disparities in the administration of juvenile justice. In K. Kempf Leonard, C. Pope, &

W. Feyerherm (Eds.), *Minorities in juvenile justice* (pp. 128–152). Thousand Oaks, CA: Sage.

Bridges, G., & Steen, S. (1998). Racial disparities in official assessments of juvenile offenders: Attributional stereotypes as mediating mechanisms. *American Sociological Review, 63,* 554–570.

Brodkin, K. (1999). *How Jews became White folks and what that says about race in America.* New Brunswick, NJ: Rutgers University Press.

Brodkin Sacks, K. (1997). How did Jews become White folks? In R. Delgado & J. Stefancic (Eds.), *Critical White studies: Looking behind the mirror* (pp. 395–401). Philadelphia: Temple University Press.

Brooks, W. M., Jr., & Willingham, T. Y. (2009). Juvenile waivers to adult court. In H. T. Greene & S. L. Gabbidon (Eds.), *Encyclopedia of race and crime* (pp. 424–427). Thousand Oaks, CA: Sage.

Brown v. Board of Education of Topeka et al., 347 US 483 (1954).

Brown, M. C., & Warner, B. D. (1992). Immigrants, urban politics and policing in 1900. *American Sociological Review, 57,* 293–305.

Brownstein, H. H. (1996). *The rise and fall of a violent crime wave: Crack cocaine and the social construction of a crime problem.* Guilderland, NY: Harrow & Heston.

Brunson, R. K. (2007). "Police don't like Black people": African-American young men's accumulated police experiences. *Criminology & Public Policy, 6,* 71–102.

Brunson, R. K., & Stewart, E. A. (2006). Young African American women, the street code, and violence: An exploratory analysis. *Journal of Crime & Justice, 29,* 1–19.

Brunson, R. K., & Weitzer, R. (2009). Police relations with black and white youths in different urban neighborhoods. *Urban Affairs Review, 44*(6), 858–885.

Bureau of Indian Affairs. (1974). *The American Indians: Answers to 101 questions.* Washington, DC: U.S. Department of the Interior.

Bureau of Indian Affairs. (1976). *Law enforcement services annual report 1976.* Washington, DC: U.S. Department of the Interior.

Bureau of Justice Assistance. (2007). *2005 national gang threat assessment.* Retrieved February 22, 2008, from http://www.ojp.usdoj.gov/BJA/what/2005_threat_assesment.pdf

Bureau of Justice Statistics. (1992). *Criminal victimization in the United States: 1973–1990 trends.* Washington, DC: U.S. Department of Justice, Office of Justice Programs.

Bureau of Justice Statistics. (2001). *Hate crimes reported in NIBRS, 1997–99.* Washington, DC: U.S. Department of Justice, Office of Justice Programs.

Bureau of Justice Statistics. (2003). *Over half of the increase in state prison populations since 1995 is due to an increase in the prisoners convicted of violent offenses.* Washington, DC: Department of Justice. Retrieved March 22, 2004, from http://www.ojp.usdoj.gov/bjs/glance/corrtyp.htm

Bureau of Justice Statistics. (2006). *Compendium of federal justice statistics, 2004.* Washington, DC: Department of Justice.

Bureau of Justice Statistics. (2008). *Demographic trends in jail populations.* Retrieved July 21, 2008, from http://www.ojp.usdoj.gov/bjs/glancetables/jailracetab.htm.

Bureau of Justice Statistics. (2010). *Felony sentences in state courts, 2006: Statistical tables.* Washington, DC: Department of Justice.

Bureau of Justice Statistics. (2011a). *Key facts at a glance: Incarceration rate, 1980–2009.* Retrieved June 17, 2011, from http://bjs.ojp.usdoj.gov/content/glance/race.cfm

Bureau of Justice Statistics. (2011b). *Key facts at a glance: Violent crime rates by race of victim.* Retrieved June 17, 2011, from http://bjs.ojp.usdoj.gov/content/glance/race.cfm

Burgess, E. W. (1925). The growth of the city: An introduction to a research project. In R. Park & E. W. Burgess (Eds.), *The city* (pp. 47–62). Chicago: University of Chicago Press.

Burns, S. (2011). *The Central Park Five: A chronicle of a city wilding.* New York: Knopf.

Bushway, S., Stoll, M., & Weiman, D. F. (Eds.). (2007). *Barriers to reentry? The labor market for released prisoners in post-industrial America.* New York: Russell Sage.

Butler, P. (1995). Racially based jury nullification: Black power in the criminal justice system. *The Yale Law Journal, 105,* 677–725.

Butler, P. (2009). *Let's get free: A hip-hop theory of justice.* New York: The New Press.

Cabaniss, E. R., Frabutt, J. M., Kendrick, M. H., & Arbuckle, M. B. (2007). Reducing disproportionate minority contact in the juvenile justice system: Promising practices. *Aggression and Violent Behavior: A Review Journal, 12,* 393–401.

Cahalan, M., & Parsons, L. (1986). *Historical corrections in the United States, 1850–1984.* Washington, DC: Bureau of Justice Statistics.

Camp, G. M., & Camp, C. G. (1985). *Prison gangs: Their extent, nature, and impact on prisons.* Washington, DC: U.S. Department of Justice.

The Campaign for the Fair Sentencing of Youth. (2009). Human rights. Retrieved July 2, 2011, from http://www.endjlwop.org

Cao, L., Adams, A. T., & Jensen, V. J. (2000). The empirical status of the Black subculture-of-violence thesis. In M. W. Markowitz & D. Jones Brown (Eds.), *The system in Black and White: Exploring the connections between race, crime, and justice* (pp. 47–61). Westport, CT: Praeger.

Carey, S. M., Finigan, M., Crumpton, D., & Waller, M. (2006). California drug courts: Outcomes, costs, and promising practices: An overview of Phase II in a statewide study. *Journal of Psychoactive Drugs, 3,* 345–356.

Carlson, P. M. (2001). Prison interventions: Evolving strategies to control security threat groups. *Corrections Management Quarterly, 5,* 10–22.

Carr, N. T., Hudson, K., Hanks, R. S., & Hunt, A. N. (2008). Gender effects along the juvenile justice system: Evidence of a gendered organization. *Feminist Criminology, 3,* 25–43.

Carroll, C. (1900). *The Negro a beast.* St. Louis, MO: American Book and Bible House.

Carroll, L. (1974). *Hacks, Blacks, and cons: Race relations in a maximum security prison.* Prospect Heights, IL: Waveland Press.

Carter, D. (1969). *Scottsboro: A tragedy of the American South.* Baton Rouge: Louisiana State University Press.

Carter, D. L. (1983). Hispanic interaction with the criminal justice system in Texas: Experiences, attitudes, and perceptions. *Journal of Criminal Justice, 11,* 213–227.

Castelle, G., & Loftus, E. F. (2002). Misinformation and wrongful convictions. In S. Westervelt & J. A. Humphrey (Eds.), *Wrongly convicted: Perspectives on failed justice* (pp. 17–35). New Brunswick, NJ: Rutgers University Press.

Catalano, S. M. (2006). *Criminal victimization, 2005.* Washington, DC: U.S. Department of Justice, Office of Justice Programs, Bureau of Justice Statistics.

Catterall, H. (Ed.). (1968). *Judicial cases concerning American slavery and the Negro* (Vol. 1). New York: Negro University Press. (Original work published 1926)

Center for the Study and Prevention of Violence. (2011). *Selection criteria.* Retrieved on July 12, 2011, from http://www.colorado.edu/cspv/blueprints/criteria.html

Cernkovich, S. A., Giordano, P. C., & Rudolph, J. L. (2000). Race, crime, and the American dream. *Journal of Research in Crime and Delinquency, 37,* 131–170.

Chabrán, R., & Chabrán, R. (1996). *The Latino encyclopedia.* Tarrytown, NY: Marshall Cavendish Corporation.

Chambliss, W. (1964). A sociological analysis of the law of vagrancy. *Social Problems, 12,* 67–77.

Chambliss, W. (Ed.). (1969). *Crime and the legal process.* New York: McGraw-Hill.

Chambliss, W. J. (1991). *Trading textbooks for prison cells.* Baltimore, MD: National Center for Institutions and Alternatives.

Chamlin, M. B., Myer, A. J., Sanders, B. A., & Cochran, J. K. (2008). Abortion as crime control: A cautionary tale. *Criminal Justice Policy Review, 19,* 135–152.

Chapin, B. (1983). *Criminal justice in colonial America, 1606–1660.* Athens: University of Georgia Press.

Chesney-Lind, M., & Shelden, R. G. (2004). *Girls, delinquency, and juvenile justice.* Belmont, CA: Wadsworth/Thomson Learning.

Chicago Commission on Race Relations. (1922). *The Negro in Chicago: A study of race relations and a race riot in 1919.* Chicago: Author.

Chilton, B. (2004). Regional variations in lethal and nonlethal assaults. *Homicide Studies, 8,* 40–56.

Chiricos, T. G., & Crawford, C. (1995). Race and imprisonment: A contextual assessment of the evidence. In D. Hawkins (Ed.), *Ethnicity, race, and crime* (pp. 281–309). Albany: State University of New York Press.

Christianson, S. (1981). Our Black prisons. *Crime and Delinquency, 27,* 364–375.

Christianson, S. (1998). *With liberty for some: 500 years of imprisonment in America.* Boston: Northeastern University Press.

Christianson, S. (2004). *Innocent: Inside wrongful conviction cases.* New York: New York University Press.

Cintron, M. (2005). Latino delinquency: Defining and counting the problem. In E. Penn, H. Taylor Greene, & S. Gabbidon (Eds.), *Race and juvenile justice* (pp. 27–45). Durham, NC: Carolina Academic Press.

Clark, L. (2007, December 13). *Minorities suspicious of ethnic groups: Poll finds stereotypes, resentment are mutual.* Retrieved from http://www.ohio.com/news/nation/minorities-suspicious-of-ethnic-groups-1.73029

Clarke, H. J. (1992). *Christopher Columbus and the African holocaust.* Brooklyn, NY: A & B.

Clarke, J. W. (1998). "Without fear or shame": Lynching, capital punishment and the subculture of violence in the American South. *British Journal of Political Science, 28,* 269–289.

Clear, T. R. (2007). *Imprisoning communities: How mass incarceration makes disadvantaged neighborhoods worse.* New York: Oxford University Press.

Clear, T. R., & Cole, G. F. (2000). *American corrections* (5th ed.). Belmont, CA: Wadsworth.

Clear, T. R., & Cole, G. F. (2003). *American corrections* (6th ed.). Belmont, CA: Wadsworth.

Clear, T. R., & Dammer, H. R. (2003). *The offender in the community* (2nd ed.). Belmont, CA: Wadsworth.

Clear, T. R., Rose, D. R., & Ryder, J. A. (2001). Incarceration and the community: The problem of removing and returning offenders. *Crime & Delinquency, 47,* 335–351.

Clear, T. R., Rose, D. R., Waring, E., & Scully, K. (2003). Coercive mobility and crime: A preliminary examination of concentrated incarceration and social disorganization. *Justice Quarterly, 20,* 33–64.

Clement, P. T. (1993). The incorrigible child: Juvenile delinquency in the United States from the 17th through the 19th centuries. In A. G. Hess & P. F. Clement (Eds.), *History of juvenile delinquency: A collection of essays on crime committed by young offenders, in history and in selected countries* (pp. 453–490). Aalen, Germany: Scientia Verlag.

Cloward, R. A., & Ohlin, L. E. (1960). *Delinquency and opportunity: A theory of delinquent gangs.* New York: The Free Press.

Cochran, J. K., & Chamlin, M. B. (2005). Can information change public opinion? Another test of the Marshall hypotheses. *Journal of Criminal Justice, 33,* 573–584.

Cochran, J. K., & Chamlin, M. B. (2006). The enduring racial divide in death penalty support. *Journal of Criminal Justice, 34,* 84–99.

Cochran, J. K., Sanders, B., & Chamlin, M. B. (2006). Profiles in change: An alternative look at the Marshall hypotheses. *Journal of Criminal Justice Education, 17,* 205–226.

Cohen, A. K. (1955). *Delinquent boys: The culture of the gang.* New York: The Free Press.

Cohen, F. (1971). *Handbook of federal Indian law.* Albuquerque: University of New Mexico Press.

Cohen, P. (2010, October 17). "Culture of poverty" makes a comeback. *The New York Times,* p. A1. Retrieved from http://www.nytimes.com

Cohen, S. (2003). *The wrong man: America's epidemic of wrongful death row convictions.* New York: Carroll & Graf.

Cohen, T. H. (2011). *Who's better at defending criminals? Does type of defense attorney matter in terms of producing favorable case outcomes?* Available at SSRN: http://ssrn.com/abstract=1876474

Cohen, T. H., & Reaves, B. A. (2007). *Pretrial release of felony defendants in state courts.* Washington, DC: Bureau of Justice Statistics. NCJ 214994

Coker v. Georgia, 429 U.S. 815 (1977).

Cole, D. (1999). *No equal justice.* New York: New Press.

Collins, C. F. (1997). *The imprisonment of African American women.* Jefferson, NC: McFarland.

Colvin, M. (1997). *Penitentiaries, reformatories, and chain gangs.* New York: St. Martin's Press.

Congressional Budget Office. (2010). *S. 678 Juvenile Justice and Delinquency Prevention Reauthorization Act of 2009.* Retrieved July 12, 2011, from http://www.cbo.gov/ftpdocs/110xx/doc11010/s678.pdf

Conley, D. J., & Debro, J. (2002). Black Muslims in California prisons: The beginning of a social movement for Black prisoners in the United States. In C. E. Reasons, D. C. Conley, & J. Debro (Eds.), *Race, class, gender, and justice in the United States* (pp. 278–291). Boston: Allyn & Bacon.

Cooper, C. (2001/2002). Subjective states of mind & custodial arrest: Race-based policing. *The Journal of Intergroup Relations, 38,* 3–18.

Cooper, C. S. (2003). Drug courts: Current issues and future perspectives. *Substance Use & Misuse, 38,* 1671–1711.

Cooper, J. A., Walsh, A., & Ellis, L. (2010). Is criminology moving toward a paradigm shift? Evidence from a survey of the American Society of Criminology. *Journal of Criminal Justice Education, 21,* 332–347.

Coppa, F. J., & Curran, T. J. (1976). From the Rhine to the Mississippi: The German emigration to the United States. In F. J. Coppa & T. J. Curran (Eds.), *The immigrant experience in America* (pp. 44–62). Boston: Twayne.

Courtwright, D. T. (2001). *Dark paradise.* Cambridge, MA: Harvard University Press.

Covington, J. (1995). Racial classification in criminology: The reproduction of racialized crime. *Sociological Forum, 10,* 547–568.

Covington, J. (2003). The violent Black male: Conceptions of race in criminological theories. In D. F. Hawkins (Ed.), *Violent crime: Assessing race & ethnic differences* (pp. 254–279). Cambridge, UK: Cambridge University Press.

Cox, O. C. (1945). Lynching and the status quo. *Journal of Negro Education, 14,* 576–588.

Cresswell, L., & Deschenes, E. (2001). Minority and non-minority perceptions of drug court program severity and effectiveness. *Journal of Drug Issues, 31,* 259–292.

Crow, M. C., & Johnson, K. A. (2008). Race, ethnicity, and habitual-offender sentencing: A multi-level analysis of individual and contextual threat. *Criminal Justice Policy Review, 19,* 63–83.

Crutchfield, R. D. (2004). Warranted disparity? Questioning the justification of racial disparity in criminal justice processing. *Columbia Human Rights Law Review, 36,* 15–40.

Cuellar, J., & Curry, T. (2007). The prevalence and comorbidity between delinquency, drug abuse, suicide attempts, physical and sexual abuse, and self-mutilation among delinquent Hispanic females. *Hispanic Journal of Behavioral Sciences, 29*(1), 68–78.

Cullen, F. T. (2009). Preface. In A. Walsh & K. M. Beaver (Eds.), *Biosocial criminology: New directions in theory and research* (pp. xv–xvii). New York: Routledge.

Curran, D. J., & Renzetti, C. M. (2001). *Theories of crime.* Boston: Allyn & Bacon.

D'Alessio, S. J., Eitle, D., & Stolzenberg, L. (2005). The impact of serious crime, racial threat, and economic inequality on private police size. *Social Science Research, 34,* 267–282.

Daniels, R. (1988). *Asian America: Chinese and Japanese in the United States since 1850.* Seattle: University of Washington Press.

Darwin, C. (1859). *On the origin of species by means of natural selection, or the preservation of favoured races in the struggle for life.* London: John Murray.

Darwin, C. (1871). *The descent of man and selection in relation to sex.* London: John Murray.

Davidson, R. T. (1974). *Chicano prisoners: The keys to San Quentin.* Prospect Heights, IL: Waveland Press.

Davis, A. Y. (1981). *Women, race & class.* New York: Random House.

Davis, A. Y. (1997). Race and criminalization: Black Americans and the punishment industry. In W. Lubiano (Ed.), *The house that race built: Black Americans, U.S. terrain* (pp. 264–279). New York: Pantheon.

Davis, A. Y. (2000). From the convict lease system to the super-max prison. In J. James (Ed.), *States of confinement: Policing, detention, and prisons* (pp. 60–74). New York: St. Martin's Press.

Davis, A. Y. (2003). *Are prisons obsolete?* New York: Seven Stories Press.

Davis, H. W. (2008). *Federal Advisory Committee on Juvenile Justice Annual Report, 2008.* Washington, DC: U.S. Department of Justice.

Death Penalty Information Center. (2008). *Juveniles and the death penalty.* Retrieved March 26, 2008, from http://www.deathpenaltyinfo.org/article.php?did=205&scid=27 3/26/2008.

Death Penalty Information Center. (2011). Retrieved from http://www.deathpenaltyinfo.org

DeFrances, C. J., & Litras, M. F. X. (2000). *Indigent defense services in large counties, 1999.* Washington, DC: Bureau of Justice Statistics.

De Gruy, L. (2010). DNA testing may unfairly target people of color.

Los Angeles Wave. Retrieved from http://www.wavenewspapers.com

De Las Casas, B. (1993). *The devastation of the Indies: A brief account.* Baltimore: Johns Hopkins University Press. (Original work published 1552)

Delgado, R. (2009). The law of the noose: A history of Latino lynching. *Harvard Civil Rights-Civil Liberties Law Review, 44,* 297–312.

Delgado, R., & Stefancic, J. (2001). *Critical race theory: An introduction.* New York: New York University Press.

Delisi, M., & Regoli, R. (1999). Race, conventional crime, and criminal justice: The declining importance of skin color. *Journal of Criminal Justice, 27,* 549–557.

Dempsey, J. S. (1999). *An introduction to policing.* Belmont, CA: Wadsworth.

Demuth, S., & Steffensmeier, D. (2004). The impact of gender and race-ethnicity in the pretrial release process. *Social Problems, 51,* 222–242.

Denov, M. S., & Campbell, K. M. (2005). Criminal injustice: Understanding the causes, effects, and responses to wrongful convictions in Canada. *Journal of Contemporary Criminal Justice, 21,* 224–249.

Department of Homeland Security. (2011). *Immigration enforcement actions: 2010.* Retrieved July 18, 2011, from http://www.dhs.gov/xlibrary/assets/statistics/publications/enforcement-ar-2010.pdf

Deschenes, E. P., & Esbensen, F. A. (1999). Violence among girls: Does gang membership make a difference? In M. Chesney-Lind & J. M. Hagedorn (Eds.), *Female gangs in America* (pp. 277–294). Chicago: Lakeview Press.

Desmond v. Blackwell, 235 F. Supp. 246 (1964).

Devine, P., Coolbaugh, K., & Jenkins, S. (1998). *Disproportionate minority confinement: Lessons*

from five states. Washington, DC: Office of Juvenile Justice and Delinquency Prevention.

Dickey, G. (2004). *Downtown opium dens attracted many.* El Paso Community College Local History Project. Retrieved December 16, 2004, from http://www.epcc.edu/ftp/Homes/monicaw/borderlands/21_opium.htm

Dillon, R. R., Robbins, M. S., Szapocznik, J., & Pantin, H. (2008). Exploring the role of parental monitoring of peers on the relationship between family functioning and delinquency in the lives of African American and Hispanic adolescents. *Crime & Delinquency, 54,* 65–94.

DiIulio, J. J., Jr. (1995, November 27). The coming of the super-predators. *Weekly Standard,* p. 23.

DiIulio, J. (1996a). My Black crime problem, and ours. *City Journal, 6,* 14–28.

DiIulio, J. J., Jr. (1996b, Spring). They're coming: Florida's youth crime bomb. *Impact,* pp. 25–27.

Dinnerstein, L., & Reimers, D. M. (1982). *Ethnic Americans* (2nd ed.). New York: Harper & Row.

Donohue, J. J., & Levitt, S. D. (2001). The impact of legalized abortion on crime. *The Quarterly Journal of Economics, CXVI,* 379–420.

Donohue, J. J., & Levitt, S. D. (2004). Further evidence that legalized abortion lowered crime: A reply to Joyce. *Journal of Human Resources, 39,* 29–49.

Donohue, J. J., & Levitt, S. D. (2006). Measurement error, legalized abortion and the decline in crime: A response to Foote and Goetz (2005). *National Bureau of Economic Research Working Paper,* no. 11987.

Donziger, S. R. (Ed.). (1996). *The real war on crime: The report of the national criminal justice commission.* New York: Harper Perennial.

Dorfman, L., & Schiraldi, V. (2001). *Off balance: Youth, race, and crime in the news.* Washington, DC: Building Blocks for Youth.

Drug Policy Alliance. (2008). *Tulia, Texas*. Retrieved March 18, 2008, from http://www.drug policy.org/law/police/tulia/index.cfm

Du Bois, W. E. B. (1891). *Enforcement of the slave trade laws* (American Historical Association, Annual Report). Washington, DC: Government Printing Office.

Du Bois, W. E. B. (1899, May 18). The Negro and crime. *The Independent, 51*.

Du Bois, W. E. B. (1901). The spawn of slavery: The convict lease system in the South. *Missionary Review of the World, 14,* 737–745. Reprinted in S. L. Gabbidon, H. Taylor Greene, & V. Young. (2002). *African American classics in criminology and criminal justice* (pp. 83–88). Thousand Oaks, CA: Sage.

Du Bois, W. E. B. (1920). Crime. *The Crisis, 19,* 172–173.

Du Bois, W. E. B. (1996). *The Philadelphia Negro: A social study*. Philadelphia: The University of Pennsylvania Press. (Original work published 1899)

Dugdale, R. L. (1877). *"The Jukes": A study in crime, pauperism, disease, and heredity*. New York: G. P. Putnam's Sons.

Dulaney, M. R. (1879). *The origin of races and color*. Philadelphia: Harper & Brothers.

Dulaney, W. M. (1996). *Black police in America*. Bloomington: Indiana University Press.

Dunlap, E., Golub, A., & Johnson, B. D. (2003). Girls' sexual development in the inner city: From compelled childhood sexual contacts to sex-for-things exchanges. *Journal of Child Sexual Abuse, 12,* 73–96.

Durose, M. R., Smith, E. L., & Langan, P. A. (2007). *Contacts between police and the public, 2005*. Washington, DC: U.S. Department of Justice.

Dyer, J. (2000). *The perpetual prisoner machine: How America profits from crime*. Boulder, CO: Westview Press.

Dyson, M. E. (2006). *Come hell or high water: Hurricane Katrina and the color of disaster*. New York: Basic Civitas Books.

Eberheart v. Georgia, 433 U.S. 917 (1977).

Eddings v. Oklahoma, 455 U.S. 104 (1982).

Egley, A., & Howell, J. C. (2011). *Highlights of the 2009 national youth gang survey*. Retrieved October 26, 2011 from https://www.ncjrs.gov/pdffiles1/ojjdp/233581.pdf

Eith, C., & Durose, M. R. (2011). *Contacts between police and the public, 2008*. Retrieved October 21, 2011, from http://www.bjs.gov/content/pub/pdf/cpp08.pdf

Eitle, D., & Taylor, J. (2008). Are Hispanics the new "threat"? Minority group threat and fear of crime in Miami-Dade County. *Social Science Research, 37,* 1102–1115.

Eitle, D., & Turner, R. J. (2003). Stress exposure, race, and young male adult crime. *Sociological Quarterly, 44,* 243–269.

Ellis, L. (1997). Criminal behavior and *r/K* selection: An extension of gene-based evolutionary theory. *Deviant Behavior, 8,* 148–176.

Ellis, L., & Walsh, A. (1997). Gene-based evolutionary theories in criminology. *Criminology, 35,* 229–275.

Ellis, L., & Walsh, A. (1999). Criminologists' opinions about causes and theories of crime and delinquency. *The Criminologist, 24*(1), 4–6.

Ellis, L., & Walsh, A. (2000). *Criminology: A global perspective*. Needham Heights, MA: Allyn & Bacon.

Emsley, C. (1983). *Policing and its context, 1750–1870*. New York: Schocken Books.

Engel, R. S., & Calnon, J. M. (2004). Examining the influence of driver's characteristics during traffic stops with police: Results from a national survey. *Justice Quarterly, 21,* 49–90.

Engel, R. S., & Smith, M. R. (2009). Perceptual distortion and reasonableness during police shootings: Law, legitimacy, and future research. *Criminology & Public Policy, 8,* 141–152.

Engen, R. L., Gainey, R. R., Crutchfield, R. D., & Weis, J. G. (2003). Discretion and disparity under sentencing guidelines: The role of departures and structured sentencing alternatives. *Criminology, 41,* 99–130.

Ennis, R. S., Rios-Vargas, M., & Albert, N. G. (2011). *The Hispanic population: 2010*. Washington, DC: U.S. Census Bureau.

Epps, E. G. (1967). Socioeconomic status, race, level of aspiration and juvenile delinquency: A limited empirical test of Merton's conception of deviance. *Phylon, 28,* 16–27.

Equal Justice Initiative. (2007). *Cruel and unusual: Sentencing 13- and 14-year-old children to die in prison*. Retrieved from http://www.eji.org

Equal Justice Initiative. (2010). *Illegal racial discrimination in jury selection: A continuing legacy*. Montgomery, AL: Author.

Escobar, E. J. (1999). *Race, police, and the making of a political identity: Mexican Americans and the Los Angeles Police Department, 1900–1945*. Berkeley: University of California Press.

Escobedo v. Illinois, 378 U.S. 478, 84 S. Ct. 1758 (1964).

Farole, D. J., & Langton, L. (2010). A national assessment of public defender office caseloads. *Judicature, 94,* 87–90.

Faust, A. B. (1927). *The German element in the United States* (Vol. I). New York: The Steuben Society of America.

Feagin, R. F., & Booher Feagin, C. (2012). *Racial and ethnic relations* (9th ed.). New York: Pearson/Prentice-Hall.

Federal Bureau of Investigation. (1930–2002). *Crime in the United States*. Washington, DC: Government Printing Office. Retrieved from http://www.fbi.gov/ucr/ucr.htm

Federal Bureau of Investigation. (1998). *National incident-based reporting system*. Washington, DC: Government Printing Office.

Federal Bureau of Investigation. (2001). *Crime in the United States, 2000*. Washington, DC: Government Printing Office.

Federal Bureau of Investigation. (2002). *Hate crime statistics, 1995–2001*. Washington, DC: Government Printing Office. Retrieved July 15, 2004, from http://www.fbi.gov/ucr/ucr.htm#hate

Federal Bureau of Investigation. (2003). *Crime in the United States, 2003 Section IV arrests*. Retrieved from http://www.fbi.gov/ucr/cius_03/pdf/03sec4.pdf

Federal Bureau of Investigation. (2004). *Crime in the United States, 2002*. Washington, DC: Government Printing Office. Retrieved from http://www.fbi.gov/ucr/cius_02/pdf/4section four.pdf

Federal Bureau of Investigation. (2005). *Crime in the United States, 2005 Section IV arrests*. Retrieved from http://www.fbi.gov/ucr/05cius/arrests/index.html

Federal Bureau of Investigation. (2006a). *Crime in the United States, 2006*. Retrieved from http://www.fbi.gov/ucr/cius2006/arrests/index.html.

Federal Bureau of Investigation. (2006b). *Hate crime statistics, 2006*. Washington, DC: Government Printing Office. Retrieved February 2, 2008, from http://www.fbi.gov/ucr/hc2006/index.html.

Federal Bureau of Investigation. (2006c). *Law enforcement officers feloniously killed and assaulted, 2006. Officers feloniously killed*. Retrieved March 18, 2008, from http://www.fbi.gov/ucr/killed/2006/felonious lykilled.html.

Federal Bureau of Investigation. (2007a). *Crime in the United States, 2006*. Washington, DC: Government Printing Office.

Retrieved from http://www.fbi.gov/ucr/cius2006/index.html

Federal Bureau of Investigation. (2007b). *Hate crime statistics, 2006*. Washington, DC: Government Printing Office. Retrieved April 23, 2011, from http://www2.fbi.gov/ucr/hc2006/index.html

Federal Bureau of Investigation. (2008a). *Crime in the United States, 2007*. Washington, DC: Government Printing Office.

Federal Bureau of Investigation. (2008b). *Hate crime statistics, 2007*. Washington, DC: Government Printing Office. Retrieved April 23, 2011 from http://www2.fbi.gov/ucr/hc2007/index.html.

Federal Bureau of Investigation. (2009a). *Crime in the United States, 2008*. Washington, DC: Government Printing Office. Retrieved from http://www.fbi.gov/about-us/cjis/ucr/crime-in-the-u.s.-2010/aboutucrmain

Federal Bureau of Investigation. (2009b). *Hate crime statistics, 2008*. Washington, DC: Government Printing Office. Retrieved April 23, 2011 from http://www2.fbi.gov/ucr/hc2008/index.html

Federal Bureau of Investigation. (2010a). *Crime in the United States, 2009*. Washington, DC: Government Printing Office.

Federal Bureau of Investigation. (2010b). *Hate crime statistics, 2009*. Washington, DC: Government Printing Office.

Federal Bureau of Investigation. (2011a). *Arkansas men charged with federal hate crime related to the assault of five Hispanic men*. Retrieved from http://www.fbi.gov/littlerock/press-releases/2011/lr040811.htm

Federal Bureau of Investigation. (2011b). Crime in the United States 2010. http://www.fbi.gov/about-us/cjis/ucr/crime-in-the-u.s/2010/crime-in-the-u.s.-2010 (Retrieved on January 16, 2012)

Federal Bureau of Investigation. (2011c). Crime in the United States by volume and rate per 100,000 inhabitants, 1991–2010. *Uniform Crime Reports*. Retrieved November 5, 2011, from http://www.fbi.gov/about-us/cjis/ucr/crime-in-the-u.s/2010/crime-in-the-u.s.-2010/tables/10tbl01.xls

Federal Bureau of Investigation. (2011d). Crime in the United States Table 43. *Uniform Crime Reports*. Retrieved November 1, 2011, from http://www.fbi.gov/about-us/cjis/ucr/crime-in-the-u.s/2010/crime-in-the-u.s.-2010/tables/table-43

Federal Bureau of Investigation. (2011e). Estimated number of arrests: United States, 2010. *Uniform Crime Reports*. Retrieved November 5, 2011, from http://www.fbi.gov/about-us/cjis/ucr/crime-in-the-u.s/2010/crime-in-the-u.s.-2010/tables/10tbl29.xls

Federal Bureau of Investigation. (2011f). Hate crime statistics 2010. http://www.fbi.gov/about-us/cjis/ucr/hate-crime/2010/index (Retrieved on 1/5/2012)

Federal Reserve Archival System for Economic Research. (n.d.). *Statistical abstract of the United States: 1929*. Retrieved from http://fraser.stlouisfed.org/publications/stat_abstract/issue/5354/

Feld, B. (1999). *Bad kids: Race and the transformation of the juvenile court*. New York: Oxford University Press.

Feldmeyer, B. (2009). Immigration and violence: The offsetting effects of immigrant concentration on Latino violence. *Social Science Research, 38*, 717–731.

Feldmeyer, B., & Ulmer, J. T. (2011). Racial/ethnic threat and federal sentencing. *Journal of Research in Crime and Delinquency, 48*, 238–270.

Fellner, J., & Mauer, M. (1998). *Losing the vote: The impact of felony disenfranchisement laws in the*

United States. Washington, DC: Human Rights Watch and the Sentencing Project.

Fernandez, K. E., & Bowman, T. (2004). Race, political institutions, and criminal justice: An examination of the sentencing of Latino offenders. *Columbia Human Rights Law Review, 36,* 41–70.

Fielding, J., Tye, G., Ogawa, P., Imam, I., & Long, A. (2002). Los Angeles County drug court programs: Initial results. *Journal of Substance Abuse Treatment, 23,* 217–224.

Finger, B. (1959). *Concise world history.* New York: Philosophical Library.

Finkelhor, D., & Ormrod, R. (2004). *Prostitution of juveniles: Patterns from NIBRS.* Washington, DC: Office of Justice Programs, Office of Juvenile Justice and Delinquency Prevention.

Finkelstein, N. H. (2007). *American Jewish history.* Philadelphia: The Jewish Publication Society.

Fischer, B. (2003). Doing good with a vengeance: A critical assessment of the practices, effects and implications of drug treatment courts in North America. *Criminal Justice, 3,* 227–248.

Fixico, D. L. (2000). *The urban Indian experience in America.* Albuquerque: University of New Mexico Press.

Flanagan, T. J. (1996). Reform or punish: Americans' views of the correctional system. In T. J. Flanagan & D. R. Longmire (Eds.), *Americans view crime and justice: A national public opinion survey* (pp. 75–92). Thousand Oaks, CA: Sage.

Fleisher, M. S., & Decker, S. H. (2001). An overview of the challenge of prison gangs. *Corrections Management Quarterly, 5,* 1–9.

Fleury-Steiner, B. (2009). Capital jury project. In H. T. Greene & S. L. Gabbidon (Eds.), *Encyclopedia of race and crime* (pp. 91–93). Thousand Oaks, CA: Sage.

Fleury-Steiner, B., & Argothy, V. (2004). Lethal "borders":

Elucidating jurors' racialized discipline to punish in Latino defendant death cases. *Punishment & Society, 6,* 67–84.

Flexon, J. L., Greenleaf, R. G., & Lurigio, A. J. (2010). The effects of self-control, gang membership, and parental attachment/identification on police contacts among Latino and African American youths. *International Journal of Offender Therapy and Comparative Criminology.* Retrieved on July 30, 2011. Published online before print December 27, 2010, doi: 10.1177/0306624X10394116

Flowers, R. B. (1988). *Minorities and criminality.* Westport, CT: Greenwood Press.

Fogelson, R. (1977). *Big-city police.* Cambridge, MA: Harvard University Press.

Foote, C. L., & Goetz, C. F. (2006). Testing economic hypotheses with state-level data: A comment on Donohue and Levitt (2001). *Federal Reserve Bank of Boston Working Paper,* no. 05–15.

Forst, B. (2003, July 28–30). *Managing errors in the new era of the policing.* Paper presented at the annual conference on Criminal Justice Research and Evaluation, Washington, DC.

Fox, C., & Huddleston, W. (2003). Drug courts in the U.S. *Issues of Democracy: The Changing Face of U.S. Courts, 8,* 13–19.

Fox, J. A., & Zawitz, M. W. (2007). *Homicide trends in the United States.* Retrieved June 18, 2011, from http://www.ojp.usdoj.gov/bjs/

Franklin, J. H., & Moss, A. A. (2000). *From slavery to freedom: A history of African Americans* (8th ed.). New York: McGraw-Hill.

Frazier, E. F. (1939). Rebellious youth. In *The Negro family in the United States* (pp. 268–280). Chicago: University of Chicago Press.

Frazier, E. F. (1949). Crime and delinquency. In *The Negro in the United States* (pp. 638–653). New York: Macmillan.

Fredrickson, D. D., & Siljander, R. P. (2002). *Racial profiling.* Springfield, IL: Charles C Thomas.

Free, M. D. (2002). Racial bias and the American criminal justice system: Race and presentencing revisited. *Critical Criminology, 10,* 195–223.

Free, M. D., & Ruesink, M. (2012). *Race and justice: Wrongful convictions of African-American men.* Boulder, CO: Lynne Rienner.

Freiburger, T. L., & Hilinski, C. M. (2010). The impact of race, gender, and age on the pretrial decision. *Criminal Justice Review, 35,* 318–334.

Frey, C. P. (1981). The house of refuge for colored children. *Journal of Negro History, 66,* 10–25.

Friedman, L. M. (1993). *Crime and punishment in American history.* New York: Basic Books.

Frontline (2004). *Four stories: Erma Faye Stewart and Regina Kelly.* Retrieved July 25, 2011, from http://www.pbs.org/wgbh/pages/frontline/shows/plea/four/stewart.html

Fulwood v. Clemmer, 206 F. Supp. 370 (1962).

Furman v. Georgia, 408 U.S. 238 (1972).

Fyfe, J. J. (1981). Race and extreme police-citizen violence. In J. F. Fyfe (Ed.), *Readings on police use of deadly force* (pp. 173–194). Washington, DC: Police Foundation.

Fyfe, J. J. (Ed.). (1982). *Readings on police use of deadly force.* Washington, DC: Police Foundation.

Gabbidon, S. L. (1999). W. E. B. DuBois on crime: American conflict theorist. *The Criminologist, 24,* 1, 3, 20.

Gabbidon, S. L. (2001). W. E. B. Du Bois: Pioneering American criminologist. *Journal of Black Studies, 31,* 581–599.

Gabbidon, S. L. (2003). Racial profiling by store clerks and security personnel in retail establishments: An exploration of "shopping while Black." *Journal of*

Contemporary Criminal Justice, 19, 345–364.

Gabbidon, S. L. (2004). Crime prevention in the African American community: Lessons learned from the Nation of Islam. *Souls: A Critical Journal of Black Politics, Culture, and Society, 6*, 42–54.

Gabbidon, S. L. (2007). *W.E.B. Du Bois on crime and justice: Laying the foundations of sociological criminology*. Aldershot, UK: Ashgate.

Gabbidon, S. L. (2009). *Race, ethnicity, crime, & justice: An international dilemma*. Thousand Oaks, CA: SAGE.

Gabbidon, S. L. (2010). *Criminological perspectives on race and crime* (2nd ed.). New York: Routledge.

Gabbidon, S. L., Craig, R., Okafo, N., Marzette, L. N., & Peterson, S. A. (2008). The consumer racial profiling experiences of Black students at historically Black colleges and universities: An exploratory study. *Journal of Criminal Justice, 36*, 354–361.

Gabbidon, S. L., & Higgins, G. E. (2007). Consumer racial profiling and perceived victimization: A phone survey of Philadelphia area residents. *American Journal of Criminal Justice, 32*, 1–11.

Gabbidon, S. L., & Higgins, G. E. (2012). Public support for law enforcement agencies recording of arrest statistics by race: A research note. *Journal of Crime and Justice*. DOI: 10.1080/0735648X.2011.641819.

Gabbidon, S. L., Kowal, L., Jordan, K. L., Roberts, J. L., & Vincenzi, N. (2008). Race-based peremptory challenges: An empirical analysis of litigation from the U.S. Court of Appeals, 2002–2006. *American Journal of Criminal Justice, 33*, 59–68.

Gabbidon, S. L., & Taylor Greene, H. (2001). The presence of African-American scholarship in early American criminology texts (1918–1960). *Journal of Criminal Justice Education, 12*, 301–310.

Gabbidon, S. L., & Taylor Greene, H. (Eds.). (2005). *Race, crime, and justice: A reader*. New York: Routledge.

Gaes, G. G., Wallace, S., Gilman, E., Klein-Saffran, J., & Suppa, S. (2002). The influence of prison gang affiliation on violence and other prison misconduct. *The Prison Journal, 82*, 359–385.

Gallagher, C. A. (Ed.). (1997). *Rethinking the color line: Readings in race and ethnicity*. Mountain View, CA: Mayfield.

Gallegos-Castillo, A., & Patino, V. (2006). *Bridging community, research, and action: An emerging center on Latino youth development*. San Francisco, CA: National Center on Crime and Delinquency.

Galloway, A. L., & Drapella, L. A. (2006). Are effective drug courts an urban phenomenon? Considering their impact on recidivism among a nonmetropolitan adult sample in Washington State. *International Journal of Offender Therapy and Comparative Criminology, 50*, 280–293.

Gallup Organization. (2007). *Sixty-nine percent of Americans support death penalty: Majority say death penalty is applied fairly*. Retrieved February 14, 2008, from Gallup Brain database.

Gans, H. J. (2005). Race as class. *Contexts, 4*, 17–21.

Gardell, R. (2010). *Federal Advisory Committee on Juvenile Justice Annual Report, 2010*. Washington, DC: U.S. Department of Justice.

Garfinkel, H. (1949). Research note on inter- and intra-racial homicides. *Social Forces, 27*, 369–381.

Geis, G. (1972). Statistics concerning race and crime. In C. E. Reasons & J. L. Kuykendall (Eds.), *Race, crime, and justice* (pp. 61–78). Palisades, CA: Goodyear.

Georges-Abeyie, D. (1989). Race, ethnicity, and the spatial dynamic. *Social Justice, 16*, 35–54.

Gerber, J., & Engelhardt-Greer, S. (1996). Just and painful: Attitudes toward sentencing criminals. In T. J. Flanagan & D. R. Longmire (Eds.), *Americans view crime and justice: A national public opinion survey* (pp. 62–74). Thousand Oaks, CA: Sage.

Gerstenfeld, P. B. (2010). Hate crimes. In Christopher J. Ferguson (Ed.), *Violent crime* (pp. 257–275). Thousand Oaks, CA: Sage.

Gerstenfeld, P. B. (2011). *Hate crimes*. Thousand Oaks, CA: Sage.

Gideon v. Wainwright, 372 U.S. 335 (1963).

Glaze, L. E. (2010). *Correction populations in the United States, 2009*. Washington, DC: Bureau of Justice Statistics. NCJ 231681.

Glaze, L. E., & Bonczar, T. P. (2007). *Probation and parole in the United States, 2006*. Washington, DC: Bureau of Justice Statistics.

Glaze, L. E., & Bonczar, T. P. (2010). *Probation and parole in the United States, 2009*. (NCJ 231674) Washington, D.C.: U.S. Department of Justice, Bureau of Justice Statistics.

Glover, K. (2009). *Racial profiling: Research, racism, and resistance*. Lanham, MD: Rowman & Littlefield.

Goldkamp, J. S. (1982). Minorities as victims of police shootings: Interpretations of racial disproportionality and police use of deadly force. In J. Fyfe (Ed.), *Readings on police use of deadly force* (pp. 128–151). Washington, DC: Police Foundation.

Goldkamp, J. S., & Weiland, D. (1993). *Assessing the impact of Dade County's felony drug court*. Washington, DC: U.S. Department of Justice.

Goldman, S. (1989, April/May). Reagan's judicial legacy: Completing the puzzle and summing up. *Judicature, 72*, 320–321, Table 1.

Goldman, S. (2003, May/June). W. Bush remaking the judiciary:

Like father like son? *Judicature, 86,* 304.

Goldstein, H. (1979). Improving policing: A problem oriented approach. *Crime and Delinquency, 25,* 236–258.

Golub, A., Johnson, B. D., & Dunlap, E. (2007). The race/ethnicity disparity in misdemeanor marijuana arrests in New York City. *Criminology & Public Policy, 6,* 131–164.

Gonzales-Day, K. (2006). *Lynching in the west: 1850–1935.* Durham, NC: Duke University Press.

Goodwin, R. (2008). *Crossing the continent, 1527–1540: The story of the first African American explorer of the American South.* New York: HarperCollins.

Gossett, T. (1963). *Race: The history of an idea in America.* Dallas: Southern Methodist University Press.

Gottfredson, D., Najaka, S., & Kearley, B. (2003). Effectiveness of drug treatment courts: Evidence from a randomized trial. *Criminology & Public Policy, 2,* 171–198.

Gould, J., & Leo, R. (2010). One hundred years later: Wrongful convictions after a century of research. *Journal of Criminal Law and Criminology, 100,* 825–868.

Gould, L. A. (2000). White male privilege and the construction of crime. In The Criminal Justice Collective of Northern Arizona University (Eds.), *Investigating difference: Human and cultural relations in criminal justice* (pp. 27–43). Boston: Allyn & Bacon.

Gould, S. J. (1996). *The mismeasure of man.* New York: Norton.

Graham, O. L., Jr. (2004). *Unguarded gates: A history of America's immigration crisis.* Lanham, MD: Rowman & Littlefield.

Graham v. Connor, 490 U. S. 386 (1989).

Graham v. Florida, 08-7412 (2010).

Green, B. L., Furrer, C., Worcel, S., Burrus, S., & Finighan, M. W. (2007). How effective are family treatment drug courts? Outcomes from a four-site national study. *Child Maltreatment, 12,* 43–59.

Greenberg, D. (1976). *Crime and law enforcement in the colony of New York, 1691–1776.* Ithaca, NY: Cornell University Press.

Greene, J. R., Piquero, A. R., Collins, P., & Kane, R. (1999). Doing research in public housing: Implementation issues from Philadelphia's 11th Street Corridor Community Policing Program. *Justice Research and Policy, 1,* 67–95.

Greenfield, L. A., & Smith, S. K. (1999). *American Indians and crime.* Washington, DC: U.S. Department of Justice, Office of Justice Programs.

Greenleaf, R. G., Skogan, W. G., & Lurigio, A. J. (2008). Traffic stops in the Pacific Northeast: Competing hypotheses about racial disparity. *Journal of Ethnicity in Criminal Justice, 6,* 3–22.

Greenwald, F. (1993). Treatment of behavioral problems of children and youth by early indigenous Americans. In A. G. Hess & P. F. Clement (Eds.), *History of juvenile delinquency: A collection of essays on crime committed by young offenders, in history and in selected countries* (pp. 735–756). Aalen, Germany: Scientia Verlag.

Gregg v. Georgia, 428 U.S. 153 (1976).

Griffin, M. L., & Hepburn, J. R. (2006). The effect of gang affiliation on violent misconduct among inmates during the early years of confinement. *Criminal Justice and Behavior, 33,* 419–448.

Grimke, A. H. (1915). *The ultimate criminal.* Washington, DC: American Negro Academy.

Grimshaw, A. D. (Ed.). (1969). *Racial violence in the United States.* Chicago: Aldine.

Growette Bostaph, L. M. (2008). Repeat citizens in motor vehicle stops: A Black experience. *Journal of Ethnicity in Criminal Justice, 6,* 41–64.

Guerrero, A. P., Nishimura, S. T., Chang, J. Y., Ona, C., Cunanan, V. L., & Hishinuma, E. S. (2010). Low cultural identification, low parental involvement and adverse peer influences as risk factors for delinquent behaviour among Filipino youth in Hawaii. *International Journal of Social Psychiatry, 56,* 371–387.

Guevara, L., Herz, D., & Spohn, C. (2006). Gender and decision making: What role does race play? *Feminist Criminology, 1,* 258–282.

Hagan, F. E. (2002). *Introduction to criminology: Theories, methods, and criminal behavior.* Belmont, CA: Wadsworth.

Hagan, J. (2010). *Who are the criminals? The politics of crime policy from the age of Roosevelt to the age of Reagan.* Princeton, NJ: Princeton University Press.

Hakins, S. (2004). *Too young to die.* Retrieved December 15, 2004, from http://www.fortunesociet.org/fa110205.htm

Hallett, M. A. (2006). *Private prisons in America: A critical race perspective.* Urbana: University of Illinois Press.

Hanson, R. A., & Ostrom, B. J. (1998). Indigent defenders get the job done and done well. In George F. Cole & Marc G. Gertz (Eds.), *The criminal justice system: Politics and policies* (7th ed). Belmont, CA: Wadsworth.

Harer, M. D., & Steffensmeier, D. J. (1996). Race and prison violence. *Criminology, 34,* 323–355.

Harjo, S. S. (2002). Redskins, savages, and other Indian enemies: A historical overview of American media coverage of Native peoples. In C. R. Mann & M. S. Zatz (Eds.), *Images of color, images of crime* (2nd ed., pp. 56–70). Los Angeles: Roxbury.

Harlow, C. W. (2005). *Hate crime reported by victims and police.* Washington, DC: U.S. Department of Justice, Office of Justice Programs.

Harmon, T. R. (2001). Guilty until proven innocent: An analysis of post-*Furman* capital errors. *Criminal Justice Policy Review, 12,* 113–139.

Harmon, T. R. (2004). Race for your life: An analysis of the role of race in erroneous capital convictions. *Criminal Justice Review, 29,* 76–96.

Harrell, A. (2003). Judging drug courts: Balancing the evidence. *Criminology & Public Policy, 2,* 207–212.

Harrell, E. (2007). *Black victims of violent crime.* Washington, DC: U.S. Department of Justice, Office of Justice Programs.

Harrell, E. (2009). *Asian, Native Hawaiian, and Pacific Islander victims of crime.* Washington, DC: U.S. Department of Justice, Office of Justice Programs.

Harrell, E., & Rand, M. R. (2010). *Crime against people with disabilities, 2008.* Washington, DC: U.S. Department of Justice, Office of Justice Programs.

Harris, D. A. (2002). *Profiles in injustice.* New York: New Press.

Harris Poll. (2004). Retrieved March 2, 2003, from Polling the Nations database at http://www.orspub.com/

Hart, T. C., & Rennison, C. (2003). *Reporting crime to the police, 1992–2000.* Washington, DC: U.S. Department of Justice, Office of Justice Programs.

Hartley, R. D., Ventura Miller, H., & Spohn, C. (2010). Do you get what you pay for? Type of counsel and its effect on criminal court outcome. *Journal of Criminal Justice, 38,* 1063–1070.

Hassett-Walker, C. R. (2009). *Black middle-class delinquents.* El Paso, TX: LFB Scholarly.

Hassett-Walker, C. R. (2010). Delinquency and the Black middle-class: An exploratory study. *Journal of Ethnicity in Criminal Justice, 8,* 266–289.

Hawkins, D. F. (1983). Black and White homicide differentials: Alternatives to an inadequate theory. *Criminal Justice and Behavior, 10,* 407–440.

Hawkins, D. F. (1986). Race, crime type, and imprisonment. *Justice Quarterly, 3,* 251–269.

Hawkins, D. F. (1987). Beyond anomalies: Rethinking the conflict perspective on race and capital punishment. *Social Forces, 65,* 719–745.

Hawkins, D. F. (2011). Things fall apart: Revisiting race and ethnic differences in criminal violence amidst a crime drop. *Race and Justice: An International Journal, 1,* 3–48.

Hawkins, D. F., & Hardy, K. A. (1989). Black-White imprisonment rates: A state-by-state analysis. *Social Justice, 16,* 75–94.

Hawkins, D. F., & Kempf-Leonard, K. (2005). *Our children, their children: Confronting racial and ethnic differences in American juvenile justice.* Chicago: The University of Chicago Press.

Hay, C., & Evans, M. M. (2006). Has *Roe v. Wade* reduced U.S. crime rates? Examining the link between mothers' pregnancy intentions and children's later involvement in law-violating behavior. *Journal of Research in Crime and Delinquency, 43,* 36–66.

Hayner, N. (1933). Delinquency areas in the Puget Sound region. *American Journal of Sociology, 39,* 314–328.

Hayner, N. (1938). Social factors in oriental crime. *American Journal of Sociology, 43,* 908–919.

Hayner, N. (1942). Variability in the criminal behavior of American Indians. *American Journal of Sociology, 47,* 602–613.

Healey, J. F. (2003). *Race, ethnicity, gender, and class: The sociology of group conflict and change* (3rd ed.). Thousand Oaks, CA: Pine Forge Press.

Healey, J. F. (2004). *Diversity and society: Race, ethnicity, and gender.* Thousand Oaks, CA: Pine Forge Press.

Healey, J. F. (2007). *Diversity and society: Race, ethnicity, and gender* (2nd ed.). Thousand Oaks, CA: Pine Forge Press.

Henderson, C. R. (1901). *Introduction to the study of dependents, defective, and delinquent classes.* Boston: D.C. Heath.

Hernandez v. New York, U.S. 352 (1991).

Herrnstein, R. J., & Murray, C. (1994). *The bell curve: Intelligence and class structure in American life.* New York: The Free Press.

Herz, D. C., & Walsh, J. E. (2004). Faith-based programs for reentry courts: A summary of issues and recommendations. *Juvenile and Family Court Journal, 55,* 15–25.

Hester, T., & Feeney, T. (2007). Assembly votes to abolish the death penalty. *Star-Ledger.* Retrieved July 29, 2008, from www.nj.com/news/index.ssf/2007/12/assembly_begins_debate_on_deat.html

Hickey, T. (1998). *Criminal procedure.* New York: McGraw-Hill.

Hickman, L. J., & Suttorp, M. J. (2008). Are deportable aliens a unique threat to public safety? Comparing the recidivism of deportable and nondeportable aliens. *Criminology & Public Policy, 7,* 59–82.

Hickman, M. J. (2003). *Tribal law enforcement, 2000.* Washington, DC: U.S. Department of Justice.

Hickman, M. J. (2006). *Citizen complaints about police use of force.* Washington, DC: U.S. Department of Justice.

Hickman, M. J., & Reaves, B. A. (2003). *Sheriffs' offices 2000.* Washington, DC: U.S. Department of Justice.

Higginbotham, A. L. (1978). *In the matter of color: Race and the American legal process: The colonial period.* Oxford, UK: Oxford University Press.

Higginbotham, A. L. (1996). *Shades of freedom: Racial politics and the presumptions of the American legal process.* Oxford, UK: Oxford University Press.

Higginbotham, A.L., & Jacobs, A. F. (1992). The law as an enemy: The legitimization of racial powerlessness through the Colonial and Antebellum criminal laws of Virginia. *North Carolina Law Review, 70,* 969–1070.

Higgins, G. E., & Gabbidon, S. L. (2008). Perceptions of consumer racial profiling and negative emotions: An exploratory study. *Criminal Justice and Behavior, 36,* 77–88.

Higgins, G. E., Gabbidon, S. L., & Jordan, K. (2008). Examining the generality of citizens' views on racial profiling in diverse situational contexts. *Criminal Justice and Behavior, 35,* 1527–1541.

Higgins, G. E., Gabbidon, S. L., & Martin, F. (2010) The influence of race/ethnicity and race relations on public opinion related to the immigration and crime link. *Journal of Criminal Justice 38,* 51–56.

Higgins, G., Gabbidon, S. L., & Vito, G. (2010). Exploring the influence of race relations and public safety concerns on public support for racial profiling during traffic stops. *International Journal of Police Science and Management, 12*(1), 12–22.

Hinton, W. J., Sims, P. L., Adams, M. A., & West, C. (2007). Juvenile justice: A system divided. *Criminal Justice Policy Review, 18,* 466–483.

Hirsch, J. S. (2002). *Riot and remembrance: The Tulsa race riot and its legacy.* Boston: Houghton Mifflin.

Hirschi, T., & Hindelang, M. (1977). Intelligence and delinquency: A revisionist review. *American Sociological Review, 42,* 571–587.

Hockenberry, S. (2010). *Person offense cases in juvenile court, 2007.* Washington, DC: Department of Justice.

Hockenberry, S., Sickmund, M., & Sladky, A. (2011). *Juvenile residential facility census, 2008: Selected findings.* Retrieved July 31, 2011, from https://
www.ncjrs.gov/pdffiles1/ojjdp/231683.pdf

Hoffman, F. L. (1896). *Race traits and tendencies of the American Negro.* New York: Macmillan.

Hoffman, M. B., Rubin, P. H., & Shepherd, J. (2005). An empirical study of public defender effectiveness: Self-selection by the "marginally indigent." *Ohio State Journal of Criminal Law, 3,* 223–255.

Hogan, L. J. (1998). *The Osage Indian murders.* Frederick, MD: Amlex.

Holden-Smith, B. (1996). Inherently unequal justice: Interracial rape and the death penalty. *Journal of Criminal Law & Criminology, 86,* 1571–1583.

Holub, H. (2011). National Latino Peace Officers Association calls on secure communities task force. Retrieved July 18, 2011, from http://tucsoncitizen.com/view-from-baja-arizona/2011/07/12/national-latino-peace-officers-association-calls-on-secure-communities-task-force/

Hooton, E. A. (1939a). *Crime and the man.* Cambridge, MA: Harvard University Press.

Hooton, E. A. (1939b). *The American criminal: An anthropological study. Volume 1. The native white criminal of native parentage.* Cambridge, MA: Harvard University Press.

Howell, J. C. (2003). *Preventing and reducing juvenile delinquency: A comprehensive framework.* Thousand Oaks, CA: Sage.

Hsia, H. M., Bridges, G. S., & McHale, R. (2004). *Disproportionate minority confinement: Year 2002 update.* Washington, DC: U.S. Department of Justice, Office of Juvenile Justice and Delinquency Prevention.

Hsu, S. (2010). Senate Democrats' plan highlights nation's shift to the right on immigration. *The Washington Post.* Retrieved July 9, 2011, from http://www.washingtonpost.com/wp-dyn/content/article/2010/05/01/AR2010050100990.html

Hubbard, D. J., & Pratt, T. C. (2002). Meta-analysis of the predictors of delinquency among girls. *Journal of Offender Rehabilitation, 34,* 1–13.

Hudson v. McMillian, 503 U.S. 1 (1992).

Huebner, B. M. (2003). Administrative determinates of inmate violence. *Journal of Criminal Justice, 31,* 107–117.

Huff, C. R. (2002). Wrongful convictions and public policy: The American society of criminology 2001 presidential address. *Criminology, 40,* 1–18.

Huff, C. R. (2004). Wrongful convictions: The American experience. *Canadian Journal of Criminology and Criminal Justice, 46,* 107–120.

Huff, C. R., Rattner, A., & Sagarin, E. (1996). *Convicted but innocent: Wrongful conviction and public policy.* Thousand Oaks, CA: Sage.

Hughes, T. A., James Wilson, D., & Beck, A. J. (2001). *Trends in state parole, 1990–2000.* Washington, DC: Bureau of Justice Statistics.

Huling, T. (2002). Building a prison economy in rural America. In M. Mauer & M. Chesney-Lind (Eds.), *Invisible punishment: The collateral consequences of mass imprisonment* (pp. 197–213). New York: New Press.

Humes, K. R., Jones, N. A., & Ramirez, R. R. (2011). *Overview of race and Hispanic origin: 2010.* Washington, DC: U.S. Census Bureau.

Huntington, S. P. (2004). *Who are we? The challenges to America's national identity.* New York: Simon and Schuster.

Hurwitz, J., & Peffley, M. (2010). And justice for some: Race, crime, and punishment in the U.S. criminal justice system. *Canadian Journal of Political Science, 43,* 457–479.

Ignatiev, N. (1996). *How the Irish became White.* New York: Routledge.

Illinois suspends death penalty: Governor calls for review of "flawed" system. (2000). Retrieved March 5, 2003, from http://www.CNN.com

In re Gault, 387 U.S. 387 (1967).

In re Winship, 397 U.S. 358 (1970).

Institute of Texan Cultures. (1998). *The El Paso Chinese colony.* Retrieved December 16, 2004, from http://www.texancultures.utsa.edu/txtext/chinese/chineseelpaso.htm

Institute on Race and Poverty. (2003). *Minnesota statewide racial profiling report: All participating jurisdictions.* Minneapolis, MN: Institute on Race and Poverty.

International Association of Chiefs of Police. (2003). *Police use of force in America 2001.* Retrieved December 16, 2004, from http://www.theiacp.org

Ioimo, R., Tears, R. S., Meadows, L. A., Becton, J. B., & Charles, M. T. (2007). The police view of biased-based policing. *Police Quarterly, 10,* 270–287.

Iorizzo, L. J., & Mondello, S. (2006). *The Italian Americans* (3rd ed.). Youngstown, NY: Cambria Press.

Jackson, G. (1970). *Soledad brother: The prison letters of George Jackson.* Chicago: Lawrence Hill Books.

Jackson, J., Sr., & Jackson, J., Jr. (1996). *Legal lynching: Racism, injustice, and the death penalty.* New York: Marlowe.

Jackson, P. I. (1989). *Minority group threat, crime, and policing.* New York: Praeger.

Jamal, A., & Naber, N. (Eds.). (2008). *Race and Arab Americans before and after 9/11: From invisible citizens to visible subjects.* Syracuse, NY: Syracuse University Press.

Jang, S. J., & Johnson, B. R. (2003). Strain, negative emotions, and deviant coping among African Americans: A test of general strain theory. *Journal of Quantitative Criminology, 19,* 79–105.

Jang, S. J., & Johnson, B. R. (2005). Gender, religiosity, and reactions to strain among African Americans. *The Sociological Quarterly, 46,* 323–357.

Jang, S. J., & Lyons, J. A. (2006). Strain, social support, and retreatism among African Americans. *Journal of Black Studies, 37,* 251–274.

Jenkins, P. (1994). The ice age: The social construction of a drug panic. *Justice Quarterly, 11,* 7–31.

Johnson v. California, 543 U.S. 499 (2005).

Johnson, B. D. (2003). Racial and ethnic disparities in sentencing departures across modes of conviction. *Criminology, 41,* 449–489.

Johnson, B. D., & Betsinger, S. (2009). Punishing the "model minority": Asian American sentencing outcomes in federal district courts. *Criminology, 47,* 1043–1090.

Johnson, D. R. (1981). *American law enforcement: A history.* St. Louis, MO: Forum Press.

Johnson, G. B. (1941). The Negro and crime. *Annals of the American Academy of Political and Social Sciences, 217,* 93–104.

Johnson, S. L. (1996). *Subcultural backlash: A new variable in the explanation of the overrepresentation of African-Americans in the criminal justice system.* Unpublished doctoral dissertation, The Pennsylvania State University.

Johnson Listwan, S., Sundt, J., Holsinger, A., & Latessa, E. (2003). The effect of drug court programming on recidivism: The Cincinnati experience. *Crime and Delinquency, 49,* 389–411.

Johnston, L. D., O'Malley, P. M., Bachman, J. G., & Schulenberg, J. E. (2007). *Monitoring the future national survey results on drug use, 1975–2006. Volume I: Secondary school students* (NIH Publication No. 07-6205). Bethesda, MD: National Institute on Drug Abuse.

Johnston, L. D., O'Malley, P. M., Bachman, J. G., Schulenberg, J. E. (2011a). *Monitoring the future national results on adolescent drug use: Overview of key findings, 2010.* Ann Arbor: Institute for Social Research, The University of Michigan. Retrieved July 4, 2011, from http://monitoringthefuture.org/pubs/monographs/mtf-overview2010.pdf

Johnston, L. D., O'Malley, P. M., Bachman, J. G., & Schulenberg, J. E. (2011b). *Monitoring the future national survey results on drug use, 1975–2010: Volume I, Secondary school students.* Ann Arbor: Institute for Social Research, The University of Michigan. Retrieved on August 2, 2011, from http://monitoringthefuture.org/pubs/monographs/mtf-vol1_2010.pdf

Jones v. Willingham, 248 F. Supp. 791 (1965).

Jones, N. (2010). *Between good and ghetto.* New Brunswick, NJ: Rutgers University Press.

Jones, T. (1977). The police in America: A Black viewpoint. *The Black Scholar,* pp. 22–39.

Jones-Brown, D. (2007). Forever the symbolic assailant: The more things change, the more they stay the same. *Criminology & Public Policy, 6,* 103–122.

Jordan, K., Gabbidon, S. L., & Higgins, G. E. (2009). Exploring the perceived extent of and citizens' support for consumer racial profiling: Results from a national poll. *Journal of Criminal Justice, 37,* 353–359.

Jordan, K., & Myers, D. (2007). The decertification of transferred youth: Examining the determinants of reverse waiver. *Youth Violence & Juvenile Justice: An Interdisciplinary Journal, 5,* 188–206.

Joyce, T. (2004a). Did legalized abortion lower crime? *Journal of Human Resources, 39,* 1–38.

Joyce, T. (2004b). *Further tests of abortion and crime*. National Bureau of Economic Research Working Paper, no. 10564.

Kahane, L. H., Paton, D., & Simmons, R. (2008). The abortion-crime link: Evidence from England and Wales. *Economica, 75,* 1–21.

Kalunta-Crumpton, A. (Ed.). (2010). *Race, crime and criminal justice: International perspectives*. New York: Palgrave-Macmillan.

Kanellos, N. (1977). *The Hispanic-American almanac*. Detroit, MI: Gale Research.

Katz, W. L. (1986). *The invisible empire: The Ku Klux Klan impact on history*. Seattle, WA: Open Hand.

Kaufman, J. M., Rebellon, C. J., Thaxton, S., & Agnew, R. (2008). A general strain theory of racial differences in criminal offending. *The Australian and New Zealand Journal of Criminology, 41,* 421–437.

Kavanaugh-Earl, J., Cochran, J. K., Smith, D. M., Fogel, S. J., & Bjerregaard, B. (2008). Racial bias and the death penalty. In M. J. Lynch, E. B. Patterson, & K. K. Childs (Eds.), *Racial divide* (pp. 147–196). Monsey, NY: Criminal Justice Press.

Kayyali, R. A. (2006). *The Arab Americans*. Westport, CT: Greenwood Press.

Kazemian, L., Pease, K., & Farrington, D. P. (2011). DNA retention policies: The potential contribution of criminal career research. *European Journal of Criminology, 8,* 48–64.

Keith, M. (1996). Criminalization and racialization. In J. Muncie, E. McLaughlin, & M. Langan (Eds.), *Criminological perspectives: A reader* (pp. 271–283). London: Sage.

Kelling, L., & Moore, M. H. (1988). *The evolving strategy of policing*. Washington, DC: National Institute of Justice.

Kempf-Leonard, K. (2007). Minority youths and juvenile justice: Disproportionate minority contact after nearly 20 years of reform efforts. *Youth Violence and Juvenile Justice, 5,* 71–87.

Kennedy, R. (1997). *Race, crime, and the law*. New York: Pantheon Books.

Kent v. United States, 383 U.S. 541 (1966).

Kim, H. (2001). The Filipino Americans. *Journal of American Ethnic History, 20,* 135–137.

Kim, H. C. (1999). *Koreans in the hood: Conflict with African Americans*. Baltimore, MD: Johns Hopkins University Press.

Kimbrough v. United States, 128 S. Ct. 558 (2007).

Kindermann, C., Lynch, J., & Cantor, D. (1997). *Effects of the redesign on victimization estimates*. Washington, DC: U.S. Department of Justice, Office of Justice Programs.

King, R. D. (2007). The context of minority group threat: Race, institutions, and complying with hate crime law. *Law & Society Review, 41,* 189–224.

King, W. R., Holmes, S. T., Henderson, M. L., & Latessa, E. J. (2001). Community corrections partnership: Examining the long-term effects of youth participation in an Afrocentric diversion program. *Crime & Delinquency, 47,* 558–572.

Klaus, P., & Maston, C. (2000). *Criminal victimization in the United States, 1995*. Washington, DC: U.S. Department of Justice.

Klinger, D. A., & Brunson, R. K. (2009). Police officers' perceptual distortions during lethal force situations: Informing the reasonableness standard. *Criminology & Public Policy, 8*(1), 153–162.

Klinger, D. A., & Grossman, D. (2002). Who should deal with foreign terrorists on U.S. soil? Socio-legal consequences of September 11 and ongoing threat of terrorist attacks in America. *Harvard Journal of Law and Public Policy, 25,* 815–835.

Klofas, J. M., Hipple, N. K., & McGarrell, E. F. (2010) *The new criminal justice*. New York: Routledge Taylor & Francis.

Knepper, P. (2001). *Explaining criminal conduct: Theories and systems in criminology*. Durham, NC: Carolina Academic Press.

Knepper, P. E. (1996). Race, racism, and crime statistics. *Southern University Law Review, 24,* 71–112.

Knepper, P. E., & Potter, D. M. (1998). Crime, politics, and minority populations: Use of official statistics in the United States and Japan. *International Journal of Comparative and Applied Criminal Justice, 22,* 145–155.

Krauss, E., & Schulman, M. (1997). The myth of Black jury nullification: Racism dressed up in jurisprudential clothing. *Cornell Journal of Law and Public Policy, 7,* 57–76.

Krisberg, B. (1975). *Crime and privilege: Toward a new criminology*. Englewood Cliffs, NJ: Prentice Hall.

Krivo, L. J., & Peterson, R. D. (1996). Extremely disadvantaged neighborhoods and urban crime. *Social Forces, 75,* 619–650.

Krivo, L. J., & Peterson, R. D. (2000). The structural context of homicide: Accounting for racial differences in process. *American Sociological Review, 65,* 547–559.

Kroeger, B. (2004, March 20). *When a dissertation makes a difference*. Retrieved March 22, 2004, from http://www.nytimes.com/

Kubiak, S. P., & Allen, T. (2011). Public opinion regarding life without parole in consecutive statewide surveys. *Crime & Delinquency, 57,* 495–515.

Kubrin, C. E. (2005). Gangstas, thugs, and hustlas: Identity and the code of the streets in rap music. *Social Problems, 52,* 360–378.

Kusow, A., Wilson, L. C., & Martin, D. E. (1997). Determinants of citizen satisfaction with the police: The effects of residential location. *Policing, 20,* 655–664.

Kuykendall, M. A., & Burns, D. E. (1980). The Black police officer: An historical perspective. *Journal of Contemporary Criminal Justice, 1,* 4–12.

LaFree, G. (1995). Race and crime trends in the United States, 1946–1990. In D. F. Hawkins (Ed.), *Ethnicity, race, and crime* (pp. 169–193). Albany: State University of New York Press.

LaFree, G., & Russell, K. (1993). The argument for studying race and crime. *Journal of Criminal Justice Education, 4,* 273–289.

La Mala, M. (2011). *Illinois is on a roll: Drops secure communities.* Retrieved July 26, 2011, from http://vivirlatino.com/2011/05/05/illinois-is-on-a-roll-drops-secure-communities.php

Lambert, E., & Clarke, A. (2001). The impact of information on an individual's support of the death penalty: A partial test of the Marshall hypothesis among college students. *Criminal Justice Policy Review, 12,* 215–234.

Lambert, E. G., Camp, S. D., Clarke, A., & Jiang, S. (2011). The impact of information on death penalty support, revisited. *Crime & Delinquency, 57,* 572–599.

Lane, R. (1967). *Policing the city: Boston, 1822–1885.* Cambridge, MA: Harvard University Press.

Langbein, J. H. (1976). The historical origins of the sanction of imprisonment for serious crimes. *Journal of Legal Studies, 5,* 35–60.

Langton, L. (2010). *Women in law enforcement, 1987-2008.* Retrieved on July 13, 2011, from http://bjs.ojp.usdoj.gov/content/pub/pdf/wle8708.pdf

Langton, L., & Farole, D. J. (2009). *Public defender offices, 2007: Statistical tables.* Washington, DC: Bureau of Justice Statistics. (NCJ 228538)

Langton, L., & Farole, D. (2010). *State public defender programs, 2007.* Washington, DC: Bureau of Justice Statistics. (NCJ228229)

Langton, L., & Planty, M. (2011). *Hate crime, 2003-2009.* Washington, DC: Bureau of Justice Statistics.

Lanier, C., & Huff-Corzine, L. (2006). American Indian homicide: A county level analysis utilizing social disorganization theory. *Homicide Studies, 10,* 181–194.

Lanier, M. M., & Henry, S. (1998). *Essential criminology.* Boulder, CO: Westview.

Lattimore, P. K. (2007). The challenge of reentry. *Corrections Today, 69,* 88–91.

Lau, A. S., McCabe, K. M., Yeh, M., Garland, A. F., Hough, R. L., & Landsverk, J. (2003). Race/ethnicity and rates of self-reported maltreatment among high-risk youth in public sectors of care. *Child Maltreatment, 8,* 183–194.

Lee, C. (2007). Hispanics and the death penalty: Discriminatory charging practices in San Joaquin County, California. *Journal of Criminal Justice, 35,* 17–27.

Lee, J., & Ruiz, J. M. (2011). Investigating discriminative bail setting: Multivariate analysis of Louisiana drug interdiction. *Journal of Ethnicity in Criminal Justice, 9,* 22–40.

Lee, M. T., & Martinez, R. (2002). Social disorganization revisited: Mapping the recent immigration and black homicide relationship in northern Miami. *Sociological Focus, 35,* 363–380.

Lee, N. (1995). Culture conflict and crime in Alaskan native villages. *Journal of Criminal Justice, 23,* 177–189.

LeFlouria, T. (2011). The hand that rocks the cradle cuts cordwood: Exploring Black women's lives and labor in Georgia's convict camps, 1865–1917. *Labor: Studies in Working Class History of the Americas, 8,* 47–63.

Legal battle looms over Arizona immigration law. (2010, July 28). CNN.com. Retrieved from http://www.cnn.com/US/

Lehrer, E. (2007). Crime's up: An old issue is about to resurface. *The Weekly Standard, 12,* 23–26.

Leiber, M. J. (2002). Disproportionate minority confinement (DMC) of youth: An analysis of state and federal efforts to address the issue. *Crime & Delinquency, 48,* 3–45.

Leiber, M. J., & Blowers, A. N. (2003). Race and misdemeanor sentencing. *Criminal Justice Policy Review, 14,* 464–485.

Leiber, M. J., & Mack, K. Y. (2003). The individual and joint effects of race, gender, and family status on juvenile justice decision-making. *Journal of Research in Crime and Delinquency, 40,* 34–70.

Leiber, M., & Rodriguez, N. (2011). The implementation of the disproportionate minority confinement/contact (DMC) mandate: A failure or success? *Race and Justice, 1,* 103–124.

Leo, R. A. (2002). False confessions: Causes, consequences, and solutions. In S. Westervelt & J. A. Humphrey (Eds.), *Wrongly convicted: Perspectives on failed justice* (pp. 36–54). New Brunswick, NJ: Rutgers University Press.

Leo, R. A. (2005). Rethinking the study of miscarriages of justice: Developing a criminology of wrongful conviction. *Journal of Contemporary Criminal Justice, 21,* 201–223.

Leonard, K. K., Pope, C., & Feyerherm, W. H. (1995). *Minorities in juvenile justice.* Thousand Oaks, CA: Sage.

Levitt, S. D., & Dubner, S. J. (2005). *Freakonomics: A rogue economist explores the hidden side of everything.* New York: William Morrow.

Light, I. (1977). The ethnic vice industry, 1880–1944. *American Sociological Review, 42,* 464–479.

Lilly, R. J., Cullen, F. T., & Ball, R. A. (2001). *Criminological theory:*

Context and consequences. Thousand Oaks, CA: Sage.

Lilly, R. J., Cullen, F. T., & Ball, R. A. (2011). *Criminological theory: Context and consequences* (5th ed.). Thousand Oaks, CA: Sage.

Lipsey, M. W., Howell, J. C., Kelly, M. R., Chapman, G., & Carver, D. (2010). *Improving the effectiveness of juvenile justice programs. A new perspective on evidence-based practice.* Washington, DC: Georgetown Public Policy Institute, Center for Juvenile Justice Reform.

Lombroso, C. (1911). *Criminal man.* New York: Putnam. (Original work published 1876)

Longazel, J. G., Parker, L. S., & Sun, I. Y. (2011). Experiencing court, experiencing race: Perceived procedural injustice among court users. *Race and Justice, 1,* 202–227.

Longmire, D. R. (1996). Americans' attitudes about the ultimate weapon: Capital punishment. In T. J. Flanagan & D. R. Longmire (Eds.), *Americans view crime and justice: A national public opinion survey* (pp. 93–108). Thousand Oaks, CA: Sage.

Lopez, R., Roosa, M. W., Tein, J. T., & Dinh, K. T. (2004). Accounting for Anglo-Hispanic differences in school misbehavior. *Journal of Ethnicity in Criminal Justice, 2,* 27–46.

Lotke, E. (1996). *The prison-industrial complex.* Baltimore, MD: National Center on Institutions and Alternatives.

Lotke, E. (1998). Hobbling a generation: Young African American men in Washington, D.C.'s, criminal justice system: Five years later. *Crime and Delinquency, 44,* 355–366.

Lott, J. R., & Whitley, J. (2007). Abortion and crime: Unwanted children and out-of-wedlock births. *Economic Inquiry, 45,* 304–324.

Loury, G. C. (Ed.). (2008). *Race, incarceration, and American values.* Cambridge, MA: MIT Press.

Luna-Firebaugh, E. M. (2003, July 28–30). *Tribal law enforcement in P.L. 280 states.* Paper presented at the annual conference on Criminal Justice Research and Evaluation, Washington, DC.

Lynn, R. (2002). Skin color and intelligence in African Americans. *Population and Environment, 23,* 365–375.

MacDonald, H. (1998). Is the criminal justice system racist? *City Journal, 18.* Retrieved from http://www.city-journal.org/2008/18_2_criminal_justice_system.html.

MacDonald, H. (2003). *Are cops racist? How the war against the police harms Black Americans.* Chicago: Ivan R. Dee.

MacDonald, H. (2004). The immigrant gang plague. *City Journal,* Summer, 30–43.

MacDonald, H. (2008). Is the criminal-justice system racist? *City Journal.* Retrieved May 6, 2008, from www.city-journal.org/

Maguire, K. (Ed.). (2011a). *Sourcebook of criminal justice statistics.* Table 2.12.2011. Washington, DC: Author.

Maguire, K. (Ed.). (2011b). *Sourcebook of criminal justice statistics.* (Table 1.82.2010). Washington, DC: Author.

Maguire, K. (Ed.). (2011c). *Sourcebook of criminal justice statistics.* (Table 1.81.2010). Washington, DC: Author.

Maguire, K., & Pastore, A. L. (Eds.). (2003). *Sourcebook of criminal justice statistics.* Retrieved from http://www.albany.edu/sourcebook/pdf/t213.pdf

Maltz, M. (1977). Crime statistics: A historical perspective. *Crime & Delinquency, 23,* 32–40.

Mandak, J. (2003, June 12). *The Patriot-News* (AP), p. B7.

Mann, C. R. (1990a). Black female homicide in the United States. *Journal of Interpersonal Violence, 5,* 176–201.

Mann, C. R. (1990b). Random thoughts on the ongoing Wilbanks-Mann discourse. In B. D. Maclean &

D. Milovanovic (Eds.), *Racism, empiricism, and criminal justice* (pp. 15–19). Vancouver, Canada: Collective Press.

Mann, C. R. (1993). *Unequal justice: A question of color.* Bloomington: Indiana University Press.

Manza, J., & Uggen, C. (2006). *Locked out: Felon disenfranchisement and democracy in America.* New York: Oxford University Press.

Manza, J., Brooks, C., & Uggen, C. (2004). Civil death or civil rights? Public attitudes towards felon disenfranchisement in the United States. *Public Opinion Quarterly, 68,* 276–287.

Mapp v. Ohio, 367 U.S. 1081, 81 S.CT (1961).

Marger, M. (Ed.). (1997). *Race and ethnic relations: American and global perspectives* (4th ed.). Belmont, CA: Wadsworth.

Marion, N. E., & Oliver, W. M. (2006). *The public policy of crime and criminal justice.* Upper Saddle River, NJ: Pearson/Prentice Hall.

Marlowe, D. B. (2011). The verdict on drug courts and other problem-solving courts. *Chapman Journal of Criminal Justice, 2,* 57–96.

Martin, D. L. (2002). The police role in wrongful convictions: An international comparative study. In S. Westervelt & J. A. Humphrey (Eds.), *Wrongly convicted: Perspectives on failed justice* (pp. 77–95). New Brunswick, NJ: Rutgers University Press.

Martinez, R. (2002). *Latino homicide.* New York: Routledge.

Martinez, R. (2003). Moving beyond black and white violence: African American, Haitian, and Latino homicides in Miami. In D. F. Hawkins (Ed.), *Violent crime: Assessing race and ethnic differences* (pp. 22–43). New York: Cambridge University Press.

Martinez, R. (2006). Coming to America: The impact of the

new immigration on crime. In R. Martinez & A. Valenzuela (Eds.), *Immigration and crime: Race, ethnicity, and violence* (pp. 1–19). New York: New York University Press.

Martinez, R., Lee, M. T., & Nielsen, A. L. (2001). Revisiting the Scarface legacy: The victim/offender relationship and Mariel homicides in Miami. *Hispanic Journal of Behavioral Sciences, 23,* 37–56.

Martinez, R., Stowell, J. I., & Lee, M. T. (2010). Immigration and crime in an era of transformation: A longitudinal analysis of homicides in San Diego neighborhoods, 1980–2000. *Criminology, 48*(3), 797–830.

Martinez, R., & Valenzuela, A. (Eds.). (2006). *Immigration and crime: Race, ethnicity, and violence.* New York: New York University Press.

Martinson, R. (1974). What works? Questions and answers about prison reform. *Public Interest, 24,* 22–54.

Massey, D. S., & Denton, N. A. (1993). *American apartheid.* Cambridge, MA: Harvard University Press.

Mauer, M. (1990). *Young African American men and the criminal justice system: A growing national problem.* Washington, DC: The Sentencing Project.

Mauer, M. (1999). *Race to incarcerate.* New York: New Press.

Mauer, M. (2004). Extended view: Racial disparity and the criminal justice system: An assessment of causes and responses. *SAGE Race Relations Abstracts, 29,* 34–56.

Mauer, M. (2006). *Race to incarcerate* (rev. ed.). New York: New Press.

Mauer, M. (2011). Voting behind bars: An argument for voting by prisoners. *Howard Law Journal, 54,* 549–566.

Mauer, M., & Huling, T. (1995). *Young African Americans and the criminal justice system: Five years later.* Washington, DC: The Sentencing Project.

Maupin, J. R., & Maupin, J. R. (1998). Juvenile justice decision making in a rural Hispanic community. *Journal of Criminal Justice, 26,* 373–384.

Mazerolle, L. G., & Terrill, W. (1997). Problem-oriented policing in public housing: Identifying the distribution of problem places. *Policing, 20,* 235–255.

McCamey, W. P., Scaramella, G. L., & Cox, S. M. (2003). *Contemporary municipal policing.* Boston: Allyn & Bacon.

McCleskey v. Kemp, 481 U.S. 279 (1987).

McCluskey, C. P. (2002). *Understanding Latino delinquency.* New York: LFB Scholarly.

McCluskey, C. P., Krohn, M. D., Lizotte, A. J., & Rodriguez, M. L. (2002). Early substance use and school achievement: An examination of Latino, White, and African-American youth. *Journal of Drug Issues, 32,* 921–944.

McCluskey, C. P., & Tovar, S. (2003). Family processes and delinquency: The consistency of relationships by ethnicity and gender. *Journal of Ethnicity in Criminal Justice, 1,* 37–61.

McGee, Z. T. (1999). Patterns of violent behavior and victimization among African American youth. *Journal of Offender Rehabilitation, 30,* 47–64.

McGee, Z. T. (2003). Community violence and adolescent development: An examination of risk and protective factors among African American youth. *Journal of Contemporary Criminal Justice, 19,* 293–314.

McGee, Z. T., & Baker, S. R. (2002). Impact of violence on problem behavior among adolescents. *Journal of Contemporary Criminal Justice, 18,* 74–93.

McGee, Z. T., Barber, A., Joseph, E., Dudley, J., & Howell, R. (2005). Delinquent behavior, violent victimization, and coping strategies among Latino adolescents. *Journal of Offender Rehabilitation, 42*(3), 41–56.

McGuffee, K., Garland, T. S., & Eigenberg, H. (2007). Is jury selection fair? Perceptions of race and the jury selection process. *Criminal Justice Studies, 20,* 445–468.

McIntosh, P. (2002). White privilege, color, and crime: A personal account. In C. R. Mann & M. S. Zatz (Eds.), *Images of color, images of crime* (2nd ed., pp. 45–53). Los Angeles: Roxbury.

McIntyre, C. C. L. (1992). *Criminalizing a race: Free Blacks during slavery.* New York: Kayode.

McMahon, J., Garner, J., Davis, R., & Kraus, A. (2002). *How to correctly collect and analyze racial profiling data: Your reputation depends on it.* Washington, DC: US Department of Justice, Office of Community-Oriented Policing Services.

Meagher, T. J. (2005). *The Columbia guide to Irish American history.* New York: Columbia University Press.

Mears, D. (2002). Sentencing guidelines and the transformation of juvenile justice in the 21st century. *Journal of Contemporary Criminal Justice, 18,* 6–19.

Mears, D. P., & Watson, J. (2006). Towards a fair and balanced assessment of supermax prisons. *Justice Quarterly, 23,* 232–270.

Meier, A., & Rudwick, E. (1970). *From plantation to ghetto* (rev. ed.). New York: Hill & Wang.

Mennel, R. M. (1973). *Thorns and thistles.* Hanover: University of New Hampshire Press.

Menninger, K. (1966). *The crime of punishment.* New York: Viking Press.

Merton, R. K. (1938). Social structure and anomie. *American Sociological Review, 3,* 672–682.

Merton, R. K., & Ashley-Montagu, M. F. (1940). Crime and the anthropologist. *American Anthropologist, 42,* 384–408.

Messner, S. F., Krohn, M. D., & Liska, A. E. (Eds.). (1989). *Theoretical integration in the study of deviance and crime: Problems and prospects*. Albany: State University of New York Press.

Miller, E. J. (2007). The therapeutic effects of managerial reentry courts. *Federal Sentencing Reporter, 20,* 127–135.

Miller, H. V., Barnes, J. C., & Hartley, R. (2011). Reconsidering Hispanic gang membership and acculturation in a multivariate framework. *Crime and Delinquency, 5,* 331–355.

Miller, J. (2001). Bringing the individual back in: A commentary on Wacquant and Anderson. *Punishment & Society, 3,* 153–160.

Miller, J. G. (1992a). *Hobbling a generation: Young African American males in Washington, D.C.'s, criminal justice system*. Baltimore, MD: National Center for Institutions and Alternatives.

Miller, J. G. (1992b). *Hobbling a generation: Young African American males in the criminal justice system of America's cities*. Baltimore, MD: National Center for Institutions and Alternatives.

Miller, J. G. (1996). *Search and destroy: African American males in the criminal justice system*. New York: Cambridge University Press.

Miller, K. (1969). *Out of the house of bondage*. New York: Arno Press and *The New York Times*. (Original work published 1908)

Miller, W. (1958). Lower class culture as a generating milieu of gang delinquency. *Journal of Social Issues, 14,* 5–19.

"Minnesota advocates for human rights express concern about immigration crackdown." (2008, January 14). *Minnesota Lawyer*. Gale document no. A173409283.

Minnesota Sentencing Guidelines Commission. (2010). *Sentencing practices: Annual summary statistics for felony offenders sentenced in 2009*. St. Paul, MN: Author.

Minton, T. D. (2006). *Jails in Indian country, 2004*. Washington, DC: Bureau of Justice Statistics.

Minton, T.D. (2011a). *Jail inmates at midyear 2010- statistical tables*. Washington, DC: Bureau of Justice Statistics. NCJ 233431

Minton, T. D. (2011b). *Selected findings: Jails in Indian country, 2009*. Washington, DC: Bureau of Justice Statistics. NCJ 232223

Miranda v. Arizona, 384 U.S. 436,86 S.Ct. 1602 (1966).

Mirande, A. (1987). *Gringo justice*. Notre Dame, IN: Notre Dame University Press.

Mitchell, A. D. (2006). The effect of the Marshall hypothesis on attitudes towards the death penalty. *Race, Gender & Class, 13,* 221–239.

Mitchell, O. (2005). A meta-analysis of race and sentencing research: Examining the inconsistencies. *Journal of Quantitative Criminology, 21,* 439–466.

Mitchell, O. (2009). Is the war on drugs racially biased? *Journal of Crime & Justice, 32,* 49–75.

Mitchell, O., Wilson, D. B., Eggers, A., & MacKenzie, D. L. (2012). Assessing the effectiveness of drug courts on recidivism: A meta-analytic review of traditional and non-traditional drug courts. *Journal of Criminal Justice, 40,* 60–71.

Mmari, K., Blum, R. W., & Teufel-Shone, N. (2010). What increases risk and protection for delinquent behaviors among American Indian youth? Findings from three tribal communities. *Youth & Society, 41*(3), 382–413.

Models for Change. (2011). *Racial and ethnic fairness/DMC*. Retrieved June 28, 2011, from http://www.modelsforchange.net/about/Issues-for-change/Racial-fairness.html

Monkkonen, E. H. (1981). *Police in urban America, 1860–1920*. Cambridge, NY: Cambridge University Press.

Moore, J. W., & Hagedorn, J. M. (2001). *Female gangs: A focus on research* (Bulletin. Youth Gang Series). Washington, DC: U.S. Department of Justice, Office of Juvenile Justice and Delinquency Prevention.

Morgan, K. D., & Smith, B. (2008). The role of race on parole decision-making. *Justice Quarterly, 25,* 411–435.

Morin, J. L. (2005). *Latino/a rights and justice in the United States: Perspectives and approaches*. Durham, NC: Carolina Academic Press.

Morrison Institute for Public Policy. (2010, May). *Illegal immigration: Perceptions and realities, Part I*. Phoenix: Arizona State University.

Mosher, C. J., Miethe, T. D., & Hart, T. C. (2011). *The mismeasure of crime* (2nd ed.). Thousand Oaks, CA: Sage.

Mosher, C. J., Miethe, T. D., & Phillips, D. M. (2002). *The mismeasure of crime*. Thousand Oaks, CA: Sage.

MSNBC (2011). *Police fear "war on cops."* Retrieved on November 18, 2011, from http://www.msnbc.msn.com/id/41235743/ns/us_news-crime_and_courts/

Muhlhausen, D. B. (2004). *The determinants of sentencing in Pennsylvania: Do the characteristics of judges matter?* Washington, DC: The Heritage Foundation.

Mumola, C. J. (2007). *Arrest-related deaths in the United States, 2003–2005*. Washington, DC: U.S. Department of Justice, Office of Justice Programs.

Munoz, E. A., & Freng, A. B. (2008). Age, racial/ethnic minority status, gender and misdemeanor sentencing. *Journal of Ethnicity in Criminal Justice, 5,* 29–57.

Munoz, E. A., & McMorris, B. J. (2002). Misdemeanor sentencing decisions: The cost of being Native American. *The Justice Professional, 15,* 239–259.

Munoz, E. A., McMorris, B. J., & DeLisi, M. J. (2005). Misdemeanor criminal justice: Contextualizing effects of Latino ethnicity, gender, and immigration status. *Race, Gender & Class, 11,* 112–134.

Myers, M. A. (1998). *Race, labor, & punishment in the New South*. Columbus: Ohio State University Press.

Myrdal, G. (1944). *An American dilemma: The Negro problem and modern democracy*. New York: Harper & Brothers.

Nation, D. (2011). *Citizens' preferences about police work: An argument for racial variations*. El Paso, TX: LFB Scholarly.

National Advisory Commission on Civil Disorders. (1968). *Report of the National Advisory Commission on Civil Disorders*. Washington, DC: Government Printing Office.

National Association for the Advancement of Colored People. (2011). *Misplaced priorities: Over incarcerate, under educate*. Baltimore, MD: Author.

National Center for Injury Prevention and Control. (2010). Youth violence facts at a glance. Retrieved October 24, 2011, from http://www.cdc.gov/Violence Prevention/pdf/YV-DataSheet-a .pdf

National Center for Juvenile Justice. (2004). *State juvenile justice profiles*. Retrieved July 15, 2004, from http://www.ncjj.org/stateprofiles/

National Coalition to Abolish the Death Penalty. (2004). *America's shame: Killing kids*. Retrieved December 15, 2004, from http://www.ncadp.org/fact_sheet1.html

National Commission on Law Observance and Enforcement. (1931a). *Crime and the foreign born* (Report No. 10). Washington, DC: Government Printing Office.

National Commission on Law Observance and Enforcement. (1931b). *Report on lawlessness in law enforcement*. Washington, DC: U.S. Government Printing Office.

National Conference of State Legislatures. (2010). U.S. Supreme Court rules juvenile life without parole sentences for non-homicide unconstitutional. Retrieved July 9, 2011, from www.ncsl.org/default .aspx?tabid=20419

National Drug Control Strategy. (2011). Available at: http://www .whitehousedrugpolicy.gov/strategy/2011ndcs.html

National Indian Gaming Commission. (n.d.). *Gaming revenue reports*. Retrieved from http://www .nigc.gov/Gaming_Revenue_Reports.aspx

National Minority Advisory Council on Criminal Justice. (1979). *Racism in the criminal courts* (draft). Washington, DC: U.S. Department of Justice.

National Organization of Black Law Enforcement Executives. (2001). *A NOBLE perspective: Racial profiling: A symptom of biased-based policing*. Retrieved July 31, 2004, from http://www.noblenational.org/pdf/RacialProfiling901.pdf

National Urban League Poll. (2001). Retrieved March 17, 2004, from Polling the Nations database at http://www.orspub.com/

National Youth Gang Center. (2008). *Frequently asked questions regarding gangs*. Retrieved March 20, 2008, from http://www.iir.com/nygc/faq.htm#q3

Neisser, U., et al. (1996). Intelligence: Knowns and unknowns. *American Psychologist, 51*, 77–101.

Neubauer, D. (2002). *America's courts & the criminal justice system* (7th ed.). Belmont, CA: Wadsworth.

Neverdon-Morton, C. (1989). *Afro-American women of the South and the advancement of the race, 1895–1925*. Knoxville: University of Tennessee Press.

Newport, F. (2010). *In U.S., 64% Support Death Penalty in Cases of Murder: Half say death penalty not imposed often enough*. Retrieved August 1, 2011, from http://www.gallup.com/poll/144284/Support-Death-Penalty-Cases-Murder.aspx

Newport, F., & Ludwig, J. (2000). *Protests by Blacks over Amadou Diallo verdict not surprising given long-standing perceptions among Blacks that they are discriminated against in most areas of their daily lives*. Retrieved from http://www .gallup.com/poll/fromtheed/ed003.asp

Newsome, M. (2007). A new DNA test can ID a suspect's race, but police won't touch it. *Wired, 16*(1). Retrieved from http://www.wired.com/politics/law/magazine/16-01/ps_dna

New York State Special Commission on Attica. (1972). *Attica: The official report of the New York State Special Commission on Attica*. New York: Praeger.

Nolan, J. J., III, Akiyama, Y., & Berhanu, S. (2002). The Hate Crime Statistics Act of 1990: Developing a method for measuring the occurrence of hate violence. *American Behavioral Scientist, 46*, 136–153.

Norris, R. J. (2011). Assessing compensation statutes for the wrongfully convicted. *Criminal Justice Policy Review*. DOI: 10.1177/0887403411409916.

Northern v. Nelson, 315 F. Supp. 687 (1970).

Norton, H. K. (2004). Virtual museum of the City of San Francisco. *The Chinese*. Retrieved from http://www.sfmusucm.org

Novak, K. J. (2009). Policy essay: Reasonable officers, public perceptions, and policy challenges. *Criminology & Public Policy, 8*(1), 117–140.

Office of Juvenile Justice and Delinquency Prevention. (2004). *Disproportionate minority contact. About DMC: Core requirement of JJDP Act*. Retrieved July 15, 2004, from http://www.ojjdp.ncjrs.org/dmc/about/core.html

Office of Juvenile Justice and Delinquency Prevention. (2008). *Statistical briefing book*. Retrieved March 20,

2008, from http://ojjdp.ncjrs
.gov/ojstatbb/crime/qa05101
.asp?qaDate=2006.

*Office of National Drug Control
Policy*. (n.d.). Retrieved from
http://www.whitehousedrug
policy.gov/about/index.html

Office of National Drug Control
Policy. (2009). *National drug
control strategy: 2009 annual
report*. Washington, DC:
Author.

Ogletree, C. J., & Sarat, A. (Eds.).
(2006). *From lynch mobs to the
killing state: Race and the death
penalty in America*. New York:
New York University.

Oliver, W. (1984). Black males and the
tough guy image: A dysfunc-
tional compensatory adaptation.
*The Western Journal of Black
Studies, 8,* 199–203.

Oliver, W. (1989a). Black males and
social problems: Prevention
through Afrocentric socializa-
tion. *Journal of Black Studies,
20,* 15–39.

Oliver, W. (1989b). Sexual conquest
and patterns of Black-on-Black
violence: A structural-cultural
perspective. *Violence and
Victims, 4,* 257–273.

Oliver, W. (1994). *The violent social
world of Black men*. New York:
Lexington Books.

Oliver, W. (2003). The structural-
cultural perspective: A theory
of Black male violence. In
D. F. Hawkins (Ed.), *Violent
crime: Assessing race and ethnic differences* (pp. 280–318).
Cambridge, UK: Cambridge
University Press.

Oliver, W. (2006). "The streets": An
alternative Black male socializa-
tion institution. *Journal of Black
Studies, 36,* 918–937.

O'Neill Shermer, L., & Johnson, B. D.
(2010). Criminal prosecutions:
Examining prosecutorial discretion and charge reductions in
the U.S. Federal District Courts.
Justice Quarterly, 27, 394–430.

Orfalea, G. (2006). *The Arab Americans:
A history*. Northampton, MA:
Olive Branch Press.

Oshinsky, D. M. (1996). *"Worse than
slavery": Parchman farm and
the ordeal of Jim Crow justice*.
New York: The Free Press.

Owusu-Bempah, A., & Millar, P.
(2010). Research note: Revisiting
the collection of "justice statistics by race" in Canada.
*Canadian Journal of Law and
Society, 25,* 97–104.

Packer, H. (1968). *The limits of the
criminal sanction*. Palo Alto,
CA: Stanford University Press.

Pager, D. I. (2007a). *Marked: Race,
crime, and finding work in an era
of mass incarceration*. Chicago:
University of Chicago Press.

Pager, D. I. (2007b). Two strikes and
you're out: The intensification of
racial and criminal stigma. In D.
Weiman, S. Bushway, & M. Stoll
(Eds.), *Barriers to reentry? The
labor market for released prisoners in post-industrial America*
(pp. 151–173). New York:
Russell Sage.

Palmer, J. W. (2010). *Constitutional
rights of prisoners* (9th ed.).
New Providence, NJ: Lexis/
Nexis Anderson.

Parade Magazine Poll. (2002,
February 10). Retrieved March
17, 2004, from Polling the
Nations database at http://
www.orspub.com/

Parenti, C. (1999). *Lockdown America:
Police and prisons in the age of
crisis*. New York: Verso.

Parker, K. F., Dewees, M. A., &
Radelet, M. L. (2002). Racial
bias and the conviction of the
innocent. In S. Westervelt &
J. A. Humphrey (Eds.), *Wrongly
convicted: Perspectives on
failed justice* (pp. 114–131).
New Brunswick, NJ: Rutgers
University Press.

Parsons-Pollard, N. Y. (2011).
*Disproportionate minority
contact: Current issues and
policies*. Durham, NC: Carolina
Academic Press.

Paternoster, R. (1983). Race of the
victim and location of crime:
The decision to seek the death
penalty in South Carolina.

*Journal of Criminal Law and
Criminology, 74,* 701–731.

Paternoster, R., & Brame, R. (2003). *An
empirical analysis of Maryland's
death sentencing system with
respect to the influence of race
and legal jurisdiction*. Retrieved
from http://www.newsdesk
.umd.edu/pdf/finalrep.pdf

Paternoster, R., & Brame, R. (2008).
Reassessing race disparities
in Maryland capital cases.
Criminology, 46, 971–1008.

Patterson, W. L. (Ed.). (1970). *We
charge genocide: The historic
petition to the United Nations
for relief from a crime of the
United States government
against the Negro people*. New
York: International Publishers.
(Original work published 1951)

Pattillo, M. E. (1998). Sweet mothers
and gangbangers: Managing
crime in a Black middle-class
neighborhood. *Social Forces,
76,* 747–774.

Payne, B. K., & Button, D. M.
(2009). Developing a citywide
youth violence prevention
plan. *International Journal
of Offender therapy and
Comparative Criminology,
53*(5), 517–534.

Peguero, A. A., & Shekarkhar, Z.
(2011). Latino/a student misbehavior and school punishment.
*Journal of Behavioral Sciences,
33,* 54–70.

Penn, E., Taylor Greene, H., &
Gabbidon, S . L . (Eds.). (2006).
Race and juvenile justice.
Durham, NC: Carolina Academic
Press.

*Pennsylvania panel advises death
penalty moratorium*. (2003).
Retrieved March 5, 2003, from
http://www.CNN.com

Pennsylvania Supreme Court. (2003).
*Pennsylvania Supreme Court
Committee on Racial and
Gender Bias in the Justice System*
(Final report). Retrieved from
http://www.courts.state.pa.us

Perez, D. M., Jennings, W. D., & Giver,
A. R. (2008). Specifying general
strain theory: An ethnically

relevant approach. *Deviant Behavior, 29,* 544–578.

Perloff, R. M. (2000). The press and lynchings of African Americans. *Journal of Black Studies, 30,* 315–330.

Perry, B. (2000). Perpetual outsiders: Criminal justice and the Asian American experience. In The Criminal Justice Collective of Northern Arizona University (Eds.), *Investigating difference: Human and cultural relations in criminal justice* (pp. 99–110). Boston: Allyn & Bacon.

Perry, B. (2002). Defending the color line: Racially and ethnically motivated hate crime. *American Behavioral Scientist, 46,* 72–92.

Perry, B. (2009). *Policing race and place in Indian Country: Over- and underenforcement.* Lanham, MD: Lexington Books.

Perry, S. W. (2004). *Census of tribal justice agencies in Indian Country, 2002.* Washington, DC: U.S. Department of Justice.

Perry, S. W. (2005). *Census of tribal justice agencies in Indian Country, 2002.* Washington, DC: US Dept of Justice, Bureau of Justice Statistics. NCJ 205332 Retrieved July 13, 2011, from http://bjs.ojp.usdoj.gov/content/pub/pdf/ctjaic02.pdf

Petersilia, J. (1983). *Racial disparities in the criminal justice system.* Santa Monica, CA: RAND.

Petersilia, J. (2002). Community corrections. In J. Q. Wilson & J. Petersilia (Eds.), *Crime: Public policies for crime control* (pp. 483–508). Oakland, CA: Institute for Contemporary Studies.

Petersilia, J. (2003). *When prisoners come home: Parole and prisoner reentry.* New York: Oxford University Press.

Peterson, D., Taylor, T. J., & Esbensen, F. (2004). Gang membership and violent victimization. *Justice Quarterly, 21*(4), 794–815.

Peterson, R. D., & Krivo, L. J. (1993). Racial segregation and Black urban homicide. *Social Forces, 71,* 1001–1026.

Peterson, R. D., & Krivo, L. J. (2005). Macrostructural analyses of race, ethnicity, and violent crime: Recent lessons and new directions for research. *Annual Review of Sociology, 31,* 331–356.

Peterson, R., & Krivo, L. (2010). *Divergent social worlds.* New York: Russell Sage.

Petrie, M. A., & Coverdill, J. E. (2010). Who lives and dies on death row? Race, ethnicity, and post-sentence outcomes in Texas. *Social Problems, 57,* 630–652.

The Pew Center on the States. (2008). *One in 100: Behind Bars in American 2008.* Retrieved at http://www.pewcenteronthestates.org/report_detail.aspx?id=35904

The Pew Center on the States. (2011). *State of recidivism: The revolving door of America's prisons.* Washington, DC: The Pew Charitable Trusts.

Phillips, U. B. (1915). Slave crime in Virginia. *American Historical Review, 20,* 336–340.

Pierce, G. L., & Radelet, M. L. (2011). Death sentencing in East Baton Rouge Parish, 1990–2008. *Louisiana Law Review, 71,* 647–673.

Piquero, N. L., & Piquero, A. R. (2001). Problem-oriented policing. In R. G. Dunham & G. P. Alpert (Eds.), *Critical issues in policing* (4th ed., pp. 531–540). Prospect Heights, IL: Waveland Press.

Piquero, N., & Sealock, M. (2010). Race, crime, and general strain theory. *Youth Violence and Juvenile Justice, 6,* 170–186.

Pisciotta, A. W. (1983). Race, sex, and rehabilitation: A study of differential treatment in the juvenile reformatory, 1825–1900. *Crime and Delinquency 29*(2), 254–269.

Platt, A. (1969). *The child savers: The invention of delinquency.* Chicago: University of Chicago Press.

Platt, A. (1977). *The child savers: The invention of delinquency* (2nd ed.). Chicago: University of Chicago Press.

Platt, A. (2009). *The child savers: The invention of delinquency* (expanded 40th anniversary edition). Piscataway, NJ: Rutgers University Press.

Plessy v. Ferguson, 163 U.S. 537 (1896).

Polk, W. R. (2006). *The birth of America: From Columbus to the Revolution.* New York: HarperCollins.

Pope, C. E., & Feyerherm, W. H. (1990, June/September). Minority status and juvenile justice processing: An assessment of the research literature, Parts I & II. *Criminal Justice Abstracts, 22,* 327–336 (Part I); *22,* 527–542 (Part II).

Pope, C. E., Lovell, R., & Hsia, H. M. (2002). *Disproportionate minority confinement: A review of the research literature from 1989 through 2001.* Washington, DC: Office of Juvenile Justice and Delinquency Prevention.

Porter, N. D. (2010). *Expanding the vote: State felony disenfranchisement reform, 1997–2010.* Washington, DC: The Sentencing Project.

Porter, N. D. (2011). *On the chopping block: State prison closings.* Washington, DC: The Sentencing Project.

Potter, H. (Ed.). (2007). *Racing the storm: Racial implications and lessons learned from Hurricane Katrina.* Lanham, MD: Lexington Books.

Powell v. Alabama, 287 U.S. 45 (1932).

Pratt, T. C. (1998). Race and sentencing: A meta-analysis of conflicting empirical research results. *Journal of Criminal Justice, 26,* 513–523.

President's Commission on Law Enforcement and the Administration of Justice. (1967). *Task force report on the police.* Washington, DC: U.S. Government Printing Office.

Preuhs, R. R. (2001). State felon disenfranchisement policy. *Social Science Quarterly, 82,* 733–748.

Price, B. E. (2006). *Merchandizing prisoners: Who really pays for prison privatization?* Westport, CT: Praeger.

Pridemore, W. A., & Freilich, J. D. (2006). A test of recent subcultural explanations of white violence in the United States. *Journal of Criminal Justice, 34,* 1–16.

Public Policy Institute of California. (2008). *Poll data.* Retrieved March 24, 2008, from Polling the Nations database.

Public Report of the Forgotten Victims of Attica. (2003). Retrieved June 4, 2004, from http://newyorkv.homestead.com/files/fvoareportfinal.htm

Puzzanchera, C., Adams, B., & Sickmund, M. (2010). *Juvenile court statistics 2006-2007.* Pittsburgh, PA: National Center for Juvenile Justice. Retrieved August 1, 2011, from http://www.ncjjservehttp.org/ncjjweb site/pdf/jcsreports/jcs2007.pdf

Puzzanchera, C., Stahl, A., Finnegan, T. A., Tierney, N., & Snyder, H. (2003a). *Juvenile court statistics, 1998.* Washington, DC: Office of Juvenile Justice and Delinquency Prevention.

Puzzanchera, C., Stahl, A. Finnegan, T. A., Tierney, N., & Snyder, H. (2003b). *Juvenile court statistics, 1999.* Washington, DC: Office of Juvenile Justice and Delinquency Prevention.

Pyrooz, D. C., Decker, S. H., & Fleisher, M. (2011). From the street to prison, from the prison to the street: Understanding and responding to prison gangs. *Journal of Aggression, Conflict and Peace Research, 3,* 12–24.

Quetelet, A. Q. (1984). *Research on the propensity for crime at different ages.* Cincinnati, OH: Anderson. (Original work published 1833)

Quinney, R. (1970). *The social reality of crime.* Boston: Little, Brown.

Racial Profiling Data Collection Resource Center at Northeastern University. (2003). Retrieved from http://www.racialprofilin ganalysis.neu.edu

Racial Profiling Data Collection Resource Center at Northeastern

University. (2008). Retrieved February 23, 2008, from http://www.racialprofilinganalysis.neu.edu

Radelet, M. L. (1989). Executions of Whites for crimes against Blacks: Exceptions to the rule? *The Sociological Quarterly, 30,* 529–544.

Radelet, M. L., Bedau, H. A., & Putnam, C. E. (1992). *In spite of innocence: The ordeal of 400 Americans wrongly convicted of crimes punishable by death.* Boston: Northeastern University Press.

Radosh, P. F. (2008). War on drugs: Gender and race inequities in crime control strategies. *Criminal Justice Studies, 21,* 167–178.

Ramsey, R. J., & Frank, J. (2007). Wrongful convictions: Perceptions of criminal justice professionals regarding the frequency of wrongful convictions and system errors. *Crime & Delinquency, 53,* 436–470.

Rand, M., & Catalano, S. (2007). *Criminal victimizations, 2006.* Washington, DC: U.S. Department of Justice, Office of Justice Programs.

Rantala, R. R., & Edwards, T. J. (2000). *Effects of NIBRS on crime statistics.* Washington, DC: U.S. Department of Justice, Office of Justice Programs.

Raper, A. (1933). *The tragedy of lynching.* Chapel Hill: University of North Carolina Press.

Rasmussen Reports. (2009). Retrieved July 1, 2011, from the Polling the Nations database at http://www.orspub.com/

Ray, M. C., & Smith, E. (1991). Black women and homicide: An analysis of the subculture of violence thesis. *The Western Journal of Black Studies, 15,* 144–153.

Reasons, C. E., Conley, D. C., & Debro, J. (Eds.). (2002). *Race, class, gender, and justice in the United States.* Boston: Allyn & Bacon.

Reaves, B. A. (2001). *Felony defendants in large urban counties,*

1998. Washington, DC: Bureau of Justice Statistics.

Reaves, B. A. (2011). *Tribal law enforcement, 2008.* NCJ 234217. Retrieved July 18, 2011, from http://bjs.ojp.usdoj.gov/content/pub/pdf/tle08.pdf

Reaves, B. (2006). *Federal law enforcement officers, 2004.* Washington, DC: U.S. Department of Justice. Retrieved February 16, 2008, from www.ojp.usdoj.gov/bjs/welcome.html

Reaves, B. (2007). *Census of state and local law enforcement agencies, 2004.* Washington, DC: U.S. Department of Justice.

Reaves, B. (2010). *Local police departments, 2007.* Retrieved July 13, 2011, from http://bjs.ojp.usdoj.gov/content/pub/pdf/lpd07.pdf

Reaves, B., & Bauer, L. (2003). *Federal law enforcement officers, 2002.* Washington, DC: U.S. Department of Justice.

Reaves, B., & Hickman, M. (2002a). *Census of state and local law enforcement agencies, 2000.* Washington, DC: U.S. Department of Justice.

Reaves, B., & Hickman, M. (2002b). *Police departments in large cities, 1990–2000.* Washington, DC: U.S. Department of Justice.

Reaves, B., & Hickman, M. (2003). *Local police departments, 2000.* Washington, DC: U.S. Department of Justice.

Reid, I. De A. (1957). Race and crime. *Friends Journal, 3,* 772–774.

Reiman, J. (2004). *The rich get richer, and the poor get prison: Ideology, class and criminal justice* (7th ed.). Boston: Allyn & Bacon.

Reiman, J. (2007). *The rich get richer and the poor get prison: Ideology, class, and criminal justice* (8th ed.). Boston: Allyn & Bacon.

Reisig, M. D., & Parks, R. B. (2001). *Satisfaction with police—What matters?* Washington, DC: U.S. Department of Justice.

Rennison, C. M. (2001a). *Criminal victimization 2000 changes 1999–2000 with trends 1992–2000.*

Washington, DC: U.S. Department of Justice, Office of Justice Programs.

Rennison, C. M. (2001b). *Violent victimization and race, 1992–1998*. Washington, DC: U.S. Department of Justice, Office of Justice Programs.

Rennison, C. M. (2002). *Hispanic victims of violent crime, 1993–2000* (NCJ 191208). Washington, DC: U.S. Department of Justice, Office of Justice Programs.

Rennison, C. M., & Rand, M. R. (2003). *Criminal victimization, 2002*. Washington, DC: U.S. Department of Justice, Office of Justice Programs.

Renowned criminologist eschews alarmist theories. (1999, September 13). *The Patriot News*, p. B5.

Rice, S. K., & White, M. D. (Eds.). (2010). *Race, ethnicity, and policing: New and essential readings*. New York: NYU Press.

Richardson, J. F. (1970). *The New York police*. New York: Oxford University Press.

Richie, B. (2002). The social impact of mass incarceration on women. In M. Mauer & M. Chesney-Lind (Eds.), *Invisible punishment: The collateral consequences of mass imprisonment* (pp. 136–149). New York: New Press.

Rios, V. (2011). *Punished: Policing the lives of Black and Latino youth*. New York: NYU Press.

Rippley, L. J. (1976). *The German-Americans*. Boston: Twayne.

Roane, K. R. (2001, April 30). Policing the police is a dicey business. *U.S. News & World Report*, p. 28.

Robinson, L. N. (1911). *History and organization of criminal statistics in the United States*. Boston: Houghton Mifflin.

Rocque, M. (2008). Strain, coping mechanisms, and slavery: A general strain theory application. *Crime, Law, and Social Change, 49*, 245–269.

Rodriguez, N. (2007). Juvenile court context and detention decisions:

Reconsidering the role of race, ethnicity, and community characteristics in juvenile court processes. *Justice Quarterly, 24*, 629–656.

Roe v. Wade, 410 U.S. 113 (1973).

Roper v. Simmons, 543 U.S. 551 (2005).

Rose, D. R., & Clear, T. R. (1998). Incarceration, social capital, and crime: Implications for social disorganization theory. *Criminology, 36*, 441–479.

Rosenmerkel, S., Durose, M., & Farole, D. (2009). *Felony sentences in state courts, 2006 – statistical tables*. Washington, DC: Bureau of Justice Statistics. NCJ 226846.

Ross, L. E. (1992). Blacks, self-esteem, and delinquency: It's time for a new approach. *Justice Quarterly, 9*, 609–624.

Ross, L. E. (2001). African-American interest in law enforcement: A consequence of petit apartheid? In D. Milovanovic & K. K. Russell (Eds.), *Petit apartheid in the U.S. criminal justice system: The dark figure of racism* (pp. 69–77). Durham, NC: Carolina Academic Press.

Ross, L. E. (2010). A vision of race, crime, and justice through the lens of critical race theory. In E. McLaurin & T. Newburn (Eds.), *The Sage handbook of criminological theory* (pp. 391–409). London: Sage.

Rossman, S.B., Roman, J.K., Zweig, Rempel, M., & Lindquist, C.H. (2011). *The multi-site adult court evaluation: Executive summary*. Washington, DC: Urban Institute.

Rudwick, E. M. (1960). The Negro policeman in the South. *Journal of Criminal Law, Criminology, and Police Science, 51*, 273–276.

Rushton, J. P. (1995). Race and crime: International data for 1989–1990. *Psychological Reports, 76*, 307–312.

Rushton, J. P. (1999). *Race, evolution, and behavior* (special abridged ed.). New Brunswick, NJ: Transaction.

Rushton, J. P., & Whitney, G. (2002). Cross-national variation in violent crime rates: Race, *r-K* theory, and income. *Population and Environment, 23*, 501–511.

Russell, K. K. (1998). *The color of crime: Racial hoaxes, White fear, Black protectionism, police harassment, and other macro-aggressions*. New York: New York University Press.

Russell, K. K. (1999). Critical race theory and social justice. In B. A. Arrigo (Ed.), *Social justice/criminal justice: The maturation of critical theory in law, crime, and deviance* (pp. 178–188). Belmont, CA: West/Wadsworth.

Russell, K. K. (2002). "Driving while Black": Corollary phenomena and collateral consequences. In C. E. Reasons, D. J. Conley, & J. Debro (Eds.), *Race, class, gender, and justice in the United States* (pp. 191–200). Boston: Allyn & Bacon.

Russell-Brown, K. (2004). *Underground codes: Race, crime, and related fires*. New York: New York University Press.

Russell-Brown, K. (2006). While visions of deviance danced in their heads. In D. D. Trout (Ed.), *After the storm: Black intellectuals explore the meaning of Hurricane Katrina* (pp. 111–123). New York: New Press.

Sachar, H. M. (1993). *A history of Jews in America*. New York: Vintage.

Sale, K. (1990). *The conquest of paradise: Christopher Columbus and the Columbian legacy*. New York: Knopf.

Saleh-Hanna, V. (Ed.). (2008). *Colonial systems of control: Criminal justice in Nigeria*. Ottawa: University of Ottawa Press.

Sampson, R. J. (1985). Race and criminal violence: A demographically disaggregated analysis of urban homicide. *Crime and Delinquency, 31*, 47–82.

Sampson, R. J. (1987). Urban Black violence: The effects of male joblessness and family disruption. *American Journal of Sociology, 93,* 348–382.

Sampson, R. J., & Bean, L. (2006). Cultural mechanisms and killing fields: A revised theory of community-level racial inequality. In J. Hagan, R. Peterson, & L. Krivo (Eds.), *The many colors of crime: Inequalities of race, ethnicity, and crime in America* (pp. 8–36). New York: New York University Press.

Sampson, R. J., & Groves, W. B. (1989). Community structure and crime: Testing social-disorganization theory. *American Journal of Sociology, 94,* 774–802.

Sampson, R. J., Raudenbush, S. W., & Earls, F. (1997). Neighborhoods and violent crime: A multilevel study of collective efficacy. *Science, 277,* 918–924.

Sampson, R. J., & Wilson, W. J. (1995). Toward a theory of race, crime, and urban inequality. In J. Hagan & R. D. Peterson (Eds.), *Crime and inequality* (pp. 37–54). Stanford, CA: Stanford University Press.

Schaefer, R. T. (2011). *Racial and ethnic groups* (12th ed.). New York: Pearson/Prentice-Hall.

Schafer, J. A., Huebner, B. M., & Bynum, T: S. (2003). Citizen perceptions of police services: Race, neighborhood context, and community policing. *Police Quarterly, 6,* 440–468.

Schall v. Martin, 467 U.S. 253 (1984).

Scheb, J. M., Lyons, W., & Wagers, K. A. (2008). Race, prosecutors, and juries: The death penalty in Tennessee. *Justice System Journal, 29,* 338–347.

Scheingold, S. A. (1984). *The politics of law and order: Street crime and public policy.* New York: Longman.

Schildkraut, D. J. (2009). The dynamics of public opinion on ethnic profiling after 9/11. *American Behavioral Scientist, 53,* 61–79.

Schlesinger, T. (2005). Racial and ethnic disparity in pretrial case processing. *Justice Quarterly, 22,* 170–192.

Schwartz, A. (2011). *DNA familial testing: Civil liberties and civil rights concerns.* Chicago: American Civil Liberties Union.

Schwartz, J. (2010). Murder in comparative context. In Christopher J. Ferguson (Ed.), *Violent crime* (pp. 276–299). Thousand Oaks, CA: Sage.

Scott, G. (2001). Broken windows behind bars: Eradicating prison gangs through ecological hardening and symbol cleansing. *Corrections Management Quarterly, 5,* 23–36.

Sellin, T. (1928). The Negro criminal: A statistical note. *The American Academy of Political and Social Sciences, 130,* 52–64.

Sellin, T. (1935). Race prejudice in the administration of justice. *The American Journal of Sociology, 41,* 212–217.

Sellin, T. (1938). *Culture conflict and crime.* New York: Social Science Research Council.

Sellin, T. J. (1976). *Slavery and the penal system.* New York: Elsevier.

The Sentencing Project. (2011a). *Felon disenfranchisement laws in the United States.* Washington, DC: Author.

The Sentencing Project. (2011b). *On the chopping block: State prison closings.* Washington, DC: Author.

Serwer, A. (2011). *Judicial override in death penalty cases: Another reason why electing judges is a bad idea.* Retrieved from http://prospect.org

Sesardic, N. (2010). Race: A social construction of a biological concept. *Biological Philosophy, 25,* 143–162.

Shane, S. (1999, April 4). Genetic research increasingly finds "race" a null concept. *The Baltimore Sun,* pp. 1A, 6A.

Shapiro, A. L. (1997). The disenfranchised. *American Prospect, 35,* 60–62.

Sharp, E. B. (2006). Policing urban America: A new look at the politics of agency size. *Social Science Quarterly, 87,* 291–307.

Shaw, C., & McKay, H. D. (1969). *Juvenile delinquency in urban areas.* Chicago: University of Chicago Press. (Original work published 1942)

Shekarkhar, Z., & Gibson, C. (2011). Gender, self-control, and offending behaviors among Latino youth. *Journal of Contemporary Criminal Justice, 72,* 63.

Shelden, R. G. (2001). *Controlling the dangerous classes.* Needham Heights, MA: Allyn & Bacon.

Shelden, R. G., & Brown, W. (2003). *Criminal justice in America: A critical view.* Needham Heights, MA: Allyn & Bacon.

Shelden, R. G., & Osborne, L. T. (1989). "For their own good": Class interests and the child saving movement in Memphis, Tennessee, 1900–1917. *Criminology, 27,* 747–767.

Sherman, L. W. (1974). *Police corruption: A sociological perspective.* Garden City, NY: Anchor Books.

Sherman, L. W. (1980). Execution without trial: Police homicide and the Constitution. *Vanderbilt Law Review, 33,* 71–100. (Reprinted in J. F. Fyfe, Ed., 1982, *Readings on police use of deadly force,* pp. 88–89.)

Sherman, L. (1997). Introduction: The congressional mandate to evaluate. In L. W. Sherman, D. Gottfredson, D. MacKenzie, J. P. Eck, P. Reuter, & S. Bushway (Eds.), *Preventing crime: What works, what doesn't, what's promising.* Washington, DC: National Institute of Justice.

Sherman, L. W., Gottfredson, D., MacKenzie, D., Eck, J. P., Reuter, P., & Bushway, S. (Eds.). (1997). *Preventing crime: What works, what doesn't, what's promising.* Washington, DC: National Institute of Justice.

Short, J., & Sharp, C. (2005). *Disproportionate minority contact in the juvenile justice system*. Washington, DC: Child Welfare League of America.

Sickmund, M., Sladky, T. J., & Kang, W. (2011). *Census of juveniles in residential placement databook.* Online (http://www.ojjdp.gov/ojstatbb/ezacjrp/).

Siegel, L. J. (2002). *Juvenile delinquency: The core.* Belmont, CA: Wadsworth/Thomson Learning.

Sigelman, L., Welch, S., Bledsoe, T., & Combs, M. (1997). Police brutality and public perceptions of racial discrimination: A tale of two beatings. *Political Research Quarterly, 50,* 777–791.

Sigler, M. (2010). Private prisons, public functions, and the meaning of punishment. *Florida State University Law Review, 38,* 149–178.

Simmons v. Roper, S.C. 84454 (2003).

Simons, D. H. (2003, June 23). Genetic tests can reveal ancestry, giving police a new source of clues. *U.S. News & World Report, 134,* p. 50.

Simons, R. L., Chen, Y. F., Stewart, E. A., & Brody, G. H. (2003). Incidents of discrimination and risk for delinquency: A longitudinal test of strain theory with an African American sample. *Justice Quarterly, 20,* 827–854.

Simons, R. L., Gordon Simons, L., Burt, C., Brody, G. H., & Cutrona, C. (2005). Collective efficacy, authoritative parenting and delinquency: A longitudinal test of a model integrating community-and-family-level processes. *Criminology, 43,* 989–1029.

Sims, Y. (2009). Jena 6. In H. T. Greene & S. L. Gabbidon (Eds.), *Encyclopedia of race and crime* (pp. 409–411). Thousand Oaks, CA: Sage.

Skogan, W. G. (2005). Citizen satisfaction with police encounters. *Police Quarterly, 8,* 298–321.

Skogan, W. G., Steiner, L., DuBois, J., Gudell, J. E., & Fagan, A. (2002). *Community policing and "the new immigrants": Latinos in Chicago.* Chicago: Northwestern University Press.

Smith, E., & Hattery, A. J. (2011). Race, wrongful conviction & exoneration. *Journal of African American Studies, 15,* 74–94.

Smith, J. (2009). Native American courts. In H. T. Greene & S. L. Gabbidon (Eds.), *Encyclopedia of race and crime.* Thousand Oaks, CA: Sage.

Smith, S. K., Steadman, G. W., Minton, T. D., & Townsend, M. (1999). *Criminal victimization and perceptions of community safety in 12 cities, 1998.* Washington, DC: U.S. Department of Justice.

Snell, T. (2010). *Capital punishment, 2009: Statistical tables.* Washington, DC: Bureau of Justice Statictics. NCJ 231676.

Snyder, H. N. (1997). *Juvenile arrests 1995.* Washington, DC: Office of Juvenile Justice and Delinquency Prevention.

Snyder, H. N. (2000). *Juvenile arrests 1999.* Washington, DC: Office of Juvenile Justice and Delinquency Prevention.

Snyder, H. N. (2003). *Juvenile arrests 2001.* Washington, DC: Office of Juvenile Justice and Delinquency Prevention.

Snyder, H. N. (2011). *Arrests in the United States, 1980 2009.* Washington, DC: U.S. Department of Justice, Office of Justice Programs.

Snyder, M., & Sickmund, M. (1999). *Juvenile offenders and victims: 1999 national report.* Washington, DC: Office of Juvenile Justice and Delinquency Prevention.

Snyder, M., & Sickmund, M. (2008). *Juvenile offenders and victims: 2006 national report.* Washington, DC: Office of Juvenile Justice and Delinquency Prevention.

Sommers, S. R., & Norton, M. I. (2007). Race-based judgments, race-neutral justifications: Experimental examination of peremptory use and the *Batson* challenge procedure. *Law and Human Behavior, 31,* 261–273.

Sorenson, J., Hope, R., & Stemen, D. (2003). Racial disproportionality in state prison admissions: Can regional variation be explained by differential arrest rates? *Journal of Criminal Justice, 31,* 73–84.

Sorenson, J. R., Cunningham, M. D., Vigen, M. P., & Woods, S. O. (2011). Serious assaults on prison staff: A descriptive analysis. *Journal of Criminal Justice, 39,* 143–150.

Sowell, T. (1981). *Ethnic America: A history.* New York: Basic Books.

Spohn, C. S. (2000). Thirty years of sentencing reform: The quest for a racially neutral sentencing process. In J. Horney (Ed.), *Policies, processes and decisions of the criminal justice system* (pp. 427–501). Washington, DC: National Institute of Justice.

Spohn, C. (2009). *How do judges decide? The search for fairness and justice in punishment* (2nd ed.). Thousand Oaks, CA: SAGE.

Spohn, C., & Brennan, P.K. (2011). The joint effects of offender race/ethnicity and gender on substantial assistance departures in federal courts. *Race and Justice: An International Journal, 1,* 49–78.

Spohn, C., & Holleran, D. (2000). The imprisonment penalty paid by young, unemployed black and Hispanic male offenders. *Criminology, 38,* 281–306.

Staff, J., & Kreager, D. A. (2008). Too cool for school? Violence, peer status and high school dropout. *Social Forces, 87,* 445–471.

Stahl, A. L. (2008a). *Delinquency cases in juvenile court, 2004* (OJDP Fact Sheet no. 01). Washington, DC: Office of Juvenile Justice and Delinquency Prevention.

Stahl, A. L. (2008b). *Petitioned status offense cases in juvenile court, 2004* (OJDP Fact Sheet no. 02). Washington, DC: Office of Juvenile Justice and Delinquency Prevention.

Stanford v. Kentucky, 492 U.S. 361 (1989).

Staples, R. (1975). White racism, Black crime, and American justice: An application of the colonial model to explain crime and race. *Phylon, 36,* 14–22.

State v. Soto, 324 N.J. Super 66, 734 A.2d 35 (1996).

Stauffer, A. R., Smith, M. D., Cochran, J. K., Fogel, S. J., & Bjerregaard, B. (2006). The interaction between victim race and gender on sentencing outcomes in capital murder trials: A further exploration. *Homicide Studies, 10,* 98–117.

Steffensmeier, D., & Britt, C. L. (2001). Judges' race and judicial decision making: Do Black judges sentence differently? *Social Science Quarterly, 82,* 749–764.

Steffensmeier, D., & Demuth, S. (2000). Ethnicity and sentencing outcomes in U.S. federal courts: Who is punished more harshly? *American Sociological Review, 65,* 705–729.

Steffensmeier, D., & Demuth, S. (2001). Ethnicity and judges' sentencing decisions: Hispanic-Black-White comparisons. *Criminology, 39,* 145–178.

Steffensmeier, D., Feldmeyer, B., Harris, C. T., & Ulmer, J. T. (2011). Reassessing trends in black violent crime, 1980–2008: Sorting out the "Hispanic effect" in Uniform Crime Reports arrests, National Crime Victimization Survey offender estimates, and U.S. prisoner counts. *Criminology, 49*(1), 197–251.

Stevenson, B. (2010). *Illegal racial discrimination in jury selection: A continuing legacy.* Montgomery, AL: Equal Justice Initiative.

Stevenson, B. (2011). *The death penalty in Alabama: Judicial override.* Montgomery, AL: Equal Justice Initiative.

Stewart, E. A. (2007). Either they don't know or they don't care: Black males and negative police experiences. *Criminology & Public Policy, 6,* 123–130.

Stewart, E. A., Schreck, C. J., & Brunson, R. K. (2008). Lessons of the street code: Policy implications for reducing violent victimization among disadvantaged citizens. *Journal of Contemporary Criminal Justice, 24,* 137–147.

Stewart, E. A., Schreck, C. J., & Simons, R. L. (2006). I ain't gonna let no one disrespect me: Does the code of the street reduce or increase violent victimization among African American adolescents? *The Journal of Research in Crime and Delinquency, 43,* 427–457.

Stewart, E., & Simons, R. L. (2006). Structure and culture in African-American adolescent violence: A partial test of the code of the street thesis. *Justice Quarterly, 23,* 1–33.

Stewart, E. A., Simons, R. L., & Conger, R. D. (2002). Assessing neighborhood and social psychological influences on childhood violence in an African American sample. *Criminology, 40,* 801–829.

Stowell, J. I. (2007). *Immigration and crime: Considering the direct and indirect effects of immigration on violent criminal behavior.* New York: LFB Scholarly Press.

Stowell, J. I., Messner, S. F., McGeever, K. F., & Raffalovich, L. E. (2009). Immigration and the recent violent crime drop in the U.S.: A pooled, cross-sectional time-series analysis of metropolitan areas. *Criminology, 47,* 889–928.

Streib, V. (2004). *The juvenile death penalty today: Death sentences and executions for juvenile crimes.* Retrieved April 30, 2004, from http://www.law.onu.edu/faculty/streib/JuvDeathApr302004.pdf

Strom, K. (2001). *Hate crimes reported in the NIBRS, 1997-1999.* Washington, DC: USDOJ, OJP, BJS.

Suavecito Apparel Co. (2004). *Zoot suit riots.* Retrieved December 16, 2004, from http://www.suavecito.com/history.htm

Subcommittee on Civil and Constitutional Rights. (1994). *Racial disparities in federal death penalty prosecutions: 1988–1994* (Staff report). Washington, DC: 103rd Congress, Second Session.

Sudbury, J. (Ed.). (2005). *Global lockdown: Race, gender and the prison industrial complex.* New York: Routledge.

Sutherland, E. H. (1947). *Principles of criminology* (4th ed.). Philadelphia: Lippincott.

Swain v. Alabama, 380 U.S. 202 (1965).

Swan, A. L. (1977). *Families of Black prisoners: Survival and progress.* Boston: G. K. Hall.

Takagi, P. (1974). A garrison state in a "democratic" society. *Crime and Social Justice: A Journal of Radical Criminology, 5,* 27–33. (Reprinted in J. F. Fyfe, Ed., 1982, *Readings on police use of deadly force,* pp. 195–213.)

Takaki, R. (1989). *Strangers from a different shore: A history of Asian Americans.* Boston: Little, Brown.

Tarlow, M., & Nelson, M. (2007). The time is now: Immediate work for people coming home from prison as a strategy to reduce their reincarceration and restore their place in the community. *Federal Sentencing Reporter, 20,* 138–140.

Tarver, M., Walker, S., & Wallace, H. (2002). *Multicultural issues in the criminal justice system.* Boston: Allyn & Bacon.

Tatum, B. L. (1994). The colonial model as a theoretical explanation of crime and delinquency. In A. Sulton (Ed.), *African-American perspectives on: Crime causation, criminal justice administration, and crime prevention* (pp. 33–52). Englewood, CO: Sulton Books.

Tatum, B. L. (2000). Deconstructing the association of race and crime: The salience of skin color. In M. W. Markowitz & D. Jones-Brown (Eds.), *The system in Black and White: Exploring the connections between race, crime, and justice* (pp. 31–46). Westport, CT: Praeger.

Taylor, B. M. (1989). *New directions for the National Crime Survey.* Washington, DC: U.S. Department of Justice, Office of Justice Programs.

Taylor, D. L., Biafora, F. A., Warheit, G., & Gil, A. (1997). Family factors, theft, vandalism, and major deviance among a multiracial/ multiethnic sample of adolescent girls. *Journal of Social Distress and the Homeless, 6,* 71–87.

Taylor, K. (2011). *System overload: The costs of under-resourcing public defense.* Washington, DC: Justice Policy Institute. Retrieved from http://www.justicepolicy .org/research/2756

Taylor, P. (1931). The problem of the Mexican. In *Crime and the foreign born* (National Commission on Law Observance and Enforcement Report No. 10, pp. 199–243). Washington, DC: U.S. Government Printing Office.

Taylor Greene, H. (2004). Do African American police make a difference? In M. D. Free, Jr. (Ed.), *Racial issues in criminal justice: The case of African Americans* (pp. 207–220). Monsey, NY: Criminal Justice Press.

Taylor Greene, H., & Gabbidon, S. (2000). *African American criminological thought.* Albany, NY: State University of New York Press.

Taylor Greene, H., Gabbidon, S. L., & Ebersole, M. (2001). A multifaceted analysis of the African American presence in juvenile delinquency textbooks published between 1997 and 2000. *Journal of Crime and Justice, 24,* 87–101.

Taylor Greene, H., & Penn, E. (2005). Reducing juvenile delinquency: Lessons learned. In E. Penn, H. Taylor Greene, & S. L. Gabbidon (Eds.), *Race and juvenile justice* (pp. 223–241). Durham, NC: Carolina Academic Press.

Tennessee v. Garner, 471 U.S. 1 (1985).

Terrill, W. (2009). The elusive nature of reasonableness. *Criminology & Public Policy, 8,* 163–172.

Texeira, E. (2005, August 28). Should the term "minority" be dropped? Word confuses, insults people some critics say. *Patriot-News,* p. A15.

Thompson v. Oklahoma, 487 U.S. 815 (1988).

Thornberry, T. P. (1998). Membership in youth gangs and involvement in serious and violent offending. In R. Loeber & D. P. Farrington (Eds.), *Serious and violent juvenile offenders: Risk factors and successful interventions* (pp. 147–166). Thousand Oaks, CA: Sage.

Thornberry, T. P., Huizinga, D., & Loeber, R. (2004). The causes and correlates studies: Findings and policy implications. *Juvenile Justice, 10*(1), 3–19.

Thurman, Q., Zhao, J., & Giacomazzi, A. (2001). *Community policing in a community era.* Los Angeles: Roxbury.

Tita, G., & Abrahamse, A. (2004, February). *Gang homicide in LA, 1981–2001.* Sacramento, CA: California Attorney General's Office.

Tolnay, S., & Beck, E. (1995). *A festival of violence: An analysis of southern lynchings, 1882–1930.* Urbana: University of Illinois Press.

Tonry, M. (1995). *Malign neglect: Race, crime, and punishment in America.* New York: Oxford University Press.

Tonry, M. (2011). *Punishing race: A continuing American dilemma.* New York: Oxford University Press.

Travis, J. (2005). *But they all come back: Facing the challenges of prisoner reentry.* Washington, DC: Urban Institute Press.

Travis, J. (2007). Reflection on the reentry movement. *Federal Sentencing Reporter, 20,* 84–87.

Trujillo, L. (1995). La evolucion del "bandido" al "pachuco": A critical examination and evaluation of criminological literature on Chicanos. In A. S. Lopes (Ed.), *Criminal justice and Latino communities* (pp. 21–45). New York: Garland. (Reprinted from *Issues in Criminology, 74*[9], 44–67, 1974.)

Trulson, C. R., Marquart, J. W., & Kawuncha, S. K. (2006). Gang suppression and institutional control. *Corrections Today, 68,* 26–31.

Truman, J. L., & Rand, M. R. (2010). *Criminal victimization, 2009.* NCJ 231327. Washington, DC: Bureau of Justice Statistics.

Tseloni, A., & Pease, K. (2011). DNA retention after arrest: Balancing privacy interests and public protection. *European Journal of Criminology, 8,* 32–47.

Tso, T. (1996). The process of decision making in tribal courts. In M. O. Nielson & R. A. Silverman (Eds.), *Native Americans, crime, and justice* (pp. 170–180). Boulder, CO: Westview Press.

Tulchin, S. H. (1939). *Intelligence and crime.* Chicago: University of Chicago Press.

Turk, A. T. (1969). *Criminality and legal order.* Chicago: Rand McNally & Company.

Turner, K. B., & Johnson, J. B. (2005). A comparison of bail amounts for Hispanics, Whites, and African Americans: A single county analysis. *American Journal of Criminal Justice, 30,* 35–53.

Tyler, S. L. (1973). *A history of Indian policy.* Washington, DC: U.S. Department of Interior.

Uchida, C. (1997). The development of American police. In R. G. Dunham & G. P. Alpert (Eds.), *Critical issues in policing* (pp. 18–35). Prospect Heights, IL: Waveland Press.

Uggen, C., & Manza, J. (2002). Democratic contraction? Political consequences of felon disenfranchisement in the United States. *American Sociological Review, 67,* 777–803.

Uggen, C., Manza, J., & Behrens, A. (2003). Felon voting rights and the disenfranchisement of African Americans. *Souls: A Critical Journal of Black Politics, Culture & Society, 5,* 47–55.

Ulmer, J. T., & Johnson, B. (2004). Sentencing in context: A multilevel analysis. *Criminology, 42,* 137–177.

United States v. Barry, 938 F.2d, 1327, 1329 (D.C. Cir. 1991).

United States v. Booker, 543 U.S. 220 (2005).

University at Albany, School of Criminal Justice. (2011). *Capital jury project.* Retrieved from http://www.albany.edu/scj/capital_jury_project.php

Unnever, J. D. (2008). Two worlds far apart: Black-White differences in beliefs about why African-American men are disproportionately imprisoned. *Criminology, 46,* 511–538.

Unnever, J. D., & Cullen, F. T. (2007). Reassessing the racial divide in support for capital punishment: The continuing significance of race. *Journal of Research in Crime and Delinquency, 44,* 124–158.

Unnever, J. D., & Gabbidon, S. L. (2011). *A theory of African American offending: Race, racism, and crime.* New York: Routledge.

Urban, L. S., St. Cyr, J. L., & Decker, S. H. (2003). Goal conflict in the juvenile court: The evolution of sentencing practices in the United States. *Journal of Contemporary Criminal Justice, 19,* 454–479.

U.S. Bureau of Justice Statistics. (2006). *Compendium of federal justice statistics, 2004.* Washington, DC: U.S. Department of Justice.

U.S. Bureau of Labor Statistics. (2010). *Labor force statistics from the Current Population Survey.* Retrieved from http://www.bls.gov/cps/cpsaat11.pdf

U.S. Census Bureau. (1995). *Top 25 American Indian tribes for the United States: 1990 and 1980.* Retrieved December 12, 2003, from http://www.census.gov/population/socdemo/race/indian/ailant1.txt

U.S. Census Bureau. (2000). *State & County QuickFacts.* Retrieved from http://www.census.gov/main/www/cen2000.html

U.S. Census Bureau. (2003). *Statistical abstracts of the United States.* Washington, DC: Author.

U.S. Census Bureau. (2004). *U.S. interim projections by age, race, and Hispanic origin.* Retrieved January 18, 2008, from http://www.census.gov

U.S. Census Bureau. (2007). *Minority population tops 100 million.* Retrieved January 17, 2008, from http://www.census.gov

U.S. Census Bureau. (2008). *Statistical abstract of the U.S.* Retrieved from http://www.census.gov/compendia/statab/

U.S. Census Bureau. (2010). *2010 Census data.* Retrieved from http://2010.census.gov/2010census/data/

U.S. Census Bureau. (2011a). *2010 Census redistricting data (Public Law 24-171) summary file.* Retrieved from http://2010.census.gov/2010census

U.S. Census Bureau. (2011b). *Census 2000 redistricting data (Public Law 24-171) summary file.* Retrieved from http://www.census.gov/rdo/data/redistricting_data.html

U.S. Census Bureau. (2011c). *Statistical abstract of the United States: 2011.* Retrieved from http://www.census.gov/compendia/statab/2011/tables/11s0225.pdf

U.S. Census Bureau. (2011d). *Statistical abstract of the United States: 2012.* Retrieved from http://www.census.gov/compendia/statab/2012edition.html

U.S. Department of Homeland Security. (2009). *Secure communities.* Retrieved July 12, 2011, from http://www.ice.gov/doclib/foia/secure_communities/securecommunitiesstrategicplan09.pdf

U.S. Department of Homeland Security. (2011). *Immigration enforcement actions: 2010.* Washington, DC: Office of Immigration Statistics.

U.S. Department of Justice. (2000). *The federal death penalty system: A statistical survey (1988–2000).* Washington, DC: Author.

U.S. Department of Justice. (2010). Assistant attorney General Thomas E. Perez speaks at the national association for civilian oversight of law enforcement. *Justice News.* Retrieved from http://www.justice.gov/crt/opa/pr/speeches/2010/crt-speech-100920.html

U.S. Department of Justice. (2011, May 16). *Arkansas man pleads guilty to federal hate crime related to the assault of five Hispanic men* (press release). Retrieved from http://www.justice.gov/opa/pr/2011/May/11-crt-626.html

U.S. General Accounting Office. (1990). *Death penalty sentencing: Research indicates pattern of racial disparities.* Washington, DC: U.S. General Accounting Office.

U.S. General Accounting Office. (1997). *Drug courts: Overview of growth, characteristics, and results.* Washington, DC: Author.

U.S. Government Accountability Office. (2011). *Criminal alien statistics.* Washington, DC: Author. Retrieved from http://www.gao.gov/new.items/d11187.pdf

U.S. Senate. (2002). *Senate hearing before the subcommittee on crime and drugs of the committee on the judiciary, United States (107–911).* Washington, DC: U.S. Government Printing Office.

U.S. Sentencing Commission. (2002). *Cocaine and federal sentencing policy*. Retrieved from www.ussc.gov/r_congress/02crach/2002crackrpt.pdf

U.S. Sentencing Commission. (2007). *Cocaine and federal sentencing policy*. Retrieved March 19, 2008, from http://www.ussc.gov/r_congress/cocaine2007.pdf

van den Haag, E. (1975). *Punishing criminals: Concerning a very old and painful question*. New York: Basic Books.

Vandiver, M. (2006). *Lethal punishment: Lynchings and legal executions in the South*. New Brunswick, NJ: Rutgers University Press.

Van Sertima, I. (1976). *They came before Columbus: The African presence in ancient Americas*. New York: Random House.

Van Stelle, K. R., Allen, G. A., & Moberg, D. P. (1998). Alcohol and drug prevention among American Indian families: The family circles program. In J. Valentine, J. A. De Jong, & N. J. Kennedy (Eds.), *Substance abuse prevention in multicultural communities* (pp. 53–60). Binghamton, NY: Haworth Press.

Varano, S.P., Huebner, B.M., & Bynum, T.S. (2011). Correlates and consequences of pre-incarceration gang involvement among incarcerated youthful felons. *Journal of Criminal Justice, 39*, 30–38.

Vaske, J., Beaver, K. M., Wright, J. P., Boisvert, D., & Schnupp, R. (2009). An interaction between DAT1 and having an alcoholic father predicts serious alcohol problems in a sample of males. *Drug and Alcohol Dependence, 104*, 17–22.

Vaske, J., Makarios, M., Boisvert, D., Beaver, K. M., & Wright, J. P. (2009). The interaction of DRD2 and violent victimization on depression: An analysis by gender and race. *Journal of Affective Disorders, 112*(1), 120–125.

Vaughn, M. G., Wallace, J. M., Davis, L. E., Fernandes, G. T., & Howard, M. O. (2008). Variations in mental health problems, substance use, and delinquency between African American and Caucasian juvenile offenders: Implications for reentry services. *International Journal of Offender Therapy and Comparative Criminology, 52*(3), 311–329.

Vega, W. A., & Gil, A. G. (1998). Different worlds: Drug use and ethnicity in early adolescence. In W. A. Vega & A. G. Gil (Eds.), *Drug use and ethnicity in early adolescence* (pp. 1–12). New York: Plenum Press.

Velez, M. B. (2006). Toward an understanding of the lower rates of homicide in Latino versus Black neighborhoods: A look at Chicago. In J. Hagan, R. Peterson, & L. Krivo (Eds.), *The many colors of crime: Inequalities of race, ethnicity, and crime in America* (pp. 91–107). New York: New York University Press.

Velez, M. B. (2009). Contextualizing the immigration and crime effect: An analysis of homicide in Chicago neighborhoods. *Homicide Studies, 13*, 325–335.

Venkatesh, S. A. (2006). *Off the books: The underground economy of the urban poor*. Cambridge, MA: Harvard University Press.

Venkatesh, S. (2008). *Gang leader for a day: A rogue sociologist takes to the streets*. New York: The Penguin Press.

Visher, C. A. (2007). Returning home: Emerging findings and policy lessons about prisoner reentry. *Federal Sentencing Reporter, 20*, 93–102.

Vold, G. B., Bernard, T. J., & Snipes, J. B. (1998). *Theoretical criminology* (4th ed.). Oxford, UK: Oxford University Press.

Wacquant, L. (2000). The new "peculiar institution": On the prison as surrogate ghetto. *Theoretical Criminology, 4*, 377–389.

Wacquant, L. (2001). Deadly symbiosis: When ghetto and prison meet and mesh. *Punishment & Society, 3*, 95–134.

Wacquant, L. (2002). Scrutinizing the street: Poverty, morality, and the pitfalls of urban ethnography. *American Journal of Sociology, 107*, 1468–1532.

Wacquant, L. (2011). From slavery to mass incarceration: Rethinking the race question in the United States. In M. Tonry (Ed.), *Why punish? How much?* (pp. 382–402). New York: Oxford University Press.

Wakeling, S., Jorgensen, M., Michaelson, S., Begay, M., Hartmann, F., & Wiener, M. (2001). *Policing on Indian reservations*. Washington, DC: U.S. Department of Justice.

Walker, S. (1989). *Sense and nonsense about crime: A policy guide* (2nd ed.). Pacific Grove, CA: Brooks/Cole.

Walker, S. (2001). *Police accountability: The role of citizen oversight*. Belmont, CA: Wadsworth/Thomson Learning.

Walker, S., & Katz, S. M. (2002). *Police in America*. New York: McGraw-Hill.

Walker, S., Spohn, C., & DeLone, M. (1996). *The color of justice: Race, ethnicity, and crime in America*. Belmont, CA: Wadsworth.

Walker, S., Spohn, C., & DeLone, M. (2007). *The color of justice: Race, ethnicity, and crime in America* (4th ed.). Belmont, CA: Thomson Learning.

Walker, S., Spohn, C., & DeLone, M. (2012). *The color of justice: Race, ethnicity, and crime in America* (5th ed.). Belmont, CA: Cengage/Wadsworth.

Walker-Barnes, C. J., Arrue, R. M., & Mason, C. A. (1998). *Girls and gangs: Identifying risk factors for female gang involvement*. Retrieved from http://www.unc.edu/~cwalkerb/present1/pdf

Walsh, A. (2004). *Race and crime: A biosocial analysis*. New York: Nova Science.

Walsh, A., & Beaver, K. M. (Eds.). (2009). *Biosocial criminology:*

New directions in theory and research. New York: Routledge.

Walsh, A., & Ellis, L. (Eds.). (2003). *Biosocial criminology: Challenging environmentalism's supremacy*. New York: Nova Science.

Ward, G. (2001). *Color lines of social control: Juvenile justice administration in a racialized social system, 1825–2000*. Unpublished doctoral dissertation, University of Michigan, Ann Arbor.

Ward, G., & Kupchik, A. (2009). Accountable to what? Professional orientations toward accountability-based juvenile justice. *Punishment & Society, 11*(1), 85–109.

Warner, S. B. (1929). *Survey of criminal statistics in the United States for National Commission on Law Observance and Enforcement*. Washington, DC: Government Printing Office.

Warner, S. B. (1931). Crimes known to the police: An index of crime? *Harvard Law Review, 45,* 307.

Warnshuis, P. L. (1931). Crime and criminal justice among the Mexicans of Illinois. In *Crime and the foreign born* (National Commission on Law Observance and Enforcement, Report No. 10, pp. 265–329). Washington, DC: Government Printing Office.

Warren, P. Y., Tomaskovic-Devey, D., Smith, W. R., Zingraff, M., & Mason, M. (2006). Driving while Black: Bias processes and racial disparity in stops. *Criminology, 44,* 709–736.

Washington, L. (1994). *Black judges on justice: Perspectives from the bench*. New York: New Press.

Websdale, N. (2001). *Policing the poor: From slave plantation to public housing*. Boston: Northeastern University Press.

Weisburd, D., Greenspan, R., Hamilton, E., Williams, H., & Bryand, K. (2000). Police attitudes toward abuse of author-

ity: Findings from a national study. Washington, DC: U.S. Department of Justice.

Weisheit, R. A., & Wells, L. E. (2004). Youth gangs in rural America. *NIJ Journal, 251,* 2–6.

Weitzer, R. (1999). Citizens' perceptions of police misconduct: Race and neighborhood context. *Justice Quarterly, 16,* 819–846.

Weitzer, R., & Tuch, S. (2002). Perceptions of racial profiling: Race, class, and personal experience. *Criminology, 40,* 435–456.

Weitzer, R., & Tuch, S. (2006). *Race and police in America: Conflict and reform*. New York: Cambridge University Press.

Weitzer, R., Tuch, S. A., & Skogan, W. G. (2008). Police-community relations in a majority-black city. *Journal of Research in Crime and Delinquency, 45,* 398–428.

Wenzel, S., Longshore, D., Turner, S., & Ridgely, M. S. (2001). Drug courts: A bridge between criminal justice and health services. *Journal of Criminal Justice, 29,* 241–253.

West, H. C., Sabol, W. J., & Greenman, S. J. (2010). *Prisoners in 2009*. Washington, DC: Bureau of Justice Statistics. NCJ 231675.

Western, B. (2006). *Punishment and inequality in America*. New York: Russell Sage.

Western, B., & Wildeman, C. (2009). The Black family and mass incarceration. *Annals of the American Academy of Political and Social Sciences, 621,* 221–242.

Whitaker, C. (1990). *Black victims*. Washington, DC: U.S. Department of Justice.

Whren v. United States, 517 U.S. 806 (1996).

Wilbanks, W. (1987). *The myth of a racist criminal justice system*. Pacific Grove, CA: Brooks/Cole.

Wilder, K. (2003). *Assessing residents' satisfaction with community policing: A look into quality of

life and interaction with police*. Unpublished master's thesis, Old Dominion University, Norfolk, VA.

Wilkins v. Missouri (1989). See *Stanford v. Kentucky*.

Williams, E. (1944). *Capitalism and slavery*. London: Andre Deutsch.

Williams, F. P., and M. D. McShane. (2010). *Criminological theory* (5th ed.). Upper Saddle River, NJ: Prentice Hall.

Williams, H., & Murphy, P. (1990). *The evolving strategy of police: A minority view*. Washington, DC: National Institute of Justice.

Williams, M. (2002). A comparison of sentencing outcomes for defendants with public defenders versus retained counsel in a Florida circuit court. *Justice Systems Journal, 23,* 249–257.

Williams, M. R., & Holcomb, J. E. (2004). The interactive effects of victim race and gender on death sentence disparity findings. *Homicide Studies, 8,* 350–376.

Williams, S. (2007, October 8). Police urged not to check legal status: Activists want immigration standing off-limits in stops; some chiefs agree. *The Milwaukee Journal Sentinel*. Retrieved March 7, 2008, from http://find.galegroup.com/ips/retrieve.do

Wilson, J. Q., & Herrnstein, R. (1985). *Crime and human nature*. New York: Simon & Schuster.

Wilson, W. J. (1987). *The truly disadvantaged*. Chicago: University of Chicago Press.

Wilson, W. J. (1996). *When work disappears: The world of the new urban poor*. New York: A. A. Knopf.

Wilson, W. J., & Chaddha, A. (2009). The role of theory in ethnographic theory. *Ethnography, 10,* 549–564.

Winterdyk, J., & Ruddell, R. (2010). Managing prison gangs: Results from a survey of U.S. prison systems. *Journal of Criminal Justice, 38,* 730–736.

Withrow, B. L. (2006). *Racial profiling: From rhetoric to reason.* Upper Saddle River, NJ: Prentice Hall.

Wolf, A. M., & Hartney, C. (2005). A portrait of detained youth in the state of Hawaii. *Crime & Delinquency, 51,* 180–191.

Wolfgang, M. (1963). Uniform crime reports: A critical appraisal. *University of Pennsylvania Law Review, 111,* 708–738.

Wolfgang, M. E. (1958). *Patterns in criminal homicide.* Philadelphia: University of Pennsylvania Press.

Wolfgang, M. E., & Ferracuti, F. (1967). *The subculture of violence: Towards an integrated theory in criminology.* London: Tavistock.

Wolfgang, M. E., & Riedel, M. (1973). Race, judicial discretion, and the death penalty. *The Annals of the American Academy of Political and Social Sciences, 407,* 119–133.

Woodward, C. (1971). *The origins of the New South, 1877–1913.* Baton Rouge: Louisiana University Press.

Wooldredge, H., Hartman, J., Latessa, E., & Holmes, S. (1994). Effectiveness of culturally specific community treatment for African American juvenile felons. *Crime & Delinquency, 40,* 589–598.

Wooldredge, J. (2012). Distinguishing race effects on pre-trial release and sentencing decisions. *Justice Quarterly. 29,* 41–75.

Wordes, M., Bynum, T. S., & Corley, C. J. (1994). Locking up youth: The impact of race on detention decisions. *Journal of Research in Crime and Delinquency, 31,* 149–165.

Work, M. (1900). Crime among the Negroes of Chicago. *American Journal of Sociology, 6,* 204–223.

Work, M. (1913). Negro criminality in the South. *Annals of the American Academy of Political and Social Sciences, 49,* 74–80.

Work, M. (1939). Negro criminality in the South. *Annals of the American Academy of Political and Social Sciences, 49,* 74–80.

Wright, B. (1987). *Black robes, White justice.* New York: Carol.

Wright, J. P. (2009). Inconvenient truths: Science, race, and crime. In A. Walsh & K. M. Beaver (Eds), *Biosocial criminology: New directions in theory and research* (pp. 137–153). New York: Routledge.

Wright, J. P., & Boisvert, D. (2009). What biosocial criminology offers criminology. *Criminal Justice and Behavior, 36,* 1228–1240.

Wright, R. R. (1969). *The Negro in Pennsylvania: A study in economic history.* New York: Arno Press and *The New York Times.* (Original work published 1912)

Wu, F. H. (2002). *Yellow: Race in America beyond Black and White.* New York: Basic Books.

Xu, Y., Fiedler, M. L., & Flaming, K. H. (2005). Discovering the impact of community policing: The broken windows thesis, collective efficacy, and citizens' judgment. *The Journal of Research in Crime and Delinquency, 42,* 147–186.

Yazzie, R. (2000, September 30). Navajo justice. *Yes!* Retrieved from http://www.yesmagazine.org

Young, V. (1993). Punishment and social conditions: The control of Black juveniles in the 1800s in Maryland. In A. G. Hess & P. F. Clement (Eds.), *History of juvenile delinquency: A collection of essays on crime committed by young offenders, in history and in selected countries* (pp. 557–575). Aalen, Germany: Scientia Verlag.

Young, V. (1994). Race and gender in the establishment of juvenile institutions: The case of the South. *Prison Journal, 74,* 244–265.

Young, V. (2007, October 25). Immigration crackdown feasts on motorists. *St. Louis Post-Dispatch.* Retrieved March 7, 2008, from General Reference Center Gold, Gale, Texas Southern University.

Young, V., & Reviere, R. (2006). *Women behind bars: Gender and race in U.S. prisons.* Boulder, CO: Lynne Rienner.

Young v. Robinson, 29 Cr. L. 2587 (1981).

Zalman, M. (2006). Criminal justice system reform and wrongful convictions: A research agenda. *Criminal Justice Policy Review, 17,* 468–492.

Zalman, M. (2011). *Qualitatively estimating the incidence of wrongful convictions—a postscript.* Retrieved from http://works.bepress.com/marvin_zalman/1

Zane, N., Aoki, B., Ho, T., Huang, L., & Jang, M. (1998). Dosage-related changes in a culturally responsive prevention program for Asian American youth. In J. Valentine, J. A. De Jong, & N. J. Kennedy (Eds.), *Substance abuse prevention in multicultural communities* (pp. 105–125). Binghamton, NY: Haworth Press.

Zangrando, R. L. (1980). *The NAACP crusade against lynching, 1900–1950.* Philadelphia: Temple University Press.

Zatz, M. S. (1987). The changing form of racial/ethnic biases in sentencing. *Journal of Research in Crime and Delinquency, 24,* 69–92.

Zimmerman, C. S. (2002). From the jailhouse to the courthouse: The role of informants in wrongful convictions. In S. Westervelt & J. A. Humphrey (Eds.), *Wrongly convicted: Perspectives on failed justice* (pp. 55–76). New Brunswick, NJ: Rutgers University Press.

Zimring, F. (2003). *The contradictions of American capital punishment.* New York: Oxford University Press.

Index

Iowa
  corrections to higher education
    spending ratio in, 2007, 248 (fig.)
  executions in, 1930-2009, 226
    (table)
  National Incident-based Reporting
    System used in, 52
  reentry court pilot sites in, 276
IQ
  biosocial thesis on race and
    offending and, 75–76
  crime relationship with, 73–74,
    326
Irish Americans
  anti-Irish sentiment and, 23
  assimilation of, 23
  Draft Riots, New York City and, 23
  Gangs of New York film and, 23
  immigration restrictions and, 23
  negative stereotypes of, 40 (table)
  potato famine and, 22
  settlement patterns of, 22–23
Italian Americans
  anti-Italian sentiment and, 22
  Catholicism issues and, 22
  Immigration Act of 1924 and, 22
  organized crime issues and, 22
  Toleration Act (1649) and, 21–22
  urban settlement by, 22

Jackson, George, 95, 258–259
Jackson, Ketanji Brown, 198
Jackson-Lee, Sheila, 199 (photo)
Jail/jails. *See* Corrections
Jang, S. J., 87, 88
Japanese Americans
  arrests data, 1933-2010, 57,
    317–319 (table)
  Hawaii labor source and, 37
  illegal activities of, 37
  immigration patterns of, 37–38
  negative stereotypes of, 40 (table)
  relocation centers for, 38, 38
    (photo), 327
  social disorganization theory of
    race and crime and, 79
  total arrests, arrests for murders,
    1950-2010, 57, 320–322 (table)
  Uniform Crime Reporting
    category of, 55
  U.S. population data, 2010, 36
    (table)
  World War II and, 21, 38
Jena 6 case of wrongful conviction,
  241
Jensen, V. J., 91, 93

Jeong, Sok, 35
Jewish Americans
  American Freemasonry and, 24
  anti-Semitism and, 23–24
  B'nai B'rith ("Sons of the
    Covenant") and, 24
  educational restrictions and, 25
  juvenile delinquency of, 24
  negative stereotypes of, 40 (table)
  organized crime and, 24–25
  prosperity of, 25
  settlement patterns of, 23–24
  White Americans classification
    of, 25
Johnson, B. D., 155, 192, 193, 305
Johnson, B. R., 87, 88
Johnson, D., 107, 233
Johnson, G., 90, 90 (fig.)
Johnson, J. B., 151
Johnson, Lyndon B.
  judicial appointments by, 199,
    201–206 (tables)
Johnson, S., 302
Johnson v. California, 261
Jonas, Glen, 132
Jordan, K. L., 158
*Judicial Cases Concerning American
  Slavery and the Negro* (Catterall),
  171
Jury nullification
  African Americans and, 161–162
  explanation of, 161, 326
  Kente cloth incident and, 161
  police testimony, 162
  United States v. Barry and, 161
  U.S. national rates of, 162, 167
  white juror color-blindness and,
    162
Jury selection
  deception strategies in, 158
  gender bias regarding, 156–157
  racial bias regarding, 156
  recommendations to reduce bias
    in, 159–160
  Scottsboro case and, 156
  venire, jury pool selection and,
    156
  See also Voir dire process
Justice Policy Institute, 153–154
Juvenile courts, 285, 326
  accountability reform and, 291
  best interest of the child goal
    of, 290
  Black child savers and, 291
  procedural safeguards in,
    290–291

as progressive reform idea,
    290, 291
  racial segregation in, 290
  rehabilitation goal of, 290–291
  "separate but equal" doctrine
    and, 290
  Statistical Briefing Book (SBB)
    and, 292, 328
  Supreme Court rulings regarding,
    290–291
  trying youths as adults and, 291,
    299–300 (table)
  See also Juvenile justice
Juvenile delinquency
  drug behavior and, 297–298
  Healthy Youth initiatives
    and, 313
  of Jewish Americans, 24
  minority female delinquency
    and, 304–306
  "street factor" in, 302
  subcultural backlash concept
    and, 302
  youth alienation factor in, 302
  See also Juvenile justice
Juvenile justice
  accountability and punitive
    focuses of, 287
  Afrocentric prevention programs
    and, 309
  Black children and, 288, 289–290
  Black child savers and, 289
  Black colleges and universities
    and, 289–290
  Blueprint Model Programs and,
    308, 309
  Center for the Study and
    Prevention of Violence and,
    308
  the child savers and, 288,
    289–290, 324
  colonial North vs. South policies
    regarding, 287–288
  comprehensive strategy
    framework of delinquency
    prevention and, 308–309
  crossover youths and, 304
  delinquency prevention and,
    307–310
  discrimination and segregation
    history of, 284–285
  disproportionate minority
    confinement (DMC) and, 284,
    300–304, 314
  Federal Advisory Committee on
    Juvenile Justice and, 304

About the Authors

Shaun L. Gabbidon, Ph.D., is Distinguished Professor of Criminal Justice at Penn State Harrisburg. Professor Gabbidon has served as a fellow at Harvard University's W. E. B. Du Bois Institute for Afro-American Research and has taught at the Center for Africana Studies at the University of Pennsylvania. The author of more than 100 scholarly publications including more than 50 peer-reviewed articles and 11 books, his most recent books include *Race, Ethnicity, Crime and Justice: An International Dilemma* (2010, Sage); *Criminological Perspectives on Race and Crime,* 2nd ed. (2010, Routledge); *Race and Crime: A Text/Reader* (2011, Sage); and the co-authored book *A Theory of African American Offending* (2011, Routledge). Professor Gabbidon currently serves as the editor of the Sage journal *Race and Justice: An International Journal.* The recipient of numerous awards, Dr. Gabbidon was most recently awarded the 2009 W. E. B. Du Bois Award from the Western Society of Criminology and the 2011 Outstanding Mentor Award from the Academy of Criminal Justice Sciences. Dr. Gabbidon can be contacted at slg13@psu.edu.

Helen Taylor Greene, Ph.D., is a Professor in the Department of Administration of Justice in the Barbara Jordan–Mickey Leland School of Public Affairs at Texas Southern University. She is an author, coauthor, and coeditor of numerous articles, book chapters, and books. Most recently, she coedited the *Encyclopedia of Race and Crime* (2009, Sage Publications) and *Race and Crime: A Text/Reader* (2011, Sage Publications) with Dr. Gabbidon. Professor Taylor Greene received the 2010 Lifetime Achievement Award from the Division on People of Color and Crime of the American Society of Criminology. In 2011, she was awarded the Academy of Criminal Justice Science's Outstanding Mentor Award. Dr. Taylor Greene can be contacted at greeneht@tsu.edu.

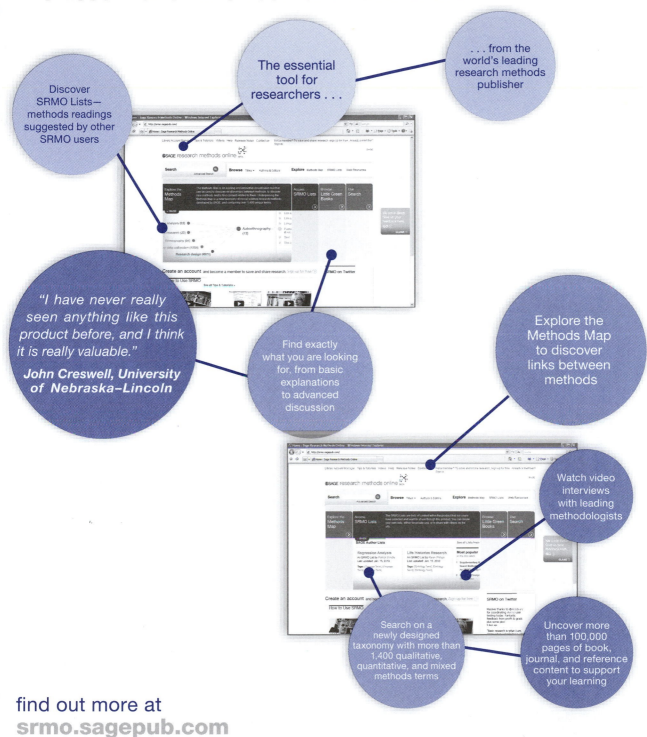